THE CONTENDER

Also by Michael Shnayerson

Irwin Shaw: A Biography

The Car That Could: The Inside Story of GM's Revolutionary Electric Vehicle

The Killers Within: The Deadly Rise of Drug-Resistant Bacteria (with Mark J. Plotkin)

Coal River: How a Few Brave Americans Took on a Powerful Company—and the Federal Government—to Save the Land They Love

My Song: A Memoir of Art, Race, and Defiance (by Harry Belafonte with Michael Shnayerson)

THE CONTENDER

ANDREW CUOMO,

a Biography

MICHAEL SHNAYERSON

TWELVE

NEW YORK BOSTON

Picture research by Carousel Research.

Twelve
Hachette Book Group
1290 Avenue of the Americas
New York, NY 10104

www.HachetteBookGroup.com

Printed in the United States of America

RRD-C

First Edition: March 2015
10 9 8 7 6 5 4 3 2 1

Twelve is an imprint of Grand Central Publishing.
The Twelve name and logo are trademarks of Hachette Book Group, Inc.

Library of Congress Cataloging-in-Publication Data

Shnayerson, Michael.
The contender : Andrew Cuomo, a biography / Michael Shnayerson.
pages cm
Includes bibliographical references and index.
ISBN 978-1-4555-2199-9 (hardcover) — ISBN (invalid) 978-1-61969-259-6 (audio download) — ISBN (invalid) 978-1-61969-260-2 (audio book) — ISBN 978-1-4555-2200-2 (ebook) 1. Cuomo, Andrew Mark, 1957– 2. Governors—New York (State)—Biography. 3. Cabinet officers—United States—Biography. 4. New York (State)—Politics and government—1951– I. Title. II. Title: Andrew Cuomo, a biography.
F125.3.C85S56 2015
974.7'043092—dc23
[B]

2014045160

For Gayfryd

Contents

Politics is a game of human beings. It all comes down to hate and revenge.

—Mel Miller, former Speaker of the
New York State Assembly

THE CONTENDER

CHAPTER 1

The High Point

The governor was having a bad week.

It was early June 2011, near the end of Andrew Mark Cuomo's first session as governor of New York State. Everything had gone right—until now. He had done all the things that governors try and often fail to do, especially in the great but broken state of New York. Balancing the budget. Cutting spending. Capping taxes. Keeping the unions at bay. Both parties were awed, compliant, and not a little afraid. The governor would never have more political capital than right now, and he knew it. Best to spend it while he could, a lesson learned from his father. Before the end of the session, he declared, he would pass a same-sex marriage bill.

This was a huge and possibly foolhardy gamble. Nationally, the issue was teetering. A handful of states had made same-sex marriage legal, but others—Minnesota, Rhode Island, New Jersey—had blocked it, and California was mired in a legal battle. A prudent governor might wait before entering the fray, and there was cause to call Cuomo prudent, even cynically so. Yet on "marriage," as his small circle of top advisers had taken to calling it, that prudence was balanced by something else, something that made Andrew Cuomo a figure to watch: a flash of passion.

As the fifty-sixth governor of New York explained to the fifty-second governor, his father, Mario, all that other stuff was *operational.* It was a word Andrew had used in his twenties, when he was his father's top aide and did whatever it took to make the wheels of government turn, including brutal firings and generally instilling fear. Now, as governor, he had to do as his father had done: set a lofty goal and lead people to it. "Same-sex marriage is at the heart of leadership and progressive government," he told his father. "I have to do this."

The bad news that week came from Dean Skelos, the Senate Republican leader. The Republicans ruled the Senate, and Skelos would be the bill's gatekeeper to the Senate floor. Skelos wouldn't block a same-sex marriage bill, he declared with an unctuous play at bipartisanship, not if the Democrats were united behind it. But they were not. Of the thirty Democrats in the sixty-two-member Senate, at least four were on record as opposing same-sex marriage. Not a single Republican was for it. Why should Skelos send a bill to the floor that would obviously fail? It would be, in the immortal words of Yogi Berra, déjà vu all over again.

That was hard to argue. Twice before, under Cuomo's predecessors, a bill for same-sex marriage had gone to the larger, Democratic-controlled Assembly, sailing through, only to be blocked by the Republican Senate. Despite months of lobbying by same-sex marriage advocates, the Senate, when it finally voted on the bill in December 2009, had shot it down 24–38, with all the Republicans and a handful of conservative Democrats piling on.

The Democrats in Albany's castlelike capitol building were convinced marriage had no chance. So were the capitol hill reporters, who filed their stories from narrow pigeonholes on the building's third floor, with its walls that seemed to be closing in, like those in "The Pit and the Pendulum." The wealthy libertarian Wall Streeters who had written six-figure checks to launch a lobbying effort for "marriage," and the legions of activists who had swarmed the nineteenth-century capitol's gloomy, high-vaulted corridors in search of wavering legislators week after week, held out little hope. Only one person in Albany seemed quietly confident that same-sex marriage would pass.

From April, when the campaign began in earnest, the governor held tight control over its many contingents. There would be no infighting among gay marriage groups and their patrons. The governor's top aide, Steve Cohen, would rule. Cohen was a former U.S. attorney who had startled the press corps by declaring that the new administration would have two speeds: "get along and kill." In private he could be a genial fellow. But when it came to promulgating his boss's agenda, there was no one tougher. Together, he and the governor changed the name of the cause. "Same-sex marriage" was now "marriage equality," with its canny appeal to justice and freedom, airbrushing away any hint of sexuality. On his own, the Catholic governor did what he could to calm his church and the lawmakers loyal to it. No same-sex marriages would have to be conducted in Catholic churches; the new bill would make that clear. With that, the governor got to work manning the phones from his second-floor office in the executive chamber.

To see Cuomo wrangling votes, coaxing one minute and threatening the next, was to see politics at its most elemental: carrot and stick. On the path from hatchet man for his father, to activist for the homeless, to a seat in President Clinton's cabinet, to New York attorney general, and now as the most powerful political leader in the state, Andrew Cuomo had made more than his share of enemies. He was brash, aggressive, often ruthless. But of all those who loathed him, none would deny him this: at the game of hardball, which was what this was, there was no one better. Now he was using those skills in the service of a cause he had come to believe in. Privately, on marriage, Cuomo figured he was a vote away, maybe two.

Of the four Democrats on record against marriage equality, Rubén Díaz Sr. of the Bronx was a hopeless cause. He was a Pentecostal minister, unbudgeable from his view that marriage was an institution established by God between a man and a woman. As far as Skelos knew, the other three Dems were no votes too. Hence his magnanimity.

Undeterred, the governor was pushing hard on those same three Democrats, one by one, with variations on a theme. "The only question is this year or the next," he told them. "And fifteen or twenty years from now, no one is going to understand lawmakers who voted no and put this off. Where in history do you want to be in this story?"

All three were downstaters, from outer boroughs of New York City. Before long two of the three would lose their seats amid corruption charges—a sorry tradition in Albany, and one that would soon grow more pronounced, threatening to tarnish the governor's record—but those misfortunes remained in the future. "You may worry about the politics of today and tomorrow," Andrew went on, "but you didn't enter into public life to be judged based on today."

The pitch was persuasive, but so was the "field." Activists had gathered overwhelming numbers of pro-marriage-equality signatures from each lawmaker's district. *Field*, they called it, as in field research. The lawmakers had been inundated with field.

By Monday, June 13, the governor had news to report. He called the press down from their pigeonholes into the Red Room adjacent to his office, with its crimson carpeting, mahogany wainscoting, and coffered oak ceiling. The room's ceremonial desk bore wheelchair marks from former governor Franklin D. Roosevelt, and a secret step that another former governor, the diminutive Thomas Dewey, could pull out and stand on to make his addresses. At six feet tall, more or less, Andrew could let the step stay hidden. There beside him were the three downstate Democrats, turned from no to yes. Making them go public locked them in, as Cuomo knew. It also pressured Skelos to honor his word that with twenty-nine Democrats united on marriage, he would let a bill go to the floor.

While Skelos absorbed the news, Andrew started phase two: wooing a handful of Republicans who might change their votes to yes if they thought the bill could pass. An hour later, he called the press back into the Red Room. More news, he announced, and went over to open the door of his private office. Out came James Alesi, Republican of Monroe County, to declare he would be a first Republican yes vote. Back in 2009, before his last vote on same-sex marriage, Alesi had been caught on camera with his head in his hands, distraught at voting no. That had been a "political" vote, he told the press now. This time he would vote from his heart.

With Alesi, the count was thirty yes votes to thirty-two no votes. Close, but not close enough.

Roy McDonald, a beefy, genial state senator from Saratoga who called himself a Lincoln Republican, was the governor's next target. His father had been a steelworker with an eighth-grade education. Patriotic and socially conservative, McDonald had worked his way up as a local banker. His three daughters were lobbying him, gently pushing him to change his vote. Cleverly, Andrew had one of his own three daughters with him when McDonald came to the governor's office. The family ties tugged, as intended. "I'm for being kind to people and letting them live their lives," McDonald said Monday. But he didn't say how he would vote.

That evening, the governor invited McDonald and other Republican senators for cocktails at the forty-room executive mansion that Andrew had reclaimed as the Cuomo home. All that gay couples wanted, he told the lawmakers, was state recognition that they were equal to anyone else. And weren't they? "Their love is worth the same as your love," he said. "Their partnership is worth the same as your partnership." McDonald liked how the governor framed marriage as a fundamental freedom. He also admired what he saw personally in Cuomo. This was a sizable political risk. The guy had guts.

Tuesday morning, McDonald stood before the cameras to say that he too would vote yes. "I'm not out to hurt some gay guy, gay woman—live your lifestyle. That's not my lifestyle, but God bless 'em—it's America." The press corps kept at him, asking if he might lose the next election because of his vote, until McDonald snapped. "I'm tired of blowhard radio people, blowhard television people, blowhard newspapers," he fumed. "They can take the job and shove it."

The count now stood at 31–31. The law was vague on whether the lieutenant governor could break the tie on a bill; Andrew wasn't banking on it. Anyway, if it did come to that, one of the converts might bail. From the start, the governor had insisted that even a one-vote margin wasn't enough. He needed a "spare tire." No Republican wanted to be the determining thirty-second vote and be blamed for the loss. The governor needed a thirty-third vote too.

Of the several Republicans the governor had been courting, Steve Saland of Poughkeepsie seemed the next best bet. A lawyer and the descendant of a prominent Jerusalem rabbi, known for his philosophical bent, Saland saw the virtue of marriage equality. He just preferred not to commit political suicide. The governor said he understood. "I need to know you'll be a yes for me," he told Saland, "but I know you want to be the thirty-third vote, not the thirty-second. Here is the deal. If I don't get that extra vote, I'll understand if you want to vote no." Saland agreed; the two shook hands.

Now it was time for the toughest prospect. Mark Grisanti of Buffalo, also a lawyer, had said flat out that he would vote no. But why? For Grisanti, an Italian Catholic lawyer in Catholic Buffalo, it was about preserving the right of the church to refuse to marry gay couples. As one Catholic to another, the governor said he shared Grisanti's concern. The new bill would have language giving priests legal protection. And so it did. The governor and Grisanti bounced the wording back and forth until Grisanti was satisfied. Now both Saland and Grisanti could claim to be the thirty-third vote, not the thirty-second. "I'll do it," Grisanti told the governor, as one of the governor's aides recalled. "I'll be there for you." And so they too shook hands. By the governor's count, the vote was 33–29. He had won—or so he thought.

The bill went to the Assembly on Tuesday, June 14. That evening, the governor went to Manhattan's legendary Palace Theater for an LGBT (lesbian, gay, bisexual, and transgendered) benefit at which the camp musical *Priscilla, Queen of the Desert* was performed. With him was his glamorous girlfriend, cookbook writer and food-show host Sandra Lee, whose thirty-one-year-old brother had come out as gay at the age of eighteen. "At one point this would have been considered a very racy play," the governor told his audience. "But given what's going on in politics today, it's pretty tame."

The next day, up in Albany, the Assembly passed the bill handily. There it stopped, while Skelos and his Republican senators anguished over whether to let the bill go to the floor after all. Skelos was trapped, and he knew it. He had urged his caucus to vote their consciences, and now two had done just that, very publicly. Not bringing the bill to the floor would be betraying them both, dooming them to almost certain defeat in their districts next election day.

That weekend, Mark Grisanti went home to Buffalo and gently suggested to his priest, among others, that he might vote yes on marriage equality. He came back shaken. First he met with Skelos and Tom Libous, the Senate's deputy majority leader. He had made a pledge to the governor. Now, he said, he just didn't see how he could keep it. It would kill him politically, he kept telling his colleagues. It would just kill him. The two were pleased to have his vote back, but breaking a pledge to the governor was serious business. "You better tell him yourself," Libous said. Grisanti blanched. "Will you go with me?"

Like a prisoner to his hanging, Grisanti went to the governor's office, accompanied by Libous. "I know I promised," he pleaded. "But I just can't do it. It'll kill me."

Cuomo darkened. "You were in my office five days ago," he said. "I looked you in the eye, you looked me in the eye, you said you were going to be with me. And now you're telling me you're not. And not because I didn't deliver the other thirty-third vote.

"You shook my hand," the governor thundered. "I'm from a world where your word means something. You made me a promise, I made you a promise. You're telling me more than about a vote. You're telling me who you really are."

Grisanti left the office stricken, with Libous in his wake.

For a long minute or two, the governor sat silent at his desk. Grisanti would vote no, so Saland would vote no. The vote would be back to a tie, 31–31, with Alesi and McDonald under such pressure that one or both might crumble. The whole marriage-equality campaign might crash for lack of Grisanti's vote. With it would go Andrew Cuomo's chance to change the history of civil rights, and perhaps his own history as well. Marriage equality would make him overnight a national figure—a presidential contender. He had time to plot another course. But this was a blow.

The governor turned to Steve Cohen, the top aide he'd put in charge of the campaign. Cohen was sitting quietly, waiting for his boss to speak. "Get me Saland," the governor ordered.

Saland appeared. He sat down. The governor looked at him intently. "Steve, we had a deal."

The Republican nodded uncertainly.

"I promised you if I didn't have the thirty-third vote, you could vote no if you wanted." The governor paused. "I'm sorry to tell you I don't have that other thirty-third vote."

There was a pause as both men pondered that.

"I think this bill should pass," the governor said, "and maybe I can get that thirty-third vote, but we had an understanding, so you should feel comfortable voting however you should vote. I will always appreciate that you were here when I needed you."

Saland had waged an internal struggle over same-sex marriage since his no vote in the senate in 2009. As a Jew, he had a sense of how it felt to be a target of bias. He had come to terms with the political cost of a yes vote. "Governor," Saland said, "whether you have the second thirty-third vote or not, I'll be there for you."

Andrew could have pressured the Republican senator. Instead, he'd invoked a sense of honor that appealed to the earnest lifelong Republican. *This is how we act as public servants, serving a higher cause.* By appealing to his better nature, the governor had won him over.

The governor had his three Democrats, and now his three Republicans. For a day, or perhaps two, he allowed himself to think he had won the vote. But he hadn't. Not yet. For now other Democrats were threatening to bolt.

One problem was money. Through the whole spring campaign, a lot of it had been raining down on possible yes-vote Republicans. The Democrats were furious. Here they were, loyally lined up behind their governor, and for what? To be taken for granted—and given none of that lucre from lobbyists and Wall Street hedge funders like Paul Singer and Daniel Loeb. Publicly, the Democrats' leader, John Sampson, was still banging the drum for marriage equality. Privately, he and a cadre of Democrats were now rooting for it to fail—a failure they would blame on the Republicans, in the hope that gay rights groups would redirect the marriage-equality money to *them*.

The vote on marriage, after a reluctant Skelos agreed to send the bill to the floor, was scheduled for Friday, June 24. This was already a stretch beyond the end of the state's quirky six-month legislative term. The day before, Sampson called Steve Cohen to say they had a problem: Carl Kruger.

Kruger was one of the three downstate Democrats who'd switched from no to yes. Sampson said Kruger was due in federal court on charges of bribery and corruption on Friday and Judge Jed Rakoff wouldn't excuse him for the vote.

Cohen reported this to the governor. If Kruger ducked the vote, one or both of the other two Democratic converts might as well. Once again, the vote's outcome was in doubt.

The governor was succinct. "Fix it," he told Cohen.

It was already after 6 p.m. when Cohen got the order—too late to call the court. Instead, he reached out to a deputy U.S. attorney in the district whom he knew. The attorney did some digging and called back bemused. Kruger was not scheduled to be in court, and in any event, his attendance at preliminary proceedings had been waived.

Cohen went back to Sampson, who seemed surprised. "Carl told us that," the Democratic leader said in his laconic way to Cohen. "I guess he was wrong."

Skelos had agreed to a vote on one condition. He didn't want a lot of Democrats giving speeches and taking credit for the bill when it passed. He would pull the bill, he said, if the Dems insisted. They did. Sampson told Cohen that no fewer than twenty-three of the twenty-nine Democrats would be giving floor speeches.

"But then Skelos will pull it," Cohen said. "The bill will fail."

"Then it's the Republicans' fault."

"No," he told Sampson. "That won't work. If Skelos pulls the bill because your members insist on speaking, I will personally talk to every reporter in this town and explain it was John Sampson who wrecked the marriage vote."

This was a fine example of what the governor liked to call the "failed tactic maneuver." Show your adversary you know what his plan is, then prove to him why it won't work.

Sampson went to his members and got their okay not to speak on the floor.

Then, and only then, did the Friday night vote proceed.

Above the senators in their ornate chamber, the mezzanine rows of public seating filled that evening with the most eclectic audience imaginable, from praying nuns to young gay activists. Among them was Steve Saland's wife: a good sign. Later, the rumor would pass that someone on the governor's staff had locked the doors to the Senate chamber to keep the Republican yes votes from ducking out.

First came Alesi's yes vote—expected, but still a relief. Then McDonald, and then Saland's deciding vote, to resounding cries. "My intellectual and emotional journey has at last ended," Saland declared. "I must define doing the right thing as treating all persons with equality in the definition of law as it pertains to marriage."

Finally came Grisanti, a yes vote after all. "I cannot legally come up with an argument against same-sex marriage," he said.

The final vote was what Cuomo had guessed from the start of these volatile twelve days: 33–29.

"New York has finally torn down the barrier that has prevented same-sex couples from exercising the freedom to marry," the governor declared. "With the world watching, the legislature, by a bipartisan vote, has said that all New Yorkers are equal under the law."

The governor signed the bill at 11:55 p.m. Thirty days to the minute later, it would double the number of Americans able to exercise that freedom, tip the national balance on marriage equality, and help nudge the president of the United States from his "evolving" view on the issue to full support. Andrew had taken a tremendous risk and made it pay off.

Not coincidentally, he had also advanced, with that stroke of his pen, as a future contender for the Oval Office.

Four years and one reelection campaign later, Governor Andrew Cuomo remains, at fifty-eight, the most tantalizing Democrat of his generation, his slightest eye twitch or throwaway line seized on as proof that he is, at last, readying a presidential run. No one who knows him doubts the day will come. The only question is when.

Cuomo, after all, has crowd-pleasing politics: near the middle, with just the occasional tack to one side or the other to keep on course. He has a gruff charisma, enough to fill rooms and dazzle his listeners—enough that *People* has twice anointed him one of the sexiest men alive over fifty. Above all, he understands how to lead a legislature better than almost any politician in America: how to wangle votes, playing on needs and vulnerabilities, building alliances and getting what he wants, with a hard-edged savvy that recalls no one so much as President Lyndon Baines Johnson. With Washington, D.C., plagued by partisan gridlock, led by a president who seems to disdain the human give-and-take of politics, is there not a strong case to be made for a President Andrew Cuomo who can coax and muscle the parties into working together again?

At the top tier, politics is as much about luck and timing as aptitude and ambition, and so Cuomo awaits his opening, which at the moment means waiting for Hillary Clinton to startle the world by saying she won't run for president in 2016, or by watching her run and make mistakes: with Hillary, it's happened before. If she does run, and win, and even win a second term, that puts Andrew in the running again just shy of sixty-seven, still well within range, and with another eight years under his belt of running the most powerful state in the Union. That is, of course, in the calculus of politics, eight lifetimes, but stipulate to this: if a path appears for the shrewdest and most tactically skilled Democratic governor in the country, he'll take it.

The next chapter remains to be written, but the prior ones are in, and the shape they take is compelling. Line up a dozen American politicians, take the most colorful biographical bits from each, and knit them into a single narrative, the iconic story of the twenty-first-century American politician. With Cuomo, those bits are all there. His story *is* the iconic story of the American politician.

It starts the way so many American political stories do, with an immigrant seeking his American dream. Andrew Cuomo's grandfather comes from Italy, works brutally hard, and lives for his children's success. Son

Mario is the one who triumphs far beyond his parents' dreams, a lawyer who runs for governor, and wins, and serves three terms.

Why, in a country that prides itself on the immigrant experience and up-by-the-bootstraps pluck, is the concept of political dynasty so compelling? Yet it is, and so the American political landscape is filled with Roosevelts, Kennedys, and Bushes, not to mention Romneys and Browns. From his father's first days as governor, dynasty for Andrew is a distant orb, hovering on the horizon. Waved off, joked about, but never quite out of sight, it beckons as the ultimate political triumph.

The Cuomo story is in many ways both typical of other American political stories and more extreme. So Andrew doesn't just work as a gofer in his father's gubernatorial campaign; he actually helps Mario win. He doesn't just marry well; he marries Kerry Kennedy, daughter of Bobby, putting the Cuomos on a par with America's reigning political family. For more than fifty years, every handsome young politician in America has been measured by how Kennedyesque he is. Marrying Kerry makes Andrew part of the clan, the two political dynasties intertwined.

Politics is public service: that at least is the idea, though it's populated at the local level by often grubby types guarding small pieces of turf. For Andrew, graduating from college in the late 1970s, it's an odd, almost quaint profession to enter. The smart ones go to Wall Street, or white-shoe law firms, or the new frontier of technology. Andrew wades in to help his father—both because his father needs him and perhaps because dutiful sons in middle-class families still apprentice to their fathers' trades. Later, his handlers will nurse a vision of Andrew the twenty-first-century Democrat, leading his party like Moses to a new, pragmatic future. But fundamentally, Andrew is old-school, steeped in New York City ward politics: his father's son.

The story of every son is the story of coming to terms with his father. For Andrew, Mario is mentor, role model, taskmaster, and moral judge. His son reacts accordingly—with a complex mix of emotions. The story of Mario and Andrew has fascinated Cuomo watchers for nearly forty years. It is, as Andrew will put it at one point, operatic.

Politics, of course, is as much about power as public service: you can't do one without the other. As his father's campaign manager at twenty-four in the watershed gubernatorial election of 1982, Andrew learns a lot about power. "The aggregation of power is essential to everything he's done," says a grizzled old pol of him.

"The difference between Andrew and his dad," says another, "is that he understands political power in a way his father didn't. He appreciates the use of political power. His father was reticent."

A third old pol, not a friend of the Cuomos, says it's more than that. "Andrew has learned from his father's mistakes, not his father's successes. He's very much a political animal, he has analyzed what went wrong with his father, and he's smart enough to plan his own strategies and not fall into those traps."

A young man with political ambitions works his first campaign, then confronts a dilemma. Which is the best way to elected office, public service or the private sector? Andrew tries both, only to jeopardize his future career in messy and questionable business deals. Just in the nick of time he pushes the private sector away and focuses on the issue he's chosen: the homeless overrunning New York City in the mid-1980s. How he makes himself a leader in the field is a textbook case for the young politician. What to do with that expertise is then the question. Run for office or seek an appointment? For Andrew, the choice is made by fate: Bill Clinton wins the White House in 1992, and Andrew, with a little lobbying from his father, lands in a high perch at HUD—the bloated, corruption-marred Department of Housing and Urban Development.

For the next eight years, Andrew works fiercely to salvage and redirect HUD. His supporters credit him with keeping the agency from being shut down altogether by ax-wielding Republicans, and there is some truth to this. His critics allege that the job is simply a means to his own advancement. At the least, he grows into a savvy public servant, able to make a federal agency work. In the process, he manages to irritate and alienate almost everyone around him.

Today, the central theme of Andrew Cuomo's image minders is that he's no longer the arrogant political son he was in those days. After HUD, so goes the story, defeat and divorce knock the stuffing out of him: in his first race, for governor in 2002, a reach in which he turns off so many voters that he has to drop out, and with the end of his marriage the next year. The marriage's failure is complex, but Kerry has an affair that hastens the end and leaves Andrew not just hurt but humiliated. Also very angry.

This too is part of the iconic story. "Very few politicians who get to the top don't go through a personal crisis they have to come out of and prove themselves by," muses Democratic consultant Robert Shrum. Bill Clinton the Comeback Kid in New Hampshire in 1992; George W. Bush an alcoholic, turning his life around at forty; Franklin D. Roosevelt after the onset of polio; Harry Truman after his haberdashery's failure in Kansas City; John F. Kennedy and PT 109—the list goes on. Andrew in 2003 is adrift, his political hopes dashed. He lives for his single-dad time with his daughters, but has no idea what to do with them, so he takes them to his mother. At night he watches television with his father, as if he's thirteen again. Later his father tells him, "After what you went through, your mother and I would not have been surprised if you spent the rest of your life in a gin mill."

Doggedly, Andrew sets about remaking himself, atoning for his hubris again and again with county leaders over dreary political dinners, sometimes just as the tag-along to his father. Then comes a bolt of every politician's greatest asset: luck. In 2004, the state's attorney general, one Eliot Spitzer, announces his intention to run for governor in 2006. Attorney general is Andrew's best possible opening, a chance to recast his harsh demeanor as the set expression of a dedicated crimefighter. He wins, and the past is forgotten, or at least eclipsed. He does well—very well—compensating for a lack of legal experience with canniness, drive, and a killer instinct for self-promotion. Then, for a second time, Spitzer vacates a seat Andrew covets: the governorship, after Spitzer's scandalous downfall. Spitzer, an archenemy, is Andrew's greatest benefactor: luck in politics almost never comes without a twist of irony.

And so the current act begins.

As governor, Andrew has proven a brilliant tactician, balancing factions, always two or three steps ahead of the lumbering lawmakers. In his youth he worked on cars, becoming a master mechanic. Friends say he focuses on fixing the engine—the engine of government now—and that that is what motivates him. Politically he calls himself bipartisan, and a case can be made that this is what bipartisan governors do: fix the car without worrying about where to drive it. But whether a governor can rise to be president without ideals and some sense of mission is a question that follows him, waiting to be answered.

Andrew is power in motion: that in itself is fascinating to watch. He's also light and dark, warm and effusive one minute, cold and calculating the next. In person he dominates a table or room, holding forth while his aides just nod: he likes to hear himself talk. Yet he's also a shrewd judge of character, flattering or cajoling until he gets what he wants. Despite his handlers' mantra about the new Andrew, he still strikes many as arrogant, even a bully. But he's also capable of thoughtful gestures done for no political gain, showing up unannounced at the funeral of an old friend's father, or playing hide-and-seek with a staffer's young son. One thing he isn't is boring.

Like his father, Andrew is an absolute ruler, making all decisions himself. He has a small circle of trusted aides, most with decades of loyalty to the Cuomo clan, less wise men than wise guys. Ideas are tolerated, but not criticism. "We don't like negatives," one says with a wince. What the governor has, as one longtime political consultant puts it, is a "complete control operation on every level."

"He doesn't tolerate criticism, runs roughshod over people, and punishes you if you get in his way," says one Republican lawmaker of Andrew. "If the ends justify the means, then you've got to admire him." Lawmakers of both parties wonder if he has any friends; publicly he seems to have only allies he controls—and enemies. "If they ever make a movie about Machiavelli," says one observer, "Andrew would be perfect in the role of the prince." In Machiavelli's argot, he is both lion and fox: the king of the forest, presiding on his throne, and the plotter in secret, doing whatever it takes.

Even admirers worry that the ironclad grip he has on his government—his strength and purpose—may be Andrew's undoing. From the start, he brings it to bear on his greatest challenge, public corruption, in a capital so rife that almost every month, another lawmaker is steeped in disgrace and forced to resign amid tawdry tales of bribery, slush funds, and shady nonprofits in a culture of pay to play. *We must clean up Albany*, Andrew declares again and again. He forms a commission to start secretive investigations, promising it will fix the mess, yet insists on naming most of its members himself and giving them veto power over any target in the executive branch—including the governor. When that committee sails into the shoals, he goes all out with a subpoena-wielding Moreland commission. Nine months later, as its probes start to bear fruit, Andrew shuts it down. He gets investigated for meddling with it—and has no one to blame but himself. "Andrew has the White House in his lap," says one former committee member. "But he can't trust the system, he has to game it, so he's going to fuck himself. He has what you need, and he is the man that America needs, but he won't be Luke Skywalker and trust the Force."

Along with tight control, the Cuomo administration is marked by secrecy bordering on paranoia. Aides communicate by the untraceable PIN-to-PIN BlackBerry messaging system. Any unsanctioned contact with the press is punished by banishment. Andrew's appearances are tightly controlled. Often the Albany press corps is reduced to interviewing a speakerphone, the governor talking through it from some other location like the Wizard of Oz. Press conferences are few, pointed questions parried. For his first two years, Andrew goes so far as to give nearly all his interviews via radio to one sympathetic journalist, Fredric Uberall Dicker of the *New York Post*, better known as FUD. The rest of the press corps has no choice but to recycle Dicker's tidbits. A falling-out between the two leads the governor to a new radio outlet, but with the same modus operandi.

Sometimes in public Andrew seems cheerful and bluff, and a wry one-liner will remind his listeners that he harbors a very quick wit. More often he comes across as wary, scowling in his speeches, shying away from crowds, his hands in his coat pockets when another politician would press the flesh and hold the babies. It's not that he dislikes his chosen profession. He just tenses at the retail aspect of it. What he loves is the power of his position, and the things it enables him to do. The more power he has, the more he can do. That may just be the political essence of Andrew Cuomo. Whether it works on the national stage is another matter. Most great American politicians have the gift of liking—or at least seeming to like—each next voter they meet.

The higher a politician rises, the more money he needs. That, too, is part of the iconic story. The challenge, in a system more porous than ever, is how to raise it without becoming a wholly owned subsidiary of those who give it. With his inauguration in 2011, Andrew helps set up a fund to finance a countercampaign promulgating his agenda. As the fund swells to $17 million, the donors remain, by law, anonymous. The ad campaign works, the unions are cowed, and Andrew's agenda takes shape. In Year 2, when donors are forced to disclose their names, they vanish and the fund shuts down.

The new pile of money is Andrew's reelection fund. His mountain of cash rises from $10 million to $20 million to $47 million, more by far than any other governor in America has raised. Big real estate developers write big checks for it, some seemingly clustered around passage of a bill bestowing tens of millions of dollars in tax breaks for the developers' new Manhattan residential towers. This is just one of the questionable deals that the Moreland commission is exploring when Andrew shuts it down. So far he manages to remain untouched by it, but the U.S. attorney for the Southern District of New York, Preet Bharara, has swooped in to take on the Moreland's investigations and pursue any possible improprieties both in how it was run and how it was shut down. The governor, Bharara implies, will not be above prosecutorial scrutiny.

Andrew is a complex fellow, with deep incongruities: a progressive in some ways but a pragmatist in others, a good guy to some and a villain to others. He has flaws—and possibly, with his need to control, a Shakespearian tragic flaw. Yet he is also a protean figure of enormous potential, winning passage of bills that matter, a master politician of charm and brute force. As fascinating as his story is so far, it grows more so at each turn, as the stakes grow higher and a gifted politician angles for the ultimate prize.

For now, despite his setbacks, Andrew Cuomo remains the most powerful and prominent governor in the country, a prince in waiting. This is the story of how he got there, and how he struggles to stay at the top of his game.

CHAPTER 2

The Men in the Family

In the heart of Queens, almost at the pinpoint center of that sprawling borough of ethnic neighborhoods east of Manhattan, lies an intersection of three quiet, curving residential streets: Pinto, Marengo, and Keno. Two of the three continue on through, so that the intersection appears to be the hub of five streets, a pleasing pentagon of open space, with only an occasional car. A nine-year-old boy will see it immediately for what it is: an asphalt green, perfect for a pickup game of baseball.

On almost every summer day of 1967, Andrew Cuomo was one of the boys playing in that intersection with his ball and mitt. The world beyond was bristling with danger and change, from war in the Middle East and Vietnam to San Francisco's Summer of Love, but the enclave of Holliswood, Queens, remained untouched by that ferment. Andrew and his friends—Frank Vitale and Bob Caracciolo, Bill Di Angelo and Frank Perillo—pondered why the Yankees were doing so badly, and why the Mets were doing worse. They were a close-knit group within a mostly Italian neighborhood, one reason why Andrew, as a politician, would always have a small, tight circle of advisers—advisers who seemed, like his baseball buddies, a bit rough around the edges, still exuding more than a little street swagger. The other reason lay one block away.

Shortly after Andrew's birth, Mario and Matilda Cuomo had moved into the new Cape Cod–style wood-frame house at 19607 Pompeii Avenue where they would raise all five of their children, from Margaret, born in 1955, to Andrew (1957), Maria (1962), Madeline (1964), and Christopher (1970). The house was one of four built by Mario's father, Andrea, and a cousin. Mario bought it for $28,000. It made a perfect home for a growing family, and to both Mario and Matilda, family was all. Friends came over, but no one really penetrated the domestic circle. Family loyalties were sacrosanct. In their respective turns as governor, both Mario and

Andrew would confide their closest secrets only to family and a few long-time advisers who had become family.

The Cuomo house was tucked into a curve on Pompeii, and seemed from the street far too small for a growing family, set as it was atop a one-car garage, with a bay window that spanned much of its front. But the living room went back to a dining table and ample kitchen—the heart of the home—and a television den, along with Mario and Matilda's bedroom. Upstairs were the children's bedrooms; below was the finished basement, with a very sixties-style pool table and bar. Andrew would spend a lot of his adolescent Saturday nights in that basement, playing pool with his pals.

Attached to the back of the house was a chimney—not a fireplace chimney, just a humble outlet for the heating system—and extending from it, at regulation height, was a basketball hoop. There, Andrew played highly competitive one-on-one with his friends and, most fiercely of all, with his father. The grass under that hoop was long gone, worn to dirt by those gladiatorial games.

The Cuomos lived in Hollis*wood*, not Hollis or Hollis Hills, and that made all the difference. Hollis, south of Hillside Avenue, was wide, flat former farmland, its row houses colonized by immigrants. By 1967, many of those new arrivals were black. The streets could be dangerous, and there was gunfire at night. Northeast lay Hollis Hills, the most affluent of the three, but with no subway station or Long Island Rail Road train stop; that put off commuters and families with children.

Holliswood was a lot safer than Hollis, and more convenient than Hollis Hills, with a subway station not far from its western border of 188th Street. It had excellent public schools, two Catholic churches and two synagogues, and those winding, leafy streets that made Holliswood feel less like a suburb than an Italian village.

Not by chance did the streets bear names like Palermo, Marengo, Sancho, Rio, and Pompeii. Holliswood's turn-of-the-century developer, Frederick W. Dunton, a bank founder, had chosen them himself. When he cleared the 136 acres of forest that would accommodate his vision, he left lots of mature trees, including some in intersections, to enhance the future neighborhood's rural feel. Dunton died in 1931 before the last of the lots were sold, and the Depression somewhat downgraded the class of homeowner he'd hoped to attract. For Andrea Cuomo, father of Mario and patriarch of a future political dynasty, Holliswood was a step up, his American dream come true. One day in 1949, while his wife was back in Europe visiting family, Andrea left his corner grocery in South Jamaica and made the decision, on his own, to buy his family a small Dutch colonial on Rio Drive. Italian husbands of that generation didn't consult their wives about where they wished to live; they just provided. And so Holliswood became the Cuomo family's world.

The house on Rio was five blocks from the Cuomo house on Pompeii. Andrew and his sisters headed over to their grandparents' a great deal, bringing groceries, or picking up a home-cooked pie. Both Andrea and Immaculata spoke limited English. Andrea, semiretired by now from the store, was as stern with Andrew as he'd been with Mario. "Puncha puncha puncha," he'd say, waving his fist. Which translated roughly as: *Life is tough, you have to keep your guard up, keeping punching all the time.* Andrea razzed Andrew as soon as he saw him. *Why are you doing it this way? What's wrong with you?* Every Saturday, Andrea took his old maroon Mercedes-Benz down to the B&G gas station on Hillside Avenue, where everyone in Holliswood brought their cars. The owner's son, George Haggerty Jr., was a pal of Andrew's. Andrea razzed him too.

"Andrea was fond of my father," recalled Haggerty Jr. "So he would pull in to chat, blocking all the pumps at the same time. When I asked for the keys so I could move it and check under the hood, I'd wisecrack and tell him I'd take it for a test ride. He would give it right back at me in his broken Italian-English that I wasn't smart enough to work on such a car. I would ask my father, 'Why does he treat me that way?' And my father would say, 'Because he likes you.' "

Andrew would grow up with the echo of his father's and grandfather's stern words, and with their grim ambition—perhaps not so much to succeed as not to fail. He would be as stern with those around him, notoriously so, and many would hate him for it, but in his mind, he would be passing on his family's work ethic—*puncha, puncha, puncha.* As for his own ambition, which so many would see as overweening, it would seem to him merely taking to heart his father's and grandfather's admonitions.

Andrea was the patriarch, but strictly speaking, he wasn't an immigrant son: by a fluke, he was born in the United States. Andrea's father, Donato, had come from Italy to Brooklyn in 1896 as a woodcutter, set on staying only long enough to make a peasant's fortune and take it home. His wife was with him, and Andrea was born in 1901, before the family's return to Italy in 1904. Back in Nocera Superiore, a mountain village outside Salerno in southern Italy, Donato used his windfall to build a new home and open a little cantina.

Andrea was too young to be pressed into army service in World War I. Instead, in his twenties, he moved to another village, Tramonti, and found work in the sprawling orchards, vineyards, and fields of a well-to-do family, the Giordanos. Andrea courted, and won, one of the Giordanos' six daughters, setting an example that the next two generations of Cuomo men would follow: marrying women wealthier than they.

That Andrea managed to win Immaculata's heart was impressive. Villagers rarely trusted strangers—"*forestieri*"—even from another village in the Mezzogiorno region, as southern Italy is known. Andrea would bring that wariness with him back to America and pass it on to his sons.

Immigration laws had tightened in the United States since Donato's trip, and Mussolini's diktats made the passage harder still. But Andrea had his trump card: a U.S. passport. With it, and hopes of greater success, he sailed to New York in 1926. Immaculata, pregnant, stayed behind until Andrea got settled and she delivered her child. In Jersey City, an uncle offered work of sorts: backbreaking manual labor five days a week, and guard duty on the weekends, all for about twenty dollars of take-home pay. Andrea took it; speaking virtually no English, he felt he had no choice.

Immaculata arrived in 1927 with an infant son, Frank. Soon came a daughter, Marie, and a second son who died in infancy. Devastated by their loss, and seeing no end to destitution in Jersey City, Andrea and Immaculata decided to leave in 1931, whatever the risks. In the grip of the Great Depression, they moved to a neighborhood in Queens called South Jamaica, where Andrea put his hopes and modest savings into starting a neighborhood grocery like his father's cantina back in Italy.

South Jamaica was a stronghold for Italian immigrants, and family markets were the heart of its neighborhoods. Andrea and Immaculata found a promising corner site at 150th Street and 97th Avenue, directly across the street from Abbott Wire, a factory that made refrigerator wiring. A sweater factory was nearby. Along with sandwiches for the workers, the Cuomos offered Italian specialties from provolone to prosciutto. The family lived upstairs. Mario, born in 1932, would recall, among his earliest memories, making forts with twenty-pound macaroni boxes in the grocery's storeroom, and making peashooters from tubular pasta and dried peas.

The corner groceries in that long-ago time offered much more than provisions. Andrea booked passage to and from Italy for many of his customers. He sold stamps, and handled letters to and from the old country; the store was many new arrivals' first mailing address. He cashed checks, and sold subway and bus tokens. He also extended credit, keeping a list of sums due in a black marbled notebook. "Not everyone had a telephone in their house," recalled Tony Gallo, whose grandparents had a corner grocery near Andrea's. "You used to have to go to the grocery store if you had to make a phone call." In its own way, Andrea's store was the start of a political dynasty.

Andrea worked almost every waking hour, so that, as Mario later recalled, his feet bled through the soles of his shoes. What went along with that dogged persistence was a strict sense of right and wrong, a code to live by. "Don't fool around with women—only your wife. Don't ever hurt anybody. And don't steal. Just do your work."

Life at the corner store was all work, joyless and without end. A young Mario spent much of his preschool time alone in the back while his parents stayed up front. When he did start school, he spoke almost no English, and was ostracized, a painful experience that stayed with him for life. Even after he mastered the language, he felt cut off and wounded by ethnic slights. He developed a temperament of brooding introspection: one part shyness, one part self-hate, as he put it, and one part guilt at the sacrifice his parents were making every day on his behalf.

Smart and driven, Mario was a star student right through law school at St. John's University. He was then shocked to learn that none of the top law firms in Manhattan would hire a St. John's graduate, even a stellar one, whose last name ended in a vowel. He ended up in Brooklyn, in a firm on Court Street, in a sea of ethnic lawyers. He never got over the rejection. Years later at a dinner hosted by Abe Rosenthal, the executive editor of the *New York Times*, feminist Gloria Steinem importuned the governor to pardon private-school headmistress Jean Harris, who had shot her lover to death in a jealous rage. "You rich people are all alike," Mario exploded. "You think she should get a pass because she's one of you. Well let me tell you, I know what it's like to grow up poor and have no one give you a break." He went on in this fashion for some time. Finally Mort Janklow, the literary agent, cut him off. "You think you're the only guy who had it hard?" Janklow told him. "I grew up in a working-class family, I worked my way through school. In fact, I went to the same junior high in South Jamaica that you did." He pointed to his host. "And Abe went to City College. Everyone at this table is self-made." Cuomo was stunned.

Mario was seventeen when his father moved the family to the house at 188-17 Rio Drive in Holliswood. Not many Italians had yet crossed the Maginot line of Hillside Avenue. More than one Cuomo relative in South Jamaica muttered that Andrea and Immaculata had abandoned their roots; their new WASPy neighbors, on the other hand, bemoaned the ethnic arrivals. One went so far as to ask the Cuomos to be sure they put lids on their garbage pails.

Andrea maintained his long hours at the store—the whole family did, often staying until late after dinner—and so it was as a family that the Cuomos returned one night to find that a storm had taken down a forty-foot-tall blue spruce in the front yard of their new home. The felled trunk stretched to the street, its root bed torn from the ground. Mario and his brother Frank assumed there was nothing to be done but have the tree removed. Andrea had a different view. "We gonna push 'im up," he declared.

The children groaned, but Andrea found rope in the house, looped it around the tree near the top, and with his sons' help pulled the tree upright. Then he dug a deep, muddy pit to give the root bed plenty of room. Miraculously, the tree survived, a living symbol of Andrea's stubborn determination. Mario was so touched by the experience that he published a children's story about it, "The Blue Spruce."

In his semiretirement, Andrea took to chiseling castle-shaped statues out of stone—a craft perhaps learned from his father—and planting them in the front yard near the blue spruce for his children and grandchildren. In 2009, long after Andrea's death, the man who now owned the Rio Drive house placed a call to Mario to offer him the last remaining castle on the property. The next day the man was startled by a call from his wife: there was a man in the front yard, digging up the statue with a shovel. It was, he realized, Attorney General Andrew Cuomo. The statue, Andrew later said, was hard to dislodge. But it meant a lot.

From one generation to the next, the deep, tangled bonds of fathers and sons marked and in many ways haunted the Cuomo clan. All fathers and sons regard each other with complex and contradictory emotions, but somehow the Cuomos had more of all of them. Andrea and then Mario inspired their sons yet often quashed their spirits. They loved their sons, somewhere deep down, but worked too hard to have much time to show it. Instead, they lectured and chastised, as if finding fault *was* showing love, which for them in fact it was. All the while the sons struggled to understand their fathers, and the hurt those fathers had left, as their sons tried to understand them. There were, as Matilda Cuomo acknowledged years later, a lot of hurt feelings.

In the summer of 1967, nine-year-old Andrew saw almost nothing of his father during the week: Mario had been drawn, as a Brooklyn lawyer, into a fierce community battle, leading local residents in a fight against city hall. He worked long weekdays and evenings, Saturdays too. He would have worked all Sunday if Matilda had let him. Sunday dinner was where she drew the line. It was sacrosanct.

Mario had made his name as a people's lawyer in another battle, representing a group of scrap-metal dealers who plied their trade in the dank, befouled neighborhood of Willets Point, Queens—once the site of the ash heaps that Nick Carraway drives through in *The Great Gatsby*. Robert Moses, the all-powerful "master builder" of New York highways, bridges, and parks, had sought to have the dealers' little patch of land condemned so that it could be renovated and added to Flushing Meadows Park, site of the 1964 World's Fair. Mario went up against Moses—and the city—in court, and won. The scrap-metal dealers could stay.

The largely Italian neighborhood of Corona, Queens, was threatened in a different way. The city wanted to raze sixty-nine homes to accommodate a high school and an athletic field. Corona seemed a lost cause, the plans set, appeals exhausted by late 1970, until a newspaper columnist named Jimmy Breslin starting writing about a community lawyer named Mario Cuomo who kept battling city hall. As Cuomo's star rose, the city began negotiating, and Mario worked that much harder.

Andrew, now thirteen, took to pulling a prank that amused him to no end. When the gruff, profane Breslin called, Andrew would answer and pretend to be Mario. It was easy, since Breslin did most of the talking and Andrew could answer, "Yup . . . yup . . . yup," just as his father would. He could even lower his voice to make it sound like his father's. Before long there would be no faking it; Andrew's voice, and his father's, would be uncannily similar: the same harsh, flat outer-borough vowels, the same rough timbre and tone. Already Andrew's was close enough that he could fool Breslin for a good minute or two, until Andrew burst into laughter and the furious newspaperman started swearing at him. It was a great shtick, if somewhat poignant: the son imitating the father who wasn't there.

In most other ways, Andrew had the same cheerful childhood as his neighborhood pals. He attended a Jesuit school, St. Gerard Majella, on 188th Street and 91st Avenue. After school he played in the streets or did errands for spare change. If a neighbor needed groceries delivered, Andrew might haul them and get a twenty-five-cent tip. "That was a big deal," recalled Tony Gallo. "You could get a slice of pizza and a drink for a quarter." Every Sunday he went with his family to church. Mario as a college student had nearly joined the priesthood, before meeting Matilda. He was a serious Catholic, also an intellectual one, who cited as his heroes Saint Thomas More and twentieth-century philosopher Pierre Teilhard de Chardin. Andrew absorbed those influences, and never stopped going to church. As secretary of HUD, he would have his driver drop him off at St. Dominic's, across from the agency, almost every morning before going in to work, for a few minutes of prayers and meditation, while the driver, a fellow Catholic, waited in the car. More than once, Andrew would ask him, "Isn't there something you want to talk to God about?"

Sunday was Andrew's favorite day. That was when his father was home. After church, father and son might play basketball in the backyard, either games of HORSE or one-on-one. Andrew was growing into a tall, athletic kid, but Mario was far more powerful. In his youth, his prowess at baseball had earned him a contract with a Pittsburgh Pirates farm team, and if not for a serious injury, crashing into the outfield wall as he went for a catch, he might have spent more than the one season he did in the pros. In his late thirties, Mario was still a formidable athlete—and a very competitive one. Under the backyard hoop, he pulled down rebounds with his elbows out, and Andrew had to learn to give as good as he got.

Often on those Sunday afternoons, father and son settled into the den together and watched sports on television, or watched shows after dinner as a family: one of his sisters' heads, Andrew later recalled, was always in front, blocking the view. Dinner itself, at the table off the kitchen, was usually one of Matilda's Italian dishes. There Mario presided as the hard-charging lawyer he was, questioning the children on issues of the day, demanding their opinions, then answering his own questions before they could. When he first ran for office, he would madden his staff with these Jesuitical interrogations. A generation later, Andrew would do the same. They were in fact a Greek rhetorical device called anthypophora, in which the speaker answers his own questions. *Was it the best deal I could get for the scrap dealers? Maybe not. Was it the best under the circumstances? Absolutely. Do I wish I could do more for them? Yes. Do I think there's any more that anyone I could do? No.* And so it went.

Later, Andrew would seem of two minds about whether those Sundays made up for the rest of the week. "My father was not physically around much," he told one interviewer. "He'll admit it, depending on the day." Mario himself told a friend, as Andrew was graduating from high school, that he wasn't sure how his son was doing. "I really don't know. I haven't spent a lot of time with him in the last four years. I guess I've taken him to two or three ball games. Matilda made me take him." And when they did see each other, there wasn't much physical affection between father and son: it just wasn't done, either by Mario or his father before him. Andrea was working too hard. Immaculata wasn't built that way either. "I won three damned governor's races," Mario said years later, "and she never said a thing about them. She never said, 'How nice.' Never gave me a hug and a kiss."

There was, in those words, more than a trace of self-pity. That was one trait Mario didn't pass down. When the journalist Ken Auletta asked a twenty-five-year-old Andrew if he had resented his father's absences, Andrew said, "I guess I never expected him to be there more than he was... What he was doing was important, and he was here when he wasn't working. It wasn't as if he was going to the ball game on Sunday with the guys." Anyway, Andrew added, "Who the hell was I to resent it? I never expected more. To resent, you have to expect something."

Andrew may have meant just that, but it didn't ring true. What son expected nothing from his father? Especially from one who set such a high bar? Mario was self-made and well-read, an intellectual, philosopher, lawyer, *and* law professor, now a public advocate who made the papers. Andrew as he grew up would try his hardest to win approval from this daunting figure. What he expected, or hoped for, was praise. Yet his efforts often went unseen by the father who wasn't there—the father who when he did come home was too self-absorbed to pay his son much mind. Ever after, Andrew would keep trying to reach that bar, yet never quite feel he'd earned his father's unconditional love at last. And mixed in with the frustration would be the resentment he said he didn't feel—resentment that drove him not only to match his father's achievements but surpass them. The key to that family dynamic was Andrea, the noble immigrant, too busy working to play with his sons. Mario was the same way. Later, as a young father, Andrew would do as his father and grandfather had done. Only after his marriage fell apart would he learn how to be a different kind of father to his daughters.

In Mario's absence, Matilda ran the household and in her calm, empathetic way had more to do with shaping her son than Mario did. "Matilda was *the* formative influence on Andrew," recalled Dino Amoroso, a longtime family friend and Brooklyn prosecutor. Andrew felt the same way. "She did the family," he told Auletta. "She used to take me to Boy Scouts meetings. She was the only woman; everyone else came with their father."

Matilda Raffa was Brooklyn-born, a daughter of Sicilian immigrants who had arrived as poor as the Cuomos but done quite well. A self-educated carpenter, Charlie Raffa had gone from cabinets to refrigerator cases, then landed a government contract in World War II to make life rafts for the U.S. Navy on a "cost plus" basis: whatever the rafts cost him, the federal government would pay, along with a profit. After the war he'd started buying commercial real estate—a store here, a vacant lot there. "One day Andrew said, 'You want to come with me? I have to run an errand,'" Tony Gallo remembered. "We're driving down Atlantic Avenue in some area of Brooklyn. Andrew starts saying, 'My grandfather owns this, he owns that.' Finally I say, 'Your grandfather owns a lot.' Andrew says, 'Yeah, but they're all empty now because the rental market is soft.'"

Still, Charlie Raffa had more than the proceeds of a corner grocery, and Mario had felt somewhat defensive in asking Matilda to marry him—enough that he spent his entire sign-up bonus of $2,000 from the Pittsburgh Pirates on an engagement ring for her. In his first years after law school, he worked long hours for maximum pay, just to prove to Matilda and her parents that he could. Andrew as a young lawyer would embark on his own phase of proving he could make good money, but it wouldn't turn out that well.

For Andrew, Mario was the challenging, hard-to-please parent, questioning his every opinion and pushing him to do better in school, as his own father had done with him. The Cuomo legend-burnishers would paint a picture of this as the typical mid-twentieth-century American father-and-son relationship: loving disciplinarian, dutiful son. The truth was darker, insisted more than one family friend: Mario was brutally critical.

Matilda was Mario's foil and Andrew's protector, warm and accepting. Andrew loved helping his mother: when her clothes dryer broke, he famously took it apart in the basement, identified the broken part, ordered the new part, and put the machine back together again. When Mario was away, Matilda told Andrew he was the man of the house, and Andrew, swelling with pride, did whatever was needed to maintain that honor, from doing errands to helping his sisters. "I was the oldest boy with all girls, taking care of the house, helping my mother with things," he said later. "I didn't have it easy. My father was not the governor of New York. He was '*come si chiama*' [breaking his balls]!"

To those who knew the family well, each parent's influence on Andrew was clearly apparent. By the age of thirteen, Andrew was a big, athletic kid, somewhat cocky, brandishing an outer-borough toughness and challenging those around him, even on occasion his teachers. That was his father, especially Mario as a young man; as a lawyer, he'd smoothed his edges, though they were still there, along with his elbows. Sometimes a quietness would come over Andrew and he could seem almost shy: a boy who could surprise with his thoughtfulness, an empathetic friend. That was his mother.

When he was twelve, Andrew's parents presented him with a baby brother, Christopher. Andrew was thrilled. "The face on Andrew when he saw that baby," Matilda later said, "it was like I had given him the world." In his family of sisters, Andrew had often wished he had a brother; now that wish had come true. He took charge of Christopher, changing his diapers, bathing and feeding him. The bond between the brothers grew only stronger with time.

"Andrew...made things okay," Christopher explained later. "Either he protected you physically or emotionally, or, you know, just told you how to get through things." Andrew taught Christopher how to protect himself. "When Johnny Toscanni used to roll me down the hill, calling me the Human Meatball, Andrew went and took care of it," Christopher recalled. "When my pop got elected and I started getting beaten up in school more often...Andrew was there...It's actually difficult to talk about him and not to cry."

Yet Andrew could also be tough with Christopher, as tough as his father and grandfather had been with him. Years later, as a television reporter, Christopher would leave his job at ABC coanchoring the show *20/20* to go to CNN because, friends said, Andrew mocked him for being a lightweight. But merely going to CNN wouldn't do the trick: one colleague recalled being shocked, after an on-air story Christopher had done, when he took a cell phone call from his brother and started cringing under Andrew's withering review.

Andrew, it was all too clear, was acting as a father to Christopher, giving him the tough love and constant support that Mario wasn't there to mete out. Mario was a role model, saving neighborhoods, but too absorbed to be the father his sons wanted him to be. For Andrew, being a surrogate father to Christopher was one way to ease the hurt he felt.

Eventually he would find another: helping save his father's political career.

After St. Gerard, Andrew could have attended the local public high school. But for upwardly striving families of Holliswood, especially Italian families, the far better choice—the only real choice—was Archbishop Molloy. One of the most admired Catholic high schools in Queens, Molloy was selective, with a rigorous entrance exam and a modest tuition that parents were proud to scrape up. Even Mario was ebullient with praise on the day Andrew was accepted.

Molloy was a half-hour commute from Holliswood: first the bus down Hillside Avenue from 197th Street, then the E or F subway to Van Wyck Boulevard. Andrew would emerge to the ceaseless traffic of the Van Wyck Expressway on one side, and on his other the large, graceless brick building that was Molloy. The school had only occupied that site and borne that name since 1957, when Archbishop Thomas Molloy relocated a small Marist school in Manhattan called St. Ann's Academy, which was spilling from its seams, to the church-owned parcel by the highway.

Molloy was still an all-boys' school when Andrew entered its ninth grade in 1971. A majority of its students were Italian—they'd overtaken the Irish—though a few Hispanic students were starting a new wave. Among its alums were dozens of standout college basketball players, a tradition that would continue right up through Russ Smith, a member of the NCAA Championship–winning 2013 Louisville Cardinals. Ray Kelly, the former New York City police commissioner, was a graduate. So was former Kings County district attorney Charles Hynes, tennis great Vitas Gerulaitis, actor David Caruso, and homeless advocate Robert Hayes.

The dress code at Molloy had softened since the early 1960s: shirt and tie and dress pants, but no blue blazer. Discipline was more relaxed too—but only by so much. No knuckles were rapped with rulers, though the Marist Brothers did have a paddle that could be applied to the backsides of unruly students, and there was a dean of discipline who could, and did, expel repeat offenders. Tony Gallo, who started Molloy at the same time Andrew did, says the more typical disciplinary measure was "skull-fucking." If a student was out of line, Gallo recalled, "The brother would say, 'Meet me in the gym after school.' It would be boxing or wrestling. He would take his collar off and say, 'Do you really want to do this?' The underlying message was: 'since we're meeting in the gym, this isn't teacher-student, it's mano a mano.' They would play with your head and make you think things out."

Molloy was a large school, with the highest academic standards, and Andrew may have been somewhat daunted by it. One classmate recalled him as "fairly quiet, not a troublemaker... but not a student leader either. Not a political leader or student government type." Andrew did take Advanced Placement courses in history and English, and then, along with generations of "Stanners," as the former St. Anners were known, he had the good fortune to take John Diorio's government class.

Diorio had come out of Manhattan ward politics and brought his fascination with government into the classroom. He took his students through the U.S. Constitution and all its amendments, the three branches of government and how they balanced each other, with a special focus on the U.S. Supreme Court. The honor of public service was a recurring theme, and to help make his case, Diorio was forever bringing in powerful local figures whom he knew from his ward days, from U.S. Senator Joe Addabbo to Judge Sol Wachtler. Andrew wasn't his top student—high 80s, low 90s—but Diorio liked him a lot. "I thought if I had a son, I would like him to be like that," Diorio said later. "He had confidence in himself, definitely wasn't a bully but he stood his ground on things. Socially, he was popular with girls—like at dances, because it was all boys here."

Despite his prowess at basketball, Andrew knew better than to try for the team: Molloy's was one of the best in the city. He did keep playing at home. At sixteen, he could throw his share of sharp elbows. Often when Tony Gallo came by on the weekends, Mario would press him into a game, and the results were almost always painful. "Hey, I'm a kid!" Gallo would cry out as Mario bulled by him for a layup.

"If you don't know how to play the game, get off the court," Mario would exclaim.

Andrew didn't try out for Molloy's baseball team either, though John Diorio thought he might have made it. With his parents on his case, he focused on his studies and, in his free time, earning money. At fourteen he launched a landscaping business. Everyone in Holliswood had a front lawn, a lawn that had to be neatly trimmed lest the neighbors start to talk. Andrew's pitch was simple but effective: "We clip you good."

For fun, when they had time for it, Andrew and his pals went from basketball in the Cuomos' backyard to Robert Caracciolo's house to play handball in his garage. At some point Robert's garage suddenly offered a huge new appeal: a 1971 black-and-white Oldsmobile Cutlass Supreme 442.

Andrew had shown an aptitude already for tinkering with machines. Probably his first exposure to muscle cars was through his next-door neighbors, the Capolongos, Dennis, Neil, and Al. One had a 1967 Corvette; another had put a turbocharger on a Corvair; a third had a 1957 Chevy. Andrew began hanging out in their two-car garage, and little by little, the Capolongos began letting him help.

For that education, Robert Caracciolo's Cutlass Supreme was a huge step forward. Now Andrew and his close pals could spend hours at a time making small adjustments, learning how to tell when the sounds were right. Of the three of them, Andrew, Tony, and Robert, Robert was the most gifted mechanic. He had a large tool collection, thanks to his father, a machinist for the New York City Transit Authority. But Andrew wasn't far behind. Eventually he would be able to diagnose a car's problem by sound alone. "In mechanics, that is really Jedi level," his brother, Christopher, would explain. "It's a gift."

One day, Matilda brought Andrew down to the B&G Esso station on Hillside Avenue where she always took her car. Andrew was about fourteen. "I want to find something for Andrew to do," she told George Haggerty, the co-owner. George turned to his son, who was Andrew's age. "Take your shirt off," he said. George Jr. took off his B&G shirt. His father threw it at Andrew. "Okay, you're working."

After school and on weekends, Andrew rode his bike down to B&G to pump gas, wash windshields, and keep the place clean. George Haggerty, who owned the station with Bob Gianino (the B in B&G) was as tough on his son and Andrew as each Cuomo generation was on the next. "You couldn't stand around," George Jr. explained. "If you did, he would find a task much worse than you could ever invent for yourself." The worst of the worst was the grease barrel.

When a car was up on the lift, the mechanic would shoot oil grease into the fittings with a pneumatic gun. The gun was connected to a hose that drew the oil from a fifty-five-gallon drum that stood in a small dark room at the rear of the garage. A vacuum mechanism inserted into the barrel drew the oil up and sucked it through the hose. But it couldn't reach the last few inches of grease in the barrel; it didn't go that low. George's father wanted to use that last bit of grease before buying another full barrel, so one of the boys—whoever was standing around—would have to go into the back room, take a plastic scoop, bend from the waist down into the barrel, and start scooping up that residue. Andrew at least was tall enough to do it on his own. George was so short that a big mechanic would have to lower him headfirst into the barrel, holding him by the ankles, to do the scooping. "It was awful work," Haggerty recalled with a shudder. "You would do anything to avoid the grease barrel: get a razor knife and square off the boxes... or take some Esso-white paint and paint the curbing again, and the arrows on the driveway and aprons—anything."

It was a different time for cars. There were so many more tasks: more oil changes, more tune-ups, more belts and hoses and radiators and thermostats to be checked and replaced. Andrew did some of this, but not too much. He was young, and it wasn't what interested him. "He was more a thinker and a tinkerer," Haggerty explained. "The more technical stuff was what we wanted to learn. How do you replace a camshaft? And if we change it and it has a different ratio, how does that affect the performance of the car? That's the stuff that grabbed us."

Andrew and George lived for the after hours, when the station closed at last—not at 5 p.m., but whenever the final jobs were done—and George Sr. resolutely headed home. That was when the younger mechanics, five or six years older than Andrew and George, brought their own cars by and popped the hoods. "It was like the midwestern hardware store where the guys congregate and talk politics and sports," Haggerty recalled. "They would bring pizzas and we would talk."

Weekends had a rhythm of their own. B&G's regular customers came by, one after another, not just for gas but to check the oil and put air in the tires. "Wash and wipe it down?" George and Andrew would ask hopefully, and if the customers nodded, it meant they would head across the street to the luncheonette for breakfast, giving their keys to the boys so the boys could bring the cars over to them. "You wanted to bring the car over, park it by the luncheonette, and give them back their keys," Haggerty explained. "Because then you would get a tip. You didn't get much of a salary; the tip was all."

Andrea came down every Saturday and parked his car sideways between the pumps, just to make the boys move it for him. Mario would come down early; he was usually good for a luncheonette run. If he didn't, then Matilda would come in with her three daughters in the car, dressed up for a trip to the mall, and Christopher, still a baby, in an open box. "She would give me a quarter, that was a good tip," Haggerty recalled. "And then another quarter because she knew her father-in-law had just been in, breaking my shoes."

Matilda was grateful to the Haggertys, but as time went on she began to worry. "Andrew was such a good worker at his part-time job at the gas station that the owner wanted to set him up in business," she recalled later. "I had to go to the man—I never told Andrew this—and I said, 'Please don't do this to us, we want him to go to law school.'" In fact, neither the Cuomos nor the Haggertys were going to let their sons become auto mechanics. George's father, like the Cuomo men, wanted to keep their boys on track. "Their feeling was that you had to work," said Haggerty, "because if you didn't, you were going to become a bank robber. They acted as if there was a competition for our very souls."

Andrew's own first car was his father's, a late-1960s maroon Mercedes-Benz four-door sedan handed down from Andrea. He would go on to a red Trans Am, then a sky blue 1975 Corvette. He bought others, fixed them up, and sold them for a profit: a 1969 Cougar, a 1969 Fiat 128, a 1973 Camaro.

Years later, Andrew would still be working on cars, but as a weekend respite from the pressures of work. "You tend to deal, day to day, with people and the complexity of people," he would reflect. "When you are dealing with mechanical issues, you are dealing with an engine. It's not emotional. You are not dealing with feelings. If there is a problem, there is a solution and it's right in front of you."

Mario was busier than ever, in a new way: running for office. With a compromise won in the battle of Corona versus city hall, he had made a first, unfortunate stab in 1973 at running for mayor—a campaign stopped before it could begin when a key Queens power broker yanked his support. A run for lieutenant governor the next year had gone hardly better. But at least it was a statewide race, and Mario, though he lost, stayed in from start to finish. That gave Andrew a chance to help.

Young, agile, and willing, Andrew was assigned to put up political posters for his father—and tear down those of Mario's primary rivals. Andrew and his pals Tony Gallo and Robert Caracciolo would meet after dinner with posters and staple guns and start shimmying up telephone poles to staple posters together around the poles. "It's a lost art," Andrew would say later. When the boys got back to Pompeii Avenue at 9 or 10 p.m., Matilda would have more food waiting. Sometimes they'd find Mario at the table with local politicos and listen in. The talk was intoxicating. The men at the table knew everyone, and as they traded wisecracks, Andrew drank in a new sense of what politics was: not the ancient history of Mr. Diorio's class, but the experience of power.

For all the posters Andrew put up, they couldn't paper over the truth that Mario in his first full-length campaign was an ineffectual candidate. He had no rationale for running, he admitted later, especially not for such a lightweight job as lieutenant governor. He hated glad-handing commuters at train stations and making speeches at union picnics. He and Hugh Carey, the man he was running to serve, had had a serious falling-out, the latest twist in an up-and-down relationship that would end in deep distrust. Yet as he lost soundly, political observers on both sides agreed: the man had a knack for public speaking. It was more than that. Eloquent and forceful, he could connect.

As much to co-opt a potential threat as to harness a rising star, newly elected governor Carey offered Cuomo his pick of appointed positions. Cuomo surprised him by choosing secretary of state, a hitherto backwater post Cuomo soon turned into a very public campaign to rein in lobbyists. No one doubted that Cuomo had a bright political future; the only question was whether he'd stay loyal to Carey or go his own way.

Andrew at eighteen was as tall as his father, and just as powerfully built. He himself would laughingly describe his features as crude. It was true that he had a prominent nose, with flaring nostrils, though as prominent noses went, it was well shaped. His eyes were dark and intense—combatively so, it often seemed—framed by thick brows and a full head of nearly black, corkscrew-curly hair. Composed, he had an earnest, almost angelic look. But when he grinned, which was often, his teeth were large enough, his grin wide enough that he looked almost roguish.

Later in life, that grin would carve deep lines that dominated his appearance. He wouldn't be handsome in any conventional sense, but that face would emanate confidence, and curiosity, and force of character. At some angles, in certain pictures, he looked rather dashing. At others, he looked harsh, almost homely. Mercurial looks were hardly a boon for a politician; smooth, pleasing features that stayed the same from side to side, angle to angle, were far better for the job. But there was a grittiness about Andrew's appearance that perhaps did him more of a favor than standard good looks. He had had opportunities because of his father, and he would have more, and yet there was in that rough demeanor a ghost of the immigrant, bent over his labor, like his grandfather Andrea, ready to work as hard as he could.

Andrew was a high school senior when his father ran for lieutenant governor and lost, but still a senior when Mario became secretary of state. Eagerly, John Diorio pressed Andrew to get his father as Molloy's commencement speaker that June of 1975. Mario delivered, which left Andrew both proud and self-conscious as his father held forth. Seeing father and son together, Diorio realized that Andrew already was mimicking his dad. Mario sat with his legs crossed and hands folded over his knees; so did Andrew. The voice, its timbre and tone: Andrew had it down.

For summer, Matilda had vowed that Andrew would do more than hang out as a grease monkey at the B&G garage. One June, he had signed on to work at Testani's, the mason who lived down the street. Testani would have his high school helpers break up old cement driveways and put the broken chunks into the back of his truck, then build new ones. Andrew didn't last more than a few weeks—no one did. He was carrying two bags of cement, and was apparently dehydrated; a friend recalled him keeling over, passed out. So back he went to the B&G.

On the evenings when he wasn't down at B&G's station, Andrew might head over with friends to the movie theater on Jamaica Avenue, the Commonwealth, and afterward to a large bar called the Community Gardens, which had live entertainment and a billiards hall upstairs. Andrew was legal: his father hadn't yet become governor and raised the drinking age. A slice of pizza at Lorenzo's across the street finished the evening off nicely.

Saturday Night Fever wouldn't appear for a couple more years, but Andrew Cuomo would have a lot in common with Tony Manero. Both were Italian-American kids from the outer boroughs, swaggering though earnest underneath, both rooted in their neighborhoods but eyeing Manhattan as Oz beyond the bridges. Andrew would probably hate the analogy as much as he did disco, but there would be something to it. He came from a higher class than Tony Manero, with some vague hopes of being a lawyer or politician, not a standout on a disco dance floor. But like Tony, he was a brash innocent with an outer-borough accent and youthful ambitions.

Andrew was in fact rougher in manner than his father, and there was an inverse logic to that. Mario, son of the first-generation immigrant, had had to be smoother than his father: from a store apron to a tailored suit. Andrew had the luxury of being able to rebel—a bit—against the suit, and the father who wore it.

That fall, at his father's insistence, Andrew enrolled in Le Moyne, a small Jesuit-taught college upstate in Syracuse. Mario thought his son could benefit from a rigorous exposure to Catholic theology, Latin and Greek, and the great philosophers. Andrew couldn't stand it. After a few days, he wanted out. His father urged him to give it a chance. In a rare act of outright defiance, Andrew said no.

Instead, Andrew returned home and enrolled at Fordham University, up in the Bronx. Mario, as secretary of state, was in Albany much of the week; once again, Andrew was the man of the house. He had to take out college loans to pay his tuition: Mario, in order to serve as secretary of state with no conflict of interest, had given up all his law clients, a noble if legally unnecessary choice that left his family scraping to make ends meet. To cover his expenses, Andrew drove the B&G tow truck on weekends for AAA emergency calls.

For all the ambition he would soon be accused of harboring, Andrew had no idea, as a freshman at Fordham, where his life would take him. But that was about to change.

CHAPTER 3

From Andy to Andrew

Fordham was one of the so-called Catholic Ivies, a top-ranked and venerable school, but few of its students had privileged backgrounds. Most were from local, working-class families and lived at home through their college years. So did Andrew, though he lived far enough from Fordham's campus in the Bronx that he had to drive there. To save gas money, he carpooled with another Fordham student from the neighborhood, Rich Mulieri. The first day Richie rolled up to the Cuomo house in his beat-up, smoke-spewing 1967 Chevy, Mario came out and gave him a baleful look. "There has to be something illegal about that." Andrew ragged him too, but was happy to save the mileage on his new blue retooled Corvette.

Fordham's Rose Hill campus was a sanctuary from the city that surrounded it, a postage stamp from an earlier time, with its Edwards Parade greensward and castlelike Keating Hall. As befitted its formal setting and Jesuitical purpose, it had a rigorous core curriculum. To balance his harder subjects, Andrew took Italian. So did Richie. On the first day of class, Richie rattled off a few home-learned phrases from his own Italian family. The teacher gave him a look. "So what slum is your grandfather from?" The Mulieris were from Calabria. Andrew, on the verge of speaking up himself, put his hand down and said not a word.

With Mario up in Albany all week, Andrew continued as man of the house, emulating his father, and so chose to major in political science. For fun, and to stay in top shape, he took up boxing.

Life off campus was for the most part no different from Andrew's high school years. He played a lot of pool with Richie and his Holliswood pals, now more often at pool halls than at home. Menthol cigarettes were for some reason in vogue: Andrew smoked Kools, his friend Bob Caracciolo favored Newports. Weekends, Andrew drove the emergency truck for B&G, handling AAA calls.

"Q-15—that was our AAA region," recalled George Haggerty. "But at night you would get other zones too." On a cold winter's night, with no one's car starting, Andrew might do two dozen or more road calls through an all-night shift. Some cars would be hopeless and need to be towed in. Andrew would tag those, bring the keys back to the shop—along with the shivering drivers—and a tow truck would then head off to bring the car in. Most, though, responded to a few expert tweaks. "You would have a little toolbox, and a thermos of coffee, and a wire brush," explained Haggerty. "A woman who was stuck somewhere, you'd pull up the hood, scrape down the battery contact terminals with the wire brush, start up the car, and give her some coffee." The coffee was the crowning touch. "With that, you were probably good for a dollar or so tip." For Andrew, fifty or sixty dollars a night was worth the cold. All through Fordham and then Albany Law School, Andrew usually did at least the Sunday shift. Which is to say that for quite a few years, from the mid-1970s to the early 1980s, AAA members who lived in the area and called for weekend help very likely got that help in the form of their future governor.

There were on occasion respites from this routine, like the hamburger-eating contest Andrew and Rich staged at the White Castle just outside the Fordham gates. Andrew ate twenty, and won. Of those diversions, the one all its participants most vividly recall was the ill-fated road trip to Florida.

"Andrew organized it," said Tony Gallo.

"It was in February, cold as hell in New York, so we went down there, I think we took Andrew's mother's station wagon," said Robert Caracciolo.

"We put the backseats down," recalled Rich Mulieri, "so two of us slept in the back while the other two were in the front seat."

The four drove eighteen hours straight to Jacksonville. By the time they reached it, Tony was sick of sleeping in the car. They stayed at a motel long enough to get refreshed. Now they were ready for action. Tony went to the front desk and asked for directions to the nearest disco.

"Disco?"

"Yeah, disco, with disco music, a disco ball hanging from the ceiling..."

"Ah!" said the clerk, and directed them "down the road a piece."

To the Queens contingent, down the road a piece meant a few blocks. Twenty-five miles later, they reached the roadhouse the clerk had suggested. A sign outside said DISCO. Inside was a nearly empty space with sawdust on the floor and a stage. "Out onto the stage," recalled Tony, "comes this band we recognized, to our horror: the Royal Guardsmen." A one-hit wonder with a bubblegum pop song titled "Snoopy vs. the Red Baron," the Guardsmen had plummeted to playing roadside dives.

"They had a stuffed Snoopy on the amplifier," Rich Mulieri recalled with a shudder.

Jacksonville was cold—alarmingly, unseasonably so—but the boys held out hope for Miami. They reached South Beach after dark and found one motel after another full up, until they tried one with fake palm trees called the Hawaii Kai. Andrew took the room key—one room for the four of them—and led the way, only to find, when he opened the door, a trio of partially clad college coeds. "Do you come with the room?" The girls were not amused.

Next morning, while the others were sleeping, Tony went out in search of cigarettes. He was stunned to find snow on the ground. "So we came eighteen hundred miles," he told the others, "to see snow?" The four went down to the beach, doffed their shirts, and posed for pictures with the ocean behind them. "We didn't want to let anyone know it was twenty degrees," Rich recalled.

"Of course we never did meet any girls that trip, at least none who gave us any hope," Tony said. "And after all, we were sharing one room. But the purpose wasn't to meet girls, it was to have an adventure." By that measure, they'd succeeded.

In his sophomore year, Andrew took on a new and daunting task: managing the Bronx for his father's 1977 mayoral campaign. Mario had jumped in at the urging of Governor Carey, whose motives were, at the least, complex.

Carey knew—everybody knew—that Mario had grown into a powerful speaker. That could be useful to the governor. New York City was teetering on the verge of bankruptcy, and Carey as governor needed a mayor of substance he could work with to save it: neither Abe Beame, the city's current mayor, nor half a dozen other hopefuls seemed palatable. Cuomo was a rising star in a city where 20 percent of the voters were Italian-American. At the same time, Carey now saw Cuomo as a serious threat: having Mario as mayor would keep him from running for governor anytime soon. On balance, while the two men might distrust each other, each was stronger with the other, and in smart politics, as Andrew was learning, political advantage trumped personal animus every time.

Mario's strongest rival for the Democratic primary was a U.S. congressman named Edward I. Koch, whose 18th District included, at that time, parts of Manhattan. Koch was known and liked among New York City voters, but Mario seemed to many to have the edge. Along with sporting the governor's endorsement, he had the backing of the small but influential Liberal Party. That ensured that his name would appear in two places on the primary ballot. There was a certain aptness to this, because there were in a sense two Mario Cuomos running. One was an eloquent liberal strongly and publicly opposed to the death penalty. That appealed to liberal voters, even if, as it happened, the mayor had no power to affect the death penalty either way, let alone have prisoners executed. The other Mario Cuomo was the outer-borough candidate—the middle-class family man. This Mario appealed to more conservative outer-borough voters like himself. Koch by contrast was a "Greenwich Village bachelor," as the Cuomo team put it, which in that time and place meant gay.

Andrew again did a lot of climbing up telephone poles with posters and a staple gun. One night Mario was on his way home from a last campaign appearance of the day, being driven back to Holliswood by Jack Newfield, the *Village Voice* political reporter, who had become so enamored of Cuomo that he and his wife actually chauffeured the candidate around. At a red light on Queens Boulevard, Newfield said to Mario, "Don't look left." Mario, of course, looked left, to see Andrew scaling down a lamppost, ripping off Koch posters as he descended. Mario was embarrassed, but not Newfield. "Mario," he said, "I want my son to be like that."

As his father's Bronx campaign manager, Andrew did most of his postering there. Al Gordon, a young campaign staffer, recalled Andrew's "incredible energy level...he would not stop. He could go through the night." Putting up posters was just part of it. At nineteen, Andrew was coming into his own as a campaign manager. "He was always strategizing," Gordon explained. "'What's the best place to go, what will be the impact, how do you make sure your time is best spent?'"

Along with this larger campaign role came a new level of cockiness: the candidate's son could throw his weight around. Richard Starkey, a media consultant, remembered the exact date—April 28, 1977—when he came out to Holliswood to do a shoot for the campaign, introducing Mario as an official candidate. "We got the whole family together," he recalled. "I was almost forty-six, and I found myself dealing with a nineteen-year-old, and he's not treating me like a respected elder, more like the help, ordering me around. I was a little taken aback. I remember saying to my wife, 'How did Mario allow his son to become so abrasive at nineteen?'"

A gentler view comes from Harold Holzer, the Lincoln historian who in 1977 was a college student working on Mario's campaign. The day after he joined, Holzer was brought to the candidate's Forest Hills headquarters and introduced to a tall, muscular nineteen-year-old in jeans and a tight white T-shirt with rolled-up sleeves. Holzer is about 99 percent sure that Andrew had a pack of cigarettes rolled up in one sleeve, very James Dean.

"I've heard a lot about you," Andrew said, and his manner, as Holzer recalled, was something less than welcoming. But Holzer, who went on to become a trusted family friend, found that first impression misleading. "He was a big kid with penetrating eyes, definitely not brash. He was imposing because of his size." In meetings, Holzer found, "We had to encourage him to be involved. He would sit back and observe, and absorb. It was eerie: he was smarter on Thursday than he was on Wednesday, he picked up things every single day."

The key meetings were often held at the Cuomos' kitchen table. Queens politicos like assemblyman Saul Weprin and borough president Donald Manes would show up, either to support Mario or just register respect so they could join the bandwagon if he won the primary. "I know the kitchen table in Queens," Andrew mused later. "I know those people, their faces. I know where they're coming from, what they're dealing with..." In 1977, Mario was still seeking their support, still running as a loyal party man. Only later would he realize he did better as a maverick. As a candidate in his own right, Andrew would go both ways at once, courting the party establishment while painting himself as an outsider.

New York City in the summer of 1977 was a scary place. Serial murderer Son of Sam was on the loose until August; Brooklyn had riots; and then one night came the citywide blackout. Koch called for law and order—and the death penalty, for which Son of Sam seemed perfectly suited, in the eyes of almost everyone except Mario Cuomo. In a crowded Democratic field, Koch clung to the lead, but just barely: on primary day, he nosed ahead of his rivals by just one point. Right behind him was Mario Cuomo, with 18.74 percent of the vote to Koch's 19.81 percent. A runoff was in order, since Koch hadn't won 40 percent of the vote.

All through the primary, Mario had felt cautious and constrained. In the ten-day runoff period, he came into his own and gave speeches with a passion that felt entirely new. Koch gave back as good as he got. It was the toughest battle that New York's political world had seen in years. Koch won the runoff, but not by nearly as much as predicted: 55 percent of the votes to Cuomo's 45. Mario's race as a Democrat was over. Yet to the fury of his party elders, he chose to stay in—as the chosen nominee of the Liberal Party. It was, he declared, a question of loyalty. Carey himself wanted Mario to drop out so he could back Koch without looking perfidious. But when Mario refused, Carey backed Koch anyway.

Whether Andrew was involved in a tawdry, still notorious maneuver in those final weeks, and if so, to what extent, is a matter of fading memories and speculation. Posters began to appear on outer-borough lampposts and highway overpasses, urging voters to "Vote for Cuomo, Not the Homo." Whether the posters even existed would be questioned eventually by the

Cuomo camp, especially after Koch's death in February 2013. And if signs *had* existed, there had been only a handful of them, done as a rogue operation by hooligans, as political consultant Bruce Gyory put it. "They didn't like the way Mario was losing on the death penalty, and I think they took it into their own hands."

The posters were apparently hand-drawn, so they might have been the work of a few freelancers. But another political consultant from that time recalled there were an awful lot of them. "Every night there were hundreds of signs, with little flowers around 'Vote for Cuomo, Not the Homo,'" the consultant recalled. "In fact, I had one of them."

Andrew denied having anything to do with the smear. As a nineteen-year-old college student, he was hardly in a position to launch a harsh new campaign slogan for his father. Mario, well known as a controlling figure who made almost every campaign decision, would have had to approve it. One school of thought is that Mario did know about it. "He might have held his nose and turned away," suggested one consultant, "but he knew about it." Confronted then and later, Mario denied he'd had any knowledge of the offensive posters and said he was "disappointed" to think anyone on his campaign had done them on his own.

Over the years, Koch's view of the matter would change. At first he was devastated and furious, and blamed Cuomo directly. "The way in which he did that was so clear and so heavy-handed that there can be no doubt of his complicity," Koch wrote in his autobiography, *Mayor*. There weren't just a few signs, either, he later said. "They put up the signs on Queens Boulevard—it was the whole boulevard."

Later, Koch reversed himself. Cuomo, he declared, was an honorable person, and he took him at his word when Cuomo said he'd had nothing to do with the posters.

But not quite. Four days before his death in 2013, Koch had dinner with a former *New York Times* journalist and political chum, Howard Blum. "I saw him at the hospital; we had dinner, just the two of us," Blum recalled. "I asked him, 'Isn't it ironic that Andrew is the champion of gay rights?' Koch had no doubt that Cuomo was behind the posters."

That view was echoed in a videotaped interview made public after Koch's death. "That matter has affected our relationship from '77 through this year," Koch relayed about Mario and himself from the grave. "We get along, and we got along as mayor and governor, but I always held it against him. I also held it against his son Andy Cuomo. Even though social relationships when we meet in public are good, underneath, he knows I know what I'm really thinking." The next words were bleeped, but they seemed to be, "You prick!"

In those last days of the general election, Andrew dared to hope his father might win after all—the momentum was palpable—and so the loss, when it came, was that much harder to bear, even if it was by an honorable 42 percent to 50 percent. In a parking lot, Andrew nearly put his fist through the windshield of a car; only a friend's intervention stopped him. Back at home, he was calm but resolute. This wasn't the end, he told his mother. "We'll make Dad a winner." That was a striking way to put it—as if the burden of the father's defeat had fallen squarely on his son's shoulders.

With Mario back in Albany as secretary of state, pondering his next move, Andrew was again left to run the household. "Andrew was my little man," Matilda said later. "Everything I needed he did for me. He took me places in the car… Once I needed a car and said, 'Mario, I have to get a car.' Did he help me? No. So I took Andrew with me. He not only kicked every tire and looked under the hood, when it came time to talk price, he hondled with the dealer."

Andrew's sisters needed guidance too—or so he felt. When either of the younger ones, Maria or Madeline, went out on a date, their escorts had to come to the house and pass muster with Andrew. One night on a dark street in the neighborhood, one of the sisters was roughed up, a lit cigarette put to her skin; Andrew was out for hours in search of the guy. Another night brought news of a rape in the Brooklyn neighborhood where Margaret, Andrew's older sister, was attending medical school. Andrew rented a U-Haul that night, packed it with her belongings, and moved her out.

Up in Albany, Carey and Cuomo eyed each other warily. By now their mutual antipathy was implacable. Yet they needed each other. Mario had lost a second race and might not be able to mount a third without help. Carey wanted another term as governor but knew his star was fading. He needed Cuomo—the scrappy underdog of the mayoral runoff who had endeared himself at the eleventh hour to many voters—to run on his ticket as lieutenant governor in the looming 1978 campaign. Mario could hardly say no if that meant his party might lose the governorship, and he had no better offers. Fine, he told Carey: he was in.

Andrew, still at Fordham, jumped in too, this time as deputy campaign manager. By now, he knew exactly how a race should be run. And to all around him it was clear by now that Andrew Cuomo had an innate, almost uncanny feeling for politics.

It was Mario's third campaign, and to his family's enormous relief, it brought him his first victory. The job of lieutenant governor was dreary—strictly glad-handing and ribbon-cutting—and Carey would prove an even more exasperating senior partner than Mario had feared, but Mario now held a statewide elected office. And Andrew had helped get him there.

As a son of the lieutenant governor, Andrew knew he'd get more attention at Albany Law than at an out-of-state school. That was a good reason not to go: if anything, he seemed eager to get out from under his father's shadow. But Albany was a sort of vocational law school for future New York politicians, and if it wasn't a top institution, it was a good one, getting better. Also, it was cheaper than some, and Andrew was paying his own way. All told, for college and law school he would take on $24,000 in student loans—a lot of money in the late 1970s—and pay them off himself. To save more money, he and his father would be living together as roommates at the crummy old Wellington Hotel, in their own version of *The Odd Couple.*

The Wellington was on State Street, a short walk downhill from the Gothic capitol building. There it remains, as a boarded-up ruin. Anyone who frequented it remembers the elevator, a creaky antique that had a sliding gate and metal mesh sides. You saw the floors going by as it rose; often it stopped with a sudden jerk and for no apparent reason, and a rider's political future seemed to hang in the balance.

Mario had settled into rooms on the top floor, the eleventh, with tired furniture and green shag rugs. "Think of Mickey Spillane's first novels," joked a Cuomo adviser of the time, Tonio Burgos, who lived downstairs. "Shades half torn, neon sign blinking in the background..." Andrew moved into one of the three bedrooms. With him came his dumbbells—by now, he was a serious weightlifter—and the first of the frozen meals that Matilda would make for the two of them, week in and week out. Saving money was one reason to live together. But this was also an experiment in father-son relations.

Often, in the beginning, the experiment seemed not to be going well. Matilda would hear from an indignant Andrew that Mario was late for dinner. "How could he do this?" The next day Mario would call to berate Matilda for the meal he'd finally gotten home to eat. "My God, I got so sick. What did he cook?"

Yet after they'd burned something for dinner, as Andrew put it, father and son would sit and talk. Andrew by now was wholly absorbed by politics; Mario was his mentor. Gary Eisenman, a new law school friend, sat in on some of those evenings and got the drift. "Mario schooled Andrew, he *downloaded* the complexities of politics to Andrew, because Mario knew that Andrew was brilliant, that he could be a great political asset and the person he could trust like no one else."

As roommates, the two did have their Felix-and-Oscar episodes. Into this grungy, already green den, Andrew brought a bright green parrot, a shrieking bird that drove Mario crazy. "It was a trained attack parrot," Andrew later explained. "I trained it myself. It was the only trained attack parrot." On Andrew's orders, the parrot dive-bombed visitors and relieved itself everywhere. "It was a nightmare, that bird," recalled Burgos. "Very loud, very smelly. It flew out the window one day because Mario left the window open. We all cheered."

The Albany workweek was a short one—Monday through Wednesday, generally—so on Wednesday evening Mario would drive home to Queens, reluctantly leaving the lair to Andrew. Serious Catholic that he was, Mario worried that his son would be led to temptation in his absence, so he hung a picture of Matilda on the wall above Andrew's bed. "So I come back Monday morning," Mario later related, "and I go directly into his room, and the picture is turned around." By now, Andrew was convinced that rooming together was his father's way of trying to slow down his sex life. To ward him off, he had Mario's driver give him a heads-up when the lieutenant governor was on his way, "in case I had a girl in my apartment."

On his first day at Albany Law, Andrew sauntered into the cafeteria, which was clearly the social hub of the school. "This big guy comes in, muscular, sits, smokes a cigarette," recalled Peter Schwarz, a classmate who would soon be a good friend. "Someone said, 'You know who that is? That's the lieutenant governor's son.'" Curious, Schwarz went up to say hello. The new kid introduced himself as Andy: he wouldn't insist on being Andrew until after law school. The two hit it off right away. When Schwarz asked if it was true about his father, Andrew made a wry face. "That's me, but let's move on."

Soon Andrew was at the center of a daily cafeteria bull session—about the Iranian hostages; about whether Edward Kennedy was better presidential timber than Jimmy Carter; and all else that came with the autumn of 1979. "He was a good listener," recalled another in the group, Bruce McKeegan. "He wasn't doctrinaire. But when he saw a weakness in your argument, he would jump in."

From among the mostly buttoned-down upstate types, Andrew early on recognized a kindred spirit from the outer boroughs. Gary Eisenman was a tall, intense kid from the Bronx who, like Andrew, wore his hair fairly shaggy, framing thick glasses that exaggerated an already intense look, and had a bit of a wise-guy city swagger. "I came to know him when he was still Andy, before his age of innocence ended and he stepped into a public life," Eisenman said. What Eisenman noted first about Andrew—what everyone noted—was his physical strength. The guy was built like a tank, Eisenman marveled, a real Italian stallion. Along with the muscles came a mental discipline: as Eisenman came to know both father and son, he saw that both were driven in the same way, pushing to change their circumstances before their circumstances changed them. "That's something I learned from Andrew," said Eisenman. "To be proactive and strive to never be a victim. Do not allow yourself the indulgence of saying, 'Oh, he did this to me.' If something goes wrong, it's because you as an individual failed to accomplish what you needed to and not outside forces acted upon you. To do that, to take personal responsibility, you have to be relentless in your efforts."

For someone who, as one friend put it, seemed to live like a shark—keep moving or die—the muscle-bound kid from Queens had a surprising gift for empathy, at least when the subject was fathers and sons. At the nearby Lark Tavern, Eisenman talked about the loss of his father and how hard it was to live without that love and guidance. From that moment on, though the two were the same age, Andrew started acting like an older brother to him. "He always sensed I really needed more support in my life at the time because of my father, and acted on it," said Eisenman. "The effect he has always had on me is that he makes me a better person." Pete Schwarz's father died in March of his freshman year; Andrew came down with three of their friends for the midweek funeral in Goshen, a lengthy drive away. Schwarz had felt depressed by his father's quite sudden death. Andrew's appearance, with those friends, was a gesture he never forgot.

Albany Law was a somewhat modest school in the late 1970s, with a hodgepodge of a campus located below the crest of the hill where New York State's government complex surveyed the Hudson Valley. It was known as a school that focused on the practice, not the policy, of law, and after graduating, many of its students happily made the short walk up the hill to some state government sinecure. Quite a few became well-known litigators in Albany or Manhattan, or judges, or even politicians.

Andrew wouldn't graduate with honors, but he did work hard. One of his professors, Michael Hutter, remembered Cuomo in his unfair-trade-practices class as a student always focused, never looking out the window. "The way we used to study was to get the hornbooks—the scholarly treatises for the subject matter," recalled Eisenman. "We'd outline the hornbooks and then put the outline on notecards. One time we were in the apartment in the Wellington and he was studying for his antitrust final. He proceeded to organize the notecards and then lay them out on the floor in the order that he felt he could understand the subject matter. All over the apartment. Then he went on his knees, read and memorized each card in that order, and got an A."

That was the exception. More often, Andrew exasperated Eisenman by hardly studying at all for a test, only to ace it the next day. He was very smart, Eisenman saw, but he worked to get the work done, not because he was learning to love the law. What he loved, aside from his blue Corvette, was basketball.

Albany Law had a gym in its main building, and Andrew immediately fell in with a loose group of students and teachers who formed their own intramural league, usually playing at 10 or 11 p.m. after the evening's studying. Andrew's team was the Gonads, shortened to the Nads after some muttering from the dean. Another was the Geriatrics, a third the Uncontrollable Urge (somehow this got past the dean). Andrew, as a forward, was the power guy on the court. "He was down the court first," Bruce McKeegan recalled. "He was the biggest rebounder, very good at grabbing." Like his father, he used his elbows a lot.

Along with basketball, Andrew played a fair amount of rugby at law school. He had the strength—and the fortitude—to take a lot of pain. One weekend, Eisenman recalled, Andrew was down in Queens, working on his blue Corvette—he called it his Blue Angel—in the family driveway. He was under the car when it slipped off the jack that was propping it up and pinned him, breaking one of his ribs. Yet he played in the next scheduled rugby game. "His pain threshold and his strength are not normal," said Eisenman. "I mean, the guy had a car fall on his chest."

For the first nights of the week, Andrew stayed with his father at the Wellington. Then he might head over to the wood-frame Victorian house at 84 Woodlawn Avenue that Bruce McKeegan, Pete Schwarz, and another friend, Mike Mine, had turned into their own frat house. Often he slept on the floor: he had back problems, likely from weightlifting, and sleeping on the bare wood floor was sometimes the only way to ease the pain.

On Thursday nights, the gang usually wound up at the Elbo Room, a local bar and law school tradition. A lot of students, including Andrew, went home for weekends, so Thursday was their Saturday night. The Elbo Room had good music, great food, and girls. Andrew did his share of flirting, but he stayed loyal to his buddies too. One of them, Domenico Biagiotti, required special attention: he had cystic fibrosis. "Soaking wet he probably weighed eighty pounds," recalled Pete Schwarz. "But brilliant. A lot of times he would be sick and not at the lectures, but he would come with us to the Elbo Room." In 1983, a year out of law school,

Domenico died. The friends reconvened for his funeral; Andrew stayed up late into the night, his eyes brimming.

Usually after a Thursday night at the Elbo Room, Andrew would make the three-hour drive home in his Blue Angel. He still had his weekend job at the B&G station, manning the AAA tow truck. And he still worked on secondhand muscle cars, selling them at a profit. By now he had a mechanic's toolkit, a metal cabinet as tall as he was, with all its hundreds of tools perfectly organized in categories and ascending size. He would bring that cabinet into each next stage of his life, and every friend who saw it would be struck by the same thought: Andrew Cuomo the politician focused on fixing broken bits of government like a mechanic, confident that every problem had a mechanical solution.

"He would work nonstop, and come back [to Albany] exhausted," recalled Schwarz of those law school weekends in Queens. Somehow, Andrew fit in another weekend job at a Brooklyn law library. "His father once told me—we were up in the Wellington apartment—he said, 'The human body only requires four hours of sleep a night,'" Schwarz recalled. "Well, not me!" But Andrew seemed to go by his father's dictum. His friends marveled at the money he made as a result. "He drove that emergency tow truck all night on the weekend," Eisenman said. "For a student he made so much money!"

Life in those first two years of Albany law was challenging, fun, and mostly routine, but not always. One weekend in Holliswood, Andrew was talking with a friend named James Spirio outside a local bar at 204th Street; the two were smoking cigarettes by the curb. Spirio moved a few steps backward, into the street; perhaps a parked truck blocked his view. One minute Andrew was talking to him; the next, the friend had been mowed down and killed by a bus. The driver was charged with leaving the scene of an accident and driving while intoxicated; Andrew testified at the trial. He was deeply shaken, his law school friends saw, both by the shock of how suddenly life could end and by what he perceived as a gross injustice: the bus driver got off.

One day in the spring of 1981, as Andrew was rounding out his second year in law school, he said to Gary Eisenman over lunch at a local diner, "Aren't you starting to get tired of Albany?" Andrew had a plan. The two of them could transfer to New York Law, a small private school in downtown Manhattan, finish their senior years away from the snows of Albany, yet get their degrees from Albany Law. Eisenman gave his friend a wry look. "And what would we want to do that for?"

Eisenman knew why. Andrew had acknowledged that his father might run for governor in 1982. With those words, Eisenman felt the tracks of his future shift. It was not the only time he would have that sensation. Andrew's friends—his close, loyal friends—would become his political posse, the grown-up version of the pals he'd played with on that pentagon-shaped intersection in Holliswood. They might go off to resume their careers and make money in the private sector. But they would find they were always on call—family forever—pulled back into the circle again and again. Being in that circle was flattering and fascinating, though as the friends would learn, it also tended to involve the giving of a lot of time, and advice, for little or no money. Still, that was better than being dropped from the circle after a critical mistake or an indiscreet word to the press. Banishment was heartbreaking.

All this lay ahead. With the end of that school year, the two law school friends moved down to the city—Eisenman to a dreary apartment in Rego Park, Queens, where his roommate would be Howard Glaser, later one of Andrew's most trusted aides, Andrew to his old room at home—and took on summer jobs. Andrew found work at a Midtown Manhattan law firm called Weiss, Blutrich, Falcone & Miller. The firm, recently founded by a close friend and campaign contributor to Mario named Jerry Weiss, was starting to represent big-league developers, including Donald Trump, William B. Zeckendorf, and Jerry I. Speyer—clients whose projects might benefit from association with a firm so close to the lieutenant governor. So close was Mario to Weiss that the very formation of the firm was said to be Mario's fallback plan. If he did run for governor and lost, he could always settle into the firm as a partner himself.

Early that summer, Andrew started dating Lucille Falcone, one of the new firm's partners. Lucille had come into Mario's orbit as a fund-raiser, a very successful one. She was also beautiful, tall with glossy black hair and piercing blue eyes—"sort of Rita Hayworth," as one friend of Andrew's put it—with a lot of sex appeal. She dressed more provocatively than the average female lawyer, observed another of Andrew's friends. Lucille was about four years older than Andrew, a sweetheart but no pushover. "Very tough, very shrewd, very up in your face," another friend recalled. She came from a working-class family, but was already on her way up: no one would stop her.

Soon Andrew was spending a lot of nights with Lucille at her Brooklyn apartment. The two made a handsome couple, an appropriate couple too. The Cuomos liked to think that Andrew might marry her. Yet the two did little to build a circle of friends together. When he wasn't working, Andrew spent most of his time under the hood of a car. By now he was a highly skilled mechanic, and to his friends, always willing to help.

One night that summer at about 1:30 a.m., Gary Eisenman was driving from Manhattan back to Rego Park when his old VW died on a desolate stretch of the Brooklyn-Queens Expressway. He left it by the side of the road and went off in search of a pay phone. He had no doubt about whom to call.

Andrew was asleep when Eisenman called, but woke up immediately. "Stay by the car," he instructed. "I'll be right there."

By the time Eisenman walked back up the off-ramp to his VW, Andrew was parked behind it in Lucille's car. Andrew popped the VW's hood; soon he had it running. "You drive Lucille's," Andrew told Eisenman over the roar of the engine, "and I'll follow you home in this death trap of yours." Only after Eisenman was home and in bed did it occur to him that anyone else would have fielded his call with sleepy annoyance and told him to call AAA. Andrew—the actual AAA man—had come as a friend right away, no questions asked.

That July, Andrea Cuomo, the patriarch of the family, died at seventy-nine of complications from a stroke. He had declined in recent years, but still tended his small garden and carved stone castles for his grandchildren. He left his wife of nearly sixty years, Immaculata, three children, and a humble legacy: the house on Rio Drive, modest savings, and a few keepsakes. Andrew inherited a gold-and-diamond ring—a small but poignant symbol of his grandfather's immigrant journey, his pride, and his hope for the future. Andrea had lived to see his son Mario rise higher than he ever could have imagined. But the Cuomo dynasty had only just begun.

CHAPTER 4

A Loyalty Like Heat

They had hoped for this. Still, to both Mario and Andrew, the news came as a shock. On January 15, 1982, Hugh Carey, fifty-first governor of New York, twice elected, announced that he would not run for a third term. Carey would forever be the governor who had saved New York City from bankruptcy. But his power was ebbing, and he knew it. Better to step down than get pushed aside. It was a painful choice, made more so by the thought that among those vying to succeed him was the lieutenant governor whom he had come to distrust and dislike.

With Carey's withdrawal, Cuomo began planning his formal entry into the governor's race for mid-March. Mario had a mixed record: two defeats for elected office before Carey had paved his way as lieutenant governor; a gift for public speaking, but little to show for it in his current job; and basically no money. He did have a secret weapon that not even he quite appreciated as yet: his son Andrew Mark Cuomo, just turned twenty-four.

Broad-shouldered and cocky, Andrew looked less like a campaign manager than a car mechanic or, if he put on a suit, perhaps a young personal-injury lawyer from Queens. At some angles, he appeared ruggedly handsome, with those dark intense eyes and sensual lips, a brash charmer. Yet he often looked stern—harsh, even—and when he did, his features rearranged themselves in a less appealing way, as the scowl of a tough guy, a fighter, ready to do whatever it took. The voice, even more than the look, cast him as the cocky and streetwise kid from Queens, those flat, thick vowels like stripes of a neighborhood flag.

Now more than just an outer-borough lieutenant, Andrew had begun sitting in on strategy meetings. But he wasn't yet his father's campaign manager—and he wouldn't be if legendary political guru David Garth took on the job. Garth had steered two winning New York mayoral campaigns—for John Lindsay and Ed Koch—and thought he could push Cuomo to the governorship. But his first loyalty was to Koch. If Koch, the current mayor, chose to run for governor, Garth would have to work with him.

At first Koch waved off the idea. A month later, astonishingly, he was in, declaring his bid for higher office little more than a year after his reelection as mayor by a wide majority. He wasn't particularly keen on becoming governor. But he did like winning races. And he didn't want Mario Cuomo to win instead. Of course he wanted Garth to handle his campaign. Cuomo would have to find someone else.

So popular was Koch that, overnight, a handful of other possible Democratic rivals abandoned the fight. Gone too were the Queens power brokers Cuomo had counted on. For months, these local pols—a tawdry group even by New York standards—had assured Cuomo of their support should he run. Now, to a man, they oozed over to the Koch camp. How could Cuomo not understand? Koch was the giant here, and power flowed to power. But Cuomo didn't understand. He was shocked and hurt and, some said, scarred for life by those defections. It was a lesson in trust and betrayal that Andrew learned too. "Politics is a game of human beings," suggested Mel Miller, former Democratic Speaker of the Assembly. "It all comes down to hate and revenge."

The traitors took more than their own clout with them. They now posed a threat to anyone in the Queens Democratic Party foolish enough to stick with Cuomo. In the almost certain event of a Koch victory, Koch's Queens backers would relegate Cuomo's backers to oblivion. One Cuomo worker recalled the Queens pols as a brutal bunch, ruthless and relentless. "They killed the wounded and ate the dead." Sticking with Cuomo was an act of political courage.

The first polls told an appalling story. Koch was 30, 40, maybe 50 points ahead of Cuomo. Family friends began urging Mario to drop out. "If you have any feeling for him," one told Andrew, "you'll convince him not to run." Instead, Mario cast about for a new campaign director. He asked political journalist Ken Auletta if he would take it on. Auletta, who at the time wrote a regular political column for the *New York Daily News*, had actually worked on two New York gubernatorial campaigns—both losing ones—for Howard Samuels, a wealthy progressive liberal. That was enough to convince him that journalists should stay out of campaigns. He told Cuomo to pick the person he trusted most, someone who could speak for him in any circumstance. By that measure, there was only one choice: his son Andrew.

At first, Andrew scoffed at the idea. "You need credibility," he told his father. "The last thing you need is, 'Oh, my *son* is going to run the campaign.'" But really there was no one else—especially for a candidate who, like Mario, was naturally wary, distrustful, and clannish. Mario did see that Andrew, smart and trustworthy as he was, would benefit from having a few gray-haired eminences around him, and began recruiting them. For a while Andrew would be their student, until he felt ready to toss them aside and run the campaign himself.

And so began one of the great come-from-behind races of the century, with a cast of Runyonesque characters battling each other door-to-door and district-to-district, a race run in the last sepia-toned days before personal computers and cell phones, in which the candidate with the most passion and best street operation prevailed against all odds. A race, too, in which a young man learned to love the game and proved—to all, but especially his father—how fiendishly good he was at it.

On a daily basis, Andrew did the grunt work of setting up campaign appearances for a candidate nearly all had written off. The turnouts were sparse, the coverage light to nonexistent. To boost his father's spirits, Andrew buttonholed volunteers into sitting in the press seats, giving them pads and pens and urging them to take notes. At the end of the conference he would take the notebooks back: he couldn't afford to buy more. If the press did show, Andrew supplied coffee and bagels. But no more bagels than necessary. All this advance work he balanced with senior-year classes and papers. He was, after all, a full-time transfer student at New York Law School.

By the time Mario formally entered the race in mid-March, he had one small cause for hope. Koch had made a huge mistake. In a *Playboy* interview, he made fun of Albany—the capital had no good Chinese restaurants—and said he couldn't imagine living upstate. Maureen Connelly, one of Koch's chief advisers, felt the mayor's lead melt away. As many as 30 or 40 points went to "undecided" overnight. Now Cuomo was only down by 10 points.

For the underdog, just finding a campaign office was a challenge. Money was tight. But also, landlords didn't want to offend the Koch camp by renting to its scruffy rival. Andrew would settle on a suite of offices, only to get a call an hour or two later saying they were taken after all.

In a temporary, one-room space, Andrew struggled to get the campaign up and running—which meant getting in money as fast as possible. Mario was broke; he and Matilda had spent the family's last $20,000 on college tuition. A day or two after Mario's formal entry into the race, Andrew, his girlfriend, Lucille, and a young worker named Mark Gordon handled the invitations to a fund-raiser. Some two thousand invitations had to be stuffed and sorted by zip code for the cheapest possible mailing rate. The three stayed up until 4 a.m. getting the work done. That morning, bleary-eyed, they walked the mass mailing over to the post office together.

Andrew needed more help—fast—and more space. At last he found a shabby office floor in the heart of Manhattan's Garment District at 15 West 39th Street. The dingy walls were flesh-colored, the windows dirty. The landlord insisted on getting his rent up front through the September primary: he didn't want to have to chase a losing campaign for the money. Into these dreary quarters, Andrew brought his "A-Team"—the "Andrew Team" of college students whom, with pleading and cajoling, he had persuaded to leave school for a term to work fifteen to eighteen hours a day at nearly no pay.

One was Gary Eisenman, his good friend from Albany Law. Another was a short, blond, toffee-nosed kid named Royce Mulholland who had come in through one of Andrew's three sisters. When Andrew met him in January, he had mocked Mulholland's blue blazer and button-down shirt and rejected his offer to help for low pay. He didn't need preppies. Then Koch had entered the race, and Andrew was grateful for anyone he could get. The third was Mark Gordon, the one who had helped with the mass mailing. Initially Gordon was shy, hardly speaking to the others. The team thought him a Park Avenue snob. Once he broke through his shyness, they realized he was a brainiac, brilliant at synthesizing information—results from previous primaries, district by district—to see where the campaign should focus its energies. "Give me lists like Gordon's," Andrew would tell the other A-Teamers. But Gordon was the only one who could deliver lists like that.

The three A-Teamers shared a folding table—and one phone—in the main room. Andrew worked in a small adjoining office. He had his own phone line, an ashtray for his cigarette habit—Parliament was now his brand of choice—and a door he sometimes closed so he could write his law school papers. Usually Mario was out all day for appearances. The two would talk several times a day by phone in a shorthand all their own; when at last Mario swept into the office, the talk simply picked up where it had left off: no hellos, no goodbyes, no words of encouragement either way.

Andrew didn't call his father Dad. He called him Mario. "You have to divide yourself as much as possible from the father-and-son-type relationship," Andrew explained. He described his relationship with his father as "businesslike." But it was family business. "Here's the beauty of it," he told one reporter. It was a phrase he used a lot. "He knows no matter how hard he comes after me, I'll be back at 8 o'clock the next morning.

He doesn't have to worry: will I quit? Will I go tell the world bad things about him?"

But in this do-or-die campaign, the relationship was far more volatile than that. "One of the strengths of [the Andrew-Mario] relationship is that it's no-holds-barred," recalled Meyer "Sandy" Frucher, one of Mario's close advisers, years later in a magazine interview. "Andrew could walk in and say, 'You blew it, you screwed up, you did this, you did that,' and the governor could turn around and say 'Fuck off.' "

"Andrew didn't stand down," recalled another young adviser, Dino Amoroso. "When Mario did the cross-exam on others, they would wither away, back up.... 'You're right.' Only to have Mario say, 'What do you mean, I'm right?' You needed to have a strong backbone."

Andrew had that backbone; he had no choice. "Andrew pushes his father, and his father pushes him in this drive to outdo each other in a positive way," suggested Todd Howe, a longtime aide. "They'll argue, they'll swear at each other, but it's always substantive. 'What do you think about this or that program?' Or 'I wanna say this about politics.' 'Oh yeah, you're just playing to the polls, that's not what the heart says.' 'Screw you, I've seen the people, you're not out there anymore!' It's really like football players pounding each other's pads to psych each other up before a game, and then the one who has to deliver the message goes out and delivers it."

On June 5, 1982, Andrew graduated from Albany Law School at a ceremony in Saratoga Springs. He failed to make cum laude or better; he earned none of the many prizes given out that day; he was merely listed among the graduates as Andrew Mark Cuomo from New York City. Unrecognized in the day's program was a higher honor inferred upon him. He was now the *full*-time manager of a losing gubernatorial campaign.

Koch, despite his missteps, was still so consistently ahead in the polls that few regarded Cuomo's candidacy as anything but quixotic. The Democratic convention that month in Syracuse would surely end the upstart's campaign. There, the party's leaders would decide whom to back for the summer's primary race, casting what they called "weighted" votes. The Democratic leader of a large, populous county with lots of Democrats got a heavier "weighted" vote than the leader of a small rural one. To receive the party's blessing, a candidate needed 25 percent of the weighted vote. Koch was predicted to win far more. The question was whether the leaders would deign to grant Cuomo his own qualifying 25 percent. They might not, it was said, unless Cuomo pledged to support whoever won the Democratic primary in the fall's general election. Whoever, of course, meaning Koch.

In the days leading up to the late June convention, Cuomo bridled at what he called the "outrageous" talk of denying him his 25 percent. Surely he'd shown enough strength, as one of the two candidates, to earn an approved primary run. He wouldn't make any pledge of future support. If the leaders denied him, he'd go the petition route: gathering fifteen thousand signatures to win a place on the ballot. Behind the candidate, helping prepare these public statements, was his new full-time campaign manager.

With money an issue as always, Andrew suggested that the campaign cut down on convention costs by renting an old mobile home, driving it up to Syracuse, and using it as both a camp and command station. He called it the Cuomo Mobile. Koch had the same idea, only his command station was a sleek, ultra-modern RV with a radio antenna—high technology for 1982. To the A-Team's great amusement, the antenna malfunctioned.

By now, Andrew had mastered the fine art of phone schmoozing from his father. He knew the value of a quick check-in with the wavering lawmaker or county executive, the mention of that man's wife and children. All smart politicians did, but Andrew did it better than most. President Nixon famously had a Rolodex at hand when he made his check-in calls, with children's names included. "How's... uh... little David?" Andrew had the names down cold for literally hundreds of party faithful, pundits, and journalists.

From calls around the state, Andrew figured that his father could count on a weighted vote of no more than 19 percent. He had two cards to play, and he had to play them just right.

One was Erastus Corning II. In a state of Koch loyalists and others too fearful to appear otherwise, the Cuomos had a rare, powerful ally in the mayor of Albany, who was also boss of one of America's longest-lived political machines. Corning's namesake and great-grandfather had founded the New York Central Railroad and served as mayor of Albany in the 1830s. Erastus Corning II was into his eleventh consecutive term when his party gathered in Syracuse in June 1982. His health was failing; he wouldn't live another year. But he was still vigorous enough to have strong feelings about Koch. He hated the *Playboy* putdown of his city, and Koch's ignorance of which upstate county he was in when asked one day on the campaign trail. Corning had the moxie to act on those feelings. Publicly, he told the Cuomos, he would direct his delegates to vote for Koch. Privately, he would let them vote as they liked. The Cuomos figured that that might bring them another 10 percent of the weighted vote. The trick was to keep this secret until the delegates voted. In the meantime, Andrew would plead for yet more weighted votes from the very Queens bosses who had abandoned Cuomo that spring.

On local television, Andrew declared that his father probably wouldn't get 25 percent of the weighted vote. That only showed how broken the system was, he added, because his father was a popular figure around the state now. "I hope we *don't* get the 25 percent," Andrew added, "because I would rather go the petition route and be able to raise the issue of being closed out by the bosses." It was a bold threat and, as Andrew knew, an empty one: the Cuomos had no money to fund a petition drive.

The message hit home. Andrew was called over for a late-night meeting at the Syracuse Hilton with four of the party leaders. One was Dominic Baranello, chair of the state Democratic Party and Koch's chief backer. The meeting was in his suite; he was lounging in his underwear, accompanied by three Democratic borough leaders: Stan Friedman of the Bronx, Donald Manes of Queens, and Meade Esposito of Brooklyn. All three would soon face corruption charges. It was a motley group.

"You've got us beat," Andrew declared. "We don't have 25 percent of the delegates. So you have to be *very* careful here."

Baranello gave him a raised eyebrow.

"My father's crazy," Andrew said. "If you don't give him the 25 percent of the delegates, he'll attack you for being big-party bosses."

Despite defecting to Koch, the bosses liked Cuomo. In truth, they felt guilty about abandoning him. Why *not* throw him 6 or 7 percent of the weighted vote, just enough to get him his 25 percent? He'd still lose, but the system would look open and honest.

Andrew told them no. "*I'm* not going to take it.... You try to give me votes, I believe it's wrong. That's *brokered*. That's *bossism*. You do that, I'll make all my delegates vote for Koch."

The bosses were startled. "*What* do you mean?" one of them said. "*What*, are you *crazy*?"

Alarmed, the bosses insisted that Andrew take a few *more* weighted votes than they'd planned on giving him. Finally, Andrew surrendered. "This will be good for you," he said to the bosses. It was a line the A-Team had come to know well, which was not to say it generally turned out to be true, or as simple as Andrew made it sound. It was more like what the scorpion might say to the frog in persuading him to let the scorpion ride on his back across the river. "This will be good for you." It might be. But it might not.

Had the bosses known that Andrew had an undisclosed 10 percent of the weighted vote in his pocket from Mayor Corning, they never would have given him any of theirs. But they didn't know.

In today's world of cell phones, the ruse wouldn't have worked. Word would have gotten out that Corning had released his delegates to vote for Cuomo if they liked. But this was Syracuse in 1982. Cuomo and his A-Team were communicating by walkie-talkie. All they had to do was keep their secret Cuomo delegates as far away from the Koch camp as possible until the vote was taken.

For the day after Andrew met with the party bosses, he instructed Tonio Burgos to rent a boat, one big enough to hold all those delegates Corning had released to vote for Cuomo. A boat was found, the delegates were herded aboard, and so began a cruise to nowhere on Onondaga Lake. Once out on the lake, Burgos killed the engine. For hours, the delegates drank cheap booze and had a fine time. Just before the vote, the engine miraculously came to life, the boat returned to shore, and the delegates staggered in to vote. Not until the final count did the bosses see they'd been duped. Mario Cuomo had not just reached 25 percent: miraculously he had 39 percent. Even against Koch's 61 percent, the "also-ran" was now a credible rival. Against the greatest possible odds, Andrew had saved his father from political death and created a possible path to victory.

At the same time, Mario was the one who had sent Andrew in to that snakes' nest to wangle those votes. Mario by now was a cunning strategist. He had a newfound confidence too. As he told his family and staff, he knew that in this race he was the better candidate for governor. He really felt it. It was Mario who would come up with the campaign's unlikely slogan: "Keep the Mayor Mayor!" Koch was so good at the job; why not keep him in it and put Cuomo in as governor? Voters would get a twofer! Mario's advisers were aghast when they first heard it. Who had ever heard of a candidate praising his rival? But as Cuomo's numbers rose, the slogan began to look like genius.

The primary was on, and for the twenty-four-year-old strategist whose father's political future still hung in the balance, the pressure was crushing. Andrew needed a place of his own, away from home and the candidate's relentless kitchen-table queries. He found, on his meager budget, a railroad apartment in Sunnyside, Queens. Andrew bought some furniture on credit, but the apartment, with its long narrow hall and small rooms, remained, as he put it, a dump—and not much of a sanctuary. Every morning at about six o'clock, he would be awakened by a call from his father. "Get up! Get up! Are you up? Get up!"

At the Garment District headquarters, Andrew now shared his office with a grumpy, impassioned union organizer named Norman Adler. No Democrat—no Republican, for that matter—could stage a race in New York City or state without union help. Mario had won the support of District Council 37, New York City's largest union of public employees, headed by the irascible Victor Gotbaum, with Adler as his political director. Gotbaum loathed Ed Koch, convinced that Koch was antiunion. "I want to make Koch bleed from the ears," Gotbaum told Adler. Gotbaum was sure Cuomo would lose—and didn't like him either—but decided to back him anyway, just to stick it to Koch. He installed Adler as his eyes and ears in young Andrew Cuomo's office. Adler's official title was deputy campaign manager.

Both strong-willed, Cuomo and Adler were doomed to clash, but in those first weeks Adler was impressed. Andrew had a lot to learn, especially about upstate. Albany was another planet to him. But the kid was a quick study, and he worked harder than anyone else. It wasn't unusual for Adler to find Andrew asleep in the office the next morning after putting in an eighteen-hour day, only to start in on a day much like the one before. Rather than bring in a folding bed, he slept on the floor, the better to ease his aching back.

Adler was just one of four seasoned strategists who now filled the single floor of office space on West 39th Street. Privately, each of these elder statesmen thought he was smarter than the others and was, in truth if not in title, Mario Cuomo's campaign manager. Andrew's job, as his father put it, was to keep the veterans from killing each other. He had a good, direct way of dealing with them, and he was cool in the crises that swept through the office on an almost hourly basis. But also, he had an advantage the others couldn't match: a direct pipeline to the candidate.

Adler saw Andrew's loyalty to his father up close enough to feel it, like heat. Andrew would have gone headfirst through a brick wall if his father had asked him to do so, Adler felt. And Andrew was unforgiving of anyone not as loyal or committed as he was to Mario's victory. Even in those early months, he would brook no negatives. He didn't want to hear them; he just shut them out. Adler wondered if the campaign could have lasted three months without Andrew's blind faith, which was, Adler thought, almost all they had. "We had no resources," he said. "It was done mostly on sheer willpower: Scotch tape and bubble gum."

Yet Adler never once heard Mario praise his son. He did hear Mario yell at him for what Adler considered inconsequential matters. Once, in the aftermath, Adler tried to cheer up Andrew and found him verging on tears. When he dared tell Mario to lighten up on his son, Mario clenched his fists, Adler recalled, gritted his teeth, and gave Adler a killing look. The message was clear: "Nobody questions how I raise my son."

More often, Andrew kept his guard up, and the two maintained a strong but fiercely competitive bond. Andrew, recalled one campaign operative, was protective of his father, and jealous in a way: he always wanted to be the one closest to him. Mario expected that, but still challenged Andrew on every point, like the Jesuitical lawyer he was. Nothing was accepted at face value: everything was questioned and questioned again.

On one level, Andrew didn't compete with his father. Mario was the intellectual, quoting his favorite religious philosophers. Andrew was smart, but not a reader, certainly not an intellectual. He cast himself instead as the practical guy, the problem solver, the mechanic. "I like to think I think the big thoughts," he told one interviewer. "But I also operationalize." There it was, that word, the sort a security consultant might use, or a police investigator with a license to kill. Mario would follow what he believed; Andrew would do what worked. The righteous end was his father's election; the means was whatever got him there. "It went beyond what a dedicated political supporter would give to a candidate," one former colleague would suggest. For Andrew, operationalizing was... whatever it took. Not for nothing would he soon be known as the Prince of Darkness.

For the first time in his life, Andrew had real power. By all accounts, including his own, he didn't always handle it well. "Mario bestowed power on Andrew, or allowed him to take it, a sign of his life and faith, but it proved a mixed blessing," a veteran of those days recalled. "Andrew doesn't share Mario's brooding nature, which tempered his father's aggression. He lacked 'emotional maturity' at the time. He had an enormous amount of power and not the temperament to wield it. It wasn't fair of his father to put him in that position."

Suddenly, Andrew, at twenty-four, was telling men twice his age what to do—or worse, telling them what they'd done wrong. Mario came beaming into the campaign office and shook hands, asked after family; Andrew took the older operatives aside to say the candidate was less than pleased. Always, he referred to "Mario," never "my father." It was, as he put it, "the son thing."

Andrew was the bad cop to his father's good cop, the enforcer and gatekeeper that Robert F. Kennedy had been to his brother Jack. And like Bobby Kennedy, Andrew soon had a reputation for being tough, even ruthless. "He has no real friends, no colleagues, only people he controls," one state officeholder said. "Everyone else he considers his enemies. To him there's only one agenda, and it's his."

That wasn't entirely fair: Andrew had his A-Team. But the moniker, which the A-Teamers invoked as a running joke, wasn't really a joke at all. If they had worked with him at first, they worked for him now. Even Gary Eisenman felt the difference. "I was perhaps his closest friend during that period, but the relationship changed. The family business was more important than his personal relationships. Mario was the priority. For the Cuomos, nothing was more important than the loyalty of the family and getting Mario elected governor."

At least Andrew was capable of staging moments of comic relief. One day he asked Mark Gordon to take a walk with him. They strolled down West 39th, chatting away, until Mark realized Andrew was steering him into a shoe repair shop. "Mark, you're getting a shoeshine," Andrew announced. Gordon should have guessed: both Andrew and his father shined their own shoes on an almost daily basis. On another day at the Garment District offices, Andrew and Mario started in on a one-on-one basketball game with balled-up paper and a wastebasket. There were flying elbows and body slams; every move was a foul. "My God," Adler recalled, "you would have thought they were playing for the NBA championship."

Not only did Andrew head up the office now, he rode in the car. The candidate's car; his father's car. On an upstate swing, Andrew had his father's undivided attention for hours. That was power—and it went to his head, as Andrew later admitted. "If you found people from '83, I'm sure they would say I was a headstrong SOB. During that whole thing I was." Norm Adler, who would become one of the Cuomos' harshest critics, took a surprisingly more sympathetic view. "What people forget about that election is that he was very, very young. The people who grew up with fathers who were senators, who went to the Kennedy School and Yale, they had a preparation for ascending in political life. But Andrew came out of Queens, he didn't see his father much . . . he had a lot to learn."

Ed Koch had made one whopping mistake already. He made another by agreeing to a dozen debates with a great debater.

At the first of those, Andrew's handiwork was strikingly apparent. First the breakfast audience at the New York Hilton was handed flyers showing Cuomo's poll numbers headed up. Then in came Cuomo to the stirring theme music from *Rocky*, and loud cheering from an audience that had a large number of planted Cuomo fans. Cuomo had taken the whole weekend off to prepare for the debate—at Andrew's insistence. Koch, convinced he had all but won the race, hadn't even opened most of the briefing books. Cuomo often rambled at his public appearances, but not here. He was right on the money at that first debate, and the money, as a result, started rolling in at last.

Despite being pummeled in the debates that followed, Koch maintained his lead as the race curved toward primary day. Usually that day was scheduled for the second week in September. The state, however, had just undergone redistricting, that once-a-decade process by which legislators redrew their voting districts, trying to include all possible supporters and exclude the rest. A week was felt necessary for voters in these redrawn districts to find their sometimes new polling places, and so primary day was delayed.

Without that week's delay, Ed Koch would have won the governorship. Mario Cuomo would have abandoned any hope of running for electoral office again—three strikes and out. And Andrew Cuomo would have likely gone into private practice as the somewhat well-connected son of a gubernatorial also-ran.

Heading into that last week, most polls had Koch ahead by 25 points. On the Cuomo team was a young, creative pollster named Robert Sullivan who thought otherwise. Sullivan saw Mario down by just 11 points, narrowing the gap each day. All through the primary, Cuomo had resisted attacking Koch. Some in his circle, including Andrew, made the case that going negative now was their only hope. "There was a desperation," Sullivan recalled. '*We have to attack Koch.*' I heard some of the talk: it was going to be really gut-ripping nasty stuff. I was begging them not to do that." To Sullivan's relief, Mario spurned his son's advice.

Cuomo's victory—a modest 53 percent to 47 percent—came early that primary night. The celebration at the Halloran House, a Midtown hotel, was giddy—a moment of pure joy among core supporters who thought Cuomo would lose but had worked their hearts out for him anyway. The candidate was more muted. Victory left him wondering if he was worthy: the self-doubts of an immigrant's son, exacerbated by Catholic guilt. He seemed to prefer brooding about the night's one setback. In a quirk of New York State primary politics, candidates for lieutenant governor ran on their own, against each other. The winner was then hitched to the winning gubernatorial candidate to make a ticket for the general election. Cuomo had hoped to run with Carl McCall, a three-term black state senator and former member of the U.S. delegation to the United Nations. Instead, the prize had gone to Al DelBello, the Westchester County executive, a Koch supporter. Cuomo was furious. He felt sure that a second Italian name on the ticket would work against him. A bit later that night, DelBello and his wife went up to Cuomo's hotel room to congratulate him. Cuomo was watching the results on television. He didn't get up; as one person in the room recalled, he never acknowledged DelBello's presence.

The next day, all those Democratic power brokers who had oozed over to Koch came back, many paying their respects at the kitchen table in Holliswood. It was another lesson learned: winning was the best revenge.

Donors started coming in too, a relief since the Cuomo campaign had no money. In that last furious week that decided the race, Andrew had spent every dime.

Money, lots of it, was what Cuomo's Republican adversary brought to the general election. Lewis Lehrman had made a fortune with his family's Rite Aid pharmacy chain. Overnight, he put millions into a television blitz that introduced him to voters as a genial family man, with trademark red suspenders. Cuomo, by contrast, had no money and no television commercials on air the first nine days of the general election campaign. The Cuomos had inspired tens of thousands of volunteers to get out the vote. Now they watched, horrified, as Lehrman simply paid to put equally large teams in place. All told, the drugstore king would spend $13.9 million to Cuomo's $4.8 million.

Mario started the race well ahead in what was, after all, a solid blue state growing more Democratic every year. Against Lehrman, with his money, Cuomo initially cast himself as the underdog—the role he loved to play. Soon he found himself actually struggling, once again, for his political life. Lehrman had more than money: he was a far better debater than Koch, and had a thought-out political philosophy. "It was one of the most substantive races I covered," recalled E. J. Dionne Jr., then the *New York Times*' Albany bureau chief. "[Lehrman] was in the Jack Kemp/Irving Kristol mode, and he ran as who he was—a real supply-side conservative." The candidates fenced so fiercely that their debate moderators barely got in a word, though Cuomo scored his best shot with a passing remark. At an October 7 debate where the two candidates argued standing side by side, Cuomo got an up-close look at Lehrman's wrist. "That's a very expensive watch," he noted. With those words, the class and party lines were drawn.

The primary had been won in that extra week that Cuomo caught up to Koch. It seemed only fair, the Republicans argued, to have the general election pushed back a week as well. A judge denied their appeal. Again for Cuomo, a week made all the difference, only this time in reverse.

With Lehrman's money, a race that had seemed easy for Cuomo grew sharply, sickeningly tighter by late October. Some polls showed him up, but now some showed him losing. Andrew pushed for airing negative ads; again, his father refused. Ads would cost money that Mario didn't have. He had promised Matilda no personal debt in this race. His staff argued that the debt would be easily repaid when he won. "Great," Cuomo exclaimed at an eleventh-hour meeting. "You want to borrow? You go ahead and borrow money. *I'm* not borrowing money."

As others weighed in, Mario fixed Andrew with a piercing look. "Is that my shirt?" he said at last. "Are you wearing my shirt? Where did you get my shirt?"

The Sunday night before the election, Andrew, in his Garment District office, worked up his last weekly graph of poll lines, using a black Magic Marker and big sheets of art paper. The prospects were bleak. The polls showed Mario losing a point almost every day; the same polls showed Lehrman rising. The black marker lines were close to crossing. At that rate, Mario might lose by Tuesday. "You could see these slopes going down," recalled one of Mario's aides. "There was very little he could do."

Like a young two-star general on the eve of battle, Andrew scanned the field, pondering where to focus his get-out-the-vote troops. A key lieutenant was Ray Harding, head of the Liberal Party, who again had provided Mario with key support and had his share of volunteers. "Get the fuck out in Westchester," Andrew told him. Westchester should have been in the bag, since Al DelBello, Mario's running mate, was Westchester County executive. Only the Cuomos had refused to put his name on any Cuomo campaign literature, since Mario so resented him. Now it was in play. Harding raced to save the day, assuming that a Cuomo victory would bring him his share of patronage jobs to dispense.

The race was tighter than Cuomo had hoped: 51 to 48 percent. Still, it was definitive. Upstairs in the Presidential Suite of a Midtown hotel after his victory speech, Mario lay on a king-sized canopied bed, loosened his tie, and took questions from reporters as a beaming Andrew stood by. Mario brushed off the close margin. "When you win, you win," he said. "That's the lesson of all political history. You will be strong if you govern well, if you act decisively."

That night, in a private moment, Andrew told his father, "No one deserved it more." His father thanked him and hugged him. Not until his inauguration, though, did Mario add, "You did this for me."

Two days after the election, Anna Quindlen, then a young reporter for the *New York Times*, found Andrew still at the shabby Garment District headquarters, fending off a constant stream of calls from job seekers.

"Everybody is after Andrew," Quindlen reported. "His secretary is compiling the most comical calls—the people who say they knew him in summer camp, the ones who say they went to third grade together.

"'I've become very popular lately,' said Andrew without cynicism but with plenty of savvy," Quindlen noted, "putting his black dress shoes on the desk and lighting a cigarette."

Good journalist that she was, Quindlen asked father and son independently for a one-word description of their relationship. Both said "businesslike." And calling his father by his first name? That was just... "the son thing," Andrew explained. "You have to divide yourself as much as possible from the father-and-son-type relationship."

Andrew had not made a decision yet about his future, Quindlen reported. "He has not taken the bar exam yet, but he bought the furniture in his Sunnyside, Queens, apartment on credit, and he needs to make the payments. He is not sure about a role in the government." When Cuomo asked Quindlen, "What do you think I should do?" and she suggested chief of staff, he sighed.

"Can't do it," he said. "The son thing, you know?"

In fact, a higher post was awaiting him—as his father's all-knowing, all-purpose henchman, his power as great as the pay was small: a humble dollar a year.

CHAPTER 5

The Enforcer

Andrew's first job in the new Cuomo administration was to help create it. As head of his father's transition team, he submitted hundreds of names by Christmas to fill the top political slots, wielding a new and heady power. Among them was a tight-knit circle of close advisers who would stay with Mario, formally or informally, through his three terms, then migrate to Andrew, forming the same circle for him.

Others fared less well. Norman Adler went in to see what his long months of union organizing might bring him. He found Andrew sitting at a big desk with flags on either side in the transition office at the World Trade Center. During the Garment District office days, he'd noticed that Andrew was something of a clean freak. He saw that more clearly now: the résumés in neat piles, the pencils perfectly sharpened, the desk strikingly clean. They talked of possible jobs, but Adler could sense the chill. There was nothing for him, at least nothing he wanted. He had had too many clashes with Mario and Andrew: not loyal enough.

Almost anyone who had made the mistake of supporting Koch in the primary was shunted aside. Even those who had then worked hard for Cuomo found the spoils scarce. Among them was Ray Harding, whose Liberal Party had given Mario its line on the ballot again—and possibly the margin of victory. Harding had committed the crime, early in the gubernatorial primary, of inviting Koch and Cuomo to lobby for the Liberal Party's support instead of just giving it to Cuomo. The party had gone on to back Cuomo anyway. But Cuomo felt Harding had kept the door open to Koch in case Cuomo's candidacy faltered. That, to him, was faith broken. To Harding's shock, the postvictory reception he got from both Cuomos was frigid, with none of the patronage jobs he'd expected. Soon, for Harding, relations with the Cuomos would get a lot worse.

Andrew handled the transition well, and the team's own members formally recommended he be given a top job in the new administration. The new governor was pleased, to a point. "The condition that I impose as a parent," he said, "is that he must promise to take the bar exam." In fact, there was another condition. Even the proud father could see that putting his son in a high post at full pay would reek of nepotism. Instead, Andrew signed on to work as his father's adviser for a symbolic dollar a year.

On inauguration night, the Cuomos walked dumbstruck through the private rooms of their new home, the forty-odd-room Queen Anne–style executive mansion on Eagle Street. Previous governors had left their marks on the nineteenth-century redbrick building: Theodore Roosevelt, the gymnasium; Franklin Roosevelt, a swimming pool; Al Smith, a zoo; and Nelson Rockefeller, the tennis courts. Governor Carey had left his own legacy: he'd painted the master bedroom's capacious bathroom pink. From then on, Mario would regale audiences with his shtick about the bathroom so big he had to hail a taxi to get from one end of it to the other. It was a charming, if somewhat disingenuous, riff: the new governor soon grew so accustomed to the mansion that he hardly ever missed a night there over the next twelve years.

Christopher Cuomo, age thirteen, put it best. "One minute we were living in *All in the Family*," he said. "The next we were in *Benson*," a TV sitcom about a black butler in a governor's mansion that aired during the 1980s. Andrew mocked his younger brother as Mansion Boy. "Remember, this is not your house," he told him. "You're not here to become some privileged kid." But Andrew was awestruck too. He chose a second-floor bedroom once occupied by Nelson Rockefeller, and took to raiding the huge walk-in kitchen refrigerator for Dagwood-sized tuna sandwiches.

Even grander than the mansion—and to Andrew, more compelling—was the state's capitol building, a nineteenth-century monument to wild architectural excess and graft. Constructed over thirty-two years, from 1867 to 1899, at a cost of $25 million—half a billion in current-day dollars—the capitol was a mishmash of Romanesque revival and neo-Renaissance, all softened and worn by time, like Miss Havisham's wedding cake in *Great Expectations*. Inside, its high gloomy corridors led to its famous Senate and Assembly staircases, with carved grotesques and gargoyles, then up to its still-ornate chambers for each governing body. The executive offices were on the second floor, a series of high-ceilinged rooms with rich molding and heavy oak doors. By contrast, the press office on the third floor was a humble hodgepodge, with dilapidated leather chairs and posters of governors past, faced by a few offices for individual reporters with walls barely wider than their desks.

Fascinated by its history and lore, Andrew as governor would oversee a thorough refurbishing of the place. At twenty-five in early 1983, he strode through the capitol building's musty halls more drawn to his new and sizable second-floor office. After Windexing his desk—the clean freak at work—he graced it with a paperweight that looked like a clump of pennies. When Gary Eisenman saw it, he joked that it must be Andrew's annual salary. Technically the office was in the personnel department, but no one was fooled by that. The son who had been his father's campaign manager was now his top adviser—and enforcer.

Ten days into his administration, Mario at last took Matilda and Andrew out for a celebratory dinner, to a Second Avenue joint called Ole. Andrew had pushed for a dinner like this after the primary victory, but his father had said no: not until after the election was won. After the election, Andrew had pushed again. No, his father said, not until after the inauguration. As they settled in to their dinner at last, the governor's new bodyguard came to their table, summoning Mario to the phone. Some five hundred inmates at the Ossining prison had seized a wing and taken nineteen officers captive. The celebration was over.

The governor's first instinct was to rush to the prison himself. Instead, partly at Andrew's urging, Mario and his team established a twenty-four-hour command post on the fifty-seventh floor of 2 World Trade Center, their new Manhattan headquarters when not in Albany. Eating and sleeping there, they stayed in constant touch with the prison authorities. The standoff lasted two days and nights but ended peacefully. The governor had had his baptism by fire, and so had his son.

Andrew appeared in news photos of the governor's team mediating the prison crisis: a first glimpse of the dollar-a-year man in action. Mostly he was invisible, doing whatever his father needed. One early assignment that came to light later showed just how tough and commanding he was from the start.

Governor Cuomo, it turned out, felt very strongly that Ray Harding of the Liberal Party had kept "the door open for Koch" in the primary, as one witness explained later to state investigators. Cuomo wanted to punish Harding by having the party hand its leadership to someone else. He made that very clear, by putting no Liberal Party members on his transition team and giving no patronage jobs to party members after the inauguration. Patronage jobs were the Liberal Party's lifeblood. For Harding, this was a calamity.

Harding met with the governor to protest his innocence. He hadn't intended to "hold the door open" for Koch, only to let the process of choosing a nominee proceed as it should. The governor seemed to soften.

He said he had "gotten misinformation." Shortly afterward, he declared that he would have nothing more to do with internal matters of the Liberal Party—it was inappropriate. Soon enough, Harding learned who would.

On January 27, 1983, two days before leaders of the Liberal Party were to vote on whether Harding rose or fell, Andrew swung into action. First he met with Harding at a Manhattan lawyer's office. Andrew repeated a proposal the governor had previously floated—that a troika should lead the Liberal Party. Harding would be one of the three, but his party rivals, Donald Harrington and James Notaro, would be the others. Harding would go from being the party's standard-bearer to being outvoted every time.

Harding proposed a compromise: a bigger ruling committee, but one he would essentially control. Andrew said he would check back.

At 5:30 p.m., Harding later testified, Andrew called to say the compromise was unacceptable. If the matter wasn't settled immediately to the governor's liking, the governor would fire all his people. Or so recalled Harding. That meant the governor would dismiss from state employment all workers known to be Liberal Party members, or at least those who were loyal to Harding. It had all the trimmings of a Stalinist purge. In his own testimony, Andrew would deny any threat to fire Liberal Party members, as would two other Cuomo aides.

According to Harding, Andrew requested that he and his two rivals come to a secret meeting that evening at 8 p.m., in a suite at Manhattan's Sheraton Centre Hotel. The meeting went on until 3 a.m., with Harding insisting he stay in charge and the others insisting he share power. It was a bitter standoff, without any seeming compromise: whichever faction gained the upper hand would banish the other.

As the early morning hours wore on, the parties agreed to put the troika solution to a vote at the party meeting on January 29. If it was voted down, then the party could vote on whether to approve Harding's plan of a larger ruling body. All sides agreed that the meeting, and the deal, would remain secret. If either side breached that trust, the names on its patronage list would all lose their jobs. Both sides knew Andrew was serious: he had made them bring lists of their respective job holders to the meeting.

At the big party meeting, Harding prevailed. No troika. Instead, the party approved his eleven-member committee, with Harding in control of six of its seats. The Cuomos were furious, the more so when a story appeared in the *New York Times* reporting that Andrew had been involved.

Within the Liberal Party, a ground war began, each side trying to vanquish the other, each threatening to fire the other's job holders. One member told investigators she had heard that Governor Cuomo had two lists, one of Harding's supporters and one of Notaro's. Only Notaro's people would be "saved," she was told. The clear implication was that Governor Cuomo would do the "saving," and that none of Harding's people would be saved along with them.

The purge never came, possibly because the press sniffed out the story. But a state commission's findings were damning nonetheless. "Threats of patronage dismissals were made to coerce [Liberal] Party members into supporting either the Harding or Notaro/Harrington faction," the investigators concluded. And no matter who had said what to whom, they added, "Aides to Governor Cuomo, according to their own testimony, intervened in the internal affairs of the Liberal Party in order to obtain a resolution of the factional dispute." Prominent among those aides was Andrew.

As his father's heavy, Andrew was an unnerving presence on the second floor, an all-purpose scout who might find fault and report back to the governor, which might result in the loss of one's job. One profile later described him at that time as "a cocky kid in a three-piece suit with a wide collar and wider ties, a mop of curly hair and a head of twenty-something arrogance. He loved to lean back in his leather chair behind an enormous desk and run a back-office operation not dissimilar to the way he played basketball... He was equally adept at showing a clenched fist as an open hand."

"He was a nasty piece of work," agreed a reporter who covered Albany at that time, "who took delight in firing and cutting down to size people decades older."

"He was just curt," recalled one staffer. "And he didn't try to dissimulate how he felt, and he didn't seem to feel sympathetic toward people like myself, who were older. I can't read Andrew's soul but I suspect he would have liked to hand-pick the people around the governor and in the executive chamber. But he couldn't; he could only pick the younger people.

"Mario was not necessarily warm," the staffer added, "but he had the self-mocking wit that covered up the fact that he was not the cuddly type. But Andrew couldn't conceal his own character."

"I did not deal with Andrew—Andrew dealt with me," recalled one aide, Bill Stern, who soon after broke with the Cuomos and so became one of the few to criticize them on the record. "He would be the one to call to say he liked this or that and comment on the job I was doing. Essentially, he is the deputy governor and he weaves a web all through government. You do not want him mad at you. He takes no prisoners."

A more charitable view came from Ken Auletta, who followed the governor through his first months in office for a two-part series for the *New Yorker.* In addition to being a good reporter, Auletta was genial, a jock—and part Italian. Soon he was having dinner with the Cuomos once a week at the executive mansion to interview the governor. Matilda was down in Queens most of the time, since Christopher was attending school there, so it was often just the guys: Mario, Andrew, and the governor's close friend and aide Fabian Palomino. The guys would cluster at one end of the long executive dining table, tucking into food the chef prepared, and Matilda's care packages: escarole soup, followed perhaps by pasta puttanesca, with olives, anchovies, hot red pepper, and lots of garlic—for Andrew, the spicier the better. Mario would serve wine from a bottle wrapped in a white linen napkin, and tell Auletta it was New York State wine, though on one occasion Auletta peeled back the napkin to find an Italian Corvo. In the privacy of his family, Andrew was at ease, kidding the others and taking their retorts with good humor. Auletta had heard the stories, but he couldn't help liking the governor's son and thinking he'd gotten a bad rap.

Out back was a basketball hoop, no different from the hoop in back of the house on Pompeii Avenue. One night before dinner, Auletta watched Andrew and his father play ball. Mario was governor, but Andrew wasn't showing any deference. "Andrew was throwing elbows, and Mario was throwing elbows, and they were jockeying under the hoop for the ball," Auletta recalled. "They were trash-talking and having the time of their lives. What you saw was not only the son's independence, but also the competitiveness of each. They were vying to win."

At one point, away from the others, Auletta asked the governor about his son. The governor beamed. "He's smart, right? He's twenty-five, but he's been around the process a long time... If I have a problem with Andrew it's that he's too mature. My concern is that he has a limited other life."

When Auletta asked Andrew about his father, Andrew answered with pride. "He was a great father," he said. "He was never home at five o'clock, or there to take me to the movies. But I guess I never expected him to be there more... What he was doing was important," he added. "He used to come home and say, 'You disappointed me.' I never wanted to disappoint him."

Even Andrew didn't know his father through and through, he told Auletta. "The areas of his life he considers private are totally, totally private. It's when his father died, who could he go to? No one. Do you go to your wife and cry? Do you go to your mother? He went for a walk alone. That's an inner strength.

"The guy's my best friend," Andrew said, "but we talk about other things."

The one occasional woman at dinner was Lucille Falcone, Andrew's glamorous girlfriend from the Manhattan law firm where he'd worked during the summer of 1981. Andrew liked her a lot, but he didn't want to go public with the relationship. One night he picked up the first edition of the next morning's *New York Times* and saw Falcone described as his girlfriend. Furious, he called the paper to demand that the description be struck from future reports. It was.

Possibly Andrew wanted to keep the romance secret to avoid jeopardizing the job Lucille was about to get with the new administration. That March, one of the governor's commissioners hired her as his assistant general counsel, a newly created position, at a salary of $80,000. That, as the *New York Times* pointed out in a blistering editorial, was only $5,000 less than the attorney general's salary, and more than the governor paid his own counsel. Rumor was that Mario himself had talked her into taking the job; he had worked with her at Weiss, Blutrich, Falcone & Miller the year before. Was this not the very sort of cronyism the new governor had vowed to avoid? When top adviser Tim Russert warned the governor the editorial was coming, he was enraged. "How could they say she's not qualified?" Ten days after joining the administration, Falcone resigned. "I am dismayed that in 1983 the press would suggest that a lawyer—who has practiced law for eight years, after graduating from a quality law school—was hired because she was 'attractive' or a 'social friend,'" she declared. "Frankly, I can only conclude that my appointment was treated in this way because I happen to be a woman."

Thirty years later, Andrew would still harbor a grudge against the paper of record. "The *Times* has always been terrible to my family," he would say. In their minds, the Cuomos were still outsiders from Queens; the *Times* was the paper of Manhattan's rich and powerful, the Cuomos felt, who looked down their noses at them.

With his critics outnumbering his fans, nicknames began to follow Andrew like tin cans on strings. "The Little Cuomo" was one, "the First Son" another, "Deputy Governor" a third. And, perhaps inevitably, "the Prince of Darkness." The barbs stung, though Andrew tried not to show that they did. When journalists asked, he said he knew he'd stir sniping and envy whatever he did. "You have to understand," he deadpanned to one interviewer about the governor, "that of all his aides, I *have* been with him the longest."

Both the governor and his dollar-a-year son were extremely sensitive to public slights, real or perceived, and soon every journalist in Albany's press corps had stories to tell of picking up the phone on a Sunday morning to be addressed by one Cuomo or the other. Adam Nagourney, then writing for the *New York Daily News*, remembered getting yelled at by the governor and told, in conclusion, "You cut off my testicle!" Shaken, he called Andrew to suggest that the son rein in his father. "He said you cut off his testicle?" Andrew echoed. "He used the singular? That's terrible." Another reporter, George Arzt, made the mistake of reporting that the governor's father-in-law owed $90,000 in back taxes. The governor called him in a fury. "You hit a poor seventy-year-old Italian immigrant who can't speak English," he fumed. "*The sewer runs to your desk.*"

One of the few in the Albany press corps who got treated unfailingly well was the *New York Post*'s new state editor, Fredric Uberall Dicker, otherwise known as FUD. Dicker had jumped from the Albany *Times Union* during the 1982 gubernatorial race, and now wrote stories that relied almost completely on anonymous sources. Most seemed to push the governor's point of view, and for capitol hill watchers the new game was to guess which Cuomo had supplied the spin. For now, Dicker was solidly in the Cuomo camp, but the Cuomos were well aware that Dicker had championed Governor Carey too, only to turn against him.

Punishing foes was one part of Andrew's role. Rewarding friends was another. One of the Cuomo camp's closest friends—and one of the governor's largest donors—was a feisty developer named Sheldon Goldstein. Soon he would become Andrew's mentor, only to pull him into a mess that almost ruined his hopes of a political career. For now, he just needed a favor.

Goldstein was a self-made millionaire, raised in Brooklyn, who in 1955 had built the first of his developments in Rockland County, not far up the Hudson from New York City. Some developers hopscotched around; Goldstein based himself in the town of Suffern, and always built nearby. By the early 1980s, when he began making campaign donations to Mario, he oversaw thirty-six partnerships and corporations, with some twenty-two hundred housing units and half a million square feet of commercial space. He did his deals in a papal-like office, in a building complex that housed many of his holdings. At fifty-three, he was known as a flashy dresser, given to gold chains and open-necked shirts, who dyed his hair jet black.

Jerry Weiss, Mario's close friend and founder of Weiss, Blutrich, Falcone & Miller, introduced Goldstein as one of his first clients to the candidate in 1982. Goldstein gave at least $49,000 to Cuomo's campaign that year, making him one of its largest individual donors. He may have given more, through relatives and limited partnerships: that would be his style in future elections. Mario eventually made him chairman of the State University Construction Fund.

Later Arco, a management company controlled by Goldstein's son, won a generous contract in Governor Cuomo's first term to manage two major state-supervised housing projects in New York City. On a government form, Goldstein would soon be obligated to note that his net worth had gone from $5.9 million at the end of 1981 to $15.7 million in 1985. To the Cuomos, Goldstein was a valuable ally.

Sometime in 1983, Goldstein became aware of a situation in downtown Manhattan that might yield him a tidy profit. The state was moving agencies out of 2 World Trade Center, where rents were high, into various cheaper downtown sites. A small-time landlord named Harry C. Partridge III had seen a chance to acquire a seven-floor commercial loft building at 400 Broome Street, fix it up, and get the state to lease it. Only he'd gotten in over his head. The building was such a wreck that Partridge kept having to put more money into fixing it up before any agencies could move in. Worried he might not be able to meet his loan payments, Partridge started planning a Hail Mary move. Maybe he could build out an eighth floor on top, get the state to rent it along with the other seven floors, and keep ahead of his loans. That was when Sheldon Goldstein stepped in. Apparently Goldstein, too, could see the potential in Partridge's Hail Mary plan. He wanted Partridge to sell him 50 percent of the building. Partridge refused, enraging Goldstein, who threatened to destroy him. In response to a state commission that looked into the matter, Goldstein admitted he had "threatened to ruin him in the state of New York as a window contractor." Not long after that came out, Goldstein left his post as chairman of the State University Construction Fund—for "personal reasons," a government spokesman explained.

Still working his Hail Mary move, Partridge persuaded a state agency to lease the eighth floor. But a routine approval from the executive chamber failed to materialize. A state executive later testified that the governor himself had raised questions about the building.

The next thing Partridge knew, Andrew was involved, asking why, with 400 Broome still in such lousy shape, the state was throwing good money after bad to lease the eighth floor. It was a fair question, though hardly fair to Partridge after the state had agreed, on paper, to do so. In late 1983, Andrew ordered the state agency in question to reverse its decision to rent the eighth floor. Partridge soon found himself charged with scheming to defraud the state out of $20 million, the value of the lease at 400 Broome over ten years. Eventually he was found innocent of all charges. By then, however, he was ruined, just as Goldstein had threatened.

While Andrew was doing his share of enforcing, he was also learning how the state worked and how to make it work better. The budget was the biggest piece, a mess by any measure. What Mario did to pull it into shape was exactly what Andrew would do twenty-eight years later.

Mario had come into office in the teeth of a recession, and the way he took on the state's hard-hit budget in that first grim year would stand as one of the brightest chapters in his three terms as governor. Proud liberal though he was, dedicated to helping government help those in need, Mario took a tough, pragmatic approach to putting the budget back in the black. There would be no increase in business, income, or sales taxes. There would, however, be spending cuts, some severe, to pull the state out of debt. To prove his bona fides as a fiscal pragmatist, Mario also insisted on getting the budget done on time, after years of missed deadlines. Andrew would do that too—though as if to outdo his father, he would get the budget in on time year after year.

Andrew in that first year took on a task that could help or hurt the budget—and his father's stature—significantly. A bridge in Connecticut collapsed, killing three and underscoring the parlous condition of the region's bridges, its mass transportation, and its roads, where as one reporter noted, potholes appeared like raisins in cereal. The answer, the governor declared, was to issue a bond for $1.25 billion for fixing the state's infrastructure. Voters would have to approve the bond in November; a whole campaign of public persuasion would have to be waged. Andrew and Tim Russert became its co-managers.

That summer and fall of 1983, Andrew's office was filled with photos of falling-apart bridges and fractured road tops, along with maps of the state's sixty-two counties, festooned with multicolored pushpins. Once again he was directing a campaign that would have a profound effect on his father, one by which Mario's effectiveness as governor would be judged.

That November, by a narrow margin, the bond passed.

Andrew had proved—if any further proof was needed—that he was a consummate political manager. The prospect of another year as his father's tough guy—for a dollar—held no appeal. He yearned to get out from under his father's suffocating, relentless control and make his own way. Tensions between the two, as a result, were sharper. One family friend recalled being at the house on Pompeii when Andrew called and the governor answered the phone.

"Is my sister there?" Andrew demanded.

"Don't you want to speak to me?" the governor asked.

"Is my sister there?" Andrew said again.

Mario, for his part, was finding that governing was harder than campaigning. He seemed to trust only a handful of insiders, and perhaps not even them. "Mario would call [Tim] Russert in and tell him one thing," recalled a staffer, "and tell [Michael] Del Giudice something else." Aides lived in fear of being viewed as betraying their boss, a toxic culture. Even Andrew, suggested one staffer, seemed unsure of himself. "The one person he wanted to please more than anyone was Mario." And Mario wasn't easy to please.

It hardly helped that the governor made almost every decision, no matter how small, himself, ignoring advice from his staff. "He's like a guy who owns a department store and cleans its windows himself," Norm Adler scoffed. The concept of delegating seemed to mystify the new governor. "Delegate what?" he said in answer to one reporter's question. "I was elected to govern. I wasn't elected to let other people govern." A few top priorities passed through the pipeline; much of the rest languished in limbo. This style of governing—by absolute control—seemed coded in the Cuomos' political DNA. Three decades later, Andrew would operate the same way.

For a twenty-five-year-old pondering what to do next after three exhausting campaigns, law was as strong an attraction as politics, maybe more so. That summer, before the bond campaign got under way, Andrew took six weeks off to study for his bar exam. He and Gary Eisenman studied together and settled on a strict daily regimen. Every morning, they'd meet at Andrew's apartment in Sunnyside, Queens, and go for a good run. Then they'd study all day, taking breaks to test each other. Andrew made Gary feel like a dolt: so much was memorization, and Andrew's memory was uncanny. Most evenings, they'd head into Manhattan for a group review class. The next morning, they'd start over again. Both passed, but Andrew did better than that. On the multiple-choice part for which he and Gary had done all that memory work, Eisenman recalled, Andrew had the second-highest score in the state that year.

As if to harden his resolve, Andrew made public, in January 1984, his decision to join a law firm—which one, he didn't yet know. He would, however, remain a part-time adviser to his father, on the same dollar-a-year basis. His first assignment in the new year was managing Walter Mondale's New York primary race in the Minnesota senator's presidential campaign. Andrew made few new friends among the Mondale staffers—arrogant and obnoxious was the consensus. "He comes in with his guys—always guys, always young guys," recalled one observer. "Now everyone did what Andrew wanted them to do. He was a dark prince in that you didn't fuck with him." Whatever he did, it worked: Andrew helped Mondale win the April primary. Not long after, he made his decision: he would go to work for legendary Manhattan district attorney Robert M. Morgenthau, one of thirty assistant DAs in the appeals bureau at a salary of $23,500 a year, writing briefs and appearing in court to argue for the prosecutors.

It was an interesting choice—the first career decision for a twenty-five-year-old who had worked until then exclusively for his father, summer and after-school jobs notwithstanding. Andrew could have joined a Wall Street firm—many would have jumped at the chance to hire the governor's son. Instead, he chose public service. A job at Morgenthau's shop was a sacrifice for any young lawyer, undertaken with a sense of mission: to protect society and punish the crooks. A stint in the DA's office, of course, might also seed the ground for a run at some first elective office: city council, perhaps, or state assembly.

For Andrew, a deepening social crisis suggested an alternate path. Both in New York City and around the state, homelessness had become a huge problem. Traveling with his father, Andrew had seen the homeless up close and was shaken by their plight. If government's role was to help those in need, as Mario proclaimed, who was in greater need than they? Yet their ranks kept growing, and neither Mayor Koch nor Governor Cuomo could see a solution.

Andrew wanted to help his father deal with a key issue, one that would cause serious political damage if left unchecked. Perhaps the governor's son might also make the issue his personal crusade, and in so doing forge a political identity of his own.

CHAPTER 6

A Cause to Embrace

If Andrew thought his new job would give him some distance from his family, he was wrong. On May 22, 1984, he received a horrifying call: his maternal grandfather, Charles Raffa, seventy-nine, had been badly beaten by two assailants during an apparent robbery in Brooklyn. The governor was en route to Albany, so Andrew was the one who rushed to the Brooklyn hospital where Raffa lay with injuries so serious that he required facial plastic surgery.

The incident was as mysterious as it was shocking, and would haunt the Cuomos ever after, stirring rumors that Raffa's assault was Mafia-connected. Twice in the future, when Mario considered running for the White House, only to back off at the last moment, the Raffa story would surface as a possible explanation. Journalist Nick Pileggi, a Mafia expert, would run down every rumor in an exhaustive article for *New York* magazine and find not one to be true. And yet the muttering would persist.

The known facts were, at the least, intriguing. Raffa had gone to a vacant supermarket he owned at 804 Stanley Avenue in the East New York section of Brooklyn. He arrived at about 9 a.m. According to the police, Raffa was surprised later that morning at the rear of the building by two men. Raffa's billfold was empty when he was found, and a ring was later reported as taken. Raffa was beaten "numerous times about the head and face" and lost consciousness, according to police. When he recovered, he staggered out to the street. "It was a terrible sight," a neighbor related. "You couldn't see his face. He was all bruised and covered with blood." No suspect was ever arrested for the beating, which left Raffa mentally and physically diminished, confined to a wheelchair.

Later, when Mario was first weighing a run at the White House, *New York Times* reporter Selwyn Raab revisited the story and found some strange details. The neighbors had noted Raffa's car, a blue 1983 Cadillac, parked in front of the supermarket at about 9 a.m. They had also noted Raffa standing near the car with a young man. Another witness, Severino Estevez, had arrived on the scene at about 9:30 and met with Raffa, as scheduled, to discuss his interest in buying or leasing the vacant store. Estevez had seen a young white man, about seventeen or eighteen years old, sitting in the Cadillac. The youth, who acted like an acquaintance or employee, joined the two men as they went into the store. Yet that was the last anyone saw of him. Soon after, Estevez left, having seen no assailants.

Several hours after the attack, New York detective Sebastian Pipitone, who served as a bodyguard for the governor, removed Raffa's car from a police station and had it washed. The car had not been searched for clues or dusted for fingerprints. "We still don't know if the car was important," said the police official who headed the investigation, "but we would have been better off if it had been left alone." Pipitone was off duty that day, yet he went to the 75th Precinct station house to remove the car. He told Raab through a spokesperson that he had cleaned the car as "a courtesy" before returning it to the Raffas because it was covered with fingerprint-testing dust. But police records obtained by Raab revealed that the car was not dusted for prints until four days after the assault.

Whether or not these details were known to the Cuomos in the aftermath of Charles Raffa's beating, the incident was deeply upsetting and, one Cuomo staffer from that period recalled, alarming. "I remember the paranoia. I remember they were more nervous about that than anything I'd ever seen."

The attack was surely reverberating two months later when Mario gave the speech that would stir giddy talk for years of a first Italian-American in the White House.

No mystery remained about who would be the Democratic presidential nominee: Walter Mondale had an insurmountable lead in delegates. The surprise was Mario Cuomo as keynote speaker, a choice made by Mondale himself. Cuomo was a fresh face, he'd pushed New York into the nominee's column, and he had that oratorical dazzle. Perhaps a bit of it might rub off on the all too stolid Minnesotan.

This was Cuomo's first time on a national stage, a huge and crucial opportunity. At his World Trade Center offices, the governor gathered his closest advisers, Tim Russert, Michael Del Giudice, and Andrew, to draft a knockout speech. They tried a metaphor Cuomo had used before, of Americans crossing the country in a covered wagon that had broken down. "That sucks," said someone, and the others agreed. But maybe it had a place somewhere.

A first draft did have an interesting device at its conclusion: Cuomo addressing President Reagan directly. "How about starting with that?" Russert suggested. They did; that was better. Now they needed an ending. So they pulled out one of Mario's stock stories, of his immigrant father working at the store until his feet bled. "That works," Andrew said. "They'll love it."

Like a football team watching game films, the inner circle watched keynote addresses at Democratic conventions going back to 1964. No matter how good the speech, the speaker always lost the crowd in the first minute or two, then fought a rising tide of chatter as he pressed vainly on. Later, Andrew would be credited with suggesting that they show a short film about Mario before he delivered his speech. The room would be darkened for the film—that was the key. With any luck, the crowd would pipe down. Such films—and darkened halls—would be standard at future conventions, but this was a first: a simple but brilliantly effective stratagem. "I think it was Russert who had the idea about the film," one insider recalled. "But it's probably like *Rashomon* at this point."

An hour before his scheduled time slot at the San Francisco convention, Mario was led off to the makeup room. When he returned, he pointed to his face. "All set!" he said with a shy smile. His handlers stared, aghast. Finally Andrew said to the others, "Well, whaddya think, guys? Maybe some putty for the eyes?" The group cracked up, and the governor, at his son's stern admonition, went back to be redone in a more natural, less corpselike way.

Out at the podium after the film, seizing the crowd's undivided attention, Mario talked of President Reagan's "shining city on a hill" and of its unseen part, where Americans not so wealthy and entitled as the president struggled to pay mortgages or even slept in the streets. "There is despair, Mr. President, in the faces that you don't see, in the places that you don't visit in your shining city."

As he went on to evoke the poor pioneers struggling to cross the frontier in their covered wagon, cameras panned across an audience transfixed. They swiveled to the speaker, emanating all his prosecutorial power on behalf of the poor and the grit they needed to get through: a new standard-bearer for the Democratic Party. In the wings, the cameras caught a tall, dark-haired, shadowy figure: Andrew, brimming with pride at his father's triumph.

In retrospect, Mario would express no less pride in his son's tenure as an assistant DA in the Manhattan DA's office. Andrew had won fifteen appeals in a row! And yet among his peers the enduring impression of him in the appeals bureau was a less than favorable one.

Andrew arrived in what would become known as the era of famous kids. Robert Kennedy Jr. was one of Robert Morgenthau's assistant DAs at around this time. So was Cy Vance Jr., son of presidential adviser and U.S. secretary of state Cyrus Vance. John Kennedy Jr. would come not long after. The famous kids stirred some resentment, but that died down with those who did their work and honored their commitment: to stay in the DA's office, on that lowly salary, for three years. Or rather, three years and then some. As one veteran explained, "If you left a day after your three-year commitment, that wasn't very impressive."

The ADAs worked in one of eight bureaus. Six were much the same: standard prosecutorial work. One was narcotics. And then there was appeals. Most new recruits went to one of the six standard bureaus and worked long hours, in and out of court all day, meeting with police officers, impaneling grand juries—and of course, dealing with defendants. Appeals was different. The thirty or so ADAs worked in near silence, researching and writing up written replies to a defendant's appeal. It wasn't easy work: a defense lawyer would come up with all kinds of bizarre rationales for why his client's conviction should be reversed, and the ADA had to counter them all. But the hours were regular, and a governor's son who wanted to stay out of the public eye could do so in appeals: he went once to court for each appeal, but that was it. Of course, compared to the other bureaus, appeals was boring.

Perhaps boredom accounted for Andrew's reported lack of interest in writing his briefs. Or perhaps his fellow ADAs envied the governor's son and let that cloud their judgment. "All I know," recalled one DA of his colleagues from that time, "is that they all say the same thing about Andrew. He basically did no work, and his office mate wrote his briefs for him." The office mate, Ralph Fabrizio, went on to become a state supreme court justice in the Bronx. His response, when asked directly if he had written briefs for Andrew, was "no." Later, though, when *Village Voice* reporter Wayne Barrett asked Andrew if he had ever written a legal brief, he was met, he recalled, with "stone silence."

However much he actually wrote of the fifteen or so briefs he did, Andrew was guilty beyond a reasonable doubt of the other rap his fellow ADAs charged him with: leaving too soon. After barely a year, he wrote to Morgenthau asking to be released from his commitment so he could manage his father's reelection campaign. "It was unusual not to do three years," the same DA explained. "Everyone will tell you that."

Mario was indeed planning to run for reelection in 1986, and Andrew would manage his campaign. But in May 1985, when Andrew left Morgenthau's office, the campaign was still in the planning stages, and Andrew was hardly its full-time manager. In fact, he had broken his commitment to Morgenthau for a job at the law firm where he had worked one summer and where his girlfriend was a partner. It was also the firm that had doubled as the governor's fund-raising machine. Jerry Weiss, Mario's close friend, counsel, and cofounder of the firm, had left it in late 1984. "Jerry's leaving," the governor said to Bill Stern, one of his commissioners. "Do you know he made $800,000 this year?" Small wonder, given that Sheldon Goldstein and a raft of other developers were now clients. With Weiss gone, the firm would no longer bear his name. Nor would it bear the name of its newest partner, who had even more clout with the governor than Jerry Weiss. It would just be Blutrich, Falcone & Miller, though everyone who dealt with it knew that its fourth and youngest partner was Andrew Cuomo.

Lucille Falcone was handling Sheldon Goldstein's banking and real estate business when Andrew joined the firm, and soon the two were doing it together. Goldstein rewarded them both with seats on the boards of two local banks he was trying to acquire. Andrew was installed on the board of the Hudson United Bank in Union City, New Jersey—a bone from the bank after Goldstein's hostile takeover bid came up short. Lucille was given a seat at the Savings Bank of Rockland, another bank in which Goldstein had taken a major interest. If Andrew wasn't on track to earn $800,000, he would at least earn $150,000, plenty to pay off his college and law school loans. Clearly pleased by his new life, he began driving around town in a Jaguar with a vanity plate that read AMC ESQ, and rented an apartment at 414 East 53rd Street, near—but not on—Sutton Place.

By now, the romance between Andrew and Falcone had cooled, enough that when one of Andrew's law school pals visited him at the firm, they seemed no more than brisk business colleagues. "He was twenty-five or twenty-six, he was still the Italian stallion, coming into this public life, becoming something of a celebrity himself," recalled Gary Eisenman. "And I think Lucille wanted to get married. She was also a little older. The end of their relationship had mostly to do with Lucille pressing him for the final commitment, and his being a little young for it."

Among Andrew's girlfriends in this period was Lisa Belzberg, a beautiful daughter of Canadian corporate raider Sam Belzberg. A smart, curvaceous blond, Lisa also dated Michael Fuchs, chairman and CEO of HBO in the mid-1980s. "I saw chemistry between them," one political consultant recalled. "It was electrifying." She would go on to marry billionaire heir Matthew Bronfman and have three children with him; she would also be linked, after her divorce, to ex-president Bill Clinton. In a very Old World way, Andrew seemed quite aware of the difference between girlfriend material and wife material. He would marry someone who was more than a romantic partner, someone who came with what amounted to a dowry for a young man of vaulting ambitions and no particular family money of his own. Meanwhile, he would let Sheldon Goldstein be his guide on how to succeed in business.

Goldstein was a fascinating wheeler-dealer—a *macher* whose fortune was growing after a series of public housing acquisitions from the federal government, at bargain prices, through the good graces of New York Republican senator Alfonse D'Amato. From the first, Goldstein seemed to regard Andrew as a protégé, teaching him the real estate business and talking of windfalls to come. Andrew seemed to regard Goldstein as a sort of Santa Claus, twinkly and generous. Like his father, he also seemed set on making a fair amount of money, not as an end in itself but to prove he could do it—and to set up a political career. If there was a seamy side to Goldstein—as his threats to ruin Harry Partridge might suggest—Andrew seemed oblivious to it.

Despite his new job, Andrew remained his father's dollar-a-year man, if more on the phone than in person. Now the job was different. There was a longer view, not just to the next gubernatorial election but to the White House. Mario after his keynote speech was the Democrats' greatest hope. Reagan had crushed Mondale in 1984; still, with Cuomo there was hope for 1988. To be a credible candidate, however, he would have to address as governor an issue of crucial concern to New York Democrats: the fast-growing legions of the homeless.

Recession had swelled the numbers, but so, unwittingly, had Mayor Koch. Responding to a lawsuit brought against the city by angry advocates, he had signed a legal consent decree committing the city to provide shelter to anyone and everyone who needed it, or be taken to court and forced to house the spillover in hotels at considerable cost. Koch had thought there might be 750 homeless each night. There were thousands. Desperate, the city had turned vast armories into emergency shelters, each with hundreds of cots, and begun renting rooms for the homeless in single-room occupancy hotels—SROs—already chopped into tiny spaces for single poor people. And still the numbers kept growing. In the fall of 1985, one of New York's richest citizens declared he had a better idea, and Andrew took notice.

Leonard N. Stern had turned a family pet-supplies business into mighty Hartz Mountain. He lived grandly, but one cold evening he found himself walking through City Hall Park and was appalled to find a large number of homeless families sleeping there. If government couldn't solve the problem, maybe a public/private partnership could.

Stern envisioned real estate developers and other city powers chipping in $100 million to build housing for the homeless on five government-owned sites in the city. The builders would build the centers at cost. They would include daycare centers and recreational facilities, in accord with Stern's belief that housing was not enough: everything from health care to child care to job counseling was needed to help the homeless get back on their feet. Stern and his partners would retain ownership of the centers, but lease them to the state. Eventually, the city's lease payments would pay back the investor. The charitable twist was that the centers would then be city-owned. As a test of his scheme, Stern proposed buying the Martinique, a dreary welfare hotel on Broadway at 32nd Street. He would take out a mortgage; over time, the city's per diems for sheltering homeless families would pay it off, and the city would then own it.

The day Stern's plan appeared in the morning papers, the governor sent an adviser to his town house. Stern heard him out and shrugged. "Okay, have the governor call me." Whether the governor lost patience with Stern or vice versa, the two failed to join forces. Instead, the governor asked Andrew to pursue the same idea.

Over at Blutrich, Falcone & Miller, Andrew began drawing up a way to make Stern's plan work by using the state's Housing and Finance Authority—basically a big pot of money designated for low-income housing. In Andrew's version, the HFA would float a construction bond, backed by its big pot of money. Then, as in Stern's plan, builders would build the sites at cost, an exercise in philanthropy but also enlightened self-interest: the sooner the homeless were dealt with, the more appealing New York would be again, and the more valuable their real estate portfolios. After ten years, the city would have paid off the bond, and like a homeowner finally paying off a mortgage, it would own the sites.

Royce Mulholland, one of the A-Teamers who would be drafted to help, got an excited call from Andrew one night. "I think I'll do housing for the homeless," he said, and explained the financing intricacies with the air of someone who'd been looking for an issue and found one. Stern would pursue his own vision with great success, but not with Andrew. "Once Andrew got involved," recalled one advocate for the homeless, "there wasn't much more between him and Stern than a nodding acquaintance." In politics, as Andrew had clearly learned, good ideas were up for grabs. The trick was to be the first one to make them work—and get the credit for them.

Andrew needed a guru, and he found one in Robert Esnard, a deputy mayor to Ed Koch. Together the two made a tour of the city's most desolate places in Andrew's Jeep Cherokee. In the painful last decade, vacant lots and empty buildings had mushroomed as businesses abandoned them rather than pay property taxes. The city was now willing and able to lure business back, and to help build schools and parks to reverse urban blight. "Unfortunately," Esnard explained, "the one thing the private sector will never do is homeless housing. And the neighborhoods don't want it either." Andrew was undeterred. "How do you begin to solve the problem of five thousand homeless families?" he asked rhetorically. "You begin with one family, one project, one community."

The site Andrew chose was in East New York, the same neighborhood where his grandfather had been beaten nearly to death. It was an abandoned lot in a low-income neighborhood, bounded by Blake, Dumont, and Snediker Avenues and Hinsdale Street. The shelter Andrew planned to build on the site would house two hundred families—up to eight hundred people. It would be a three-story rectangular building around a large open courtyard with a playground. Only families would be housed here, mostly young mothers and small children. The two-room apartments would be accessible only from the courtyard, to residents with passes, and guests would go no farther than visiting rooms. HELP I, as Andrew dubbed it, wouldn't just house these homeless families: as in Leonard Stern's vision, there would be counseling for addiction issues, job training, child care, and more. A continuum of care—that was the phrase Andrew began to use.

Designing a new site, instead of putting the homeless into some sad old hotel, was a thrilling prospect for Andrew. He loved poring over blueprints and brainstorming on how to make HELP I efficient but elegant. It wasn't so different from tinkering with a car engine, except he got to create the engine from the ground up. "Andrew can look at a spoon for a hundred hours, contemplating it," A-Teamer Royce Mulholland said, only half joking. "Is it round? Is it concave? What other uses could it have?"

At first, Andrew wondered if the best design for HELP I might be a cinderblock box. The families that stayed there shouldn't get too comfortable; the whole point was to move them out within a year to live on their own. But soon Andrew was consulting top architects, proudly describing how beautiful HELP I would be, and how good design was essential to the project. At a news conference to announce HELP I held at Gracie Mansion with the governor and Mayor Koch looking on, he showed beautiful renderings. This, he strongly implied, was how to do housing for the homeless.

In the tight-knit world of advocates for the homeless, Andrew and

HELP I stirred mixed reactions. "Here's my beef with Andrew," explained one. "He thought Help was unique. The only way it was unique was because he got a lot of favors from Daddy's administration to ease the way. There were nonprofits that waited years to get approvals from the state or the city, and because he was Mario's son, he was the hot knife through butter. Then Andrew in his arrogant way would go around town saying, 'I did this, why can't everyone else do it?' But no one else could get the city and state agencies to move as quickly as the governor's son.

"For many of us," the advocate added, "this was our life's work. And it was always clear that Andrew was on a political track. Yet he would portray himself as the savior of the homeless. That's the gist of it. And he was not a humble public servant. I hated him."

In the spring of 1986, with HELP I rising, Andrew was again profiled by the *New York Times*, this time in his fourteenth-floor office at Blutrich, Falcone & Miller. In the entranceway, the reporter noted a blowup of a newspaper article headlined "No Special Favors for Clients of Governor's Son." Within the office hung the portrait of Saint Thomas More that had belonged to his father. "Am I still an adviser to the governor?" Andrew echoed. "Yes. But at the same time I am Andrew Cuomo and I am an independent person and that is very important to me now."

HELP I was giving Andrew that independence, and as the reporter noted, he had achieved it by "getting the support of bankers and builders and others by relying on the Cuomo name, by being aggressive, by concocting intricate scenarios and deals, and by pressing again and again and again until a needed supporter gave in." But the reporter did not have to look far to find a critic of that style. William Stern, who had worked on the governor's 1982 campaign and then briefly served as head of the state's Urban Development Corporation, had broken with the Cuomos and now spoke harshly of Andrew. "Andrew believes in winning, that winning is its reward," Stern said. "He plays the game of politics at the cutting edge. He's very charming and that masks an ability to be ruthless."

In his dollar-a-year capacity, Andrew was focused on another Cuomo win: his father's 1986 campaign for reelection. Victory was all but inevitable. The challenge, as Andrew knew, was to win by such a commanding margin that the national Democratic leaders saw fit to back the New York governor as the party's nominee for president in 1988. Four other New York governors had made that leap: Martin Van Buren, Grover Cleveland, and the Roosevelts, Theodore and Franklin. Why not Mario?

The state's Republicans had a weak field of possible rivals for the governorship to start with, but that wasn't good enough for Andrew. Privately, he struck a deal with New York's Republican senator, Alfonse D'Amato, who was also up for reelection that year. The Cuomos would do little or nothing to support D'Amato's Democratic rival, Mark Green, if D'Amato recruited the weakest possible Republican candidate to oppose Cuomo. After the election, the state's Democratic senator, Daniel Patrick Moynihan, would confirm as much. "Of course there was a nonaggression pact between Governor Cuomo and Senator D'Amato," he would declare. "That's not a theory; it's a fact." The straw man chosen as Mario's Republican rival was Andrew O'Rourke, Westchester County executive, a charming self-made man from the poor Irish neighborhood of Hell's Kitchen who against the Cuomos' now mighty political machine had not a shred of hope.

For Mario the risk developed, unexpectedly, with the race for lieutenant governor. The shotgun marriage between Mario and his first lieutenant governor, Al DelBello, had ended when DelBello, completely marginalized, resigned in disgust. The Cuomos were backing a bland assemblyman named Stan Lundine, but a spoiler had emerged. Abe Hirschfeld was an eccentric, possibly crazy real estate developer who had made his fortune with open-air parking garages ("Cars don't catch cold," was his mantra) and taken to tilting at political office with little more than money and chutzpah. Few pundits thought Hirschfeld could win, but if he did, his victory would be calamitous for the Cuomos. It would show the governor not in control of his own state party, a bad harbinger for a White House run. Worse, if Mario ran for president anyway, he would show he was willing to risk saddling his state with Hirschfeld as governor. Ruthless tactics were needed, and Andrew knew just what they were.

First, Andrew emptied the campaign offices of envelope-stuffers and filled them with election lawyers. Hirschfeld had gathered 70,490 signatures to win a place on the ballot. That was 50,490 more than required by law. Andrew, undaunted, had the lawyers start checking every signature, not only for forged signatures but lapsed voter registrations. It was a costly gambit, and one that would make Mario look bad if he lost. But Andrew persevered. If they could show enough forged signatures to make a case that Hirschfeld's petitions were "permeated with fraud," as the legal jargon had it, then even if the valid signatures outnumbered the invalid ones, a judge could disqualify them all. The beauty of "permeation with fraud" was that there wasn't a measurable standard. The judge could decide. Judge Vincent Bradley in the state supreme court in Albany heard both sides, and listened to witnesses brought in by the busload at the Cuomo campaign's expense to testify as to how they had come to sign the Hirschfeld petitions—not at gunpoint but nearly so. Then he made his decision: Hirschfeld was off the ballot, due to technical errors. The next morning's newspapers ran pictures of Hirschfeld weeping at a news conference. He appealed the decision and lost.

Andrew, now fully in control as campaign manager, dealt with Andrew O'Rourke, his father's Republican rival, by ignoring him altogether. The challenger of 1982 who had demanded that Ed Koch air his views in a string of debates wasn't going to make the mistake of letting the little-known O'Rourke raise his profile by sharing a stage with the governor. There would be no debates, no shared stages, no exchanges at all. O'Rourke took to carrying around a life-size cardboard cutout of Cuomo, "debating" him at every campaign stop.

Columnists mocked the strategy—classic Rose Garden—and predicted that Cuomo would be viewed as arrogant and vindictive if he staged a presidential run two years later. "I'm not the arrogant one," Cuomo replied earnestly, "I'm the one fighting for openness." Cuomo, who had raised about $10 million to O'Rourke's $1 million, won in a landslide, 64.3 percent to 31.77 percent.

Cynical or not, Andrew's strategy had given his father the smashing victory he needed to contemplate a White House run. Yet for Mario there was a bitter aftertaste. Along with talk of a President Cuomo had come speculation that an Italian couldn't win. Cuomo had already stated that he had no plans to run, but as he declared, "If anything could change my mind about running for the presidency, it's people talking about 'an Italian can't do it.'" Though Andrew sympathized, ethnicity would never seem as important to him, personally or politically, as it was to his father. Mario was the son of immigrants, bearing their slights and insecurities as his own; Andrew was the third generation, the all-American boy.

But there was more—and Andrew was at the heart of it. In the campaign's August doldrums, reporters had raised questions about Blutrich, Falcone & Miller, and Andrew's role in it. Here was the governor's campaign manager working as a partner of a firm with powerful real estate clients who wanted favors from the state. Wasn't there a conflict of interest here?

Andrew had told the press the line was clear. With his arrival in May 1985, the firm had stopped representing new clients with business before state agencies—agencies whose heads were appointed by his father. But he felt it entirely proper to represent clients with *other* matters before the state. "Otherwise," Andrew suggested, "you would have to say, 'Andrew, you shouldn't represent anyone who has any interaction with the state.' Then I couldn't represent anyone who wants a driver's license or has a tax problem."

That might be so, but the real estate titans who had signed on as clients seemed to feel that the firm had useful political clout all the same. Bill Zeckendorf admitted he'd retained the firm because "we thought they could help us politically." Donald Trump acknowledged that the firm was representing him "in a very significant transaction" concerning a lease negotiation. A *New York Times* editorial followed, along with an attack by columnist William Safire on Andrew Cuomo as "the new rainmaker." In a phone interview for the column, Safire asked the governor if Blutrich, Falcone & Miller's clients were hiring Andrew because his father was governor of the state. "An outrageous, unfounded conclusion," Mario thundered. Safire asked the governor if his son might be better advised to hang his shingle in another state, simply to avoid the appearance of conflict of interest. "That," reported Safire, "triggered another blast—hell of a nerve, etc.—which shows the Governor to be a) a loving father b) a feisty interlocutor c) blind."

Weeks after his outsize win, Mario was still boiling at what he saw as baseless attacks on Andrew. He lashed out at the Albany press corps, accusing them of conspiring against him—a "cabal," as he called it. In evening phone calls to reporters, his ire spilled over. "You set out to hurt me and you succeeded," he told a *New York Times* reporter. "I hope you sleep well." Andrew was as quick to phone reporters as his father, and to criticize them—off the record, of course—but generally he kept his feelings in check. He knew that losing his temper meant losing the debate—and Andrew didn't like to lose. Already he was learning as much from his father's failings as from his strengths.

One of those failings on Mario's part was blindness with respect to one of his largest campaign contributors. Even as the governor was railing at the press for raising questions about Blutrich, Falcone & Miller, and Andrew's ties to some of its clients, his son was working as Goldstein's lawyer to pull off a deal that would make Goldstein much, much richer than he was, and make Andrew wealthy as well. This was a deal that would involve opening up a private wilderness larger than Manhattan and having the state build a new Thruway interchange for easy access to it. It was, in fact, a taxpayer-financed project that would benefit the developer buying up hundreds of acres both in and around the forest—Sheldon Goldstein—in a gambit that evoked nothing so much as the movie *Chinatown*.

CHAPTER 7

In Search of a Killing

The mystery began with a seemingly innocuous phrase in Governor Cuomo's State of the State speech in January 1984.

Going down his list of pledges for the year, the governor promised highway improvements that might have great economic benefits—"for example, the construction of a new Thruway interchange near Sterling Forest."

This was news to the governor's Thruway Authority, as well as to the local officials of Orange County, which encompassed most of Sterling Forest, a one-hour drive north of Manhattan on the west side of the Hudson River. The very idea was surprising. As a rule, interchanges were built to alleviate intolerable points of congestion. Sterling Forest wasn't a destination for many motorists. It was, in fact, a *forest*. The interchange would be a huge boon, however, for the local developer who hoped to build thousands of homes in and around the forest. Andrew would be his lawyer, his point man, and, if plans proceeded, his partner in transforming the forest into Sheldon Goldstein's fiefdom.

Sterling Forest was unique: the last vast chunk of primeval wilderness in private hands within a fifty-mile radius of New York City. At twenty-two thousand acres, it was larger than Manhattan, yet virtually unchanged since the Iroquois had hunted its oak and pine woods and fished its pristine lakes. The steep-sided ridges and narrow, swampy valleys had put off pioneers; even now, only 15 to 20 percent of the forest could be built upon. Still, several thousand buildable acres remained, whole new communities for city commuters. In short, a fortune to be made.

Originally a conglomerate called City Investing had bought the forest from W. Averell Harriman, the diplomat and onetime governor of New York. It had a bold vision: it would turn the forest into a corporate utopia of research-and-design parks, with engineers dreaming up future products in glass-walled boxes tucked among the trees, then going home to their wooded enclaves. A few of those parks were built, and a few dozen homes went up, but the forest remained mostly undeveloped.

By the early 1960s, City was pushing for a highway interchange to make the forest more accessible. The New York State Thruway ran along Sterling's eastern edge, but without a nearby exit: the few corporate parks that had gone up in the forest were forced to use the smaller Route 17-A instead. One administration after another nixed the pitch for a new interchange that would allow cars to cloverleaf off the Thruway onto 17-A at a point where the Thruway crossed over it. "My objection," explained Governor Hugh Carey's Thruway chairman, Gerald Cummins, adding his veto to the others, "was that it was an exit for a private development, and that was not our function."

Unconcerned, Governor Cuomo pushed through a bill for the project, issued a no-bid contract for the work, and during an appearance at the Orange County fair on July 24, 1985, signed the bill authorizing the first $5 million to be spent.

From his papal-like office in Suffern, Sheldon Goldstein for years had nursed his own vision for Sterling Forest. He could see its lakes ringed by residential units, its outskirts dotted with shopping malls built and leased by one or another of his dozens of corporate entities. Work wouldn't start on the Thruway interchange for some time—there were permits to obtain and processes to endure—but Goldstein could see the vast potential. Why not buy the whole forest? It would be like buying his own kingdom. In January 1986, he made a bid of $35 million for the whole twenty-two thousand acres.

At about this time, investigative journalist Wayne Barrett of the *Village Voice* began looking into the Sterling Forest interchange plan and how Goldstein might benefit from it. Barrett had taken a special interest in the Cuomos—both father and son—and established with both a combative camaraderie. In a long, intense interview with Barrett, Andrew acknowledged that he was acting as more than Goldstein's lawyer in submitting the $35 million bid to acquire the whole of Sterling Forest. "At one point in 1986," Barrett later wrote, "the Sterling Forest acquisition was clearly the biggest deal in Andrew Cuomo's life. He was not merely representing Goldstein... Cuomo was scheduled to get both legal and real estate brokerage fees on the sale, and Goldstein was going to allow him to retroactively invest those fees... in the firm's booming real estate department."

With that as the plan, Andrew started visiting the forest as due diligence. Bruce Bean, then general counsel for the City Investing subsidiary that owned the forest, recalled him as "very aggressive, very self-confident."

Andrew didn't yell, exactly, but he did talk very forcefully, Bean noted. Sterling Forest manager Ken Heim took Andrew in his Jeep down various back trails. On one, they came up to a big tree fallen across the way. Heim had neglected to bring a chainsaw. "I guess we'll have to turn around," he told Andrew.

"Let's move the tree," Andrew replied, and jumped out of the Jeep. Heim looked at the tree; he looked at Andrew. "It was a full-sized tree," he recalled. "No one was going to lift that tree." For a minute or two Andrew huffed and puffed, with Heim trying to help. The tree didn't budge. Finally a grim-faced Andrew got back in the Jeep. He was about the most determined man Heim had ever seen.

In the end, the deal to buy the whole forest never got past the talking stage. Bruce Bean never received a firm commitment from Goldstein's Lynmark Development Associates. City Investing's new CEO now thought that with the interchange moving ahead, the forest was worth north of $150 million, perhaps as much as $250 million. Very likely those rising numbers discouraged Goldstein from making a formal bid.

As a fallback, Goldstein acquired an option on one of the corporate park inholdings: the 160-acre parcel owned by International Nickel, or INCO, toward the southern end of the forest. Just when Sheldon Goldstein acquired that option was a matter of some interest. Had it preceded, by chance, Governor Cuomo's State of the State speech in January 1984? Then, like the California speculators in *Chinatown*, he might have controlled the land for a fraction of its value, knowing that its worth was about to jump with the Thruway interchange.

Goldstein exercised his option to buy the INCO parcel in August 1987, and had his lawyer, Andrew Cuomo, speak to the *New York Times* to tamp down speculation on the timing of the acquisition. Andrew didn't say exactly when Goldstein had taken that option. He just said that Goldstein had taken his option after Mario's State of the State speech in 1984, so that no one could accuse of him of having an inside track. Under rigorous questioning, Andrew warned that even the mention of his name in the article would create an unfair impression of impropriety when in fact he had violated no ethical or legal standard.

INCO might be the only property Sheldon Goldstein had managed to buy within the forest. But just north of the forest was a parcel of 110 undeveloped acres that he had purchased in 1981. Three other parcels a bit north of that, purchased between 1978 and 1982, totaled nearly 600 acres. In 1985, Goldstein had also begun talks in the town of Chester about developing a twenty-eight-store mall on 30 acres. All these would rise in value a great deal if the forest was opened up to Thruway traffic and subdivisions.

The INCO parcel was a nice consolation prize. Unlike the forest at large, it already had a power and utility grid. Goldstein started drawing up plans to build 150 houses on the property's steep hillsides, overlooking the aptly named Blue Lake. It was a development that would only become marketable with the interchange, but permits for the interchange were in the works. The news of a major new development in Sterling Forest was not received well, however, by the state of New Jersey.

INCO was near Sterling's southern tip, still in New York but just above the New York–New Jersey state line. The sewage from more than four hundred new residents of the planned INCO development, even if carefully treated, would empty into a river that flowed into New Jersey's Wanaque and Monksville reservoirs, a source of drinking water for 1.8 million New Jersey residents. Appalled by the risks that Goldstein's plans appeared to entail, New Jersey took drastic action. Roughly two thousand of Sterling's twenty-two thousand acres lay in Passaic County, on the New Jersey side of the state line. The county seized those two thousand acres by eminent domain, and vowed to do all it could to stop the INCO project from moving ahead.

That summer, the Thruway Authority seemed poised to break ground on the new interchange, only to find rising opposition on every side. The nearest town was Tuxedo, old-money and WASPy, from which that badge of formal wear took its name. Many of Tuxedo's residents were alarmed by the traffic and tax hikes the interchange would bring. Conservation groups were worried too: real estate prices would rise, complicating efforts to preserve more land in the area. New Jersey's state government was still focused on the sewage issue. All these forces might have been straight-armed by the governor of New York State. But not so easily the U.S. Department of the Interior.

There was one place, and one place only, that the interchange could go: where the Thruway passed directly over Route 17-A, the smaller road to which it would be linked. Some land for the interchange would be needed, and that land, as it happened, was state parkland. As a further wrinkle, the land had been given to the state by the federal government, which reserved the right to approve of any change in usage.

Interior took a serious look, and didn't like what it saw. The Cuomo administration had commissioned an environmental study of the interchange project, whose estimated cost had ballooned to $8.5 million. The study only considered the impact of the interchange on the land immediately *under* it. This was at best a myopic approach. What effect would all this new traffic have on the forest? On the nearby Appalachian Trail? On the lakes and rivers of Sterling Forest, and the reservoirs of northern

New Jersey below? The state's report was silent on all of these issues. Interior decided to study each and every concern, in a process that would take at least nine more months. Could the interchange survive that scrutiny? Apparently not: one day in December 1988, the Cuomo administration declared the project dead. Reporters seeking comment from senior officials found no one available.

Andrew had lost out on a first fortune dangled before him by Sheldon Goldstein. But Goldstein had another scheme up his sleeve, one that might be easier to bring off. Instead of years spent fighting to build houses on pristine forest lakes, wrangling in court over sewage treatment plans, Goldstein had a get-rich-quick scheme that involved a savings and loan bank in Florida, and some fancy lawyering for Cuomo to do.

Oceanmark. That was the name of the bank. It was a name that would come to haunt Andrew Cuomo, infuriate his father, and nearly ruin the family's hopes of a political dynasty.

Sheldon Goldstein was too brash and ambitious a real estate mogul not to jump into the S&L game at its peak in 1986. Every developer with property to flip, and every two-bit banker, not to mention every con man and white-collar criminal with greed in his heart, wanted in on the grand casino that savings and loan banks had suddenly become. A wave of deregulation had allowed S&Ls to put their depositors' money in any speculative investment they liked—virtually on red or black—at no risk, as that capital was backed by government insurance. For anyone smart enough to do the numbers, it was a thrilling new opportunity.

Savings and loans, also known as thrifts, were the modest banks on every Main Street of America that made home loans. Let other banks earn higher interest with higher-risk consumer and commercial loans. Thrifts did mortgages, and did just fine. The catchphrase of the industry was "3-6-3." Thrifts paid 3 percent on the savings-account money they took in from depositors. They loaned that money out at 6 percent in the form of mortgages. And by 3 p.m. their bankers were out playing golf.

By the early 1980s, that formula no longer worked. Savings and loans were so hard hit by higher-interest-paying money markets that their depositors left in droves. To keep the thrifts alive, the federal government let them offer higher rates to compete with the money markets, and make go-go investments on their own—like in commercial real estate. For that matter, they could make those investments anywhere they liked, not just in their hometowns. And the federal government would back the investments with federal insurance. So the S&Ls could take up to $100,000 of each depositor's account, invest it as they pleased, and either make a profit or get the government to cover their losses.

For a brief Wild West period, any old Joe—or Sheldon—could buy an S&L anywhere, pull in his pals as investors, and make fail-safe investments in increments of $100,000. Heads they won, tails the U.S. government lost.

This was the backdrop in 1986 against which Sheldon Goldstein, with Andrew as his lawyer and protégé, jumped into Oceanmark, a brand-new S&L in North Miami Beach, in 1986.

The story of Andrew's run at Oceanmark is only passingly told in the newspaper articles of late 1987 and early 1988, generated by the lawsuits that Andrew and the owners of Oceanmark threw at each other. The court record of those suits no longer exists. Lynn Fenster Smith and her brother Jeffrey Fenster, Oceanmark's founders, may still have their own copies of the court record but are no longer interested in talking about the legal battle that consumed them, in one form or another, well into the 1990s. By chance, however, a Washington-based journalist, Sam Dealey, spent months in the late 1990s reporting a story on Cuomo for the *American Spectator*, with fellow journalist James Ring Adams. An obsessive reporter, Dealey gathered far more documents than he needed, including key filings from the still-extant case record—and kept them all.

The story, according to the first pair of lawsuits filed by Lynn Fenster Smith and her brother, began in 1986, when the two got a call from a New York developer unknown to them: Sheldon Goldstein.

Oceanmark was a newly chartered S&L, privately owned with a small amount of stock. The Fensters owned about 24 percent; the rest was in limited circulation. Goldstein said their bank had great potential, but clearly could benefit from more capital. He offered to acquire a hefty chunk of the outstanding stock. "Goldstein made it very clear that he would be contacting a series of passive investors," the complaint alleged, "each of whom had an interest in making individual investments in South Florida that might result in a fair return." At no time did Goldstein acknowledge that he represented a "New York group" of investors acting in concert to acquire a *controlling* interest in the bank and enact a prearranged scheme, according to the complaint.

During those talks, the complaint continued, Goldstein allegedly advised Lynn Fenster Smith that she would need to visit the New York law offices of Andrew Cuomo, to sign certain relevant papers. In his office, Andrew presented her with proxy documents granting two of Goldstein's other investors the right to vote extra chunks of stock and wield more control over the bank if needed. "Under extreme pressure from Mr. Cuomo," the complaint alleged, "Ms. Smith executed the draft proxy materials after extracting the express promise of Messrs. Cuomo, [Herbert] Kreiger and [Howard] Ellish that they would not be effective or enforceable unless they were reviewed, approved and signed by Jeffrey Fenster, Ms. Smith's brother and attorney." Jeffrey Fenster never did sign those documents, according to the Fenster complaint. "Mr. Fenster's refusal to execute the documents was based, in part, upon defendant Andrew Cuomo's insistence that the documents remain secret, and that they not be disclosed to federal regulatory agencies."

All seemed to go well until the end of an Oceanmark board meeting on July 21, 1987. As the meeting's minutes later recounted, a "guest" was announced. Andrew Cuomo, twenty-nine, identified as "esquire of New York, New York," made a proposal. It was a proposal that startled and alarmed the board.

Cuomo proposed that Oceanmark merge with another thrift, Financial Security Savings and Loan Association, of nearby Delray Beach, which happened to be losing $6 million a year. He explained that he had a "new investment group" that would infuse Oceanmark with $6 million of capital, a hefty supplement to the $3 million that Oceanmark had on hand. Oceanmark could use some of this capital to buy Financial Security.

Why would a healthy thrift like Oceanmark want to buy a thrift that was losing roughly $6 million a year? Because, Andrew explained, Financial Security had a very interesting real estate portfolio: basically a number of distressed properties whose aggregate market value of $31 million or so had dipped, with foreclosures, down to perhaps $5 million. But that was still $5 million that selling them off would bring.

If Andrew had gone on to say that this $5 million would flow back into Oceanmark, he might have been applauded. To the dismay of Oceanmark's board, he proposed that the $5 million would go directly to the new investors: Sheldon Goldstein, Andrew himself, and however many others constituted what Lynn Fenster Smith would come to call the "New York Group."

Andrew acknowledged that Financial Security, which had no other assets, would expire as a result of this legerdemain, leaving Oceanmark the sole survivor of the merger. Cuomo maintained that Oceanmark would emerge stronger because financial securities losses could be set against Oceanmark's future income. That wasn't how Oceanmark's board members saw it. From their own back-of-the-envelope jottings, they felt Oceanmark would go under too, in perhaps twenty-four months' time. The only winners would be the New York Group, who would make off with that $5 million package of real estate and sell their Oceanmark stock while it was high.

Lynn Fenster Smith's lawyer, William Friedlander, has since died, but in 1998 he laid out the New York Group's modus operandi as he saw it in an interview for the article that Sam Dealey and James Ring Adams were preparing for the *American Spectator.*

"They weren't interested in our bank," Friedlander explained. "They were interested in Financial Security S&L Association, which was an upside-down S&L with a negative net worth, but with a tremendous amount of real estate that they held as the result of the foreclosures... But...to make a play for Financial Security, they would have come under intense scrutiny because it was a failing institution."

Friedlander explained exactly what he thought the New York Group planned to do. "They would take over Oceanmark, without disclosing that they were gaining control, so there would be no regulatory review—the Fensters had already been approved. They would then merge Oceanmark with Financial Security so it would be Oceanmark rather than the New York Group that was acquiring Financial Security. They would get by the regulators that way without disclosing who they were or what they did."

As Lynn Fenster Smith would learn through documents procured by her lawyer, the New York Group was larger than she had believed it to be. It was composed of more than twenty investors, most of whose names she hadn't known. A key document, seemingly drawn up by someone in the New York Group, listed all the investors' names, how much money each was investing, and how many shares of Oceanmark each would have as a result. Goldstein's two sons were members; so was Lucille Falcone, along with a loose network of Goldstein colleagues, including Andrew Cuomo. Goldstein was to get the most shares—fifteen thousand. Andrew was to get two thousand shares.

The Fensters knew that Goldstein, Cuomo, and a few others together owned 37 percent of Oceanmark's stock. But as the Fensters later claimed in their federal complaint, they didn't know about the "scheme." "Members of the New York Group would each acquire shares in Oceanmark Savings through separate checks, making it appear to plaintiff Lynn Fenster Smith and to Oceanmark Savings (as well as to federal agencies) that they were making separate investments in the bank, and that they were not acting in concert with one another. At the appropriate time, the New York Group would begin to act in concert with one another." After taking over Financial Security and making a quick profit on its real estate portfolio, the Fensters alleged in their complaint, "it was the intention of the New York Group to allow the combined financial institution to become insolvent."

From exchanges between Goldstein and his protégé that were part of the then extant court record, the New York Group apparently kept the merger plan a secret for some time from their partners at Oceanmark. In a memo to Andrew dated April 16, 1987, Goldstein wrote excitedly of his plan to do "the savings and loan deal in Del Ray Beach," adding, "It could be a super deal because we could tie it into Oceanmark and have a $200,000,000 or better bank at one shot . . . The big problem with this bank is the $35,000,000 to $45,000,000 in bad real estate," Goldstein wrote. But he thought "we may be able to slough the real estate and pick up $4,000,000 to $5,000,000. All in all this could be our first big piece."

In that same memo, Goldstein wrote, "It is imperative that you and I sit down together and discuss the whole Venture deal, and on Monday I will put out the call for the $500,000."

Lynn Fenster Smith and her brother would come to abhor both Cuomo and Goldstein, but for a while they regarded the flashy developer as a welcome new partner, and listened to him brag about his style of business. "Shelley would gin up an investment and he would put out a call for money," Jeffrey Fenster related later to Sam Dealey. "And Shelley had a thing that no one would ever lose money. He always gave them their money back if they lost money." It was a credo that cut both ways, Lynn Fenster Smith explained. "The first time you didn't bring your money—he told me this—you didn't get to go again. And the first time you ever got worried about your money or didn't want to stay there, he would literally write you a check and you would never get called again."

That memo from Goldstein included an intriguing postscript—one that underscored his role as Andrew's money mentor. "I really don't know what you did on your taxes," Goldstein scolded. "I called and found out you filed for an extension. Please, please let's put it together or some day it will come back and bite us."

Goldstein might be the dealmaker, but Andrew was critically involved. In a memo to Goldstein and other members of the New York Group dated June 4, 1987, he laid out in detail the plan to effect a stock swap between Oceanmark and Financial Security, sell off the real estate for a quick $4–$5 million profit, and take the tax advantages from the paper losses on those assets. Documents outlining the merger were drawn up by Andrew personally. "If you have any questions you can contact me at home over the weekend," Andrew advised, and provided his home phone number.

With their own board clout, the Fensters managed to block the merger by August 1987. That, as Lynn Fenster Smith recounted in an affidavit, led the New York Group to try to buy her and her family out. In the federal complaint, the Fensters alleged that Goldstein had "made overt threats of violence" against the plaintiffs if they didn't sell their shares, "stating before several witnesses that 'his friends can't understand why he doesn't just cut the Fensters up with a razor,' or words to that effect."

When the family refused to sell, Smith alleged in the complaint, the New York Group set about trying to push her out, along with her brother. Now they pulled out those proxy statements that Smith had signed in Andrew's New York office—the ones that gave two of the New York Group members extra voting power. The Fensters declared the proxies null and void: Jeffrey Fenster had never signed them, and in any event, they hadn't been exercised since they'd been drawn up more than a year earlier. By Florida state law, the Fensters argued, the proxies were unenforceable.

Waving that logic aside, the New York Group declared at a December board meeting that it was now in charge, by virtue of those proxies, and would vote the Fensters off the board at the very next meeting. It made that declaration, the Fensters' lawyer later claimed, without notifying federal regulators of a change of control—a violation of federal rules.

The Fensters felt the bank they had started only a year or so before was about to be seized from them in an outrageous and illegal maneuver. That December 1987, they sued in both state and federal court, asking the judges for an injunction to stop what they deemed the racketeering activities of the New York Group.

That holiday season was a strange one for Andrew, a roller coaster of good and bad news. In late November 1987, Sheldon Goldstein was subpoenaed in the case about 400 Broome Street. He managed to avoid testifying, however. The trial ended in mid-January with Partridge's conviction for perjury but nothing else; his acquittal would come on appeal. In the court record for 400 Broome, the heavies seemed to be Goldstein and Andrew Cuomo, but they were not on trial.

Andrew's thirtieth birthday was that December 6, and he celebrated it with about twenty-five friends, all of them male. A group picture shows Andrew at the center, on one knee, like the captain of a football team. Nearly all the friends in the picture were linked in one way or another to the Cuomo political camp.

The one notable absence from the photo was Jeff Sachs, a former operative for Governor Carey who was helping Andrew on HELP I. Sachs was perhaps Andrew's best friend at this point, but that was hardly by chance. Sachs had more social connections than anyone else in the group. He was there that night: he was the one taking the picture. The party was in his apartment.

The lines between personal and political friendships were not just blurred, but gone altogether. Politics, and the business that arose from it, *was* Andrew's personal life. He was, as one friend put it, a totally pragmatic person now. Unless there was a purpose to the friendship, he didn't have time, and the friends he did nurture were all compartmentalized: this one for that, that one for this. That wasn't a criticism, the friend added: it was just the way Andrew was, the way that any thirty-year-old aspiring to be president had to be. It was partly ambition, partly self-protection. "If he's compartmentalized," suggested the friend, "then there's no one who knows him completely, no one who can connect the dots completely. Andrew is the only one—and that is total control."

Days before Christmas, HELP I opened at last. Andrew had vowed proudly at Gracie Mansion in early 1986 that his first homeless shelter would be done by year's end. He admitted he had been too optimistic. Still, he objected when a reporter asked him about the delays. "I don't want to see an article saying it's behind schedule," he said. "That's not true. That's not fair." But it was: Andrew had clashed with local unions, and the union heads had come to resent his tendency to plant press items that made them look bad. The shelter had also cost far more than expected: $14 million. That was a lot of one-night SRO hotel stays. Still, it was done, and it looked beautiful. "This is my Christmas present," one homeless mother of three declared as she toured the three-story building before moving in to one of its two hundred apartments. Like most of the other fourteen homeless mothers who moved in that day with their children, Margaret Cammarota had come from an SRO hotel. Between HELP I and the hotel, there was no comparison. By Andrew's reckoning, a night's stay at HELP I would cost the city $52 a night, versus $63 a night for an SRO hotel. On a day-to-day basis, HELP I made financial sense. Whether the builders could be repaid their $14 million in ten years was an open question.

From its opening day, HELP I had a daycare center and a job training center, allowing mothers to start the search for work. It had a playground and courtyard too. Andrew had sweated over every detail of the shelter's design—perhaps a bit obsessively. Years before the concept of branding had grown ubiquitous, he had brought it to HELP I. "Andrew was very into the logo," one colleague recalled, "and coffee mugs that said Help." He even designed the baseball uniforms for the HELP I team. Later, that spring, when the team held its first day of practice, Andrew came by to coach. The kids had never had baseball mitts; they had to be taught how to use them. One in particular just seemed hopeless. Andrew would toss the ball gently at him; the ball would hit his chest. Or his head. Someone suggested that the kid might have poor vision. "We take him to get an eye test," recalled Royce Mulholland. "He's legally blind!" They got him glasses. "Turned out he could catch after that."

Within hours of HELP I's opening, the Fenster Family Group filed its first suit against Andrew Cuomo, Sheldon Goldstein, and others in Florida's Broward County Circuit Court. The suit alleged that Cuomo and the rest of his New York Group had invested in Oceanmark under false pretenses, concealing their plan to vote as a bloc and take over the thrift. They had cooked up a plan to merge Oceanmark with Financial Security Savings and Loan, long before informing the Fensters. And Andrew Cuomo had allegedly given false information to regulators at the Federal Home Loan Bank Board, claiming that the Fensters had approved the merger. Within days, Smith filed a second suit, this one in federal court under the Racketeer Influenced and Corrupt Organizations Act, better known as RICO. Based on the same facts, that suit charged Cuomo and Goldstein with nothing less than "a pattern of racketeering activity."

Andrew reacted to the suits as he would to awkward news again and again: by distancing himself from it. He said he no longer represented the New York Group, and neglected to mention that he had been a member of it. He merely admitted he had served as the group's lawyer while the Oceanmark merger with Financial Security was under consideration. The merger was just "a business deal gone sour," he said. "They want to use my name to give them leverage and I think it's a ploy," he declared. With that, he filed his own suit in return, demanding $10 million from Smith for libeling him—a claim later upped to $50 million. His suit alleged that Smith had threatened "that unless her unreasonable demands were met, she would undertake a campaign to embarrass, undermine and defame the Cuomo family." To a reporter, Cuomo added, "She said to my former clients, 'If you don't accept the offer, I will name Andrew as one of the twelve, and it'll be embarrassing.' She said it in front of people."

With the lawsuits resonating, the New York Group again tried to buy out the Fensters. That offer too was rebuffed. "The stock is not for sale to Cuomo and Goldstein at any price," declared the Fenster family's lawyer, William Friedlander. "Not at $1.65 per share, not $160, not at $1,600. We want them out of the bank. We want them to leave us alone. We are not angling for a stock price."

In his later interview with the *American Spectator*, Friedlander explained why he had added the Federal Home Loan Bank Board and the Federal Savings and Loan Insurance Corporation as defendants in the federal suit. He hoped to goad them into investigating the New York Group and its failure to file a change-of-control notice when it acquired 37 percent of Oceanmark's stock and started trying to push the Fensters off the board. Oddly, the agencies had shown little interest in looking into that.

The two sides met in a federal courtroom in Fort Lauderdale on January 7, 1988, before Judge Jose Gonzalez, to consider the Fensters' plea for an injunction to stop the New York Group from taking over Oceanmark at its next scheduled board meeting, on January 27, 1988. Gonzalez denied their motion, but seemed curious about why the agencies had failed to investigate the change-of-control issue. He set another court date, for January 21, and encouraged the agencies to act in the meantime. "I think the federal agencies should do that for which they are paid," Gonzalez said drily.

On that next court date, the New York Group seemed to gain the upper hand. Judge Gonzalez ruled that the Fensters had no grounds to sue under federal change-of-control rules. He also declined to stop the New York Group from taking over Oceanmark at its next board meeting. When that meeting occurred, the Fensters were indeed voted off the board, leaving the New York Group in charge. But not for long.

On April 18, 1988, the lawsuit was settled, and hardly in the New York Group's favor. Apparently a cold-eyed look at their case had convinced them its merits were few. As a result, Lynn Fenster Smith was reinstated as acting chairman. The dissident shareholders were sent packing, with a pledge to sell their stock back to the Fensters at roughly the price they'd bought it for: $10 a share. This was far from the big money Goldstein had envisioned; this was no money at all. In return, Cuomo dropped his libel suit. In what would become a signature tactic, he wrung a conciliatory statement from Lynn Fenster Smith, one that seemed written by Andrew himself. "I regret any personal hardship this purely business dispute may have caused Mr. Andrew Cuomo . . . I have always considered him an outstanding professional and count him as a friend."

The play wasn't over quite yet, however. Quietly, the Federal Home Loan Bank Board had begun investigating after all, poking around to see if Oceanmark had been subject to an illegal change of control. On June 17, 1988, the FHLBB reached its own settlement with the New York Group.

The FHLBB's language was careful and lawyerly, but left no doubt that the New York Group had acted in ways not altogether appropriate; otherwise the settlement would not have been needed, and the board would not have issued the cease-and-desist order it did. The FHLBB noted, though, that the New York Group did not wish "to contest any issues concerning control," so the agency would "forbear from the initiation of proceedings against the stockholders for their acquisition of the stock of Oceanmark."

Assuming, that is, that "the stockholders hereafter comply with the provisions of this agreement."

By the agreement, the stockholders—Cuomo, Goldstein, and other members of the New York Group—would not acquire any more Oceanmark stock without the FHLBB's approval, and would sell all the Oceanmark stock they owned within six months. They would agree not to sell their stock to any relatives or "to individuals or companies that would be presumed to be acting in concert with the stockholders." Any stock still held after six months would revert to Oceanmark. The stockholders would also agree not to meddle with Oceanmark in any way. They admitted no wrongdoing.

The agreement was signed by Goldstein, Cuomo, and two other members of the New York Group. It was not signed, however, by any Fenster family members. Nor, apparently, were the Fensters made aware of the settlement.

This was striking. A federal watchdog agency had issued a formal settlement, yet one of the two parties affected by it was never told about it. Nor, seemingly, was any effort made by the FHLBB to assure that the terms of the settlement were met—because two years later, the New York Group would still have its Oceanmark stock, having failed to sell it back to the Fensters for $10 a share. Still ignorant of the FHLBB settlement, the Fensters would be back in court, arguing that at least the New York Group be kept from using the stock it still owned to influence Oceanmark's board, and that it be put in trust. So the Fensters would be fighting over the disposition of stock they should have already owned, had the FHLBB agreement been enforced and they been made aware of it.

When the Oceanmark suits had first made news, Andrew's father had lashed out at its instigators, declaring his son "as honest as the day is long." All this, he added, was "the price [Andrew] pays for my being governor. It's frustrating for me."

Andrew *had* paid a price for being his father's son, though not perhaps the price Mario meant. Sheldon Goldstein was Mario's top donor. Directly or indirectly, the governor had foisted him on Andrew and given his blessing for Andrew to join Goldstein on his merry way to big money. Only instead of making big money, Andrew had been burned—badly—by this real estate operator who seemed to enjoy bullying people to get what he wanted, and not minding if the governor's son became collateral damage in the process.

Later, one family friend would recall a stretch of four or five months when father and son didn't speak—a direct result of the Oceanmark debacle. If so, the son had at least as much right to be angry at his father as his father did at him.

What Andrew needed badly was a change of course from murky business deals and legal work for dubious clients. He needed to cleanse himself of the Goldstein taint and plunge full-time into some activity so admirable that he could reinvent himself. The answer was obvious: quit the law firm and dedicate himself to housing for the homeless. With any luck, that might also lead to some bright political future.

CHAPTER 8

Cuomolot

The news had horrified Westchester. Andrew Cuomo, son of the governor, would be solving the county's homeless problem. Not by shepherding the homeless out of one of New York City's most affluent bedroom communities, but by building shelters for them, each with at least fifty units, in four Westchester communities: Greenburgh, Mount Pleasant, Mount Vernon, and White Plains.

Andrew and his HELP group hadn't bothered to consult the good people of those four towns. He had just drawn up plans and gotten the blessing of Westchester's county executive. All he had to do now was get the four towns to agree to it. First on the list was Greenburgh, where a public meeting was scheduled for the evening of January 22, 1988. By the time Andrew walked into the gym for that meeting, he knew he was in for the roughest night of his life.

A collective roar of rage from more than seven hundred residents greeted him. Fists were shaken, oaths shouted; one elderly lady made a beeline for him, screaming in Italian, and spat in his face. Undeterred, Andrew strode to the podium to explain the many virtues of what he'd come to call WestHELP.

The homeless weren't going away, Andrew told the crowd. But WestHELP could help by getting homeless people off the streets. It would offer not just beds for the night but social services, to get parents working again. The goal was to reduce the ranks of the homeless—and everyone wanted that, right? The shelters would take in only families, which meant mostly single mothers with small children. Who could be against mothers with small children? Best of all, the shelters wouldn't cost the towns any more than the fleabag hotels where they were currently housing their homeless. In fact, they would cost less. "This will work," Andrew told the crowd. "I'll prove it to you."

The crowd roared back its answer.

On the stage with Andrew was one of his only supporters, a salty former U.S. Air Force pilot with a bronze star for his fifty combat missions, and the name to match: Tony Veteran. The town's Democratic supervisor, Tony was more liberal than most of his constituents, but they loved him for his foulmouthed candor and nonpartisan style. Tony had seen the merits of WestHELP right away. It had to be better than putting the homeless in single-room occupancy hotels, and he wasn't bothered by the political risk of helping Andrew push it through. Without Tony Veteran, WestHELP in Greenburgh would have died that night, taking Andrew's new life with it.

Surprisingly, Andrew's other big Westchester backer was the Republican his father had trounced in the 1986 gubernatorial race: County Executive Andrew O'Rourke. A gentle, gracious fellow, O'Rourke had shrugged off his stinging loss; the governor, for his part, had made amends by helping O'Rourke keep a General Motors operation from leaving Westchester County. But O'Rourke also nursed a compassion for the poor, bred from his hardscrabble childhood in Hell's Kitchen, and felt strongly that they sometimes needed a hand. After his father's untimely death, O'Rourke himself had survived on welfare for much of his youth. One night in the fall of 1987, Andrew took O'Rourke to dinner at the "21" Club and sketched out his WestHELP plan. O'Rourke signed on.

Like HELP I in Brooklyn, WestHELP would be financed by bonds. Andrew would use the money from those bonds to build the shelters; the county would pay the operating costs, and over time pay off the bonds; after ten years, the various villages would own their shelters and could do with them as they wished. Greenburgh, a cluster of six villages in western Westchester, was to have the largest shelter—108 units—for its sizable homeless population. Tony Veteran helped Andrew choose the site, a county-owned parcel next to a community college, in a fairly wooded area. They hoped that would minimize the number of homeowners who cried out, "Not in my backyard!" It didn't.

After the Greenburgh debacle, Andrew spoke at one public gathering after another, some with as many as a thousand people, nearly all of them furious with him. William O'Shaughnessy, a courtly Republican broadcaster who owned two Westchester radio stations and had become a close, admiring friend of Governor Cuomo, looked on in amazement as business leaders told Andrew to forget the shelters and instead put the homeless in boats on the Hudson River, or in tents on the nearby Ward Pound Ridge Reservation, a huge preserve.

"One night, there was a guy named Burt at a community meeting with about two thousand people in a high school," O'Shaughnessy recalled. This was Burt Siegel, leader of the opposition. "Burt was beating the shit out of Andrew, reading from Mario's own published 'Forest Hills Diary' about how imperative it was to listen to the community. Finally it's about 12:45 a.m., Andrew takes a break, steps out to light up a Parliament. The dew is coming up on the cars. And out comes Burt. 'I'm sorry I had to do that to you,' Burt says. Andrew says, 'That's okay,' and puts his arm around Burt. And they got Greenburgh."

Andrew did get Greenburgh, but not that fast, and not that peacefully. As opposition stiffened, Andrew got tough too. Local officials opposed to WestHELP found themselves on the receiving end of angry calls. Late one night, Andrew told Greenburgh legislator Paul Feiner that he would break Feiner's bones if he kept insisting that the number of units in the shelter be reduced from 108 to 60 or 70. There would be no compromise, Andrew insisted. When Feiner hemmed and hawed, he started seeing articles knocking him for opposing the homeless, and calls from civic groups came in, all prepped with the same attack lines.

According to *Newsday*, another wavering legislator, John DeMarco, made the mistake of showing up at a county meeting red-faced and disheveled, stirring rumors he had a drinking problem. Soon enough, he got a call from Andrew. "John, you're in real trouble now," Andrew told DeMarco, or so DeMarco recalled; Andrew denied this, as well as the call to Feiner. "I've got your back to the wall. I can help you, but you better go along with this project." Incensed, DeMarco voted against WestHELP anyway. Andrew denied ever threating anyone. He called DeMarco's and Feiner's stories "total fabrications."

"He was a hard charger at that stage in his life," a sympathetic friend of Andrew suggested later. "And sometimes the hard charging kept him from laying the groundwork. He was taking it on the chin for that." Even the governor grew concerned, the friend admitted. "Mario was proud of Andrew, but critical privately, because *he* was getting yelled at when he came to Westchester." More than once, the governor had to tell his son to use the carrot more than the stick.

The residents hated WestHELP, but even more so the implication, from Andrew and his forces, that they were racists for objecting to it. They viewed Andrew as a hypocrite. "If you like these shelters so much," Burt Siegel would cry out, "why don't you put them in your neighborhood?" There was some truth in that: Andrew wasn't proposing a WestHELP shelter in *his* backyard. But race did play a part in the outcry. Lois Bronz, a black local official and WestHELP supporter, addressed a gathering of some six hundred nearly all-white residents and felt she was down in the

Deep South, facing a crowd of segregationists, for whom homeless meant black. "How can you guarantee me my daughter won't get raped by one of these homeless men?" one mother demanded. Bronz met her gaze and said, after a pause, "I can't guarantee that."

Despite the uproar, Greenburgh's board, with Veteran's arm-twisting, voted in favor of the 108-unit WestHELP shelter. But the ground breaking would have to be delayed: a white upper-class enclave known as Mayfair Knollwood, situated near the proposed shelter, began gathering signatures for a petition to secede. If they could form their own village, they could change the zoning that governed the site.

As Greenburgh's fierce debate wore on, its sister towns reacted in varying ways. Mount Pleasant's supervisor felt ambushed: no one had told him of WestHELP's plan to put a fifty-unit shelter in his town until he read it in the papers. He and his board passed a resolution "unequivocally opposing" the plan. Now it was Andrew's turn to be angry. "I can't believe it!" he told one interviewer. "I didn't even *present* this! How can they vote on it when it wasn't even formally proposed? The bastard. He doesn't let me *speak.* I ask him three times to speak to him, and then he says it was poorly presented. There is nothing before the town! *Nothing!* They don't even have anything to act on! That bastard!"

Mount Vernon was a different case. At least half of the town's residents were African-American and Hispanic. They were wary of WestHELP too, because the Mount Vernon site Andrew had in mind was on their turf—the south side—imperiling their property values. The town's middle-class white population felt threatened as well. Why was it their town that got targeted for a homeless shelter instead of Bronxville or Pelham, the wealthy white towns next door? One night, Andrew met with a dozen or so residents of Mount Vernon at a private home, hoping to win them over. It soon became clear he'd done his homework. "The man knew everyone's name," recalled a participant. "He would make his point, then turn to make eye contact with each next person, and invoke his name."

A profile in *New York* magazine in early 1988 perfectly caught Andrew's restless energy as he pressed ahead with WestHELP. With the writer, Jeanie Kasindorf, in the passenger seat of his 1975 Corvette Stingray, Andrew drove to Bill O'Shaughnessy's Westchester radio station, smoking Parliaments and, like his father, both asking and answering the questions. "Here's what people know about me," he told Kasindorf. "Governor's adviser. Campaign manager. HELP. Then there's all these little unconnected dots, little questions." Like the stories suggesting he'd used the family name to get legal clients, and the stories about the Florida

S&L lawsuits. "Hopefully, someday it will be like this: HELP. Campaigns. Governor's adviser. And no more unconnected dots."

For over two hours at the Westchester radio station, Andrew fielded questions from angry callers, chain-smoking and sipping 7UP. He struck Kasindorf as earnest, calm, and polite—but he didn't seem to be changing many minds. That evening, Kasindorf watched him take on a crowd of seven hundred at Woodlands High School. "For the first time in the three weeks I've spent with Andrew Cuomo, he looks younger than his years," Kasindorf wrote. "He sits on the stage with Westchester County officials, gray-haired veterans of this kind of fight, and frequently rubs his hands over his face, as if he's not sure what has hit him. He keeps his answers short and doesn't try to 'jump in,' afraid that it will only increase the crowd's anger. By eleven o'clock, when there are only about 200 people left, he becomes more forceful. 'Where is the humanity,' a man asks, 'of putting 108 families in one little spot?'

" 'Where is the humanity,' Andrew says, 'of welfare hotels?' "

In Andrew's WestHELP campaign there were three motives, separate but intertwined. He did want to help the homeless: no one denied him that. He was at his best harnessing his brute strength to a worthy cause, and he seemed to know that, even then. Unquestionably, he hoped WestHELP would bring some political payoff, though he had no idea what it might be. No one who met him could remain unaware of his vaunting ambition. But the third motive was perhaps the keenest: to help push his father to the White House.

That help was needed. A year into his second term, Mario had struggled to meet the expectations his own soaring rhetoric had set. He had proven a good steward of the budget. He had rebuilt roads and bridges, and improved New York City's transportation system. Oddly for a self-described liberal, he was also building a record number of new prisons. But he hadn't envisioned, much less built, some innovation that might define his governorship. Thomas Dewey had created the State Thruway and the state university system. Nelson Rockefeller had made the state university system the country's largest and transformed the Albany skyline with his Empire State Plaza. Hugh Carey had saved New York City. Mario Cuomo's most striking accomplishments were a mandatory seat belt law and a rise in the drinking age from eighteen to twenty-one that reduced highway deaths. These were hardly the planks on which to stand as a candidate for the presidency.

Mario's thin agenda indicated a deeper problem. The mesmerizing orator who spoke of New York as a family had proved a poor paterfamilias as head of state. He scorned his legislators as mediocre at best, corrupt at worst, and loathed compromising with them to get bills through. "He called them his monkeys," recalled one state politician. "Now, to a great extent he was right. But if you want to get something done, you either have to use absolute power, or you do like Rocky—Governor Rockefeller—did: put your arm around them and give them a choice. 'I'll do it in a nice way or not.' Eighty percent of the time, people will respond to that." As his former union organizer and now unabashed critic Norm Adler put it, Mario didn't understand the nature of shared power. He was the governor; why didn't everyone just do as he said? Andrew would be a strong, dominating governor himself, but he would know that at the end of the day the other party needed its own small share of the pie or bitterness would fester and gridlock ensue.

Against this backdrop, the homeless presented Mario with a staggering problem—and perhaps a great opportunity. In his five years as governor, the number of homeless needing shelter in New York City each night had doubled, to more than five thousand families and ninety-eight hundred individuals. For a governor whose eloquent call for compassion had come to define him, this was bad. Homelessness might end his political career.

Yet there was Andrew with not only a promising approach to the issue but one of the few programs in Mario's governorship that could be called truly innovative. HELP, and now WestHELP, would make a story to tell on the presidential campaign trail—if the number of shelters could multiply fast, helping thousands. The problem was that for all the effort Andrew had devoted to it in more than two years, just one shelter had been built so far, HELP I, the one in East New York. For all the press conferences and interviews, just two hundred families, and their successors, had been housed so far. Mario wasn't going to win the White House on that.

So far, this was just inside baseball. At the start of this presidential election year of 1988, Mario remained a red-hot prospect, even after declaring early the previous year that he wouldn't be running. He was a national figure now, thanks to several seminal speeches. More important, he was seen as a moral leader. Compared to Michael Dukakis, the staid Massachusetts governor plodding toward the Democratic nomination, Mario was a beacon of brilliant potential: presidential timber indeed.

Mario hadn't ruled out a draft, and loyalists had kept that hope alive. But when he deigned to talk about the presidency at all, Cuomo seemed daunted by it—not so much by campaigning as by governing. "Leadership isn't a multiple-choice test on the issues," he told one interviewer. "Any idiot can study and pass that. Leadership is making the people feel confident in you." Cuomo seemed unsure he had that confidence in himself.

He seemed haunted still by his parents' immigrant story, as if as a result he might be too new an American, or too much a denizen of Queens, to lead the nation. At other times he seemed to compare himself to presidential greats and think he might be made of similar stuff. The *New York Times*' Jeffrey Schmalz recalled a Sunday morning with him, the governor "making his own coffee in the kitchen of the executive mansion, then walking through the residence pointing out the nicks in the woodwork left by Franklin D. Roosevelt's wheelchair." Cuomo also mused about Lincoln. "Lincoln had bad press, too," he noted. "He wasn't appreciated until after he was gone."

The darker theory for Mario's reluctance to run was that he must be protecting some family link to the Mafia—a link that would emerge if, and somehow only if, he declared his candidacy. The very notion infuriated the governor. He seethed at the implication that all Italian-Americans must be related to Mafia gangsters. The very word "Mafia" struck him as suspect. "You're telling me that the Mafia is an organization," he said in one interview, "and I'm telling you that's a lot of baloney."

Yet Matilda Cuomo's father, Charles Raffa, eighty-three, remained in a wheelchair, physically and mentally incapacitated from the still-unsolved beating he'd sustained four years before. He would die later that year, on October 19, taking to his grave any knowledge he might have of the mystery.

Whatever his reasoning, Mario put an end, in April 1988, to the draft-Cuomo movement. "This was not the pitch to swing at," Andrew explained, implying that 1992 might be a better at-bat. It was an odd judgment, given the weakness of Democratic front-runner, Dukakis—and, for that matter, the uninspiring Republican front-runner, George H. W. Bush. This was about as clear a path to the White House as any politician could hope for—and yet Mario had said no. Andrew, said one family friend, was deeply frustrated—devastated—by his father's decision. In the end, all he could do was make WestHELP work, and hope the path to the White House in 1992 was as clear as it was now.

For all his confident predictions, Andrew had to be wondering, by early September 1988, if WestHELP might fail altogether. In Greenburgh, a bitter secession fight wore on, stopping the town from breaking ground on the grandest of Andrew's shelters, with its 108 units on thirty acres. There would be no shelter in Mount Pleasant—that bid was dead, thanks to the supervisor whom Andrew had failed to court. There was progress in White Plains, but the city's common council still had to weigh in, and that might take months, now that organized opposition had emerged.

That left Mount Vernon. After a noisy and acrimonious hearing, Mount Vernon signed on: a tangible victory at last.

With that, Andrew announced his departure from Blutrich, Falcone & Miller. From now on, he said, he would be working full-time on HELP. The job change would reduce his salary to $50,000; gone was the Jaguar with the AMC ESQ plate. But Andrew had no regrets. "You don't change the world but it's a good thing," he explained. "It feels right." His father spoke of the decision with pride. "That's the kind of guy he is," the governor said, "and we love him for it." Tonio Burgos, one of the governor's close advisers, put it another way. "Whether it's a campaign, whether it's HELP, he likes moving something from A to B to C," Burgos suggested. "Planning, coordinating, moving something—that's what he loves."

In making the switch, Andrew denied that he was laying the groundwork for a political campaign. "Anyone who says the way to run for office is by proposing a homeless facility sees politics much, much differently than I do," he declared. But distancing himself from Blutrich, Falcone & Miller and its most notorious client clearly had some political benefit. A *New York Times* story noted that Andrew had told friends he hadn't spoken to Sheldon Goldstein in eight months, and was resigning from the board of Hudson United Bank, the thrift that Goldstein had tried to take over when Andrew was his lawyer. Goldstein, Andrew clarified, was no longer his client, though the firm still represented him. HELP, at any rate, was Andrew's all-consuming mission now. His political future, whatever it might be, hung in the balance. So did his personal life.

Not every thirty-year-old bachelor would have chosen, for his first date with a Kennedy daughter, to take her to HELP I, less so on a Harley-Davidson motorcycle, but Andrew had a pretty good hunch that that was exactly what would most impress Kerry Kennedy. On their way, they rolled by the Bedford Stuyvesant Restoration Corporation, the country's first community development center, established in 1967 by Kerry's father, then–New York senator Robert F. Kennedy. In a very real sense, it was the direct precursor of HELP I.

The seventh of Robert and Ethel Kennedy's eleven children, Kerry was two years younger than Andrew, a vigorous athlete like most of her siblings, and a graduate of Brown and Boston College Law School. She was an ardent human rights activist who had led delegations to troubled countries from El Salvador to South Africa; she was just setting up the Robert F. Kennedy Center for Human Rights. More sensitive than some of her siblings, Kerry had just suffered a personal loss that left her especially vulnerable. Her longtime boyfriend, whom she'd met when both were undergraduates at Brown, had dropped dead of a heart attack during a snowball fight on the Washington Mall. The two had fully intended to marry; Kerry was bereft, and open to a big, strong, protective guy who not only knew the values her father had lived by, but seemed to embrace them.

On their first date, Kerry recalled later, Andrew led her around HELP I, proudly pointing out aspects of its design—the central entrance for residents, through the courtyard and office, so that outsiders couldn't sneak in; the simple but efficient apartment units. At every turn, he asked her to suggest improvements. "It was striking to me that there was no sense of self-satisfaction," Kerry told an interviewer later. "Mario gets incredible fulfillment out of study and literature and intellectual debate. Andrew gets fulfillment out of making things better. He leaves things better, faster, sleeker."

By the end of the tour, Kerry was smitten. "Not only was he handsome and funny and great to be around and committed to this issue—that was obviously very attractive to me—but really I remember what just impressed me was the personal relationship he had with the families there." She did roll her eyes a bit when she first saw his apartment: the always fastidious Andrew had his living room furniture covered in clear plastic. The first night she cooked dinner for him there, she opened the oven to find the original foam packing material still in it. Andrew had avoided using it for fear of dirtying it up. But there were worse traits than being a clean freak, Kerry decided.

As the romance deepened and a Kennedy-Cuomo pairing became more than idle speculation, the two political families viewed each other with wariness and curiosity, though perhaps not in equal measures.

To the Cuomos, the Kennedys were American royalty, for all the reasons they were to everyone else. Marrying into that charismatic clan would make the Cuomos royal too, insofar as any American political dynasty could be seen as such. It would also draw them into a private world of wealth and privilege, a planet away from Queens. The Cuomos played stickball on the streets of Holliswood; the Kennedys played touch football on their oceanfront lawn at Hyannis Port. Andrew had driven a AAA truck for extra money and taken out student loans. Bobby, the late senator's oldest son and Andrew's counterpart, spent his spare time training falcons; the Kennedys could saunter into Harvard as they pleased, and go on to the Kennedy School of Government. Andrew was awed by that. Over the next fifteen years he would invoke the Kennedy name so often and with such delight that his listeners would be startled by it, and not forget.

The Kennedys were somewhat less impressed. The Cuomo swagger didn't square with the old-guard reserve imparted so sternly by Joseph Kennedy to his children, and from them to theirs. Yet the Kennedys were also more relaxed than the Cuomos, not just quick to throw a ball around but happy to join in rambling dinner debates and to brandish high ideals. "Andrew refused to do anything fun, anything without a clear benefit to his career," a family acquaintance said years later. After three generations, the Kennedys were at ease with who they were and not shy about their shortcomings; the Cuomos, as one journalist noted, were "tight-knit and tightly wound, fiercely protective of any chink that might be perceived as a sign of weakness or vulnerability." One insider, asked what the family thought of Andrew as a match for Kerry, sighed and said, "You just try to be supportive."

For Kerry, a turning point came when Andrew agreed to fast with her for three days to protest pesticide use on table grapes and show support with labor leader Cesar Chavez. As Kerry later explained, "I thought, 'Well, he builds housing for the homeless and he fasts for Cesar Chavez'... Look, he was very handsome, very charming, very funny... It was a traditional crush."

Clannish as they were, and especially sensitive as they surely felt with the courtship progressing, the Cuomos were appalled to find the family dragged, by early 1989, into court for a messy estate battle after the death of Matilda's father. It was a story that aired deep sibling rivalries, jealousy, resentment, and greed—all over a sum of money the Kennedys could only have viewed as piddling.

Matilda and two of her four siblings had filed the suit, challenging her father's will. By the terms of the will, Matilda was bequeathed \$700,000. But Charles Raffa had left as many as fifty properties in New York, New Jersey, and Italy. Many were empty lots or derelict buildings; still, they added up, to a figure some press reports pegged at \$13.8 million, though family members cautioned it was closer to \$5 million. Matilda's suit targeted her brother Sam, who had been named executor of the estate. Various sources close to the family painted a picture of Sam as a bitter figure, jealous of his brother-in-law the governor, and aggrieved that his own career as an attorney for the county of Nassau had yielded such modest rewards. Matilda declared him "untrustworthy" in her suit and suggested, among other things, that a \$100,000 trust fund set up for her by her father had vanished after Sam took over his father's affairs.

In a story for *New York* magazine by writer Peter Blauner, family members described a handwritten codicil to the will, signed in a spidery scrawl by Raffa just months after his savage beating. The document made Sam his executor. For Matilda, family members said, the codicil was "the straw that broke the camel's back." Matilda couldn't let stand what she perceived as an outrageous and improper seizure of her father's assets. But as a family friend noted, it was also a matter of money. "To some people, [her share of the estate] might not seem like all that much money," a friend said. "Not enough to go to court over. To Mario and Matilda Cuomo, it's a fortune. They haven't got any money."

The suit was settled. But the Kennedys had to wonder: were these Cuomos, with their brooding egos and their battling relatives, really the right fit for America's first family?

For all the arm-twisting he was still doing in Westchester, Andrew found time to strategize for Democrat David Dinkins, the courtly black Manhattan borough president now running for mayor. Dinkins was pitted against Ed Koch for the Democratic primary, and Andrew leapt at the chance to help deny his father's nemesis a fourth term in office.

Dinkins was a weak candidate, but his timing was right: corruption charges had tarnished the Koch administration, and racial tensions fanned by the mayor had opened the way for an African-American with a soothing, inclusive message. The question for Dinkins in the primary was whether to go on the attack against Koch or stay above the fray. Andrew weighed in on that.

"We had a picture of all the people in the Koch administration that got indicted," recalled Dinkins's campaign manager, Bill Lynch, years later. "They had done an ad about that, and we were deciding if we should use it. I remember a meeting: the two media consultants, Andrew and myself. Should we use it? Of course the consultants wanted to use it. The race was neck and neck. And I was the arbitrator, the campaign manager." To Lynch's surprise, Andrew was against it. "His point was that with an Afro-American candidate, it would not play well in the larger community." Translation: an angry black man scared white voters, and possibly black voters too. Impressed, Lynch nixed the ad.

Lynch's staff was less sanguine about Andrew. "Loyalists were pissed," recalled one staffer. "Andrew was arrogant, he came in as if he were the great white hope. He'd dominate a room, so there was resentment on our part. We thought: who is this guy? We felt maybe it was Mario's idea to send his son over to help the black people who didn't know anything." Whatever the rationale, Andrew's presence seemed to help: Dinkins beat Koch, and went on to defeat Republican Rudy Giuliani that fall. Andrew would be owed a favor, and Dinkins would grant him one, only to regret it later on.

With Kerry up in Boston working as executive director of the Robert F. Kennedy Center for Human Rights, and Andrew in New York pushing HELP, the couple spent the next year in a commuter courtship. That continued right up to Valentine's Day 1990, when Andrew proposed over dinner at an Italian restaurant in Manhattan, giving her an emerald-cut diamond ring. Later, he described the talk as "sober," adding, "I just sort of said, 'Look, we have to understand what you want out of life, and what I want out of life. And what I don't want out of life.' I said, 'I have no desire to make a lot of money. It doesn't interest or excite me. That makes a very big difference in what your life will be about. I want to make enough money that my children would have the opportunities that life can afford one, but I didn't come from money. In some ways your life is a little simpler... There is nothing wrong with a solid middle-class background.'" It was perhaps a more revealing account than Andrew realized. In it was an echo of his mother's frustration: that Mario *hadn't* made enough money for his family. At the same time, it echoed his father's scorn for the materialistic life, and pride in a life of public service and intellectual rigor. Yet was this not the politician having it both ways? Eschewing wealth while marrying into it? And in that sense, doing what his father had done? If nothing else, marrying into the Kennedy clan would make taking the high road a little easier.

The engagement was announced in mid-February 1990, to a lot of breathless press about the joining of two prominent political families. "This is a story that has everything," the *New York Times* gushed. "Love. Politics. History." Kerry was giddy too. "I think this is the happiest day of my life," she said. As for Andrew, he described himself as "a very lucky man," and waved off questions about a prenuptial agreement as "tacky."

"Tacky" was perhaps not an inappropriate word to describe the latest twists in the Oceanmark story, which in the spring of 1990 suddenly threatened to become a real embarrassment to the prospective groom.

According to a new suit filed that spring by Oceanmark's brother-and-sister cofounders, the New York Group had held on to its stock after all, and was steering the bank into the shoals, with each year's losses worse than the last. The founders wanted new federal regulators to take a look. Back they went to Judge Gonzalez, who saw enough merit in their claim to schedule a trial for July 1990—right after Andrew's wedding date. Meanwhile, all relevant characters could be deposed, including Andrew.

The first time Andrew was deposed, he called in sick with vomiting, diarrhea, and a headache; that evening, he showed up at a black-tie affair, as the *New York Post* duly reported, calling him "one sick puppy."

The second time, Andrew's lawyers came into the deposition room to announce that the New York Group would settle. It had something far more important to protect than its investment in a Florida S&L. At stake was Andrew's political future. One damning deposition might well destroy it.

And so came the new agreement, dated May 1990, and signed by Andrew, Sheldon Goldstein, and others. It called for the New York Group to put its Oceanmark stock into a trust for five years. The New York Group would then get its stock back. No more bickering over change of control; no more lawsuits.

The only problem with this settlement was that it was fraudulent, according to the claims asserted by the Fensters in the lawsuit that followed. By the secret agreement struck in June 1988 with the FHLBB, all this stock was due to have been sold within six months or, if unsold after that time, donated back to the bank. By the new agreement, the New York Group had just regained stock it should no longer have owned. But since the Fensters had never learned of the original FHLBB agreement, they remained in the dark about this.

For Andrew, the settlement was a win-win. His two thousand shares of Oceanmark, which he might have imagined had gone up in smoke, were once again his, if locked up in trust for five years. At $10 a share, that was a $20,000 windfall—not a fortune, but cheering nonetheless. Far more important, he'd dodged that deposition, and the publicity that would have followed if the case went to trial, just as he was about to marry into the Kennedy clan.

The first time he visited Hickory Hill, the Kennedy estate in Washington, Andrew found himself at a boisterous gathering, with most of the Kennedy brothers at one end of the table, when the subject of Oceanmark came up. "So what did you do with that bank in Florida?" Bobby asked.

"Andrew then goes into this ten-minute speech of nothingness, not making any sense," recalled RFK sibling Douglas. "The whole table stops, we're listening to this very defensive explanation. Finally he finishes, and there's a lull, and one of the brothers says, 'So what did you do with that bank in Florida?' And everyone laughs but Andrew."

Proposing to Kerry was a big step for Andrew, and by the time he did it he had given it a lot of serious thought. He'd asked others to give it serious thought too. "I'm planning to ask Kerry to marry me," he said to the journalists and PR flacks whom he used as a sounding board. "How do you think it will play?" Some of the journalists were acquaintances at best. Appreciative as they were of candor, the preproposal talk struck them as odd. Why would he share this intimate plan with them before he broached it to Kerry? And why worry about how the media would perceive it?

From the moment Kerry accepted his proposal, Andrew took on the planning of the wedding like a political campaign. Three-inch binders covering its every aspect were worked up by trusted aides. Later, Kerry would admit to friends that his manner shook her a bit, but at the time she gushed at how manly and confident he was, taking charge. Wasn't that what every bride wanted? To her family, a red flag went up when Andrew decreed that there would be no toasts, either at the wedding reception or at dinner the night before. No toasts? The Kennedys were astonished. Toasts were the best part of a wedding, the more irreverent the better. But that, it seemed, was exactly why Andrew forbade them. He didn't want the risk of any off-color stories. *This is no fun*, the Kennedys muttered among themselves. But they too tried to put their doubts aside.

McFadden's, a journalists' bar on Second Avenue around the corner from the then headquarters of the *New York Daily News*, was the setting for a bachelor party that drew a network of friends, colleagues, and Kennedys. John F. Kennedy Jr. threw hoops all night at a basketball machine, and Senator Ted Kennedy talked happily with the New York governor who was about to become Kerry Kennedy's father-in-law.

Most of Andrew's friends that night were journalists, one guest recalled. Mike McAlary, the *Daily News* reporter whose scoops and nightly gallivanting had won him a wide circle of admirers, was a formidable character. Others were more in the gossip-column category: Andrew, mused a friend, seemed to enjoy the company of sycophantic reporters. Then there were the political PR types. Dan Klores, a powerful public relations man who often handled the personal crises of prominent New Yorkers, had become a close friend; he was there. So was John Marino, who had worked for two governors—Carey and Cuomo—and was now managing Mario's third gubernatorial race. Both Klores and Marino were as close to the Cuomos as any outsiders could be: lifetime members in good standing of the Cuomo kitchen cabinet, who would see Andrew through all the ups and downs of his burgeoning political career.

The most memorable moment of the evening came courtesy of developer Donald Trump, who made an appearance by video. Clearly Trump hadn't gotten the memo about no toasts. Mired in a messy divorce, he offered the about-to-be-married Andrew some sage advice. "Whatever you do, Andrew, don't ever, ever fool around." No one missed the spin: after his breakup with Lucille Falcone, Andrew had made the most of his bachelor years. Monogamy was going to be a new chapter.

The wedding, at St. Matthew's Cathedral in Washington, D.C., on June 9, 1990, was as close to a royal affair as an American nuptials could get. Kerry's choice of church was poignant: St. Matthew's was the setting, twenty-seven years earlier, for President John F. Kennedy's funeral mass. The bride wore a white satin gown with beaded skirt and sweetheart neckline, carrying a bouquet of gardenias and white roses. Her mother stood at her side in a pink chiffon suit. By Kennedy tradition, the three hundred guests applauded when Kerry entered the church trailing fifteen bridesmaids and eleven flower girls and boys. She walked up the aisle unescorted, a poignant moment in itself. As a mass was performed, the bridal couple sat at the altar in white chairs surrounded by white roses and snapdragons. Already, the press had a catchword for the new political chapter the wedding would bring: Cuomolot. "Just looking at the two of them," Matilda Cuomo said, "their values and their priorities are so much the same. You just know that this marriage will last a lifetime."

Initially, the newlyweds moved into Andrew's bachelor apartment on East 53rd Street. Eventually they found a six-bedroom house in the upscale Queens enclave of Douglas Manor—a major real estate purchase made with a little assist from the bride's side of the family. When they'd finished redecorating, they covered a second-floor wall with letters that President Kennedy and Kerry's father, Bobby Kennedy, had written her over the years.

Andrew had his Kennedy bride—and as much as their union might seem a modern marriage of convenience, conjoining two political families like European kingdoms, friends discerned a deeper bond. Kerry understood what it meant to lead a public life and hide one's vulnerabilities when the going got rough. In all the ways he needed, she could be his helpmate. Lucille, suggested a friend, had lacked that understanding. "As bright and beautiful as she was, she was still a nice Italian girl from Brooklyn. She didn't know that world. There was nothing that Andrew could learn from Lucille about how to manage the complex dynamics of political climbing, and living in that fishbowl we call politics. Kerry was the right person at the right time for him. It wasn't just that she offered him entree. It was that she *understood.* And they were kindred spirits who fell in love because they share this bond."

It was a real marriage—if, perhaps, not a marriage for life.

CHAPTER 9

Waterloo in White Plains

A new chapter was unfolding for Andrew: the start of his marriage, talk of children, and a rhythm of days spent commuting with Kerry into Manhattan. Andrew went to his HELP office, and Kerry rode up to the next floor, to an office Andrew had found for her, where she managed the Robert F. Kennedy Center for Human Rights. Almost everything was going well—except with WestHELP and the simmering townships of Westchester. Unfortunately, that was where Andrew had staked his reputation and political future.

Not every neighborhood was so skeptical of Andrew's plans for the homeless. Two HELP shelters had arisen in the Bronx, there was one now in Bellport, Long Island, and two more in the tough Brooklyn outpost of East New York, right by HELP I. At the five-year mark for HELP, February 1991, Andrew could point to a network of a thousand units encircling Manhattan, a staff of four hundred, and an annual operating income of about $30 million in federal, state, and local funds.

Like his father, Andrew was trying to run a sprawling operation virtually on his own. Grudgingly, he came to see he needed a CEO, and found one in Richard Motta, a forty-five-year-old business executive tired of soulless work in the private sector.

Minutes into a first meeting with Andrew, Motta realized that HELP's accounting system consisted of a checkbook and a secretary who wrote checks. Motta started by bringing fiscal order to the two new shelters in the Bronx. Like the other HELP sites, they were overseen on a day-to-day basis by a group like the Red Cross; in the case of the Bronx sites, it was Volunteers of America. One day, Motta walked into Andrew's Manhattan office to find him screaming into the phone. "Goddammit! I told you to answer the phone 'HelpBRONX,' not 'Volunteers of America.'"

Motta gave him a quizzical look.

"I promised the people of the South Bronx it would be run a certain way," Cuomo replied, still heated up. "And these goddamn people are answering the phone wrong." The slightest failure to promote the brand—the HelpBRONX brand—infuriated him.

With Motta's gentle prodding, Andrew managed to delegate oversight of his growing empire. He stayed in charge of surprise inspections, though. "Andrew would get the senior staff together once very six months," Motta recalled. "He'd say, 'We're going on a road trip.' The VP of finance, the executive VP, the VP of operations, we'd all get into Andrew's Ford Explorer. We called it the White Glove Inspection. He would run his hand along the top of the doors—in homeless shelters!" Woe to the on-site manager if Andrew found dirt on his hands.

One day on an inspection in HelpBRONX, Andrew climbed up to the shelter's clock tower. Every shelter had one of these ornamental towers: it was the HELP logo, the sign of the brand. It was, of course, Andrew's idea. Years later, his staffers in Albany would have TEAM CUOMO T-shirts: more branding, with Andrew the brand creator and promulgator.

"No one ever went up there, because it's five flights up," Motta recalled of Andrew's climb up to the clock tower. But Andrew did. "There was pigeon shit all over—and he went crazy," Motta said. "No one was ever going to see it but him. But to Andrew it was everything. The only way you could build another shelter, he felt, was to get recommendations from the last ones we'd done. So we had to be cleaner than the rest of the neighborhood."

Andrew was vigilant, and the HELP centers in New York City were as a result clean and well run, models for the brand. And yet Westchester remained an agonizing struggle, one that for all his pushing, Andrew still might lose—and with it the perception that HELP was a success.

One of the Westchester four, Mount Vernon, was up and running, with forty-six families and not a single incident of crime associated with it. That did nothing to charm the naysayers in Greenburgh. In April 1990, Andrew stood up at more mass public meetings and took more abuse. Look at Mount Vernon, he told the angry crowds. The homeless in its shelter were young mothers with small children. What threat were they? "Someone got these women pregnant," one resident cried out in an all too typical response. "What happens when the men come around and they can't get in? They'll come through the woods. They'll rape our children."

Finally, despite fierce opposition, Greenburgh scaled its last hurdle, the county legislature, and County Executive Andrew O'Rourke signed its HELP shelter into law. The shelter opened in January 1991, almost three years to the day since Andrew had addressed that first angry crowd in Greenburgh.

The score was two victories, in Mount Vernon and Greenburgh, and one defeat—Mount Pleasant—with the balance to be tipped either way by White Plains.

With White Plains up for grabs, Andrew let a reporter follow him around for what became a vivid profile of the thirty-three-year-old on a roll. "See that?" Andrew said as he barreled down the Major Deegan Expressway, gesturing with a lit cigarette at a dreary housing project near Yankee Stadium. "That's how we used to build low-income housing." The former grease monkey and future governor cut from lane to lane like a racecar driver. "That was bungled," he declared. "That. Did. Not. Work!"

The reporter was struck by Andrew's compelling if somewhat coarse features. "It's a mercurial face, homely at one moment, ferally handsome the next. There's a suggestion of a panther in the way he moves, with wide, rolling shoulders, supreme confidence, a dangerous hint of stayed aggression. His manner says: This is a young man on intimate terms with power."

There was something winning about Andrew's focus, even if ultimately it was all about himself. The reporter sat in on a meeting at HELP to review progress on the White Plains shelter. Andrew sat wreathed in blue cigarette smoke at an oval table, handing out documents like playing cards to the lawyers, architects, and staff around him. "The pack of Parliament Lights at his left hand," the reporter noted, "empties as Cuomo fires questions, anticipates problems, demands to know every detail, from the content of the vending machines to the color of the bathrooms to the height of the fence around the project. And he's quite serious about the fence. 'Barbed wire,' an unsmiling Cuomo says, 'will help ease neighborhood fears.'"

At the end of his fly-on-the-wall time, the reporter asked Andrew why he was doing all this—HELP and WestHELP. Wasn't it about building a platform to run for political office?

No, Andrew said. "If you're in office, you have to pay the price. You have to remember: I had power. I had notoriety. I don't want it." He paused, noting the apparently skeptical look on the reporter's face. "I can't convince you. I can't convince anybody." But still, when the reporter asked if Andrew would rule out running for any office, he hedged. "It depends," he said with a small smile. "It depends on the position. I'll never say never."

First he had to win over White Plains.

Early on, Andrew had tried to charm White Plains' feisty mayor Al Del Vecchio. The two had even gone fishing together. But Del Vecchio, a thickset, Bronx-born college professor of thermodynamics, came to resent Andrew's approach. "He attempted intimidation," Del Vecchio recalled. "And I'm no shrinking violet."

Del Vecchio wasn't opposed to having his city build housing for the homeless. He knew that putting them up at the old Coachman Hotel was a stopgap measure at best. Why not just rehab the Coachman, then, if helping the homeless was what Andrew wanted to do so much? Why build a spanking-new center with fifty units? The mayor thought he knew: because fixing up the Coachman would bring none of the glory that a new, beautifully designed building would. "He said he had no funds for the Coachman, as I recall," Del Vecchio said. "I said, 'Ask Poppa for the money.' "

Del Vecchio came to regard Andrew as untrustworthy. "I told him I wouldn't buy a used car from him," he recalled. Andrew wouldn't give up. And so the campaign rose and ebbed, with various sites and plans considered. Eventually a compromise was struck. The city would give HELP a small, dreary site hard up against a steep slope. Andrew's shelter there would have 36 units, not the 50 he'd proposed. As part of the deal, Andrew would also buy and rehabilitate the old Coachman and put another 120 families there. All that was needed was for the White Plains Common Council, presided over by Mayor Del Vecchio, to vote for formal approval of the plan. A meeting date was set for September 3, 1991.

A videotape of that marathon meeting, along with the next day's vote, shows the WestHELP founder in a dark suit, boyish and sleek, as the formidable young lawyer he was, playing every legal and psychological angle, rattling off zoning ordinances with aplomb, addressing the council members by name, humoring them one minute, lecturing them the next. In Mayor Del Vecchio, as the videotape shows, Andrew had met his match.

"Mr. Mayor, my grandfather used to say, if you're not right, yell," Andrew said after an early outburst from Del Vecchio. "I don't have to yell."

"But you have to insult, and lie," Del Vecchio retorted.

"When you say I lie, when you say I'm a lowbrow, that's not an insult," Andrew said. "It's on the merits."

"I take you as I find you," Del Vecchio shot back. "This meeting started out on a very nice basis until you decided to play games."

"If that's how you read it, I apologize, sir, for any umbrage you may have taken."

The game the mayor accused Andrew of playing concerned the Coachman Hotel, and what exactly Andrew had done, or not done, to guarantee he would buy and rehab the hotel as part of the deal. Yes, Andrew said, he had an enforceable contract with the hotel's owner to buy the Coachman. As soon as the city voted to let him proceed with the new HELP center, he would plunk down $100,000 to buy the Coachman.

Charlie Goldberger couldn't believe his ears. The lawyer for the Coachman's owner was at home, watching the meeting on public-access television. Andrew Cuomo did not have an enforceable contract! Goldberger drove right over to the meeting and explained to the council that all Andrew had was a letter of intent, more than a year old, not an enforceable contract. Nor had Andrew put down his 10 percent deposit. He hadn't put down a dime. What was enforceable about that?

The two sides huddled, then reconvened. "My attorney's position is that the contract is enforceable," Andrew declared. Basically, he said, Goldberger was trying to make him put down that $100,000 before the council voted on the new site. How fair was it for Andrew to be made to put down all that money, or even a portion of it, before knowing if he had the new site?

Taking his father's Jesuitical style to almost comical lengths, Andrew declared of that letter of intent, "If I put a lot of money on the table would it be more enforceable? Yes. Is that what [Goldberger] communicated to you? Yes. Does he think this body might be instrumental in getting that done? Yes. Is it a coincidence that he's here tonight? No. Do we have a contract that's enforceable? Yes."

The meeting went on so late into the evening that the vote was put off to the following night. Andrew came to the follow-up meeting having reached an agreement with the Coachman's owner and his lawyer. He brought with him a deposit for $10,000. That was what he would hand over as soon as the town approved the new site, with the rest to follow.

Seven members, including the mayor, sat on the White Plains Common Council, each with an equal vote: four Democrats, three Republicans. Andrew had assumed his plan would fly with that Democratic majority. There was, however, a twist.

The site chosen for the new WestHELP center was not ideal. By local ordinance, any building by a steep slope required its own special council vote. Not just a majority vote, but a supermajority: five votes out of seven. Andrew needed that 5–2 vote first.

Mike Coffey, who owned a small moving company, was the Republican Andrew targeted for his swing vote. Rita Malmud, one of the Democrats, knew Coffey had indicated a willingness to swing. As the debate entered its final hour, she saw Coffey stiffen and started trying to signal her fellow Democrats: *Give Coffey what he wants so he'll vote yes with us on the supermajority vote.* They seemed oblivious.

Mike Coffey had heard something that got his back up. Earlier in the process, Andrew had promised that the WestHELP center would house no homeless with drug or alcohol addictions. From something Andrew said, Coffey realized that Andrew could not deliver on that promise, not if he was going to get money from state social services. The state services would insist he treat homeless addicts too. Andrew had failed to acknowledge this. "He didn't give any humble explanation as to why," Coffey recalled. Coffey felt Andrew was trying to con him.

The council room was packed when Mayor Del Vecchio called the vote on the steep-slope issue. When Coffey voted no, there were audible gasps, and cries of outrage from WestHELP supporters. Now there would be no vote for the new WestHELP center. The dream was dead.

"Everything erupted," Del Vecchio recalled. In seconds, Andrew's shock gave way to rage. "A couple policemen had to escort him out," Del Vecchio recalled. "He was yelling as they walked him down the stairs."

Del Vecchio found himself feeling sorry for the governor's son. "After working so hard, to see this fall apart in a few seconds—it was a big disappointment for him." Even Coffey, the swing vote, felt bad. "It was a tough vote for me because Cuomo's was the only program that worked, rather than what the Republicans were doing, just dumping people into welfare hotels," Coffey recalled. "But Andrew Cuomo could not live up at the public forum to what he had agreed to do."

With the White Plains defeat, WestHELP had to be deemed overall a failure, two of its four sites blocked. Yet the other two were up and running, and if together they only offered 154 units of homeless housing—a drop in the bucket—they did at least suggest a new and better approach to homelessness, with lessons to be learned.

The very month White Plains died, Andrew got a call from an aide to New York City mayor David Dinkins. The homeless were overwhelming Manhattan, imperiling the Dinkins administration. The Lower East Side's Tompkins Square Park, a homeless encampment, had been cleared by police one violent night in June, a similar tent city at Columbus Circle a week later. The city was up in arms, sick of the homeless but aghast at the brutal removals. In desperation, Dinkins had trotted out that oldest stalling tactic in the book: a blue-ribbon commission. He wanted Andrew to head it up.

The mayor's staffers were for the most part wary of Andrew. They knew of his reputation as a hard charger, a my-way-or-the-highway guy.

They also worried that he would serve as a stalking horse for his father, who had proved not much of an ally to Dinkins. But First Deputy Mayor Norm Steisel met with Andrew and liked what he heard. The city officials in charge of the homeless were jealous, he felt, because HELP was working. Of course, as the governor's son, Andrew had gotten state funding. So what? He had fresh ideas and, as far as Steisel could tell, no ulterior motives. Why not see what he could do? So Andrew was named despite the grumbling. It was a decision the mayor came to regret almost at once.

The whole point of blue-ribbon commissions was to buy time for calm, considered choices to be made. Yet within days of convening it, the mayor announced a bold new plan to be undertaken in tandem with whatever the commission proposed. He would choose up to twenty-four city-owned properties throughout the five boroughs as new sites for the homeless, each with up to 150 beds. When the sites were identified, cries of rage went up from all twenty-four neighborhoods.

"I don't think it's necessary for the commission to pronounce the mayor's plan dead," Andrew told a reporter shortly before his blue-ribbon commission's first public meeting, "because it was dead on arrival." Andrew went on to say he wanted nonprofit groups to build and run many of the shelters, not the city. Essentially, he wanted the city to do it the HELP way: his way. The *New York Times* called Andrew's comments "a potentially devastating political setback" for the mayor.

Even as he met with his commission, Andrew was tending to a matter of greater urgency. On October 11, 1991, when asked by supporters at a breakfast meeting to think about a run for president, Mario had replied, "How can I not think about it?" Over the following days he confirmed he was giving the race serious thought, and his actions bore that out. His staff began issuing position papers, feeling out major fund-raisers, even shopping for office space.

All this shook up the wide, so far unexciting field of Democratic nominees, including Senator Bob Kerrey of Nebraska, Senator Tom Harkin of Iowa, former senator Paul Tsongas of Massachusetts, and a fresh-faced governor of Arkansas named Bill Clinton. The party's elders were intrigued, but mindful of the New York governor's wavering in 1988, a drama of indecision so protracted that Mario had come to be known as "Hamlet on the Hudson." The Democratic Party's national chairman, Ron Brown, flew to Albany to urge the governor to make a firm decision by election day of that year, November 5. The governor vowed to abide by that. Instead, he slid through mid-December, right up until the December 20 filing deadline for the New Hampshire primary. And so unfolded one of the oddest days in late-twentieth-century American political history.

The governor spent the morning and early afternoon closeted with advisers, ostensibly dealing with two very different matters the governor viewed as linked. One was the state budget. Talks over the upcoming budget had stalled over a looming $5 billion deficit. A budget veto by the Republicans was now in the offing. This was exactly what it seemed: a minor matter of state politics.

At the same time, two chartered planes were sitting on the tarmac at Albany County Airport, waiting to fly the governor and his press corps to Concord, New Hampshire, where he would pay his $1,000 filing fee for the upcoming presidential primary and announce that his run for the White House had officially begun.

Andrew's position was clear: he wanted his father to run. All that morning, recalled one close adviser, Andrew pushed his father to take the leap and issue the statement that he was in fact filing for the New Hampshire primary. Yet right up to 2 p.m., when the governor began to write a statement for the press, Andrew had no idea what his father would say. "I don't know," he kept saying as loyalists asked. "I don't know."

Finally the governor appeared in Room 250 of the state capitol to say that he had decided not to run. "It seems to me I cannot turn my attention to New Hampshire while this threat hangs over the heads of the New Yorkers that I've sworn to put first," the governor said, referring to the budget impasse with state Republicans. From then on, the image of those planes on the tarmac would all but define Mario Cuomo as an American political figure: the orator of such promise who might have been president but chose not to run.

In years to come, Cuomo loyalists would note a tendency for Governor Andrew Cuomo, at public events where his father was present, to extoll him as the greatest governor in the history of New York State. At one such event in the fall of 2013, to launch a basketball program for inner-city kids, no fewer than five speakers would take up the theme after the dinner plates were cleared at the cavernous Cipriani restaurant on East 42nd Street. The toasts would go on so long and so fervently that the hedge funders in the audience would start rolling their eyes and checking their iPhones. Andrew's own address, last of the five, would be so emphatic that it struck one listener as almost satirical. What did it say, that listener would wonder, about the man being honored that so many lengthy tributes were required? Was this not an indication, perhaps, that what lurked within the former governor was a fragile ego? And that on some level the son was exasperated with him?

Why Mario had let his tarmac moment pass would remain one of those great political imponderables. Had he worried that the harsh light of the national press might uncover embarrassing secrets about his father-in-law and whatever had led to Charlie Raffa's brutal beating? Did the arduousness and constant travel of a presidential campaign daunt a man who had come to love spending every night in the governor's mansion? Or was it, as more than one loyalist suggested, that on some deep level Mario felt he wasn't up to the job of president?

This much was for sure: no one would ever say of Mario's firstborn son that he didn't want the job enough, or lack the stomach for the race. Twice now Andrew had come close, through his father, to the power of the presidency. If he had a chance to seize that power on his own—both for the good he could do with it and perhaps to make up for his father's indecision—he would never, ever let that moment pass.

The mayor's panel on homelessness, Andrew Cuomo presiding, met once or twice as a group of nineteen that fall, but the meetings were hardly necessary. Andrew knew exactly what he wanted to recommend: basically the opposite of what the mayor wanted to do.

Mayor Dinkins's dead-on-arrival plan for twenty-four more homeless sites fit into his larger view, a liberal Democratic view that the government should do more—whatever it took—to help those in need. That was Mario Cuomo's view too. But it wasn't Andrew's. HELP in its way was a Republican program: less government, more outsourcing. Basically, Andrew felt the city should give nonprofits the money and freedom they needed to build shelters with neighborhood input. Andrew's other idea was purely Republican: vouchers. Instead of congregating all the homeless in group shelters, he wanted some to get rent vouchers and live where they liked. In the current economic downturn there were empty apartments; vouchers might work.

Andrew wrote up the report with a genial Republican businessman and homeless advocate, George McDonald, and his wife, Harriet. After one session, McDonald recalled, "Andrew and I walked out together, and I said I knew Dinkins would not like what we would propose: fire all the union people and contract out the services of about three thousand people to not-for-profits. We're walking down the steps, and I say, 'What if he won't do it?' Andrew gave me a piercing look. 'We go to war.'"

To McDonald, Andrew's approach to the homeless squared perfectly with his own: work over welfare. "The big part of it was personal responsibility: switch homeless people from being victims to being responsible. What treatments do they need to become responsible? Give them the choices, and hold them accountable. That was a cultural shift."

Somehow the report's findings leaked to the press in late January 1992, before they reached the mayor. Cuomo well knew the value of leaks by now: getting grateful journalists to go with his spin; reaping credit without seeming to blow his own horn; leaving his opponents sputtering in surprise as the news cycle passed them by. Leaks would be a Cuomo signature, fully on display by the time he occupied the New York attorney general's office. Only then his opponents would be white-collar criminals and their high-priced defense lawyers. Here the other side was the mayor who had hired him, asked for his help, and come to his bachelor party. The mayor had extended a hand; Andrew had bitten it off, not only dismissing the mayor's own approach but making him look like the last to know that his own commission would undermine him. For his part, the mayor waved off "any perceived embarrassment," calling it "little enough to pay to solve a very difficult and knotty problem that nobody else has solved."

The harsh findings, though, stung the mayor and his senior aides. For months after, Dinkins claimed to be following the commission's findings while putting them up on a shelf for more study, maybe permanent study. Finally, in September 1992, faced with a nightly overflow of the homeless and constant lawsuits, the proud mayor buckled, and a new city homeless agency arose from the rubble: the very independent agency, working with nonprofits to build small shelters with social services, that Andrew had pushed nine months before.

Mario was out of the race for the White House, but not exempt from presidential politics. A few days before Andrew threw his fiery report into the Dinkins camp, explosive news rocked the Cuomo family. The governor of Arkansas, moving to the front of the pack after Mario's decision not to run, had had to respond to the allegations of one Gennifer Flowers, a former nightclub singer who claimed she had had a twelve-year affair with him. Bill Clinton had gone on *60 Minutes* on January 26, 1992, to deny the affair, with Hillary staunchly beside him. Flowers had then produced tapes of conversations with Clinton. One of them included an exchange she had had with Clinton about Mario Cuomo.

In the exchange, Flowers said she didn't care for Cuomo's "demeanor."

"Boy, he is so aggressive," Clinton responded.

Flowers then said she wouldn't be surprised if Cuomo "didn't have some mafioso major connections."

"Well, he acts like one," Clinton rejoined.

Clinton had reason to resent Mario Cuomo. By letting his name remain in play as long as he had, the New York governor had held Clinton back and kept potential donors from jumping in. In his public apology, Clinton indicated as much. "At the time the conversation was held," he said, "there had been some political give-and-take between myself and the governor and I meant simply to imply that Governor Cuomo is a tough, worthy competitor." The Arkansas governor went on to say, "If the remarks on the tape left anyone with the impression that I was disrespectful to either Governor Cuomo or Italian-Americans, then I deeply regret it."

Mario was underwhelmed. "What do you mean 'if'?" he replied in his best Jesuitical manner. "If you are not capable of understanding what was said, then don't try apologizing." Cuomo added that "this is part of an ugly syndrome that strikes Italian-Americans, Jewish people, blacks, women, all the ethnic groups."

The incident may have left a sour aftertaste for the Cuomos, but Mario was too shrewd not to see the political advantage that might be had from helping a presidential front-runner nurse a guilty conscience. That April, with the Cuomos' backing, Clinton made a commanding first-place showing in New York's Democratic primary. Now he owed the Cuomos that much more.

The debt came due that December.

Clinton won, and in the aftermath of political favor repaying, Andrew landed a spot as a member of the president-elect's transition team. It was a temporary posting, a grunt job, as Bob Blancato, chair of the Italian American Democratic Leadership Council, recalled. Blancato was on the team too. "You'd spend ninety-six hours working, paid nothing, working your ass off...to produce a snapshot of federal agencies and their conditions and make a report." Cuomo's assignment was to evaluate HUD, the Department of Housing and Urban Development. "Everyone wanted to be the first to get their report in," Blancato recalled, "and this is indicative of Andrew's political skills and ambition. Turns out he and I end up in the elevator together, both of us have our reports, and we're going upstairs to deliver them to transition headquarters. He knew I was on another team, and we got out together, and we kind of smiled at each other. Technically he got in the elevator first, so he was first. But to show what a good political guy he was, we went down together and handed in our reports at the same time." But both knew who was first.

Andrew may not have joined the transition team with any specific hopes, but by December 16, his father had some for him. Henry Cisneros, the former mayor of San Antonio, had just been named as the president-elect's pick for secretary of HUD. "I got a call that afternoon from Governor Cuomo, whom I did know from a range of capacities, in fact would have supported him for president," Cisneros recalled. Cuomo came right to the point.

"You'll hear from a lot of men that their sons walk on water, but in the case of mine, he actually does," Mario said, in Cisneros's recollection. "He has studied all the options of being in government—Treasury, Justice, Commerce. The one job he wants is at HUD, the section that deals with homelessness. That's the job he wants." Andrew was aiming high for a young man with no federal government experience: he wanted to be one of the four assistant secretaries directly under Cisneros.

In his next meeting with the president-elect, Cisneros brought up Cuomo's call. "Here's an opportunity to do something that Governor Cuomo would really like," Cisneros told Clinton. "I know there's been some tension between the families. This would really bring the families together."

Clinton could see the logic right away. He had heard that Andrew could be a bull in a china shop, but it would be Henry's shop. Clinton held off until Cisneros could line up the rest of his top appointments. The names were announced together in early February; Cuomo's was the one that made the headline.

Andrew strode into his Senate confirmation as if he knew its outcome already. He probably did, for there among the members of the Senate Banking, Housing, and Urban Affairs Committee peering down at Andrew was a family antagonist, New York senator Alfonse D'Amato, who might have quashed the nomination right there. Yet D'Amato greeted him warmly.

D'Amato and the Cuomos, father and son, tended to circle each other with a wariness bordering on paranoia. The senator and the governor, it was true, had struck their peace pact in 1986 and both had profited from it. But suspicions were never far from the surface. Was it an Italian thing? A New York thing? Perhaps a bit of both. Not long before, amid racial tensions in New York City, the Dinkins administration had accused D'Amato of saying that blacks were "jungle bunnies" who ought to go back to Africa. Governor Cuomo had then exacerbated the situation. "That was like the senator saying send all the Italians back to Italy." D'Amato denied ever using the term and was furious at Cuomo for piling on. He vowed to take his revenge, and would do just that a year later by backing New York Republican George Pataki for governor and engineering Cuomo's defeat.

Yet here was D'Amato at Andrew's hearing, purring and demurring. One reason, perhaps, was the esteem in which they held their mutual friend Sheldon Goldstein.

D'Amato's history with Goldstein said a lot about how "Senator Pothole" got things done. It said even more about the scandal-ridden agency that Andrew was about to join. And perhaps a bit about the Cuomos.

Goldstein had given generously to Al D'Amato's first U.S. Senate campaign, in 1980. He had then bought seven low-income housing projects, at bargain prices, from HUD's New York regional head, one Joseph Monticciolo, who worked closely with D'Amato. Goldstein and his colleagues made a $17 million profit from selling those projects. So Senator D'Amato and his top donor both did well—and so did Monticciolo, who upon leaving HUD ended up as head of something called Eagle Capital, started for him by Goldstein and other investors. The other investors together contributed $1 million, while Monticciolo contributed nothing but earned a $125,000 annual salary and 15 percent of the business, whatever that was. All this led to an ethics investigation of Senator D'Amato, whose members eventually declined to recommend any disciplinary action. But it was in that climate that Senator D'Amato, newly reelected, chose to put only the gentlest of queries to the governor's son whose ties to Sheldon Goldstein were as strong as his own.

D'Amato didn't even bother to bring up the Oceanmark case. "You could nitpick anyone to death," D'Amato mused years later. "Our staff never attempted to dig for dirt, it didn't amount to anything except it could make newspaper headlines. There were innuendos, but they were talk, and talk is cheap.

"I could have derailed it," D'Amato added about Andrew's nomination. "What purpose would be served: because I had had a dispute with the dad? I'm going to have a war with your son? Silly."

For any young politician of high ambition, life didn't really begin until his own party took the White House. Only then did the plums start falling from the trees. Bill Clinton had made that happen for the Democrats, but he had done more than that. He had brought both houses of Congress with him. A president and both houses: that was the triple crown, a once-in-a-generation chance to enact serious, lasting change. Now Andrew was part of that moment, a plum in his hand as HUD's assistant secretary of community planning and development. He would bend all his energy, and all his ambition, to make the most of it—and in so doing, make the most of it for himself as well.

CHAPTER 10

Mr. Cuomo Goes to Washington

The first executive decision Andrew made in Washington had nothing to do with HUD. He and Kerry had moved into Hickory Hill, the Kennedy estate in McLean, Virginia, where Kerry had grown up amid constant sports, roughhousing, and bombing down pool slides with her ten siblings. They would be welcome there, Kerry's mother, Ethel, assured them, until they found a house of their own. With Andrew's arrival, however, one Kennedy tradition would change immediately.

Hickory Hill was a rambling estate where Bobby and Ethel Kennedy's daughters had run as wild as their sons. In their teen years, the boys had brought endless girlfriends over, and the girls—Bobby's daughters—had competed as hard in the dating realm as any other, none more so than Kerry. So welcoming was the Kennedy clan that the exes of either sex simply stayed on as friends, with Kerry's many former boyfriends remaining especially close to Bobby Jr., Max, and the rest.

Andrew put a stop to that. No more former boyfriends. Not even Tim Haydock and Bob Nixon, whom the Kennedys regarded as family. That was the word, and Andrew was dead serious about it. The exes were banished, the Kennedy sons left sputtering. The new rule reinforced the doubts the family had had about Andrew from the start. He wasn't fun, he didn't *get* fun. He was, to put it mildly, a spoilsport. Unlike the Kennedys, too, he didn't mask his ambition with charm, and no one, not even his in-laws, would stand in his way.

Much of the time, Andrew and Kerry had Hickory Hill to themselves: Ethel spent most of her summer in Hyannis Port, and part of the winter in Florida. For all the terrible moments the family had endured in that house, it was a bright, happy place, still echoing with the voices of an era. Soon after Andrew took up residence as the new man of the house, that changed. "Andrew shut that down," recalled one of the RFK siblings,

Douglas. Not only were there no more gatherings, but the shades and curtains were drawn. "That house had been the brightest, it had had the most lights," Douglas said. "Now everything was darkened."

Early every morning, Andrew donned a black leather jacket and helmet and rode his Harley-Davidson motorcycle from Hickory Hill to the hulking cement bunker that was HUD.

There were those who admired the ten-story, brutally modern Marcel Breuer building on 7th Street SW that in 1968 gave the then new HUD its home. Others found its slablike bulk and deep-set windows depressing. Breuer had settled on a curvilinear X-shaped design. The goal was daylight to the greatest possible number of offices. Still, the building seemed cheerless. Employees called it "the Dogbone." They especially hated the wide front plaza that had no plantings and nowhere to sit. One of Secretary Cisneros's first moves was to design concrete planters where workers could sit, under gaily-colored round plastic canopies that to the new secretary had a fiestalike feeling. Andrew itched to change them. But he couldn't. He wasn't the secretary—not yet.

The secretary and his deputy, along with their staff, were on the tenth floor. The four assistant secretaries were on the seventh floor. From where the central elevators opened on the seventh floor, Andrew walked an outwardly curving corridor, motorcycle helmet in hand, to his windowed but modest office.

That walk alone reminded Andrew that he and the other assistant secretaries were, like the secretary they served, a breed apart: the "politicals." The offices they passed were occupied by civil servants, there for life. Art Agnos, a newly appointed political who had served as mayor of San Francisco, gave his whole staff—civils and politicals—a pep talk about being a team. One of the civils approached him later to explain there were two teams, not one. "You're the A team, and we're the B team," the civil said with a knowing smile. Agnos protested, but the civil service manager shook her head. "You don't get it," she said. "You're the A team, we're the B team. We be here when you come, and we be here when you go."

Early on, the Clinton politicals heard about the slipper people. Civil service staffers could choose the eight hours of each day they put in. Some liked to arrive by 6:30 or 7 a.m. in order to leave by 2:30 or 3 p.m. By long practice, they padded down to the cafeteria for breakfast in their bedroom slippers, sometimes with curlers in their hair. An early-arriving political would see them shuffling by. At their desks, the slipper people passed judgment on memos and requests; their answer was usually no.

In his first week as assistant secretary of CPD, Andrew reeled in managers from across the country for a summit meeting meant to air their concerns, and also to make clear that they had a new, very demanding boss with big plans for the department. This was a boss who wanted to hear "yes," not "no." The civils applauded politely and went home unconvinced. They had heard a lot of promises. Many had been with HUD from the start, civil rights activists of the 1960s who had dared to hope that HUD might break the cycle of urban poverty and end racism in America. They were old, gray-haired activists now, their ideals dashed, their hearts broken, biding their time to retirement.

HUD was an acronym created by an acronym: LBJ. It was a hodgepodge of housing programs, some started by President Lyndon Johnson, others going back to the New Deal in the depths of the Great Depression. One cynical old-timer would call HUD the biggest ATM machine in the world. "In itself it doesn't do anything," he would say. "It doesn't provide housing, it doesn't provide homeless shelters. What it does is provide funds to nonprofits, and state and local governments, to do those things." Within that ATM were four main accounts, four piles of money for programs to help the poor and homeless in various ways. For a young manager with high ambitions, CPD was clearly the best of the four to oversee.

President Harry Truman had said it with his Housing Act of 1949: housing was not just about a home here and a project there. It was about neighborhoods, and the cities in which they grew. Whole slums needed clearing, new blocks built. This was urban planning, with social services, to help lift cities up. That was what Community Planning and Development was formed to do at HUD. It doled out big community development block grants to virtually every city and state in America, large or small. In doing so, it dealt with the mayors of those cities. For them, and their city officials, the assistant secretary of CPD was more than the public face of HUD. He had the power of the purse, not only for CPD money but for other programs at HUD as well. "Almost any program at HUD that was going to localities, there was a tendency to run it through CPD," one HUD veteran explained. "They had the channels, the bookkeeping; you couldn't just drop checks from a plane." Which meant that of the four main assistant secretaries of HUD in the new Clinton administration, Andrew was politically the most powerful.

Unfortunately, HUD was still reverberating from a series of scandals, and scorned as broken beyond repair. The story of HUD regional head Joseph Monticciolo and his bargain sale of low-income housing projects to Sheldon Goldstein was but one small case of systemic corruption that occurred under President Reagan's HUD secretary, Sam Pierce Jr., who reportedly spent most of his office hours watching television. Pierce's successor, ex–Republican congressman Jack Kemp, oversaw a Reform Act under President George H. W. Bush and earned high marks from both parties. By then, though, the damage was done, the staff demoralized. "You know what this place is like?" Kemp told his staffers. "It's like ten floors of basement."

Though the scandals had festered under President Reagan, HUD to Republicans represented the worst of the Democrats' New Deal and Great Society rolled into one. Partly their bias was philosophical: spending billions of taxpayer dollars on housing for poor people was not the most constructive government handout, Republicans felt. Partly it was political: the inner-city blacks whom HUD served more than any other constituency were mostly Democrats. More than a few Republicans saw HUD as nothing less than a national get-out-the-vote machine. Even Democrats, especially those on committees that oversaw HUD, were appalled by the agency: HUD was such a mess that it had never once, in its nearly thirty years, produced a clean audit. HUD could neither account for its money nor say which buildings it owned and what shape they were in.

On both sides of the aisle, the growing sentiment was to solve the problem of HUD by shutting it down.

If Andrew couldn't change CPD overnight, he could at least set a new tone—and that he did. He got to his office early, striding past the slipper people, and then, just like his father, pulled out his shoeshine kit and buff-shined his black wingtips. If one of his civil service staffers arrived for a meeting with shoes dull or scuffed, Andrew was not above pulling out the kit to shine theirs too.

Also like his father, Andrew was a list maker, setting priorities by hand in a black three-ring binder and holding staff meetings to parcel them out, then strike them when they were done. He had, as one observer put it, "an almost militaristic devotion to strategy and detail." His brother, Christopher, added, teasingly but not in jest, "Organization is like candy for Andrew, even his socks. He has plastic bins all over his house."

"Andrew was going 150 miles an hour," recalled a staffer. "Anytime someone said, 'Let's do that next year,' he would say, 'Let's do it right now.' If you tried to slow him down or dissuade him, you were no good."

"He does not rest easy in his chair," one reporter noted during a visit early on. "He leans forward, he leans back, jabbing the air with his index finger. When he talks, he hits his syllables hard and quick, his voice sliding from a new whisper to a head-snapping hurl."

Andrew's civil staffers soon realized that their boss was capable of withering criticism. "He yelled at me in a way that my own parents haven't yelled at me," one recalled later. Another recalled Andrew's shoving a report in his chest and barking, "Give me something in plain English." One staffer was struck by Andrew's extremes. "He was sort of at your feet or at your throat. He would be charming with you in person and then talk about you like a dog when you weren't there." If you were with him, the staffer explained, he might bad-mouth someone else. "*Joe Shuldiner, what a dope.*" The staffer would be literally speechless: Shuldiner was one of the other assistant secretaries. "I would just sit there. They were my betters! I couldn't comment on them." Those below Andrew came in for harsher abuse. They were "fuckheads" or "dumb fucks" if they underperformed. "He threatens to fire them daily," one staffer reported at the time. "[He] has a huge foul mouth which he often puts his foot in . . . I have to tell you, this guy is a monster."

Within weeks, Andrew had brought in a small circle of trusted advisers. One was Mark Gordon, the brainy A-Teamer from 1982, who became Andrew's first chief of staff. Another veteran from 1982 was Howard Glaser, a recent Harvard Law School graduate. Glaser, unlike Gordon, was a tough, combative aide-de-camp. He would remain Andrew's trusted number two guy through both Clinton terms and resurface for the governorship, handling one hot issue after another, as much a day-to-day head of the state as Andrew himself.

The old-timers understood that Andrew had to shake things up. They had just one complaint. "You were never given the chance to show you were as energetic and innovative as he is," one remarked. "You never had that opportunity. You had a stigma placed on you from the beginning. Personally he's very arrogant, and stereotypes people."

Andrew didn't deny the arrogance rap; he just explained it. "You come in, you tell the truth—you're right: the place stinks," he said. "The civil servants say, 'Whoa, you're criticizing us.' That's right—because it's true. I'm not blaming you, civil servant, it was the manager, it was Congress that passed the laws that put you in place. But if it sounds like a criticism, that's because it is. And by the way, everyone out there knows it doesn't work. You may not like hearing it, but everybody knows. Actually, I'm getting you something: it's called credibility. And now maybe we can do something with it."

Henry Cisneros had heard the stories of Andrew as his father's enforcer. He did not see any of that. Every Monday morning, Cisneros and his four assistant secretaries met to plan the week, and Andrew was unfailingly courteous and cheerful. Also fun. One of Henry's staffers was a very petite woman named Bert Benavides; Andrew would pick her up by her elbows, almost over his head. "He wasn't necessarily the most important of the assistant secretaries," Cisneros recalled. "But he was first among equals. He carried himself with a kind of charisma. When Andrew was in the room, you knew there was a special person there, in part because of his father, in part because of his marriage, and in part because he was tall, strong, and well-groomed. Even though others had more important jobs, they deferred to Andrew."

In Cisneros's own conversations with Andrew, Mario was a touchstone. "I was a great admirer of his father," Cisneros recalled. "So it was a rare conversation we had that didn't relate in some way to his father. There would so often be 'this is how the governor would handle this.'" For Cisneros, the Kennedy connection was just as strong, if not more so. Andrew and Kerry invited Henry and his wife to events at Hickory Hill. Andrew could show Henry the giant oak tree where Dolley Madison hid her picture of George Washington when the British burned the city in 1814. He could show his boss the framed documents and letters that lined the wall going up the stairs: the copy of the Emancipation Proclamation signed by Abraham Lincoln; Thomas Jefferson writing to Lewis and Clark; President Eisenhower writing to President Truman. And of course the sunroom, where President Kennedy and Attorney General Kennedy mediated the Cuban Missile Crisis. Cisneros, who revered the Kennedy legacy, was thrilled.

Along with jump-starting CPD, Andrew remained his father's close adviser—at a dollar a year or not—and so, just weeks into his new Washington life, he found himself serving as a go-between for Mario and the White House on the startling, unexpected question of whether President Clinton would name the governor of New York as a next U.S. Supreme Court justice.

Justice Byron R. White, whose appointment by President Kennedy had raised hopes of a staunch liberal tenure but led instead to a more centrist voice on the Court, announced his retirement in March 1993. Mario was at the top of a short list of prospects to replace him. Did he want it? That was what the White House wanted to know, to avoid the embarrassment of offering him the seat, only to have the famously indecisive Cuomo waffle or, worse, decline. And so ensued a flurry of calls between the president's senior policy adviser, George Stephanopoulos, and Andrew, acting as his father's surrogate.

"Andrew wanted his father to do it," a close Cuomo adviser from that time recalled. "He was encouraging the [Clinton] administration, saying, 'My father will not reject you.'" The White House remained cautious.

Mario would make a great Supreme Court justice—of that there was no doubt. And the choice would reflect well on Clinton. But Clinton had won the election that Mario might have won if he had taken the swing. And Mario was a brooding, complex man. How could Clinton know—really know—that Cuomo wouldn't turn him down out of some dark urge for revenge?

In his memoir *All Too Human*, Stephanopoulos recounts the dance between President Clinton and Mario over the Court seat. The president called Cuomo on March 29 and failed to reach him. Calls went back and forth until the two connected while Clinton was on Air Force One. According to a later account in the *New York Times*, Mario asked the president not to consider him. That was when the dance got interesting.

Over the next several weeks, Stephanopoulos talked several times with Andrew, who insisted his father was now willing to take the seat after all. Relying on that message, Stephanopoulos arranged for the president to call Mario at 6 p.m. on Sunday, June 14. Fifteen minutes before the two were to speak, Mario called Stephanopoulos to say he wouldn't accept the nomination after all. In his memoir, Stephanopoulos recalled that while he was speaking to Mario, Andrew called to say, regretfully, that his father had had a 180-degree change of mind since the day before.

Possibly. But from the close adviser to Mario comes an alternate version. Days before the call that never happened, the adviser heard on good authority that the governor truly didn't want the nomination. The adviser called the governor to confirm that. The governor was noncommittal. The adviser knew what that meant. "Well, that's a story that ought to be out there, right?" From the governor's end, there was only silence.

The adviser felt he had been given his cue, and he called an AP reporter to say the governor didn't want the nomination—period. When the story appeared, the adviser was told sternly to call George Stephanopoulos and say he had been talking out of turn, without the governor's blessing. That admonition came, directly or indirectly, from Andrew. And so the dance continued, until the last possible moment, when the governor had to force Andrew to end it.

The adviser's point was that Mario, for whatever reason, hadn't wanted the seat from the start. Andrew had wanted it for him—and had kept on lobbying on his behalf, telling Stephanopoulos that he represented his father's views when in fact he was out there alone, pushing his father's nomination and hoping that when the president called, his father would say yes after all.

Andrew's own motives, the close adviser felt, were at least as complex as his father's. "There are those who believe that Andrew very much wanted his father elevated to the Supreme Court because that would put him out of the way." In or out of elected office, the presence of Mario Cuomo in New York would be disruptive to the son hoping to run for governor or senator himself. But immured instead in the U.S. Supreme Court Building? Perfect, for both father and son.

Homelessness had defined the young Andrew Cuomo; it had brought him to HUD; now as the Clinton administration's expert on the issue, it put him front and center with a president in need of a national response to what had become a national problem. Clinton started cautiously, calling for a coordinated study involving seventeen federal agencies, with no one of them in charge. That was all the opening Andrew needed.

Brandishing his HELP credentials, Andrew seized control of the process—HUD was, after all, the agency among those seventeen with arguably the strongest claim to the issue—and started traveling around the country to hold interagency conferences, soliciting different perspectives. He then wrote the report he would have written if he hadn't talked to anyone at all. One staffer marveled at her young new boss's political savvy. "It was supposed to be authored by twelve [agency] secretaries," she recalled. "He didn't really care what they wanted. He knew what he wanted it to say, and he happened to be right. My job was to keep the junk out of it. Someone maybe didn't want it to be focused on the continuum of care . . . and every agency wanted its own pet project. We had to resist all that."

By now Andrew had his eye on a far bigger political prize: empowerment zones. Poor areas, both urban and rural, would be marked off and given big block grants to pull them up. Other administrations had toyed with the idea, without much success. Perhaps its time had come: Cisneros was a big fan. The new secretary let Andrew run with EZs, and Andrew ran them right to the White House.

The vice president, it turned out, loved empowerment zones. Like Andrew, Al Gore was a policy wonk, and happily agreed to chair the multi-agency EZ initiative himself. Soon the two were immersed in acronyms and line items, speculating on where the various zones might best go. With the vice president's backing, the numbers got big very fast: hundreds of millions of dollars, maybe billions. HUD would do the urban EZs, while the Agriculture Department did the rural ones. Andrew made certain, with the help of a burgeoning press department, that he would be the one most strongly associated with EZs.

With the passage of EZs into law in August 1993—nine to start with, each getting federal block grants of up to $100 million—Andrew held a cocktail party at Hickory Hill. The vice president attended. So did a host of top-tier Clintonites: Senior Adviser for Policy and Strategy George Stephanopoulos, Labor Secretary Robert Reich, Assistant to the President for Economic Policy Robert Rubin, Chairman of the President's Council of Economic Advisers Laura D'Andrea Tyson, Environmental Protection Agency Director Carol Browner, Director of the Office of Management and Budget Leon Panetta, presidential adviser David Gergen, U.S. Attorney General Janet Reno, and White House Chief of Staff Mack McLarty. Waiters served petit fours with "EZ" piped in chocolate icing. As the crowd polished them off, Andrew invoked the father-in-law he'd never known. Empowerment zones, he declared, were the next step in Robert Kennedy's war on poverty.

The EZs were a hefty addition to Andrew's portfolio. Big chunks of money would flow to the states right away, not as cash, but as commitments. Businesses still had to apply, and grants would be doled out over time. Over the life of the program, with all tax incentives figured in, it might reach $6 billion. That was a lot of power. Another secretary of HUD might have grabbed them for himself: they were secretary-sized, even tenure-defining. But Cisneros let Andrew have them. Already he had begun to regard Andrew as a sort of younger brother, and to take pride in his triumphs. The EZs, he acknowledged, made Andrew the most important assistant secretary at HUD. He admired Andrew's yen for the mechanics of management. "Andrew had, and still has, a great feel for how you get from the idea to execution," Cisneros observed. "He didn't argue for doctrinaire liberal positions—he put them to the test."

Andrew embarked on a rigorous travel schedule around the country, talking up empowerment zones and offering local leaders help in applying for them. The leaders were impressed, not just by the talk of EZs but by Andrew's advance team. It was larger than any they'd ever seen for an assistant secretary of HUD. When Andrew himself arrived, he was flanked by four or five staffers with two-way radios, and security agents with earbuds. It was like the president had arrived. Except that at thirty-five, Andrew Cuomo still looked like an overgrown kid.

Andrew's star was rising fast. That December, he and Kerry were invited to the White House for dinner and a screening of the movie *Philadelphia. Time* magazine ranked them as one of Washington's power couples of the new administration, adding impishly, "Not much fun but great last names."

Unfortunately, Andrew and Kerry were having little in the way of fun with each other in their new home in McLean. Perhaps, as in any marriage, each bore some of the blame. For Kerry, the top priority was her human rights work; the mundane tasks of keeping up a household were of considerably less interest to her. She was, as one family friend put it, no Matilda Cuomo. Andrew bridled at that. He found her cooking and cleaning less than adequate, her wardrobe dowdy. As for her friends, he disapproved of most, so few were invited to the Kennedy-Cuomo home for dinner. Even Kerry's best friend, Mary Richardson, who would soon start dating, and then marry, Kerry's brother Bobby, wasn't welcome at the McLean house. Kerry had to see her on her own.

Andrew now socialized with the president himself. When a columnist for the *Wall Street Journal* wrote an admiring piece about Andrew, the president dashed off a note of congratulation; Andrew put it up in his office. The president sent him a clipped-out crossword puzzle that he'd completed in ink, with "Cuomo" as one of the answers. That went up on the wall too, along with a page from the final Housing Act of 1994—authorizing the EZs—signed by the president. For Christmas, the president sent Cuomo a board game called Triopoly: three-dimensional Monopoly. "I'm good," the president wrote, "but you get Triopoly."

For Andrew, this was more than about getting in his ultimate boss's good graces. The president his father had scoffed at not long ago was dizzyingly charismatic. He was at least as well-read as Mario, and as passionate in his politics but also, like Mario, very pragmatic. Later, Andrew would speak of Clinton as one of his three mentors, along with his father and—quite seriously—John Diorio, his high school government teacher back at Molloy. What others saw was Clinton *supplanting* Mario as Andrew's number one mentor—becoming in effect a new father figure. Clinton was only eleven years older than Andrew but he was, after all, the president. Age was beside the point.

Awed as he was, Andrew was aware of the craft behind the charm. To friends, he would demonstrate the Clinton touch in all its variants: holding a shoulder, gripping an arm, a forearm, taking a hand or patting a knee. Andrew, as one reporter noted, seemed to understand both the lure of the Clinton touch and the humor of it. Clinton, Andrew said, knew every nuance of what he was doing. "The effect of touching you there," he demonstrated to the reporter, "or touching you here." Implicit in the shtick was an awareness that Clinton was always, on some level, acting.

The gravitational pull was palpable. Back in his office, Andrew frequently quoted Clinton to his staffers. He still revered his father—he always would—but he sometimes seemed a bit impatient with the aging three-term governor who'd botched his chances for higher office. At an event in 1994 that all three men attended, Mario was scheduled to speak before the president. Andrew scribbled a note to his father, sternly telling Mario not to go on for too long. Acting shocked, Mario passed the note to the president. Clinton grinned, and scrawled on it, "Clinton's 8th Law. Blood is thicker than water. But the paycheck is thicker than blood." Andrew promptly framed the note and added it to his office wall.

Andrew worked hard to keep the president impressed, and he succeeded. The report he'd been asked to prepare, crafting a national policy on the homeless, came out in February 1994 to widespread praise from advocates and policy wonks, and consternation among Republicans. The government's estimate of six hundred thousand homeless in the United States was too low, Andrew argued. Including those who passed in and out of homelessness due to health issues, or job loss, or family circumstances, the figure in America was more like seven million. Far more federal help was needed, far larger budgets for agencies like HUD and programs like the empowerment zones. The previous year, Henry Cisneros, at Andrew's urging, had increased the homeless budget by 50 percent, to $837 million; in 1994 the administration would nearly double it, to $1.5 billion. The higher Congress raised your budget, the more points you won. Republicans groaned. But Clinton took notice.

Spending money wasn't the only measure, however. Saving it, by making agencies more efficient—that helped too.

By now, Andrew knew that HUD's systems for managing money were thoroughly bollixed. In came funding requests, out went the funds, but through wires as crossed as an ancient telephone switchboard's. Andrew came up with what he called the Consolidated Plan. It merged twelve bureaucratic processes into a single streamlined system. Before, social services in a city like New York—for everything from housing programs to the homeless to economic development—would submit funding requests on their own, each oblivious to the others and *their* needs. Andrew, with backing from Cisneros, was the first to suggest that the groups communicate with each other and submit one unified block grant plan. The Consolidated Plan sped up the process of fund-granting. It also made the groups accountable for what they spent: for the first time, Washington could see where the money went. The Consolidated Plan won an Innovations in American Government Award from Harvard's John F. Kennedy School of Government. For all the churn of programs from one administration to the next, it would last through eight years of President George W. Bush and the Obama administration after that. To the extent that any program at a federal agency could be deemed permanent, the Consolidated Plan would be.

It did have political ramifications, however.

That first year the plan was up and running, 1994, New York City's homeless programs did as instructed, bundling their fund requests rather than sending them willy-nilly as in the past. The request totaled $60 million for twenty or so programs. "We sent in the application—and nothing happened," one advocate related. "We were competing with other localities, and one by one, they began to hear about their grants. But not us. Then we were told: the NYC application had been turned down completely. We were mystified."

A month passed—a month in the new tenure of New York City Republican mayor Rudy Giuliani, who, by dint of his position, might have handed out the funding to the various programs. At last the money came, but not through Giuliani. Instead, Andrew himself meted out the funds to the various programs, denying the Republican mayor that bit of positive press in his home state.

In the fall, Mario ran for a fourth term as governor of New York—to his son's dismay. Voters were tired of the Cuomo brand, Andrew told his father. Mario himself was tired. Better to step aside, let a fresh face run, and win the enduring gratitude of the state Democratic Party, which might prove useful, both father and son knew, for a future Andrew candidacy. Besides, Andrew was in Washington. He had a day job. He simply could not be his father's full-time strategist again.

Mario listened, but seemed not to hear. If there was another candidate opposed to the death penalty, his signature issue, he might bow out, he said, but there wasn't. One of his staffers from that last campaign felt that that was just an excuse. The soaring rhetoric of the first terms was gone, replaced by a dogged determination to go the distance and burnish the legacy. "We were all about validating what we'd done." The problem was that Mario hadn't done much—and his son almost certainly knew it.

In fairness, Mario's governorship had run early on into the buzzsaws of crack cocaine, the homeless, and AIDS. The economic downturn of the early 1990s had not helped. But Mario had made his plight worse. He had tried to do too much, and ended up doing too little. "Mario wrote two-hundred-page speeches," one lawmaker recalled. "If you got 20 percent done by the end of the year that was a miracle. Versus Rockefeller's list of five things, and they would all get done."

The vaunted triumphs were often less than they were cracked up to be. Mario liked to say that the state had generated half a million jobs, but the bull market of the 1980s had done that. He claimed year after year of balanced budgets, but one senior lawmaker from those days questioned that. "I would swear that a significant number of them were *not* balanced," suggested former Speaker of the Assembly Mel Miller. "You can balance a budget by saying, 'This year income tax will bring in $29 billion instead of $28 [billion],' when it fact it may end up just bringing in $28." In terms of bricks and mortar, Mario had built prisons—lots and lots of prisons. He had modernized the rest stops on the New York Thruway. After that, the list petered out pretty quickly.

In truth, the legacy was modest—and that, for the governors Cuomo, father and son, would be from now on the elephant in the room. Years later, in his memoir, Andrew would profess guilt at having not done enough to help his father win a fourth term. The truth was that Mario's run was over, with no one to blame but himself, and no one, not even his son, would be able to put him in office again.

George Pataki, the tall, lanky Republican state senator from Westchester who took Cuomo on, had a record as middling as his demeanor. But behind him was the Cuomos' bête noir, Senator Alfonse D'Amato. The fragile alliance between him and the Cuomos was sundered; D'Amato was out for revenge and power, and in Pataki he had found the perfect package, an inoffensive lawmaker smart enough to let the senior New York senator guide him.

For starters, Pataki railed at Cuomo for "Air Cuomo"—the governor's frequent use of state helicopters to transport family members. Helping stir the pot, whenever he could, was the *New York Post*'s political columnist Fred Dicker. Once again, Dicker had admired a sitting governor, only to grow disenchanted. Dicker's columns were generated almost entirely by off-the-record sources. They were a morning ritual in Albany: everyone read them, then tried to guess who the secret sources were. For a long time one or another of the governor's inside circle had served as those sources, throwing mud on whichever lawmaker displeased them that week. But now Dicker was listening to the Pataki camp, and slamming the governor. More than a few legislators would feel that Cuomo's loss, by just a few points, was due to Dicker, that if Dicker's honeymoon with Cuomo hadn't ended, Mario might have won a fourth term. They would watch in fascination as Dicker's honeymoon syndrome played out with one governor after another, until Andrew took on the challenge of charming the excitable fellow—the same columnist who'd slimed his father—and trying to make the honeymoon last.

For his fourth gubernatorial campaign, Mario traveled the state grudgingly, and voters seemed to feel it. Always he insisted he be back in Albany for the night: he had grown so accustomed to the executive mansion that he loathed missing a night in his capacious bedroom, with the huge long bathroom he had once derided as grandiose. Andrew rarely traveled with him, but he did call once or more a day, often with sharp rebukes for what his father was doing. He railed at the two-and-a-half-inch-thick campaign book of accomplishments that Mario insisted on having drawn up and given to reporters. "That's stupid," he hissed at one of the governor's aides. "You don't give reporters a two-and-a-half-inch-thick book. Who's going to read that? You give them three or four things." As his poll numbers plateaued, the governor took to telling audiences, "Andrew says I should focus on a couple areas." But then he would drone on, regardless, with his overly long list of to-dos.

If Mario had convinced himself that he could win a fourth term, he was disabused of that notion. For two days after his loss, he remained in the mansion. Finally in a rueful interview he acknowledged the impact of voter discontent. "It's very difficult to say what the people wanted," he said. "Maybe the people just didn't like Mario Cuomo."

An era was over, and Mario knew it. From now on, the only Cuomo in public life would be his son.

CHAPTER 11

Rise to Power

Larger forces were at work that fall of 1994. Turned out of office, along with Mario Cuomo, were enough Democratic senators and congressmen to flip both houses to the Republicans and their fiery leader, Newt Gingrich, whose budget-cutting Contract with America now radiated the power of an electoral mandate. At the very top of Gingrich's list of spendthrift federal agencies deserving summary execution was HUD. If he needed any more reason to act, two nonpartisan federal agencies came out with scorching condemnations of it. According to the General Accounting Office (GAO), the entire agency was in a "high risk" category, on the verge of hopeless dysfunction, the bureaucratic equivalent of flatlining.

Some weeks after the Republicans' midterm victory, Henry Cisneros accompanied Vice President Gore on a plane ride. Gore was somber. Profound changes were in the offing, he told Cisneros. "Some departments are going to be faced with the idea of whether they should exist or not." Cisneros didn't need to ask: he knew HUD was one of them.

Cisneros managed to wangle a meeting with Gingrich and get the new Speaker of the House's thoughts on what might constitute meaningful, ax-exempting change at HUD. He took what he heard back to his assistant secretaries and asked them to come up with recommendations over a December weekend, while he was away. Andrew was the one who proposed an all-weekend session to draw up what came to be known as the Blueprint, basically turning HUD on its head.

"A lot of this was Andrew's vision," acknowledged Joe Shuldiner, at the time the assistant secretary for public and Indian housing. Power would be pushed down to the forty regional offices. *They* would bundle the funding requests of all the nonprofits in their respective areas. They, in turn, would push the local housing authorities to turn the cities around. Some sixty aid programs across the country would be merged into three funds. Along with more responsibility out in the field would come more accountability. Over time, that would allow HUD to get by with a far smaller staff: from 11,900 down to perhaps 10,000. Or so suggested the Blueprint.

Later, the story would go out that Andrew had whipped the whole Blueprint into shape and written it up. This was not quite true. The other three assistant secretaries had helped draft it too; others would put the rough ideas in proper bureaucratese. But Andrew's jottings were what Cisneros was presented with that Monday morning, and the secretary was impressed. The recommendations weren't "more money, more government," as Cisneros noted approvingly. They were about decentralizing and scaling down. He was all for practicality; so was Andrew. Here was a chance to be practical, just in a slightly left-leaning way, motivated by the conviction that HUD was worth saving as the one department in the whole federal government dedicated to the poor.

Cisneros was at home on a mid-December evening when friends at the White House tipped him to a key meeting scheduled for the next morning to weigh draconian cuts, HUD among them. Alarmed, he made copies of the Blueprint and at 10:30 p.m. drove to the Old Executive Office Building to slip them under the doors of the economists and policymakers due at the next morning's meeting. The policymakers were duly impressed, especially by that bold goal of cutting HUD's staff significantly. HUD was so gargantuan that even then its spending would be out of control. Still, the Blueprint showed an agency facing up to its flaws and embracing new ways. With that, the crisis was at least postponed. And Andrew, as first among equals, could take the lion's share of credit for saving a federal agency.

Andrew had another, more personal triumph to savor on January 11, 1995. That evening at Georgetown University Hospital, Kerry gave birth to fraternal twin daughters. "It was really a breeze," Kerry declared. The chosen names honored the matriarchs on both sides—Cara Ethel and Mariah Matilda—along with the start of a new political dynasty: the Kennedy-Cuomos.

Kerry hoped the twins would give the marriage a wonderful added dimension. It certainly needed one. From Andrew's first days at HUD, the couple had been in marriage counseling. Kerry had had the sinking sense that she and Andrew were far more different than she realized. She was a serious athlete, happiest skiing or sailing. Andrew had an athlete's build, but not much interest in the sports she liked. Nor did he like going to Hyannis Port, which Kerry loved more than anything else. Perhaps he resented spending time on the Kennedy family turf; it was the one place where he had no control.

The Blueprint had brought only a temporary stay of execution. By the spring of 1995, Republican leaders, including Gingrich, were putting HUD in the crosshairs again. They kept cutting its budget, then damning it for not doing what the Blueprint had promised. Judy England-Joseph of the federal General Accounting Office, who had overseen the most damning of those two HUD studies and understood the agency as well as anyone in Washington, felt that in retrospect the Blueprint was basically a public relations document. There was, she acknowledged, "a real belief about *trying* to do something. But it was not going to move forward at that moment."

Like the other assistant secretaries, Andrew now had to make the case before Senate and House subcommittees for protecting his programs and their budgets. That was a challenge, because hardly anyone on those committees much liked him.

As he had done in prepping for law school exams, Andrew focused his formidable memory on absorbing every relevant fact and figure. Untypically for an assistant secretary, he appeared alone before the committees, or with a single aide. He rattled off numbers with great aplomb, and made his case with passion. The problem, which became a syndrome, was that he pushed too hard. "Cuomo took an agency that wasn't known for being political...and it became political," recalled a Republican Hill staffer. "The narrative was that we were throwing women and children on the street by our tactics." In fairness, some of that bluster was needed. After the appropriations committees got their "top line" budget numbers, they had to divide that money among thirteen groups of federal agencies. Some agencies were grouped logically—Agriculture and Interior, for example. So the chunk for their group could be carved in a way that pleased them both. HUD had the ill fortune to be grouped in a mishmash of unrelated agencies. As the staffer noted, it was the ugly stepchild of its group. "Veterans Affairs has a constituency stronger than any other—members climb all over each other to take care of vets," explained the staffer. "NASA was very popular. EPA we could give two shits about, but they had those water grants. What did we care least about? HUD." Appropriations committee members got used to Andrew fighting the budget number they handed down to him. If they wouldn't give him what he wanted, he would appeal to the Office of Management and Budget—or to the White House. He would not be denied. For lawmakers and their Hill staff, that left a sour taste.

As Andrew became an all too familiar figure on the Hill, he found himself pitted against a sort of doppelgänger: a young Italian-American as fierce and ambitious as he was. Rick Lazio was a boyishly handsome Republican congressman from Long Island who, like Cuomo, had built his political career on the issue of housing. At thirty-seven, the same age as Andrew, Lazio was embarked on his second term and newly installed as chairman of the House Banking Subcommittee on Housing and Community Opportunity. This gave him the power of authorization, to vote yea or nay on new programs, as opposed to appropriation, which had the power of the purse over programs once they were approved.

"From day one they were rivals," recalled one congressman who worked with both Lazio and Cuomo. "But it goes beyond just political rivalry. The view was that if Lazio wanted something Cuomo would be against it, and vice versa."

Lazio took a dim view of the Blueprint, which fell within his purview. It was, he said, an "illusory" transformation. He was practical enough, however, to see that killing HUD wasn't a useful option. The agency had a lot of long-term housing contracts that could not be broken. It also filled a lot of needs that should not be ignored. The agency could be broken up, its pieces parceled to other agencies, as some of Lazio's Republican colleagues had suggested. But HUD by any other name would still be HUD. And since housing was the subcommittee Lazio had drawn, saving HUD was the best way to advance his career. Lazio was eager to do that—just on his own terms.

The debate involving HUD and how it would change to survive had an end point: a massive housing bill, working its way through committees. The Republicans felt that public housing should not just be for the poor. They wanted at least some working-class residents in the mix. Democrats argued that government's job was to help the neediest—period. Cuomo and Lazio rarely talked one-on-one. Their scorn was relayed through their staffers, to the point that a Lazio staffer decided to take matters into his own hands.

In early 1996, the Lazio staffer issued a draft amendment to the burgeoning public housing bill. It called for the elimination of one specific position at HUD: the assistant secretary of community planning and development. "It was 100 percent goof," recalled the staffer fondly. "We wanted to see Howard Glaser's hair on fire," he said, referring to Andrew's top aide. "We ended up seeing Andrew's hair on fire too." As the bill made its way to the floor, phones started ringing off the hook. Cuomo's staff called Lazio's staffers; they called Lazio himself. No one answered. Finally, they called Joseph Kennedy II, Democratic congressman from Massachusetts and Andrew's brother-in-law. Kennedy was a member of the House Banking Committee, with oversight of HUD. Kennedy, in turn, finally reached a Lazio staffer. "Did you write this amendment?" Kennedy demanded. The staffer admitted he had, but it wouldn't be offered. "We're just shit-stirring." There was a pause on the line. "Thank you for your honesty," Kennedy said.

Andrew simply took himself too seriously not to have his chain pulled. That winter he found himself satirized, with Hogarthian precision, in *Primary Colors*, the thinly veiled fictional send-up of the Clintons and their circle, published anonymously but soon revealed to have been written by journalist Joe Klein. Andrew was clearly Jimmy Ozio, the savvy, ambitious son of New York governor Orlando Ozio. "He was a big guy, curly hair, handsome in a lurky kind of way," writes the novel's narrator. Also so attuned to the nuances that when Governor Stanton, a.k.a. Clinton, asks him if he likes barbecue, Ozio shoots back, "Hamburgers and hot dogs?" The narrator is impressed. "Jimmy's game was elegant: you play southern, I'll play northern. We'll see who cuts the shit first."

Not for some time would it be possible to measure the success of those nine empowerment zones after hundreds of millions of dollars were poured into them. But the process of how the zones had been chosen could be judged—and was—by HUD's inspector general, a woman whose name Andrew would come to know all too well.

Later, when the tensions between Susan Gaffney and Andrew led to all-out war, Andrew's loyalists would accuse Gaffney of engaging in a partisan witch hunt, and there would be some evidence, if only anecdotal, of that. But it was also true that Gaffney had been appointed by President Clinton. And in her withering reports, beginning with the one on empowerment zones in August 1995, she would be so meticulous that no one ever accused her of inaccuracies, only of overstepping her bounds.

Gaffney concluded that Andrew's review of all those EZ applicants had been a sham. There wasn't enough paperwork to prove that any fair and rigorous system of judging had been followed. There were no detailed written rankings or rationales, just group discussion, with the final decisions made by gut. Andrew's gut, that is, and the secretary's. The inspector general suggested that the process appeared to be "open to favoritism." What she refrained from saying was that a program disbursing more than $1 billion, with little or no oversight, was one wide open to the back-and-forth of politics, and the rendering of big favors with future interest due. In a bristling reply, Andrew declared that the IG had exceeded her authority, and blasted what he called a "lack of accountability" on her part. Who, that is, was investigating *her* motives?

Later, Gaffney recalled that in a meeting that followed this exchange—a meeting of the two of them—Andrew somehow got on to his notion of effective punishment. Criminal sanctions, she recalled him saying, were often less effective than punishment through "adverse publicity, reputational harm, budget-cutting and legislative action." It was a philosophy she would come to know well.

Andrew was facing scrutiny from another quarter, this one potentially more harmful. Those pesky Fensters were back.

At some point after the New York Group's May 1990 settlement with Oceanmark, the Florida S&L's founding family had learned of the secret FHLBB enforcement decree—the one obligating the New York Group to sell all its Oceanmark stock in a timely fashion. Back they went to court, this time to get hold of that stock after all.

The timing was, for the Fensters, fortuitous. By the spring of 1996, Henry Cisneros's personal life was threatening his political one: a former mistress was making allegations that might obligate him to leave government. For Andrew, that meant two words in bright neon letters: job opportunity. If Andrew was to be considered a candidate for secretary himself, the last thing he needed was for the Oceanmark story to leak out again, in far more detail than before.

The parties reached their new settlement in April 1996. The Fensters agreed to ignore the FHLBB agreement of 1988. The New York Group could keep its stock. Every last share of it, however, had to be traded in for nonvoting shares. Most members of the New York Group signed the settlement that month. The last holdout was Andrew, who waited until September 3 to sign. By then, he knew his boss was almost certainly leaving. He had to make Oceanmark disappear.

There were perhaps valid reasons to fault Henry Cisneros's tenure as HUD secretary. Little or nothing had come of the Blueprint. HUD had implemented no new national strategy, aside from empowerment zones, on which the jury was still out. The Republican Revolution was in full swing, and there was nothing Cisneros could do about it. Congress had reduced the number of new housing vouchers to zero, the first time that had ever happened; not one additional poor person in the United States was getting a voucher to help pay his rent. In a brutally hostile climate, Cisneros at least had razed a number of dreadful, outdated housing projects, a campaign he called Hope VI: Republicans loved viewing the footage of emptied HUD buildings getting blown to smithereens. He had pushed immigration issues that affected Latinos, a special point of pride.

He was also enormously popular, both in the building and in the White House, where the president counted him a truly close friend. Almost certainly he would have become one of the rare cabinet members who served a second term. And then Andrew would have had to decide whether to spend those next four years as assistant secretary of CPD at HUD, working for Cisneros, or running for office—likely in a race against Alfonse D'Amato in 1998 for the New York senator's seat.

Andrew was spared that choice. In the first of what would be three similar turning points, the occupant of a higher office Andrew coveted would be forced to leave because of personal peccadilloes, and Andrew would have the luck to be next in line. There was a lot in politics a shrewd up-and-comer could anticipate and manage, and there wasn't a shrewder up-and-comer than Andrew. But then there were sudden twists no one could control, and a young politician could do no more than hope they went his way.

That Cisneros had had a mistress was long known. The answers he had provided on the subject in his background check for secretary were the problem: more money had gone to the mistress than he had acknowledged. Even if he survived an ongoing investigation, his legal bills left him no choice but to seek a high-paying job in the private sector. By the time he announced his decision to leave in the aftermath of President Clinton's reelection in November 1996, Andrew had been strategizing for months.

Andrew clearly had the vice president's backing. The two continued to work closely together on empowerment zones, and Andrew had coached Gore for his campaign debate against Jack Kemp, a turn that had gone well. The president was a fan too, but he was cagier. Andrew thought a good deal about how to sell himself to Clinton for the cabinet post. "We strategized together about how to put him out there for secretary of HUD," recalled Greg Craig, a prominent Washington lawyer with close ties to both the Clintons and the Kennedys. "Three or four others are always in waiting for any cabinet post. Andrew didn't want to campaign, but he wanted the job, and he didn't want to make any mistakes, so we had two or three conversations."

The most worrisome rival was Norm Rice, rounding out his second term as mayor of Seattle. Rice was an early Clinton loyalist; he had transformed Seattle's shabby downtown into a tourist mecca; and he was black. Big trouble.

As White House staffers looked more carefully at Rice, at first no red flags went up. Then came word from HUD that Rice was the subject of a fresh investigation. As mayor, he had helped arrange a $24 million, HUD-insured loan for a downtown development project involving Nordstrom, the department-store chain. The concern was that he might have somehow misspent that money. With the investigation hanging over his head, Rice was suddenly a liability.

The loan in question had come out of CPD long before; the memo first raising concerns about it had been written by a Seattle HUD official in 1994. The memo had languished for nearly two years, only to be snatched up by...someone. Another HUD staffer, a civil servant who worked closely with Andrew, recalled unequivocally, "It was Andrew." In fact, recalled the staffer, Andrew asked Susan Gaffney to initiate the probe, or "audit," as agency jargon had it for investigations undertaken by the inspector general. Andrew and Gaffney weren't enemies yet, the staffer explained. The staffer recalled being in the same room when Andrew, as he heard it, said to Gaffney, "'I have a real concern here about Seattle and this grant we did. I think there's some hocus-pocus here, I'd really like you to look into it.' And she was like, 'Yes, I will.' It was going to be an audit, not an investigation." Soon after Andrew was named secretary, the investigation went away. "I don't think anything happened with it," the staffer recalled. "Or we looked at Nordstrom and concluded they ought to keep their files better."

In Cisneros's recollection, the process was more benign. For a moment, he said, there was a "boomlet" of interest in Rice. "There were champions for him: very articulate, good reputation. But Andrew's name came to the fore. He was the only logical one within the HUD team." And Cisneros felt good about that. "He knew the department, had been part of the work I had begun, so there was a reasonable chance that a lot of our initiatives would go forward."

Years later, Rice, now CEO of the nonprofit Seattle Foundation, declined to comment.

Andrew had not won his seat—not yet. He still had to persuade his family's old nemesis, Senator Alfonse D'Amato, to support him. The president wouldn't think of nominating Andrew as secretary without the blessing of the chairman whose committee oversaw HUD.

D'Amato was relieved to think that Andrew wouldn't be a threat to his Senate seat in 1998. Still, having Andrew as head of the agency with which he had done so much political business was disconcerting. That was a lot of power. What if Andrew came at him to avenge his father's loss?

Frank DeStefano, a longtime housing staffer on the Hill who now worked for Andrew at CPD, was close to D'Amato as well as the Cuomos, and found himself the go-between for a peace-pipe dinner. A staffer for D'Amato, Mike Kinsella, was a great Italian cook, so the dinner was held at his place. Andrew didn't come, but DeStefano came as his ambassador—unacknowledged, so he could claim deniability if need be. D'Amato did come, but neither he nor Kinsella acknowledged that DeStefano was representing Andrew. Late that afternoon when DeStefano left Andrew's office for the dinner, Andrew grabbed him at the door. "Frankie," he said, "don't let them screw me." The dinner went well, and D'Amato liked what he heard; positive words about Andrew were spoken. At the door on his way out, D'Amato grabbed DeStefano by the arm. Could Andrew, and for that matter Mario, be trusted? Really? "Frankie," he said, "don't let them screw me."

There was one last hurdle. President Clinton worried that with Cisneros leaving, he might want another Hispanic for HUD. Better yet, a Hispanic woman. Aída Álvarez, a high-ranking HUD staffer, was a consideration. On the Thursday night before Christmas, with the president weighing various cabinet picks, DeStefano got a call from a White House friend. "This thing is going the other way," the friend reported. "It doesn't look good for Andrew." That was when a member of the White House inner circle—possibly the vice president—suggested an answer to the missing Hispanic problem. Federico Peña, the outgoing secretary of transportation, was well liked. Why not have him stick around and become secretary of energy? Peña's name ended with the right vowel. So he could fill the cabinet's Hispanic slot, freeing HUD up for Andrew.

That night at 11 p.m., DeStefano got another call from his White House friend. The vice president had come in to lobby personally for Andrew. He had made a kind of humorous move by jumping into a chair and saying, "This is Andrew's seat!" Clinton, his Hispanic quota filled, was won over, and put the call in to Andrew.

Like any other cabinet nominee, Andrew spent the next weeks paying courtesy calls to the committee members who held his fate in their hands. The Senate Banking Committee had Democrats whom Andrew knew well: John Kerry of Massachusetts, Chris Dodd of Connecticut, Daniel Patrick Moynihan of New York, and more. Every Democrat was a yes vote. But there were tough old Republicans who told Andrew bluntly that they thought HUD should be scrapped. One was Lauch Faircloth of North Carolina, who had actually introduced a bill to kill the agency.

Senator D'Amato, chair of the Banking Committee, set the strongly positive, bipartisan tone. The numbers were, after all, impressive. Andrew's CPD had gone from serving 20,000 homeless annually to more than 280,000, with all the continuum-of-care services he had championed, yet with only a doubling of the homeless budget. The so-called HOME program, which the Clinton administration had inherited, had built 2,000 units of housing in 1992—and 110,000 units by the end of 1996. Empowerment zones were up and running around the country, with more than $1 billion passing through them to local businesses. Meanwhile, Andrew's Consolidated Plan had streamlined a dozen bureaucratic processes into one. Somehow, while serving so many more people, he had also managed through attrition to cut the CPD staff by 25 percent.

It was a formidable record, but the challenges were even greater. As D'Amato somberly put it, HUD was spending billions more every year to house the neediest Americans. The biggest budget buster was its long-term contracts with landlords for low-income housing—the vouchers that Republicans were loath to renew or increase in number. The contracts were expiring; rents were rising; more money was needed to keep roofs over those people's heads. In just four years, D'Amato noted, HUD had gone from spending $3.6 billion on housing to $10.2 billion. Yet its budget had been cut in that time, from $25 billion to $20 billion. At that rate, it would soon spend its entire budget on housing and have no other money for empowerment zones or anything else.

There were, amid the gloom, a few light moments. At hearing someone mention that Andrew was not yet forty, Senator Moynihan feigned amazement. "My God! He's—"

"Thirty-nine, yeah," Andrew finished for him.

"He can't—"

"I look young," Cuomo said.

When it came his turn to speak, Andrew thanked his wife, "who is my partner and who has decided that we can do this and that's why we're here before you today.

"I'm also glad that my brother, Christopher, could make it. A little tardy, but he made it anyway, Senator. It's the thought that counts, I guess," Cuomo cracked.

In the end, the vote was unanimous, with no mention made by any of the Republicans of the Oceanmark suits that had mired Andrew in charges of fraud, brought him a cease-and-desist letter from federal bank regulators, and involved him in dubious stock maneuvers. Senator D'Amato was aware of Oceanmark but chose not to bring it up. The other senators may have been unaware of it. The page of Andrew's ethics disclosure that called for him to list any civil or criminal proceedings in which he was a defendant, or any inquiry or investigation by a federal, state, or local agency in which he was the subject of inquiry or investigation, listed only "Smith v. Cuomo et al shareholder dispute and litigations settled." The Smith in question was Lynn Fenster Smith of Oceanmark.

Even had they known, the other Republicans might not have brought up Oceanmark. HUD was desperate, and lawmakers on both sides of the aisle agreed: Andrew was HUD's best hope. He was confirmed by a 99–0 vote.

The swearing in, Andrew's mother-in-law declared, would be followed by a huge reception at Hickory Hill. Frank DeStefano, the Hill staffer who had helped calm the waters between Senator D'Amato and the Cuomos, found himself pressed into duty for the transition. The idea of Andrew heading off from the White House to a party at Hickory Hill hosted by Ethel Kennedy struck him as off-key. "With all due respect," he told the Cuomos, "it's a bad idea."

Mario Cuomo, down in Washington, D.C., for the occasion, took issue with that. What was wrong with a party afterward? he demanded.

"Right now he has a reputation for being arrogant," DeStefano said to the former governor, with Andrew in the room. "He should go right to the HUD building and meet with the goddamn staff. They're the ones who are going to make or break him over the next four years."

And so Andrew was sworn in at the White House and then went directly over to HUD to try to make a fresh start and a good first impression on the staff that now stood at 10,400, in the most dysfunctional agency in the government, in the ongoing Republican Revolution.

The lunch, hosted by his mother-in-law at Hickory Hill, was held at a later date.

CHAPTER 12

Mr. Secretary

Andrew had worked at the concrete bunker that was HUD for four years. And yet when he rode over from the White House ceremony on a brisk February day in 1997, he seemed to see it through fresh eyes. Why, in front of the building, was an ugly construction mess still ringed by a chain-link fence, with visitors forced to cross it on wooden planks? "What kind of message does this send?" Cuomo exclaimed to his newly appointed deputy chief of staff, Todd Howe, a Mario man from the 1980s. "We're in charge of housing, and the headquarters is under construction for years?"

Andrew strode through the double glass doors that set off the secretary's wing on the tenth floor and summoned his new aides into the conference room of the capacious corner office that Henry Cisneros had left after a tearful goodbye party. "It's February 6," he declared. "Three months from this date, I want that plaza completed. Get the GSA director on the phone, find out why no work has been done on it for months, fix the problems and *get it done*."

All too soon, Andrew was forced to confront HUD's deeper problems. One of his first meetings was with Senator Kit Bond, Republican of Missouri and chairman of the appropriations subcommittee that oversaw HUD among other agencies: the holder of HUD's purse strings. HUD was a mess, Bond said bluntly, starting with the fact that its budget for the next fiscal year was on course to be late—again. If the senator didn't see progress pretty soon, he'd dismantle the agency and send its parts to other, better-functioning agencies. What Bond did not say was that many Republicans savored the prospect of HUD being put out of business with Andrew Cuomo atop it. Son of a Democratic governor and Kennedy in-law? Thirty-nine-year-old cabinet secretary with an eye on the White House? The sooner Cuomo could be dispatched, the better. Throughout Andrew's stormy tenure at HUD, that would be a subtext.

Andrew knew, from his father, how crucial budgets were. You either beat them into shape or they beat you. More than anything else, they defined you, made you powerful or made you weak. In Washington, even more than in Albany, money was the measure. "Cuomo had one focus: money," recalled a staffer who worked for him on those budgets. He felt that his reputation in Washington would depend on whether he got more money or less.

Grimly, Andrew set benchmarks, and deadlines, and accountability if the deadlines were missed. When aides seemed stunned by weekend calls, Andrew would tell them, "You can sleep when the administration is over." Early on, he hired a twenty-seven-year-old administrative assistant and had her work until 8 or 9 p.m. every night. "You're going to scare her off," a colleague admonished him. "Nah," Andrew said. "If she makes it through the first week I'll know she's good—and she'll stay." She was, and she did, infused after that first week with a die-hard spirit.

The new admin assistant wasn't the only one who responded well to tough love. One night, Andrew had some of his aides over to Hickory Hill, and got to talking about his heroes. One was his father; another, he said, was Vince Lombardi. Why Lombardi? Because, Andrew explained, he got more out of people than they believed they had to give. "He would say, 'You can,'" recalled Fred Karnas, who headed up the interagency council on the homeless that Andrew basically controlled. "I would say, 'I can't,' and he would say, 'Yes, you can.'"

"He was tough, and you made it or you didn't," recalled Julian Potter, then deputy assistant secretary for CPD. "If you did, you got back as much as you gave." He was, added Potter, as tough on himself, and there were consequences. "He never did anything fun," she said. Once she asked him, "Do you ever go to the Smithsonian?"

Andrew looked at her. "What building is that?"

In his first appearance as secretary before a House subcommittee, Andrew ticked off the ominous budget numbers he had gathered. On top of its $19.2 billion budget for the fiscal year starting in October 1997, the agency needed an additional $5.6 billion if it was to avoid what Andrew termed the greatest crisis HUD had ever faced. The money was needed for vouchers that provided rent subsidies for the poor, the disabled, and the elderly, either in buildings whose landlords accepted them or in projects run by city housing authorities. Section 8s, the vouchers were called. Nearly two million of those housing voucher contracts would expire in 1998 alone. The vouchers couldn't be renewed at the same rates. Costs had risen. Landlords wanted higher rents to cover those costs. The tenants couldn't make up that difference. HUD would have to do that. If Congress didn't give it the $5.6 billion Andrew was requesting, more than 4.4 million Americans could be homeless within the next year. There was a bit of hyperbole in this. Congress had managed to cough up $3 billion the year before to keep voucher holders from becoming homeless; they were unlikely to let them starve now. But Andrew at his bully pulpit was a force to behold.

Andrew gave his budget numbers, the president approved them, and the death by a thousand cuts began: subcommittees trimming a number here, a program there, en route to the final—real—budget. Still, the first brutal deadline was met, and in the end Andrew would get most of what he sought.

With a bit of breathing space, Andrew started traveling around the country to housing authorities, Native American reservations, and the many other principalities of the sad kingdom known as HUD. With him was Clarence Day, his 24/7 security man. Clarence had provided security for four secretaries of HUD before Andrew. More than any of the others, he came to feel, Andrew seemed to connect with the lower- and middle-income people HUD helped. "There was something about him and his personality," recalled Clarence. "He was an exceptional man—really into what he was doing." When they stayed at hotels, Clarence took the room next to Andrew's. "One thing I want you to remember," Andrew told him early on. "I don't ever want to be in a room alone with a female while we're traveling." Clarence made sure of that.

Along with mayors and other elected leaders on those trips, Andrew met HUD field staff. To one and all, he gave the same message. "What is HUD?" he would start in his Socratic fashion. "It is scandal. It is inefficient. It is wasteful. It is the constructor of public housing institutions. It is the destroyer of neighborhoods. It is the place where good taxpayers have their dollars ripped off. I'm going to change everything you believe about HUD. But first of all, I'm going to acknowledge all of this. Acknowledge it, then resolve it."

The difference in tone between this secretary and the last one was drastic. Cisneros was gentle, solicitous, and universally loved. Andrew was blunt, tough, and demanding. "People looked at us like, 'You're too aggressive, too energetic, you're rocking the boat,'" recalled Todd Howe. Arrogant too: Cisneros would never have sent out the memo that Andrew did, early on, demanding that he be called Mr. Secretary, not Mr. Cuomo. Apparently some of HUD's older hands, confronted by a secretary young enough to be their son, had called him Andrew. No more of that. Anyone who called him Andy might as well pack his bags. The new secretary regarded that as an insult, and responded accordingly.

Politically, Cisneros and Andrew were different in another way. Cisneros made an effort to be bipartisan, but clung to Democratic ideals. Publicly, Andrew espoused those ideals, but made a point of cultivating powerful Republicans—Senator D'Amato for one, Senator Bond for another—and always seemed to weigh the political benefit or cost of whatever he did. His future and HUD's were aligned, and it was already clear to all that Andrew was focusing all his energies into furthering both. "The brilliance of Cuomo is this: he is probably the most effective secretary that HUD ever had," recalled Joe Ventrone, a Republican Hill staffer at the time. "And the most hated."

The most hated, that is, outside his close advisers: Howard Glaser, Mark Gordon, Todd Howe, and Gary Eisenman. Jon Cowan was a recruit from Cisneros's public affairs office, but ardently loyal to his new boss, enough that he would be named Andrew's chief of staff. Karen Hinton, a vivacious southern blond from Mississippi, oversaw the press office, and provided grist for the gossip mill when she and Howard Glaser left their respective spouses to marry each other. Jacquie Lawing, a Gore campaign worker in 1992 and then a staffer for Cisneros, was another outsider who made it to the inner circle, running homeless programs among other duties. She seemed to come in for more harsh words from her boss than the others; more than once, recalled one high-ranking staffer, Andrew made Lawing cry. "If Andrew said, 'I need a kidney,' she'd say, 'Where do I go to give it?' " recalled the staffer. But all took tongue-lashings from time to time. Was it tough love? Or Stockholm syndrome? That was hard to say, but a willingness to take abuse was definitely a job requirement for the inner circle.

Along with these close advisers, there was a next concentric circle of attorneys and other advisers—a gang of thirty-somethings, as one put it, to a secretary not yet forty himself. For all the pressure he put on them, Andrew instilled a real esprit de corps. Inviting them to his corner office after hours, he would break out cigars, noting which had come from President Clinton, and recounting White House experiences with the president and vice president. The next day he would tell them that the report they had knocked themselves out on wasn't good enough and had to be redone. The Double Down, they called it. "To me the message wasn't about being unreasonable," recalled Matt Franklin, a former deputy assistant secretary at HUD. "It was about the limitations we put on ourselves about what we can accomplish in the world. I saw firsthand how he wouldn't be constrained by that."

That was one world. The other lay outside the double glass doors of the secretary's tenth-floor wing. The career people who worked in the rest of the building were all but ignored by the new secretary. "He told his assistant secretaries, 'You deal with the career people, they're damaged goods,'" recalled one staffer. "He had no relationship with the rank and file. He didn't want to go down to these old white heads sitting there to be told, 'You can't do it this way, you have to do it that way.'" In fact, the white heads had a lot of institutional knowledge and knew how the housing laws worked. Sometimes they had to tell the secretary that some new plan violated a law or regulation. Andrew didn't want to hear that. So for him, recalled the staffer, "The vast majority of HUD did not exist."

By now, Andrew seemed to regard his in-laws with the same disdain. He hated the gatherings in Hyannis; he always felt odd man out. The joshing around, the freewheeling talks—Andrew was just too tightly wound to join in. One night, typically, the family began singing songs, each member singing a favorite. "The Kennedys are terrible singers, but it's one of the great joys," explained Douglas Kennedy. "One time Joe [Jr.] is up there, and he sings 'Danny Boy,' and everyone is happy about it. Except Andrew. He's on the couch with his arms folded, looking disgusted by the whole thing. Everyone is calling for someone else to sing a song. 'Andrew, you sing,' someone says. But he says, 'No, I'm not Irish.' So someone else says, 'Sing something Italian.' Andrew still won't, so I sing 'Volare.'"

Andrew stopped going to Hyannis at one point, a family member recalled. But he made sure to be with the clan at any gathering covered by the media. Early on, the family noticed that at every visit to Arlington Cemetery to honor their father or uncle, Andrew situated himself just so. "He would always find the exact perfect place to stand so he could be in the newspaper the next day," recalled a relative. "So if that meant grabbing [Ethel's] hand and walking to the grave, or standing next to John or Caroline, he would get himself in the frame. That was his whole thrust."

At the end of December 1997, the Kennedys would endure another death in the family. Michael Kennedy, not yet forty, sixth of Robert and Ethel's eleven children, died in a skiing accident in Aspen. Two days later when the family gathered to mourn at Hyannis Port, Andrew was there. The press were up the street, but the family remained cloistered in grief. "It was a different kind of death in the family," one close observer explained. Other than by name, Michael had not been a public figure. "It was not something we were sharing with the world."

A television was on, and suddenly there on the screen were Andrew and his brother, Chris, speaking to the press about Michael and the impact his death had had on his family. They had just walked up the street on their own to give the interview.

Most of the family were too stunned to say anything to Andrew when he returned, but Rory managed to ask, "Andrew, why did you do that?" Two days before, she had been on a ski slope in Aspen, trying to save her brother's life with CPR.

Someone had had to do it, Andrew replied. In fact, the family was lucky that he was there to handle the moment.

Speechless, Rory fled to her room upstairs.

"We had tried to be gracious," one family member said. "In my family, no matter how much someone is an enemy, you can be gracious with them." That was how Ted Kennedy conducted himself as a U.S. senator; it was how the next generation tried to act too. With Andrew, the siblings were forced to concede, graciousness just didn't work. "Andrew always interpreted graciousness as weakness," Doug Kennedy explained. "No matter what anyone did to be nice to him, it was going to be interpreted as political."

For Douglas and—so he says—his siblings, that news conference after Michael's death was the turning point. "That's where I started to think, 'This is just a bully.'"

The new secretary had a big-picture vision for HUD. He called it 2020, a catchall for all the ways he planned to transform the agency. Formalizing a plan like that would take months. What he needed right out of the box was a hit, some headline-grabbing initiative that might offer a first taste of what 2020 would entail and show that HUD had started a new chapter.

Going after slumlords of HUD housing projects—that would work. Andrew hadn't forgotten a trip to Las Vegas in August 1994, when he toured a HUD-funded housing project owned by one of HUD's largest and most notorious landlords. One area was supposed to be a playground, he told reporters. The playground was there, all right, along with an overpowering stench. "I was trying to identify the source," Andrew recalled, "and then I saw a broken sewer pipeline in one part of the playground."

By late April, HUD had moved to debar more than a dozen landlords whose buildings were in horrible disrepair, including one of the real kingpins, Allan S. Bird, whose $500 million California-based real estate company controlled more than a hundred properties nationwide. Bird earned $24.5 million a year from HUD for managing them, yet appeared to do little to address their squalid conditions. Bird and the other slumlords, Andrew declared at a press conference, would never be allowed to do business with HUD again.

The slumlord campaign was good optics. Unfortunately, another all too similar campaign was being conducted by HUD's inspector general,

Susan Gaffney, that same irritating woman who had written the report knocking the way Andrew chose empowerment zones.

Back in 1994, Henry Cisneros had encouraged Gaffney to launch a multiyear probe of crime in HUD-affiliated public housing authorities. The IG wasn't just a watchdog with an assistant or two. Gaffney oversaw a staff of over five hundred. In addition to being HUD's ombudsman, questioning agency matters and writing up "audits," she had scores of investigators empowered to use guns for campaigns outside the building. For Operation Safe Home, as the probe came to be known, Gaffney's investigators started going to housing projects, rousting out drug dealers and scofflaws, uncovering illegal firearms, citing slumlords for overcrowded apartments, and the like. "They were out at all hours of the night doing all sorts of questionable things that were not even remotely connected to what they were trying to find," recalled Saúl Ramirez, Andrew's deputy secretary. True or not, Gaffney had started holding her own press conferences for Operation Safe Home. How dare she run this rogue operation out of his agency! And so began Andrew's campaign to control the inspector general, first by wooing her, and then, when that didn't work, doing his best to destroy her.

To Gaffney, this came as a total surprise. She was just doing her job. Nor had she intended any personal slight with her stinging report on empowerment zones, back when Andrew was head of CPD. Every federal agency had an inspector general—an in-house but independent critic, reporting not to the agency head but to Congress. IGs had separate staffs and separate budgets. The audits that constituted most of their work almost always found fault: that was what they were meant to do. The agency heads didn't have to make the changes the IGs suggested, but they did have to pay attention; those audits could stir a lot of press, and ire on the Hill. Usually the agency heads gritted and smiled, and the relationship between them and their IGs was cordial, if not warm. That was not, however, to be the case with Andrew and his IG.

At first, Andrew seemed to value Gaffney strongly. Inordinately. He called her often, both at the office and at home on weekends. He wanted her counsel on how to reform the agency. With Gaffney's first press conference for Operation Safe Home, the tone began to change.

This wouldn't do, Andrew told her. He was the secretary. He couldn't have the IG going off on her own, making arrests in housing projects and staging her own press conferences for them. "On the one hand he felt he ought to be there at the press conferences—lots of arrests, lots of coverage," one staffer recalled. "But just about everyone who got arrested was black." The optics were terrible.

Gaffney reminded Andrew that inspectors general were independent. Andrew didn't seem to understand that. He still felt she worked for him. Operation Safe Home would have to be run through his office, he told her. For that matter, he wanted Gaffney to issue her audits through his office too. Later, senators at a subcommittee hearing would express amazement at this. Yes, Gaffney would sigh in response, everyone knew this was flat wrong, "and yet," she would add with dry humor, "we are starting de novo in HUD in these discussions of what the IG Act is about."

The irony was that Gaffney had liked Cuomo quite a bit early on, perhaps even nursed a crush, two staffers later suggested. She admired his energy and, according to one staffer, occasionally pined, "Oh, he's so handsome." When Andrew had asked her, toward the end of his term as assistant secretary, to look into Seattle mayor Norm Rice, she had cheerfully obliged, one staffer recalled, perhaps not even fully realizing that in doing so she was helping win Andrew his cabinet seat.

Boyish, with short-cropped sandy hair and glasses, Gaffney appeared not to have much of a life outside the building. Never married and living alone in her early fifties, she spent weekends at her little house in Arlington, Virginia, cultivating roses—and her privacy. A certain tinge of sexism crept in to colleagues' descriptions of her. One described her as hyper, another as shrill; that, at least, was how she seemed to strike men. She did have a tendency to raise her voice when she was stressed, which was often. But she was a serious government wonk, with years of experience in IG positions at various federal agencies. Most recently, at the Office of Management and Budget, she had had a title that would have fit right into David Foster Wallace's unfinished novel, *The Pale King*, about the IRS: chief of the Management Integrity Branch. With President Clinton's appointment of her as HUD's IG in 1993, she had worked four years, peaceably enough, with Henry Cisneros.

As a career civil service person, Gaffney kept her politics to herself. Andrew and his loyalists felt sure she was a closet Republican, doing her audits as an agent provocateur, expressly to see Andrew fail. In fact, both the key Senate and House committees to which she reported were in Republican hands; they, more likely than she, felt a touch of schadenfreude toward Andrew. Gaffney was actually a liberal Democrat, a staffer recalled, just one whose job happened to pit her against Andrew Cuomo. Shrill as she might be, she was in her own way pretty tough, and was not going to be rolled.

Backed by the Republican subcommittees that funded HUD, Gaffney kept on with Operation Safe Home. That was when the dirty tricks, as she would come to call them, began.

In the early spring of 1997, an anonymous letter found its way to the secretary's office. It accused Gaffney of discriminating against African-Americans and other minorities on her staff. With her Operation Safe Home campaign, she was also accused of spending "millions of dollars of taxpayer money rounding up young African American boys in housing projects so she can look [good] on television while serious white collar abuses by her own staff and rich building owners go uninvestigated."

Andrew refrained from showing the letter to Gaffney, or even telling her about it. Instead, his aides tried to provoke a government investigation of its charges. They failed, and Gaffney became aware of the letter. She went right to the President's Council on Integrity and Efficiency to demand that the council start its own investigation to see if any of the allegations were true. The council found no grounds for the charges and closed the case.

Andrew tried another tack. He had senior aides meet with Gaffney and accuse her of sharing confidential information with reporters. As a consequence of this breach, the aides demanded she sign an agreement that all press from her office be channeled through Andrew's press office. When Gaffney refused, a formal complaint from the secretary's general counsel's office was lodged against her in regard to the "confidential information" leaking out of her office.

Gaffney called the general counsel to ask what exactly the information was. He couldn't give her specifics. She then tried Andrew. After calling several times, she finally heard back. "Susan, it is too serious," Andrew told her solemnly, in Gaffney's later recollection. "You are better off not knowing what the facts are. It involves your immediate office, and there are some things you are better off not knowing about."

Gaffney did the only other thing she could think to do. Her office tipped off a reporter from the *Washington Post* about the formal complaint. Intrigued, the reporter called the HUD general counsel's office to ask about it. Days later, the complaint was withdrawn.

Gaffney was perhaps not entirely without blame. As tensions rose, she reminded Andrew that as IG, she oversaw his security. She wanted Clarence Day, the gentle security guard so loyal to each of the four secretaries he had served, shunted aside. She seemed to want to assign Andrew a new security guard—one who would be loyal to her and keep her apprised of Andrew's every move. Andrew quashed that one, then threw her another curve. In July, he announced that HUD would create a new "enforcement center," headed by a former FBI agent, to stamp out waste, fraud, and abuse by those receiving HUD funds. This was a fine idea, except that waste, fraud, and abuse were exactly what the inspector general, with all her investigators, was in charge of combating. Not only that, but the "enforcement center" would be in New York City, leaving Gaffney, in Washington, cut off at the knees.

This was a tactic Andrew would use repeatedly, marginalizing a foe by setting up a new office or agency that mirrored the foe's own, then taking over his or her turf. The mirror move failed this time when HUD's employee union realized it meant losing jobs. Eddie Eitches, head of the HUD union, felt the plan was just a way for Andrew to shore up his home state base with New York patronage jobs, from the construction workers who would build the center to the lawyers who would staff it. "The only reason [the move] is being done is for Cuomo to contract out to his friends and prepare for future political ambitions," said Eitches, according to an August 1997 e-mail written by subcommittee assistant Shanie Geddes. "The most disturbing fact, however, is that Cuomo told the union the reason it is in NY is because [Long Island Republican congressman Rick] Lazio dictated it had to be there [to fuel his own] future political ambitions," Eitches continued in the e-mail. Asked if that was true, Lazio marveled, "Why in the world would I want an enforcement center in Manhattan? If I wanted one I'd want it in my district."

By late 1997, Andrew was forced to retrench. There would be an enforcement center, he vowed, but in Washington, not Manhattan. As for how much it would poach on Gaffney's turf, that remained to be seen.

The slumlord campaign was a great success, with lots of press generated by an ever-larger press office—a press office considerably larger than that of any previous HUD secretary. Going after bad guys made for good press. Clearly, too, enforcement suited Andrew's character. His father had started as the lawyer of the downtrodden, fighting to right wrongs, and Andrew had inherited that same sense of moral mission. For both father and son, the quest for justice was the perfect expression of politics and personal ambition: both a raison d'être and a great way to play to the crowd. In scanning for more of the same, Andrew's eye alighted, naturally enough, on HUD's humblest relation, the Office of Fair Housing and Equal Opportunity (FHEO).

An offspring of President Johnson's Great Society campaign, the FHEO fought discrimination not just in public housing but wherever any American was denied housing or equal treatment on the basis of race, religion, or national origin—and, after amendments, gender, disability, or family status. Andrew was passionate about the FHEO. Had white racists put poisonous snakes in the front yard of a black Mississippi woman to drive her out of the neighborhood? The FHEO could go after that. Was a

Hispanic family denied an apartment in a "white" building? That was an FHEO case too.

Complaints like this came in every day to the FHEO, piling up like old *New Yorkers*. There simply wasn't the staff to respond to each case. Andrew changed that. He gave the department more staff, redesigned the way it responded, and drew up performance metrics. He wanted every complaint addressed. Even more, he wanted stories he could serve up to the press.

And so began, for the FHEO staffers, the relentless push for "hot cases." If more than a week passed without a hot case issuing up from the department, the secretary's office would call down to ask why. The staffers weren't media-savvy, and they sometimes brought cases that, while significant, weren't good media stories. Perhaps this week's story of a family denied housing was too similar to last week's. Maybe a victim of discrimination was, inconveniently, a felon.

A drawback with most hot cases was that legally they were premature. The evidence wasn't all in. Andrew was a lawyer, yet he seemed not to appreciate that most basic legal principle: there were two sides to every story. When his own general counsel raised concerns about a hot case, he didn't listen. He just got mad. "He would yell," recalled one staffer. "Sometimes his eyes would just pop out." Often he stood up abruptly and left the meeting where the latest hot case was being discussed. More than once, a hot case Andrew insisted on publicizing led to embarrassment, as a landlord's lawyer objected angrily—and rightly—to the way the case had been fed to the press by the FHEO.

The pressure for hot cases put Andrew on a collision course with Eva Plaza, the FHEO assistant secretary. Plaza, a lawyer, had worked with distinction in the Justice Department, but HUD was a different world. She was cautious, deliberative. Not Andrew. He ruled with a sort of swagger. "I was shocked by someone that brash," said one staffer. "I've dealt with a lot of macho guys in my family, I can spot them a million miles away. I was just surprised that someone like that had gotten to be secretary."

At the large staff meetings he liked to convene, Andrew's style, like Mario's, was to challenge his aides. Some, like Jon Cowan, Todd Howe, Gary Eisenman, and Howard Glaser, thrived on that: it was a kind of office blood sport, mano a mano, the gladiators going at it while the audience looked on. Others, like Plaza, just froze. "He would ask her a question about fair housing, what we were doing, and she would answer nervously and perhaps not fully," recalled one staffer. Andrew would then turn to another staffer and ask him the same question, a stinging rebuke for Plaza.

Andrew's treatment of Plaza became an ongoing spectacle. "I saw his wrath," recalled another staffer. "I would sit in a meeting and put my head down, and I'd say, 'Not here.'" But Andrew wouldn't relent. "It was almost like he smelled blood," recalled another staffer. "Andrew had a little bully in him," said a third, "and bullies tend to pick on the not so strongest people."

That was in meetings. One-on-one with Plaza, Andrew was worse. One staffer sitting in on a call between them heard Andrew ask her a question. When she couldn't answer it, he shouted, "Do your job!"

Other staffers, unprepared, or just hesitant, came in for similar treatment. "He could come on like a thug, in your face, talking down," recalled one staffer. "'*What is this?*' '*Where did you get this from?*'" He wanted action, and anything less ticked him off. "Process does not count as progress," he would exclaim. "Don't tell me you had a meeting, don't tell me you called them, don't tell me you're going to get together and you sent out a memo. That's process. Where's the progress? Where are the results?" He had a point. In fairness, he almost always had a point. But that point could be really sharp. "When you can't respond," recalled one staffer, "that's the cruelest thing."

Slumlords and hot cases were headline-grabbers on their own. But they also fit into the agency-wide overhaul Andrew announced in late June 1997, the plan he called HUD 2020.

Andrew started by acknowledging that HUD was built on a massive conflict of interest. The same agency that put roofs over people's heads, often by persuading landlords to accept housing vouchers, was also obligated to punish landlords who didn't provide that housing cheaply and cleanly enough. Out there in the field, it was hard to wear both hats. A regional head of HUD was inclined to feel grateful to a landlord housing poor people, and not to want to look too closely at how that housing was maintained. Andrew proposed to change all that.

The new HUD would be carved into halves. It would have a new breed of "community builders" to help people find housing and foster urban renewal: in short, the good cops. The bad cops, monitoring the programs and meting out enforcement when landlords took advantage, would now be known as "public trust officers." Both would be out in the field, reporting back to headquarters in Washington.

In addition, HUD's eighty-nine separate financial systems would be transformed into one. HUD's massive portfolio of some twenty-nine thousand buildings around the country would be inventoried and assessed for the first time. The department had no idea which were in grievous disrepair, and how so. A new computer system would do all that. Focus and efficiency would reign. Most critically for restoring credibility, HUD's army of 10,400 employees would be slashed to 7,500.

Staff cuts were clearly needed: HUD was bloated. Still, under Henry Cisneros, HUD had dropped from 13,400 to 10,400 employees simply by attrition and buyouts. The further drop planned was music to Republican ears. But how exactly had Andrew divined that magic number? The GAO's Judy England-Joseph had no idea. As far as she could see, Andrew had seized on it arbitrarily, out of the blue, like magic. "'Where did it come from?'" she recalled asking Andrew. "'Can you show me?' He couldn't."

That October, HUD's 10,400 employees got notices putting them in one of three categories. The majority kept their jobs. Some of the rest got reassigned. The dregs were put in limbo and told to start looking for new jobs. The name of their category was "New Horizons."

The workers contemplating their new horizons weren't fired. Instead, they sat at their desks with nothing to do, or got moved in clumps. "It was nerve-racking," one HUD civil servant recalled. "You would find new people in your office, just moved wholesale." Presumably the departments those workers had left could operate more efficiently without them, though as one staffer points out, the main result was that programs got outsourced. The displaced workers, the ones now sitting in some other department, kept getting paid to do nothing at all.

The drive for the magic number was inspired by Vice President Al Gore's Reinventing Government campaign. Gore had pushed for downsizing across the gamut of federal agencies—though again, the downsized didn't depart, only migrated. "You had directors who'd been there a long time, who'd had their satraps through half a dozen administrations," explained one staffer. Gore's initiative sent the old-timers off to the Turkey Farm, as it came to be known. The old-timers were told they would be part of the reinvented government, but that tended not to happen. Instead, they were left on the Turkey Farm, in limbo, until they retired. A lot of Andrew's unwanted civil service staffers got sent to the Turkey Farm, noted a former staffer. "Every white-haired guy who didn't give Andrew the right answer ended up there at the Turkey Farm with an old desk and no phone."

To Susan Gaffney, the whole downsizing campaign was ill-advised. The magic number of 7,500, she wrote in an audit in November 1997, was "arbitrarily derived" and "built on an unsupported premise, namely, that the department can adequately function with a staff of 7,500." Gaffney warned that reaching the magic number would put HUD in "serious jeopardy."

Then a curious thing happened. Over the next months, through attrition and buyouts but no firings, HUD's ranks fell to 9,100. In May 1998, Andrew signed a document abandoning the magic number of 7,500. For reasons never explained, the new magic number was 9,000.

That aspect of HUD 2020 had solved itself. The plan's crown jewel would fare less well. Creative and yet crassly political, the program Andrew called "Community Builders" would embody his own strengths and flaws: a harbinger of things to come.

CHAPTER 13

A Nemesis to Contend With

On his one-year anniversary as the youngest HUD secretary ever, the *New York Times* took a long, appraising look at Andrew and liked what it saw. "It's Andrew Cuomo's Turn at Bat, and Some See Makings of Slugger," ran the page-one headline. The *Times* noted that despite the "high risk" tag still tied to the agency, Andrew had accomplished a lot. Partly that was his tireless zeal to streamline and consolidate programs, root out waste and abuse—and burnish his image in the process. Partly it was his canniness at compromise with the party in power. "Cisneros got dribs and drabs from us," one Republican aide said, because the previous secretary dug in his heels. "Cuomo is smart. He sees the writing on the wall and changes strokes midstream."

Andrew's mentor—the president—admired his performance too. Clinton had some personal problems that were about to get worse: on January 26, 1998, he held a press conference to declare he hadn't had sex with Monica Lewinsky. Soon Ken Starr, the Captain Ahab of special prosecutors, would embark on his investigation of Clinton's affair with his intern, leading to impeachment proceedings. But the president, like Andrew, was adept at compartmentalizing. Business at the White House went on as usual, including Wednesday night political gatherings at the White House residence to which Andrew was now invited. "The president really respected his judgment," recalled Doug Sosnik, White House political director at the time. "And that's the best test, ultimately, of what a president thinks of someone—whether he wants to engage and listen to him."

The meetings were held in the second-floor Yellow Oval Room of the president's personal residence, which opened onto the Truman Balcony with a view of the Jefferson Memorial in the distance. Along with Sosnik, the political gang included Rahm Emanuel, John Podesta, Paul Begala, Ann Lewis, and Sylvia Mathews, as well as pollster Mark Penn.

The president presided, Vice President Gore beside him, with just two cabinet members rounding out the circle: Commerce Secretary William Daley, and Andrew. The president was more centrist than Andrew—at least the Andrew of that time—and he liked hearing Andrew's more liberal take on issues. He also seemed to admire Andrew's willingness to take on Penn. "One time Penn scoffed at a policy choice by saying, as he usually did, 'I tested that, my way is better,'" one member recalled. "And Andrew challenged him directly. 'Everything you test, you find that your own ideas are the way to go.'" The circle knew that Clinton abhorred confrontation, so taking on Penn in front of the president was a real risk. But that, said the observer, was typical of Andrew in those meetings. "He gave honest and fearless advice."

Impressed by his savvy, the president awarded Andrew his next budget triumph. For the next fiscal year, starting in October, HUD would get its first increase for housing vouchers in three years: $2.7 billion, pushing the overall HUD budget up to $27.2 billion. That was big.

Along with advocating for new vouchers, Andrew was prosecuting more bad landlords. A top target was Bruce Rozet, whom Andrew accused of one fraud or another at ninety HUD-sponsored housing projects, making this the biggest case in HUD's history. At an April 15, 1998, news conference, Andrew mentioned that a company that had done business with Rozet, providing management services for some of his projects, had reached a settlement with HUD for paying kickbacks. The management company was Insignia Financial Group; the settlement was $7.5 million. And therein hung the start of a tale that would weave through Andrew's political career, a tale of money and very odd bedfellows.

Insignia's chairman, Andrew L. Farkas, was enraged by the HUD settlement, and Andrew in particular. He felt he'd been railroaded for a practice widespread in the housing industry—not kickbacks at all, merely a commission paid for getting the service contract on a housing project—and denied doing anything illegal. Had he been told that day in 1998 that he would become one of Andrew Cuomo's personal friends, and one of his larger campaign contributors, he would have laughed bitterly.

Farkas had bought, among other Rozet properties, the Sierra Nevada Arms in Las Vegas. That was the one Andrew had visited in 1994, with a playground into which human waste was spewing. HUD had seized the property in 1997 and was preparing to file charges when Andrew learned that the new owner came from a wealthy Manhattan family: Farkas's grandfather, George, had founded the Alexander's department-store chain. Andrew Farkas had attended the private Trinity day school, then Harvard—a different world from Archbishop Malloy and Fordham.

Farkas might have challenged HUD in court. He might even have won. He was, however, on the verge of selling Insignia to a company in Denver. The market was up; prices were high. Farkas had started Insignia with just $5.5 million in 1989, and he stood to make more than $900 million by selling it. He couldn't jeopardize that sale by fighting kickback charges. Through clenched teeth, he agreed to the $7.5 million settlement without any admission of wrongdoing. Farkas hadn't yet met Andrew. Nor did he have any desire to do so. Andrew, as he put it, was his "sworn enemy."

If there was anything Andrew loved more than bringing bad landlords to justice, it was dreaming up new programs and making them work. Of the many he had in mind for HUD 2020, the one that most excited him—the signature on the canvas—was the wildly ambitious, ultimately ill-fated Community Builders.

A new program like this needed congressional approval and funding—a heavy lift in a Republican-ruled Congress. To this end, Andrew paid an early visit to Senator Kit Bond. With Bond was his aide Jon Kamarck, a rumpled conservative who probably knew HUD better than anyone else on the Hill. Andrew arrived alone—good optics—and proceeded to read impassioned letters from voters in Bond's home state pleading for HUD to bring Community Builders to them. "Senator Bond was immediately skeptical," recalled one former Hill staffer. "He thought Andrew might have gotten the letters drawn up for him."

Even so, Andrew had a compelling message. He envisioned Community Builders as a modern Peace Corps, with all the idealism that President Kennedy had instilled in the original. He wanted recruits from all over: teachers, graduate students, nonprofit professionals, even lawyers and politicians, anyone smart and excited by the vision. Once trained, this new elite would break out of HUD's silo culture and go directly to the poor and needy, helping however they could.

Bond and Kamarck listened closely. They liked a lot of what they heard, with one caveat. Andrew kept referring to this *new* elite corps. Why couldn't he staff up Community Builders from inside the agency? Surely he could find seasoned hands within. And how would it look for him to be hiring new troops when he was cutting career people?

Andrew scowled. A Hill staffer recalled him saying he had a "moribund" agency. "He kept going on about the HUD staff: they're not very competent, they just know how to fill out forms, they don't know about housing..." Bond and Kamarck were taken aback. "I respectfully disagree with you, Mr. Secretary," Kamarck said. "I know a lot of people at HUD who really care about housing." It was an odd twist: a Republican defending HUD to the agency's Democratic secretary. But in truth, Republican lawmakers who oversaw HUD tended, at least then, to care about it and want it to succeed, if only to preserve what was for them part of their political turf.

With the Republicans' wary approval, Andrew started hiring his community builders. Nearly all were from outside. To avoid adding career civil servants to the rolls, he hired them all as "politicals," or "schedule C's," with two-year contracts. Off they went to Harvard's Kennedy School of Government for four-week training sessions. The first Community Builders Fellows class, drawn from some 9,000 applications and numbering 230, would graduate that September 1998. Within a year there would be nearly 400 in all. In his enthusiasm, Andrew seemed not to appreciate the ill will his campaign was causing agency-wide.

Instead of adding these new recruits to HUD offices around the country, Andrew envisioned giving them their own storefronts. Each storefront would have an orange kiosk with a computer touch screen, like an ATM, with twenty-four-hour information on how to find HUD-owned buildings in the neighborhood, or how to file a complaint of racial discrimination. Inside would be the community builders, ready to help. With his usual flair for marketing, Andrew called the storefront plan "HUD Next Door." For a prototype at Washington's Union Station, he and Todd Howe spent weeks deciding the color of the awning. Not royal blue, exactly, not sky blue either. *Duck canvas navy blue*—that was it. And for the storefront's façade, a matte tan color, ditto the walls inside, with carpeting that picked up both the brown and blue. Andrew wanted the carpet's pile to be supple and soft, so children could play on it while their parents talked with the community builders. As for the kiosks, more than a color choice was needed. Andrew had to be sure the kiosks worked. In 1998, that was a challenge.

That first HUD Next Door, situated near Union Station, was expensive: $687,000. A third of that, however, was a one-time design fee that future storefronts would use. Andrew's goal was a storefront for each of HUD's eighty-one field offices. It was a bold step. "The context is: this is the agency the GAO rated as high-risk," recalled one senior staffer. "There was incredible pressure on Andrew to say this is too much of a leap."

Expensive as it was, Community Builders might have worked, and worked well, if not for Andrew's insistence on hiring new people. "You bring in people who have no experience in the area they're going to," suggested Judy England-Joseph of the GAO, "and if you don't bring your own rank and file along so they understand what you're doing, there's just huge pushback." As predicted, tensions rose when the newcomers were given higher civil service rankings than the old-shoe field staff. HUD's union head, Eddie Eitches, was amazed. "They were all 13s, 14s, and 15s—and they knew nothing! So they were being taught by career 11s and 12s." Yet the community builders were being regarded by HUD's tenth floor as the new elite. Even more infuriatingly, they were given the power to decide how HUD funds should be doled out in each region.

"How else were you going to attracted talented people?" demanded Andrew's old friend Gary Eisenman. But the results were disastrous. "We ended up having to promote the old field staff to erase the disparity," said one HUD staffer. "Everyone got a promotion."

To shield Community Builders from the inevitable attacks by his arch-nemesis Susan Gaffney, Andrew hired three outside consultants to assess the program and the rest of HUD 2020. All were well known: Booz Allen, James Champy, and David Osborne. Andrew warned Gaffney that their reports, due at the end of March, would be very positive, and that if she criticized Community Builders in the meantime, she would be "humiliated." All told, Gaffney later figured, Andrew spent $412,000 on the consultants.

The reports did praise 2020, though David Osborne, part of Vice President Gore's Reinventing Government campaign, later acknowledged some frustrations. "As a company, we helped design reinvention strategies. He kept asking us to *review* his strategies." Not to chart a course, just to validate the one he had chosen. Osborne saw a sincere effort, but one not too well thought out, especially when it came to Community Builders.

"The office storefronts turned out to be gimmicky," Osborne recalled. "You can't put a storefront on the front of a terrible bureaucracy and have it work." Especially not if the chain of command was as flawed as HUD's was. "If you as a community builder need to respond quickly to community needs, you need the programs in D.C. to respond to you. But if they're not accountable to you, why should they?" And if community builders didn't have the full force and commitment of Washington behind them, what good could they do?

On May 7, 1998, Gaffney told Senator Connie Mack's housing subcommittee that, regrettably, staff cuts and office consolidations for 2020 had put HUD on an irreversible course. "We must move forward, because HUD is not staffed to turn back at this point." And yet its goals remained unclear. "Each document defines HUD's mission as 'Empowering People and Communities' and 'Restoring the Public Trust,'" Gaffney said in exasperation. How was anyone to measure such a broadly defined mission? Though she didn't say so, she seemed to suspect that that might be the point.

Gaffney was tough, but she wasn't a street fighter. That spring she left herself open to a nasty counterattack.

At the urging of her Republican overseers, Gaffney began planning a new chapter of Operation Safe Home, a multiyear investigation of fraud in the public housing authorities of three American cities. She was given a special budget of $9 million and told to choose the cities herself. Gaffney talked to FBI investigators who had done some fieldwork on the issue, then came to Andrew. The three cities the FBI had suggested were San Francisco, New Orleans, and Baltimore. What did the secretary think of that?

"I realized of course that the mayors in these three cities were African American, and there could therefore be a perception problem," Gaffney later told the subcommittee. Also, all three mayors were Democrats. "I consulted with the secretary about this well before any selection announcement was made," she explained. "The secretary said he wouldn't expect any problems with Baltimore or New Orleans. But San Francisco could be a problem, because everything in San Francisco is perceived in racial terms. I said we needed to look at the San Francisco Housing Authority, but didn't have enough staff to do it right. He responded, 'Well, you'll just have to go forward.' "

The three black mayors got notice of the probe in April 1998. They were incensed. "It is un-American to target only those cities with African American, Democratic administrations," declared Baltimore mayor Kurt L. Schmoke. "I just don't understand why the largest housing authorities in cities with white mayors get a pass."

"It stinks, it smells, it looks suspicious," said New Orleans mayor Marc Morial. Perhaps, he added, race was only one factor. "Are we victims of a war between the secretary and the inspector general?"

Andrew now lined up squarely with the three black mayors. "This is in our opinion either illegal or unethical," he told the *Los Angeles Times*. "It is not a situation that can or should be tolerated."

Gaffney was stunned. She believed Andrew had set her up.

Republican congressman Jerry Lewis, chair of the House subcommittee that signed off on HUD budgets, vigorously defended Gaffney. "There is little doubt in my mind she has no racial bones in her body," he said. But neither he nor Gaffney could explain why the probe had failed to include any of the four U.S. cities with the largest housing authorities, whose mayors all happened to be white. Under mounting pressure from the White House and black mayors around the country, the probe was put on hold.

Gaffney was all but unhinged by how she felt Andrew had treated her. One staffer recalled wandering into her office at that time for a surreal experience. "She laid a trip on me about Cuomo: he had insulted and berated her... He had called her on a Saturday morning and reamed her out for three hours, the gist of which was, 'Tell me what it would take me to get you out.'" She seemed vulnerable, freaked out, almost paranoid. It was infectious. "By the time I left her office," the staffer recalled, "I was looking over my shoulder to see if anyone in the secretary's office was following me."

One charge of racism might be fended off. Two set a pattern hard to shake. With the black mayors still hyperventilating, the discrimination complaint filed against Gaffney by one of her staffers, Philip Newsome, could be the final straw.

Newsome was a black investigator in the IG's office with twenty years' experience in the field. After a turn as deputy assistant IG for investigation, he had hoped for a promotion to assistant IG. Instead, in December 1997, Gaffney had awarded the higher post to a white colleague. That same day, Newsome learned he would not receive a performance-based bonus. He filed a complaint in February 1998 with HUD's Equal Employment Opportunity office, charging Gaffney with racial discrimination. Whatever its merits—HUD and IG staffers could be found on either side—Newsome's case elicited considerable interest in the secretary's office.

As protocol dictated, Newsome's complaint was assigned to an outside investigative firm. The firm charged $2,700 to look into the charges, a touch under the $3,000 that such cases usually cost. Its deadline was August 11, 1998.

Later, the firm would report having started its work by June 11. Somehow, Howard Glaser, Andrew's top aide, got the impression in mid-July that no investigator had been assigned. That, he decided, was grounds to terminate the outside investigator's contract. The secretary's office then hired two outside law firms to look into the case. Neither was on the government-approved list, and they charged unprecedented rates: $50,000 for each firm.

A report later done by the General Accounting Office found Glaser the central figure in these maneuvers. Glaser was Andrew's enforcer, known in the halls as "the Hammer." According to the GAO, Glaser chose the lawyer from each firm that he wanted on the case. One was Deval Patrick of Day, Berry & Howard, a former assistant AG in the Department of Justice's Civil Rights Division who would later become governor of Massachusetts. The other was Kumiki Gibson, an attorney with Williams & Connolly who had also worked in the Justice Department's civil rights division and as counsel to Vice President Al Gore. Patrick and Gibson were heavy artillery, distinguished lawyers both—and both arguably inclined to feel the same way about the case as those who had hired them, never mind that both were black.

Merely stating that two law firms were investigating Gaffney for racial discrimination was the equivalent of a guilty verdict in the court of public opinion. Andrew's top press officer, Karen Hinton, told the press that "a dozen of [Gaffney's] employees have made racial complaints against her... the bipartisan U.S. Conference of Mayors has passed formal resolutions on a pattern of racism by the IG and... Deval Patrick, the former assistant attorney general for civil rights, is now investigating her on the most serious charges of racism in the department's history." The charges were unspecified and unproven. Aside from Newsome, no one in the IG's office had come forward.

The word the GAO used more than once in its follow-up probe was "extraordinary." The GAO investigators found it extraordinary that Howard Glaser had intervened to fire the compliance firm and hire two law firms at unprecedented rates for such work. They found it extraordinary that the secretary refused to be interviewed, and that other HUD employees came to their interviews with outside counsel in tow.

In his own interview with the GAO, Glaser said that Gaffney had driven at least seven other IG staffers to make race-based complaints. Yet when the GAO investigators asked to speak to those seven staffers, they were told that all wished to remain anonymous. Glaser did acknowledge that the controversy over the three black mayors had led him to put the Newsome investigation on a new, faster track. There were, after all, two scenarios of racial discrimination now, not one.

Shortly after the two outside law firms were hired, Gaffney heard about them and demanded a face-to-face meeting with Andrew. The racism charges were bad enough, but there was more. Gaffney had warned Andrew that his planned enforcement center could not be what he wanted it to be. He wanted it to stage criminal investigations and have subpoena power. Gaffney had warned him that he had no such powers. Only the IG could do criminal investigations; only she held subpoena power. She had made Andrew stipulate, on paper, that he understood this. Now, in public statements, he was again saying the enforcement center would handle criminal matters. The racism charges were personally upsetting. But this latest end run threatened the very structure of the agency.

Gaffney confronted Andrew head-on. "I reminded him that... if he started the 'dirty tricks' again," she later testified, "I would fight."

The next week, Gaffney walked into a committee hearing on the Hill and fired away. "It is to me somewhat jolting, maybe shocking, that the current secretary of HUD has exhibited an extremely hostile attitude towards the independence of the HUD OIG," Gaffney declared. "He has, in fact, let this hostility lead to a series of attacks and dirty tricks... Recently the tempo of those attacks and dirty tricks seems to be escalating, and their focus seems to be increasingly that I am a racist.

"I think there is more than good reason to believe that the purpose of these attacks...is to force me to leave HUD," Gaffney continued. "I have stayed at HUD because I fear that if I leave, the secretary would replace me with someone whose loyalties are primarily to the secretary...I am trying to fight the good fight, but within the administration, it is clear that I am not in Secretary Cuomo's league. So someone needs to help. Someone needs to convince the secretary that I am not an adversary. I am trying to do my job."

That December, the two outside law firms assigned by Glaser to the Philip Newsome case concluded that Newsome was a victim of racial discrimination by the inspector general. They recommended that President Clinton fire her. Whether unconvinced by their reasoning, or perhaps distracted by the looming prospect of impeachment hearings, Clinton declined to do so.

The secretary's office, meanwhile, hired a separate outside lawyer, Donald Bucklin of Squire, Sanders & Dempsey, to determine whether anyone had acted incorrectly in handling the Newsome complaint, specifically in hiring the first two law firms to investigate it. The fee for this additional investigation was $100,000.

Bucklin concluded, on December 23, 1998, that Andrew's office had handled the Newsome case appropriately. The other two law firms had acted appropriately too.

The GAO's report, submitted later, reached a very different conclusion. It found no justification for ending the first outside investigation of Newsome's case, and for hiring the expensive law firms. It took particular issue with Glaser's contention that many IG staffers had experienced discrimination at Gaffney's hands but declined out of fear of retaliation to come forward. Staffers had come forward in the recent past, the investigators found. Since Gaffney's arrival in 1993, about 2 percent of IG staffers had registered racial complaints. Interestingly, in the Office of the Secretary, the incidence of racial complaints had gone from 10.3 percent in fiscal 1997 to 17.5 percent in fiscal 1998.

Newsome himself saw no impropriety on Andrew's part in the handling of his case. "At no time did the Secretary have control of or influence over my actions or me," he e-mailed years later. "The accusations that I was somehow 'in concert' with Secretary Cuomo against Susan Gaffney are simply not true to any degree." While declining to detail the charges he had made against Gaffney, he remained adamant that they constituted prejudice and abuse. "I've tried to forget about the entire ordeal," he wrote, "yet I sometimes still find myself waking up in the middle of the night in a cold sweat over it...As a professional criminal investigator, I had an advantage over those [who] opposed me. I was trained to focus on the evidence. It was evidence, not a hunch, feeling or assumption that led me to file a complaint."

Despite the three outside law firms that all supported Newsome's story, HUD's Equal Employment Opportunity office never did act on the complaint. The complaint has since been destroyed, according to a response from the department to a Freedom of Information Act request. One IG staffer later said the EEO found no grounds for action in Newsome's complaint. Newsome said the EEO planned to issue a finding of discrimination, but didn't because his attorneys instead took the case to court.

Newsome's lawyers did take the case to court—federal district court—in early 1999. With that, Andrew's relationship with his inspector general hit a lull. For the moment, she seemed too tired to fight.

Appearances to the contrary, Andrew did find time for more than battling his inspector general. That fall of 1998, he played a vital role in helping pass the most important housing reform act in half a century.

For at least three years now, Rick Lazio had been standing on the House floor hectoring friend and foe alike on the need for public housing reform that would mix in working-class families with the desperately poor. America's urban housing complexes had never been intended only for the poor, he argued; they were meant to help "lunch pail" job holders too. Lazio remained Andrew's doppelgänger, the other young New York politician of Italian descent with gubernatorial ambitions. Andrew didn't necessarily disagree with Lazio's lunch-pail argument. But he didn't want Lazio to be the one who redefined his turf and got the credit for it.

Andrew came up with a clever way to co-opt Lazio. In a program called "Officer Next Door," police officers would get 50 percent deductions on foreclosed houses in low-income neighborhoods with Federal Housing Administration loans. The officers would be a stabilizing presence, as well as good role models. It was a great idea that found its way into the final bill, though with unforeseen consequences. Officers began subletting the properties, or flipping them, and living elsewhere. "It was enough that we all said, 'Wait a minute,'" a HUD staffer recalled. "The police weren't living there, that's for sure."

Still, "Officer Next Door" helped Lazio shape the housing bill with middle-class tenants. What Andrew wanted in return was vouchers, and here he scored an unequivocal triumph.

Vouchers were actually a Republican idea that over time had migrated across the aisle. A poor tenant in a HUD-subsidized building was more or less trapped there. Better, perhaps, to have HUD subsidize him directly: to give him a voucher that covered part of his rent wherever he chose to live. These were the so-called mobile Section 8s that the Republican Revolution of 1994 had put a stop to: no new vouchers, period. If Lazio was going to get his middle-class tenants, Andrew wanted the first new mobile Section 8s in four years. Andrew didn't just want a few thousand new vouchers. He wanted more than one hundred thousand.

Senator Bond and the rest of the housing-focused Republicans were shocked. Each voucher was worth about $5,000: that was how much a recipient got to defray his rent over the course of a year. Andrew wanted vouchers not just for the poor, but welfare recipients looking for work, the homeless, the elderly, and the disabled. The price tag of those hundred thousand-plus vouchers was $585 million. But not just $585 million once: $585 million each year, in perpetuity. And that was a moving target. What happened in a tight housing market when rents went up? Either the voucher holders would be priced out or the federal government would have to give them *more* money.

Senator Bond countered at ten thousand vouchers.

Unfazed, Andrew held out for more than one hundred thousand. At a key conference, a Hill staffer was startled to find two or three of the secretary's top aides hovering outside the door, there to make the case for more vouchers. "As staff came out, they would buttonhole them," the staffer recalled. "They were quite animated." The staffer had never heard of this happening before—or, for that matter, the spine-stiffening calls to Democratic staffers at home. "You can say, oh, he's very passionate," the staffer added. "But it was like being confronted by thugs." To the staffer, the subtext was always apparent. "Andrew was probably the most political HUD secretary I've dealt with," he declared. "His personal ambition touched everything he wanted."

Eventually, Senator Bond upped the ante, to about fifty thousand new vouchers. Andrew wouldn't cave. Back he went to OMB. When OMB stood firm, so did he. "I demand to see the president," he declared.

Any cabinet secretary, as Andrew knew, had the right to argue his budget case at the eleventh hour before the president, if he chose to risk the president's ire and spend that political capital. Andrew did. He wanted one hundred thousand more vouchers, he told President Clinton. Anything less would be a blanket surrender. The president noted that if he gave Andrew all those vouchers, he would have to take the money from other agency budgets. What could be more important, Andrew said, than helping the poorest of the poor?

With that, the president acquiesced. In the final bill, Andrew got ninety thousand vouchers. That number overshadowed Rick Lazio's press releases celebrating—and taking credit for—the epic housing reform act. By the only yardstick that mattered—money—Andrew had just notched a big win.

That was the public Andrew. The private Andrew was doing less well. Two months after the Cuomos' third daughter, Michaela, was born in 1997, Andrew and Kerry were talking divorce—not whether to get one, but when.

According to several family members and friends, Kerry had stepped down from her job in order to raise the kids, and worked on a book about human rights leaders at night after they went to sleep. She felt she was shouldering too much of the load. At the same time, she often went on human rights trips, leaving the children at home. One friend recalled getting a call from her the night before Kerry was to go to India. Could the friend help care for the three Cuomo daughters while she was gone? Kerry had made no provisions. The stresses of marriage and parenthood might have been alleviated, Kerry felt, if she and Andrew spent more time with their families, particularly her own. More childcare options, more camaraderie, more love and support, but no, Andrew did not agree.

Through his time as HUD secretary, Andrew had hardly lost the drive for more: more power, more glory, more visibility. So far, no particular office beckoned. That changed in November 1998 with the startling news that New York's senior senator, Democrat Daniel Patrick Moynihan, seventy-one, would not run for a fifth term in 2000. With Senator Alfonse D'Amato's defeat that same week by Democratic congressman Charles Schumer of Brooklyn, the state's political landscape changed overnight.

On the list of some dozen possible contenders for Moynihan's seat, the youngest, and possibly the most potent, was Andrew Cuomo. Andrew's name, reported *New York Times* columnist Bob Herbert, was the one most frequently mentioned among Democrats. Andrew would have a tough choice to make if Vice President Al Gore ran for president in 2000. A Gore victory might bring Andrew an appointment as chief of staff. Gore might even tap him as his running mate; there was talk of that. "Does he give that up," Herbert wondered, "for what undoubtedly will be a brutal fight for the Senate?"

By early January, the senate scenario for Andrew was moot. Hillary Clinton was quietly mobilizing for a Senate run of her own, and Andrew could hardly run against the woman whose husband he worked for. All he could do in the short term was hope that Gore's presidential prospects rose, and that his own fortunes rose with them. If not, then for the longer term—2002—he had a new target: the governor's mansion in Albany. And for that, he had an early card to play: showering hundreds of millions of dollars of government money—HUDbucks—on one of the state's most Republican regions, the storied Erie Canal Corridor.

It would prove a quixotic—and darkly comic—campaign.

CHAPTER 14

A Last Chance for Change

Over five days in August 1999, a festive entourage made its way east along the Erie Canal by boat and bicycle. A beaming Andrew, his wife, Kerry, and their twin daughters, Cara and Mariah, marveled at the sylvan backdrop they glided past, and the sleepy canalside towns with their redbrick buildings and high-steepled churches, markers of a time gone by. To the local lawmakers who came aboard at each next stop, Andrew rhapsodized about his love of the canal, and DeWitt Clinton, his favorite New York governor—after his father, he hastened to add, the lawmakers breaking into peals of laughter—whose vision for the canal had become a reality back in 1825. After decades of somnolence, it was coming to life again, Andrew assured his audiences—this time as the engine of tourism it deserved to be.

At each stop, Andrew sweetened his speeches with yet another major grant, or loan, or both. Sixteen million dollars here, thirty million there: pretty soon he was talking real money, at least to the economically depressed towns of the Erie Canal Corridor. That week, Andrew and his boat mate, Agriculture Secretary Dan Glickman, together handed out $193.1 million in federal dollars to scores of corridor towns. Yet there was more. By the giddy math of Andrew's press releases, tossed off at each next stop like confetti, every canal town would benefit. In all, HUD was handing out $237.3 million, Agriculture was adding $160.2 million, and the cumulative $400 million or so was being leveraged by public/private partnerships to . . . $800 million. That was big-time, transformative money—enough, perhaps, to revitalize the whole western sweep of the state. And, in the process, help get Andrew Cuomo elected as New York's next governor.

The Erie Canal! Its very name evoked the early American frontier, and the challenge of taming it with an almost unimaginable triumph of engineering in any era, let alone a barely postcolonial one. The Erie Canal had helped make America a world power. Then had come the railroads, auguring the canal's long decline, until the interstate highway rendered it not just unneeded but quaint.

Governor Mario Cuomo had had plans for reviving the canal system as a tourist attraction. But George Pataki had shown little interest after becoming governor in 1995 in taking up this pet project of his predecessor, and so it was left to Andrew at HUD to revive his father's vision, christening it the Canal Corridor Initiative. For Andrew, the opportunity to do good was inspiring, the political payoffs irresistible.

Steve Groat, then the mayor of Clyde, a town midway on the Erie Canal once known for its Mason jar factory, went in the fall of 1997 to a slide show narrated by Andrew himself. Scores of local officials from up and down the canal were there, their excitement rising as Andrew gave a passionate pitch for what the Canal Corridor Initiative could do for them. Their towns would get more than $100 million in block grant money from HUD. They would qualify for much more as loans under something called Section 108. The idea, as Andrew explained, was that towns could take out the loans by putting up future block grant money as collateral. The future block grant money was guaranteed, so HUD wasn't taking a risk by making those loans. But what about the towns? If a town defaulted on its Section 108 loan, did that mean it would lose its future block grant money? It did.

Still, for a region as desperate as the canal corridor, Andrew's plan was galvanizing. Groat, a spark plug of a fellow, compact and hyper, saw nothing less than salvation for his long-suffering town. With the Mason jar factory long gone, a GE plant too, Clyde had come to seem a permanent outpost of the old and jobless, its wide streets empty, its storefronts blank. Why open a store when the shopping mall was just twenty minutes away? Now all that might change.

Eagerly, the town fathers of Clyde applied for a grant of $350,000 to build a dock and pump-out station on the canal, with a little canalfront park. Maybe now canalgoers would stop for the night. The town fathers got it, though the money ran out before they could add the pump-out station, and so hardly any more canalgoers tied up for the night. In the stillness of Clyde, the park and dock did look very pretty, however.

An hour and a half west in Holley, a grant of $560,000 built a dock that did include a pump-out station, along with a little canalside park, bathrooms, and a gazebo. Those touches were done by the balmy August day in 1999 when Andrew disembarked at Holley to view them. The park had even been expanded, with another grant. Now it included a little nature trail wending its way back through the woods. The trail was only a hundred yards long, so the Cuomos could easily walk it. At its either end were monuments of local Medina sandstone, each five feet tall, suitable for a national park or the Appalachian Trail. And what did the monuments proclaim? The Andrew Cuomo Canalway Trail.

The canalfront improvements were beautifully done. Aside from the labor expended to create them, though, hardly any jobs had come of the Canal Corridor Initiative. For that, the towns needed to apply for those Section 108 loans. Unfortunately the process was so complicated that almost no one managed to wade through it. Poor as they were, desperate for investment, the canal townspeople encountered so much red tape on those Section 108 loan applications that they just gave up. That was a pity, because most of the money Andrew had announced with such fanfare—nearly all of it, in fact—*was* Section 108 loan money.

Perhaps sensing a problem, Andrew hired a Cornell professor named Susan Christopherson to analyze the job potential of the Canal Corridor Initiative. In September 1999, Andrew came back to the region, visiting the canal town of Amsterdam with Vice President Gore in tow. There he announced Christopherson's findings. HUD's investment in the canal corridor, Christopherson concluded, was "likely to yield over 17,000 additional jobs [in tourism]."

The next year, at Andrew's behest, Christopherson came out with a follow-up. In addition to those tourism jobs, the corridor program was now also likely to create ten thousand more jobs in manufacturing and business services.

Christopherson was a big fan of the program, but she did have to clarify more than once that these numbers were projections. "They aren't actual jobs," she told Andrew. "I'm just using a model." No one would know for sure if those jobs materialized before they did. "Whaddya mean?" Andrew asked her. She explained in detail and he said he understood. Still, the HUD press releases touting the studies didn't say the initiative *might* create those twenty-seven thousand jobs. They said that according to estimates, it *would*. Two years later, when Andrew was making his first run for governor, his campaign website would make a wilder claim. "As HUD assistant secretary and then as Secretary," it would declare, "Cuomo began and implemented the Canal Corridor Initiative that resulted in billions of dollars in public and private investment *and created 27,000 jobs*." Hardly any of those jobs had materialized. As for the billions of dollars in investment, that was just wishful thinking.

In their inevitable audit, Susan Gaffney and her IG investigators looked at twelve of the fifty-three towns that had benefited from the Canal

Corridor Initiative. They found that few had managed to get any Section 108 loan money. The program had projected 1,338 jobs for those twelve towns; only 153 had been created. Of those, one town had created 100. Eight of the towns had created no jobs at all.

The Erie Canal was a good tryout, at least. If Andrew was going to use a cabinet seat in Washington as a springboard for the governorship, however, he would need to do much more. To New York voters, his track record at HUD—making it work better, boosting its budgets, perhaps soon getting it struck off the high-risk list—was all inside-the-Beltway stuff. The best way to reach those voters was to build a more national profile, weigh in on weighty issues—in short, start to look like a governor. To that end Andrew began taking poverty tours around the country in the winter and spring of 1999. With his first, to the coal-mining counties of West Virginia, he struck an unmistakable comparison to the father-in-law he'd never met.

Robert F. Kennedy's own immersion in Appalachia had transformed him, from a tough, even cynical U.S. senator into an advocate for the poor. Three decades later, the Clinton economy was booming, but the good times were passing many by, as Andrew sermonized to *New York Times* columnist Bob Herbert, the secretary's journalist du jour. After his own trip to coal country, Andrew had a new, national message. The time to help the poor was now, when the country was best able to do it. "You fix the hole in the roof when the sun is shining," Andrew told Herbert, "not when it's raining."

Poverty, as any politician knew, was not a winning issue. "When you advocate for the poorest people in this country... you're going to end up looking like an old-style liberal," Andrew told another reporter. "That's what happened to my old man." Nevertheless, as head of HUD, poverty was the card he had to play. The question was whether he could get the White House to play too.

First, Andrew published a glossy report entitled *Now Is the Time: Places Left Behind in the New Economy.* Then he enticed the president and vice president to join him on a quick swing to Edinburg, Texas, a dusty and desperately poor town near the Mexican border. The poor were poor enough, the backdrop suitably dire. Now the challenge was to get the president to do a national tour of places left behind, one with real media impact. The White House wanted to help—if only as part of the president's postimpeachment campaign of rehabilitation—but needed an upbeat message that would resonate on both sides of the aisle. Helping the poor? Too liberal. Someone, probably Andrew, came up with the better spin: *finding economic opportunities in overlooked markets.*

The most overlooked of all possible markets were tribal lands, where unemployment rates were tragically high, alcoholism and drug abuse endemic. The reservations made a powerful backdrop, and HUD had responsibility for them. If he *were* to come, though, the president couldn't just make a speech and move on. He needed new programs to announce, new grants and access to housing loans to hand out: no tour like this would work without them.

Andrew needed a guide, and he found one in Jackie Johnson, a member of the Tlingit tribe who had become his deputy assistant secretary for Native American programs. Johnson took Andrew to Alaska, to some of the country's most remote tribal villages. The trip got Andrew fired up. Always, mixed in with ambition, was a real sense of social mission. He wanted to do something, he told Johnson. "Jackie," he demanded, "where are the neediest of the needy?"

"I'm not taking you there," Johnson told him.

"Wait—where is it? Which is the neediest place?"

The answer was Pine Ridge, South Dakota, but Johnson was adamant. She wouldn't take him there. Why, Andrew wanted to know. "Because everyone goes there, and takes a look, gives them a glimmer of hope, and leaves them with nothing," said Johnson. "I'm not going to expose them that way."

Instead, Johnson took Andrew to New Mexico. He saw more tribal lands, and a lot more poverty. Now he was obsessed. "He kept saying, 'I want to do stuff in Indian country,'" Johnson recalled. He meant the broken heart of Indian country: Pine Ridge. Finally Johnson agreed to take him, but on one condition. "'We are actually going to do something that has a lasting effect.' He said, 'Okay, I'm committed.'"

Amid the low, rolling hills of southwestern South Dakota, Andrew and Johnson met with the tribal elders of Pine Ridge. Andrew saw small houses occupied by several families. He saw children with vacant looks, living in dirt. "When we came back to the Housing Authority," recalled Paul Iron Cloud of the Oglala Sioux Tribal Housing Authority, "he broke down and cried."

The elders were skeptical that this fancy suit from Washington could do anything to improve their lot. But over a period of two years, Andrew worked with Johnson to draw up a list of new programs and policies. HUD would give tax credits to Fortune 500 companies to invest in Indian country, training workers. Internet access was another need: in the late 1990s, there was virtually none. Simply putting an ATM on reservation land was a major innovation.

With the president agreed to do the tour and make Pine Ridge one of his stops, Andrew and Jackie Johnson rallied the U.S. Department of Defense to commit seven thousand soldiers to build modular houses, along with roads: nation building at home. In all the soldiers built seventy-two houses and stayed the whole summer, right through the president's visit.

No president since Calvin Coolidge had made an official trip to an Indian reservation. Clinton's was scheduled for an annual Native American conference, held at Pine Ridge that year, so that elders from tribes all over the country would be there.

Andrew flew in the day before to inspect everything—too much was at stake for him not to do that. Besides, these were the optics he did better than anyone. Once, he had arrived at a scene like this, taken one look, and ordered the stage and seats turned in the opposite direction: the backdrop was better. This time he approved, then flew back a hundred miles to the town where the president had just arrived by Air Force One, so that he, with Kerry, could accompany him the next day to Pine Ridge by presidential helicopter.

On the dais, Andrew spoke first, stressing his theme that the poorest corners of America had enormous, untapped buying power. The Indian leaders dutifully applauded. Then he introduced Kerry, who recalled her father's vivid impressions of his own poverty tour some thirty years before. Finally the president addressed the crowd. "We're coming from Washington to ask you what you want to do," he said, "and tell you we will give you the tools and support to get done what you want to do for your children and their future."

It was Clinton at his empathetic best. But then he and Andrew and Kerry were gone, the presidential helicopter a vanishing speck in the sky, the tour, after a final stop in the Watts district of Los Angeles, over and done. What, years later, had come of the white men's latest promises?

Jackie Johnson felt Andrew had delivered. "It may not be everything that everyone expected," she said, "but it was an investment, a partnership." True, the plan of pulling in Fortune 500 companies had not panned out. Some of the families that had moved into those seventy-two houses had failed to make their mortgage payments and been foreclosed upon. But at least those seventy-two houses had been built, along with a new boys-and-girls center at Pine Ridge, and Internet cafés both at that center and others.

Paul Iron Cloud was more measured. "The president gave us a chance to do a lot of programs," he acknowledged. "We had to just put them together, but it takes money to do things. A lot of it was putting together programs with no dollars." Fifteen years later, multiple families were still crammed into falling-down houses; addiction and depression still reigned.

"Our kids come to school, put their heads on the desk, and go to sleep," he said. "Because of parties."

In casting about for other national issues to address from his bully pulpit, Andrew found one as poignant as poverty, and in some ways more dramatic, both for the passions it stirred and the lives it might save. He was barely back from his Pine Ridge trip when he took it up as his new cause.

Strictly speaking, gun control as a federal issue fell within the purview of the U.S. Justice Department and other enforcement agencies. But guns, especially illegal handguns, brought terror and death on a daily basis to HUD's public housing authorities. How could a HUD secretary do his job and *not* deal with guns?

Already, Andrew had waded into the issue with a gun buyback program, for which President Clinton had pledged $15 million to buy back up to three hundred thousand guns, no questions asked. Clarence Day, his security detail, drove a truck loaded with thousands of guns down to Virginia one day and watched with Andrew as they got melted down. "You know what?" Andrew said to Clarence. "I feel good today. I know that these weapons will not kill another person in this country."

It was noble work, but a new political rival was nursing a far grander plan. In his first term as New York's attorney general, Eliot Spitzer had noted a wave of lawsuits against gun makers, filed by various cities and counties, for expenses incurred as a result of gun violence. It was a creative approach, and the gun makers were feeling the heat. By July 1999, he had started advocating a compromise: if the manufacturers put new limits on gun distribution, along with new safety measures, the suits might be put aside. A new code of conduct—that was the phrase Spitzer used. It was a phrase that Andrew would borrow for his own turn as attorney general, and then use so much that it came to define his whole approach to enforcement. Instead of indicting one or two bad apples, get a whole industry to change by signing a new code of conduct. Unfortunately for Spitzer, the gun industry balked.

As Spitzer tried to restart his talks, Andrew saw his chance and took it. With a sign-off from the White House, he reached out directly to the gun makers, offering both carrot and stick. He could bring a class action suit too, larger than any of the local lawsuits, on behalf of HUD and its public housing authorities. Or the gun makers could negotiate. And so the paths of two fiercely driven politicians, one a cabinet secretary and one an attorney general, crossed for the first time.

Eliot Spitzer and Andrew Cuomo were in some ways polar opposites. Spitzer had enjoyed a childhood of privilege, his father a wealthy New

York developer, the family ensconced in the affluent enclave of Riverdale overlooking the Hudson. Eliot attended the private Riverdale Country Day School, then Horace Mann, with Princeton for his undergraduate years and Harvard for law school, nothing but the best for a son who might be the first Jewish president one day.

All this was reason enough for Andrew—scrappy child of the Hollis-wood streets, his student loans for Fordham and Albany Law paid off in full by the sweat of his own brow, his swaggering style itself a diss to the rich and fancy—to loathe Eliot Spitzer. "Eliot was the consummate *Harvard Law Review* lawyer, Andrew was up at Albany Law getting a degree because it would be a good thing to have," suggested a top Spitzer aide of several years. "These were two people who were not going to like each other a lot."

Perhaps it was what the two had in common that really pitted them against each other. Both were sons of highly successful men, driven to outdo their fathers. Each was accustomed to being the smartest guy in the room, and bristled at any challengers. Both, too, were press hounds, with the highest political hopes. New York State—or at least its government—simply wasn't big enough for the two of them.

Surely it irked Andrew that in a matchup of these two supremely ambitious New Yorkers, Spitzer was arguably ahead—and two years younger to boot. Both had done the requisite tour of duty in the Manhattan DA's office, but Spitzer hadn't just fielded appeals and left early; he had fought organized crime as head of the office's labor-racketeering unit. While Andrew worked for a small firm that doubled as his father's fund-raising machine, Spitzer had gone on to Skadden, Arps. Andrew swelled with pride at his cabinet seat—he liked to see himself described as the nation's housing czar—but it was an appointed post, made possible, if he was honest about it, with pull from his father. Spitzer had won the 1998 attorney general's race by a whisker, but still, it was a statewide office, an *elected* office. Both men knew which résumé was more impressive.

When the news broke in mid-December of Andrew's end run to the gun makers, Spitzer professed to be pleased. His own approach could be the "dagger," with federal pressure from HUD the "meat ax," he told one reporter. Each could help the other. But by early January 2000, the honeymoon was over. With Andrew, Spitzer told a friend, the objective was the press release, not the actual result. Everything Andrew did, Spitzer felt, was to line up his run for governor.

Tensions heightened between the two at a meeting in the Old Executive Office Building in Washington to see how the dagger and meat ax would work together. Spitzer felt his own initiative was still the best course, even though for the moment it had stalled. He would restart the talks, he said—his way—backed now by the clout of the federal government, and keep Andrew apprised. When Andrew suggested that HUD representatives be included on Spitzer's negotiating team, Spitzer resisted, his voice rising. He planned to reach a deal with gun industry officials at an upcoming gathering in Las Vegas.

"The Vegas meeting won't work if we have twenty-five people there," Spitzer declared.

HUD was the federal government, Andrew replied; it was the top of the food chain. Of course HUD should be there.

Spitzer resisted that. "How as secretary of HUD are you any more qualified than the attorney general of New York and our negotiating team to represent the interest of the parties?"

The gun lobbyists agreed. HUD wasn't needed at the negotiating table. "All they were looking for," one lobbyist scoffed about Andrew and his team, "was an opportunity to stand before a microphone...As far as Mr. Cuomo was concerned, the motivations were 100 percent political." Soon enough the plan fell apart anyway, and with it Spitzer's inside track on the issue.

Unbeknownst to Spitzer, Andrew now opened a back channel to an unlikely ally: Ed Schultz, the CEO of Smith & Wesson. As one of Andrew's negotiators put it later, Schultz hadn't grown up in the gun industry; he was a business guy more than a gun guy. He wanted to be helpful, as long as it didn't hurt his bottom line. "Would I put locks on our guns if it might save one child?" he asked himself. "The answer was yes."

The talks stayed secret not only from Spitzer but from the rest of the gun makers. HUD lawyers held furtive meetings with the Smith & Wesson executives and worked late into the night. Andrew was a relentless boss, but he knew how to motivate his troops, and somewhat to their own surprise, they rose to the task. He also had a sense of humor. "Kevin and I had made some mistake," recalled Max Stier, who with Kevin Simpson led the legal team, "and Andrew called us into his office." The lawyers found him looking very serious.

"I'm chagrined about what we did," Simpson blurted out.

Andrew fixed him with a look. "Chagrined?" He pulled out a dictionary and looked up the word as the lawyers looked miserably on. Then he broke into a smile. "Yes," he said. "*Chagrined*."

Spitzer was more than chagrined when he heard about the talks in late February. He called the White House; the White House declined to call back. Caught in the crossfire, Ed Schultz marveled at the egos on each side. "It is two rich kids trying to be captain of the team," he told the *New York Times*. "They are rivals. There is no question that each one of them wanted to have their own party and each would have been happy to have the party without the other one there, if they could arrange that."

Andrew couldn't quite get away with that. But he came close. At 10 p.m. on March 16, Spitzer got a call informing him that a deal with Smith & Wesson had been struck, and did he want to attend the press conference the next morning? Not only had Andrew run with his idea; he had made it work! But if Spitzer gave any thought to skipping the press conference, he soon put it out of his head. The only thing worse than attending would have been not to go.

The deal was short-lived, however. Down on Ed Schultz's head came the collective wrath of the American gun industry—and that of the country's gun owners, stoked by the National Rifle Association. Though none of the other gun makers would admit it, the most damaging aspect of the settlement was that Smith & Wesson clearly felt it could absorb these modest changes without losing sales. The traitor in their ranks had to be brutally punished. And so he was. A boycott killed sales. Overnight, at gun shows around America, the name Smith & Wesson became anathema. Soon Ed Schultz was gone and Smith & Wesson was on its way to being acquired by a new corporate owner, who promptly tore up the agreement.

Aside from raising the profiles of two young New York politicians, the campaign for safer guns had accomplished nothing at all.

At the start of his last year at HUD, Andrew gathered his staffers for a solemn meeting. "It seems to me we have a choice," he said. "We can sit on our laurels to the end, close up shop, and walk out the door knowing we've done a lot. Or we can decide to do more and decide what our top priorities are."

Since sitting on laurels was probably not the right choice, Andrew's top aides took turns arguing for one course of action versus another. It was, as one recalled, a sort of moot court. Everything on their new to-do list served at least one of three overriding goals. Bigger budgets? As always, a must. Getting HUD off the at-risk list? Absolutely. But the third was perhaps even more important, because it served as a measure for the whole administration: raising home ownership rates for minorities, the poor, and the lower middle class.

President Clinton had championed the goal of higher home ownership, and overall he had great numbers to tout. More Americans owned their homes in 1999 than ever before: 66.8 percent of households, after steady rises from 64 percent when Clinton had taken office. The rates of minority ownership, however, lagged far behind: about 45 percent, and the president, and Andrew, wanted to change that. "This was going to be Andrew's great legacy," recalled a HUD staffer. "He wanted minority ownership to be at record levels. He pounded away at this incessantly."

For Andrew, the blame or credit had everything to do with a power that Congress in 1992 had chosen to bestow on the HUD secretary: the power to regulate the so-called gods of Washington, Fannie and Freddie.

Fannie Mae and Freddie Mac, the two giant quasi-federal mortgage companies more properly called "government-sponsored entities," or GSEs, acted to keep money flowing through the country's mortgage market. They did this by buying up residential mortgages from regular lenders and then packaging them as securities on the secondary mortgage market. Like blood, that capital cycled through the system. By selling their mortgages to Fannie and Freddie, the lenders had more money to make more mortgages, and the secondary market thrived. As part of their charter, Fannie and Freddie had to cover the losses for any mortgages they bought whose borrowers defaulted: that reassured all the players and helped keep the system stable. As long as the vast majority of mortgages they bought stayed solid, Fannie and Freddie would not only prime the pump of real estate but make profits—considerable profits—on their loans.

In April 1999, HUD issued a study of the GSEs that concluded they weren't buying enough mortgages issued to low- and moderate-income borrowers. Fannie and Freddie at the start of the Clinton administration had spent 30 percent of their money buying up low- and moderate-income borrowers; by 1999 they were up to 42 percent. But why not 50 percent? Andrew figured that no fewer than twenty-eight million low- and moderate-income families would be served if the GSEs hit the 50 percent goal. There were heated words between Andrew and Fannie's powerful head, Jim Johnson, who felt increasing the number of low- and moderate-income borrowers would increase the number of defaults, but Fannie did buy up more of those loans, and so did Freddie.

To later critics, Andrew's push for Fannie and Freddie to buy up even more of the low- and moderate-income mortgage market was all the evidence needed that he had fueled the housing crisis. These were the subprime loans that would start to tank in ever-growing numbers as poor borrowers defaulted. But an inconvenient truth stood in the way: Andrew's high goals for the GSEs did not induce them to lower their standards for mortgages they bought, at least not at that point. No-money-down mortgages and other dubious devices were kept at bay. Default rates did rise modestly from 1999 through 2000, but then began to dip and kept declining through 2004. Only after President George W. Bush set even higher affordable housing goals at the start of his second term did Fannie and Freddie start gorging on subprime loans, with a resulting rise in default rates.

A decade later, after the bubble had burst and mountains of subprime mortgage securities had melted along with the real estate market, two *New York Times* reporters would investigate whether the ex–HUD secretary running for governor a second time should be held responsible for some or all of the housing crisis. They would find he might have done more to avert it—he did have that regulatory power—but he would have had to possess a prescience absent from nearly all the relevant players: Congress, the banks, the U.S. Treasury and Federal Reserve, the GSEs, even the president.

Andrew did bear blame, however, for failing to stop a sneaky practice of the mortgage industry called "yield spread premiums." To draw in new business in those go-go years, lenders paid mortgage brokers a premium for each new client. Only they didn't take that premium out of their own pockets. They charged the borrower—without telling him. Up ticked his interest rate, just enough to cover the broker's premium. This was a kickback, pure and simple.

Andrew vowed to eliminate the yield spread premium. But the mortgage brokerage industry was one of Washington's most powerful special interests. By March 1999, when he rolled out a new set of policies for HUD's Federal Housing Administration, he had had a change of heart. Yield spread premiums were not "illegal per se," he ruled. Brokers didn't even have to disclose them. Some 150 class action suits were stopped by that phrase.

The yield spread premium not only enriched brokers at the expense of their clients, but it goosed the subprime market by giving those brokers an incentive to write up more and more dubious mortgages. In the end, roughly 90 percent of all subprime mortgages would have yield spread premiums baked into them.

The ghost of subprime past wouldn't come back to haunt Andrew until he ran for governor in 2010, after the housing market had crashed. But as he laid the groundwork for a first gubernatorial campaign from his corner office at HUD, he faced his share of other ill portents.

One was his likely Democratic opponent, Carl McCall. At sixty-four, McCall had a seemingly perfect résumé for the New York governorship. Son of a welfare mother, he had graduated from Dartmouth, run for and won a state senate seat, been appointed U.S. ambassador to the United Nations, earned private-sector credibility as a vice president of Citicorp, and come back to public service as head of New York City's Board of

Education. Now he was the New York State comptroller, overseeing the $120 billion state pension fund, which made him in effect the biggest individual investor in the world.

Within a broad swath of the state Democratic Party, there was a sense that McCall wasn't merely the best candidate to block George Pataki from a third term as governor but the one whose turn it was to run. If he did run, and win, he would go down in history as New York's first black governor, a stirring incentive for a lot of voters, and not just black ones. He even had the Mario Cuomo seal of approval: back in the 1982 Democratic gubernatorial primary, Mario had supported McCall for lieutenant governor, and seethed when the voters gave him Al DelBello instead.

If McCall had a flaw, it was lack of desire, that raw ambition that any politician needed to jump in, much less win. He had failed to run for governor against George Pataki in 1998. That same year, he had begged off from a go at Daniel Moynihan's U.S. Senate seat, months before Hillary Clinton had even entered the race. His hesitancy extended to fundraising—he didn't much like it—and political views, of which he seemed to have none. As political columnist Michael Tomasky put it, McCall's reason for running was, "It's my turn." Andrew's, for better or worse, was, "It's not my turn but I'm running anyway." McCall was running for a lifetime achievement award. Andrew was running for the job.

Andrew had his youth, his keen ambition, and the Cuomo name. Against him he had... his youth, his keen ambition, and the Cuomo name. At the Democratic state convention in Albany in May 2000, Andrew met a cool reception. His arrogance preceded him; so did the legacy of slights and slams doled out to many in the Mario Cuomo years, either by Andrew or Mario himself. One assemblyman, asked if he planned to attend Andrew's reception that night, said, "You mean the guy whose father forgot to endorse me when I was the only anti-death-penalty Democrat in my race? I don't think so."

McCall got a standing ovation, with cries of "Run, Carl, run." The same crowd listened with studied politeness to a speech from Andrew. The son had all the cadences of his father's oratorical style, and the gestures—like the hand to the tie, as if to say, "This is what I believe"—and even some of the soaring rhetoric about the haves and have-nots. These old Albany pols weren't buying it. The Andrew they knew was his father's hatchet man, aiming to jump from a cabinet seat he'd won with his father's help to a governorship he felt was his because of his family name. A governorship? Without even the modesty to run for any lower office first? What nerve!

Andrew had not declared, and neither had McCall. The race was two years off—an eternity in state politics. A better offer might come in. Not as Al Gore's running mate: that hope, if Andrew held it, was dashed well before the Democratic National Convention in August 2000. For all the cigars and reinvention talk they had shared, Gore was hardly about to choose someone who had never run for elected office. Chief of staff, though, that was a prospect. At the Los Angeles convention, Andrew gave a speech for Gore. Not a keynote speech, like his father's in 1984, just one of the warm-ups. As he moved afterward from one caucus to another, a delegate stopped him to say he'd heard the speech.

"I am going to put you on the spot," Cuomo teased him. "Who gave a better speech this morning, me or Ted Kennedy?"

"Ted Kennedy," the delegate said without missing a beat.

Andrew froze.

At the top of Andrew's problem list for electoral office was another Kennedy—his wife. By then the marriage was more a business relationship than anything else. Kerry wanted a divorce, and she wanted it now.

Andrew pleaded with her to hold off. "At least stick with me through the campaign," he told her. Andrew was right about one thing, as one family friend noted. "It was unthinkable that he could run without her—and without the Kennedy support."

By now, Andrew had all but officially declared himself a candidate for the New York governor's race in 2002. In his last year as HUD secretary, he would make forty-six official trips, twenty-five of them to New York. California would be his next most visited state; he would go there four times. He was giving speeches—anywhere, whenever asked. "He never, ever, ever turned down a request from us to speak at an event, even if it was short notice, even if he had to fly across the country," a former Democratic National Committee official later said. "He was relentless, and I would say he became our most requested speaker, after the president and vice president."

Distracted father or dedicated cabinet secretary: perhaps it was all in how one chose to view him. Max Stier, the young government lawyer who'd just helped negotiate the Smith & Wesson deal, was a new arrival and so had a fresh view on Andrew as secretary. After seven years at HUD, Stier sensed, Andrew was still fired up, with a clear vision of what he hoped still to do. It was as if he could see around corners. At the same time, Andrew was trying to protect what he'd done from being taken apart by a George W. Bush administration if Gore lost. Stier signed on to help with that, and, with another lawyer named Kevin Simpson, took on the delicate task of handling the nemesis who now seemed to devote all her time to dashing Andrew's legacy.

On February 17, 2000, Susan Gaffney told the House Budget Committee that Andrew had basically failed to put HUD back on track. HUD 2020 was a mishmash of name changes and new programs—more programs, that is, after Andrew had vowed to *reduce* their number—with not enough staff to get them up and running. A clean audit, for the first time in HUD's history? Yes, Andrew had managed that—and celebrated with a staff party to which he brought a Mr. Clean impersonator. But he had paid a contractor more than $2 million to get HUD's books in shape. Staff cuts? Yes, but then outside contractors had been needed to manage all those HUD programs, and all too often, chaos had ensued.

The wink was what made Stier and Simpson wonder if Gaffney had gone over the edge. The two were in a meeting with her and two of her top aides. It was, as Stier recalled, a contentious meeting. Simpson had warned Stier earlier that he would have to leave early to make a flight. "He got up to go," recalled Stier, "and he looks at me, and gives me a wink, because he's saying, 'Sorry, it's all yours.'" To the astonishment of all in the Cuomo camp, Gaffney soon after filed a formal complaint against Andrew and most of his inner circle, accusing them of sexual harassment and discrimination. Exhibit A: the wink.

There were, in fact, no strictly sexual allegations. The complaint, as Simpson termed it, was largely a rehash of her "greatest hits." She accused Andrew of verbally abusing her in weekend phone calls; she said she was subjected to baseless allegations made to investigators, and leaks aimed at planting disparaging information about her with the media. She termed this "sexually discriminatory" harassment.

The complaint, filed with HUD's Equal Employment Opportunity office in October 2000, was soon withdrawn.

In the surreal aftermath of *Bush v. Gore*, Andrew felt his fate hanging with those famous chads, up one day and down the next. But with Gore's concession on December 13, that story was done.

Andrew might have worked straight through the holidays, doing all he could to end his tenure with a flourish. Kerry, though, insisted he join her on a family vacation that Christmas. They took their daughters to Waikiki and checked in at the Royal Hawaiian, a luxury palace of pink adobe. Kerry's brother Bobby came too, with his wife, Mary, and their children. The plan was for the fathers to teach their kids to surf, but it didn't work out that way. Forced to start readying the handover of HUD to a new administration, Andrew spent most of the time on the phone to Washington.

Once back at his office, he focused on burnishing his HUD record, as a prelude to the New York governor's race. So appeared *A Vision for Change: The Story of HUD's Transformation*, a 150-page softcover book with many color pictures, fourteen of which featured or included Andrew. The book was well done, and perhaps of some value to future administrations. But the cost—reportedly $750,000—was substantial.

On his last week in office, Andrew issued a final broadside: a three-page press release touting the major triumphs of his tenure. At the top of the list was his greatest goal achieved. "The General Accounting Office (GAO) has taken the Department of Housing and Urban Development off its 'high risk' list," the release declared, "as a result of significant management reforms set in place under Secretary Andrew Cuomo's leadership." Andrew himself was quoted. "HUD's department-wide high risk designation is now a thing of the past," he declared.

This was glaringly, whoppingly untrue. The GAO had removed a single HUD program from the 2001 list. The programs that accounted for 75 percent of HUD's budget—single-family mortgage insurance and rental housing assistance—remained on the high-risk list for gross waste, fraud, abuse, and mismanagement. A GAO follow-up in 2002 would find those programs still high-risk—essentially dysfunctional, the budgets misspent and unaccounted for. As one example, the 2002 report showed pictures of shockingly derelict single-family properties acquired by HUD through foreclosure. So neglected were they, the report would note, that they could "contribute to a neighborhood's decay, particularly as they age."

Even the removal of that one HUD program from the list was not quite what it seemed. It had as much to do with the GAO's changing sense of how to define "high risk" as with anything Andrew had done. The GAO had decided that tarring a whole agency as high-risk—the Department of Defense was another—might do more harm than good. Better to focus on its particular programs. Andrew had seized on a change in semantics, and made it sound like a major win.

Andrew eventually conceded a loss or two. "In my business you never win anything 100 to 0," he ruminated later. "Perfection is 90–10. I started with a Republican Congress that said, 'We're going to eliminate HUD.' Four years later Congress gave HUD the best budget in twenty years. They implicitly and explicitly affirmed the progress."

There was plenty to admire about Andrew's tenure without the "high risk" canard. He had taken what he came with—his expertise in homelessness—and as an assistant secretary had made the "continuum of care" a national standard, its budget doubling and doubling again. He'd squeezed order from the chaos of application grants, and forged his Consolidated Plan. Perhaps most significantly, he'd set up those nine empowerment zones in his first term, and more after that.

A pair of professors would write a whole book assessing the different zones, and decide that some had done well, others not so much. Success, they concluded, wasn't a function of how much money each zone received, but of how clean and well organized its local government was. The EZ in New York City's South Bronx failed to meet expectations, the professors judged. Harlem's EZ was more of a success, bringing in various big-box stores and national chains. Yet in the process it had killed off many a mom-and-pop store. On balance, declared future New York governor David Paterson, the Harlem EZ had failed. "I think that the community has very negative [feelings] about the Empowerment Zone," he suggested, especially those who had applied for loans to start their own businesses. "They didn't need to get a new Empowerment Zone to create hope and then get rejected on the same criteria as they were rejected by the bank."

As secretary, Andrew had had the power to do much more—and he had done his best. He could take partial credit for a major housing reform bill. He had created a system to track every HUD-affiliated property in the country and fix what needed to be fixed. He had lobbied successfully for higher budgets, doled out higher block grants, started new programs, and won some ninety thousand new housing vouchers after four years of none at all.

Less successful were some of the fancier moves, the initiatives with catchy names and clever optics. HUD 2020 was at best a work in progress. Org chart boxes were shuffled and changed, but not the org itself. Community Builders, its crown jewel, had sucked up nearly 10 percent of HUD resources, only to create an army of... publicists basically, futzing around in the field and embittering the old guard. As time went on, the program had come to be seen less as an agency changer than as an army of political foot soldiers for Andrew's inevitable political campaign, whatever it might be. Within weeks of assuming power, the Bush administration would kill it. "If you saw all the time and effort that he invested," sighed Betsy Julian, southwest regional director for HUD in Andrew's tenure, "and then it was just gone with the stroke of a pen."

You're the A team, we're the B team. We be here when you come, and we be here when you go. In the end, Andrew hadn't changed the culture of HUD. But every day, for eight years, in his own relentless way, he had tried.

As for the war with his inspector general that had consumed so much of his time, Andrew was partly to blame. So, though, was Gaffney, as stubborn as he, and perhaps not right after all on the merits of the Philip

Newsome case. The black investigator charging her with job discrimination was about to win a court settlement of $490,000.

"Without going into specifics," Newsome relayed by e-mail, "the outcome speaks for itself. When is the last time you've heard of the Justice Department settling for practically the statutory maximum if they thought they were on the right side of an argument?"

If Gaffney *had* discriminated against Newsome, then maybe Andrew's motives in taking up the case had been less cynical than some assumed. Maybe he hadn't just used Newsome as a pawn against the inspector general who so bedeviled him. Maybe he'd actually tried to right a wrong.

If he had, no one would ever know. For Andrew was his own worst enemy: no one who knew him, friend or foe, believed he did *anything* without considering the politics involved.

As he packed up his clothes at the McLean house that January, readying his move to New York, Andrew planned every detail of the party at which he would announce his informal candidacy for governor. A wealthy political friend, Denise Rich, would host it at her lavish Manhattan apartment. Then came the stunning news that as one of the last acts of his presidency, Bill Clinton was pardoning Denise's husband, the fugitive financier Marc Rich, who had faced charges of tax evasion, wire fraud, and trading with Iran during the U.S. embassy hostage crisis.

A bit of shifting was quietly and quickly done. Kenneth Cole, the wildly successful shoe designer married to Andrew's sister Maria, offered to host the party at his Rockefeller Center shoe store. Caroline Kennedy Schlossberg, one of Andrew's many Kennedy in-laws, volunteered to cohost. Denise Rich was quietly deep-sixed.

Hearing that Carl McCall planned to announce his own candidacy in early February, Andrew stole his thunder by staging his party three days before. He had heard the mutters—that he shouldn't block the path of the first potential black governor of New York State—and so he came to the party equipped. There to introduce him was Martin Luther King III, a prominent name in the black community, if not any sort of leader. Nearby was Russell Simmons, the hip-hop impresario, whose famously tough upbringing in Hollis, Queens, fascinated the up-and-coming politician from Holliswood.

There too was a major contingent of Cuomos and Kennedys, including Mario and Matilda and, on the Kennedy side, Kerry's mother, Ethel. If hip-hop had come booming out of the speakers, the Kennedys might not even have noticed it, so focused were they on making the launch of Andrew's campaign a success. They could hardly help but react to one song that did get played, at rousing volume: "Sympathy for the Devil," by the Rolling Stones. As its first blurry chords filled the room, the Kennedys looked at each other, disbelieving. Could Andrew really have done this? Yet on the song went, to its telltale line: "*I shouted out, 'Who killed the Kennedys?' / When after all it was you and me.*"

Seemingly oblivious, Andrew smiled, made the rounds, and then, when the music was shut off, gave a short, punchy speech—a Kennedyesque speech. The crowd broke into applause. Andrew Cuomo had the name, he had the CV, he had the drive. Andrew Cuomo for governor!

Why not?

CHAPTER 15

Running into the Ground

One early spring day in 2001, Andrew drove a journalist to Brooklyn. After more than two decades in politics, he was trying on how it felt, at forty-four, to be a candidate himself for the first time. With the campaign so new and the rhetoric still fresh, he seemed ruminative on the ride out, almost philosophical about the larger journey he was embarking on. What did it take to be the kind of person voters and the media wanted? Did he want to be that person? And what did it take to avoid being tainted by the process of running for office?

The journalist was Michael Wolff, then of *New York* magazine. As the 2002 gubernatorial campaign unfolded, he would see Andrew a dozen times, maybe more, for long, soul-searching sessions en route from one appearance to the next, sometimes late at night. Wolff would like him; no one was immune to Andrew's charm when he turned it on. At the same time, Wolff would marvel that Andrew Cuomo, in his first race for elected office, was the most undisciplined, disorganized candidate he had ever seen.

They met that day in front of the Wall Street law firm Fried, Frank, Harris, Shriver & Jacobson, where Andrew was now "of counsel." The firm had given him an office, moderate pay, and the freedom to come and go as he pleased, all helpful to a candidate getting his campaign in gear. It was the sort of arrangement more typically made for a gray-haired eminence winding down his public life. Andrew was young, and his legal experience was slender for a serious firm like Fried, Frank. But his was not a typical case.

Everything was in flux. Kerry and the three girls were still in Washington, D.C., so the twins could finish their school year there. (The youngest, Michaela, was still a toddler.) Andrew was bunking at 101 West 79th Street: his brother, Chris, had a small apartment in the building, his sister Maria and brother-in-law Kenneth Cole a larger one. Kerry wanted the family's next home to be a house in Westchester; Andrew was lobbying for Manhattan. But as he noted to Wolff, the costs of a three-bedroom apartment and three private-school tuitions in Manhattan would be a heavy hit, even for members of the Kennedy clan. In fact, Kerry would win that debate, and the family would soon move to the affluent, low-key Westchester town of Bedford, though Andrew would seem a bit embarrassed by that address. When asked on the campaign trail where he lived, he said Mount Kisco, a neighboring and more humble town. Challenged later, he would admit that while he used the Mount Kisco post office, he lived in Bedford.

"The whole family has traded up," Wolff noted of the Cuomos. "He's married a Kennedy, his sister [Maria] has married [shoe designer] Kenneth Cole, and another sister [Margaret] married the millionaire video producer of 'Buns of Steel' [Margaret was, in her own right, a radiologist]; his brother is a television personality who hangs with Hamptons socialites. [Christopher was a correspondent for Fox News who would move on to ABC and CNN.] Even Mario and Matilda live on Sutton Place now."

It was true: the Cuomos had left Queens at last, and lived in one of Manhattan's most elegant enclaves. A family always acutely aware of its social standing had climbed the ladder from immigrant to middle class to political royalty. "Your kids won't go to Fordham and Albany Law School," Wolff teased. "I know that," Andrew replied. However much Andrew might still feel the outer-borough kid with the chip on his shoulder, he wasn't spending much time in Queens anymore.

Andrew's feelings about money seemed, like those about class, complex. At Fried, Frank, he was doing quite well. Tax returns obtained by the *New York Post* would reveal that in 2001, Fried, Frank paid him roughly $400,000, or about $526,000 in current-day dollars. Yet he presented himself as hard-pressed, and sounded bitter. Any young politician who ran for office before making his pile might sound that lament. But there was an echo here of Mario's own ruefulness about how little money he'd earned, first as an Italian lawyer from Queens, then as a public officeholder. No one appreciated the Cuomos enough for what they did for the world.

Andrew drove Wolff out to his favorite place in East New York: HELP I. The journalist was duly impressed. Thirteen years after its opening, the model for Andrew's continuum of care was a clean, up-and-running place, its single mothers taking computer training, their young children in day care as they worked toward new lives off the streets. Just as spiffy was the four-story building across the way that Andrew had built for permanent housing. All told, HELP now housed thirty-five hundred people in New York and Pennsylvania.

Wolff found Andrew a smart, wry, hardworking guy, eager to prove himself. He might, as Wolff wrote, even be one of that rare species, the real thing, an alchemy of idealism and cunning: Bill Clinton, for one, Bobby Kennedy for another.

Still, was HELP I, plus a cabinet seat, a record to run on? For governor? As his first elected office?

Old hands had tried to hold him back, urging Andrew to let Carl McCall have his turn. Jack Newfield, the *Village Voice* political writer who loved the Cuomos so much he'd served as Mario's driver in 1977, told Andrew over dinner one night at Ballato, an Italian joint in lower Manhattan, that running for governor against the great black hope was a huge mistake. With him was Joe Spinelli, one of Mario's most trusted advisers. "Run for comptroller," Spinelli pleaded. "You won't ostracize the whole black community." The actor Denzel Washington was at a nearby table. It was a sign! Even Denzel would be pissed. Andrew shook his head. "This is a movie, and it has different acts," he said. "I think this is a second or third act and it will evolve for me."

"Andrew was naïve about the black constituency," suggested one reporter who covered the campaign. "I think he just thought he was more qualified than Carl and never anticipated the level of resentment. It shouldn't have been any surprise at all. He just figured he'd learned it all from his father and he could do it."

For better or worse, Mario's presence hung over his son's campaign like a poltergeist. No one could fail to sense the Hamlet in it all: the son out to slay the king who had killed his father, politically at least. "Andrew very much wanted to repair the family legacy," recalled Fabian Palomino, Mario's oldest friend, in a newspaper interview later. The Cuomos felt they'd been evicted from their home—the executive mansion—in the middle of the night. They wanted it back. Perhaps the son was not just out for revenge, but to supplant and outdo his father, to show *him* who was king. Later, when the campaign faltered, the shouting between father and son would suggest, at the least, that very strong, contradictory feelings still roiled beneath the surface.

At the outset, Mario had hundreds of strings to pull for his son, and despite his protests to the contrary, he pulled them all. That was what Cuomos did. Not every county executive and small-city mayor responded as hoped. Such was the level of enmity toward Mario from many state Democratic functionaries that McCall's advisers formed a committee of them. Al DelBello, the former lieutenant governor whom Mario had ignored so completely in his first term that he finally had to resign, led the charge. "I worked for Mario," went the mantra. "I knew Andrew. I'm for Carl McCall." It was a powerful pitch, delivered with passion. "The joy on people's faces in those meetings was incredible," recalled one participant. "Throughout the eighties and early nineties, there were people treated badly by Mario. This was their way of serving a cold plate of revenge."

The black community had no beef with Mario. Most still admired him. But they were angry that Andrew dared challenge their chosen candidate, and they felt an implicit racial slight in the very fact of Andrew's campaign. With McCall's credentials, recalled Democratic state senator Kevin Parker, "it should have been a walk in the park except that he was African American. He would never say that. He would be mad at me for saying that. But it's the truth."

"I think what it came down to," said George Arzt, Ed Koch's closest adviser, "is they forgot the tremendous symbolism of the race."

Andrew had the family name and, as far as he was concerned, the experience to do the job. He had the fire in his belly, unlike McCall. He even had donors lining up, and good early poll numbers. He had something else just as important for taking on Carl McCall: he had the Kennedys.

By now, Andrew had been married to Kerry for more than a decade. For all the tensions in their marriage, the pride of being a member of the Kennedy clan had clearly not abated. "He shoehorns his wife into almost every conversation," Michael Wolff noted, "in a way that suggests that he either thinks the Kennedy thing is the biggest political asset he's got going for him, or she's been after him to get some credit for herself *(It's not all about you!)*." The aura included his own children. At one appearance that spring, his youngest daughter wandered out in front of him. "Upstaged by a Kennedy," Andrew quipped to the crowd. His daughters, he proudly noted, even had Kennedy mannerisms and gestures.

Kerry was present for many of those campaign stops and often spoke, sometimes at greater length than her husband. "It's rare in this age of cynicism to find someone you really believe in... who you feel comfortable saying, 'I am going to devote myself to getting this person in office,'" Kerry declared in an interview during the campaign, "and that is how I feel about Andrew." That was true, as far as it went: the campaign had made her appreciate Andrew's capacity for hard work, and she had no doubt that he would make a good governor. Her problem with her husband was strictly personal. He hadn't done the modest things she had asked of him as the father of their daughters: visiting their schools, for one; reading a book on parenting, for another. Kerry was done being the nag. Either Andrew would work on the marriage or he wouldn't and the two would divorce.

A deal was a deal.

The Kennedy name provided more than glamour and fund-raising clout. Jack and Bobby were virtual saints among black voters. The Civil Rights Act was President Kennedy's direct legacy. Bobby's whole campaign had been a cry for social justice. Surely their legacy would inoculate Andrew against resentment in a race against a black candidate. Or so Andrew seemed to think on the day he visited the New York attorney general at his office at 120 Broadway to ask for his endorsement.

Andrew and Eliot Spitzer were hardly allies after their bruising fight over handguns. But both were pragmatic enough to weigh how a Spitzer endorsement might play out for each. The day before their meeting, Spitzer got a visit from Andrew's security detail to check out the office. Spitzer marveled at that. A security detail? For a preprimary candidate? To check out the attorney general's office?

In their talk, which was pleasant enough, Spitzer made clear he was leaning toward McCall. "It would be wonderful to have a nominee for governor of New York who's black," Spitzer told Andrew, "and as a matter of pure politics, Carl has proven himself a good vote getter—he got a lot of votes in his reelection run in 1998." That was for McCall's second term as state comptroller, which would end in 2002. "How are you going to beat him?"

Andrew grinned. "Blacks have three pictures on the wall," he said. "Jesus Christ, Martin Luther King, and JFK. And I am a Kennedy now."

Spitzer was stunned.

Years later, Andrew denied the three-pictures story to *New York* magazine writer Jennifer Senior. "That is total... that just never happened... This was one of those rumors at that time."

But Spitzer wasn't the only one to report hearing Andrew offer the three-pictures theory. Mark Green, then the New York City public advocate, heard it too. Spitzer and Green were both perhaps biased as prospective rivals. But then there was Martin Connor, at that time the Democratic minority leader of the New York state senate; he was quoted as saying he'd heard it. *Daily News* reporter Joel Siegel quoted—anonymously—an upstate county chairman saying Andrew had told him the story. As for Michael Wolff, he recalled Andrew telling him the three-pictures story too, more than once.

Bill Lynch, the longtime political consultant who had signed on as one of Carl McCall's advisers, assumed the story was true but offered a gentle view of it. "It was a story said by black folks about black folks," Lynch suggested, not long before his death. "Andrew felt he knew blacks so well that he knew that's what they would say, so it wasn't a smear."

Whatever his logic, Andrew had badly misjudged his appeal in the black community. Virtually no black leader publicly endorsed him. Several, like longtime U.S. congressman Charlie Rangel, whose district included Harlem, told him bluntly to run instead for lieutenant governor—essentially, to stop being a brat and pay his dues. Andrew was rocked by the rejection. From then on, he would feel a certain anxiety about the black vote, and an enduring hurt. Four years after losing the race, he would find himself on a street corner with state senator Liz Krueger, a staunch Manhattan liberal, preparing to march in a parade. "Liz, I want to ask you a question. Do you understand why black people were so mad at me for running against Carl McCall?"

"Yes," Krueger would say, "I think I do."

"Why?"

"I'm a white Jewish person!" Krueger would retort. "I'm pretty sure I understand it, but I'm not African American, you need to talk to Afro-Americans about it."

Andrew would give her a look that seemed to say, "I couldn't do that." From then on, Krueger felt, Andrew seemed daunted by blacks. "Many of us have learned: if you want to get something done when he doesn't want to do it, you have to get black people to yell at him."

As the early months wore on, Andrew hit the wrong note with potential supporters, black or white. One officeholder later told *Salon*'s Jake Tapper he had taken a call from Andrew out of curiosity. Though leaning toward McCall, he felt open to the candidate's pitch. "I was absolutely offended by how crass he is. He said, 'The blacks are sticking together so much, we have to be as vocal as they are.' "

Andrew had hoped for support from the Clintons, but as 2001 unfolded they remained oddly quiet. As New York's new junior senator, elected in 2000, Hillary had at least as much clout to wield on Andrew's behalf as the ex-president, but she stuck to her day job. Some time later, a top adviser just coming on to Andrew's campaign asked the obvious question: where's Hillary? "What I heard from several sources," the adviser recounted, "is that she just didn't like him."

One of the few local pols who did come out publicly for Andrew was a New York City councilman who won his office in November 2001: Bill de Blasio, the future come-from-nowhere mayor of New York. Another was Ray Harding, the gargantuan Liberal Party vice chairman who had backed Mario in 1982 only to find himself targeted by both Cuomos, father and son, for his perceived disloyalty.

Harding had survived that putsch and was still in power, with the Liberal Party ballot line still to offer. Oddly enough, he remained fond of Andrew, inordinately so. "From 1977 until the day he died he loved Andrew," a longtime ally of Harding's recalled. "He would refer to some speech Andrew gave when he was HUD secretary as one of the greatest speeches he'd ever heard." The old pol regarded Andrew as a surrogate son, with a world-class political mind. Of course he would give Andrew the Liberal Party line, Harding assured him. Andrew just had to make the same promise his father had, the same promise Harding extracted from everyone he backed: that he stay in the race through the general election, even if he lost the primary, so the Liberal Party could garner fifty thousand votes and keep that ballot line. Would he do that, Harding asked?

Yes, Andrew assured him. Of course he would.

Day to day, the Cuomo campaign lurched along in need of a strategist like . . . Andrew Cuomo. Unfortunately, the candidate *was* the strategist: a classic mistake. He could keep his father's campaigns on track, but not his own. Schedules got screwed up, and when the candidate finally showed, he talked all over the place, anywhere but on message.

"He was a terrible candidate," Wolff recalled, "and not just because he couldn't stop talking. He overrode everyone. He was a guy in the center of chaos, a pig in the mud." Andrew loved the game so much that he couldn't control it. And while a few of his father's old-timers, like Michael Del Giudice and Joe Percoco, were there to wring some kind of order from the mess, others were first-timers, like Andrew's multihyphenate friend Dan Klores (journalist-adman–political consultant). Mario issued warnings, but they went unheard.

So eager was Andrew to make each next appearance that Wolff began to wonder if he had another motivation besides winning the race. "Anything to get out of the house, was my impression." One day Andrew brought Wolff home. When he introduced Wolff to his wife as the journalist who'd just profiled him for *New York* magazine, Kerry stiffened. She hadn't read the article, she said. Andrew seemed more sheepish than hurt, as if he'd said the wrong thing. That woman was cold, Wolff felt, and so was the vibe between the Kennedy-Cuomos.

At the end of the evening, Andrew would insist on driving Wolff home to his apartment. Again, Wolff sensed that Andrew was seizing any excuse to avoid going home. He was also schmoozing with intent, closing the sale. Like his mentor Bill Clinton, he had mastered the touch.

"When we got to my building," Wolff recalled, "he would put a hand on my wrist, and keep it there, and the monologue would begin." On and on it went, Wolff locked into place by the hand on his wrist. "He could... not... stop... talking."

Wolff's instincts about the marriage were sound. Kerry had put her human rights work on hold in order to campaign with Andrew. She'd won endorsements for him, made frequent appearances, and raised millions of dollars—probably the bulk of what he had raised, one insider suggests. Yet Andrew was gone all day, every day. The only times Kerry saw him were when she made a campaign appearance with him. At one point, Kerry insisted on another family vacation, this one a fishing trip in Florida. Another family with children joined them. Andrew stayed indoors the whole time, talking on the phone, while the father of the other family took the children fishing. Most weekends, various Kennedys and their children would gather at Bobby Kennedy Jr.'s Westchester house, near Andrew and Kerry's Bedford house. There would be swimming and softball and capture-the-flag for a whole gaggle of Kennedy-Cuomo kids. "But no Andrew," recalled a family friend.

Kerry was done. She had promised to see Andrew through the campaign, and that she would do. Then she would demand a divorce.

Through much of 2001, Andrew was up in the polls, by as much as 23 points. The McCall camp wasn't so much rattled as annoyed. Instead of a free ride to the general campaign against the Republican incumbent, they had to spend lots of money, wrangle for every union endorsement and county chairman's support—and then hope they did well enough to knock Andrew out at the state convention, eliminating him from the primary.

The polls did disclose an odd little trend line, one not going Andrew's way. In early focus groups, recalled Richie Fife, a McCall adviser, "People would watch a tape of Andrew and would react negatively. One said, 'He sounds like Mario, but there's no heart.'" That was good for McCall, with every contingent but one: prospective donors. "People would say, 'We're not afraid of Carl,'" recalled Fife. "'If we don't give him money and he wins, we can put our arms around him the next day and we'll be fine. We're scared of Andrew.' The irony is that Andrew had no power—not yet—and he *still* scared people. Whereas McCall, who had held one powerful position after another, scared no one."

Then came 9/11.

"That changed the dynamic of the race," recalled *New York Times* reporter Adam Nagourney. "That overlaid everything."

Amid the smoke and wreckage, President Bush exhorted the nation to keep strong, Mayor Rudy Giuliani rallied New Yorkers, and even bland Governor Pataki showed grace under pressure. But where was Andrew Cuomo? In the hours after the attacks, the gubernatorial candidate confronted a new reality—not about the twin towers, but about his own political status. He had none. "Andrew was totally closed out," recalled Pataki adviser Bob Bellafiore. "Every elected official could put on a baseball cap and get a televised tour of the site. Andrew couldn't."

Worse, the whole electorate had changed—in one hour. Instead of two political parties, there was one nation, indivisible. The power of the flag was palpable, inspiring. In this new world, Bush was the stolid but decent man, doing his best. So was Pataki: steady, stoic, great with cops and firemen. In short, a good disaster governor. Andrew was the one out of step, his harsh demeanor all wrong. In the wake of 9/11, McCall's adviser Hank Sheinkopf took to calling him Andy, and the moniker stuck. Andy was a churlish young man, a schoolyard bully. "The more the people of New York are exposed to Andy," Sheinkopf chortled, "the less they like him."

As steeped as Pataki was in post-9/11 bipartisanship, he hadn't lost his political smarts. In early 2002 he surprised both his Democratic rivals by winning the endorsement of 1199, the health care workers' union that almost always backed Democrats. So powerful was 1199 that it could tip elections; candidates for state office courted union president Dennis Rivera as they would the pope. For Pataki, the endorsement came at high cost: he had to push through a bill that gave Rivera $1.8 billion in raises for health care workers. But the trade-off was worth it, a major blow to both Cuomo and McCall.

Andrew started hammering away at Pataki. He accused the governor of dawdling on plans for the 9/11 memorial site, a charge that didn't play well in the post-9/11 world. He called for an end to the status quo, and an era of change, an odd theme to push after twelve recent years of his father as governor.

Mostly he railed on about Air Pataki, accusing the governor of using state aircraft for personal reasons. This was an old brickbat used by both parties. The fact was that New York State was too large for any governor to travel efficiently by car from Manhattan to Albany to Buffalo and back, but rules were rules, and state aircraft for personal use was technically forbidden. The answer was to build a little business into every flight schedule. No one had stretched that practice more than Mario Cuomo—in just four of his twelve years as governor, Cuomo family members took 729 flights on state aircraft. For that matter, Cuomo family members had often ridden the state choppers without *him*. "I was on a number of those flights when Mario was not there," recalled a political aide, "but Matilda was there, or Andrew, or Christopher. This was their plane and their helicopter." So egregious was the use of state aircraft for family members that after leaving office Mario had agreed to reimburse the state $29,000. Accusing Pataki of misusing state aircraft produced a lot of eye-rolling in Albany.

Andrew's campaign was stalling, but thanks in part to the Kennedy clan, he had $8.8 million to paper that over—more than McCall, who had had a two-year head start while Andrew was in Washington. In what would become a pattern, most of Andrew's campaign money came from large donors. For that, among others, he could thank his finance chairman, none other than Andrew Farkas, the rich city kid whose company had been hit with that $7.5 million fine by Andrew's HUD.

The transformation of Andrew Farkas from foe to friend was a marvel and mystery to all. It had begun with a chance meeting in the summer of 2001. Andrew had come to the Manhattan office of a powerful developer to pitch for a campaign contribution. A friend of the developer's had happened by and sat in on Andrew's pitch. At some point, Andrew realized that the stranger was a still-angry Farkas. Gamely, he asked for a meeting with him. Farkas felt sure his nemesis would fail to follow up, but by the time he got back to his office, Andrew had left a message for him.

A tense meeting ensued. Farkas said the HUD case had been utterly without merit. Andrew heard him out, expressed sympathy, and asked that they put the case behind them. Not, said Farkas, until Andrew met with the Insignia managers whose lives had been turned upside down by the suit. Again, Andrew surprised him by following through. Farkas's troops were less won over than he: they gave him, as Farkas put it, "mixed reviews."

Since then the two had become, to their mutual surprise, close friends. Whether Andrew Cuomo by now could form a friendship that didn't bring him political dividends was a question perhaps only he could answer. Whether a friendship built on dividends *could* be a friendship was for philosophers to decide. What was irrefutable was that Andrew Farkas had become a strong admirer—and supporter—of Andrew Cuomo. Through his network of family and colleagues, he generated more than $300,000 in contributions to the gubernatorial candidate. By 2006, when Andrew ran for attorney general, the overall campaign contributions from Farkas and related business and family entities would exceed $800,000.

Andrew did his part too, helped by Kerry. Now as a candidate he sought out a new breed of young Silicon Valley multimillionaires, pulling them in with fund-raiser talks at fancy San Francisco apartments. John Belizaire, a twenty-nine-year-old who'd grown rich from the sale of a software company he cofounded, went to one of those talks and soon after found himself dining at Aqua, a top-tier seafood restaurant in San Francisco's financial district, with the candidate—and Kerry Kennedy. "A lot of our conversation was, 'Why is California the leading high-tech state and not New York?'" Belizaire recounted later. As a Brooklyn native, he was impressed—enough to persuade his former business partners and their wives to give a collective $235,000, the candidate's biggest campaign bundle yet. Often Kerry was a key player in these gets, making the follow-up call herself and saying, in closing, "Look, we need 25 [thousand dollars] and can you send it by the end of the week?"

The money was still rolling in on April 16, 2002, the day Andrew officially entered the primary race.

The next day, it all but stopped.

"It was probably midafternoon," recalled one of the reporters on Andrew's campaign bus. The bus was en route from Utica to Buffalo. The candidate was at the back, shooting the breeze with a clutch of journalists. Beside him was Kerry, showing support on this kickoff statewide tour. The talk was casual, but on the record; no one had said it wasn't.

Andrew started in on Pataki's stewardship of the state post-9/11. He wasn't buying the line that the governor had shown such sterling leadership. Not like Mayor Rudy Giuliani. Giuliani had shown grit; he'd made the tough decisions. *He* was a leader. "There was one leader for 9/11: it was Rudy Giuliani," Andrew declared. "If it defined George Pataki, it defined George Pataki as not being the leader.

"He stood behind the leader," Andrew added. "He held the leader's coat. He was a great assistant to the leader. But he was not a leader."

The reporters looked at one another. Had they heard that right? Andrew hadn't spoken with any particular bitterness. He was just holding forth, feeling good, enjoying the sound of his own voice. But the statement was so jarring, and so revealing. New York was still raw from 9/11. Whether or not Pataki had done a good job in the aftermath—and most New Yorkers thought he had—Andrew just seemed tone-deaf to diss him. Even his press aide, Peter Ragone, felt it. "That's not a big deal, is it?" he asked one reporter as the rest slid back to their seats and started typing furiously on their laptops. "Very big news," the reporter said, and slid away to start filing his own story.

Adam Nagourney, the *New York Times* man, filed his story within minutes. He had no doubt the story would run. The only question was whether it would make the front page. It made the first page of the Metro section: big enough. In it, Nagourney had Giuliani's stunned response. "I held his coat as often as he held mine," the mayor said of the governor.

"We were inseparable." Andrew, Giuliani added, was introducing partisanship into a tragedy that had so far been largely free of politics. "If he fights the campaign with this strategy, George Pataki should win unanimously," Giuliani said. "I don't get it."

The coat-holder quote would come to be viewed—universally—as a campaign killer. "I don't know if he would have won the nomination against McCall," said Nagourney, "but if he had any chance it ended that afternoon. It just felt so wrong. It played into this idea of being a little craven and amateurish. It was too opportunistic and revealing."

That was the day the press corps stopped taking Andrew seriously as a candidate. By midsummer, most of the boys on his campaign bus would have peeled away. The irony, suggested one of Carl McCall's operatives, was that as undiplomatic as the coat-holder comments were, they weren't all wrong. "Pataki *was* holding Giuliani's coat," the operative said with a laugh. "It *was* Giuliani who took center stage with 9/11. And Pataki was in the background."

Kevin Finnegan, a savvy young political operative, had the bad luck to join the Cuomo camp the day before the coat-holder comment. He had come from 1199, where he had helped trade the union's Pataki endorsement for all that health care money. Feeling a bit guilty—he was a true-blue union Democrat—he had signed on with Cuomo to help win him a majority of the weighted vote in the upcoming state Democratic convention. For a day or two Finnegan thought the coat-holder comment might actually play well among Democratic primary voters. But the press was in a feeding frenzy. "It was like we were already headed straight down," he recalled later, "as soon as I got there."

Finnegan started working the phones in search of weighted votes from the local Democratic chieftains. Many of his calls weren't returned. He pushed Andrew to do some outreach himself. A lot of Andrew's calls weren't returned either. "It became pretty obvious," Finnegan recalled, "that we weren't going to get to 25 percent." The nonresponders infuriated Andrew. "Destroy him," he would tell Finnegan about some state committee person who didn't want to give Andrew his vote. "*Destroy him.*"

His back to the wall, Andrew began using the line he had wielded so well two decades before, on behalf of his father, at the 1982 convention. *Carl is going to win big, give me some votes so I'm not embarrassed.* Only this time, almost no one took the bait.

On the eve of the convention, to be held at a Midtown Manhattan hotel, Andrew's camp started passing the word that he had chosen to skip the whole thing. His spinners said he wasn't worried about getting 25 percent of the weighted vote—not at all. He just felt the whole convention was ward politics at its worst. He would go the petition route instead, get his fifteen thousand signatures from the people of New York, and fight McCall for the primary win in September as a reformer of the system.

If Andrew's faithful felt let down, McCall's camp was apoplectic. In shunning the convention, Andrew would deny their candidate his rightful triumph, and the victory lap that came with it. "Let me tell you the difference between me and him," McCall declared with uncharacteristic vigor. "I have never run from a fight."

Particularly galling were Andrew's claims to have 25 percent of the weighted vote even as he washed his hands of the whole affair. Insiders noted that he had been scrambling through the last weekend to line up delegates—hardly the modus operandi of a candidate who felt sure he had 25 percent. Now, as part of his announcement, he declared he was releasing his delegates. "What, all two of them?" McCall cracked.

More than symbolism was involved. McCall had thought that if Andrew failed to get his 25 percent, he would slink off a loser, giving McCall a free ride to the nomination and letting him spend that time and money whacking Pataki. Now, assuming Andrew got his signatures, McCall would have to spend the next three-plus months campaigning against *him*. Even if McCall prevailed in the primary, he would be weakened for the general election, against an already strong incumbent.

A curious scene unfolded the next day at a Manhattan nightclub near the Midtown hotel where the convention was starting. Andrew's handlers called it a "counter-convention." "I want to be the candidate placed on the ballot by the people, not the party," Andrew told the throng of loyalists. Never mind that he was heir to two of America's best-known political families, and that Carl McCall was the son of a single mother who'd worked his way up. Andrew was the outsider now.

On the stage behind the candidate was a fascinating political tableau, faces and names that evoked the civil rights movement of the 1960s. One was Martin Luther King III. Another was Robert F. Kennedy Jr. In their rousing introductory speeches, they talked of needing "vision, not division." King declared that Andrew would "fight for the civil rights of education," and told the crowd that Andrew's life had been "threatened" by the Ku Klux Klan, a drama nowhere mentioned in twenty years of coverage about him. Kennedy talked of "the soul of the country." Kerry Kennedy spoke too, on behalf of the women of New York. "We must harness our outrage," she declared, "and use it to create change." The women of New York, she added, "rank dead last [in the nation] in health and wellness." Political columnist Eve Kessler, there on the scene, found that hard to believe. "Really?" she wrote later. "Worse than Mississippi?"

The staging and rhetoric seemed meant to portray Andrew not as the next governor Cuomo, but as the next Robert F. Kennedy, keeper of the flame. That, as Kessler put it, seemed "a meretricious use of American scripture," cynically drawn up as a campaign strategy against a black rival who'd just kicked his butt. "Every successful reform movement is driven by the people," Andrew told the crowd. "You need the people to rise up!"

Notably, the biggest name in the room—Mario Cuomo—did not address the crowd. Not one speaker mentioned his accomplishments. The three-term governor, after all, was the very embodiment of the political establishment that Andrew was vowing to replace.

Over at the Sheraton, the convention mood was muted. When the counting was done, McCall had 100 percent. No one took much satisfaction in that. The man who wasn't there that night had ruined the show. He'd skipped it to avoid being drubbed, and to wangle another chance to win. In so doing, he'd hurt the party's chances of winning the governorship that fall. David Axelrod, then an adviser to McCall, later a senior advisor to President Obama, grudgingly called the walkout "a fairly shrewd move," one that might turn "hamburger into steak." But to do it, Andrew had had to abandon all the party leaders who *had* cast their weighted votes for him.

Between Andrew and those burned supporters, relations would never be quite the same, though Andrew would act as if *he* were the one who had been betrayed and harbor ever after a certain wariness of them. That wasn't a singular case. With the Cuomos, loyalty was expected, but sometimes withheld in return. When it was, the loyalist was always the bad guy, the one not loyal enough. The Cuomos were never to blame.

Only fifteen thousand signatures were needed to qualify for the primary. Multiply that by two or three to shake out unregistered voters and the petition route was still a breeze for a candidate as well connected as Andrew: signatures were easier to come by than votes. Andrew decided to make a bigger statement. He would get one hundred thousand signatures, and not just from mostly downstate. From all over. It would be more than a petition drive. It would be a grassroots campaign, the people taking back their state, with Andrew the reformer leading the charge. In ungrassroots-like fashion, however, the signature gatherers would be paid.

"We had like a thousand people on the payroll," recalled one Cuomo operative. "In any given week we'd have three hundred to four hundred of them out on an hourly basis—paid—gathering signatures." Andrew couldn't pay for each signature; that was against the law. But he could pay by the hour. The grassroots troops were mostly black and Hispanic high school and college students, recruited by the Cuomo camp and happy to have the summer work. On average, the petition drive cost the campaign $150,000 a month.

Unfortunately, McCall's poll numbers were moving up, and Andrew's were moving down. Fund-raising was hard; the Silicon Valley high-tech twenty-somethings were proving less receptive than before to calls from the candidate soliciting their opinions and cash. By mid-July, the campaign hit a budget shortfall. Down from the top came a halt to all unnecessary expenditures. Including, as it turned out, paying the signature gatherers.

After a week without pay, students started asking about their checks. They got muttered excuses. The full-time staffers, for their part, started worrying for their own safety. A lot of those students were big. Then came the second week of no checks. A large college student came up to the staffer running the grassroots operation. "What's going on?" he demanded.

The staffer said he didn't know.

"Well I'll tell you what's going on," the student said, leaning menacingly close to the staffer. "I'm not going anywhere until I get paid."

The nervous staffer found Michael Del Giudice, the longtime Cuomo loyalist, who happened to be on the premises. Del Giudice paid the kid from his wallet, then called Andrew. Within a day, the checks resumed. Still, the staffers were dismayed—because it wasn't as if the campaign had run out of cash, or the candidate had had to reach into his own pocket. The incoming contributions had just dwindled enough that they failed to cover the whole budget. Andrew was the one who had decided that his grassroots army—not, say, the advertising buys—would take the hit.

Andrew was crisscrossing the state all this time, trying to prop up his sagging campaign. The poll numbers made him miserable, and that made him an angry boss. "He wasn't a screamer," explained one staffer. "But he was a prick... his way of dealing with staff or things he doesn't like is to play mind games with people and make them feel small, and let others do the dirty work of telling someone something they don't want to hear." The staffer remembered Andrew's tone all too well: "Oh, you want me to go Buffalo? Why should I go waste my time asking people to vote for me when you incompetents can't organize the trip right?" Incompetence was a theme. "You guys are just chasing the soccer ball," he would tell his staffers. "You guys are just scrambled eggs. You call yourselves professionals?"

Almost always, when he got to the next stop, Andrew was disappointed. "We would send him up to Orchard Beach—a picket line, say—and try to get the press to follow," recalled Kevin Finnegan. "But we weren't getting good press. Or any press." It was like 1982 all over again, Andrew putting the reporters' notebooks on empty chairs. Only now he was the candidate.

A repeat of that campaign's rise from the dead seemed unlikely. That July, New York's senior senator, Democrat Chuck Schumer, formally endorsed McCall, joining a majority of other prominent state Democrats. A decade later, when they found themselves targeted by Governor Andrew Cuomo, some of those Democrats would wonder what they had done to deserve his enmity. Had they not supported him for governor in 2010? They had. But not in 2002. Eric Schneiderman, then a New York state senator, later the state attorney general? Tom DiNapoli, then a state assemblyman, later the state comptroller? The list went on. Back in 1982, when the Queens pols abandoned his father, Andrew had learned that revenge is a dish best served cold. Now a different generation of New York Democrats was abandoning him. He would not forget the names on that list. Not a single one.

The Clintons were, of course, exempt from retribution. They were too powerful. But Andrew could only have seethed at their silence as the campaign wore on. The Clintons, as skilled as Andrew in the art of off-the-record leaks, let slip that Carl McCall, in their opinion, would fare better against Pataki than Andrew, delivering key blocs of blacks and union members, perhaps winning the governorship. A primary victory by Cuomo, on the other hand, would only exacerbate racial tensions. "She doesn't need any of that rubbing off on her—she knows that," said one of Hillary's advisers. "She's better off if it's Carl, and so's the party." In Clinton world, as in Cuomo world, comments like that didn't come out by chance, though for the record, Hillary insisted she was neutral.

With the vast preponderance of black leaders lined up for Carl McCall, Andrew had to take what he could. Martin Luther King III did his share of stumping. So did Charlie King, Andrew's chosen candidate for lieutenant governor. King was one of his former regional directors for HUD, a fellow lawyer at Fried, Frank, a county Democratic chairman—and black. The optics of the two of them together were anything but subtle. On a tour of black churches, Andrew brought Cornel West, the left-leaning black philosopher. "Carl is a decent man, but he is a hesitant brother," West said of McCall to the congregations. "He's a timid brother." E. J. Dionne of the *Washington Post*, along for the tour, found it astonishing that McCall's moderation might be used against him. But what else could Andrew do?

Andrew had maintained a lead in most polls all year. In early July, he led by as many as 15 points. But in August his numbers plummeted, giving McCall a 16-point lead. The shadow race was emerging as the primary neared. Voters were paying more attention, and in Andrew they just didn't like what they saw.

In desperation, Andrew tapped his secret weapon: the former governor. Mario had kept a low profile until now, lest voters feel that with Andrew they were getting a fourth Mario term—with many, he had worn out his welcome. He still held sway, however, among die-hard Democrats most likely to vote in primaries, and so off he went on the hustings. Between the now bitter rivals, that stirred a sharp exchange. "If you were out in the street, in a battle, and you were kind of losing, you might run home for Dad," McCall scoffed. Andrew quickly inflated the taunt into an all-out attack. "It's one thing, you want to attack me," he said. But "even by the normal New York standards, attacking my father... is going too far."

Between father and son there was tension as well. "Mario had this forty-page manifesto for how to right the ship," recalled an aide. "He wanted someone on the campaign to read it and take it seriously. He decided I was the person, but he did this with five or six others on the campaign. It reflects on the complexity of that relationship that Mario was pitching staff on strategy." Andrew was hardly about to read the manifesto, let alone change his whole campaign to comply with it, so the tensions grew. "There were some very intense conference calls," recalled one reporter on the campaign. "His father was screaming, 'You have to drop out now.' "

Michael Wolff sensed tension too. Father and son would appraise each other, in each other's absence, with a pragmatism verging on coldness. They admired each other's political strengths, Wolff thought. But it wasn't clear, at least at this moment, that they actually liked each other.

By late August, the whole staff was wretched. Kevin Finnegan realized just how bad he felt one day on the way to work, when he started wishing to get hit by a cab—not killed, just forced to stay home for a couple days.

The toll wasn't just emotional. "My staff was running up thousands of dollars in campaign expenses," recalled one staffer, "putting things on their credit cards, and not getting reimbursed." One of Finnegan's campaign workers was a kid just out of college who'd rented a car on his credit card at Finnegan's request. Now Andrew was saying he wouldn't reimburse him. Finnegan was livid. He knew the campaign had $3.3 million left in its coffers. "We didn't have a chance to win," he recalled. "Why piss it away on media and not do the right thing and reimburse workers who were out thousands of dollars?"

Finnegan lit out for his house on the east end of Long Island without telling anyone he'd gone. No sooner was he home than the phone rang. It was Mario. Finnegan told him why he was so upset. Mario, he recalled, was in total agreement with him. "If he goes through with this," Finnegan recalled the ex-governor saying, "I'll represent his employees in court to get the money back." So Finnegan came back.

In a Hail Mary move, Andrew brought in his old inner circle from HUD: Howard Glaser, Karen Hinton, and Jacquie Lawing. "They came in as a shadow campaign staff," recalled one staffer. "So it was a weird dynamic. They were sort of running it but we were still here." Campaign manager Josh Isay wondered aloud how to handle staff meetings. Was he still the campaign manager? Should he even act as one? In a case of bad timing, Isay had gotten married earlier that summer; he found out he was being marginalized from an item that appeared on the *New York Post*'s Page Six while he was on honeymoon.

For the two weeks leading up to the primary, Andrew, through his longtime handler Joe Percoco, asked everyone on staff to forgo their salaries. This was not received well, in part because the staff knew about the $3.3 million still in campaign coffers, in part because Andrew himself had contributed nothing to his campaign. His family, yes: Mario and Matilda together gave nearly $200,000, while Maria and her husband, shoe designer Kenneth Cole, gave roughly $80,000. But not Andrew. Why should his staff make more of a financial sacrifice to the campaign than he?

Desperate times, it seemed, called for desperate measures. One August day, a tawdry story about McCall's chosen running mate, a businessman named Dennis Mehiel, found its way to Fred Dicker of the *New York Post.* The would-be lieutenant governor had fathered two out-of-wedlock children with two women while he was married to his first wife. While Dicker weighed whether to print it, McCall's camp privately charged Andrew's camp with having leaked it. The charge was denied, rather implausibly. Who else would have done it? Not Pataki's people: if anything, they would have sat on the story until close to the general election and maximized the damage to McCall then, assuming McCall won the primary. If Cuomo won, of course, the story would be moot. To spite Dicker, Mehiel fed the story to an AP reporter who then scooped the *New York Post.* To Cuomo watchers, the only real surprise was that Andrew appeared to have made his peace with Dicker, whose vitriol in 1994 had surely contributed to Mario's loss that year.

Andrew was a poll hound, long accustomed to wheedling the latest results directly from pollsters the weekend before they appeared. The Monday numbers he heard over that last weekend in August were devastating. McCall was ahead by 53 to 31 percent, a stunning spike in less than a month. Andrew seemed unable to see that voters tuning in as the primary loomed found him harsh and unlikable. There had to be another reason. "That was the exact three, four weeks that his ads went up and mine went up," he later declared of McCall. "His ads were very good. Mine stunk."

Eight days remained: the endgame in which campaigns typically unleashed their most stinging negative ads. Later, Andrew would say he agonized over whether to hold his fire, not wanting to stir more resentment in an already racially charged race. His actions seemed to belie that.

Secretly that last weekend in August, Andrew reached out to Congressman Charlie Rangel, one of McCall's top supporters. It was time to talk. If Andrew needed any more confirmation of that, it came Saturday when he made an appearance at a county fair. The Clintons came too, yet somehow failed to find him in the crowd. The next day, New York's junior senator went further. Hillary walked with McCall down Brooklyn's Eastern Parkway in the West Indian American Day Carnival Parade. Andrew was in the parade too, Clintonless.

One of Andrew's emissaries was John Marino, an old and trusted family adviser. Another was Bill de Blasio, the towering city councilman whose unwavering support for Andrew had forged a bond. Prescient as both were, neither Andrew nor de Blasio could have predicted that twelve years later they would be squaring off as mayor and governor. Together, Marino and de Blasio told the McCall camp their man would withdraw—under three conditions.

First, Andrew wanted a high-profile role in McCall's fall campaign. Second, he wanted McCall to pledge his future support. Specifically, he wanted McCall to endorse him if he chose to run for governor in 2006. Third, McCall had to say publicly that Andrew's withdrawal had been brokered by ex-president Clinton.

Alternatively, Andrew could stay in the race these last eight days and spend his $3.3 million war chest smearing McCall with negative ads that would leave him in tatters for Pataki.

McCall was a genial, low-key fellow, everybody's friend. Not on this day. The chutzpah of this kid! Three or four months earlier, as one of his former advisers noted, McCall might have made a deal—back before he'd spent all his money fighting Andrew, back when he could have saved that money for the fall. But not now. What was done was done. And Andrew had nothing but gall. "Nothing was offered to anyone," McCall declared. "And President Clinton didn't broker an agreement."

Andrew's campaign manager, Josh Isay, was left to make the routine denials. "I don't know where that came from," he said of the list of conditions. "It's not true."

Andrew's withdrawal remained a secret to all but a few aides on either side. No one else on his staff had any idea that he was about to back out. Many spent all of Monday night preparing fliers to hand out in the final days. They stayed up until dawn on Tuesday, got some shut-eye, and awoke to Andrew's news conference at a Midtown Manhattan hotel.

A soothing mood of unity was meant to drape the occasion, a goal somewhat hindered by the fact that Andrew's rival wasn't there. Charlie Rangel, the Harlem congressman, stood on one side of Andrew. On the other stood ex-president Clinton, coaxed into dignifying the occasion with his presence. "Today is a day you should be very, very proud of, Andrew," the president declared to a hastily gathered crowd that included Kerry Kennedy, Andrew's parents, and his sister Maria, all in the front row. This was the right decision, Clinton intoned, good for the party, and Andrew would live to fight another day. The only political career that was over, the former president joked, was his own.

Andrew spoke solemnly, like a prisoner at his own sentencing. "While it's harder for me to step back than step forward, today I step back," he said. "We need healing now, maybe more than ever before. I'm not going to start dividing now."

Yet later that same day, Andrew called the *New York Times*' Bob Herbert, the black liberal columnist who had so admired Andrew's Kennedyesque quest to help the poor. Herbert was surprised to hear Andrew say he had lost because he'd had to pull his punches against his black rival. "I believe in my heart," Andrew said, "that if I did a negative ad I would have won."

Herbert asked Andrew if perhaps his personality had had something to do with his plummeting poll numbers. Andrew disagreed. *He* wasn't a negative. "The negative here is that I was running against the first African-American. It was his turn." Herbert suggested Andrew might have been viewed the same way even if his rival was white. "No, no," Andrew replied. "It was about this. I was an arrogant interloper, interfering on his turf. I came from Washington. Came here. Didn't wait in line and came here and said 'I'm going to run.' And got in the way of the first African-American."

Herbert hung up dismayed. "If Mr. Cuomo does not acknowledge that his arrogant, abrasive, controlling and—in the view of some—even mean-spirited qualities played a big role in his defeat by Mr. McCall," he wrote, "then . . . his political career is doomed."

If anything, other postmortems were worse. ABC White House correspondent Jake Tapper wrote in *Salon* of Andrew that "his grating personality has sullied what could have been a promising campaign," and called the withdrawal "a rare moment of grace" for someone more typically "blaring his obnoxiousness for all to suffer." To a lot of voters, Tapper added, "he seemed like an asshole. And sometimes a politician's problems are truly that simple."

Norm Adler, the union organizer who had overseen a very different Cuomo primary in 1982, said in effect that Andrew was finished. "This was his time and his place, and he blew it," Adler opined. "He spent $14 million of other people's money. Would you give him money to run another campaign?"

Tomorrow was another day, but this day, a *New York Times* reporter declared, marked for Andrew, who had started his campaign with such confidence and clout, nothing less than "a spectacular humiliation."

Andrew wasn't the only loser that day. Unmentioned at the news conference was his misty-eyed admirer, Ray Harding. So close was Andrew's withdrawal to primary day that the Cuomo name would remain on the Liberal Party ballot line, both for the primary and the general election. Cuomo wouldn't be running, so the only voters who would pull the Liberal Party lever were the addled and the ignorant. Andrew had promised Ray Harding that, like his father, he would stay in the race, doing his part to get the Liberal Party the fifty thousand votes it needed to keep its line. A promise was a promise, and Andrew had broken his. Without its line, the party that had helped pull Mario from the ashes in 1977 and possibly given him his margin of victory in 1982—the party, in short, that had played a vital role in elevating Mario Cuomo—was dead, killed by Andrew.

Carl McCall, as it turned out, was just more collateral damage. A last poll before the primary had him up by 63 percent to 18 percent. A mammoth primary victory might have reinvigorated his campaign, made him look like a winner, possibly *made* him a winner against Pataki. Instead, for the second time, Andrew had deprived him of that. "What a selfish motherfucker," one of McCall's aides recalled in disgust. "How dare he! I had never heard of that before." Now, too, the money was gone. "Fund-raisers who might have given to Carl had given to Andrew instead," explained campaign aide Bill Lynch in an interview before his death. "And all the resources McCall had were spent on the primary. Andrew dried up those resources." In the end, Pataki won it in a walk.

Some weeks after the primary, journalist Ken Auletta ran into a friend who knew Andrew well. "How is he?" Auletta asked. Depressed, was the answer. On a whim, Auletta took Andrew's number and gave him a call. They met for coffee at a Starbucks in Rockefeller Center. Andrew was clearly morose; Auletta had expected that. What surprised him was Andrew's level of self-involvement. Auletta recalled a young man less brash than ebullient. A kidder, an optimist. Now he seemed consumed by the tragedy of his loss. "We spent probably an hour and a half," Auletta later recalled. "I don't think he asked me a single question about me or anything else."

Michael Wolff, the *New York* magazine writer, sought out Andrew too. "I felt bad," he recalled. "I called him and told him I had a great idea for him. He should write a book about . . . political failure. That didn't go down well." Not long after, Wolff ran into him on a Midtown street. "No one was paying attention to him." The two went to Michael's restaurant and had a pot of tea. Like Auletta, Wolff found Andrew steeped in despair—and self-pity.

Mario, survivor of more than one electoral defeat, seemed more philosophical. That fall, legendary campaign manager Bob Shrum was in Milan with his wife, having dinner at the Four Seasons hotel, when his wife took notice of the bandleader conducting the live dinner music. "That guy looks like Mario," she said. It *was* Mario. The ex-governor was waiting for a friend and on a whim had taken up the baton. After his impromptu conducting, Mario joined Shrum and his wife at their table and they talked for some forty-five minutes. Shrum found him judgmental about the campaign, defensive about Andrew, but sure his son had another, better campaign in him. A different campaign. "He definitely thought this was not the end."

If so, Andrew was in no position to feel it. The day after the primary, Kerry demanded a divorce—this was the end. She had lived up to her side of the deal, she told friends, being the loyal candidate's wife throughout the campaign, not letting a hint slip of the true state of their marriage. Enough was enough. It was time for Andrew to grant her an amicable divorce.

"One can live magnificently in this world," Tolstoy had famously written, "if one knows how to work and how to love." Andrew had just shown he was a failure at the work he had thought he could do. Now his marriage was crumbling. Soon it would end altogether, in a tabloid feeding frenzy.

CHAPTER 16

Hitting Bottom

In their troubled twelve-year marriage, the Cuomo-Kennedys had made few friends together. Andrew was still nonplussed by most of Kerry's friends, and, not counting his brother, he had almost none of his own. Campaign donors, journalists, consultants, and fixers—those he had. Not many friends, though, if friendship meant a relationship purely for pleasure. Bruce and Ann Colley were a rare exception. They were a couple both Andrew and Kerry liked.

Ann Colley sat on the board of the Hudson Riverkeeper, the nonprofit started by Kerry's brother Bobby Kennedy Jr. to clean up and protect the river. She worked for a very rich man, hedge funder Louis Bacon, a big Republican donor who was also an environmentalist. As for Bruce, his father had made a sizable fortune based on McDonald's franchises: with a partner he owned nearly one hundred of them. By the early 2000s, the two couples saw each other a lot. All four would have been shocked to know how their friendship would end.

Bruce was a few years older than Andrew, though with his longish blond hair and WASPy good looks he seemed almost cherubic beside his new pal. "Andrew was a Rottweiler," suggested one insider. "Bruce was a golden retriever—a nice guy who liked to party. He was always happy. You could cut his leg off, he'd still be happy." His father, after making his fast-food fortune, had taken up the equestrian life, becoming master of the hounds at the fox hunt in North Salem, New York. Bruce had come to share his father's love of horses, and let it lead him to polo. He played at Mashomack, the tweedy club in Dutchess County where members dined in a candlelit room papered with Hudson River scenes. He played in the Hamptons and as a Harvard man at the annual Harvard-Yale match. He even played on occasion on teams fielded by Prince Harry.

Ann was from an older, North Carolina family. She oversaw Louis Bacon's philanthropic initiatives, and sometimes staged events at Robins Island, his 435-acre private barony in Peconic Bay, just off the Hamptons. Along with fund-raisers, the financier liked to host English "driven pheasant" hunts there. The Colleys were part of all that, and so, by 2001, were Andrew and Kerry.

Colley opened a Chelsea restaurant called Man Ray that year, and Andrew and Kerry became regulars, drawn in part by the glittery investors: actors Johnny Depp, John Malkovich, and Sean Penn. As they drew closer, the two couples went skiing together with their children in Aspen. A stranger, sitting down to a meal with the four in Aspen, would have assumed that Kerry was married to Bruce Colley, not Andrew. Colley and Kerry shared a love of skiing and sailing, of horses and the outdoors. Andrew seemed uninterested in all that. Only politics engaged him; that was the bond he still had with Kerry. He took his work very seriously, one friend from those days recalled, and he wasn't much fun. "On rare occasions he would have a drink, and a good chuckle about someone, usually at their expense. But that was rare."

The Cuomos and the Colleys were still friends when Andrew ended his primary race that September day of 2002. The next day, as agreed, Kerry asked him for a divorce. Later, when her children asked her why she had chosen to end her long marriage to their father by having an affair, she would say she couldn't discuss it. So there was no talk, then or later, of the years that had led her to this point.

Hearing the request he had known to expect, Andrew begged Kerry for more time. The race had flattened him; he was too depressed to handle a divorce too. Let them wait, he pleaded, until the twins' birthday, after the holidays. The twins' birthday was January 11. Kerry went along with that, even after Andrew was feted with four different parties for his own December birthday. How depressed could he be if he could go to four birthday parties? Still, she waited, as they'd agreed, until January 12, 2003. That day she hired a divorce lawyer and told Andrew he had to leave. He refused.

For some weeks after that, Kerry tried persuasion. Finally she resigned herself to living separately with Andrew under the same roof, until the girls were out of school for the summer and she could shelter them from any stories in the tabloid press by taking them to Hyannis.

As far as Kerry was concerned, she was on her own, free to act as she wished. That spring, she felt her feelings for Bruce Colley change from friendship to what was widely reported as an affair.

When friends asked Andrew what he was doing that winter and spring of 2003, he was apt to say, with mordant humor, "Trying to stay relevant." He became a visiting fellow at the Kennedy School of Government at Harvard. With his friend Russell Simmons, the rap impresario, he lobbied for an end to the so-called Rockefeller drug laws: brutally harsh prison sentences for nonviolent repeat offenders, even if the offense involved a single marijuana joint. He gathered essays from prominent Democrats and a few Republicans for a collection titled *Crossroads: The Future of American Politics*. In his own essay, he blamed 9/11. While President Bush "exemplified leadership at a time when America was desperate for a leader," he wrote, on the Democratic side there was "chaos." The time Andrew seemed to be harking back to was his campaign for governor; the crossroads was his own.

The Cuomos and the Colleys continued meeting for dinner at Man Ray, but less often now. Andrew was growing suspicious. Kerry was seeing Bruce Colley on her own; that seemed odd. According to tabloid reports, Andrew checked her cell phone records and found an inordinate number of calls between them. Finally he called Ann Colley and compared notes. She had been getting suspicious too. They decided to confront their respective spouses at the same morning time, in their separate houses. Later, the tabloids would have Kerry confessing immediately. What she said, according to one close observer, was very different. "What I do is none of your business. Tell the kids we're divorcing, hire lawyers, and move out."

Andrew's pride was stung. But in a way, the news was a gift: it gave him the power of being the wronged party, with righteous indignation to spare.

The story was still a secret, both from the children, who were finishing their school terms, and from the outside world. Kerry told her daughters the day after their school terms ended—June 23—and a week later sent out, at last, the press release about an "amicable" divorce. Reached by a reporter, Andrew said, "We agreed not to go beyond the statement, and I'm going to honor that."

Within twenty-four hours, all bets were off, and the Cuomos were convening a family meeting. There, along with Mario and Andrew, was Dan Klores, Andrew's longtime adviser and public relations man; his brother, Chris; and the family lawyer. There was talk of whether to mention Kerry's affair, with at least one participant advising against it. The consensus was: go for it. Within hours, Andrew's divorce lawyer, Harriet Newman Cohen, issued a stern public statement: "Mr. Cuomo was betrayed and saddened by his wife's conduct during their marriage. Despite that, for the sake of their three daughters, Mr. Cuomo has been trying to keep their marriage together for some time. But he will try to accommodate Ms. Kennedy Cuomo's decision to leave the marriage. In the interest of the privacy of the party's children and the family, Mr. Cuomo will make no further comment."

With that, the Kennedy-Cuomo marriage exploded, and the tabloid frenzy began.

Initially, the partner in Kerry's "conduct" remained a mystery figure. By Friday of the July Fourth weekend he was unmasked. Colley called the *New York Post* to "categorically" deny the affair and profess his love for Ann. "Why is he denying this so strongly," muttered one friend of both couples to the *Daily News*, "when he knows it's true?"

By then, Kerry was up in Hyannis Port, safe from the tabloids but not from the news splashed across their pages. She read Colley's denials with pained surprise. She had expected him to deny the affair, but not with such fervor. Colley for his part felt blindsided by all the press and, as he told one friend later, simply felt that defending his marriage was what one should do. He hoped Kerry would realize that he still adored her, and that she knew he hoped they would be together after all this mess was sorted out. What had started as a sweet, almost giddy romance was now all but squashed by the tabloid media.

Andrew remained at the house in Bedford. At one point he came outside to grant a short interview to one of the tabloids whose reporters were at the property's edge, waiting for comment. "I'm thinking about the kids right now, that's what's important," he said from his driveway. The reporter noted that he wore shorts, a T-shirt, and flip-flops, and that he still had a wedding ring on. "This is not a good situation," Andrew added, "to go through this in the public eye. They've seen it in the papers, [and] kids pick up on things, the little conversations. It's really tough on them." He seemed not to appreciate his own role in the spectacle: without his public swipe at Kerry's conduct, the separation would have been a one-day story.

By now, the story was out of control. Andrew went up for the holiday weekend to Martha's Vineyard to stay with his sister Maria and brother-in-law Kenneth Cole. Kerry remained in Hyannis Port with the children. At the local Fourth of July parade, Kerry snapped pictures of her children on a float and did her best to create an air of normalcy. From the Vineyard, Andrew told the press he had asked his friends to say nothing. "I don't know how you can call yourself a friend if, by definition, you are not and I have asked you to say nothing." To the Kennedys, the comments were a sham. Cuomo operatives were feeding the press every day, the Kennedys felt sure.

Bruce Colley, for his part, made no pretense of telling his friends not to talk. What struck them was his strangely blithe reaction to the scandal. "He kind of thinks this is a big game and a lot of fun," one friend told the tabloids. His first wife, Susan Hory Colley, said her ex was a sweet guy who hadn't meant any harm. "Bruce has fooled around... it's part of who he is," she said, "but I love him and we're still best friends." Ann Colley was less understanding, but the real target of her fury was Andrew. "Ann was as mad at Andrew—maybe even more so—than she was at her own husband," a source told the *New York Post*. "She knew what her husband was like, but she didn't want everyone else to know. And she felt like Andrew allowed that to happen."

Shortly after learning of the affair, according to the tabloids, Andrew had called Bruce Colley and told him to stay away from his children. Colley bristled. "If you threaten me or do anything," he reportedly said, "I'll sue you." To friends at Man Ray, he reportedly retailed the conversation and told pals he wasn't afraid of Andrew.

Then, Colley told his friends, three big, muscular guys showed up at Man Ray the next night. They took the table next to Colley's, and at first just stared at him. Then, Colley explained, they addressed him directly. They said he had "fucked with" a friend of theirs and he had better watch out.

The next week, Colley slunk away to Argentina for an urgent polo match. Kerry went to Italy and then Mexico City for a human rights conference. The extramarital romance appeared to be over, and so did Cuomolot.

Kerry remained with her daughters in the family's Bedford home, while Andrew spent the next nine months at the Manhattan apartment of his friend Jeff Sachs, before renting a two-bedroom place of his own at One West Street in the financial district. He had hit bottom, and had no one but himself to blame.

Andrew had two top priorities now, and politics wasn't one of them. He needed money, private-sector money, enough to cover child support and build up some savings after fifteen years of public-sector salaries. He also needed to disappear, at least from public view. The brash son of Mario was a brand that voters had shunned in droves: Andrew could see that as well as anyone. The breakup of his marriage had only heightened the perception that Andrew Cuomo was toast. Once, he had inspired admiration and fear. Now he was a subject of pity and derision. He needed time to take his own measure, to see if he could pull himself up. He needed, in short, a wealthy patron to see him through this nadir. He had one in Andrew Farkas.

Risk-taker that he was, Farkas had taken his profits from the $910 million sale of Insignia's residential properties and formed a new venture, Island Capital Group. It was a real estate merchant banking firm, which meant that instead of just loaning money to real estate gambits he liked, Farkas took an ownership share: more risk, more reward. He also now managed some $1.5 billion of trophy real estate assets owned by others, like the royal family of Dubai. Farkas—or Farkie, as his friends sometimes called him—loved yachting, and that had led him to his latest real estate idea. A new era of mega-yachts had dawned, yet there was a dearth of mega-marinas that could accommodate them. By early 2004, Andrew was a vice president at Island Capital, tasked with remedying this alarming problem.

One stop was St. Thomas, in the U.S. Virgin Islands, where Andrew went as Farkas's representative to help negotiate one of these mega-marinas. He was met by a crowd of furious locals who lived in a public housing complex across the street from the planned marina and had learned that their access to the bay would be blocked. Andrew heard them out, and persuaded Farkas to protect their access. There was a faint echo, in that, of Mario saving the scrap-metal dealers of Willets Point. Except that Andrew was saving the day for mega-yacht owners.

Watching in the wings was the royal family of Dubai, which wanted mega-marinas and all that came with them—restaurants, shopping malls, and more. They liked Andrew's style. He found himself jetting over to Dubai on a regular basis on behalf of a new entity called Island Global Yachting, advising the family's real estate arm, Nakheel, on how to finance the marinas. One goal was to encourage the building of regal homes on the marina front. The plan was to prime the pump by bundling mortgages for these homes into securities through Dubai's secondary market. Andrew was doing what he'd done at HUD—only instead of using that market to help low-income black families buy houses in the United States, he was helping Arabs buy homes in Dubai.

As an advocate of social justice who'd made his name helping the homeless, Andrew may have felt some embarrassment at the turn his life had taken. "He hated the job," confided a family friend. In fact, he had every right to earn good money working for a wealthy financier, especially after all those years in public service. True, the money was very good indeed: he reported an adjusted gross income of $819,473 for 2004, his first year at Island. But why not? The issue, if there was one, was whether Farkas would later benefit directly from his two and a half years as Andrew's employer. That was a question for the future.

Andrew was keeping his head low, but he hadn't just put his political ambitions aside. He was like a boxer: there *was* no other career. He was down on the mat, the crowd jeering. In his punch-addled brain, all he could think was how to change his game, take the time to recover, and then schedule the next fight. Muhammad Ali had Angelo Dundee to coach him back to triumph, Mike Tyson had Cus D'Amato. Andrew Cuomo had Jennifer Cunningham.

Andrew had met Cunningham over dinner at union man Norm Adler's Albany apartment back in 1982. Since then, the willowy intern for District Council 37 had gone far. After several years as a lawyer for Paul, Weiss, she had become deputy counsel to state assembly Speaker Sheldon Silver—a powerful position in itself—then gone to 1199 SEIU, the health care workers' union, where as head of politics and legislation she had overseen a staff of fifty, essentially becoming the voice of New York's most powerful union. This arguably made Jennifer Cunningham the most powerful unelected woman in New York State politics. Norm Adler would grow almost teary in singing her praises. "She's very articulate, writes like a dream, she's self-possessed without being cocky... reads widely and quickly... and is probably one of the best looking operatives in politics. Also, she snorts when she laughs. I can see why Andrew would like and respect her. Why she liked and respected him I don't know."

Andrew would have loved to have Cunningham in his corner for 2002, but he was too late: Pataki had wangled that early endorsement from 1199, tying up Cunningham too. Andrew would not make that mistake again.

Often, when Andrew called someone he hadn't reached out to for a long time, he opened with "Hi there, this is Andrew Cuomo. C-U-O-M-O." It was a nice self-deprecating bit, though the humor of it was that the person on the other end of course knew who he was, so it wasn't so modest after all. The first time he called Cunningham, in late 2002 or early 2003, she figured out the reason for his call before he'd finished his opening shtick. Andrew never called out of the blue about anything. He wanted to run again for something, bloodied as he was, and this time he wanted the backing of 1199.

They had lunch; they had dinner. Andrew talked about how much he'd learned. Cunningham, as one of her colleagues recalled, gave it to him straight. "You have total credibility issues," she told him. Which was to say, on the issue of credibility, he had none. No one was going to believe that he'd undergone some personal transformation in getting trounced.

Andrew had angered almost every Democratic power in the state, black and white, upstate and down—and for good reason. That anger still glowed red-hot.

Andrew wasn't brash, at least not with Cunningham. He had a rueful charm, and voiced a blunt appeal hard to resist: he needed her help. She—and only she—could give him another chance. She knew he had a lot of fences to mend. She could help set up those meetings. Those seething Democrats—they would listen to her. Not only that, but she could get him 1199. The first step was to run for the right office. Not governor—he knew how presumptuous he had been to think he could start at the top. Attorney general—that was the right fit. "Almost no incoming," he said, meaning enemy fire, "and all you do is get the bad guys."

Andrew was right: once you won it, the job was apolitical. Everyone admired an AG who fought for truth, justice, and the American way. Just look at Eliot Spitzer. True, Spitzer was still occupying the seat. But there was chatter—a lot of chatter—that Spitzer would run for governor. Andrew had learned he couldn't start too early, certainly not in trying to woo and win the endorsement of 1199.

Cunningham was an attractive divorcée, a few years younger than Andrew, and together they might have raised eyebrows even if her ex wasn't a New York state senator. In fact, she and Eric Schneiderman were happy coparents to their daughter, Catherine, and Cunningham remained Schneiderman's chief campaign adviser. But ever after, Andrew would seem to regard Schneiderman with a special animus, and this odd political troika did seem somehow to account for that. One close observer from that time would feel sure that Andrew and Cunningham had become lovers, but Cunningham, asked directly, would deny it with a laugh. "There were rumors," she recalled. "But they simply weren't true."

All through 2004, as Andrew earned his big Island Capital paychecks, he went tirelessly after work or on weekends to every county barbecue and fair that would have him, usually driving with his barrel-chested advance man, Joe Percoco, mending fences wherever he could. Mario was a big help: at every public appearance he made, he had Andrew at his side. The crowd came for Mario; whether they liked it or not, they got Andrew as well, sharing the mike with his dad. Often Andrew did more than talk. He gave out money, drawing on the roughly $3.3 million that remained in his campaign coffers from 2002. In all, between the end of 2002 and the end of the 2006 race, he would reportedly dole out some $500,000. That mended a lot of fences.

Spitzer's announcement came on December 7, 2004: the sheriff of Wall Street would run for governor. So popular was Spitzer by now that his victory seemed preordained. Not so the AG race his plans provoked: it was wide open. Andrew was one of a half dozen contenders jockeying for placement. Another was Bobby Kennedy Jr., who along with his name brought more than two decades of serious environmental advocacy. The prospect of the not-yet-former brothers-in-law going head-to-head was mind-boggling. "We'll see what Bobby does and leave it at that," Cuomo said. Worrisomely, the president of 1199, Dennis Rivera, appeared to have made up his mind. "If Bobby Kennedy decides to be a candidate for attorney general, I could not perceive a more charismatic, energetic candidate," Rivera said. "He is what the Democratic Party needs, not only to be attorney general but to help give guidance and direction to a party that at this moment is searching for its identity and sense of direction."

Kennedy wasn't the top choice just of Rivera. Polls put him high above the rest of the field, including Andrew. Tensely, Andrew tried to persuade Kerry that Bobby should stay out of the race. "You have to get Bobby out of it," one friend recalled him saying to Kerry. "It'll be really ugly." Kennedy told friends he was eager to run against Andrew. Yet by late January 2005, he declared he wouldn't be running after all. Publicly, he said the job would be too consuming, keeping him from his six children.

With that, Andrew pushed Cunningham to have him address the leadership of 1199 at its next monthly meeting. Some seventy members, including Rivera, watched skeptically as Andrew strode to the podium. They were, to a man, McCall supporters from 2002. They hadn't forgotten who spoiled his run. Cunningham was in the audience too. Andrew began to speak—and she began to get goose bumps. "It was a little like you closed your eyes and you remembered the best of Mario," she said later. "He's one of those who . . . even if he's speaking to people who've given up on the promise of government, he can win them over. And since so much of the attorney general's job is about justice and fairness, it was a perfect match."

Later, Cunningham would recall being shocked when Rivera approached her after the talk and said, "Why don't we move towards an endorsement?" Cunningham was perhaps underestimating her clout as 1199's political director. Andrew had been working hand in glove with her since 2004, if not sooner. The endorsement was his to lose. With the union's blessing after his "barnstormer of a speech," the *New York Times* noted, "Mr. Cuomo catapults to the head of a crowded field."

Summoning all of his fierce determination, Andrew now shouldered two full-time jobs, working for "Farkie" as he ramped up his AG campaign.

He also managed to fit in a new and exciting romance, to television food star Sandra Lee.

Sometime in the summer of 2005, Andrew went to a garden party at the Bridgehampton home of Domna Stanton, a socially prominent New Yorker, Democratic fund-raiser, and academic. Domna's daughter, Alexandra, a lawyer by training and venture capitalist by profession, had worked as a special assistant to Andrew at HUD, and was by now a close social friend. She was also a friend of Sandra's. It was she who invited Sandra and introduced the two.

Blond, beautiful, and brassy, Sandra was a dazzling presence in Domna Stanton's rambling but cozy home, which included a converted barn. Andrew was charmed too by her rags-to-riches story. A daughter of teenaged, troubled parents in Los Angeles, Sandra at two years old had been dropped off one day with her younger sister Cindy at their grandmother's house in Santa Monica on what they thought was a routine visit, only to have their mother disappear for the next several years. When she'd finally returned to take them back, their mother had a new husband, and all too soon, another child. Sandra's childhood and adolescence were a blur of forced moves, desperate straits, and physical abuse by her stepfather, who, she later wrote, regularly beat her with his belt. By the age of twelve, she was her family's caretaker, minding her younger siblings and cooking dinner every night. As her mother succumbed to depression and prescription drugs, Sandra was forced to take care of her too. One of her few consolations was the nightly game of turning humble groceries into good comfort food. From that came the skills and ambition that would make her a television food star, one whose national audience faced the same nightly challenge and knew that Sandra had struggled as much as they did to make ends meet.

A natural-born salesman and entrepreneur, Sandra launched a window curtain business, Kurtain Kraft, and eventually landed as a client the giant KB homes, a Fortune 500 company. That led her to moonlight for KB as a television spokesperson. The company's chairman and CEO, Bruce Karatz, was intrigued and soon fell hard for her, leaving his wife of thirty-five years and marrying Sandra in 2001 in a lavish Beverly Hills ceremony overflowing with bridesmaids and extras dressed as nymphs.

Karatz was significantly older than Sandra and clearly doted on her, doing whatever he could to help her realize her dream of becoming a lifestyle guru, the next Martha Stewart. Through him, Sandra met Hollywood superlawyer Bert Fields and his art consultant wife, Barbara Guggenheim. They in turn led her to Tina Brown, at that time editor of *Talk* magazine, who introduced her to *Talk*'s backer, Hollywood producer

Harvey Weinstein. As impressed by her as the others, Weinstein signed her to a Talk/Miramax multiple book and television show deal.

By the time Andrew met her, Sandra was a market force to be reckoned with. She had published more than a dozen cookbooks, hosted a hit cooking show, *Semi-Homemade Cooking*, on the Food Network, and would, at the age of thirty-nine, embark on a memoir. But her marriage was foundering. Soon Karatz would be fighting charges that he'd profited by backdating stock options; eventually he would be found guilty of multiple charges and sentenced to five years' probation. In the divorce, Sandra reportedly would win a settlement "in the mid eight figures," a not unlikely sum given that Karatz would earn, in 2005 alone, $135.53 million.

That night, Andrew came to the party with his three daughters. "He walked in with three beautiful girls," Sandra recalled. "It was as if they were one unit. They came in, bouncing, bubbly, bopping off him like popcorn. Just one big ball of fun." Apparently that was how Sandra first saw him: as a single dad, not as a potential boyfriend. As one mutual friend explained, Sandra spent the next weeks trying to fix up Andrew with one or another of her girlfriends. Finally Andrew could take it no longer. He wasn't interested in those other girls, he told her. She was the one he wanted to date.

Both cautious after their divorces, and with Andrew's three daughters to consider, Andrew and Sandra kept their romance a secret for some time and maintained separate residences. Eventually they were outed, according to one report, by Mario and Matilda, who told them it was high time they let the girls in on the secret. In 2008, they would move at last into a four-bedroom home in the Westchester town of New Castle, purchased for $1.22 million. The buyer of record would be Sandra. Coincidence or not, Andrew again had found love with a woman substantially wealthier than he. She brought the money, he brought the political promise: the equation seemed to work.

By June 2006, Andrew had cleaned out his office and hit the road full-time. More often than not, Jennifer Cunningham was with him. "She really ran the AG campaign," said Kevin Finnegan, the embittered Cuomo operative from 2002 who had gone back to 1199. "She took him all over the state, used our troops; it was an 1199 operation."

Cunningham did more than get him places; like the good coach she was, she changed his whole style. "She really resurrected him," said Finnegan. "Partly it was by getting him to shut up."

No more boys on the bus with hours of schmoozing to get the candidate in trouble. Press access was tightly controlled—and would remain so. Gone was the arrogant Andrew who seemed to disdain rivals and staffers alike. The new Andrew listened, he didn't boast or snap; he actually seemed capable of respecting others and not radiating the sense that he was the smartest guy in the room.

A Cuomo transformed? Or a politician repackaged? That was the conundrum that so intrigued the state's political establishment. Cunningham felt the changes were real: that was why she had taken him on. Finnegan, who had seen Cuomo at his worst, tended to agree. "He's different now," he conceded. "Andrew was not afraid to take anyone on, he thought he could beat them all. He doesn't think that anymore."

Hank Sheinkopf, a Democratic operative of some forty years who had worked for Carl McCall and often maddened the Cuomo clan with tart on-the-record remarks, also felt the change was real, if more pragmatic than personal. "Andrew became the antithesis of what he was in 2002—he reverted to his father's style of doing things. Surround yourself with the most loyal people, bring no outsiders in, keep the circle very close, do not discuss your personal life, be very focused on the government, and create yourself as the moral authority. And don't presume in public that you have any other ambitions but to do the present job well. The logic being that if you do the job well there will be something higher. His father did it—he's the model."

Along with the chastened tone and tight circle was a new, unwavering discipline. The rumpled, shoot-from-the-hip, streetwise braggart that journalist Michael Wolff had met in 2001, who ran the most undisciplined campaign Wolff had ever seen—that Andrew Cuomo was gone.

With Kennedy out of the race, Andrew set about dispatching his next-strongest rival, former New York City public advocate Mark Green. The two had a lot in common. Both were brash enough to irk many of their Democratic colleagues, and both had lost bruising contests after offending the black and Hispanic political establishment—in Green's case, the mayoralty of New York City in 2001, by a razor-sharp margin, though the greater factor may have been the $74 million dumped into the general election by Republican victor Mike Bloomberg.

Once again, a Democratic state convention loomed, with all the back-room horse trading for weighted votes. With 1199 in his corner, and an unloved rival in Green, Andrew and his operatives worked the phones, telling local leaders they wanted to stop Green at the convention: no 25 percent. No 25 percent for any of the other candidates either. Hank Sheinkopf knew exactly how it worked. "Tell Reggie LaFayette, the head of Westchester, tell the boys in Brooklyn, gin up [Brooklyn district attorney] Joe Hynes and friends to attack him on ridiculous things..." Andrew *was* going to win this one, and the local pols knew the cost of backing a loser. "The style of this is to demand absolute loyalty," Sheinkopf suggested, "and in most cases to give nothing in return."

Four years before, Andrew had boycotted the convention, railing at "bossism" and launching a "people's" petition drive. Now he was working the strings from inside as nimbly as any nineteenth-century ward captain.

The full-court press worked: Green got less than 25 percent of the weighted vote. The other candidates who had made it to the convention came up short on weighted votes too. Both, like Green, would have to go the petition route. One was Sean Patrick Maloney, a former Clinton White House staff secretary running as openly gay. The other was Charlie King, the black candidate for lieutenant governor in 2002 who had campaigned with Andrew. King felt more than disappointed. He felt betrayed.

King's history with the Cuomos went back way before 2002. He was a close and longtime family friend. As a young lawyer and rising Democratic functionary, he had played a lot of basketball with Mario. "After my father died," King later said, "Mario Cuomo was the closest thing I had to a dad." In 1999, Andrew at HUD had made him a regional director for New York and New Jersey. In his 2002 race for lieutenant governor, King had campaigned as Andrew's running mate, knowing he was alienating droves of McCall supporters, only to be left hanging when Andrew bailed. His friendship with Andrew had withstood that turbulent week, but it had been sorely tested in early 2005, when King realized that Andrew was readying to run for attorney general. King had already staked *his* claim. How could Andrew reward King's years of loyalty to the Cuomo clan by challenging him?

Publicly, Andrew kept silent as the campaign unfolded; he knew better by now than to criticize a black rival. Privately, he started squeezing supporters King thought he'd lined up. He emerged from the convention with 67 percent of the weighted vote—an amazing comeback for the Cuomo who had scraped in vain for 25 percent in 2002. Eliot Spitzer did even better, vaporizing his one Democratic rival for governor. Barely had the votes been counted when Andrew's aides began pushing Spitzer's aides for a Spitzer endorsement. To their fury, Spitzer declined. He had known and liked Mark Green for twenty years. He knew and disliked Andrew Cuomo. Besides, dealing with the Cuomo team was like dealing with the Delphic oracle: you never knew what they would say next. Better to stay above the fray and wait to endorse whoever won the September primary.

Even without Spitzer's blessing, Andrew was far and away the front-runner. As such, he took a page from his father's 1986 playbook, shunning most of the candidate debates to a chorus of whining from his rivals. The *New York Times* was impressed neither by his Rose Garden strategy nor, as Mark Green put it, by his "sackcloth and ashes" campaign of spiritual resurrection. In late August, it endorsed Green—and urged voters to avoid a candidate whose chief concern as attorney general would be "burnishing a political resume." That, the *Times* declared, was exactly what Andrew had spent his time doing at HUD. Here, said Andrew, was more proof that the daily paper of record had a personal bias against his family.

Andrew did better—far better—with the black political establishment. Miraculously, the spoiler of 2002 was now embraced by every black leader from U.S. congressman Charlie Rangel to former Manhattan borough president Percy Sutton. "What more dedicated, honest, and sincere guy can you find than Andrew Cuomo," Rangel intoned. Along with Andrew's fence-mending efforts, political reality played a role: this time, he looked like a winner. A week before the primary, Charlie King, stuck in the single digits, reluctantly dropped out and endorsed Andrew. "Well, this is a bittersweet moment for me," King declared. "But it's the right moment to do what I'm going to do: endorse Andrew Cuomo." King would land on his feet as black community leader Al Sharpton's chief of staff. "It was with Andrew's blessing," Bill Lynch, the late Democratic political operative, would explain. "Charlie is like an agent of Andrew's."

The good news about King was offset by a stinging exposé, on the eve of the primary, by investigative journalist Wayne Barrett in the *Village Voice*. Over a twenty-year period, Barrett had followed the Cuomos more closely, and critically, than any other reporter. He'd dug deep into the Cuomos' ties to Blutrich, Falcone & Miller, and spent weeks on the Sterling Forest story. Now he had come up with a long exegesis on Andrew's friendship with Andrew Farkas. Barrett focused on the $1.2 million that Andrew had earned, in sum, from his time at Island Capital, then gave the backstory of HUD's lawsuit against Farkas and his real estate management company, the talk of payoffs, and the $7.5 settlement. On close reading, neither Andrew nor Farkas had done anything wrong. The two hadn't known each other when HUD sued Insignia Financial Services; the "payoffs" were a formerly accepted practice called fee-splitting; the $7.5 million settlement resolved the matter; and Andrew had committed no ethical missteps in going to work, years later, for Farkas, unless earning big money was a crime. Still, when put together, the facts emitted a rank odor. Here was the former HUD secretary who had called Farkas a slumlord, now deep in the guy's political debt as he stumped to become the next state attorney general. Bad optics, as Andrew clearly realized. In full damage control mode, he spoke at length to Barrett, while urging him to delay publication of the story until after the primary. By now, the two were used to jousting this way. The more Barrett dug up, the more Andrew wanted to talk: to defuse the threat, but also to try to pull an antagonist around to his side. The *Voice* went to press as scheduled; the story stirred talk; and Andrew won regardless, by a resounding 53 percent to 33 percent over Green.

At first blush, Andrew's Republican rival for the general election looked formidable indeed. Jeanine Pirro, the former Westchester County district attorney, was tough and attractive. Her office had prosecuted more than four hundred thousand cases, she declared, with a 98 percent conviction rate on felonies. Andrew, by contrast, had worked some fifteen months as an assistant district attorney in Robert Morgenthau's shop more than twenty years before, possibly delegated the writing of his appeals, then handled a few dodgy real estate deals for wheeler-dealers at Blutrich, Falcone & Miller before leaving the law altogether. As Pirro discovered, Andrew had actually submitted a disclosure form with the New York State Ethics Commission listing himself as a "nonpracticing" lawyer. "You wouldn't hire as your own lawyer to protect your family an attorney who certified that he doesn't practice law," Pirro crowed. "Well, nineteen million New Yorkers don't want a nonpracticing attorney general either."

Pirro's record was unimpeachable. Not so her personal life. Her husband had been convicted of filing fraudulent tax returns. Pirro professed ignorance of the matter, but it hung over her candidacy. Two weeks into the general election came more embarrassing news. Pirro had considered bugging her husband's boat because she thought he was having an extramarital affair; she might have asked former New York City police commissioner Bernard Kerik to have it done for her. Pirro denied breaking any laws, but Kerik could hardly corroborate that; he was the subject of an ongoing investigation for his own ethical lapses.

A pattern was forming. Andrew in his first term at HUD had hoped to rise, and seen his opening when Henry Cisneros's mistress issues forced him to step aside. Now Pirro's own marital mess was clearing the way for his first electoral victory. In time, a popular governor thought to have a lock on the office for years would let his sexual appetites undo him; the lieutenant governor who took his place would have personal failings of his own; and into the breach would come Andrew Cuomo. "Andrew is a very lucky guy," declared one of Spitzer's prosecutors. "At every stage he benefits from sex."

Eliot Spitzer, soon to be that popular governor, felt he had no choice but to endorse the primary winner in the race to replace him as attorney general. A top aide had tried to dissuade him. "You do not want Andrew as AG," the aide pleaded. Already, the Cuomo camp resented Spitzer for not endorsing Andrew earlier. A late endorsement wouldn't make an ally of him; it would only ease him into the office from which he could be a constant threat to the governor. "Andrew is unprincipled," the aide told his boss. "You don't want him in a position where he can go after you." Spitzer thought the aide was worrying too much. "I'm stronger than Andrew," he said. He was also more popular: the sheriff of Wall Street was one of the most popular figures in the country. Surely that would keep Andrew in his place. In the end, Spitzer did endorse Andrew, holding his nose as he did.

Spitzer was right: he *was* too powerful for Andrew to take on. But that might change.

As Andrew's victory began to feel inexorable, a golden late afternoon light seemed to bathe his father. In a sense, this campaign had meant more to Mario than any other. His son's political future was on the line: there would be no more campaigns if Andrew lost this one. Yet victory, if it came, would be Mario's vindication too. The Cuomo brand had left a bitter aftertaste. The upstate cities, once proud, named for beacons of the classical world—Ithaca, Rome, Syracuse—were still poor, unhelped to any noticeable degree by Mario. Still, when he spoke now at county barbecues and fairs, he felt the love returning.

From the start of this campaign, Mario had worked the phones. Andrew denied that: he told a *New York Times* reporter that Mario had made perhaps ten calls in all to local leaders. The reporter promptly called twenty-two local leaders and found that every one had received a call from Mario. That irked Mark Green. "Andrew didn't have to lie," he said later. "He could have said, 'I don't know,' or 'Yes, my father made lots of calls, wouldn't any father?' "

Perhaps Andrew couldn't accept how much he needed his wise but exasperating father. "A former governor in his 70s squiring around his son the former cabinet secretary is a good definition of tense," one campaign report had noted on the campaign trail. Over breakfast with one operative, Mario with Andrew beside him had said, "He's thick-skulled; he won't listen to me. Tell him what to do." Andrew had flared at that. "Oh Mario, give me a break. I've been in politics twenty years." Hank Sheinkopf, the political consultant, sensed Mario's resentment too. "I think by that time, [Mario] truly just wanted to help. But there was always that backhanded comment: 'Make sure it's okay with Andrew because sometimes he doesn't like me helping.'"

Each needed the other. It had always been that way; it was that way now. Pirro was a weak opponent, but Andrew knew at heart that he wouldn't have risen from the political dead without his father. This was his father's campaign too.

Happily for the Cuomos, the margin of victory that November was wide. So was Eliot Spitzer's for governor, and Hillary Rodham Clinton's for her second full term as U.S. senator. With Democrat Chuck Schumer as the state's senior senator, Democrats now held all of New York's most powerful seats, ending the twelve-year Republican rule of Mario's nemesis George Pataki.

Surely they would work in perfect harmony, guiding the state together.

CHAPTER 17

Attorney General with a Vengeance

The handoff took place in the attorney general's lower Manhattan office, with a twenty-fifth-floor view of the World Trade Center. Eliot Spitzer had watched the towers go down from here. He had held the office through difficult times, and reinvigorated it—reinvented it, really, taking on systemic Wall Street corruption. The man to whom he was yielding it had no legal experience to speak of, not on this level. With a firm handshake, Andrew Cuomo inherited hundreds of lawyers, a duty to protect the state, and a mission to keep the office as powerful and active as Spitzer had made it. The new governor offered his new attorney general his very best wishes. What he meant was: *Good luck, bub.*

Andrew at least knew he needed a lot of first-rate help. For weeks, he had churned through lists of the state's best prosecutors. He had no choice: many of Spitzer's troops would be leaving, some following the new governor to Albany, others peeling off into private practice. He found a right-hand man in Steve Cohen, a former prosecutor for the Southern District who worked for Mario while in college and law school.

Cohen had drifted away from the Cuomo circle, so much so that his name found its way to one of the lists by chance. "Wait, is this the Steve Cohen we used to know?" Andrew asked. Cohen was called in to help in a general way; five days later, Andrew showed him the new org chart and pointed to a place on it right below Andrew's name. "How about if I put you here?" For Cohen it meant giving up a lucrative salary in private practice, with his wife and children. But the opportunity was irresistible, and he took it.

Cohen was soft-spoken, genial but tough. He would earn a reputation as the governor's best strategist, the one willing to challenge the boss if he thought Andrew's approach was wrongheaded. His candid advice was usually imparted one-on-one. In meetings, even Cohen deferred. He knew better than to upstage Andrew.

Andrew's org chart said a lot about the new attorney general as manager. He had taken Spitzer's upper echelons and flattened them. Cohen would be right below him, followed by a horizontal line of deputy attorneys general. Theoretically, the deputies reported to Andrew. In fact, they reported to Cohen. Andrew knew that the top lawyers he was trying to hire would all want to report directly to him. Otherwise, why give up the jobs they had? But they couldn't all report to the AG; they would eat up all his time. This way, each would feel first among equals.

The plan that suited Andrew's needs also created a bottleneck. The horizontals could pitch cases to Cohen; it was then up to him to pass them to Andrew. Cohen felt strongly that he was a facilitator, not a gatekeeper, but that wasn't how the horizontals saw him. Just trying to get input on the cases they'd been assigned was a challenge. "It didn't work at all," one former staffer muttered. "Steve was impossible to get hold of, and you had to get his approval for every fucking subpoena, so people couldn't get anything done."

Below that horizontal line of direct reports to Cohen lay hundreds of lawyers from the Spitzer era who felt abandoned, basically left to shovel coal. Under Spitzer, they had found cases on their own and pushed them up the chain of command for approval. The chain was long, but it did lead to Spitzer, who tried to take the line attorneys' recommendations and make those cases the AG's agenda. In Andrew's shop, almost no cases came from below.

A lot of what the AG's office did *was* coal shoveling. The state was sued a lot, by everyone from prisoners to grumpy state employees; the AG took those cases on. It issued legal opinions to towns and cities; it handled appeals from state courts; if the governor had legal questions or issues, it weighed in on those. The AG did almost no criminal cases: those were handled for the most part by the state's district attorneys, one for each of the sixty-two counties.

What brought glory to the office were the relatively few cases the AG launched on his own: the so-called affirmative cases. These were the cases to right wrongs, stop injustice, and make the world a better place. If an insurance company or bank cheated its customers, that might be an affirmative case for the AG. If citizens were affected by a polluting power plant, or their civil rights were violated, the AG might step in. Wall Street scoundrels, shady developers, corrupt public officials—all were fitting targets of the AG's affirmative cases. Those were the cases that made public attorney salaries worthwhile. For an ambitious AG, they were also the cases that made news.

Steve Cohen was still unpacking when one of Andrew's new top hires knocked on his door. Ben Lawsky was a tall, intense former assistant U.S. attorney, all of thirty-six, who liked working for strong characters: he'd served as chief counsel for Senator Chuck Schumer before coming into Andrew's orbit. He and Cohen had been sifting through the cases that Spitzer's team had left pending—or as Eric Corngold, another top new hire, put it, seeing what was bubbling in the pot. "You have to hear this," Lawsky said.

The case, not yet filed, concerned college student loans. Campuses were steering students to certain "preferred lenders," and getting rewarded by the lenders in return. Not in outright cash—nothing so crass. Instead, the lender might invite the helpful college administrators to a Caribbean conference, all expenses paid. Or contribute to the college's scholarship fund. Or install free software programs for students to apply for those loans. The students were sheep: they went to the lenders their colleges suggested, unaware that they might be paying higher-than-market rates.

As soon as he got the picture, Andrew called in the line attorneys working the case. He asked them what they had done. They had written to one or two of the banks that were involved, asking for answers within thirty days.

"Why did you send a letter instead of a subpoena?" Andrew asked.

Because, the lawyers said, the banks had agreed to cooperate.

"Why are you giving them so much time?"

Lots of documents were involved, the lawyers said. Dozens of boxes.

"Why haven't you gone to the schools right away?"

The lawyers had no good answer for that.

Andrew wanted answers that week, not next month. And not just from one or two colleges. From fifty, across the country. This whole "preferred lender" business was a racket. He wanted it stopped.

"But it's January," one of the line attorneys said. "The whole loan process is under way for next September."

"Isn't this exactly when we should do it," Andrew said, "so we don't have another whole cycle of people hurt by it?" He might be new to the job, Andrew added, and he might not know what kind of subpoena to serve the universities, but he knew to move fast, and press hard—before students newly accepted to college locked in their four-year loans.

To the shock of the old guard, Andrew not only called for answers from a national cross section of colleges, he ordered a multimedia consumer alert set up with an 800 number. "But who will answer all those calls?" one of the lawyers said weakly.

"How about you!"

The new speed was fast, with an emphasis on get it done, and with all the attendant press Andrew could stir. The student loan story got headlines right away; dragged into the light, the colleges and lenders began settling as soon as they could. The press was useful; it also showcased the new hard-charging AG to best advantage.

As at HUD, Andrew exercised tight control over all this burgeoning coverage. No one was allowed to speak to reporters without permission, and usually just off the record even then. Indictments and arrests were announced by Andrew; if he was unavailable for the inevitable press conference, they were postponed until he could preside. Hogging the limelight was one of his motives, but so was trust, or the lack thereof. Robert Hernan, an assistant AG in the environmental protection bureau, later marveled at Andrew's seeming inability to trust anyone but Cohen and the horizontals. "I have served under five attorneys general," Hernan declared, "and I never encountered that kind of micromanagement and lack of trust in the staff attorneys."

Communications at the top tiers were carefully guarded too. The executive staffers were required to use BlackBerry cell phones, and to send any sensitive e-mails via BlackBerry's unique PIN-to-PIN messaging system. Instead of being relayed via a server, which kept a record of all e-mail that passed through it, PIN-to-PIN messages went directly from sender to recipient. Once the messages were deleted, they were gone.

All this control could be oppressive. But there was for many of the new hires an excitement about working for Andrew. "There's this side of him that is inspiring," recalled one staff attorney, "that fosters loyalty and makes you want to work for and with him. And you can never shake that. Every now and again I'll say to my wife, 'Maybe I should go back and work for him,' and she says, 'Are you crazy? Do you remember what he did to you, and how it felt?' "

Then too, like all good bosses of the dictatorial sort, Andrew rode himself as hard as he did his staffers. He got to his office early, stayed late, and worked weekends, with an attention to detail that bordered on the obsessive. As at HUD, he still spit-shined his shoes, wore a perfectly pressed suit, and set the papers on his desk just so. That much his staffers came to expect. But what was it with that leather binder? As they watched in surreptitious fascination, Andrew would wax it too, to a fine and glossy sheen.

From the start, Andrew wanted to focus on public corruption. Spitzer had made his reputation as the sheriff of Wall Street. Though Andrew would be on the lookout for Wall Street cases too, the badge he aimed to earn was as sheriff of Albany's State Street, doing a clean sweep of the capital. The Albany *Times Union* had given him his opening with a legal campaign the previous fall. First it had asked both parties to disclose their "member items." There were the funds that each lawmaker slipped into the state budget for his district's special needs. A new fire engine for one town, a new high school for another—these were member items. When the leaders had stonewalled, the *Times Union* had gone to court and won a ruling that both parties immediately disclose all six thousand of their member items. That was a great step toward cleaning the capital of conflicts of interest. But more was needed. Even now, there was no way to assess which of the six thousand annual member items were legit, and which were quid pro quos between a lawmaker and some constituent. Joe Bruno, the Republican majority leader of the state senate, was facing a federal investigation over the $500,000 in grants he had directed to a profit-making technology company in which a close friend was an investor. It was an all too typical case.

Andrew declared that his office would study all member items, even those below $15,000, for legitimacy and conflict of interest. He would also enforce a Spitzer ruling that lawmakers disclose their member items and the identities of their recipients. The new disclosures wouldn't prohibit lawmakers from wangling member items as before, but at least they would be accountable. That was a start.

To go further, Andrew needed to follow the money that lawmakers took in and doled out, to see where the conflicts or outright corruption lay. He called in Jerry Goldfeder, one of the few experts in this relatively arcane field, at least as far as it applied to New York State, to kick some ideas around. Halfway through the meeting, Andrew realized the answer was simply to hire Goldfeder.

"But you know I worked for Carl and Mark," Goldfeder said. Goldfeder had served as the campaign attorney for Carl McCall and Mark Green, both political rivals of Andrew.

"But I've known you a long time," Andrew said.

Goldfeder took a week to think it over. "Nah," he said, "can't do it." Switching over from private practice would be a sacrifice, but also, Goldfeder wasn't persuaded that the AG's public integrity unit could be made as strong as Andrew imagined.

"Just come back and meet a few people," Andrew said.

When Goldfeder returned, Andrew introduced him to some of his new hires. "She's not afraid of change," he said of one, and pointed to another. "He's not afraid of change." When Andrew was on a charm offensive, there were few who could resist. Overcoming his doubts, Goldfeder signed on.

Another recruit to the public integrity team was Ellen Biben. For an assistant Manhattan district attorney, Biben was surprisingly low-key, almost demure, with long blond hair and argyle sweaters. She struck some of her colleagues as looking more like a Park Avenue wife than a prosecutor. She came, in fact, from a fairly privileged Upper East Side background and probably didn't need to work, but she loved the job, put in long hours, and was a stickler for detail. The only evidence of an affluent life away from the office was her penchant for taxis: as far as her new colleagues could tell, she never, ever took public transportation.

Biben could hardly strike a starker contrast with Linda Lacewell, the somewhat carelessly dressed ex–assistant U.S. attorney who became Biben's partner in nearly all of Andrew's most significant investigations. Lacewell had prosecuted Sammy "the Bull" Gravano, the mafioso, on drug charges, then plunged into Enron. At first she seemed as civil as Biben, but when provoked—by, say, a witness she felt was lying to her—she would turn fierce, her voice rising to a shout. "She freaks people out," muttered one defense attorney forced to deal with her. Even her colleagues were taken aback. "Linda will bite your head off in front of your lawyer," one admitted. Biben was the good cop, Lacewell the bad cop. And by now, Andrew knew exactly where to point them.

From his first days in Albany, Andrew had heard the rumors about the New York State retirement fund. The fund was a pot of $154 billion for the pensions, current and future, of New York's state workers. By comparison, those six thousand member items that Andrew had just scrutinized were a mere $200 *million* in all. Other states had committees to tend their retirement funds, the better to keep their investing decisions transparent and conflict-free. Not New York. The New York state comptroller alone had the power to decide which firms and advisers would get to invest chunks of that $154 billon for handsome management fees.

Until the previous December, the state comptroller had been Alan Hevesi, a former Democratic state assemblyman. He had won the elected post of comptroller in 2002, only to resign, shortly after his reelection in November 2006, for pressing state employees into service as chauffeurs for his disabled wife. As AG, Spitzer had deemed the case closed before moving on to the governorship. Andrew wasn't so sure. Two decades before, an aide to another New York comptroller, Edward Regan, serving during the Mario years, had bluntly explained what a financial firm needed to do to get pension fund money to manage: make campaign contributions to the comptroller who held the purse strings. "Those who give," the aide declared, "will get." From what Andrew heard, not much had changed since then. Hevesi, through close advisers, appeared to have extracted extra fees, favors, and campaign contributions from the firms and hedge funds he assigned to manage tranches of that $154 billion.

There was a fine line here, as Andrew knew. The game could and did involve legal placement agents who for their labors got middleman fees. Andrew would have to prove that the fees were exorbitant or covered more than the business done. And if campaign contributions had rained down later on Hevesi from those same management firms, Andrew would have to prove that they were paybacks for fund business, not just politics as usual.

The new AG was not dissuaded. First, he knew Hevesi from Queens. He didn't trust him. In fact, to avoid any appearance of personal vendetta, he told Cohen to keep him out of the loop. "I want this to be done straight," he told Cohen. "Don't even tell me how you do it." Before signing off, he did say he felt that Hevesi's chief adviser, political consultant Hank Morris, hadn't just taken legitimate fees as an independent adviser. The sense Andrew got was that Morris had wielded control: you either hired him, and did what he wanted you to do, or you got no funds to manage. Oddly, it wasn't all about Morris enriching himself, at least not directly. Morris had told one financial firm that if it wanted a piece of the pie, it should give Ray Harding a consulting contract for $500,000. Ray Harding! The old chieftain whose Liberal Party had lost its ballot line after Andrew bailed before the primary in 2002. All the more reason for Andrew to keep his distance from it.

By May 2007, Biben and Lacewell had piles of documents. In a case as nuanced as this, though, the documents could be read either way. The investigators needed a narrator: someone they could flip who would give a grand jury the inside story. As in any organized crime case, that usually meant starting with someone at the bottom and working their way up the ladder. Perhaps they had one. Jack Chartier had been Hevesi's chief of staff. He had proven useful to Spitzer's team on the chauffeur business, and gained immunity. He had had nothing to do with investment decisions, but he had used the power of the comptroller's office to help a woman he had a crush on: onetime *Mod Squad* television actress Peggy Lipton. Enamored of her, and distressed by her story of struggling to get by, he had turned to one of the firms that won a portion of the fund to manage. The firm gave her a loan: gallantry on Chartier's part, perhaps, but quite improper. Chartier agreed to talk.

On May 7, Andrew went public with the investigation. His office had found "very troubling, serious, systemic conflicts of interest" in the way the comptroller's office had managed that $154 billion. Showing a penchant for useful clichés that would become a trademark, he called Jack Chartier "the tip of the iceberg in some ways." Andrew made a point of exonerating the new comptroller, Tom DiNapoli, from any suspicion: the popular Long Island Democrat and former assemblyman was running the fund just fine. Still, Andrew felt that no sole steward should oversee it, and DiNapoli respectfully disagreed. By the time Andrew became governor, DiNapoli would be one of his bêtes noirs.

By late spring, an unexpected shift had occurred. Andrew, the unlikely and untested attorney general, was finding his way. Eliot Spitzer, the most heralded New York attorney general of the modern era, elected governor by an awesome margin, was floundering. For Andrew, nearly every day brought headlines on the widening student loan investigation. "This is like peeling an onion," he said. "It seems to be getting worse the more we uncover." The new governor watched the headlines mount and voiced some frustration to his aides. All that student loan stuff—it had been waiting for Andrew when he arrived. Who had heard that first anecdotal evidence and acted on it? Spitzer's team, not Andrew's! At which Andrew's staffers rolled their eyes. "Eliot has this fixation," Cohen said later. "Everything is Eliot; anything we did was because he started it. How are you going to do anything in the first six months that hasn't been started before? Only Eliot would say, 'You see, that was me.'"

Spitzer's own first months had been a series of disasters, interspersed with a few clever but futile moves. Flush with his 69 percent electoral victory, he had declared, "On Day One, everything changes." He meant an ethical change for the capital scarred by scandal. That, he felt, would require seizing the Senate majority from the Republicans. They were the ones blocking any reform of the state's porous campaign finance laws, from which he felt all corruption flowed.

Spitzer might have been right, but his battle cry smacked of hubris, and he chose a dubious way to go at the Republicans. Shortly after taking office, he persuaded a Republican state senator in Long Island to give up his seat by offering him a political plum of a post in public safety. A special election was then held for the seat, and a Democrat won. That moved the party to within a seat of gaining the majority—and embittered the Senate Republicans, who cried foul.

Yet almost immediately, Spitzer managed to alienate his own party too. Another special election was held early on to fill a vacated post: that of state comptroller, after Alan Hevesi's resignation for using state employees as his wife's chauffeurs. The Assembly, not the public, got to vote on that one, and Tom DiNapoli was the overwhelming favorite. Spitzer objected. He didn't like DiNapoli—perhaps the only subject on which he and his attorney general would agree. But when he tried to ram his own recommendations through, his own Democratic Assembly rebuffed him, seating DiNapoli and handing the new governor a sharp political defeat. The Republicans had already felt the sting of Spitzer's white-hot temper. Now the Democrats did too.

Spitzer came to see Senate majority leader Joe Bruno as the block to all he wanted to do. According to Bruno, the governor warned him, "I am going to hit you so hard you're going to go down and never get up." Spitzer denied saying that, but his sentiments were clear.

With his majority shaved to one seat, Bruno was vulnerable. Recent allegations of shady business dealings had only made matters worse. Then, on July 1, 2007, the Albany *Times Union* ran a front-page story that seemed to spell his doom. Bruno had taken almost weekly trips that spring to Manhattan on state aircraft—trips that included a lot of political fundraising and a bare smidgeon of state business. The article implied that the trips might violate state ethics regulations.

Were the trips legal? That was the question that Andrew as attorney general set out to resolve.

Four days later, the story did a backflip. Bruno's travel itineraries had not just appeared out of thin air. They had been fed to the *Times Union* by the governor's office. In fact, the governor's staff had induced the state police to engage in what the *New York Post* now declared "an unprecedented state police surveillance program." No other official had been targeted to this extent—only Bruno. The *Post*'s Fred Dicker quoted a "senior state official" as saying the governor had sought to "set up" Bruno by having the state police record his comings and goings on a state helicopter.

Clearly this was part of the story that Andrew was already investigating. And so the attorney general began looking into exactly how those travel itineraries had found their way to a *Times Union* reporter.

In the scandal soon to be known as Troopergate, Andrew would engineer an astonishing act of prestidigitation, shifting his audience's attention from Bruno to Spitzer, and in so doing wounding—just enough—the governor he was meant to protect.

"It was an Alice in Wonderland world from the start," one of Spitzer's aides later grumbled. Nothing went according to protocol, but no one noticed, and the governor's aides found themselves oddly powerless to do anything about it. All they could do was watch as Andrew took the story and turned it on its head.

There was at the outset the salient question of who should investigate what. No one asked Andrew to investigate Bruno's trips, though when the AG said he would do so, the governor and his staff could hardly discourage him. In fact, they cheered him on. Then came the ricochet. Bruno was the one who asked Andrew to investigate how his travel itineraries had found their way to the Albany *Times Union*. Later, when he found out, the governor could hardly object, not when his own aides were implicated and saying no would stir cries of cover-up. In fact, the more logical choice to investigate these troubling stories was the inspector general. Andrew simply beat her to it. So aggressive was he that she found herself reduced to rubber-stamping his report.

One former Spitzer aide noted that as attorney general, Andrew should have at least called the governor to let him know he would be looking into the ricochet story: how the travel itineraries found their way to the Albany *Times Union*. After all, the governor was, strictly speaking, the AG's client. Andrew said not a word. And so for the next three weeks the governor presumed that Andrew was investigating Bruno, when in fact Andrew was investigating *him*.

Andrew's Troopergate team consisted of three of his top new hires: Ellen Biben, the good cop; Linda Lacewell, the bad cop; and Jerry Goldfeder, whom Andrew had enticed to head his public integrity unit after suggesting that Goldfeder was afraid of change. Change they got: for three weeks in July, the team barely slept as they raced to finish the Troopergate report while the story was fresh.

Later, the office's style of interviewing witnesses would come under scrutiny. Members of the state police would say they were discouraged from seeking legal counsel or bringing lawyers with them for their interviews. "Essentially what he told me was that as law enforcement officials we understood that if someone comes with an attorney, there is a presumption that they have something to hide," Pedro Perez, acting superintendent of the state police at the time, would recall of a conversation he had with Andrew himself. "And I said that is not, in fact, the case. In our system, having an attorney present does not create a sense of guilt. There's a right to an attorney. I was taken aback." Another state police superintendent and a lawyer for the state police would both corroborate the charge. A spokesman for Andrew would flatly deny it.

The Troopergate report was issued on July 23, 2007—a Monday. Whether or not the intent was to have the news reverberate through the week, that was the effect. Its wording was measured, its tone calm, increasing its sting. Here, after all, was the attorney general admonishing the governor. That didn't happen every day.

About Bruno and his helicopter trips, the AG was succinct. He found that on each of ten trips Bruno had taken to date in 2007, some business had been done. Not much—on May 17, Bruno had flown down to Manhattan on the state helicopter and participated, when he arrived, in two short meetings that qualified as state business. He had gone on to a fundraiser that evening, stayed over, and flown back the following morning. The rule was a porous one, the report acknowledged, and should be tightened. But Bruno had abided by it, such as it was, and the attorney general had no legal cause to upbraid him.

Of the report's fifty-three pages, Bruno and his trips—the original impetus of the investigation—took up just thirteen pages. The rest was a scathing dissection of how the governor's aides had pushed to gather and disseminate Bruno's travel plans.

The report did acknowledge that no campaign of surveillance had been conducted against the majority leader, contrary to Bruno's suspicions and the reporting of the *New York Post*. The governor's aides, however, *had* pushed the superintendent of state police to gather Bruno's travel records, and not just the flight itineraries readily at hand. Rather, the state police had been asked to go back and piece together Bruno's whereabouts from hour to hour during his state aircraft trips.

Darren Dopp, a Spitzer adviser, had had the idea to gather those records. Whether Dopp then simply handed the records over to a reporter from the Albany *Times Union*, or waited until the reporter submitted a so-called FOIL—Freedom of Information Law—request to get them, was to Andrew the crux of the story. Dopp said the FOIL came first; Andrew suggested by an exacting timeline that it did not.

For the governor and his aides, this was Alice in Wonderland indeed. Joe Bruno was a public servant, taking trips on state-owned helicopters at taxpayer expense. What was wrong with investigating how that money was spent? And if such an inquiry was untypical or, as Andrew's report deemed it, unprecedented, so what? Why did that mean such an inquiry couldn't be made? And why did the information handed over have to be prompted by a FOIL request? Couldn't the governor's aides disseminate such public information to the media whenever they wished? Seemingly not, according to Andrew.

After spending most of the report castigating the governor and his aides for their transgressions, Andrew recommended that the governor punish Dopp and two others. For Bruno, he served up not one word of criticism even though it appeared that Bruno was gaming the system with trips that failed the smell test. That was why the *Times Union* had seen fit to report them in the first place.

Perhaps Andrew did feel constrained by the regulations on state aircraft from faulting Bruno at all. To longtime Cuomo watchers, however, there was another possible reason why Andrew had gone easy on the Senate majority leader: Air Cuomo. Prosecuting Bruno might have provoked damaging mentions of those hundreds of flights Mario and his family had taken at the state's expense. Of greater concern, it might have called attention to those twenty-four round-trip flights that Andrew had taken from Washington, D.C., to New York in his last year at HUD, when he was gearing up for his first gubernatorial campaign.

Most maddening, the Spitzer staffers knew there was no justification for Andrew to have issued a report at all—not when his digging had determined that no laws had been broken. "There was no one to sue, no one to indict," as one Spitzer aide noted. "And the attorney general is not a historian; he has no obligation to write the definitive history. Once he determines no laws have been broken, he's done." But no one questioned Andrew's decision to write a report. The press just ran with the results.

Of the governor's aides, none more keenly felt the surreality of the situation than Darren Dopp. A onetime AP reporter, Dopp had become Mario's press officer on the road—day trips only, so that Mario famously could spend every night at home in the executive mansion. He was still on the road with Mario in 1994, as the governor struggled to make his case for a fourth term and tensions sparked between father and son. Dopp, a soothing and gentle sort, often ended up mediating their quarrels.

Dopp had gone on to be Eliot Spitzer's communications director through both his terms as attorney general, then followed him to the governor's office. He knew everyone in New York State politics, and counted himself a confidant of both Spitzer and Andrew, a feat he managed, in part, by always having the latest political gossip. Only now he was the subject of the latest gossip, and, horrifyingly, the attorney general he so admired had concluded he was the villain of the tale.

In the days leading up to the report's release, Andrew had asked the governor's office for permission to interview Dopp, and Dopp had wanted to talk. Dopp felt that if he could just talk directly to Andrew, his friend of two decades, he could explain the whole situation and make Andrew see that he had done nothing improper, regardless of when the FOIL request was made. "He's not going to fuck me," Dopp pleaded to the governor's lawyers.

Yes, the Spitzer lawyers replied, that was exactly what Andrew would do.

Andrew couldn't force Dopp to talk, because he lacked subpoena power: so far, he had found no evidence of criminal activity. Despite

Dopp's pleas, the governor's lawyers refused to let him. They felt he had showed a disturbing tendency to tell his story slightly differently each time. That might just be the way his mind worked, but it left him vulnerable, if two versions varied, to being accused of perjury. Instead, the governor's lawyers interviewed Dopp themselves and drew up a statement based on what he had said, to be signed by him, notarized, and submitted to Andrew. They did the same with another aide, Rich Baum.

In the report that came out that next Monday, neither statement was mentioned or excerpted. Nonetheless, Andrew recommended that Dopp be punished. At a press conference, an ashen-faced Spitzer embraced the report and announced that Dopp would be suspended for at least thirty days without pay. With that, he hoped this matter might at last be put behind him.

Out, within days, trickled the news that Dopp and Baum had opted not to sit for interviews with the AG's investigators. In retrospect, a Spitzer aide would agree that Dopp, Baum, and the governor himself should have sat for interviews after all. The worst they had to hide was that they had used the FOIL request as a pretext for handing over Bruno's travel plans, and that the governor, despite his denials, might have urged them on. So what? Instead, Dopp's and Baum's refusal to sit for interviews gave Republicans a rallying cry for investigating the matter further. The state ethics commission, which did have subpoena power, became the first of several bodies to heed that cry.

In all, Troopergate would generate eight additional investigations. The AG's office would not formally participate in any of those, though it would hand out documents and interviews as requested. Andrew himself would keep nosing around, going so far as to call Dopp at home to talk him into testifying at last. Dopp's wife would field the calls, and pass on Andrew's message: *They're shooting you in the back*. Through his wife, Dopp would send his reply: *I can't be disloyal. Even if they are crapping on me, I can't do it.*

None of these subsequent investigators found any laws broken, unless Dopp's faulty memory constituted perjury, a sideshow at best. But the drip-drip of investigations forming, and witnesses being subpoenaed, would keep the governor's wound from healing—keep him, in fact, from coming to Albany much at all for the rest of his short, unhappy tenure.

That, whether he meant it or not, would be the legacy of Andrew's report on Troopergate—a report so measured that no one could accuse him of piling on, even as it made the governor look far worse than the facts warranted. Had that been Andrew's intent?

Later, one insider from the attorney general's office would pause when asked that question. Andrew, this person would say, never told his investigators how to proceed, or what conclusions to reach. He didn't have to. "Nobody had to tell them how to deal with this investigation as it related to Spitzer and Bruno," the insider mused. "If you didn't know, there was no reason for you to be there."

Andrew had wounded the governor, just as the governor's aides had warned he would. But none could have imagined how soon the end would come.

CHAPTER 18

Managing the Meltdown

Perhaps it was giving Andrew too much credit to say that his Troopergate report showed perfect political pitch. Perhaps his team had merely done its best, and the report was the result. Still, it did strike a balance that benefited an ambitious attorney general. Andrew had jumped right in: a show of vigor, to be sure. Yet he'd been content to investigate without subpoena power. He could have asked the governor for it; Spitzer would have seen no choice but to grant it. Why hadn't he? "That would have been too naked," one AG insider suggested. "If you don't have subpoena power, there's a limit to what you can do. So you do what you can, and let others carry forward, so you're not seen as trying to bring down the governor."

Without subpoena power, the report was bound to be incomplete. That too benefited an attorney general eyeing the governor's seat. The beat would go on, this time *with* subpoena power. Andrew may not have anticipated that. But he did nothing to quiet the clamor. Not once did he come out and say enough was enough, no laws were broken, let the governor get back to work.

With such a triumph, more than a touch of Andrew's old swagger returned, and the culture he created in the AG's office reflected that. As at HUD, long hours and unwavering loyalty were de rigueur—and not always enough. "Here's the thing about Andrew," explained one of his former staffers. "He's fiercely smart, and he can be very charming—and very mean. You would get called into Andrew's office. If you were unprepared, if you could not answer his questions, he looked at you like you were a moron." He might not criticize you to your face, suggested another staffer. But he would rap you when you left the room. "When you're a bully you insult people to their faces. This was to the back."

All it took was one strike. "If you screwed something up for Andrew, you were out," said a staffer. "He didn't want to be the bad guy, though. So he tells Steve [Cohen], and Steve becomes the bad guy." Once, Andrew had been cast in that role—by his father. Now he was the boss and Cohen swung the hatchet.

Even among his four top lieutenants, Andrew ruled by fear as much as encouragement. Ellen Biben and Linda Lacewell, his good and bad cops, lived in fear of prompting their boss's ire, suggested one former staffer. "I think he liked Ellen more than Linda, but he admired Linda more. So they were always paired together." But not always praised equally. "When the sun shines," said one longtime adviser to Andrew of his management style, "it shines very brightly and makes people want very much to keep pleasing him. Just as quickly, the sun leaves, and it makes some people strive that much harder to get the sunshine back."

So it was with Andrew's two top men. For a while, said one staffer, "[Ben] Lawsky became the darling of the office. We all hated him because he was the attorney general's guy, and very abrupt. He and Andrew would watch the same TV shows from their homes at night, and text each other while they were watching. Like automotive shows. Lawsky was Andrew's bitch, so everyone liked Steve [Cohen] because Steve was so affable. In truth, Steve was the one who fucked everyone, and Lawsky didn't, even though he was abrupt. And it was only their opinions that mattered."

Close as he was to both, Andrew could play one against the other, just as his father had done. "With Ben and Steve, one was usually more in than the other," explained one staffer. "And it went back and forth. One might piss off Andrew, so Andrew would go to the other one." Whichever one was out of the room was a potential target for criticism. "Andrew said something negative about everyone," said one staffer. "About Lawsky, about Cohen, even. No one was competent. Every day it was a different person. That's a thread—a subtext. The story is how they were all cowed by Cuomo."

Some would say the key with Andrew was *not* to feel cowed—to stand up to his Jesuitical grilling and tell him where he was wrong. "The truth is, he's one of these guys who has six ideas and only one of them is good," explained one insider. "You have to be willing to tell him the other five aren't right." Whether anyone really took him on, told him he was flat wrong—that was perhaps wishful thinking on the part of his staffers. They didn't so much stand up to Andrew as venture, ever so gently, that he might be right in a different way.

Like towel snappers in a high school locker room, Andrew and his top aides could pick on weak targets. One was a lawyer named Hank Greenberg. "They treated him terribly, they made fun of him," recalled a staffer. "Hank would say, 'On the one hand, on the other.'" They thought this showed such weakness. Andrew and Cohen and Lawsky would make fun of him all the time to everybody. They were merciless." Jerry Goldfeder, the election law expert, became another target. "Jerry thought he was very close to the AG," one staffer recalled. "But there's no such thing as a friend for Andrew at work."

Not everyone chafed under Andrew's management style. Blair Horner, a longtime public activist, took up Andrew's challenge to come in from outside and help improve transparency in Albany. Andrew envisioned a database that would show, in one place for the first time, campaign contributions to lawmakers from all the usual suspects, and choices those lawmakers had made that might benefit those donors. Andrew called it "Project Sunlight." Despite Republican opposition, he managed to get $700,000 for it, and a staff for Horner to see it through.

As a gadfly, Horner was inclined to be skeptical of power. Now, from inside, he grudgingly came to admire Andrew as a master of statecraft, up on the nuances and always prepared. The AG expected others to be too. "In these executive staff meetings...you did not want to be in that room if he asked you a question and you didn't know the answer," Horner recalled. "I liked that: taxpayers don't pay public officials to sit around and figure out the answers. This was a clear example where the person in charge really was in charge. He drove the staff, he drove the focus of the organization, and he was clearly on top of what was going on."

One old Mario hand saw an analogy between Andrew and another attorney general: Bobby Kennedy, the father-in-law Andrew had never had. Each had made his bones as a family enforcer, letting the principal be the hail-fellow-well-met while the enforcer made the demands and delivered the bad news. Both, as a result, had been seen as arrogant and harsh, even brutal. Both had then managed the rare and difficult transition to being principals themselves, reinventing themselves as conscientious public servants. Both, in the process, had become their own men.

Andrew's Cagney and Lacey, as he called Ellen Biben and Linda Lacewell, were busy bees that summer of 2007. Even as they were finishing the Troopergate report, they were assembling the pieces of the pension fund puzzle. The picture was still incomplete, but the outlines suggested an epic pay-to-play operation. *Those who give will get.* It wasn't just one story, however. It was half a dozen.

The common denominator in all these instances was Hank Morris, a seasoned political operative whom everyone in New York State politics knew. Morris had steered Alan Hevesi's rise to comptroller in 2002, and benefited in the intervening years by putting himself squarely between

Hevesi and any firm angling for pension fund money to manage. The well-known Carlyle Fund, for one, had channeled $12.3 million to a small financial services company that happened to employ Morris, and passed the money directly to him. Around that time, Carlyle got $1.3 billion of the pension fund to manage. Morris also steered firms to contribute to Alan Hevesi's reelection campaign. To Biben and Lacewell, the fees looked like kickbacks. So did the political contributions.

The problem was that Morris was now a licensed placement agent. And wasn't this what placement agents did? Took middleman fees for advising the comptroller on which firms to go with? It was. And weren't political contributions to city and state comptrollers entirely legal? They were. The key was that the firms had to have a choice. They had to be able to hire a placement agent other than Morris, if they liked, and have just as much chance of landing state business. They also had to be free not to make political contributions to get and keep that business. From what Andrew and his team could see, the firms here had no choice.

Proving Morris was a gatekeeper wouldn't be easy. Proving his fees were illegal would be harder still.

By the end of his first year as AG, Andrew had proven he was up to the job. Whatever his motives, he had handled Troopergate with masterful restraint. The pension fund story was getting bigger by the week. The student loan scandal was the gift that kept on giving: America's college students were prey, it was now clear, to a whole host of financial predators. Small wonder that Spitzer was jealous of the press that student loans kept stirring.

Despite the obvious tensions, Spitzer invited Andrew to the governor's mansion one night that fall for drinks, just the two of them. Andrew might be forgiven for walking in warily, though if he did, the governor soon put him at ease. He wasn't bitter—at least that night he wasn't. "These things are like football games," he said, meaning the whole foolish mess that had become Troopergate. "You go out and play as hard as you can, then the next day you start over." If he had his frustrations with the report—in the end, he felt it was a lot about nothing—he bore Andrew no ill will for how it had turned out. He wasn't a grudge-bearer, he told Andrew, a self-description that might have surprised many in Albany. He wasn't angry at all.

In fact, Spitzer mused over their second drink, he and Andrew had a lot in common. "The two of us are both products in different ways of New York politics. In your case it was in your blood. In my case, I was a kid from the shtetl." Spitzer's father was in fact one of the wealthiest real estate developers in New York. But Spitzer had apparently chosen to omit a generation or two from his family saga. For Andrew, whose father was imprinted with his own father's immigrant experience, it was surely a mind-boggling comment.

Gracious as he was that evening, Spitzer could only look with dismay at the role reversal the year had brought. As a year-end profile of the two men in the Albany *Times Union* put it, "Spitzer's first year has been one that many fellow Democrats would just as soon forget, marked by fights, plummeting poll numbers and a travel records scandal that will likely drag on for at least part of 2008. Cuomo, though, has become a celebrity, successfully taking on questionable lenders, Medicaid fraud artists and polluters with a zest that has brought him national acclaim."

Spitzer had stumbled badly. Even so, he had no cause to think he would leave the executive mansion anytime soon. He was one year into his four-year term, with all the perks and power of incumbency; he was governor of a solidly Democratic state; and he was one seat away from a new Democratic majority in the state senate. There was only one person who could bring him down before the next gubernatorial election, and that person wasn't Andrew Cuomo. It was Spitzer himself.

The story came in fragments that March week of 2008, each more shocking than the last: the governor who was leading a secret life as Client #9 in a high-priced prostitution ring; the cops who traced him to a hotel room in Washington, D.C.; the public resignation with Silda, his wife, standing by him in shocked humiliation.

Some would wonder if Andrew had given the governor some final nudge: passed along a rumor of call girls to the authorities, perhaps. Years later, one of Spitzer's top former aides dismissed the thought out of hand. No one, he declared, ever felt that Andrew was complicit in any way. Anyway, the aide added with a sigh, the governor alone was responsible for his conduct and its consequences, and he knew that. Spitzer himself never blamed Andrew.

For the hard-charging AG, the sad spectacle spelled opportunity nonetheless. Spitzer was handing over the state's highest job to his lieutenant governor, David Paterson. Paterson would serve out the rest of Spitzer's term and doubtless run in 2010 for election in his own right. But Paterson had serious shortcomings: for one, he was legally blind, the result of a childhood infection. Andrew's exuberance got the better of him. "The black thing is dead," he blurted out. As one staffer explained, "Translation: we can go get this guy, we can destroy him, and no one will accuse me of being a racist like they did with Carl McCall."

Like Andrew, David Paterson was a second-generation New York politician: his father, Basil, had been a state senator and deputy mayor of New York City. David was a longtime state senator himself, a force in Harlem like his father before him, very smart, very charming, very experienced. Also, by reputation, a little reckless and irresponsible.

"Not a focused guy," sighed one senior state lawmaker. "No attention span, can't work an issue, can't think three steps ahead, and he just doesn't have the patience and work ethic." Paterson's personal life was a bit shaky too. In a move apparently meant to preempt the sort of criticism Bill Clinton had met for his answer to the marijuana question, the new governor declared that he had done his share of recreational drugs, including cocaine, *and* had affairs. "David likes to go out and stay out late," said a prominent Democratic political consultant. "Maybe twenty years ago you could get away with that, but no longer."

From the state's Democratic establishment came, with Paterson's ascension, a collective *uh-oh*. The mere image of a nearly blind governor feeling his way across a stage or signing legislation with his nose to the document itself was disconcerting. As for a hearty-partying David Paterson up to his usual hijinks, it was a chilling prospect. It was not too much to imagine the Democrats losing the governorship in 2010. So began the whisper campaign that would dog the new governor through his difficult, unraveling term. The right choice for governor next time—the only choice—was Andrew Cuomo.

More than a state government was teetering. Nationally, the real-estate-fueled boom had gone bust. Subprime mortgages were going belly up, taking down the securities based on them; the banks that dealt in those securities were going into death spirals. In retrospect, Andrew would come under attack for not using his power as attorney general—New York attorney general, with Wall Street on his turf—to march the villains off to jail, and there would be some truth to that. But it was also true that he was one of many overseers, at every level, trying to ride out a storm that in its power almost no one predicted.

By early 2008, Andrew had targeted a root cause of the crisis: the appraisers. Too often, the appraiser determining the value of a house was in league with the bank that wanted to grant a mortgage on it. The bank wanted to grant as large a mortgage as possible, to get its money working and earn the biggest possible profit on it. So the bank would nudge the appraiser to set the highest possible value on the house. The appraiser wanted more business from the bank, and thus happily complied. The result was an overvalued house the homeowner couldn't sell when the market started to cool.

Andrew made a deal with Fannie Mae and Freddie Mac, the government mortgage companies that had bought so many billions of dollars of subprime mortgages from lenders since he as HUD secretary had encouraged them to do just that. From here on in, Fannie and Freddie would only buy mortgages from lenders that used independent appraisers. It was a smart move, if one made too late to stop the market's collapse.

At first, neither Andrew nor his staff quite appreciated the significance of what the big banks did on the eve of Valentine's Day 2008. Auction-rate securities were an arcane market. Many investors had never even heard of them. But their collapse was the canary in the coal mine for the country's looming credit crisis, and the AG's office was soon racing to deal with them.

In the simplest sense, auction-rate securities were a handy way for institutions like state and local governments, or not-for-profits, to raise capital for new projects: a new building, say, or a new hospital. What made them uniquely appealing to buyers was the auction aspect. Every week or so, they got put up for auction, so their rate got adjusted within a certain range as the market rose or fell. As a result, even though they were long-term securities, they had short-term pricing, which made them almost as liquid as cash—with interest rates still a bit higher than real cash alternatives like treasuries and money market funds. Big institutional buyers liked that; they could use auction-rate securities to leverage their investment funds. The banks liked them too. As middlemen, they got fees not only for selling the securities initially but also for handling the ongoing auctions. Even individual investors liked them: a family saving for college could put its money to work at those higher-than-treasury rates, yet presumably have access to its money at the very next auction. Everybody liked auction-rate securities. They liked them right up until that February day when the auction-rate security market tanked.

To help keep those auctions ticking along, the banks had always used a bit of their own money, acting as buyers of last resort. In recent months, though, as the real estate market sagged and more investors fled, they had secretly bought more and more of the securities—until the day they decided to abandon the effort. Overnight, the $330 billion market froze up as a large proportion of auctions failed, and bank windows shut with their customers' money inside.

"What's the SEC doing about it?" Andrew asked Eric Corngold, his executive deputy attorney general for economic justice. The SEC was looking into it, Corngold said, but doing nothing yet.

"So they can spend the next two years investigating," Andrew scoffed, "and meantime you have people who can't get their money out."

He told Corngold to get right on it, and the subpoenas started flying. The banks were incensed. So, to Corngold's surprise, were the federal regulators. "You can't do this," regulators told him. "These banks are hanging by a thread." Andrew was undeterred: this looked like fraud.

The attorneys general of several states were on the case already, coordinating their efforts for maximum impact. When they asked Andrew to join, however, he refused. He felt, Corngold explained, that going it alone would bring faster results.

At a press conference in late July, Andrew announced that New York was suing UBS, a major investment bank. It was a shocking case: seven executives of the bank had sold their personal holdings of auction-rate securities in the days before the market for them froze, disparaging the securities among themselves while continuing to urge their customers to buy them.

Within days, Andrew launched investigations of seven other major players in the auction-rate security market: Citigroup, Merrill Lynch, Goldman Sachs, Lehman Brothers, JPMorgan Chase, Morgan Stanley, and Wachovia. The New York attorney general behaved as though he were the lone prosecutor, despite the fact that the SEC and state regulators were working on parallel investigations. In fact, Massachusetts had filed suit against UBS the month before, in a complaint of some one hundred pages that included shocking e-mail exchanges between UBS bankers indicating that they knew before February that auction-rate securities had become a doomed market.

After word came down from the Federal Reserve to go easy on the banks, Andrew hammered out a settlement with Citibank, and one by one the other banks capitulated too, agreeing to buy back securities worth tens of billions of dollars, and paying tens of millions of dollars in fees.

Impressive as the numbers looked, the deals Andrew made with the banks were fairly generous. "The settlements basically said up to $10 million it was fraud, and over $10 million you should have known better," recalled Joseph Fichera of Saber Partners, an expert on auction-rate securities. Meaning anyone who bought less than $10 million in auction-rate securities was presumed to be an individual investor fleeced by the banks, and thus was made whole, while institutional investors like corporations and pension funds that had more than $10 million of them were presumed to be sophisticated enough not to have seen through the scam, and so were left hanging. But an institutional fund might have relied upon the same misrepresentations made by the banks to the under-$10-million crowd. And weren't both categories equally injured? "This didn't make much sense," Fichera said. Except in one sense: they were settlements rushed at one of the most precarious times in the market—the summer of 2008—just before the Lehman bankruptcy in September.

A former prosecutor in Spitzer's AG office felt that the banks managed to hold on to a lot of that auction-rate security money because Andrew's deals were done too quickly and superficially. "Cuomo never understood that market," he declared. "That was 99 percent a case of Wall Street screwing Main Street at an institutional level. All they did was make it so some retail investors got taken out of these bonds, which created no pain for Wall Street banks." In many cases, noted one investment banker, the banks convinced the issuers of those securities to restructure and refinance them.

"It was really about stopping the bleeding of the headlines," said one financier. "Andrew came in as a hero to help the little guy, and then structured the deal so the banks could recoup their money and shift their burdens back to the issuers. He got the headline he wanted, and then he moved on."

In the summer of 2008, with the market slipping but the crash yet to come, Andrew sought to fix another of the factors thought to be harming the financial system. When banks bundled subprime mortgages like sushi rolls, then sliced and sold them on the secondary market, they needed one of the three major ratings firms to evaluate those securities: Moody's, Standard & Poor's, and Fitch. Over time, the banks had come to game the system by "rating shopping." A new security was shown to the three firms, and whichever firm gave it the highest rating was the one the bank hired for that issue, paying only after it made its choice. This was more than a conflict of interest. It was a fraud perpetrated on the buyers of those bonds, who relied on the ratings for honest information. As the housing market grew more and more inflated, the ratings firms vied with each other to plant seals of approval on ever more dubious subprime securities.

Instead of singling out bad guys and bringing them to court, Andrew advocated a new approach. Wall Street players would sign on to a code of conduct swearing off some dubious practice. Better to change the system than play Whac-A-Mole, as he put it. Flanked one day that June by executives of all three ratings firms, he announced a six-part agreement that would end the rampant conflicts of interest.

Only it didn't—not really. The firms would be paid equal up-front fees, but that wouldn't make them equal competitors. It would just give them all more money. The firm chosen would still get later fees for services, and thus still have an incentive to give a rosy rating that got it the business. On the other side of the equation, the banks would now have to provide more information to the ratings firms so the firms could rate their securities more accurately. The catch was that the ratings firms didn't have to *ask* for that information. And they didn't, because the more information they got, the lower their rating might have to be. An in-depth report on the settlement in the *New York Times* suggested that its terms, in any event, would last only three years. Presumably by then the code of conduct would take root and the agreement could simply dissolve. Financial writer Charlie Gasparino wrote in the *New York Post* that Andrew did no more than force raters to make "marginal added disclosures." The raters' conflicts of interest with the banks, he wrote, remained "firmly intact."

In his dealings with Wall Street, Andrew was operating in a very different way from the rampaging AG he had replaced. Spitzer's prosecutors investigated a shady practice for months before gathering enough evidence to issue subpoenas. The indictments that followed were so airtight that a company might lose half its share value in days. "Cuomo would just get an idea, send out a subpoena, announce it, and settle it," a Spitzer-era prosecutor fondly remembered.

Andrew's settlements tended to involve these "codes of conduct"—Spitzer's phrase but adapted to Andrew's desire for quick results. "It was incredibly efficient," the Spitzer-era prosecutor said. "You could do that with three people. But it's a bad thing if you think that the role of the regulator is to actually discover stuff and make it public."

In the clubby world of New York prosecutors and white-collar defense lawyers, Andrew's alleged use of leaks in this game of subpoena-and-settle was no longer surprising, merely appalling. "Spitzer was very happy to be in front of the press and claim credit and perhaps go over the line," one defense lawyer acknowledged. "But what I did not find him to do was to leak things to the press beforehand. Whereas with Cuomo I always seemed to find out what was going to happen [to my clients] from reporters."

Damaging as the leaks were, all a company had to do to stop the rain was settle and let Andrew take the credit. "New York under Spitzer had been the most feared financial regulator in the country," declared the former Spitzer prosecutor. "What Cuomo did to the office of AG was move it immediately out of the galaxy of things the companies were worried about: he could be bought off with a cosmetic fix."

Andrew had taken on three bad actors in the sagging real estate market: the appraisers, auction-rate securities, and the ratings firms. In the case of Richard Grasso, he faced a murkier challenge. For better or worse, the way he chose to resolve it was antithetical to what Eliot Spitzer as AG would have done.

Five years after the former head of the New York Stock Exchange (NYSE) had walked away with his gargantuan retirement package, Grasso remained a symbol of Wall Street excess, and the case that Eliot Spitzer had filed as AG to get that money back was still in the courts.

Grasso had worked at the NYSE for more than thirty-five years and done a good job, but the payout—$139.5 million, bizarrely paid not upon retirement but right then and there, along with $48 million to be paid later on—seemed exorbitant to almost everyone except Ken Langone, the Home Depot cofounder and NYSE board member who chaired the exchange's compensation committee. Andrew as AG had kept the case going, but it had taken an odd turn. The not-for-profit NYSE had become a for-profit company, merging with the electronic market Archipelago Holdings. Grasso argued that as a result, the AG could no longer pursue him on behalf of the NYSE. In doing so, the AG was spending public funds on a prosecution that no longer served the public's interest because the NYSE was no longer a nonprofit entity. When the appellate division of New York's Supreme Court sided with Grasso in 2007, quashing four of Spitzer's six causes of action, Andrew seemed to lose heart. An appeal was duly filed with the appellate division—but a settlement seemed in order.

One day in the spring of 2008, Andrew summoned Grasso, Langone, and their respective lawyers for a meeting in the AG's downtown office. "We've got to settle this," he declared. He wanted Grasso to give up most but not all of his compensation package, and for Langone to concede that he hadn't run the NYSE's compensation committee as well as he should have. Langone grew emotional, as he later related. "I don't care what everybody else in this room does," he declared. "You're getting nothing from me. This may consume the rest of my life, but my children are going to know their father didn't roll over."

Later that day, Langone got a call from Andrew. "He tells me the stock exchange, which is named in the suit, has offered $35 million to settle," Langone later recalled. "I say, 'It's Dick's money, but General—[Andrew] didn't like being called General—if he gives you a fucking nickel, I'll never talk to him again. I'm in this fight for two reasons: that justice prevail and because I stand by my judgment.' "

Andrew stood firm too—until the appellate division hit him with a one-two punch. On June 25, 2008, it upheld its previous dismissal of most of the AG's causes of action. A week later, it dismissed the remaining two. Grasso had won, and Andrew saw no reason to fight another day. "We have reviewed the court's opinion and determined that an appeal would not be warranted," announced a Cuomo spokesman. "Thus, for all intents and purposes, the Grasso case is over."

One AG was relieved. Another was apoplectic. *Can you believe this?* Spitzer told friends. Letting Grasso go like that? Not even letting the appeals process play itself out? The spin from the AG's office was that Andrew had run out of options. According to a lawyer familiar with the case, that was half right. The case could not be automatically appealed—"as of right," as the jargon had it. "But you can also apply for 'leave' to appeal," as the lawyer explained. "I would hazard the opinion that leave would have been granted if the AG had sought it." And if he needed encouragement, he had it in spades from one of the four appellate division judges, Angela Mazzarelli, who filed a blistering dissent.

Instead, Andrew had let Grasso keep his $190 million, and let Langone, the facilitator, off the hook too. Apparently he had come to believe that Grasso deserved the money. When he called Langone to chat about the ruling, Langone recalled saying to him about the appeals judges, "They did the right thing." To which Andrew, according to Langone, replied, "I know."

Langone, an emotional man by his own admission, was gratified by Andrew's decision not to pursue that final appeal. Rock-ribbed Republican though he was, he would go on to be a significant campaign donor to Andrew, giving $50,000 for his reelection fund in 2013. By early 2014, he would become chairman of Republicans for Cuomo. He liked what Cuomo was doing to try to keep the wealthy from leaving the state, he said: keeping a lid on taxes. He also liked how Andrew had acted in letting the Grasso case go. At the same time, the end of the Grasso case showed a young public servant, in his first elected job, dealing carefully with two very rich and powerful New Yorkers who might be of considerable use in his future.

Like small dark clouds on the horizon, other wealthy New Yorkers were already making major contributions to Andrew and, like Langone, crossing party lines to do so. Between 2001 and 2009, developer Donald Trump would chip in $64,000. In 2010, David Koch, the libertarian billionaire whom Democrats reviled, would give $87,000. What did they want? That was always the question.

Andrew's first move after watching Lehman sink into oblivion was to see what legal basis he might have for going after short sellers—those cold-eyed investors who hastened the market's drop by betting that already reeling banks would fall further. They were, he said in disgust, like "looters after a hurricane." There was nothing to be done about them, at least by the AG. Short selling might be ugly, but it was legal.

Andrew watched aghast as the federal authorities raced to stave off a global collapse by pouring $700 billion into the country's largest financial institutions. Hardest hit was the insurance giant American International Group, or AIG, which had made ungodly profits by insuring mortgage-based securities. The cowboys at AIG had assumed they would never have to pay out on those insurance policies: real estate was too solid to go down. Back in August 2007, Joseph Cassano, head of AIG's $441 billion portfolio of so-called credit default swaps, had crowed, "It is hard for us, without being flippant, to even see a scenario within any kind of realm of reason that would see us losing one dollar in any of those transactions." Now real estate *had* crashed, and AIG was stuck paying out billions on cratered securities. It couldn't make those payments without government help: first $85 billion, then another $38 billion, eventually $182 billion in all.

Surely there was criminality to pursue in all this, but Andrew was apparently made aware of certain realities in a private meeting shortly after the meltdown with Timothy Geithner, the young president of the Federal Reserve Bank of New York. As reported by the *New York Times*' Gretchen Morgenson and Louise Story, the two met at Andrew's lower Manhattan office, where Geithner cautioned Andrew about being too aggressive in drawing up indictments: the economy was on the verge of collapse, and saving it was a higher priority than putting scalps on the wall. Geithner was speaking not only as the head of the New York Federal Reserve, but as AIG's prospective creditor; he wanted to be sure AIG survived its financial heart attack. If it died, it would take the government's money with it—and very possibly the global financial system as well.

When asked about AIG later, Andrew's office would deny that his hands had been tied in any way. "The attorney general went on to lead the most aggressive investigation of AIG and other financial institutions in the nation," the office declared. That was true as far as it went. But Andrew didn't challenge the way AIG did business. He didn't eliminate credit default swaps, the privately traded paper that AIG had trafficked in, endangering the real estate market, or the insurance AIG had written on those swaps. He might be America's most powerful attorney general, but he was still just one of many figures, most of them federal, struggling to pull the economy back from the abyss. Whatever Geithner did or didn't do to rein him in, he couldn't fight those battles himself. He needed an angle that worked for him. He found it in bonuses—those outrageous bonuses and perks that AIG was doling out even as the government was giving it tens of billions to keep it alive.

The details were shocking. Days after the federal government had committed $85 billion to AIG from its newly christened Troubled Asset Relief Program (TARP), AIG had sent seventy "top performers" on a junket to the St. Regis resort at Dana Point, California, at an overall cost of $440,000, including a $23,000 bill from the spa. A partridge hunt in England for other AIGers had cost the company about $90,000, not including $17,000 for the private jet.

In early October, Andrew summoned the new CEO of AIG, Edward Liddy, to demand an immediate end to junkets. His authority for this was hazy, but the optics for AIG were just horrendous. Liddy readily agreed, and a slew of upcoming junkets was scratched.

This, Andrew soon learned, was chump change. AIG's previous CEO, Martin Sullivan, had left the previous June with a golden parachute that included a $5 million bonus, $15 million in severance, and other benefits that brought his package up to $47 million. This, after presiding over quarter after quarter of multi-billion-dollar losses. More egregious was the departure earlier in the year of Joseph Cassano, the crowing overseer of AIG's credit default swaps. He had left with a $34 million bonus, a $1 million per month consulting arrangement, and $69 million in deferred compensation and bonus pools.

On a crisp fall day in mid-October, Andrew called an outside press conference a block from the New York Stock Exchange to demand that AIG reel back these bonuses and other payments, or face legal action. The term of art was "clawbacks." Andrew wanted to claw back those ill-gotten gains.

Liddy agreed to halt planned bonuses to top executives from a $600 million fund, as well as $19 million in remaining payments to departed CEO Martin Sullivan. He wasn't sure about clawing back anything from Cassano. The no longer strutting head of AIG's credit default swap division was holed up beyond Liddy's reach—and Andrew's—in a three-story town house with a private garden on a bucolic square in London's Knightsbridge district. He hadn't volunteered to give any of his money back. Still, Andrew vowed to get it. "The days of extravagance, bonuses, stock options, those days are over," Andrew declared. "The taxpayers are now paying the bill and they're not going to pay for post-mortem parties."

These were bonuses already allocated. Worse were bonuses the banks seemed set on bestowing for 2008. The country's nine major banks were now fortified by all of those TARP billions; any bonuses they gave would in effect be federal bailout money, passed on to their employees. The bank denied it: no less than Goldman Sachs stiffly declared that bonuses would be paid from earnings, not TARP money. But that was absurd. Money was fungible.

In late October, Andrew fired off a trenchant letter to all nine of the major banks that had taken TARP money. He gave them a week to come up with detailed lists of what bonuses they planned to pay, and to whom. Andrew made his own feelings clear. As far as he could see, there shouldn't be *any* bonuses for banks so strapped they'd had to take bailouts.

Soon after his unexpected victory in November 2008, with the financial crisis hanging over his head, President-Elect Barack Obama made the surprise move of nominating for secretary of state his ex-rival Hillary Clinton. With that, a new race began for who would succeed her as New York's junior U.S. senator. Very much in the race, though never declared, was Andrew.

The race had an electorate of one: the governor. It was he who had the authority to fill unexpectedly vacated U.S. Senate seats. But the cheerfully indecisive David Paterson was open to opinions, and as he wryly put it, none of the likely prospects was shy. And so began a jockeying for his vote that pitted Andrew, among others, against a glamorous contender from out of the blue, Caroline Kennedy.

The race should have ended as soon as it started, when Governor Paterson, according to one source familiar with his thinking, privately offered the seat to Bobby Kennedy Jr. Kennedy was sorely tempted: it was, after all, the seat his father had held. But Kennedy's wife, Mary Richardson, was experiencing drastic mood swings, and Kennedy was wary of leaving the family's six children in her care while he traveled back and forth to Washington. "I'll tell you who you should ask," Bobby told the governor. "My sister Kerry." During her decades of human rights work, Kerry had become a strong public speaker. "The other person who might be interested," said Bobby, "is Caroline." If Paterson had chosen Kerry, he would have had a battle-tested Kennedy in the seat, to the acclaim of almost everyone except her former husband. But the thought of Caroline—daughter of the slain president—intrigued him more.

At fifty-one, Caroline had no political experience whatsoever. But that hadn't stopped Kennedys before. She did appear to have the new president's gratitude and affection for having penned a *New York Times* op-ed of strong support at a critical moment in his campaign. As friends and supporters quickly stepped up to note, she could use that access to get New York its due in political spoils. Anyway, she was a Kennedy, and a prominent one at that.

Publicly, Andrew declared he already had a job, and was happy doing it. Yet loyalists began a whisper campaign for a Senator Cuomo before Hillary was even formally offered secretary of state. Paterson and his aides were annoyed. "He's not being helpful," one terse aide put it.

Why Andrew would consider the job was a bit of a mystery. He was on a roll as attorney general, overseeing Wall Street at a critical time and getting more done than most U.S. senators. With Spitzer gone, his path to the governor's mansion seemed clear, and as he knew as well as anyone, the governors of most states, including New York, ran budgets and wielded far more power than U.S. senators.

"It wasn't necessarily the case that there would be an opening for governor," suggested one top political operative. Paterson still had the power of incumbency; he might just build a formidable lead. For Andrew, a U.S. Senate seat would be a new and attention-bringing challenge. "There are very few deck chairs on the highest level, and they change so infrequently," the operative noted. "So if you can't go up you go sideways."

There was perhaps another reason—a very personal one. Caroline was Andrew's former in-law, not only his cousin but a stalwart of the Kennedy clan. Six years after his separation from Kerry, there was still bad blood between the Kennedys and the Cuomos—enough that Kerry began saying publicly what a great choice Caroline would make. The last thing Andrew wanted was a Kennedy in the top tiers of New York's political world, eclipsing him with her Kennedy glamour. Better to thwart her by taking the job himself.

By December 1, Obama had formally tapped Hillary, and the whisper campaign intensified. Caroline set out on a tour of the upstate cities—Syracuse, Rochester, Buffalo—that any New York senator would have to know well. Asked if she had ever visited those cities before, her aides declined to answer. A flurry of calls from Andrew's top aide and enforcer, Joe Percoco, apparently preceded her. According to one report, Percoco told upstate officials and labor leaders not to throw their support to Caroline—though he did so coyly, without mentioning Caroline's name, or Andrew's. "Don't you think [the new U.S. senator] should be someone who understands upstate?" Percoco opined. "Don't you think it should be someone with experience?" As the recipient of one of those calls recounted later, "It was, 'I can't say he wants you to tell people he wants it, but you should, wink-wink, nudge-nudge, know that he kind of wants it.'"

Whether or not Percoco included the upstate newspapers on his call list, they greeted Caroline, as the *New York Times* put it, "like a cold front coming down from Lake Ontario." The *Rochester Democrat and Chronicle*'s editorial page bluntly compared Caroline to Andrew and said that on the "upstate barometer, between the two it's Cuomo hands down."

In person, accompanied by a media caravan, Caroline did nothing to thaw the upstaters. She seemed vague on issues, and disinclined to provide any details of her financial worth. She also had a bad case of teen speak, sprinkling her sentences with "you know"s and "um"s. Asked at one point how she regarded her apparent chief rival for the job, she replied, "I'm, you know, actually, Andrew Cuomo is someone I've known for many, many years, and we've talked, you know, throughout this process, so, you know, we have a really good relationship and I admire the work he's doing now and what he's done."

For all her gaffes, Caroline got the ink, and Andrew was marginalized, even as he took on a fat new target: Ezra Merkin, one of the feeders for just-exposed financial scoundrel Bernard Madoff. The lack of press interest frustrated him. "It's driving him crazy," one Andrew loyalist admitted. Andrew felt he'd made a tactical error in not coming right out for the job, rather than choosing discretion. What could he do now without looking mean-spirited? "He's boxed in," said the aide. "He can't do anything except fume, and he is fuming."

Caroline was doing her own quiet strategizing. Her uncle Senator Ted Kennedy was beloved by labor; calls went out to all the state union leaders arguing that Caroline was the inevitable choice and urging them to get on board now. When Paterson got wind of this latest move, he was as irked with Caroline's people as he was with Andrew's. He *hadn't* made a decision, he stressed, and while Caroline was a leading contender she wasn't a lock. She "has a tremendous relationship with the president, and that's certainly a plus," Paterson noted. "She does not have much legislative experience, which is a minus."

Paterson himself was in a box. If he chose Caroline, he would seem to have caved and made the expedient choice. By the state's election laws, Caroline would then have to run on her own in 2010, and again in 2012. Was she really capable of two grueling, back-to-back state campaigns? A loss would hurt the governor and possibly handicap him in his race for reelection. Andrew was the smarter choice, but there was a catch. By another of the state's election laws, Andrew's successor as AG would be chosen by the Assembly's Democratic majority leader, Sheldon Silver—not a great political ally of Paterson's. Andrew had just shown how wounding an attorney general could be to the governor. Paterson might face the same treatment from Andrew that Spitzer had received, but he actually felt comfortable with Andrew. He might not feel the same about an AG chosen by Silver. That would argue for keeping Andrew where he was. Caroline or Andrew? It was for Paterson an agonizing choice.

On January 20, as a newly inaugurated President Obama began grappling with how to save the economy, Paterson declared that he was ready, at last, to make his choice. The next afternoon, Hillary was sworn in as secretary of state. Concurrently, she resigned from the U.S. Senate. Paterson appeared about to choose Caroline when she called him with shocking news. She had decided to take her name out of the running.

Recent polls had shown Andrew to be a strong favorite over Caroline for the job. That may have jarred her, but so did a family crisis. The day before, Senator Ted Kennedy, already fighting brain cancer, had suffered a seizure and been hospitalized.

Paterson was stunned. Through the rest of the day, the governor's team held talks with Caroline's camp—talks described as frantic. Caroline wavered, but by that Wednesday evening she was firm. She told Paterson that she would at least do him the courtesy of letting him reject her the next morning, rather than having her make the public announcement and thus reject *him*.

At 11 p.m., Caroline called Paterson again, and he asked her not to withdraw, according to Caroline's camp. According to Paterson's camp, in that call she said she would stay in. The governor turned in early—he'd been up late at the inaugural parties the night before, one insider explained—and thus was asleep at midnight when Caroline decided to issue a statement to the media after all: she was bowing out of the race. Paterson was so angry reading the news the next day that someone on his staff called Col Allan, editor of the *New York Post*, and claimed that Caroline was lying and that in fact the governor had rejected *her* because of various personal issues. When the *Post* published the allegations, the Kennedy camp attacked them as lies, and by Friday morning, amid a barrage of claims and counterclaims, the governor was forced to back down.

"Andrew was in his office, around 11 a.m., he's watching it on TV," recalled a Cuomo acquaintance. "I'm in the office, I can see this is the greatest thing that ever happened to this guy. He's watching the dismemberment of the guy he wants to unseat."

For Andrew, it was the best possible outcome. No Kennedy to contend with, and a governor who had so bungled the Senate seat search that he was now widely viewed as inept.

Throughout this strange political chapter, the governor had been under relentless pressure to name a woman to the seat. Now he turned to a dark horse, Kirsten Gillibrand, a U.S. congresswoman whose district included at that time much of the Hudson Valley and Albany. Gillibrand would prove a highly competent senator—ironically, a very good choice. But Andrew had moved on. He had the governor firmly in his sights now. There could be no weaker incumbent than David Paterson at the end of the Caroline Kennedy debacle—and no stronger rival to take him on.

CHAPTER 19

Man of the People

Andrew and his top investigators had searched high and low for a legal rationale to block year-end bonuses at all the big banks. The TARP money changed everything, they felt. If a bank or firm was getting federal bailout money, it had new obligations. Andrew came up with the creative argument that as AG, he might have the right to sue the banks for fraud if they misspent taxpayers' money—on bonuses, for example. The legal term was "fraudulent conveyance."

Privately, Andrew had to admit fraudulent conveyance was a stretch. But this wasn't about going to trial. All Andrew needed was a justification to try the banks in the court of public opinion. The public was out for blood.

In early December 2008, a new bonus outrage bubbled up, tied to Bank of America's imminent $50 billion acquisition of Merrill Lynch. Bank of America's Ken Lewis was buying a pig in a poke: Merrill's losses, already epic, were ballooning in the fourth quarter of 2008. Overall, Merrill would lose $27 billion for the year. Yet Merrill's CEO, John Thain, had decided to bestow $3.57 billion in year-end bonuses, mostly to his senior officers. Bank of America's shareholders would take that hit.

When all this came to light in January 2009, Andrew hauled in Lewis and Thain for interviews of four and six hours respectively. The more Andrew's investigators dug, the murkier the story became. Basically, Ken Lewis had tried to back out of the Merrill deal at the last minute, only to have his feet held to the fire by the federal government. Bad as the merger might be, the feds reasoned, letting Merrill collapse like Lehman Brothers would be worse. For the sake of the global economy, Bank of America was forced to go through with the deal.

Eventually Andrew would file a fraud suit against Bank of America, charging that Ken Lewis and others had hidden more than $16 billion in losses from shareholders to close the deal with Merrill. The suit would drag on until March 2014, when the bank and Lewis agreed to settle. Lewis would pay $10 million and be barred for three years from serving as an officer or director of a public company. Bank of America would pay $15 million and agree to enact corporate reforms. The two parties would also pay the state's legal costs. They would pay no damages, however, and admit to no wrongdoing. It was an all too typical case of how Wall Street outrages tended to peter out in lengthy trials—and why Andrew's "code of conduct" approach, though mocked by his predecessor, had something to be said for it.

By February 2009, Andrew had shamed most of the banks that had taken TARP money into slashing bonuses. Overall, the big banks' bonus pool for 2008 would drop from $32.9 billion to $18.4 billion. It was still too much, in Andrew's opinion: zero seemed like the right number to him. Contractual agreements limited his options. He could, however, demand the names of the biggest bonus earners and disclose them: punishment in the public square.

Ben Lawsky spent Friday, March 13, 2009, in court trying to persuade a judge that Bank of America should release the names of its own biggest bonus earners, including those formerly with Merrill who'd carved up the $3.57 billion that Thain had sent their way. That night at around 9 p.m., Lawsky was drinking with colleagues at the bar of Bobby Van's, a steakhouse near the office, when he got a BlackBerry message that made him realize he had taken his eye off the ball. The ball was AIG.

AIG had just mailed out $165 million in payments for a "retention plan." These were bonuses by another name, given on the rationale that AIG could only retain its top performers by essentially bribing them to stay. This was a nasty surprise from a firm that had seemed willing to make amends. Its CEO, Edward Liddy, had agreed to freeze that $600 million in regular bonuses and deferred compensation. Now it appeared he was raiding the kitty after all, just changing "bonus" to "retention payment." Worse, Lawsky learned, the U.S. Treasury and Federal Reserve had approved the retention payments. Once again, the feds had their own agenda.

Andrew had Lawsky demand the names of all those new bonus recipients. AIG responded with a list of numbers but no names. Andrew turned up the pressure by sending a letter with the numbers to Congressman Barney Frank, Democrat of Massachusetts, chairman of the House Committee on Financial Services. At a formal meeting the next day, Frank read the numbers aloud. The biggest retention payment was $6.4 million, the next six recipients received more than $4 million each, and so it went:

in all, it was quite a piece of political theater. Embarrassed, AIG meekly relayed to Andrew the names of its "retention plan" recipients.

So outraged was the public now—from President Obama on down—that Andrew could have riveted the country by naming those names. But that very phrase—*naming names*—gave him pause. Senator Joe McCarthy had made himself a demagogue for the ages by naming names. If what Andrew wanted was to claw back the retention payments and get banks to rethink their bonus systems, perhaps it was better to withhold those names and give AIG's top performers a chance to do the right thing by sending their bonuses back.

That Friday, March 20, Andrew told AIG that its top retention-payment earners had the weekend to decide whether to comply. On Monday, nine of AIG's top ten bonus recipients, along with fifteen others, agreed to give back their retention payments, $50 million in all. As promised, Andrew slid the names in a drawer: he would no longer threaten to release them, or any others.

The rest of AIG's high earners had no intention of returning their retention payments: $115 million in all. Most of that balance, about $85 million, went to employees outside the United States. "We have a very aggressive theory about our jurisdiction," Andrew said, "but we don't have a theory that gets us to London." London was where AIG's financial products division was based. Roughly seventy employees of the division had received $1 million each. For the same reason, Joseph Cassano, the London-based overseer of AIG's credit default swaps, would get his $69 million in deferred compensation and bonuses.

The $50 million that would be clawed back was not insignificant. Whether it had any effect on how AIG and other banks paid their bonuses was harder to discern. The bonus season of 2014 would look an awful lot like 2008. "Did anything get changed about the way bonuses were paid?" echoed one of Andrew's investigators. "It's a great philosophical question. I'm not sure."

Andrew was on firmer ground with the pay-to-play games of the state pension fund than with Wall Street bonuses. Bonuses after the meltdown were egregious, but legal. Pension fund kickbacks were a crime.

For two years, the AG's office had used its subpoena power under the 1921 Martin Act—the cudgel that Spitzer as AG had unearthed to whack financial fraud—to follow the money from the state pension fund. Ellen Biben and Linda Lacewell had connected a lot of dots. Clearly, Alan Hevesi's longtime political guru Hank Morris had set himself up as the gatekeeper and taken extra millions of dollars in outsized fees. The case remained a challenge, however. Lacewell and Biben needed a higher-level storyteller than the Peggy Lipton–beguiled Jack Chartier. They found one in David Loglisci, the fund's chief investment officer.

Loglisci was a smart young guy in a position to know who had made what promises to whom, and why. The odd thing about him was that he himself seemed not to have profited. Hank Morris was bossing Loglisci around, telling him what investments to make and squirreling away his millions; Loglisci, as far as the lawyers could tell, was putting through all the deals without getting a cut. "Where's his benefit?" was how Andrew kept putting it to Biben and Lacewell.

The benefit turned out to involve Loglisci's brother Steve, who had tried for some years to finish and market a comic film he called *Chooch*. The film's story involved Mexican prostitutes and a nine-pound dachshund named Kiwi Limone. David Loglisci had tried to be helpful by having a few of the pension fund suitors help underwrite *Chooch*. In all, the firms had contributed $288,841 to the film, which starred unknown actors and was so terrible that when the comptroller's staff organized a pizza party to screen it, they couldn't sit through it to the end. When Andrew announced a 123-count indictment for the whole pay-to-play scheme on March 19, 2009, Loglisci was named as a defendant, along with Hank Morris.

The indictment hit the news the same week that Andrew was clawing back bonuses from AIG. Together, the two stories made for Andrew's finest turn in public life to date. An admiring if wry profile in the *New York Times* conceded that Andrew had "found his moment like few politicians in the United States." As AG, he had "given voice to disgust with the abuses and self-regard within the nation's financial industry." With the "muscular" use of his office, he had "sent his subpoenas to those in plush offices, and dragged out the names of bonus recipients from American International Group and Merrill Lynch, to loud applause from many voters." Questions of whether all this might lead to another gubernatorial run were duly waved off. But as the profile noted, Andrew was certainly doing all an aspirant needed to do. "No fund-raiser is too parochial, from Buffalo to the Bronx. He purrs into phones with legislative leaders and chest bumps with assemblymen."

By mid-April, the bonus story was old news: quietly the banks could start putting aside beans for next year's bonuses, when, absent public outrage, they could be bigger again. The pension fund scandal, however, had ramped up. One company after another, confronted by evidence that their dealings with Morris and Hevesi amounted to kickbacks, settled for millions, including the powerful Carlyle Group.

Of all the financiers contacted by Andrew's office, only one refused to acknowledge any wrongdoing. The 123-count indictment seemed to faze him not at all.

Steven Rattner was a cofounder and managing principal of the Quadrangle Group, a private equity investment firm. He had begun his career as a reporter for the *New York Times*, only to realize he was at least as smart as the financial figures he was interviewing. To the enduring envy of his journalistic colleagues, he had left to become an investment banker, first at Lehman Brothers, then at Morgan Stanley, then at Lazard Frères & Co., where he had become deputy chairman and deputy chief executive officer before striking out on his own. He now managed Mayor Michael Bloomberg's billions, among others.

Along with Bloomberg, Rattner counted among his closest friends *New York Times* publisher Arthur Ochs Sulzberger Jr., with whom he reportedly exercised in a basement gym early every morning. Rattner and his wife, Maureen White, lived in a baronial Fifth Avenue apartment, where they gave frequent Democratic fund-raisers. By February 2009, Rattner was spending a lot of his time in Washington, as President Obama's so-called car czar, doing the ruthless financial engineering to save General Motors and Chrysler from bankruptcy. He was, in short, a powerful man with friends in very high places.

Rattner had met with Andrew once, in the late 1990s, at the then HUD secretary's dining room, and found the experience distasteful. Andrew wasn't yet running for governor, but he was clearly cultivating Rattner for a big future campaign contribution. Some months later he ran into Rattner at a social event. "We should go out and have a bottle of wine, just the two of us," he said. Rattner was used to being hit up for money by ambitious Democrats, but there was something about Andrew that put him off. He gave no money to Andrew's first campaign in 2002, nor to his run for AG in 2006.

Rattner had hired Hank Morris as a placement agent, and Morris had done well, wangling $150 million of pension fund money for Quadrangle to manage. When the AG's office asked him to come in and talk about it in 2007, Rattner was happy to comply. He answered questions about David Loglisci and *Chooch*, stressing that he had helped Loglisci's brother get a distribution deal as a favor, not as a quid pro quo for pension business. He said as much before a grand jury, and won immunity in return. Two years later, Rattner was down in Washington, D.C., trying to save the auto industry, when his partners at Quadrangle found themselves under renewed scrutiny for the firm's pension fund dealings. The documents Quadrangle turned over—particularly the e-mail chains—offered a very different version of Rattner's *Chooch* dealings.

A self-taught whiz of a mechanic, Andrew could—and still can—diagnose a car's problems by sound alone. *Jim Garrett*/New York Daily News/*Getty Images*

The Cuomos of Queens, 1977. From top: Matilda, Mario, Margaret (below her mother), Maria, Madeline, and Chris, with Andrew in foreground. *Jim Garrett*/New York Daily News/*Getty Images*

Mario and his winning campaign manager in the 1982 governor's race. *William Sauro*/New York Times/*Redux*

Father and son going one-on-one at the governor's mansion in 1983. New York Times/*Redux*

Andrew's 1990 wedding to Kerry Kennedy sparked a new media moniker: Cuomolot. *Corbis/AP*

The twins, born January 11, 1995, were named after the matriarchs on both sides: Cara Ethel and Mariah Matilda. Michaela was born two years later. *Brian Diggs/AP*

Andrew with Vice President Al Gore in 2000: two policy wonks in a pod. *Mike Segar/Reuters/Newscom*

"Andrew could be anything he wanted to be in American politics." —HENRY CISNEROS

Andrew Cuomo's Quest for Camelot

He has the passion and the pedigree to be the next governor of New York. For Andrew Cuomo, politics is a love affair.

By Abigail Pogrebin
Photo by Oliviero Toscani

IN AN AIRY CORNER OFFICE, BEHIND AN UNcluttered desk, former New York governor Mario Cuomo is drinking hot chocolate and reflecting on his eldest son Andrew's run for his old job. It's a loaded proposition: Andrew helped his father win the seat no fewer than three times, and—if Andrew wins the Democratic nomination—he'll be facing the same man who prevented his father from serving a fourth term in 1994, New York's sitting governor, Republican George Pataki. "I'm just guessing that Andrew learned a lot from watching me," the former governor says. "But he learned a lot more about what not to do than what to do. I was not a good politician. I was not prepared for it. I didn't behave well. I didn't see the people I should have seen. I didn't try to construct relationships with people."

Regret and ambivalence are recurring chords in Mario Cuomo's life: not making more money, not spending enough time with his children ("I wasn't there as much as I should have been," he admits), not running for president, not accepting a Supreme Court appointment. It's in the diaries he published and in his thoughts today. "I think Andrew probably suspects that I should have been bolder in making my decisions," Cuomo continues. "Just generally in life, that I should have taken more risks.... And he may—although we have not talked about it—he may be saying to himself, 'I'm not going to make the mistakes he did. I'm going to be bolder and more assertive.' It may be so." ▸

AUGUST2001 talk 61

Cuomolot seemed secure during Andrew's first gubernatorial run in 2002. It wasn't. *Courtesy Oliviero Toscani/*Talk *magazine*

Amid plummeting poll numbers, Andrew abandoned the governor's race in September 2002.
Beth Keiser/AP

Andrew's marriage to Kerry exploded in a tabloid fireball in early July 2003.
Patrick Andrade/AP

In his 2006 race for attorney general, Andrew blamed Eliot Spitzer for not supporting him sooner; Hillary Clinton made a pro forma appearance. *Henry Ray Abrams/AP*

The doting single father—and new attorney general—with his twins and Michaela in 2007. *Enid Alvarez*/New York Daily News/*Getty Images*

Andrew's first oath of office as governor on New Year's Day 2011, with Sandra Lee. *Mike Groll/AP*

A victory lap after passage of New York's marriage equality act of June 2011. *Jemal Countess/Getty Images*

Andrew managed to get the president to come to him—not vice versa. *Pablo Monsivais/AP*

Former president Bill Clinton with Andrew at Ed Koch's 2013 funeral. Until his death, the former mayor believed the Cuomos had smeared him in 1977 with homophobic posters. *Spencer Platt/Getty Images*

The governor and his daughters courting support in Buffalo in 2013; for all the public money he showered on western voters, they spurned him the next year. *Jason Reed/ Reuters/Newscom*

Outgoing New York City mayor Michael Bloomberg, Sandra Lee and the governor, and President Bill and Hillary Clinton at the January 2014 swearing-in of new mayor Bill de Blasio (not pictured). Smiles mask a complex web of contradictory feelings and alliances among the group. *Anthony Behar/SIPA/AP*

Andrew and Sandra celebrate a desultory reelection win in November 2014; Andrew spent $23 million to beat an all-but-unknown foe. *Kathy Willens/AP*

"We look at the e-mails," recounted one of Andrew's senior staffers. "It becomes pretty clear that those e-mails really corroborate a version of events that is more than mildly inconsistent with what Rattner's position has been." One in particular urged the CEO of the Quadrangle subsidiary to treat Steve Loglisci and his movie project carefully, because Quadrangle was trying to get pension fund money to manage from Loglisci's brother. "As for Steve Loglisci," Rattner wrote, "I would appreciate it if you could dance along with this for another couple of weeks while I try to figure out what we need to do." Rattner went so far as to ask Hank Morris if the pension fund deal hinged on getting distribution for *Chooch*.

From the start, Andrew had viewed Rattner as just the sort of Manhattan rich guy he'd learned from his father to detest: snobbish, entitled, looking down his nose at the Cuomos from Queens. Andrew didn't care that the Rattners were big Democratic donors—not at this stage in his career. From the new e-mails, he felt sure that Rattner had knowingly misled his investigators. If so, Andrew had him on securities fraud and perjury, and neither the mayor of New York nor the publisher of the *New York Times* would deter him from filing those charges.

Until June 8, 2009, Andrew said nothing publicly about David Paterson, the governor he was hoping to replace. Then came the Senate uprising of that day. So ham-handed was the governor's response that Andrew felt he had no choice but to weigh in.

Unnoticed by most of America, perhaps, the previous election season had brought, along with America's first black president, a change in the majority of the New York state senate. Down 30–32, the Democrats had gained two seats—one thanks to political hardball by then governor Spitzer, the other from Republican majority leader Joe Bruno's decision to step down. They were on top, 32–30, and sailed that way through the legislative session of 2009—until that June day when the Republicans pulled a fast one of their own. They lured two Democrats across the aisle—making one of them, Pedro Espada Jr., Senate president. A week later, the other one, Hiram Monserrate, was persuaded by his former party to cross *back*. Now the Senate was deadlocked at 31–31, and with both sides in high dudgeon, its work came to a halt.

Procedurally, the lieutenant governor would cast the deciding vote. Except there *was* no lieutenant governor: that was the seat Paterson had vacated in order to become governor, and vacant it remained. On July 9, 2009, Espada also returned to his party, awarded for his treason with the title of Senate majority leader, and so the crisis eased. Clearly, though, a lieutenant governor was needed—not just to cast a critical vote but to keep Espada from seizing the governorship on a technicality if Paterson left the state. That was how crazy things were.

The governor started looking for one to appoint. Upon which Andrew, as attorney general, warned the governor that this was illegal. Paterson went ahead anyway, naming Richard Ravitch to the post.

Ravitch was a wise old bear of New York politics, gruff and gravel-voiced, who had often jumped from his family's real estate business to one government post or another, and in the process earned respect as an astute budget cruncher. He seemed a perfect choice to help guide the state back to financial health. There was one blot on his résumé: Mario had taken a dislike to him back in the 1980s, for reasons he never revealed, and fired him as head of the Metropolitan Transit Authority. Once banished, always blamed. Andrew vowed to block the appointment.

Andrew based his objection not on family history—so he said—but on constitutional grounds. The state constitution called for the governor and lieutenant governor to be elected at the same time—by the voters. For Paterson as governor to fill the seat on his own would be, Andrew argued, "a political ploy that would wind through the courts for many months," contested inevitably by the party not in power. On the merits, he might be right. But the state was awash in red ink, its Senate paralyzed. Why not have Ravitch serve on an interim basis and help the government get back on track, then stage a special election for lieutenant governor?

For an AG eyeing a run for governor the next year, that was a plan that might backfire. Maybe Ravitch would run for governor himself. True, he was seventy-six years old, his ambitions of elected office seemingly behind him. But Andrew was leaving nothing to chance. Better to keep the lieutenant governor's seat open. The vacancy would keep the governor off balance and remind everyone how inept he was.

When the inevitable suit contesting Ravitch's appointment did come, filed by the Republicans, it went up to the state-high Court of Appeals. The vote was close—four to three—but the majority was unequivocal: of course the governor had a right to fill a vacancy so vital to the operation of the state. The drafters of the state's constitution would never have envisioned leaving the seat unfilled for such a long time.

Taking up his duties at last, Ravitch fired off a series of budget proposals to help the listing ship of state. Andrew opposed them all. As attorney general, his opposition might seem irrelevant. It wasn't, for by the fall of 2009, Andrew was acting less like an attorney general than a governor in waiting.

The Senate uprising wasn't Paterson's fault. It was the work of two greedy lawmakers, Pedro Espada Jr. and Hiram Monserrate, the one under investigation by Andrew for embezzlement, the other indicted for violently assaulting a girlfriend. Both would soon be found guilty as charged. Paterson had simply failed to quell the revolt, adding to the image of a feckless leader. As his poll numbers plummeted, the prospect of his running for a full term as governor in 2010 seemed unrealistic at best. Undaunted, he insisted that that was exactly what he intended to do.

Andrew could hardly demand that the governor change his mind. But he could have his loyalists work the phones, and that they did. "The Cuomo play is both pushing him and coaxing him out of the race through fear or otherwise," a Paterson ally explained at the time. "The governor has been the recipient of a fairly continuous, concerted effort to undermine him, to keep him on the ropes, to keep his poll numbers down." The grapevine reverberated with talk of a *New York Times* article that would blow the lid on Paterson's personal life and peccadilloes. The story never appeared. "Whether Andrew created it or not I don't know," said another Paterson aide. "Whether he fanned the flames—sure."

In mid-September, Andrew gained a powerful ally in his quest: the president of the United States. On the eve of a presidential trip to the state in mid-September, the White House political director, Patrick Gaspard, conveyed a blunt message to Paterson. The president wanted the governor to abandon his campaign for reelection. Paterson's certain loss threatened to pull other Democrats down and weaken the party's hold on the state. Rumors that Republican ex-mayor Rudy Giuliani was contemplating a run for governor made the problem more urgent.

Paterson was still reeling the next day when President Obama alighted from Air Force One in Albany. Paterson, as governor, was there on the tarmac to greet him, but after an awkward half hug, Obama turned away and headed off for his day trip in a group that included Gaspard...and Andrew.

To Albany's press corps, this riveting act of political theater begged an obvious question. What role had Andrew played, if any, in getting the White House to nudge Paterson? One former aide to Paterson noted Andrew's multiple ties with Gaspard: through the Clintons, through Obama, also through 1199, the health care workers' union where Gaspard had succeeded Jennifer Cunningham as the union's political strategist. Cunningham, of course, had been Andrew's political Svengali for the AG campaign. "It was definitely worked on in tandem."

To almost everyone's surprise, Paterson refused to heed his president's wish. He was running, he declared; he intended to win.

Tensions between Rattner and the AG's office were growing. The prosecutors now felt that Rattner had lied to them when they interviewed him in 2007; they felt he had lied to the grand jury as well, downplaying his role and motivation in helping the producers of *Chooch*. As far as the prosecutors were concerned, Rattner had only helped in order to win a chunk of state pension fund money to manage.

Rattner had a very different take. Back in 2008, he had instructed his then legal team to turn over all relevant documents. They did that, so they said, but somehow their data dump failed to include the e-mail chain so illuminating to the side story of Rattner and *Chooch*.

Rattner found the whole situation Kafkaesque. He hadn't known exactly what his first lawyers withheld, he told Linda Lacewell. So how could he be guilty of perjury, as she now charged, for misrepresenting information in the withheld documents? Lacewell was adamant, contending that Rattner had knowingly misled the AG's team. They were going to get him, and no settlement was even possible. He would have to plead guilty to a felony or misdemeanor—a criminal charge. He was going to jail.

Rattner's new lawyers saw no point in having him cooperate any longer. The investigators would just pounce on any small, unintended nuance to help make their case. When the two sides next faced each other, Rattner pleaded the Fifth—sixty-eight times. He knew that this too, would be used against him, but he saw no other way to go.

Through that fall of 2009, the threats escalated. The U.S. Securities and Exchange Commission was now conducting its own investigation. Rattner was warned that if he didn't plead guilty, he would be jailed—by the AG—and pay a huge fine to the SEC as well.

That October, Ray Harding pleaded guilty to steering a state assembly seat to Alan Hevesi's son Andrew and taking money in return, another piece in the pension fund puzzle. Facing four years in jail, he told investigators all he knew. "That's a major development for us," Andrew declared, enough, he said, for Harding to merit probation instead of hard time.

Sympathy wasn't Andrew's default mode, but he just couldn't put Ray Harding in jail. At his sentencing in 2011, on a single misdemeanor count, Harding was spared jail time and allowed to keep the money that Hank Morris and Alan Hevesi had steered his way. A year later he was dead.

Andrew had tried nudging David Paterson to abandon the governor's race. Now it was time for a hard shove or two.

In late October, Paterson went to Yankee Stadium with four others for the opening game of the World Series. Within days, the *New York Post*'s Fred Dicker came out with a sizzling story that Paterson had gotten the tickets, each with a face value of $425, at no cost. A spokesman for the governor first said the tickets had been a gift from Yankees president Randy Levine. "He's a liar," said Levine of Paterson. "I never talked to him."

Paterson's personal aide David Johnson, it turned out, had procured the tickets by demanding them from the Yankees. Free tickets weren't illegal per se, but the Yankees were registered to lobby the state in regard to their new stadium. That meant the free tickets violated the state's gift ban. Andrew jumped on the story. According to one Paterson aide, he gave the governor stern legal advice. "Andrew told David that he should step aside or risk legal damage."

Again Paterson stood firm. Embarrassing as the ticket flap was, he was still running for election.

The incident that finally brought Paterson down needed no piling on from Andrew, though once again he offered stern counsel. David Johnson, the aide implicated in the Yankee tickets business, had visited a girlfriend the previous Halloween and gotten into an altercation, one so bad that the girlfriend had sought an order of protection. Right before the hearing where she planned to seek a final protective order, the girlfriend got a call from the governor himself. Whatever he told her, she chose not to appear at the hearing, and the case was dismissed.

It now appeared that the governor of New York had engaged in witness tampering, as well as intimidating a victim of domestic violence. When the news broke, Paterson did what he should have done in the first place: he suspended Johnson without pay and asked Andrew, as attorney general, to look into allegations that the state police had made harassing calls to the girlfriend, warning her to drop the case. The only question now for Paterson was not whether he should abandon the governor's race, but when.

Andrew was still undeclared. Unofficially, though, he was doing everything in his power to clear the path for his imminent candidacy. That included working the phones with anyone who might help talk Paterson into doing the right thing. One was Ravi Batra, an Indian-American lawyer who had strong ties with the black establishment. Batra was flattered to find, in the attorney general, a new friend to schmooze with about the beleaguered governor. "I remember calling Andrew at midnight on his cell, just saying I had had a very long and tiring day." That was how close the two had become. "The day David got out, that ended," Batra said with a rueful laugh. "And I have discovered from many of his aides and abettors the same scenario. I was useful to him as long as I was hurting David. After that, he didn't need me."

At last even Paterson's closest aides converged in his Manhattan office to tell him the jig was up. Paterson seemed relieved at letting the governor's race go. To those who had called on him to quit right away, he was unyielding. He would serve out his term, he vowed, and in that period would find a saving grace, setting policies without worrying about their political costs.

Andrew was amazed. Until the announcement, he had felt sure Paterson would ignore all advice, including his own, and stagger through the campaign. Weakened as he was, Paterson would still stir memories of the nasty Andrew who had shortchanged Carl McCall. Having Paterson out was a huge boon. Andrew, it seemed, had just locked up the governor's race without even entering it.

Now all he had to do was keep from blurting a coat-holder comment—and remember to smile. Against a bellicose, no-holds-barred opponent, neither would be easy.

CHAPTER 20

Going for Governor

To the surprise of no one, Andrew announced on May 22, 2010, that he was a candidate for governor. He had no Democratic challengers and a war chest of at least $16 million, already more than most state office incumbents in America commanded. Using the infamous Tweed Courthouse in Manhattan as his backdrop, he vowed to root out corruption in Albany. Lobbyists, special interest groups, politicians of both parties—all would come under his withering scrutiny. Fiscally, he would fight for a property tax cap and balance the state budget with no new taxes. Transparency would be his watchword. As for redistricting, that hoary process that would unfold in 2012, as it did every decade, Andrew pledged to be the first governor of New York to see it done equitably. No more gerrymandering by incumbents—especially Republicans, who in a state as true-blue as New York desperately needed to draw those district lines to their advantage in order to stay in power. More than anything, Andrew would preside over a government that knew how to create new jobs.

To journalists old enough to remember the Mario years, there was a striking irony to Andrew's campaign pledges. In many respects, Andrew was running against his father's record and the government his father had made. He said New York was overtaxed; who was more to blame for that than Mario? He railed against late and bloated budgets; Mario had had more than a few of those. Mario, the anti–capital punishment candidate, had built scores of prisons around the state; now they were a drain on the budget, and Andrew resolved to close many of them. As for the jobs Andrew hoped to create, the upstate cities had staggered with rampant unemployment and abject poverty through Mario's last terms, so hard hit they'd missed the whole bull market that followed. Whatever Andrew did to help them, it would have to be the opposite of what his father had done.

At the head of the list of Andrew's powerful supporters was, not surprisingly, the health care workers' union, 1199. Union chief Dennis Rivera's early endorsement in 2006 had put the wind at Andrew's back for attorney general. Fourteen months before declaring for governor, Andrew had given the keynote speech for the New York State Black, Puerto Rican, Hispanic and Asian Legislative Caucus, and spotted 1199's new political director, Kevin Finnegan, in one of the front rows. Finnegan was the one who had worked for Andrew in 2002 and grown so disgusted with how the campaign was handled that he'd quit not once but twice. Perhaps he needed some courting. That night, Andrew delivered his entire speech looking intensely—and only—at Finnegan. "It was really weird," Finnegan later recalled with a laugh. "He told me two years later, 'You know, I gave that speech looking at you the whole time.'"

There was no reason to fear: Andrew got his nod from 1199 early on. But so, to his consternation, did one of the nominees running to replace him as attorney general. "Eric Schneiderman?" he echoed. "Eric Schneiderman?"

Andrew summoned Finnegan to his AG's office. "He yelled at me for forty-five minutes," Finnegan recalled. "Never did the tone go to normal." In the room was Andrew's enforcer, Joe Percoco, who looked about ready to whip out a shillelagh.

"This hurts me," Andrew ranted. "You want me to be governor, this undermines everything you want me to do."

"Andrew, we think you're going to be the greatest governor," Finnegan said, "but we need to support Eric."

"I want George Gresham here," Andrew fumed.

The next week Finnegan brought Gresham, the new president of 1199, for a second meeting at Andrew's office. Again Andrew vented. Gresham heard him out and promised to think it over. A week later Finnegan called to say that 1199 was backing Schneiderman, and that was that. For weeks afterward, Andrew turned his head whenever he saw Finnegan, which was often, since Finnegan was leading so many rallies on Andrew's behalf. Only with time did the sight of all those health care workers in their 1199 purple shirts—the workers mobilized *for* Andrew, *by* Finnegan—appear to mollify him.

What was it about Schneiderman with Andrew? There were various theories, every one of which offered a window into the complex psyche of Andrew Mark Cuomo.

As a New York state senator with a district that stretched from Manhattan's Upper West Side into the Bronx, first elected in 1998, Schneiderman had doubtless irked the Cuomo clan by backing Carl McCall in 2002. By this most obvious theory, Andrew nursed a political grudge and wanted payback. But to be that angry still at a state senator for his eight-year-old endorsement of a rival seemed extreme even for the Cuomos.

More plausibly, Andrew bridled at the prospect of a strong-willed, independent attorney general taking his place—an attorney general like him. Better than anyone, he knew what a vigorous AG could do to a governor, while purporting to serve him: a shiv to the soft underbelly was one metaphor that came to mind.

"He knew that Eric might not be that controllable," suggested one political operative. "And maybe he didn't want another white male liberal, though that would be the least nefarious assumption."

But of course, it could have been personal too. Schneiderman was Cunningham's ex, the other man in the troika, even if his relationship with her had long cooled into coparenting and political campaigning. Back in 2005 and 2006, when she'd managed Andrew's AG campaign, Cunningham had helped guide Schneiderman's reelection campaign for state senate too. Andrew brooked no rivals, personally or politically. He wanted Schneiderman *gone*.

Perhaps, as one friend of Schneiderman's suggested, there was another aspect to the relationship: that old outer-borough resentment of Manhattan money and class. Schneiderman had grown up on the Upper West Side, his father a partner at the Wall Street firm of Cahill Gordon & Reindel—the kind of firm that would have rejected a young Mario, and Andrew too, if he'd applied. A progressive Jew of the Upper West Side mold, the father had been a key backer of WNYC, City Opera, and NARAL. Andrew from his early years had Jewish friends; some of his closest advisers were Jewish, including Howard Glaser, a cohort that Larry Schwartz would soon join. "But these aren't German Jews," a political insider noted. He was referring to a stereotypical view that German Jews tended to be more affluent and sophisticated than Jews from, say, Russia. The Sulzbergers were German Jews. So were the Schneidermans. Eric attended the private Trinity School, then Amherst, then Harvard Law School. That was what the children of upper-middle-class progressive German Jews on the Upper West Side did. To judge by those he surrounded himself with, Andrew was more comfortable with people who came "from the bottom up," as one of his top gubernatorial aides would put it with a laugh. "Working-class toughs."

Andrew had no primary rival, so he could save most of his $16 million and spend his time handing out voluminous policy papers, telling journalists when they asked about one issue or another to go off and read the books. With that kind of war chest, he also had no need to grovel before the unions and real estate pashas who normally financed a gubernatorial run. As a result, he had no vested interests to serve—a good thing. All of this made for just the sort of primary season Andrew liked—soporific—in all respects but one: Bill Samuels's quixotic race for lieutenant governor.

Samuels, like Andrew, was the son of a charismatic New York Democrat, though his own father, Howard, had entered politics after earning a fortune inventing such kitchen staples as the Baggie and Hefty garbage bags. Howard Samuels's 1974 run for governor was the one in which Mario Cuomo ran as lieutenant governor; both lost in the primary. His son Bill had built a software company, but politics was his passion. On the state level, Bill Samuels had just helped the Democrats regain the Senate, only to see Pedro Espada hijack his dreams of a liberal Democratic agenda. Partly out of passion, partly guilt, Samuels had decided at sixty-seven that he would run for lieutenant governor—unaligned with Andrew or anyone else—to help push Espada out and make a Democratic Senate majority do the things he knew it could do.

Samuels was the first to admit that the campaign was a ploy. He had no interest in being Cuomo's lieutenant governor. He just wanted to oust Espada and elect up to four more Democrats. He would commit $500,000 of his own money to the plan, but he wanted Andrew to pony up a chunk too, from that $16 million.

There was a gray area here, since Andrew as AG had just charged Espada on various counts of self-dealing. But if the dapper little fraudster was still clinging to his post as Senate majority leader, why shouldn't Andrew as a candidate take him on? So ensued the first of six meetings between Samuels and a changing cast of Cuomo insiders, graduating up to a deal memo meeting with Joe Percoco, the enforcer, on June 1, 2010.

Samuels confirmed that he would give up his fledgling campaign to be lieutenant governor, freeing Andrew to run with a candidate of his choice. In return, Samuels and the Cuomo team would do all they could together to oust Espada from his seat in the primary that September and replace him with an honest man. In the general election, they would work to protect four endangered Democrats, assuring a clear Democratic majority in the Senate. Then change in all its overdue forms could come, starting with campaign finance reform and fair redistricting, both of which the Republicans had kept under lock and key as long as anyone could remember. Samuels would spend his $500,000 in the primary; Andrew would then give at least $1 million of his $16 million war chest to New Roosevelt, Samuels's new progressive think tank, to help reelect those other Democrats.

"I want Cuomo to be not just another governor, but a great governor," Samuels told Percoco. The enforcer nodded, and stepped outside to call Andrew with the terms. When he came back, he said the deal was done, though he seemed more interested in what Samuels really wanted for his $500,000. A role on the transition team? No, Samuels said, he had no interest in handing out patronage jobs. Cochair of the gubernatorial campaign? Samuels hesitated. Yes, he said, sure, why not.

With the agreement notched and on paper, Samuels publicly gave up his campaign on June 5 in front of Pedro Espada's house in Westchester, pledging to do all he could to unseat him. That September, Espada lost the primary, in no small part due to the field operation that Samuels funded in the Bronx to support a challenger.

Thrilled, Samuels now waited for the call from Percoco naming him cochair of the Cuomo campaign. He waited for the $1 million to flow from the Cuomo campaign coffers to New Roosevelt for those four senatorial campaigns. He waited, and he waited, and heard exactly nothing from the Cuomo campaign. That November, without Cuomo's $1 million to help tip the scales, the Republicans would win back their majority. To Samuels, it would be clear that Andrew, for his own political reasons, had let them win, breaking, in the process, his written promise to Samuels.

Without a primary rival, Andrew worked the kind of campaign he liked best: of the Rose Garden variety. He gave interviews by conference phone, unseen and remote—very Wizard of Oz, as one reporter put it. Those freewheeling press chats of 2002, like the one that had led to the coat-holder comment—those were history. "The only guy that can defeat Andrew Cuomo is Andrew Cuomo," one aide confided. "And he's not going to let that happen again. Nothing will stand in his way—nothing that he can control."

Formally, David Paterson was still the governor, serving out his accidental term, but by midsummer 2010 he and his aides had to acknowledge that Andrew was calling the shots. He was working closely with Larry Schwartz, a top aide to Paterson who had once worked for Mario; together, Andrew and Schwartz were pretty much running the government day to day. "I think people underestimate how challenging the job is when you can't see," one Paterson aide explained. But also, Paterson simply couldn't prioritize. "Too much information, too many events..." Also, the aide said with a sigh, "Not a great relationship with the truth."

Andrew's campaign might have stayed on autopilot right through the general election if not for a September surprise. Rick Lazio, his old sparring partner on the Hill, was cruising to an easy win in the Republican primary, and Andrew could hardly envision an easier matchup. But then Lazio lost, to a Buffalo businessman named Carl Paladino, and the cards went up in the air.

Paladino was a political neophyte, but he'd tapped into a vein of indignation among upstate conservative voters tired of high taxes and high unemployment. Paladino promised to lead a "people's revolution" and "take a baseball bat to Albany." He might, as one of Andrew's surrogates declared, be a "wacko," but when a postprimary poll showed Paladino within six points of Andrew, the Cuomo team was gripped by fear—the fear that Andrew might have to leave his Rose Garden and fight a more public campaign. The thinking, as one of his aides later put it, was, "Are we going to have to show our faces here, and do events, which would be tragic? Andrew knew it would work against him to be in public, so he preferred not to be."

The way to deal with Cuomo, as even Paladino knew, was to goad him into an angry or a foolish response. Gleefully, the burly developer challenged Andrew to "come out and debate like a man." He circulated a flier with a computer-generated image showing Andrew in the shower, washing the muck of Albany corruption off his naked upper torso. Around Andrew's neck was a gold chain—again computer-generated.

Paladino was Italian too, but the two were antithetical types: Paladino the braggart, shooting off his mouth. Andrew the tightly wound introvert, weighing every utterance. The gold chain was clearly meant to cast Andrew as low-class: the swaggering outer-borough kid. Andrew seethed at the stereotyping, as thin-skinned about it as Mario. *The Sopranos*, HBO's popular series, was only the latest example of it, implying that all Italians were mafiosos. When a reporter described him as a "double espresso" of a politician, Andrew called him to complain that this showed anti-Italian bias. Having two Italians pitted against each other only exacerbated the issue. He couldn't have said it, or perhaps even thought it, but if someone had passed a law prohibiting more than one Italian from entering a campaign, Andrew would have approved. Assuming, of course, that he was the first one in.

With his aides gathered, Andrew pondered what, if anything, to do about Paladino's attack. By accident, as the meeting started, one aide's phone redialed the last call made on it—to *Daily News* reporter Ken Lovett—and the line stayed open, offering Lovett, and soon all his readers, a seat at the table. "If a guy says you have no cojones," Andrew wondered aloud, "how do you punch him back—call him an asshole?" The team had plenty of "stuff" on Paladino, but worried it might backfire, making Andrew look mean.

Fortunately for Andrew, Paladino was the one who lost his cool. The press learned he had a daughter from an extramarital affair, and camped outside her door. At a subsequent press conference, Paladino blamed the *New York Post* and took on its pugnacious political columnist Fred Dicker. "You send another goon to my daughter's house and I'll take you out, buddy."

Why, Paladino wanted to know, was the press focused only on his extramarital affair? Andrew had had affairs while he was married too, Paladino claimed in interviews. The Republican candidate never produced any proof of this, except to note in a TV ad that "Andrew's prowess is legendary." Later he backpedaled, saying he only meant to say Andrew should face the same questions as were put to him. But after the Dicker dustup, he looked a little unhinged.

Doing his best to ignore his rambunctious rival, Andrew focused on winning key supporters. One of the most important was New York mayor Michael Bloomberg, whose centrist views as often tipped him toward Democrats as Republicans. Privately, the mayor resented Andrew for going after his close friend and money manager Steven Rattner on what he felt were dubious grounds. But the mayor tried to put that aside on the September morning that Andrew came to Gracie Mansion for an hour-long breakfast. The mayor and would-be governor sat outside in Indian summer weather and seemed to forge a bond. The meeting led to a formal endorsement, before the cameras, outside city hall.

The bond was more political than personal. "It is true they spent time together, and it went fine," a mayor's aide later said. And the mayor not only endorsed Andrew, but moved up the endorsement a day to offset the poll that would briefly show Paladino closing the gap. "But the narrative that the mayor fell head over heels is a bit stretched," the aide explained. "Andrew was going to be the governor. We wanted a relationship; it served the mayor's interests to work well with the governor and to endorse a Democrat in a blue city."

When Andrew won that November, the mayor called to congratulate him, and his staff began working with the governor-elect's aides. "It was very specific and precise," a mayor's aide recalled. " 'Here are ten things we want to do.' " Back from Andrew's aides came answers just as precise: " 'We can do this, we can't do that.' " The mayor knew he wouldn't get all he asked for, but Andrew's aides appeared to be promising at least half the items on the list. "So we think... 'great,' " recalled the aide. It was the last time the mayor and his staff would feel that way.

Andrew's other challenge, in those preelection weeks, was wooing black voters. As far as New York's black political leaders were concerned, he had said far too little, for far too long, on behalf of the black community. "Where have you been these last four years?" blasted Elinor Tatum, publisher of the community's leading newspaper, the *Amsterdam News*. "You have showed us nothing that makes us want to stand strongly behind you. We feel as though all too often, you have taken us for granted and you have less than 40 days to turn this ship around."

Trying once again to placate a leadership that never seemed satisfied, Andrew headed to Harlem one morning to shake hands at a St. Nicholas Avenue subway entrance. There to heckle him were a dozen or so backers of a fringe candidate for the newly formed progressive Freedom Party. After a few awkward exchanges with schoolchildren, Andrew slunk into a community center, then sped away as soon as he could. Aside from a few crackpots, black voters were going to vote for Andrew. They had nowhere else to go. That was some consolation, at least.

If Andrew didn't quite annihilate Paladino, as he had hoped, he still won by a thumping majority: 62 percent. Another winner that day was Eric Schneiderman, eking out a narrow victory, with the help of his ex, Jennifer Cunningham, to succeed Andrew as attorney general.

Also in the winner's column were a majority of Senate Republicans, dashing Bill Samuels's dreams. The new governor was delighted. At the top of his own agenda was cutting the budget, and somehow cutting taxes too. For that, he would be far better off with a Republican Senate than a Democratic majority of mostly downstate lawmakers railing about cuts to their daycare centers. The dreams of Democratic reformers would have to wait.

Traditionally, departing governors all made their share of midnight appointments. It was a way to stay in the loop: grateful new job holders would pass on the gossip and bestow a favor or two. Andrew would have none of it. All appointments, he told Governor Paterson, would have to be cleared through him. If Paterson felt strongly about someone on the list, he should underline the name. Andrew would see what he could do. It was, as one Paterson sympathizer put it, emasculating.

Paterson did have the power to issue certain executive orders. One in particular would leave Andrew a tricky, complex issue to resolve, which grew more divisive and heated by the day.

By late 2010, the state was almost evenly divided over fracking, the newly expanded drilling method used to extract natural gas. As outgoing governor, Paterson could have given it a green light, pleasing industry, opening a new market, and providing New York with a deeply needed economic boost. He might have wrecked aquifers and landscapes in the process, if the warnings about fracking proved true. He could have taken that chance. Or he could have banned it outright, at least for some time. Instead, Paterson split the difference. Vertical drilling, tried and proven, could proceed. Only the horizontal kind, in which drills bored deep underground and then turned sideways into the shale, posing potential risks to water and human health, would be put on hold. Andrew would be left to make a decision that was politically a complete no-win.

Andrew's term as attorney general was drawing to a close, its list of victories long. The principal players in the pension fund scheme, though, remained at large, none more irksomely to Andrew than Steve Rattner.

For all their threats, Andrew's investigators had a modest hand to play with Rattner, and they knew it. The immunity granted back in 2008 could only be quashed if they could prove he had perjured himself and knowingly withheld key documents, among them the e-mails related to *Chooch*. Andrew's best chance was to hope that the SEC, in its own investigation, found Rattner guilty of civil violations and made him pay an outsize fine.

That scenario had already played out at Quadrangle, the firm from which Rattner had parted amid bitter feelings on either side. Quadrangle had agreed to a $7 million fine from the AG's office, and a $5 million fine from the SEC. Warily, Rattner started his own talks with the SEC. By mid-October, he was ready to settle, without admission of guilt, for $6.2 million. "Rattner comes back and says, 'I settled, so I assume you don't want to proceed with me,'" explained one source in Andrew's AG office. "And we say, 'That's a little too clever for us.'"

Rattner's argument was that the $6.2 million constituted his profits from the pension fund business done at Quadrangle, and by law that was all he should pay. Andrew disagreed. He felt Rattner had taken far more in profits, and the punishment ought to be commensurate. The SEC, he felt, had a history of settling cheap and moving on. As a separate matter, there was Rattner's conduct with the AG's investigators—perjury, as far as they were concerned. Andrew wanted Rattner to be punished for that too. In addition to the SEC's $6.2 million, what he wanted from Rattner was an admission of guilt—and $26 million.

At Andrew's request, the SEC held off until after the election to finalize its $6.2 million deal with Rattner. Andrew had hoped to announce his own deal with Rattner before the election, as a vote-getting triumph. He did wring a preelection guilty plea from Alan Hevesi—the seventh and most significant in his pay-to-play campaign; Hevesi would go on to serve nineteen months of hard time. Not long after the election, Hank Morris pled guilty too. He agreed to return the $19 million he'd illegally earned, and was sentenced to twelve to eighteen months.

Rattner signed on to the SEC's $6.2 million settlement, and agreed to a two-year ban in the securities industry. He might have agreed to pay a comparable sum to the New York AG's office. Another $6 million—sure. But there was no way he was going to prostrate himself before Andrew and hand over the wildly exorbitant sum of $26 million.

For all their threats of prison time, Andrew's investigators had been unable to conjure up a criminal case. Instead, on November 18, 2010, Andrew filed two civil suits against Rattner for allegedly paying kickbacks to obtain $150 million of the state pension fund to manage. Each sought $13 million in damages. In addition, Andrew filed to have Rattner banned for life from the securities business in New York State—a sharp stick in the eye of the man who now managed $5 billion for Mayor Michael Bloomberg. He told Rattner's lawyer he wanted to settle the case—but for no less than $26 million.

For Rattner, the AG suits were liberating. No longer constrained by the hope that private talks might solve the problem, he went on the *Charlie Rose* show to tell his side of the story. The next day, Andrew angrily told two *New York Times* reporters that Rattner had lied. "The operative word is lie," he declared.

One day in mid-December, a friend of Rattner's asked where the financier's case stood. "Nowhere," Rattner said glumly. The friend gave him a look. "It's nice to have problems you can solve with money," he said. Rattner found himself wondering if writing a big check might be worth the hit for moving on with his life—and getting Andrew Cuomo out of it.

Christmas shoppers were thronging the streets when Rattner called a Cuomo confidant he knew. "Do you think Andrew wants to settle this or not?"

"Funny you should mention that," the contact said. "I got a call from the Andrew camp saying, 'Do you think Steve wants to settle this?' "

Rattner said he would talk—on one condition. He refused to deal with Andrew's pit bull investigator, Linda Lacewell. He wanted to deal directly with Andrew, face-to-face.

The pictures were down from the walls at the AG's offices on lower Broadway when Rattner arrived with a single lawyer. Andrew had Lacewell on speakerphone from Texas, but no one else in the room. Charming one moment, bullying the next, the departing AG made clear he wanted to settle—though there was a point below which he simply couldn't go: Lacewell wouldn't let him. "You need to help me here," Andrew told Rattner, indicating the speakerphone. It was classic good cop/bad cop.

There was no resolution that day. For the first time, however, Rattner heard a compromising note from the AG. Clearly he wanted to claim victory and put a bow on the whole pay-to-play investigation before his AG tenure ended on December 31. Perhaps, too, he wanted to keep his newly elected successor, Eric Schneiderman, from making the deal and getting the credit. Andrew did say he had come up with a new criminal charge he thought would stick—so one option was slapping Rattner with it and letting the new attorney general handle it as he wished. That, Rattner thought, was a bluff. Still, dealing with the devil he knew might be his best bet. Neither of the two expert negotiators came out that day with a figure, but by the end of the meeting, both knew what it was: $10 million.

Adamant that the case not ruin any more of his life, Rattner took his family that holiday week to the Turks and Caicos islands in the Caribbean. He might as well not have left home. The phone rang constantly. Along with the money, Andrew wanted admissions of guilt and workplace bans. Rattner, sensing Andrew's eagerness, refused. In the end, as with the SEC, he made no admissions. He did accept a five-year ban on appearing before a New York pension fund—not a concession, he felt, since he had no wish to do that work anyway. What he cared about was buying and selling securities. With New Year's Eve ticking down, Andrew agreed to forgo any securities ban. Rattner could keep managing Mayor Bloomberg's money. As part of the deal, the two agreed not to disparage each other: the press release for the settlement would not list any allegations, and Mr. Cuomo and Mr. Rattner would agree to put the matter behind them.

For nearly four years, Andrew had haunted the wily financier without surcease, accusing him of perjury, demanding he plead to charges, threatening him with serious jail time. Almost certainly he had cost Rattner a chance at secretary of the treasury; instead, when the car czar should have been basking in the Obama administration's undying gratitude, he had become an embarrassment, and quietly resigned his post to come home.

Yet in some ways Rattner admired his nemesis. The man did work hard. When the eleventh-hour talks began, Andrew himself had gotten on the phone with Rattner again and again. And those weren't short calls. He had threatened, but unlike his furious sidekick, he never raised his voice or grew irrational. He wanted to get the deal done.

What Rattner most admired about Andrew was that the AG had gone after him in the first place. Another Democratic attorney general might have paused at the prospect of targeting a major fund-raiser for his own party—a fund-raiser who, moreover, counted the billionaire mayor of New York and the publisher of the country's most powerful newspaper among his closest friends. Andrew hadn't flinched.

All in all, including Rattner's $10 million, the attorney general who might never have written a brief could say that as a result of his pension fund investigation the state had recovered $170 million for hard-to-prove fraudulent deals—success by anyone's yardstick.

For the entire Cuomo clan, New Year's Eve 2010 was a tearful return to Albany's executive mansion after sixteen years—a New Year's Eve like no other. Mario and Matilda, Andrew's three sisters and his brother, Chris, the grandchildren—all milled about with the family's closest advisers, most of whom recalled coming to the mansion with Mario after his own gubernatorial triumphs. Drew Zambelli, Joe Percoco, Michael Del Giudice, Steve Cohen, Howard Glaser—and Paterson adviser Larry Schwartz, the go-between known as "North," soon to be formally part of the new regime. Here, too, were close friends, if "friend" was a word that applied to Andrew's top fund-raisers: Jeff Sachs for one, Andrew Farkas for another. "It was like *Evita*," recalled one guest. "It was the return."

There, too, was Sandra Lee. The governor-elect's girlfriend would not preside as de facto first lady or have a staff, she had already clarified. Whether or not she would stay most nights at the executive mansion was not a question she chose to answer. Her primary residence, a spokesperson sniffed, would continue to be the home she shared in Westchester with Andrew and his daughters. Clearly the first couple's personal lives were beyond the scope of the governor's new transparency.

About sixty people in all—forty of them members of the Cuomo clan—dined at the mansion on chicken and pasta. After, at 10:09 p.m., Andrew and Lieutenant Governor-Elect Robert Duffy took the oath of office before Court of Appeals chief judge Jonathan Lippman. If Andrew had any regret, it was only that Eric Schneiderman was taking an oath of office too: he was New York's new attorney general—and Governor Andrew Cuomo's lawyer.

Behind Andrew stood his father, looking on with feelings too complex to be called simply pride. Mario had always called his son smarter and more capable than he, but if forced to parse "smart," he would have said clever, strategic, cunning perhaps—not intellectual. Mario was the intellectual; Andrew, by his own description, was the "operational" guy. Andrew knew which of the two, the intellect and the doer, his father held in higher regard than the other. Now it was his turn to prove his father wrong, to prove that the son could match—and perhaps outdo—the father.

CHAPTER 21

A State in Need of Saving

By 8 a.m. on Saturday, January 1, 2011, Andrew was presiding from the same modest office his father had occupied for twelve years. In that castle of a capitol building, the room's humble dimensions made no sense without the backstory. Historically, the capacious corner Red Room next door was the governor's lair, which he shared with aides like a king with his court. The last to use the room that way was Al Smith, one of Andrew's favorite New York governors. Franklin Roosevelt had made the Red Room a ceremonial chamber for press gatherings and bill signings, using the small adjacent office as his inner sanctum for small and intimate meetings. On its other side, that room opened into a series of others, down the same high-ceilinged hall, like a railroad apartment on some baronial scale: if all the massive mahogany doors of each office were opened, a journalist in the Red Room could see straight down to the general counsel's office. Intentionally or not, the rooms created an unmistakable pecking order.

Closest to Andrew's sanctum was the secretary to the governor—Steve Cohen, who would soon lead the marriage-equality campaign. After four years as Andrew's right-hand man in the AG's office, Cohen had signed on for another stint of glory at government pay on one condition: that it be mercifully short. He would help get the governorship up and running, but leave at the end of the first legislative session for the private sector. Through the next months he would patiently remind the governor of that timetable, then calmly, resolutely act on it, accomplishing a rare feat among Cuomo loyalists: the exit without rancor from the boss.

The office next to Cohen's was for Larry Schwartz, the Paterson adviser who had more or less run the state with Andrew while Paterson futzed around. He was one senior policy adviser. The other, next door to him, was Howard Glaser, Andrew's "Hammer" from the HUD days.

Inevitably, Glaser and Schwartz would vie for the boss's favor. That was the point. "It was the same thing Mario did with Michael Del Giudice and Tim Russert," explained one insider. "Both Mario and Andrew like to play people off each other."

On that first morning, Andrew gathered his whole senior staff in the Red Room. Along with Cohen, Glaser, and Schwartz, there was General Counsel Mylan Denerstein, a Brooklyn district attorney until Andrew had charmed her into joining his AG's office by coming to meet her at the Brooklyn Marriott for breakfast; Chief of Staff Ben Lawsky, the young hard charger in the AG's office who'd led the student loan cases and liked to watch car shows on TV with the governor; and special assistant to the governor Linda Lacewell, the fierce and occasionally terrifying prosecutor who'd co-led the pay-to-play investigations with Ellen Biben. Biben, neatly coiffed, was also there. Rounding out the inner circle were Joe Percoco, the faithful front man and fixer—Andrew's last call before he went to sleep, as one insider put it—and Drew Zambelli, the anxious pollster and media spinner from Mario's time, always on guard for the next attack on his boss. Like his father, Andrew would keep his circle tight, rely for guidance on these loyal advisers—and make all decisions himself.

A little before noon, Andrew strode across the second floor, the walls hung with portraits of governors past, to take another inaugural oath, this one public, in the Governor's Reception Room, also known as the War Room for its ceiling murals dramatizing New York's historical conflicts. Judge Lippman was again the officiator; now he also administered oaths to newly elected Attorney General Eric Schneiderman and Tom DiNapoli, the widely liked comptroller. All too soon, the governor would take on both men. Whether he would do that out of personal spite or as political sport neither would quite know, only that the murals overhead would seem prescient.

As he strode up to the podium to take his oath, Andrew was accompanied by Sandra Lee and his three daughters—but not, he suddenly realized, his parents, still seated in the front row. Turning, he gestured to his parents to follow. In his inaugural speech, he invoked his father's tenure, lionizing Mario as "one of the greatest governors in the history of this state." Mario, meanwhile, stood behind Sandra Lee, oddly eclipsed by her taller figure.

After a short, sober speech, with promises to right the state's economy and root out public corruption, Andrew gave Sandra and each of his daughters a kiss on the cheek. When he leaned over to do the same to his father, Mario pushed him away and gave him a little slap on the arm.

Perhaps it was paternal affection, though one pair of guests seated nearby had a different impression. It seemed to them that the slap on the arm was less one of warmth than impatience with his son's public sentiment.

Among those impressed by Andrew's inaugural speech was Rex Smith, the rather dashing editor in chief of the Albany *Times Union*. Smith had seen the Cuomos up close for decades. He knew how they worked the phones, schmoozing or threatening as the moment warranted. He was both impressed and amused when Andrew came in to meet the editorial board and embraced the Boston Irish chief editorial writer as if they were old pals; they weren't, but if Andrew made the most of a passing acquaintance, why not? That was what political pros did, and Andrew was a pro, all right. Smith's editorial the next day caught the capital's optimism about this new governor, tough and even cynical as he might be. "It's not a time for a rhetorician," the *Times Union* declared, in a seeming putdown of Mario. "We need a smart professional politician to remake a system that isn't performing. It's a job that exactly matches Andrew Cuomo's capacity... Now, armed with the tools voters have given him, we'll see what kind of a mechanic Andrew Cuomo really is."

For old Albany hands, radical change came just four days later. As far back as anyone could remember, New York's governor had given his State of the State speech in the Assembly chamber, an august and intimate venue that held hardly more than lawmakers and other top officials. No more, Andrew told his staff. He wanted to open up the speech to a larger audience, the better to get his message out. He would give it in the auditorium of the capital's convention center, where hundreds more could hear it directly, and the media, accustomed to a snoozy nonevent, could beam it across the state.

There was perhaps another reason for the change of venue. As attorney general, Andrew had come into the Assembly chamber for the State of the State followed single file by the lieutenant governor and the comptroller. He would earn modest applause, so too the lieutenant governor. Then would come Tom DiNapoli, the comptroller, to rousing cheers. "They love Tom," said an insider. "It was really noticeable. I always thought that grated on Andrew." Now, instead of filing into the chamber, the lawmakers took the center's underground corridors to the auditorium's side entrance. There they found Joe Percoco in the wings, shaking each person's hand before he went onstage. "Not because he's happy to see them," the insider noted. "It's more like, 'You're coming to my party.' That stagecraft stuff—Andrew is masterful at orchestrating that."

The chill the lawmakers began to feel as Andrew took the stage was a literal one: the new governor had ordered the thermostats turned way down, to assure that his audience stayed awake and focused. Andrew had decided that his State of the State would be new not just in venue but format. It would be a PowerPoint presentation.

The crisis, Andrew began, pointer in hand, was not just grave but growing: the next fiscal year's $10 billion deficit would be, if unchecked, next year's $14 billion deficit, and the following year's $17 billion. The state was saddled with higher Medicaid bills than any other state in the nation, high education bills with poor results, and high, almost unequaled taxes that too often drove residents and businesses away. The $10 billion deficit was going to have to be cut without borrowing or imposing new taxes. That, in turn, would mean cutting the biggest, most bloated chunks of the budget. Health care. Education. Pensions. State agencies across the board would be cut; some might be consolidated with others. To that end, Andrew boomed, he would start by putting together insurance and banking oversight with consumer protection into a new department of financial services. At that, the new attorney general, Eric Schneiderman, looked up. Had he heard what he thought he heard? That sounded a lot like part of the job he had just been elected to do.

Schneiderman had already taken one shot across the bow. On December 22, 2010, nine days before the end of Andrew's own tenure as AG, $56 million remaining in settlement money from health insurers had been moved from the AG's office to the state Department of Health, to be overseen by the governor-elect. This was a case that Linda Lacewell had investigated, a company called Ingenix that had lowballed medical reimbursements for out-of-network patients across the country. Now Andrew, not the new attorney general, could reap the political dividends from spending it on health-related issues. Later, when Schneiderman's office requested an analysis from the Department of Health on how that $56 million had been allocated, no reply was forthcoming.

Taming the budget, Andrew declared as the slides whisked by, would take a bipartisan spirit. "Right now the budget process is like ships passing in the night." Up on the screen three crudely drawn boats came and went. "Hold on a second," Andrew deadpanned. "Bring those ships back. I think I recognized someone. Is that—zoom in on that man on that battleship—yes it is, Senate majority leader Dean Skelos. And look, it's Commander Sheldon Silver!"

As the crowd erupted in laughter, Andrew pointed to the third ship, under bombardment. "Oh, and there I am. And here are the special interest groups. You notice, Dean, how all of the missiles from the special interest groups went into my battleship? I would humbly suggest as the new governor that maybe, just maybe, we try doing it a different way this year, what do you say?"

Ethics reform was the other big push, Andrew acknowledged. As a start, he wanted full disclosure of all outside income earned by New York's lawmakers, a suggestion met by silence. Lawmakers in each house were paid annual salaries of $79,500, a pittance even for the six-month legislative session from January through June, and hardly enough to tide them over the rest of the year, when they did state business from their districts. Many supplemented their meager incomes as lawyers, and they were not barred from representing clients who might have business before the state. No disclosure of clients was required, nor any potential conflicts of interest. About the only restriction was that they not, in their spare time, work as lobbyists importuning their fellow legislators. The opportunities for corruption were not just rife: they were endemic. Andrew wanted to change that.

True reform, Andrew thundered on, would only come about with honest redistricting: that every-decade process of redrawing the lines of the state's sixty-two voting districts. Back in 1812, Massachusetts governor Elbridge Gerry had let his Republican legislators redraw the state's district lines as they pleased, to maximize the number of Republican voters in each. They had produced bizarrely shaped districts, including one that looked like a salamander; a Federalist wag had nicknamed the process "gerrymandering." Ever since, incumbents had been gerrymandering their turf to hold on to their seats. New York in 2011 had its own odd districts. One looked like Abraham Lincoln riding a vacuum cleaner, another like a great big frying pan. Still others were chopped in separate, unconnected parts.

In the senate, the artists behind these vivid creations were Republican leaders who clung to power in a solidly Democratic state. Former New York City mayor Ed Koch, now an elder statesman, had spent much of the previous campaign season pushing to make redistricting equitable at last, and sixty of the state's sixty-two senators—including all the Republicans—had signed on to his plan. "We're going to have an independent monitor," Andrew said of redistricting. "We're going to listen to Ed Koch's warnings."

Reform had a third leg, as all in the room knew. Andrew gave it a short, single sentence. "*And we need public financing of campaigns.*" Such a limp avowal was, to many, a sign that campaign finance reform would remain a distant goal. Yet without it there could be no hope of cleaning up the capitol. The state's rules on political donations were so lax that big donors could pretty much buy the legislation they wanted.

From the speech's highlight—the shtick with the boats—the audience came away with two impressions. Andrew's boat was bigger than the others: let Skelos and Silver take note. And somehow, Andrew was going to deflect those special interest missiles that came raining in on any new governor. That, it turned out, was the agenda of the new, seemingly innocuous Committee to Save New York.

Ever since his father's first days in office, Andrew had seen how the game worked. A new governor came in determined to cut the entitlements that sapped the budget: health care, education, and pensions. Before he could say boo, unions representing those interests would blanket the airwaves with television commercials that made the governor look like a heartless enemy of teachers and students, state workers and retirees. Andrew had a different idea, as he warned Dean Skelos. His old pal Dan Klores, adman and media *macher*, had set up the Committee to Save New York as a nonprofit of the 501(c)(4) category. A 501(c)(4) had to spend most of its money and effort promoting some issue or policy that promoted the social welfare; that was why it qualified for tax breaks. Unlike a 501(c)(3), however, it could coordinate with political campaigns, before and after an election, as long as it declared those actions and paid taxes on them.

Within days of the State of the State, the CSNY was running slick ads that praised the new governor for standing tough to get the state back in shape. In that first year of Andrew's tenure, the CSNY would spend more money than any other lobbying group in the state: nearly $12 million. For the first time in New York politics, the unions were outspent—and outmaneuvered.

Who was paying for all this? As a 501(c)(4), the CSNY didn't have to disclose its donors. A few came forward on their own, like Rob Speyer, president of Tishman Speyer, one of New York's most venerable real estate firms. In his twenties, Speyer had worked for Andrew at HELP. Four other real estate powers disclosed their donations. All these upstanding citizens doubtless shared Andrew's vision of balancing the budget and getting New York back on track. Directly or indirectly, all five also benefited from dealings with the state.

The CSNY was brilliant politics. But for the governor who'd just vowed to enact ethics reform, it raised a few questions. Blair Horner, the public gadfly who had worked for Andrew in the AG's office and admired his management style, was an outsider again and startled by the CSNY. First, he felt, it was misrepresenting itself. "They were saying they weren't lobbyists, and they were." Horner filed a complaint with the Commission for Public Integrity and won that round: the CSNY was forced to register as a lobbying organization.

Horner felt just as strongly that the CSNY should disclose all of its donors. "These were well-funded developers and others who had business before them," Horner said of the governor and his team. "At a minimum we should know who they are." But the CSNY declined to name the rest of its members, and that, the commission ruled, it could do.

Despite all those commercials, Andrew knew that his draft of the budget, due February 1, would be a bitter pill. On the eve of submitting it, he invited the leaders of the legislature for dinner at the executive mansion to wash it down.

That there should be any honeymoon at all between the leaders and their governor was striking. Most Albany insiders had thought the only question was which leader would vivisect Andrew first: Sheldon Silver, leader of the Democratic Assembly, or Skelos. The two were opposites in many ways, but both were tough, cynical, and highly skilled at outmaneuvering governors. Silver was an Orthodox Jew who had lived his whole life on Manhattan's Lower East Side. Skelos was from a Greek-American family in Nassau County. Silver was a liberal on most issues, always ready to spend more on education and health care, and to raise taxes, if needed, to do it. Skelos was a classic tax-cut Republican, also a stern right-to-lifer. Silver was known as the master of delay. Skelos did whatever it took to keep his party in power, even as New York grew bluer and bluer.

In a different climate, both men might have resisted Andrew's agenda. But both had more to gain by helping the new governor than by sparring with him—at least for now. Both parties were still living down the debacle of 2008 and 2009: the Republicans for losing the state senate, the Democrats for botching their big chance to run it well. Both knew that serious cuts would be needed to stanch the $10 billion deficit. And both knew that Andrew held the carrot they wanted more than anything else: the power to let them, if he chose, handle redistricting *their* way in 2012, to help each win reelection again—and again—for the next ten years.

Andrew, of course, had just declared his fervent support for fair and independent redistricting. The leaders weren't worried. They had time.

For the two minority leaders, just getting invited to the dinner was a big deal. Brian Kolb, the Republican leader of the Assembly, had spent a decade in the minority wilderness, reduced to fighting for pencils and parking places. A classic upstate Republican on social issues, he didn't expect much, just a say in the process. The impression he came away with was that Andrew would give him that.

John Sampson, newly named leader of the dispirited Senate Democrats, was a more complicated package. A Brooklyn state senator since 1997, he was still trying to put a major scandal behind him. The previous October, a scathing three-hundred-page report from the state inspector general had implicated him, among others, in a tawdry bidding war over which casino developer would be allowed to install video slot machines at the Aqueduct racetrack in Queens—a plum worth tens of millions of dollars a year. Questioned by the IG, Sampson had answered, "I don't recall" more than a hundred times. Still, he came away from that dinner at the executive mansion with the same sense Kolb had: his voice would be heard.

It was the last time the minority leaders would feel that.

From the head of the table, Andrew saw opportunity. Silver and Skelos were each willing to bend, not only with redistricting over their heads but because Andrew's poll numbers were too high for the leaders not to work with him. He had promised a new era of transparency, but as the budget talks began, an old Albany phrase would seem more accurate: "Three Men in a Room." From time immemorial, Albany's deals had been cut not by the legislature in its august chambers, but by the governor and the two legislative leaders behind closed doors. They were the Three Men in a Room.

As Andrew walked his guests to the door, he sensed already how all this would play out. Different issues would have different alliances. Silver's Democrats would tip one, Skelos's Republicans another. In between, like a fulcrum, was the new Independent Democratic Conference, a group of four breakaway Senate Democrats disgusted with their party's losses and embarrassments, voting for the first time as a bloc on their own. Jeff Klein of the Bronx, the IDC's founder, was socially liberal: his bloc of four would throw its weight behind marriage equality. But on fiscal issues, it might part ways with its party and support Andrew's more conservative plans. The beauty of it, as Andrew might say, was that with the senate so narrowly split, he could nudge the IDC to either side as needed, looking bipartisan as he did.

Publicly, Andrew had said little about the IDC, and nothing to counteract the impression that it had formed organically from those four Democrats' frustrations with their party. In fact, he had been "deeply involved" in the IDC's formation, as insiders later acknowledged, and now had a back channel to Klein, guiding him in ways that would occasionally undercut the Democrats' agenda. Andrew didn't trust Klein; then again, he trusted almost no one. He could use Klein, as Klein used him. That was enough.

Andrew's draft of the budget, dripping with draconian cuts, was met by an angry chorus of union leaders, those in public education the loudest. This time they were drowned out by all those television commercials from the CSNY touting Andrew's prudent stewardship.

In that drowned-out chorus was New York mayor Michael Bloomberg. The budget would cut almost $1 billion from state aid to the city. The city could handle the pain, Andrew's staff told the mayor's staff blithely: it had $2 billion in reserves. For Bloomberg, who had planned to use that money to close the city's own deficit of $2.4 billion, this was the first sign that Andrew, whom he had backed, had already betrayed him.

Back in the campaign, when Bloomberg had breakfasted with Andrew at Gracie Mansion, the two had agreed that once in office, Andrew would work with the mayor on a laundry list of issues dear to Bloomberg's heart, starting with revenue sharing by the city and state.

With Andrew's inauguration, the mayor's staff had tried for weeks to stage a meeting. "We literally couldn't get on the calendar," one of the mayor's inner circle recalled. Finally a time was set, and the mayor's staff came to Albany bearing three-ring binders with all their proposed bills. On the governor's side of a conference table were Howard Glaser, Larry Schwartz, Ben Lawsky, and Steve Cohen. "This was the beautiful partnership we had envisioned," recalled the staffer. "We go in, and we talk. And we get no feedback whatsoever."

To the mayor's team, teacher layoffs were the story that showed how Andrew really operated. They were on the table—with a $10 billion deficit, everything was on the table—and Bloomberg wanted some way to assure that the teachers who got let go were not the best ones. Unfortunately, the teachers' unions were wedded to LIFO: Last In, First Out. The newest teachers would be let go first, regardless of how good they were. Teachers with the most years of service had the most seniority, regardless of whether they put their students to sleep. Bloomberg wanted to get rid of LIFO. So did Andrew, or so he'd said.

"The romance had not entirely faded," recalled one insider of Bloomberg's relationship with Andrew after that jarring first meeting of "no." The staffs might now detest each other, but Bloomberg still hoped for the best. He made a point of meeting with Andrew one-on-one to be sure the governor shared the mayor's view: LIFO must be scuttled. Having Andrew on board was key, because LIFO was a state law. The legislature would have to pass a new law undoing it. "I can't make miracles," Andrew told Bloomberg. "You need to get Shelly and Skelos on this."

Bloomberg was ready: he had made generous donations to Skelos and started his own campaign of suasion with both leaders. The mayor bought airtime, importuned editorial boards, and finally coaxed Skelos to bring a bill to the floor. Suddenly almost every Republican was for it, and one or two of the new IDC members. A vote was taken; the bill passed. The Senate had officially killed LIFO. If the governor lent his weight, the Assembly might kill it as well.

Within minutes, to the shock of the mayor's team, a press release appeared from the governor's office: Andrew was proposing his own legislative reform of LIFO, one that would start with fixing the system by which teachers were evaluated. "It was bullshit!" recalled a member of the mayor's team. "It's him declaring the Senate bill dead on arrival."

Why had the governor done this, when he had agreed with Bloomberg that LIFO must go? Canny tactician that he was, Andrew had realized that LIFO could serve as a pawn in the greater game of getting his budget passed.

Perhaps, in some abstract sense, Andrew did think LIFO should go. But it didn't matter. It had no political heft. It was Bloomberg's fight, a New York City issue; why was Bloomberg even bringing Andrew a fight he didn't want? As Bloomberg had started making headway on it, rounding up Republicans, the governor had realized that LIFO presented a golden opportunity.

Andrew had a budget that no one would like: that, he couldn't avoid. But he had won over some of the unions by now, including all-powerful 1199, the health care workers' union, which had held its fire because Andrew had given it a seat at the table of his Medicaid team, stakeholders from every side of the issue working together to cut $2 billion from the state's share of Medicaid costs. Other unions were finding themselves drowned out by the Committee to Save New York. The one group that posed real danger was the teachers' unions. So, as one of the mayor's aides later explained, Andrew went to the head of the most powerful teachers' union, Michael Mulgrew of the United Federation of Teachers, and gave him LIFO as a cat would deliver a dead mouse.

It was a trade-off. Alarmed as the unions were to contemplate a budget of painful school cuts, they were even more anxious to see Bloomberg on the verge of eliminating Last In, First Out: it would rob them of power over teachers and school administrations. By his deal, Andrew would protect the unions by killing LIFO in the legislature—if they kept mum about the budget.

Andrew's own bill appeared just days later. It proposed to go slow with LIFO, fixing teacher evaluation first. For twenty-four hours, the mayor's advisers did all they could to get out the word that Andrew's bill was a sham; he had no intention of scuttling LIFO. They failed: it too passed the Senate, but died in the Assembly—as planned. "It had an assembly sponsor but it was never going to go anywhere without the governor pushing hard, because of Shelly," one insider explained. The larger lesson was clear. The governor and his aides, the mayor's team felt, were completely incapable of having a straightforward relationship.

It was too soon to discern a troubling pattern in Andrew's dealings with other powerful politicians. That he would take on each and all, a bull in the pasture head-butting every challenger to show who was boss—only later would that become clear. But Eric Schneiderman, the new attorney general, could hardly doubt that one of the governor's first measures had been crafted to cut him down to size.

What *was* this new Department of Financial Services that Andrew had mentioned in his State of the State? As an exercise in streamlining, it seemed sensible enough: oversight of the banking and insurance industries was put under one roof. In charge was Ben Lawsky, a very capable fellow: no problem there either. As drafted, though, Lawsky's DFS would have the power to conduct criminal investigations. That would make Lawsky a sort of second attorney general, under Andrew's command, pushing Schneiderman to the margins. "That was the 'oh shit,'" explained an AG insider. "We organized very quickly to put *that* idea down."

Schneiderman won that round: no criminal investigations, though Lawsky did retain subpoena power. But if there was any doubt that Andrew intended to clip Schneiderman's wings, it vanished when Schneiderman asked for authority to pursue criminal cases of public corruption. Back when Andrew was attorney general, his top aide Steve Cohen had asked Governor Spitzer for that very power, arguing the AG should have it. Request denied. Now, despite Andrew's vow to stop public corruption, he no longer saw the virtue of empowering the AG to pursue it. Steve Cohen himself relayed that message, seated now on the other side of the desk.

All power and all control—that was Andrew's management style. To his inner circle, there was nothing new about it. The micromanaging, the top-down decisions on every matter, no matter how local, the tight control of even the most innocuous news emanating from the second floor—this was Andrew as he'd always been, only more so. Others were taken aback. "Nothing can be decided without going to the second floor," marveled one senior member of a previous administration. "You speak to commissioners, you speak to people in the administration—nothing can be decided." The commissioners were even proscribed from talking to the press on their own. Another Albany old-timer called it "controlled to a degree not even seen in Mario's day." A new press flack for one of the government's agencies shared with a lawmaker just how extreme the second-floor culture now was. "If a reporter calls, I cannot take the call until I talk to one of three people on the second floor," the flack confessed, meaning Larry Schwartz, Howard Glaser, or Joe Percoco. "I must write up everything I say, and write up and code every 'ask' for information, all through a centralized operation."

The advisers setting that tone were not merely dedicated to shielding their boss. They were his pit bulls. "The door will open to the extent that they're worried about you," one former lawmaker suggested. "They'll fuck their friends and help their enemies and vice versa, based upon fear. You're dealing with a computer program that operates a certain way. To the extent you perceive differences [among them], you are reading stylistic differences. There is only one decider, and that is Andrew. He makes *all* the decisions."

Norman Adler, the longtime union operative and onetime Cuomo aide, was neither the first nor last to wonder how this style would play in the White House. "It's a bad way to prepare someone to become president," he said. "When you run on a national stage, there are no secrets, no way to protect yourself, and if you try to do that, you get into more trouble."

Once again, as at HUD and at the AG's office, Andrew pushed his staff hard, to the point of exhaustion and misery, but never more than he pushed himself. The work went right on as he left the capitol Thursday nights for his home with Sandra in Westchester, making calls on his BlackBerry, leaving his untraceable PIN-to-PIN e-mails. "He might leave at 7 p.m.," said one member of the second floor, "but he's in a car doing PINs, calling legislators, for that next ninety minutes.

"I can't tell you how many times I look at my state BlackBerry," the aide added, "and there are PINs he's sent at 4:30 a.m."

Many of those calls were to union chieftains, as Andrew haggled over budget cuts. The state workers' unions were one of his last hurdles: he had warned them from the start that he wanted them to find savings of $450 million or he would cut up to ninety-eight hundred jobs. The Public Employees Federation and the Civil Service Employees Association were upset but knew he meant business: there were, as one reporter noted, spreadsheets all over their offices, to the low hum of crunching numbers.

The one constituency that seemed impervious to either the carrot or the stick were the black downstate Democrats, who knew what pain the budget cuts would inflict upon their voters. One night in late February, Andrew braved their ire with a speech to the Association of Black and Puerto Rican Legislators. At the top of their list were education cuts, which they felt—correctly—would affect poor school districts far more harshly than affluent ones. Adding insult to injury was Andrew's avowal to end the so-called millionaires' tax imposed as an emergency measure by Governor Paterson in 2009. The tax, on the state's highest earners, starting at $200,000, was due to "sunset" at the end of 2011 as the economy recovered. To please the Senate Republicans—his budget partners—Andrew had declared that the millionaires' tax would end on schedule, even though its end would leave a hole of an estimated $4 billion. To the downstate Democrats, that made no sense at all. Why not keep the millionaire's tax on the books—the rich could afford it—and steer that money to poor schoolchildren, instead of making all these cuts?

As Andrew spoke, a pair of hecklers began shouting. "Tax the rich!" they cried. "Stop the cuts!" Finally Andrew stopped to address them directly. "How are you tonight, Charles?" he said. He meant Charles Barron, who had formed his own Freedom Party the previous year to run against Andrew for governor. "I don't see who it is," Andrew said, peering into the darkness, "but I know who it is."

Andrew did have one sop to throw the irascible downstaters: a pledge of honest redistricting. The drawing of those lines by Senate Republicans had disenfranchised blacks and Hispanics since the days of Governor Gerry. Either people of color were stranded in largely Republican districts, or they were crowded into districts so heavily Democratic that their clout was diluted. "Cracking" and "packing" were the terms of art. Assembly Democrats did the same thing. And so both parties benefited, each giving the other the right to draw its own lines, which was why 96 percent of incumbents won reelection time after time. The solution was simple: lines that contained districts of roughly equal population, regardless of political party. But to draw *those* lines would require a truly reform-minded governor.

To the joy of downstate Democrats, Andrew Cuomo seemed that governor. As promised, he had just submitted a bill for independent redistricting—basically the same bill that Ed Koch had championed. This was also the bill that all thirty-two Republicans had pledged to support before the election, only to start backsliding as soon as the votes were counted. Brazenly chucking their campaign pledges, the Senate Republicans had used procedural sleight of hand to block Andrew's bill. But the governor vowed to the downstate Democrats that he would get it through.

Nothing, it seemed, would stop Andrew from achieving this noble goal. But all was not quite as it seemed. "When Cuomo stands up for the independent panel, he gets credit," explained Hank Sheinkopf, one of Albany's most venerable political consultants. "He doesn't have to do it. In fact, he didn't do it. Yet most people out there vaguely following the news thought he was for reform."

Andrew was teaching a master class in strategy. To the angry downstaters—and to the rest of the Democratic Party—he seemed to have embraced an issue of vital importance to them. A year later, when he had gotten all he could from the Senate Republicans and gave them redistricting their way, he would say he had had no choice. The legislature had the right to draw those lines as it liked. He could veto what they did, but they could draw them again. The only way to change the process permanently was by constitutional amendment: getting two successive legislatures to approve it, then putting it to the voters in a referendum. That was true. But then all the talk of establishing an independent commission *without* a constitutional amendment was hokum. Had he learned this only later, in 2012, when he gave up the fight for one? Or had he known it in 2011 and simply made a show of trying to establish one? "You stick up the Republicans to get what you want," suggested Sheinkopf, "then when you get what you want, somehow everyone forgets about the independent commission."

To cut that $10 billion deficit to zero, balance his budget, and get it in on time, Andrew had to do more than whack the unions. He had to win over the legislature too. For that, he had one mighty persuader his father had never had, one that sounded like some medieval form of torture: the Paterson extender.

History might record it as the Pataki Extender, from a 2004 lawsuit won by the then governor, but Paterson had seen its potential and made a cudgel of it. When the legislature held up his budget in 2010 and resisted his cuts, Paterson issued a temporary budget every two weeks with more cuts in it. Lawmakers could either accept that temporary budget as is or shut the government down. Lawsuits had followed, but the governor had won them. Paterson had already decided not to run for reelection: he could take the heat from furious voters if the government closed its doors. Legislators couldn't. Eventually, Paterson had worn the opposition down.

By mid-March, Andrew went further. He was prepared to offer one extender, and one only, if all sides didn't manage to cut that $10 billion deficit by the April 1 deadline. That meant Andrew would submit a single extender budget with all the cuts *he* chose, for the entire fiscal year, and give lawmakers a Hobson's choice: accept it whole or shut the government down. With a governor sporting a 74 percent approval rating, the lawmakers knew who would get blamed if they chose the latter.

Albany had a catchphrase for the twenty-four hours of frantic haggling a governor and his lawmakers engaged in to settle the budget's thorniest issues: the Big Ugly. Side deals were struck behind closed doors, measures inserted that benefited one or another lawmaker's district, trade-offs made among the three legislative leaders that often shocked their own troops the next morning. Andrew's first Big Ugly took new liberties with a once rarely used tool of governance: the "message of necessity." Ordinarily, lawmakers had three calendar legislative days to review pending legislation before casting their votes. By attaching a message of necessity, a governor could demand a vote be taken as soon as a final version was distributed. Messages of necessity were meant for true emergencies, such as if, say, Russia attacked New York State. The only reason anyone could imagine that Andrew had attached a message of necessity to various bills of his first budget was to assure that it came in at $132.5 billion, under the deadline of April 1.

By the last week of March, Andrew was able to sheathe his threats of an extender budget. He had won most of the cuts he wanted, including painful ones for public schools, and gotten lawmakers from both parties to sign on. "Cuomo has taken almost complete control in Albany in a way no governor has since Nelson Rockefeller bought his power," the Albany *Times Union* gushed. "[He] has all but dictated the details of a devastating $10 billion deficit reduction plan that, in prior years, the Legislature would have declared dead on arrival."

A balanced budget, the $10 billion deficit wiped out! Not only that, but Andrew had produced New York's first on-time budget since 2005. On-time budgets were like supermoons: the last before that had been reached in 1983, under Mario's guidance.

Budget gurus like E. J. McMahon of the Empire Center for New York State Policy were somewhat less impressed. The budget did nothing to scale back New York's huge and growing pension obligations; instead, it let the state make its contribution to the pension fund in promissory notes—IOUs—which didn't count as charges against the budget, but rather as costs in the hazy future. Nor did it do anything to ease the share of Medicaid and other mandated costs borne by local governments. For that matter, another expert opined, the budget didn't really cut the deficit at all. "He didn't cut ten billion [dollars]," the expert mused. "The budget division imputed a level of growth to expenditures that showed there would be a $10 billion deficit. But expenditures didn't grow anywhere near that. So it wasn't an executive or legislative decision to save $10 billion. It was a projection based on one set of estimates that turned out not to be true."

Still, it *was* a budget, an on-time budget and, to laymen, a balanced one, and in the nation's most dysfunctional capital, that was enough. For his first gubernatorial triumph, Andrew strode into the capitol's Red Room flanked by Silver and Skelos to announce the good news. Days before, he had warned both of them that he was weighing an extender. Now the three stood together, all smiles. "I'm hoping that this spirit of love and euphoria that I feel is infectious and grows and continues," the governor declared. "Do you feel it, Dean?"

"I feel it," Skelos chimed.

Not everyone did. Four days later when the governor took his seat at the Red Room desk for the signing, the two minority leaders, to their great surprise, were steered away by Joe Percoco, the governor's fixer, to the front row of audience seats, away from the whirring cameras and flashing strobe lights. Senate Democratic leader John Sampson and Assembly Republican leader Brian Kolb seethed. What governor had ever pushed the minority leaders out of the picture for a budget signing? None—ever! Political opposites though they were, Sampson and Kolb were one that day in their indignation. It was, as one of them put it, the ultimate disrespect to leaders who between them represented millions of New Yorkers. Worse, the slight was planned: the names of each leader were preprinted and put on the backs of their chairs, like tails on donkeys. The message being beamed by the media was Cuomo the inclusive governor, reaching across the aisle to get the job done. The governor the minority leaders were seeing here seemed, to the contrary, petty and divisive. Both seriously considered walking out; both later wished they had.

As a body, the lawmakers were exhausted, relieved, and awed. The governor had courted and cajoled them, with a kind of brute force no recent governor had displayed. Spitzer, with his outbursts, had come closest, but from the start he had seemed more petulant than scary. Andrew *was* scary. More than any of his predecessors, he understood power and how to use it.

Of all the governor's budget proposals, the only one left out was the one he had started the session by championing: a 2 percent property tax cap. In the end, the property tax cap passed into law on its own—with the support of Shelly Silver, the Assembly majority leader famously opposed to any such thing that kept schools, and the teachers' unions, from getting all the money they needed. Silver did get something in return: he extended rent regulations for New York City. Still, he had caved on a core issue. "That was unbelievable," a prominent Democratic senator marveled. "That was Shelly saying, 'I can't win against this guy.'"

Andrew knew how to rule. He also knew how quickly he had to build on this first success. "I'll be judged on whether I was a great governor based on my first eight months in office," he confided to one lawmaker. It was true. With the budget behind him, he was halfway there. Now, after this stern economizing, he had to lead with his heart, both to show he had one and to win the hearts of those who'd voted him in.

He knew just the issue. The timing was right. All he had to do was coax three reluctant Senate Democrats into voting for marriage equality, then find four even harder-to-get Republican votes.

He might as well have confronted seven camels and tried to teach them how to dance.

CHAPTER 22

Like Midas

Andrew was an unlikely hero for the same-sex marriage campaign. Whatever the truth of the old story—"Vote for Cuomo, Not the Homo"—he had done nothing of consequence for gay rights as attorney general.

Yet there he was one day in April, the budget done and gone, chairing a meeting in the Red Room with members of five gay rights groups set on changing the law at last. The governor told them how it was going to be. Steve Cohen, the governor's secretary, would be their boss. They would do what he said. There would be no rivalries, no angling for credit. To make that point very clear, the groups would work together under a new name: New Yorkers United for Marriage.

Bill Smith wasn't sure what to think about that. A seasoned activist at thirty-six, he had no problem with Andrew's blunt demeanor. Smith had worked on his first campaign, in Alabama as a college student, with an older operative named Karl Rove, and come to view him as a mentor even as their politics diverged. He liked the rough-and-tumble of the game. He just wasn't sure how Andrew would swing the votes with a Senate that in 2009 had voted down same-sex marriage 38–24. Meanwhile, the Tea Party's rise was stalling progress in Minnesota, Maryland, and Rhode Island. Even in New Jersey the movement had hit a wall with the election of Chris Christie: the new Republican governor was adamantly opposed to marriage equality. What made the time right for New York?

Not long after, the governor invited Smith to his office for a private meeting. As deputy executive director for the Gill Action Fund, Smith was one of the campaign's top operatives, and his years with Rove had given him insights into the Republican mind that would be useful for bringing around wavering Republican senators. Still, Smith expected the meeting to last five minutes, ten at most. Instead, he spent an intense hour with Andrew. He gave him a rundown on all that Gill Action was doing, starting with hiring a Republican pollster and lobbyist. Finally Andrew held up a hand. "We don't know each other that well," he said, "but I'm going to be really honest and tell you where we are and what we need to do."

Step one was to pull those three reluctant Democrats into line. Once they were on board, Andrew would stage the news conference with all twenty-nine Dems who were now yes voters. That would squeeze Skelos, who had said he would let gay marriage go to the floor for an up-or-down vote if the Democrats came together. Then, and only then, would they target Republicans who might be induced to switch their votes if they thought a bill would pass. And not just the three essential ones needed to tip the vote. That was the meeting at which Andrew explained the spare tire rule: you always lined up an extra vote so that the vote-tipping lawmaker didn't feel so exposed. Here that would mean getting a fourth Republican, for a 33–29 vote.

For the three balking Democrats, Andrew ticked off which county executives and local officials might be persuasive with each: "influencers," as he called them. He seemed to know every influencer in the state. On the Republican side, the governor had prospects whom Smith hadn't even considered, and strategies for each. Smith was still reeling when he called his fellow activists to say how the meeting had gone. "This guy is a hell of a poker player," Smith declared. "He is so far beyond where anyone knows he is on this." For the first time, Smith dared to think the campaign might prevail.

This was good news, the activists agreed, but the timing spooked them. Andrew wanted to hold off from submitting a bill until June—the end of session, after pushing other bills through. Why submit a bill, he reasoned, before he had the votes for it? Governor Paterson had taken the same tack in 2009, only to have the vote slide from June, when the Democrats staged their coup, to December, with disastrous consequences. Was this 2009 all over again? Andrew was adamant that that wouldn't happen again. Trust me, the governor told them. Just trust me.

It never occurred to Bill Smith not to trust the governor. Andrew seemed that determined and sure. Smith just worried about the lawmakers. Were they conning the activists again, taking the campaign's money and secretly planning to kill the bill? Passing it would mean an end to all that beautiful money; killing it might keep the money coming for next time. The possible Republicans were more trustworthy in a way: the political hit they would take from a yes vote far outweighed whatever money they might get, so theirs, Smith felt, would be votes of conscience, not cash. Later, one prominent Republican would disagree. "They did it for the money," he would say of his yes-vote colleagues. Not much money would come in before the vote. But in the months afterward, the four Republican senators who voted yes would take in far more money than they had before, ten or twenty times more. Did the prospect of that economic windfall sway votes? It was hard to say.

Money would matter—that much was true. But Andrew felt sure a bill would pass, and not because of the legislators and who tried to buy their votes. "The push of the people is what pushes the politicians," he liked to tell his staff. "That's what gets things done." On marriage equality, Andrew felt that push. It was only a matter of time.

On April 15, 2011, Alan Hevesi was sentenced to jail for a minimum of one year and maximum of four on a felony corruption charge. The former state comptroller had pled guilty to a wide range of misconduct, from taking free luxury trips and illegal campaign contributions to steering sham consulting fees to Hank Morris. It was the last scene in the pay-to-play drama that Andrew had led from his first days as attorney general. Along with that $170 million, the far-ranging investigation had netted eight guilty pleas. Hevesi was the second offender to go to jail, after Hank Morris, and the highest-ranking official in New York's modern history. Also, at seventy-one, the oldest. "I know that I caused enormous damage to the integrity of my former office," Hevesi told the court. "I will never forgive myself. I will live with this shame for the rest of my life."

Andrew had vowed to pass in his first year a sweeping ethics reform bill, one that would end pay-to-play with the state pension fund, but also force lawmakers to disclose outside income specifically, tighten campaign finance rules, and form a vigorous new panel to investigate legislators *and* the executive branch.

That last, if enacted, would be a huge step. As it was now, each branch had an ethics commission of its own, governed by its own leaders. Even as the list of indicted lawmakers grew, the legislature's ethics panel slept on, declining to punish a single lawmaker. On the executive side, the Spitzer-inspired Commission on Public Integrity had roused itself to slam Governor Paterson for those Yankees tickets, but that was a rare and shining moment.

Andrew warned Skelos and Silver not to block his ethics bill: if they did, he would convene a Moreland commission to paw over all their big campaign contributions and start connecting dots. The 1907 Moreland Act was peculiar to New York State, an enormous power vested in the governor to form a subpoena-wielding commission for the purpose of investigating any department, board, bureau, or commission in the state.

The one body a Moreland commission couldn't pursue was the legislature, but there were, perhaps, ways around that. Rather than put Moreland's limits to the test, the leaders agreed to give Andrew his bill and its crown jewel, a new investigative body Andrew had taken to calling JCOPE, for the Joint Commission on Public Ethics. JCOPE would have the unprecedented power to investigate both the executive *and* legislative branches for any kind of public corruption. There was, however, a catch. The leaders agreed that JCOPE would be independent, but together they would control its fourteen seats. The governor and lieutenant governor would get to fill six of them. Three of the governor's picks would be Democrats, the other three Republicans. Each of the majority leaders, in turn, would fill three seats. Each of the minority leaders would get one.

That might have seemed fair, if not for the veto rules. Any investigation of the legislative branch could be nixed by three votes, any investigation of the executive branch, just two. All that any of the three men in a room had to do to block an investigation they didn't like was have their handpicked members veto it. So as Blake Zeff, a political operative turned pundit, observed, JCOPE was a board that would investigate public corruption—only not any corruption in the legislature or the governor's office. "That leaves as targets the comptroller and the attorney general. Brilliant!"

JCOPE would occasionally hold open meetings, but most of its deliberations would be secret. Through his minions, then, the governor could control the process, suggest new targets of investigation, and veto any investigations he disliked—all behind closed doors. "This reminds me of J. Edgar Hoover," one lawmaker said in disgust. He wasn't far off.

That June, reluctantly, the legislature passed Andrew's ethics bill, with JCOPE as part of it. Despite JCOPE's obvious flaws, it might improve upon those snoozing commissions, and the bill overall seemed sound. Among other things, it set deadlines for lawmakers to disclose outside income and clients. Never one to miss the chance for a lofty title and acronym, Andrew called his bill the Public Integrity Reform Act, or PIRA. But for a governor who'd made ringing pledges of ethics reform, two elephants remained in the room.

One was redistricting. Andrew had stood by his pledge to veto any partisan plan to redraw the lines: he would settle for nothing less, he said, than an independent committee. But through the spring he made no effort to start such a committee. As for the party leaders, they settled into a not uneasy stalemate: neither, after all, wanted the independent committee that Andrew professed to want. Did even he want it? When it would surely mean an end to the Senate Republicans' newly rewon majority? The Senate Republicans, that is, with whom he was getting so much done? All that spring, whenever he was asked about it, Andrew said yes!—*independent redistricting!*—then let it slide, month after month.

By June 7, Democratic senator Michael Gianaris of Queens, for whom equitable redistricting had become a holy cause, began to despair. All he could do was hope that the governor responded to positive reinforcement. "We are here to say that we are not going to let this go away," Gianaris said in a hearing that day. "We have a governor who has stood strong, made clear his commitment to this issue, and has promised on more than one occasion that he will veto any redistricting bill that comes before his desk that was drawn by the legislature in the traditional, gerrymandered partisan way we have seen in the past. And with his continued commitment, I think we're heading towards a much fairer and evenhanded process going into next year."

With the end of the session, a legislative task force on redistricting would spend the summer crisscrossing the state like a traveling medicine show, holding meetings and drawing up maps the legislature might review, but also reject. Andrew would appear almost Zenlike, neither embracing the task force nor shutting it down. On all sides, the subject of redistricting appeared to inspire magical thinking.

The other elephant in the room was campaign finance reform. It too was essential to any plan for curbing corruption in Albany. Currently, a donor could give a statewide Democratic candidate up to $19,700 in a primary race and $41,100 in a general election. He could do it through an LLC—and then form another LLC, and give $60,800 through *that*, ad infinitum. A donor family could give $132,738 in the primary, and $270,413 in the general. Any donor could also give as much as he liked to a state party's "housekeeping fund." Arguably, New York had the most porous campaign finance rules in the nation. Yet in that first triumphant season, with his poll ratings as high as 77 percent and his power greater than it would likely be again, Andrew had kept a curious silence on the subject. Not everything could be done at once, his right-hand man Steve Cohen would say to good-government types who asked: let campaign finance be Year 2.

That June, as Andrew began chasing votes on marriage, one of his least favorite fellow Democrats came up with a plan of his own for campaign finance reform. Tom DiNapoli, the garrulous comptroller whom everyone but Andrew seemed to like, proposed a voluntary public campaign financing system that would apply only to the next comptroller's race. A test case, as it were. The plan would give each candidate six times the amount he raised in private contributions through matching public funds, up to a $2,000 limit in private donations. Under the anything-goes rules, DiNapoli's own race for comptroller the previous year had cost him $4.09 million; his Republican challenger had spent $6.97 million. That was madness. By starting the test now, before the next cycle, all candidates for comptroller would, like racehorses, be equally handicapped and fair elections might follow.

The legislature applauded its favorite comptroller, but declined to pass his bill. The truth was that neither party thought much of caps on campaign contributions: incumbents did better without them. Three years later, DiNapoli's plan would come back to haunt him, as Andrew took him up on it at last, in a way designed not to solve the problem but to punish and humiliate him.

What *was* it about DiNapoli that so irked the governor? That was a mystery the comptroller surely pondered. From his restless pursuit of Alan Hevesi and cronies, Andrew had come to believe no one official should have oversight of the state pension fund; perhaps he resented DiNapoli for not just resigning when the governor made his feelings clear. Or perhaps Andrew resented that in his official capacity DiNapoli had questioned cuts to the new budget and resisted the changes that Andrew was floating to trim state worker pensions. Whatever it was, the governor seemed to regard him with spite. Already with his inner circle, he referred to him by a nickname: Chipmunk Balls.

To Bill Smith, the weeks leading up to the vote on "marriage" were a blur. And then came the moment that he and his army of activists had fought so long to see. Smith came to the Senate chamber that Friday night barely able to breathe, until those third and fourth bill-tipping votes were heard and the chamber erupted in cheers.

Within minutes, Smith got a call on his cell to come to the Red Room. Other activists came too, and looked giddily on as Andrew, at the ceremonial desk his father had used before him, signed the bill into law. Then it was on to the executive mansion, where an impromptu party lasted well into the night. At one point, Andrew came over to Smith and clapped him on the shoulder. "You know what, Bill?" the governor asked. "You are very good at what you do." Smith was astonished. For the governor who had just changed the course of history to remember Smith's name, let alone think to praise him, was proof for Smith that here was a governor who could operate on multiple levels at once, from the global down to the individual.

That Sunday, Andrew joined the forty-second annual gay pride parade in Manhattan, holding up a banner with Mayor Bloomberg, City Council Speaker Christine Quinn, and other politicians and waving to the crowd.

All were warmly greeted, but Andrew was the unmistakable star, the roars rolling with him as the parade made its way to Christopher Street. "Finally we got someone who does what he believes in," one exuberant onlooker declared. "A lot of past governors and even the president haven't come through. He did."

With Andrew was Sandra, a rare joint appearance. Staffers were agreed that she'd pushed the governor hard on marriage; among the millions rooting for a change in the law was her gay brother, Johnny. Stepping out from the parade for a moment, the governor told a *New York Times* reporter, "I think you're going to see this message resonate all across the country now. If New York can do it, it's O.K. for every other place to do it." The new law made New York the sixth and largest state to legalize gay marriage. Republican governor Chris Christie, asked what he thought of the hullaballoo, waved off the thought that his state might be next. "I believe marriage should be between one man and one woman," he said. "I wouldn't sign a bill like the one that was in New York." Time would tell—very clearly—which governor had a better awareness of where the country was going.

"So, Governor," teased Maureen Dowd, the *New York Times* columnist, in an interview days later, "are you afraid you're going to hell?"

One Catholic to another, no explanation needed: the church had taken stern exception to Andrew's marriage-equality bill. For that matter, it bristled at his pro-choice stance on abortion, and his living in sin with Sandra Lee. In February, a Detroit-based advisor to the Vatican had publicly declared that because Andrew was living in "public concubinage" with Lee, he had no right to receive communion. As the marriage-equality campaign heated up, New York archbishop Timothy Dolan had fought it fiercely, calling gay marriage a perversity against nature. Dowd's question was wry, but not rhetorical.

"There are forms of hell, Maureen," the Jesuit's son retorted. "The question is, which level?"

Being at odds with the church, Andrew hastened to add, was troubling, but he had come to accept that that tension would probably remain through his political life, given that he was, in his words, an aggressive progressive—a liberal, that is, refashioning government to have goals and effective service, not a supplicant to big government. He still attended church with his three teenage daughters; he'd last received communion at his inaugural-day mass. But his faith was perhaps better illustrated by the picture of Saint Thomas More that his father had given him as a graduation present from Albany Law School—the picture he had carried with him from one office to the next.

Goading him a bit, Dowd asked if Andrew had taken on marriage equality as a stratagem, not out of the goodness of his heart. He told Dowd he hadn't thought he'd win. So... stratagem? Not really. It was, rather, a stance born out of scores of talks with voters, pleading for a bill that could change their lives. Signing that bill—with the ink wet, as he said, lest it somehow go away—had given him great satisfaction. But that was nothing compared to the gay pride parade.

"I have never been in anything like that in my life, period," he said. "Not when I worked with Clinton. Not with my father. In my 30 years in government, I never felt what I felt in that parade. Just the difference we made in people's lives, how we touched people and made them feel good about society. It was really magic."

Yet Andrew was hardly oblivious to the politics of the issue. Overnight, the vote had put him on the national stage. That, in turn, had led to talk of Andrew as a presidential candidate for 2016, perhaps even in a showdown with Christie, his rival across the Hudson. When Dowd popped the inevitable question about whether he'd run for national office, Andrew was ready with aw-shucks charm. "If I'm breathing in 2016," he told Dowd, "I'll be happy."

These were the words of a master deflector with epic ambitions. The giveaway was his travel schedule. Not once in his first six months had Andrew left the state. Trips, especially to Washington, D.C., would have made him seem a candidate in the making for higher office. That was what presidential hopefuls did. Andrew instead had kept his head down. It was a lesson learned from his father: focus on the job at hand and let the future take care of itself. Yet keeping a low profile also kept him a fresh commodity and piqued curiosity. And so not traveling became a kind of double fake-out. It tamped down talk of 2016, even as it kept him fresh for later on. He could say he really wasn't running. And he wasn't. Or did that mean he was?

For now, this much was clear: Andrew had had an extraordinary debut. He had accomplished nearly all he set out to do, from wiping out the budget's $10 billion deficit to passing an ethics reform act and changing the national course of marriage equality. It was not too much to suggest that the U.S. Supreme Court would be led, in its landmark ruling two years later, by the sea change New York had helped bring. In Albany, it was a session that inspired awe, even among downstate Democrats who resented his budget cuts. "I don't think any governor has ever had a first year like he had," marveled Democratic senator Kevin Parker. "Everything he wanted to do—it was like Midas."

As for the issues Andrew hadn't resolved, maybe—just maybe—the canny tactician had left them unresolved on purpose. Keeping redistricting in limbo played to his advantage. This way it remained a carrot to dangle over the Senate Republicans, perhaps to squeeze more from them before tossing it their way. As for campaign finance, the old, porous system worked just fine for an incumbent governor: already big contributions were flowing into Andrew's 2014 reelection fund, building a chest against chance. Let the do-gooders howl; nothing the governor did would be enough for them anyway. Maybe next year for campaign finance reform. Maybe the year after that.

The wild cheering for marriage equality had just died down when a more nettlesome issue reemerged, one that would not so easily be played on Andrew's political chessboard. On July 1, 2011, the state's Department of Environmental Conservation, or DEC, came out with its eagerly awaited report and recommendations on fracking. For the first time in his governorship, Andrew found himself looking at an issue that had the potential to turn out very badly—irreversibly so. Roughly half the electorate passionately supported it; the other half just as passionately decried it. Politically, fracking was a no-win.

Vertical fracking—drilling for natural gas—had been going on for decades in much of the country. The great innovation was *horizontal* fracking. Drills went deep underground, then angled sideways, shooting a high-pressure mix of water, chemicals, and sand to dislodge natural gas and oil from shale formations. Horizontal fracking did a great job tapping natural gas. Unfortunately, it also seemed capable of poisoning drinking water with toxic chemicals like benzene and arsenic, turning farms into brown fields with salty wastewater, and shrouding townships with sewage-like odors from chemical ponds. Most alarming, it appeared to add climate-warming gases, principally methane, to the atmosphere.

The DEC had undertaken this latest study of fracking at Governor Paterson's behest: he was the one, in December 2010, who had blocked the state's approval of fracking at the eleventh hour, and the free-for-all that would have ensued. Not enough about horizontal fracking's effects on the environment and human health was known, Paterson observed, and the risks were high.

Now, with Paterson's moratorium about to lapse, energy companies were restless and eager to drill. But scary stories were wafting north from Pennyslvania, where fracking was well under way. Parents were reporting children with respiratory illnesses—sick and dying barnyard animals too.

At neighborhood meetings, residents held up Mason jars of foul-looking water, taken, they said, from their sinks and streams.

The DEC's new report suggested a middle course. It advised going ahead with fracking, but very carefully, and only on private lands. Fracking would not be allowed in the upstate watershed that fed New York City, nor in watersheds that fed other cities and towns. No fracking in public parks and wildlife preserves either. Instead, it would start in the counties of the impoverished Southern Tier, along the New York–Pennsylvania border, over the gas-rich Marcellus Shale deposit. Over the last few years, the hard-hit farmers of the region had eagerly sold their mineral rights to the land agents who materialized like zombies, sent by the energy companies. But if fracking appeared too risky for public lands and watersheds, why would it be any less so in the Southern Tier?

Andrew was torn. He was still an environmentalist; even now, he was using his bully pulpit to call for the closing of the Indian Point nuclear plant in Westchester. Yet the economic benefits of fracking might pull New York's poorest counties from their decades-long depression, as well as fatten state coffers. The energy companies were pushing him hard; so, from the other side, were the fast-growing ranks of antifrackers. After reading the DEC report, Andrew told his DEC commissioner to start drawing up rules for fracking's first, small steps in the state.

For a governor wreathed in triumphs, fracking was a minor nuisance as yet. The only real threat to this new administration was Andrew himself.

Tough, nasty, vindictive—those judgments came from both sides of the aisle, though lawmakers in the minority of either chamber were, to be sure, more vocal. "I think he overplays the toughness," one lawmaker said. "Talk to lobbyists, legislators—they'll almost unanimously say the guy is a real prick, and he will do whatever he can to punish you, only you won't know it because he won't do it to your face. So if your community doesn't get a grant for a hospital that you've been advocating for... 'It wasn't competitive,' they'll say. Or if you call an agency to get things expedited and they don't expedite things when you call... Who knows? I'm not saying he's the only governor who's done that, but he's more prone to do it, and with no fingerprints."

Most politicians made it their business to cultivate their peers. By now, Andrew had gone out of his way as governor to alienate the four most prominent other politicians in the state: Senators Kirsten Gillibrand and Charles Schumer, Attorney General Eric Schneiderman, and Comptroller Tom DiNapoli. The governor had treated them warily at best, if not with outright antagonism. "I've never met someone so *mistrustful* of people, one of the four marveled. "How can anyone who feels that way get into politics?" So equally shared was that view that no one could say which of the four had articulated it.

On a day-to-day basis, the governor's inner circle punished uncooperative lawmakers with damaging leaks to the *New York Post*'s Fred Dicker. Uncooperative journalists, as in Mario's time, got hectoring calls, sometimes from the governor himself. The flip side was that Andrew, like his father, was available to reporters—the pliable ones, at least—whenever they needed him. But invariably those talks were off the record. It was if the whole Albany press corps had taken oaths of *omertà* with this fierce, controlling governor. Some felt complicit in a kind of conspiracy, a network of underground wires that all led to the governor's second-floor office. They could talk to the governor—yes. But most of what they heard they either couldn't use or could only attribute to sources close to the governor.

The stern, punitive climate that Andrew fostered was disquieting enough. The bigger problem was that Andrew by all accounts really did make every last decision, minor as some might be. He really did surround himself with a small tight circle that ran the state: Howard Glaser, Larry Schwartz, Joe Percoco. All were loyal and seasoned, efficient and tireless. But not one was an academic, let alone an intellectual. Not one wrote papers for scholarly journals or put in time at think tanks. They were all, like Andrew himself, "operational" guys. Bob Shrum, the venerable Democratic campaign manager, called Andrew "Mario without the poetry. I think he's almost proud of that. I actually think that could be something of a weakness if he runs for president. We respond to the poetry."

With such a death grip on the government, Andrew had filled his cabinet and lower levels mostly with lesser lights, leaving the occasional first-rater struggling to get anything done. Jason Helgerson, his Medicaid director, had brought his expertise as a Wisconsin state director and led the Medicaid Redesign Team: he was a standout in the Cuomo administration. Dr. Nirav Shah, the health commissioner, was another, with a serious academic background. But that, suggested a seasoned hand in the health care field, was about that. "Those are the only two stars. He has the poorest crop of commissioners I've ever seen. He has had huge trouble getting people to work for him. Cuomo and his small group can't figure out why they can't get good commissioners. Because the commissioners can't make any decisions!"

Below each commission head and agency director, Team Cuomo installed a loyalist whose main job was to provide a back channel to the second floor. "They often forget to invite the commissioner to meetings," the health care expert explained, "because he's not really necessary." At every agency and commission, the agenda was dictated from above. "The agencies are not empowered to do anything that's not an idea from the second floor," the health care expert said. "And if it's the second floor's idea, they jump and say, 'We have to do it, even if we don't believe in it.'" As a candidate, Cuomo had vowed to replace administration hacks with a real brain trust. But that would have meant enlisting independent minds. Even the governor's top advisers would admit that independence, in the Cuomo administration, was not a welcome trait.

Andrew had just had a phenomenal first session. If he ruled with an iron hand, feared more than loved, if he punished his enemies and let it be known he took pleasure in that, if he micromanaged to the point of strangling his staffers, and made every decision himself, what of it? He had just whipped the country's most dysfunctional capital into shape. Fear worked. Wielding harsh power worked.

But that was a hard way to sustain a kingdom, much less a querulous state. Soon, the strengths that had brought him this far—the brute force, the dark ambition, the political cunning—would threaten to become liabilities, and the challenges he had met would seem modest compared to the ones he faced ahead.

CHAPTER 23

Making Enemies

From his first day in office, Andrew knew that the mother of all memorial events loomed on the horizon—the tenth anniversary of 9/11—and that he would want to be involved in the planning of it. *Very* involved. Mayor Bloomberg, for his part, felt he had the planning in hand. In his nearly ten years in office, he had made the rebuilding of the twin towers site and the commemoration of 9/11 victims two of his highest priorities, not just as mayor but as chairman of the National September 11 Memorial & Museum at the World Trade Center Foundation. He had raised roughly $450 million in private monies for the memorial and museum, $15 million of that from his own pocket. He needed no help at all from the fledgling governor. But he knew he had to play nice.

The call came from Larry Schwartz, one of the governor's two chiefs of staff. Schwartz was polite, but left the mayor's team sensing that the governor wanted to run the show himself. Bloomberg rolled his eyes at this, but these were early days, and he still hoped to build a rapport with Andrew. So his team invited Schwartz to city hall for a full-fledged, bells-and-whistles briefing. The hope, as one staffer explained, was that Schwartz would be reassured the mayor wasn't trying to shut the governor out. But perhaps Schwartz would also see that the planning was so complex that Andrew wouldn't want to deal with it.

Schwartz seemed satisfied, and the more so at being included after that on the team's weekly 9/11 conference calls. The mayor's advisers thought they were home free—until a call from Schwartz a night or two before the event. "I get this screaming phone call from Larry saying, 'What's this poem that Andrew has been assigned to read?' " one aide recalled. "He's crazed. I can barely understand what he's saying." Finally the aide gleaned that Andrew was furious at being asked to read aloud a passage from President Franklin Roosevelt's famous declaration of the Four Freedoms from his 1941 State of the Union speech. The speech, Schwartz ranted, had been read before at an earlier 9/11 anniversary by Governor Pataki. Apparently that soiled it.

Since this particular aide wasn't on the 9/11 team, he wasn't sure what the program entailed. He said he would "check it out."

"I don't want you to fucking check it out," Schwartz shouted. "I want you to fucking fix it."

The aide learned that all speakers would be doing short readings only. Moreover, all would be reading passages used at previous anniversary gatherings. The ceremony was a ritual, to be *repeated*. Schwartz stayed furious long enough to fire off a few scorching e-mails to Patti Harris, the mayor's top aide, but the temperature cooled once he understood that none of the speakers would be giving a political speech. Especially New Jersey governor Chris Christie, who was already being discussed as a Republican rival for 2016. Finally Andrew agreed to read the Four Freedoms, only to be slighted again, or so he felt, on the day of the event.

Early that Sunday morning, Mario tried to access the World Trade Center site, to be rebuffed by security. Soon after, when he tried to enter the 9/11 Memorial area, he was blocked again. Tensions remained high until a Port Authority official intervened to see him through. When Andrew heard this, he was livid. The mayor was snubbing his father! The whole Cuomo family felt dissed.

How exactly had Mario been snubbed? a mayoral aide later inquired. He had been asked to go through a metal detector, and apparently refused. "It was crazy shit!" the aide marveled. "The mayor's attitude was: I go through a metal detector every day at city hall. So does everyone. So it's not a snub to make Mario go through a metal detector. Our attitude was wonderment and dismay."

Andrew's was molten resentment.

In their first year as partners in running the state and city of New York, Andrew Cuomo and Michael Bloomberg had found each other annoying so often that stories of their mutually bruised feelings made the rounds of New York's political class and even the *New York Times*. "They Fume and They Bicker While Running City and State," ran the *Times* headline in mid-December 2011, over a story that noted the governor and mayor had not appeared together at one news conference all year. Instead, they scoffed at each other's "egos, moods and stunts," the slights and retorts conveyed through their aides-de-camp. "The governor portrays the mayor as inflexible, sanctimonious and someone who treats the democratic process as an inconvenience," the story suggested. "Mr. Bloomberg is said to see Mr. Cuomo as the epitome of the self-interested, horse-trading political culture he has long stood against." Cuomo, according to confidants, thought Bloomberg acted like a king, bullying anyone who balked at his plans. "Mr. Bloomberg's camp, in turn, saw the governor as willing to hold hostage an important piece of legislation to squeeze the city on other issues."

With the 9/11 fight simmering, the two spent much of the fall fighting over taxis—and not who had first hailed one in the rain. It was a standoff that showed the governor at his worst: willful and machinating.

Bloomberg had set out to solve the age-old problem of finding a taxi in the outer boroughs. Yellow medallion taxis stuck to Manhattan, their drivers fearful of venturing to poor and sometimes dangerous neighborhoods beyond. Unlicensed livery cars filled the gap, but with drivers who might be unreliable or worse. Bloomberg wanted a new fleet of up to thirty thousand properly permitted outer-borough livery cars. In June 2011, he had helped push a bill through the state legislature. Oddly, the governor refused to sign it. Instead, as one mayoral adviser put it, "he proceeds to just bloody torture us for months."

Andrew's advisers liked to say that the governor went out of his way to avoid even the appearance of favors granted in return for campaign contributions. "Giving a big donation to Andrew," one adviser said, "is the best way to assure you *don't* get special treatment." Yet the politics here did seem to create an unfortunate appearance. Vehemently opposing Mayor Bloomberg's livery car bill was the yellow-taxi industry. One of its major players, Medallion Financial, had given at least $49,000 to Andrew for his governor's race, and $37,000 for his AG race. One of Medallion Financial's longtime board members, as it happened, was Mario, who for his services was paid about $53,000 a year.

Typically, the governor signed new bills within days or weeks of their passing. Instead, of course, he could veto them. With the livery car bill, Andrew simply took no action, month after month after month. "He couldn't veto the bill because of Mario," one observer noted: that would look bad. But he could leave the bill open, knowing that lobbyists from the taxi industry would swarm, wringing so many concessions that the bill's own backers might kill it in disgust.

The bill was still sitting on the governor's desk in December when Andrew found a way to use it as a bargaining chip with Bloomberg on another issue. The mayor's staff was astonished. As one staffer put it, "We have a deal, we have a bill, no way they're pulling it!" Andrew responded by pulling the bill, then denying it even existed. Assembly leaders decided enough was enough. Andrew would have to sign the bill in ten days or go on record as vetoing it. In the end, after whacking down the number of livery cars the bill would sanction, from thirty thousand to eighteen thousand, Andrew signed—on such short notice that Bloomberg was iced out of the press conference and forced to participate by speakerphone. Privately, the mayor ranted to his aides; publicly, he stuck to protocol. "The governor and I are going to have big smiles on our faces tonight," he told reporters. "This is something that was three decades in the making, but tonight it is getting done."

In the fall of 2011, with the legislature still out of session, Andrew focused on getting JCOPE up and running. By December, he had chosen his six of the fourteen commissioners: three Democrats and three Republicans, as per the rules. Only he didn't stop there. Privately, he pushed for Ellen Biben, top prosecutor from his AG tenure, to be JCOPE's executive director. Biben had glided to a nice perch in the new administration as state inspector general. After Andrew's bruising battles with Susan Gaffney at HUD, he knew how troublesome an IG could be, and happily exercised his power to choose the state's IG himself. At JCOPE, Biben would give the governor more of the same: unquestioning loyalty. The push came via Larry Schwartz, who urged Democratic minority leader John Sampson to have his one JCOPE member support Biben. Sampson had chosen Ravi Batra, the Indian-American lawyer with close ties to the black establishment. Batra told Sampson he had already made up his mind to vote for her, given her pedigree as an alumna of New York district attorney Bob Morgenthau's office. Others fell into line, but not without misgivings. They had been assured that JCOPE would be an independent body. They knew exactly what Biben was: the governor's eyes and ears.

Getting JCOPE up to speed was perfect work for a restless governor in the legislative hiatus. Unfortunately for the lawmakers, an issue arose that December that Andrew couldn't handle on his own. It needed a vote before the lawmakers' scheduled return—in fact, before the end of the year.

This was the season of Occupy Wall Street, the ragtag rebellion of the poor and the young against the moneyed One Percent. By late October, an Albany faction of roughly two hundred protesters had taken up residence in Academy Park, across the street from the capitol, pitching about fifty tents and settling in, it appeared, for the long haul. Their grievances were the same general ones they had aired on Wall Street: social and economic inequality. But in Albany they had found a perfect, timely target: the millionaires' tax set to expire on December 31. Why not keep the One Percent paying that $4 billion a year to New York State's coffers, and use the proceeds to help the oppressed? From the encampment they called

Cuomoville, the Occupiers mocked Andrew as Governor One Percent for his adamant refusal to prolong the tax—a moniker that started to stick.

Overnight, the governor who had wielded such iron control over Albany looked rigid and brittle. He could have wandered over to chat with the protesters and pulled the story his way. Instead, he urged Albany mayor Gerald Jennings to enforce a curfew and have scofflaws removed. Initially, Jennings agreed. Then wiser legal counsel prevailed; the protesters, he decided, could stay after all. During the past year's campaign, Andrew had thought of asking Jennings to be his lieutenant governor—Jennings had supported him back in the ill-fated 2002 gubernatorial campaign—but gone instead with Rochester mayor Robert Duffy. In a snide leak to Dicker, one of Andrew's top advisers declared, "It's fair to say that after Jennings's performance with the demonstrators, the governor thinks he made the right choice."

In truth, the millionaires' tax was a tough nut. Its vanishing would be cheered by the wealthy New Yorkers forced to pay it for three years as a stopgap when the Great Recession hit. Governor Paterson had promised the tax would be temporary; Andrew felt duty-bound to honor that pledge. But as the Occupiers noted, its sunsetting would cost the state $4 billion.

Andrew had his own reasons for wishing the tax might stay on the books. He'd promised to restore $805 million to education in 2012. The millionaires' tax would solve that problem. Then, too, the ongoing year's budget, triumphal as it was back in April, was opening a $1 billion gap, one likely to grow to more than $3 billion in 2012–13. Without the millionaires' tax, where would that money come from?

As the protesters milled outside, Andrew cracked open the tax codes in search of a compromise. The legislative chambers were dark, but Silver and Skelos were willing to meet with him: Three Men in a Room, the whole tax code before them.

The fix Andrew found was both simple and clever. He would *not* let the millionaires' tax sunset as planned. Nor would he keep it as it was. Instead, he would cut it in half. The rich would see their taxes go down, just not as much as they'd hoped. The tax that remained would still generate $1.9 billion—enough for Andrew to make good on his education pledge and help plug the expanding gap. Some of that money would even be used for a modest *middle-class* tax cut. Less taxes for all! Skelos and Silver could sell the compromise to their different constituencies as a tax cut, while neglecting to note that a top-tier tax intended to last three years would extend another three years after all.

As soon as the leaders had worked it all out, Andrew called a one-day emergency session of the legislature and handed out his still-wet tax bill with—no surprise by now to the lawmakers of either party—a message of necessity. The Senate was forced to vote on the nineteen-thousand-word bill less than half an hour after receiving it. Susan Lerner of Common Cause, one of the state's good-government watchdogs, was staggered. The entire tax code had just been recast by Three Men in a Room and the lawmakers were supposed to just rubber-stamp it?

Brian Kolb, the minority leader in the Assembly, was in conference on the bill with his fellow Republicans when he got word the governor was calling. "Tell him I'll call him back as soon as we're done with conference," Kolb said.

The governor, Kolb was told, wanted to talk to him now.

Clearly, Andrew had heard rumblings of discontent from the Republican side of the aisle. Kolb had members who wanted to sunset the rest of the millionaires' tax as planned: $2 billion was $2 billion. The governor was not pleased. The threat he made to Kolb, as one staffer recalled, was quite explicit. *You tell your members I will come into their districts—anyone who doesn't support this bill*, he told the minority leader. Andrew would use his bully pulpit, and his popularity among Republicans, to turn voters against any lawmakers who failed to support his bill. He would definitely come after Kolb, supporting a rival in the leader's next election.

These weren't votes Andrew needed. He had his majorities for the bill in both chambers. Kolb just had a few malcontents. But the governor didn't just want a majority on his millionaires' tax bill. He wanted *all* the votes.

"The governor wants me to give you a message," Kolb told his members when Andrew had rung off. Kolb duly relayed it. *You tell your members . . .* After a pause, he added, "I want you to know that if you vote no, I'll be standing right beside you." Kolb voted no, as did a handful of colleagues; in all, the bill drew eight no votes from the entire legislature.

Apparently one or more of Kolb's Republicans saw fit to communicate the governor's threat to the press. Suddenly Kolb's office phone began lighting up, as one staffer later put it, like a Christmas tree. Kolb was on the floor without a cell phone; when he got back to his office, Andrew was on the line. He was furious the press had found out about his threat.

What, Kolb said wonderingly, was he supposed to do?

"You can shut this down," the governor said.

"I'll just say what happened," Kolb said.

"You can't do that."

At the other end, Kolb could hear Joe Percoco next to the governor, whispering into his ear.

"What would be really helpful is if your press people shut up," Andrew said. "You've fueled the fire!"

Grudgingly, Kolb agreed to call the press corps and tamp down the story. He made fifteen calls, low-keying the dissident votes and giving noncommittal quotes. But the damage was done.

Kolb had only done what the governor told him to do. And yet Andrew was enraged. "He wants to control it," Kolb mused to a colleague later. "He wants to control it all."

On the first anniversary of his inauguration, the governor, in a dark suit and tie, greeted hundreds of visitors in the executive mansion's receiving hall. Beside him stood Sandra Lee, elegant in a sleeveless white dress, her blond hair up in a simple chignon. State workers thanked Andrew for bringing dignity back to the country's most dysfunctional capital. Young couples praised him for seizing the initiative and getting things done—big things, like marriage equality. Children told him they planned to run for governor too. "I think he's been doing a very good job," one nine-year-old said, "and he's so lucky he gets to live in such a big house."

Insiders might nurse their beefs, but to the public, Andrew stood as the can-do leader of a new, hard-driving, honest administration, credible and competent. Nowhere was that more evident and impressive than in the capitol building itself. There, in addition to his day job, Andrew was presiding over a full renovation of the 1899 landmark with an energy that surprised even his closest advisers.

Like so much else in Albany, the restoration had begun years before—in the Pataki administration, in 2000—and moved slowly to remove the dust and decay of decades. The red terra-cotta roof still had leaks; skylights were blacked out from World War II; the Hall of Governors, with its portraits of governors past, was steeped in gloom; the ceiling mural of historical state conflicts was obscured and all but forgotten. New York State history buff that he was, Andrew had seized control of the project, determined not merely to clean up the place but make it a visitors' destination. The governors' portraits were refurbished, text blocks added below, the walls painted in colors historically correct, the floors waxed and buffed just so. By early 2012, the restoration was nearly finished, two years ahead of schedule, at a cost savings, the governor proudly noted, of more than $2 million.

Some lawmakers ridiculed the governor's insistence on choosing paint colors, and called it a metaphor for how he ran the state, the micromanager at work. For Andrew, it symbolized something else: appearances mattered. "I walk into your home, you haven't said a word, you've communicated a lot to me: what you have on the walls, what it looks like," Andrew told the *New York Times*. "This building makes a statement about the state government."

Historian and Cuomo family friend Harold Holzer, enlisted to help, admired Andrew's energy for what was in fact an extra full-time job—or three—as chief architect, art historian, and restorer. So dedicated was Andrew that he lent items from his personal collection of New York gubernatorial history, including documents from nineteenth-century governors Morgan Lewis and Martin Van Buren. At its unveiling, the Hall of Governors would be missing only one governor's portrait: that of Mario Cuomo. Mario had refused to sit for one, either during or after his governorship. It was one of Albany's little mysteries, for which Andrew had no answer. "Some things are above my pay grade, and that's one of them," he told a reporter. "You're talking to the wrong Cuomo."

The capitol was the least of it. For his second State of the State speech, in early January 2012, Andrew made clear that major changes were in the offing, changes that would do more than close a budget gap. In Year 2, Andrew wanted to pull the state's economy out of its decades-long torpor at last.

Out of protocol, the governor invited Mayor Bloomberg to attend the address; out of protocol, the mayor came; and so it was that the mayor found himself in a car with aides, headed in from the Albany airport, when a call came from Larry Schwartz, Andrew's "secretary" now that Steve Cohen had gone back to private practice. The governor wanted the mayor to know that in his speech he was going to announce a vast new convention center to be built in New York City, adjacent to the Aqueduct racetrack in Queens.

The mayor was stunned.

"Think about the gall," suggested one of the mayor's aides in retrospect. "To announce this package of billions... and huge construction... you tell the mayor minutes before?"

To his curious and slightly confused audience, Andrew explained that a Malaysian gaming company called Genting would build the complex at no cost to the city or state. It would generate tens of thousands of jobs and help jump-start New York's economy. It would, as he put it, "complete the vision" of the Aqueduct racetrack where it would be built. Genting had just unveiled the first part of that vision: thousands of "video lottery terminals" for gamblers, adjacent to the Aqueduct track, the end of a long and messy contest among bidders for that VLT business. VLTs were gambling lite, but already generating heavy profits. Andrew neglected to mention that along with the convention center, the rest of Genting's vision for Aqueduct would include full-on casino gambling, not yet legal statewide. He did, however, call for full-on gaming to be legalized.

"It's not a question of whether we should have gaming in New York," Andrew declared. "The fact is we already do." The state had four Thoroughbred horse-racing tracks, but the proceeds from those were small change compared to what full-fledged casinos might bring. It had quite a few harness-racing tracks with "racinos"—VLTs, as at Aqueduct—but they too were small-bore compared to casinos. It had six Indian-run casinos on reservation land, but the state got only a smidgeon of the revenues it felt it was owed by those. To maximize the gains that gaming could bring, New York needed full-fledged casinos overseen by the state. That would require an amendment to the state's constitution: approval by two successive legislatures, followed by a public referendum. The governor promised to start that process in 2012.

Among the princely benefits that Genting's complex would bring was this one: it would obviate the need for the ugly and much-maligned Javits Center in west Midtown Manhattan. That, Andrew explained in his speech, would free up eighteen acres of state-owned land overlooking the Hudson River, a real estate bonanza in one of Manhattan's fastest-growing neighborhoods.

Most in the audience recalled that another Governor Cuomo had built the Javits Center, amid cost overruns and links to mobster-affiliated contractors. Unsightly as the center was, it had gone on to be profitable, with an 80 percent occupancy rate—profitable enough to be in the midst of a $500 million renovation. Only later would lawmakers learn that razing Javits was a requirement of the deal: Genting wanted no competition. Andrew would be tearing down his father's eyesore and building something more beautiful of his own.

Genting fit the Year 2 theme of jump-starting the state's economy. But how had a major building plan, with future profits of billions of dollars, won the governor's blessing without competitive bidding? The answer wouldn't come for some months. When it did, it would rock the governor like nothing before.

In those opening weeks of his second session, buoyed by triumphs and still-high poll numbers, with even the millionaires' tax turned to gold, Andrew wielded almost absolute power. With it he sought more control, which gave him more power. His conduit was Ellen Biben, his handpicked inspector general, about to take her seat as his handpicked executive director of JCOPE.

Early in her tenure as IG, Biben had gained enormous power, clearly at Andrew's behest, when all the deputy inspectors general of all the government's many agencies ceased reporting to the IGs of those agencies and started reporting instead to her.

Then came the follow-up. In a memo of understanding generated in early February 2012, Biben took over the state tax department's investigation operations and deputized all her IG troops as special tax commissioners. Now every last one of them had the power to inspect the tax records of any state employee under suspicion.

The implications were immense. Before, a small number of IG investigators at the Department of Taxation and Finance—and *only* at that department—had had access to the tax records of the state's two hundred thousand workers. Now no fewer than sixty-three employees of the newly expanded IG's office would have that access. Strictly speaking, a state worker needed to be under investigation for the IG's myriad investigators to pull a tax record. But anyone linked to that target was fair game too. For that matter, what was to prevent a governor from using this vastly increased power to conduct fishing expeditions against his political enemies? Nothing in the wording of the policy.

Both sides of the aisle were aghast. One high-ranking Republican senator went so far as to call the new policy "very, very dangerous." But Andrew had picked his moment well. The party leaders could ill afford a showdown with the new budget unfinished and redistricting unresolved. And so they seethed in silence. Later, a court ruling would rein in the new policy. Only ten key IG staffers would be allowed to go through tax records. For the lawmakers, this was cold comfort, since the IG reported to Andrew. It did nothing to stop the governor from fishing as he pleased. And as the lawmakers knew from fawning stories on how he spent his leisure time, the governor liked to fish.

On February 28, 2012, JCOPE officially seated Ellen Biben as its executive director. There too was JCOPE'S new chairwoman, Janet DiFiore, the Westchester district attorney. Andrew had supported her when he was attorney general.

To Ravi Batra, the member named by Democratic Senate minority leader John Sampson, any hope that JCOPE would be a dignified, independent body was dashed as soon as everyone took their seats in a conference room at the foot of capitol hill. Biben and DiFiore had staffers sitting right between the commissioners at the table. "I don't want a staffer sitting right next to me, watching what I write in my notes," Batra explained. "Second, when staffers are sitting with us, they're equal with us. One of the oldest lessons of power is protocol. The commissioners' power was destroyed the first day of JCOPE."

At that first meeting, Biben told the commissioners she intended to keep JCOPE impartial. Batra took her at her word, but others at the table were troubled. Not only were Biben and DiFiore the governor's handpicked choices, but JCOPE would report to the inspector general's office. That in effect made it part of the executive branch, reporting directly to Andrew.

Batra's concern was philosophical. "An ethics commission is not a prosecutor's office," he declared. "An ethics commission is more like the church. It talks about your morality and soul. Prosecutors deal with black and white: a crime or not a crime." JCOPE, he felt, should be less about deterrence than uplifting lawmakers to be moral. Yet all its leaders were prosecutors.

As he worked to balance his second budget and get it in on time, Andrew made another power grab, this one in the name of efficiency.

Lawmakers were startled to find, in the governor's draft, a little 130-word paragraph in legalese, repeated hundreds of times. The inclusion gave the governor power to pull funds from one agency to another after the budget was done. The point, as he explained, was to get the most use from the money. A dozen small piles might be merged to get a big job done—a new road, say, or a bridge—and also be leveraged to borrow that much more. Already, Andrew had a public/private program in mind called New York Works that would spend more than $25 billion on such projects.

Efficient, yes. But proper? Not really. Money authorized for one use, Comptroller Tom DiNapoli observed, could not just be used willy-nilly some other way. Pressed by seventeen good-government groups to drop that 130-word paragraph of boilerplate from the budget, the governor instead put tighter constraints on his power grab. In the end, it passed.

For that small pushback, DiNapoli found himself a target. The Department of Financial Services, led by Andrew's top aide Ben Lawsky, suddenly determined that the time was meet and right to audit the technology used by the office of the state comptroller. It was shocked—shocked!—to find outdated systems. "Meanwhile," said an observer sympathetic to DiNapoli, "Cuomo has made the comptroller's budget neutral—so there's no money for new technology!"

The governor had another unpleasant surprise for DiNapoli in his draft of the budget. Part of the state comptroller's job was to audit most contracts worth $50,000 or more in the ninety days before they were signed:

an impartial set of eyes focused on keeping the state's expenditures sound. The governor proposed to do away with that protocol. Better and more efficient, Andrew argued, to get contracts signed quickly, start the work, and do the auditing later. As the *New York Times* noted in an editorial, waste and corruption were all too common in New York State, and so-called preauditing by the comptroller had blocked more than enough dubious contracts to justify the practice. But Andrew was adamant.

DiNapoli had an enemy in the governor, no doubt about that. He found it both jarring and baffling. "I supported the guy!" he told colleagues. "I don't get it!" He meant he'd supported him *lately*. Not in 2002. Perhaps more to the point, DiNapoli had violated the first rule of Team Cuomo: never disagree with the boss. This was true even if, as was the case here, Andrew wasn't DiNapoli's boss. The comptroller was a force unto himself. The rule still applied, since Andrew was, as far as he was concerned, everyone's boss. "I *am* the government," he had explained not long before in a radio interview. Reminded that the government included the legislature, which was not under his control, Andrew had qualified his statement. "On the executive side," he said. That was the more interesting slip. In fact, the governor did not oversee the entire executive branch: the comptroller and the attorney general were both powers unto themselves. Perhaps that was why the occupants of each office—DiNapoli and Attorney General Eric Schneiderman—got under the governor's skin.

With DiNapoli, tensions grew as Andrew drafted the next year's budget, due as usual by April 1. The governor's new goal was to trim, at last, the state's pension obligations. To Andrew's annoyance, the comptroller disapproved of his plan.

Andrew knew better than to try to cut pension money already promised. His pitch was to curb the benefits of *future* workers. Instead of having them kick in just 3 percent of their earnings to their pension plans, they would pay between 4 percent and 6 percent. The age of eligibility would be bumped up from sixty-two to sixty-five; the percentage of full-time pay they would get after retiring would decline by 17 percent. Since they didn't yet exist, these future workers could hardly complain, and the state would save a bundle: $113 billion over thirty years, or so said Andrew.

Sitting as he did on the $140.3 billion state workers' pension fund, DiNapoli questioned whether there was really a crisis here. The fund was doing better than those of many states, well enough to meet its obligations. Why punish future workers? He worried, too, about Andrew's call for workers to invest their pension money in self-managed 401(k) funds rather than the state fund. Workers who knew little about investing would be vulnerable to serious losses.

DiNapoli felt he had to speak out against Tier VI, as Andrew's proposed layer of future cuts was now formally known. The governor retorted that this was none of DiNapoli's business, since any change in state worker pensions was the legislature's to make, not anyone else's. "The comptroller is irrelevant from a voting point of view," Cuomo snapped, "because he doesn't vote."

"I may not have a vote in it," DiNapoli shot back, "but I do have a voice in it."

As the days ticked closer to the March 31 budget deadline, Andrew again threatened to pull out the Paterson extender. If the legislature failed to pass some form of Tier VI, Andrew would put his own version up for a take-it-or-leave-it vote. If the lawmakers voted it down, that would close the government. There wasn't any more extreme move than that, but Andrew would do it, he warned: pension reform was that important. It was, in fact, the "central power struggle of Albany," as he put it, pitting special interests against taxpayers. "Pension reform," he said, "goes right at the heart of the beast."

As part of the budget fight, Andrew was still vowing to end partisan redistricting at last. But any reader of the Albany tea leaves could see he was readying to let both parties draw their own lines again. The only question was how much he'd squeeze from the anxious Republican Senate before he let them off the hook.

By early March, he had nixed the legislative committee's first set of lines as "hyperpartisan" and submitted his own version. Back from the legislature came a revised draft. "It was about 98 percent the same as the first," recalled one disgusted lawmaker. "But suddenly it wasn't hyperpartisan anymore—Cuomo was saying it was better, though it didn't pass the straight face test."

Andrew put it more philosophically. "If there were acceptable lines—not the current lines, which are unacceptable—if there were acceptable lines, and if there was a real constitutional amendment and if there was statutory language that could protect the people if the legislature changes their mind and want to pass a constitutional amendment, that would be a possible resolution," he now said, opining, as had become his custom, on *New York Post* political columnist Fred Dicker's local radio show. Reasonable though that might sound, it was very different from his mantra of the previous summer: that he would veto any plan not done by an independent panel.

This was more than a compromise. It was a ten-year concession. By Andrew's new plan, lines for the next decade would be drawn as before, hopefully a bit more equitably, but by the same old process. At the same time, a constitutional amendment would start making its way through the legislature. *If* the amendment passed, then in 2022, when once again the time came to draw those district lines, an "independent" panel would do that work. The legislators, however, would get to determine the makeup of that panel, and if they didn't like what the panel produced, then after two tries they could modify the plan—to what end, who knew?

For the lines now being drawn, Andrew still had the power of the veto. And while the Republican Senate held its collective breath, waiting for those lines to be approved, the governor had power—absolute power—over them. It was not an opportunity to be missed.

First and foremost, the governor got Tier VI, with its trimmed-down benefits for future state workers. The new retirement age would be sixty-three, not sixty-five. It would save $80 billion, not $113 billion, over thirty years—or so said Andrew; Tom DiNapoli had his doubts. Still, it was a victory, and one that showed grit: not many governors went up against their state workers' unions.

The budget, as always, was a party bag of bills, not just one. This year, as last, Andrew got nearly all he wanted. One victory was a constitutional amendment for gaming approved by the legislature. The amendment would bring seven casinos to hard-hit regions, assuming the next legislature approved it too, and the public voted yes. Another on the list was a plan at last to evaluate teachers by quality, not just seniority. Andrew lost his bid to pull funds as needed from any state agency as he wished—potentially putting every public project across the state under his control—but he did get the right to combine funds strictly for "back office" purposes. He also won his battle to approve contracts for state work without a preaudit from Tom DiNapoli, the put-upon comptroller. DiNapoli called it a mistake, but his warning went unheard.

In his campaign for office, Andrew had vowed to usher in a new era of transparency. Yet the Big Ugly of 2012 was hashed out, as always, behind closed doors: Three Men in a Room. On March 14, 2012, bleary lawmakers waited for Cuomo, Skelos, and Silver to hand down the bills one by one as Wednesday night turned to Thursday morning. The pension bill—Tier VI—was the last to arrive, so late that the vote to approve it came at 7:26 a.m., as the sun was rising. Yet all four bills were tagged as "messages of necessity," like state emergencies, to be voted on so quickly that lawmakers barely had time to peruse them, much less ponder them. Not to worry, they were told: the lawmakers merely had to vote as their leaders told them. "Sleep deprivation is something they use in warfare to confuse people to get them to do inappropriate things," noted Republican assemblyman James Tedisco. "When it's three or four or five o'clock in the morning, you want to get home and get to your family and go to sleep. People lying on couches asleep—that's not the way to govern."

At some point in that long night, the governor gave Skelos and Silver the silver platter they'd wanted all along: redistricting their way. Not only did the bill call for drawing the lines as usual for the coming elections of 2012 and the decade following, but the party leaders also used highly dubious electoral math, based on a constitution from 1894, to resolve that a new district be added to the sixty-two constituting the state. This new sixty-third district, technically number 46, would be in the upper Hudson Valley. Its lines enclosed a Republican stronghold. Essentially, Andrew was giving the Republicans an extra vote to help assure their senate majority.

As lawmakers pored over the 253 copier-hot pages of the Big Ugly's biggest deal, outlining street by street the proposed lines of the Senate and Assembly districts, angry cries arose from those who had dared to hope that justice would prevail at last. There was no way to justify the "packing" of poor blacks and Hispanics into gerrymandered districts that gave them one assemblyman instead of the two their population deserved, or the "cracking" of such districts so that each half was absorbed by a larger district, with a commensurate loss of representation. Yet the die was cast, the lines drawn: for the next decade, pools of the poor, the black, the Hispanic, and in some cases just plain old white Democrats would be modern-day equivalents of the colonists under King George III: taxed without representation.

"Have you no shame?" exclaimed Queens Democrat Michael Gianaris, Assembly leader of the years-long fight for fair redistricting, to Senator Michael Nozzolio, the Republican point man on the bill. The Republicans could take the bill, said Gianaris, "and shove it." In the Senate, Democrats led a walkout. The vote, as a result, was 36–0: the thirty-two Republicans plus the four members of the Independent Democratic Conference, the wedge group formerly known as Democrats.

To Mayor Ed Koch, for whom redistricting had been a last hurrah, it was a bitter blow, enacted by "the most devious Legislature in America." He had tried his best, he said, to no avail. "The ghouls won." To Koch, the most villainous of the Three Men in a Room that night was Dean Skelos. The Republican leader had pledged to reform the plainly corrupt process; so had his colleagues. In the end, he had broken his promise. "Not an honorable person in my book," Koch said. Skelos's reply was a model of prevarication. "When that whole situation came up, it was the swirl of the campaign. And after the election I explored it and my belief was the constitution would not allow it," he said, meaning an independent panel without a constitutional amendment. "The governor has indicated on numerous occasions that it is a legislative function. We cannot delegate that away, period."

Andrew, surprisingly, agreed: drawing those district lines was a legislative function. Why then had he ever suggested forming an independent panel to draw the lines, when he knew he couldn't impose one on the legislature? Had this just been a ploy to mollify the liberal wing of his party?

Andrew did have one last weapon he could have used if he wished. He could have vetoed the bill and let the line drawing go to the courts. He hadn't for a reason he chose not to announce. The truth was that Andrew distrusted his fellow Democrats, at least those in the Senate, none more so than its leader, John Sampson. The Democrats, especially the downstate Democrats—more pointedly the black and Hispanic downstate Democrats—were being indicted one after another. Skelos and his fellow Republicans might resist the governor's social agenda, but they, at least, were grown-ups. Andrew preferred working with them, so much so that he had just given his blessing to bad legislation, and a decade at least of inequity for the Democratic voters of his state, to get done what he needed to do, with the lawmakers he trusted—or, perhaps more accurately, those whose goals more closely tracked his own and whom he could herd his way. "In a Senate controlled by Democrats, he never would have gotten a property tax cap," admitted downstate Democratic senator Kevin Parker. "We never would have allowed him to pass a budget in the way he did. He knew the kind of legislation he needed to do."

But now the trade had been made. The Republicans had their majority, likely for the next decade, despite their dwindling numbers across the state. They had helped the governor win legislation that they for the most part wanted anyway, starting with Tier VI. Who, then, was the real winner here? "I'll tell you a story about the senate majority," said a senior lawmaker. "The day the governor signed the bill on the districts, Skelos told his troops, 'Stand up straight, pull up your pants. We're going to do it our way now.'"

To Democrats, Andrew's deal on the districts was a great betrayal, not only of his campaign vow on the issue, but of the whole party. By their reckoning, an equitable drawing of the lines would have put them, next election day, squarely in the Senate majority with thirty-six or thirty-eight seats. Their leader had pulled the rug out from under them. "The truth is," opined the *New York Times*, "this deal guarantees that the back-room politics that have infected Albany for generations will govern for another decade."

"I failed, I failed," Andrew lamented about redistricting to reporters in his office the morning after. "I supported an independent commission for these lines," he said. "I lost." But the governor was adamant that long-term reform would come. "My legislative proposals were asking for the moon," he said, with his usual penchant for clichés. "Fight as hard as you can, and then understand there's going to have to be some amount of reasonable compromise."

For the most part, when Andrew wanted to make his thoughts known, he shared them with the *New York Post*'s Fred Dicker, whose admiration of the governor's prowess was absolute. In his column after the Big Ugly, Dicker lauded Andrew's "tour de force of political dexterity" and his "quadruple victory."

To fellow journalists who had covered a governorship or two, Dicker's enthusiasm had a déjà vu feel to it. Every new governor, beginning with Mario, had provoked in Dicker a sort of extended professional swoon. In exchange had come almost daily leaks from the second floor, all from unnamed sources. Then suddenly, with each governor, the honeymoon had ended. Some stance or failing had enraged the columnist. Afterward, the governor who could do no wrong could do no right, and so each leader had come to the end of his tenure heaped with Dicker's scorn.

When, Albany's press corps wondered, would Dicker's honeymoon with Andrew end? Clearly the columnist remained an ardent fan. Unbeknownst to his colleagues, Dicker was about to sign on with a major New York publisher to write the governor's biography. For Andrew, it was a double play. Having Dicker as his Boswell would keep him close. It would also serve as an alternative to another recently announced biography of the governor—this one.

Just how sensitive the governor had grown to knocks from the rest of the press became clear in mid-April 2012, as Dicker was announcing his biography. Liz Benjamin, a seasoned Albany reporter and longtime rival of Dicker's whose *State of Politics* blog was required reading on the hill, along with her "Capital Tonight" commentary on the YNN cable network, had apparently earned the second floor's ire with a number of blog items about the governor and his administration. In a thirty-five-page dossier, a top Cuomo press aide had annotated passages of the offending items with stern critiques. Several passages were noted as "generally snarky," while one was deemed an "example of poor reporting/inadequate fact-checking." The dossier had been discarded, retrieved by a New York City politico, and passed on to the online site BuzzFeed and its pundit Ben Smith. "This is a glimpse at the old Andrew Cuomo we all knew and hated," the dossier purveyor remarked. "He has worked hard to keep this scary dark side at bay, but every now and again it reveals itself, and it's ugly. The secret dossier on Liz Benjamin is the stuff of Richard Nixon and Eliot Spitzer." The press aide, Richard Bamberger, retorted that "the only news here is how my discarded papers, garbage literally, wound up in the possession of Ben Smith."

The dossier dramatized how quick the governor was to take offense—Liz Benjamin's blog posts were hardly snarky. That, in turn, showed an administration both wary and guarded. Andrew boasted that his governorship was "the most transparent and accountable in history," but by the spring of 2012, few outside his inner circle would agree.

Secrecy pervaded the second floor in ways both large and small. Three Men in a Room still hashed out all the legislative bills—that was how the government worked, and Andrew had done nothing about it. At the other extreme, reporters' FOIL requests for public documents were all but ignored. One FOIL request for the appointment calendars of senior administration officials, showing with whom they met during the 2011 budget process, gathered dust for nearly a year before the calendars were coughed up. When a reporter for the Albany *Times Union* FOILed records of all state aircraft trips taken by Andrew as governor, the administration first produced a heavily redacted version, then blamed a low-level administrative aide for redacting too much. The governor, it turned out, was basically commuting from Albany to his Westchester home; possibly, given his vigilance as attorney general in analyzing then Senate majority leader Joe Bruno's helicopter trips, Andrew had initially balked at disclosing his own.

As for Andrew's time as attorney general, it was utterly shrouded. Requests for his schedules as AG at first elicited no response, then word that all his schedules appeared to have been discarded. Fifteen months after the end of his AG tenure, he had sent almost no records to the state archives, as other AGs had done. Eliot Spitzer had sent 919 boxes, most within months of becoming governor, including his daily schedules and files on key issues and official correspondence. A spokesman for the governor decried the "gotcha" motives of Albany reporters and had no answer for when the AG records would be received. Ironically, as the Albany *Times Union* noted, this was "Sunshine Week," Andrew's own declared annual celebration of newly wrought government openness.

Close up, Andrew had his flaws. But as a newcomer to the national stage, he looked a big winner—and he was. The governor who'd whipped the country's worst-run capital into shape, pared its $10 billion deficit, balanced two on-time budgets in a row, *and* passed marriage equality—here was a contender indeed. And with that recognition came, inevitably, more talk of 2016. The *Washington Post*, in a rundown of the country's top ten governors, put Andrew at number one. Not only was Cuomo the most popular governor in the country, the *Post* noted, "but he's also doing it in a tough state where politics is cut-throat and the budgeting process is a minefield. A Siena College poll released this week had him at 73 percent approval... At this point, it's hard not to call him an early favorite for the 2016 Democratic presidential nomination." *Time* put him on its new list of the hundred most influential people in the world, with a write-up by former Pennsylvania governor Ed Rendell. "Andrew Cuomo has shown no fear in calling out one of his party's strongest allies, the teachers' unions, by putting in place an evaluation system based on teacher performance," Rendell wrote. "He has lowered business taxes that have long burdened the state. Now he must find a way for New York to take advantage of its rich store of natural gas deposits while at the same time protecting the environment." But Rendell clearly thought he could do it. Cuomo, he declared, is a "pro-growth Democrat and one of his party's rising stars."

Usually, Andrew waved off 2016 with a wry one-liner. But with the budget behind him and his poll numbers high, he chose to riff on the subject in a late April press conference. "I've seen this movie before," he said, meaning the premature talk and the peaking too soon. "Once you start saying let's start talking political, my own politics, my own aspirations, it can become not just distracting in that it takes time, but it can become confusing and frustrating and is this now a political agenda or a governmental agenda? So... what I am doing is about making this state the best state I can make it and being the best governor I can be, regardless of politics... that is really, really where I am in my heart. And that's where I'm going to stay."

Andrew's response was just right: neither closing the door nor opening it further, acknowledging the reality that he did stir talk of 2016 and could be a candidate, while saying he wasn't, at least... not yet. Most important, he was signaling to the diaspora of Democratic powers and donors that anything might still happen, and not to commit all their money and mojo to Hillary Clinton so soon in the game. If nothing else, Andrew was part of the conversation, and not going away. Or was that reading too much into a rambling remark?

A good way to look presidential without saying a word on the subject was to host the president on a campaign swing. Early that May, President Obama visited a computer-chip research facility in Albany, part of a push by Andrew to make the capital region a center of nanotechnology. The governor, who had done little to help Obama in 2008 and had been known to invoke the president's name with gently mocking gestures, duly praised Obama's efforts to pull the country from recession. Obama, in turn, praised Andrew's "extraordinary leadership" and "outstanding work." Being on that stage with the president, the national press corps in thrall, Andrew could bask in the presidential glow and still put on a show of being dedicated to his day job.

Part of what made the optics so optimal was that the president came to Andrew, and not the reverse. Nearly eighteen months into his first term, Andrew, like his father, had established a strong predilection for staying put. Not only did he steer clear of Washington, D.C., but he rarely made public appearances in Manhattan. Like his father, he shied away from socializing with rich potential patrons, or did as little of it as he could. One Wall Street dealmaker got a call from Andrew asking him to set up a fund-raiser on one of the governor's rare Manhattan evenings: major donors only. Sure, said the dealmaker.

"Can we make it just drinks?" Andrew said.

The dealmaker was stunned. "No way!" he said. If he was going to ask his friends to write big checks, they had to know they had him for dinner. Andrew relented and stayed as promised, but was clearly happy to leave: he was no Bill Clinton, buttonholing every last guest in the room. Oddly, when this same dealmaker had cause to ask Andrew for a favor in return—getting him to make a brief appearance in New York with a major political figure—the governor never called back. Some time later, the dealmaker ran into him again. Andrew was bluff and hearty as before, but made no mention of the favor denied.

Was it reticence to press the flesh? Or perhaps a certain discomfort with wealthy New Yorkers? One donor recalled an odd request from Andrew. There were four people Andrew wanted him to call, big-money prospects in the donor's field. "I can call them," the donor told him, "but so can you. I mean, you're the governor. They're going to get on the line faster with you than they are with me." But Andrew didn't want to make those calls if he could help it.

The son's reluctance was, of course, the father's: that old outer-borough chip on the shoulder. For Mario, those early rejections from white-shoe law firms had never lost their sting. Either Andrew had inherited that class resentment or learned it on his own growing up in Holliswood.

Like his father, Andrew stuck close to Albany, in the realm he knew and could control. Do your work and the rest will follow. So far, that approach was pulling him along, toward the presidency, as briskly as any governor could go in a current whose upcoming eddies and blockages no one could predict. The first crisis of his governorship was right around the bend, though. How he handled it would say a lot about who he was, and what kind of leader he might be.

CHAPTER 24

The Great Allure of Gaming

Charlie Hayward never intended to cross the governor, much less be an impediment to his vision of a $4 billion convention center at Aqueduct racetrack. He just had the bad luck to be CEO of the New York Racing Association, which managed the track. That was not a good place to be in the spring of 2012.

Hayward, sixty-one, was an unlikely head of NYRA, which also ran two other New York Thoroughbred horse-racing tracks, Belmont and Saratoga. A big teddy bear of a fellow, rumpled and earnest with a tendency to talk nonstop, he didn't consort with Whitneys and other such denizens of the Thoroughbred horse-breeding world. Nor had he come from the louche side of racing. He was a book guy, not a bookie: former president and CEO of Little, Brown. But Hayward had nursed a nearly lifetime love of horse racing. So when he jumped into the horse world from publishing, his literary friends were not surprised. For four years he served as president and CEO of the *Daily Racing Form*. In 2004 he had come to NYRA as its CEO.

Hayward had felt Andrew's wrath just weeks into the new governor's tenure. He needed thirty more phone clerks to handle an upswing in betting, but couldn't entice union employees to fill the positions: they liked working the windows, where winners gave tips. So Hayward had hired phone clerks in Oregon. No sooner had he done it than Andrew fired off a sizzling letter to the press, rapping NYRA for outsourcing. He wanted all thirty jobs back in the state—right away. "Look," said Michael Del Giudice, a fellow NYRA board member and one of Mario's longest-serving advisers, to the crestfallen CEO, "Andrew is like a younger brother to me, but if there's ever a moment when he can take political advantage, he'll cut someone off at the knees, me or anyone else."

Perhaps a meeting the previous fall should have tipped Hayward off.

He had a drink with John Sabini, head of the state's Racing and Wagering Board, an entity under the governor's thumb. After a drink or two, Sabini grew candid. "You guys have to watch your every step," he told Hayward. "He's out to get you." He meant Andrew.

What, Hayward wondered, did Andrew have against him? Only later would he come to suspect that he and NYRA might be seen as hindering the governor's grand plans for a convention center at Aqueduct—and the even larger plans of Andrew's favorite new corporate ally, Genting. Perhaps a meeting that fall should have tipped him off.

One October day, Hayward and NYRA chairman Steven Duncker received a visitor: Tan Sri Lim Kok Thay, chairman of the Genting Organization, Malaysia's third-richest man. Kok Thay was in town for the grand opening of forty-five hundred video lottery terminals at Aqueduct. He arrived with his son, and excitedly laid out a far grander scheme, the one Andrew would announce weeks later at his State of the State speech. Kok Thay's vision, however, went further than what Andrew would publicly relate. Along with the convention center, Genting wanted a full-fledged casino at Aqueduct, assuming the state constitution was amended. The casino would arise from the track itself.

What about the track? one of the NYRA executives asked.

That was where the scheme got really interesting. The racetrack at Aqueduct would be history—covered over. The horses and their winter season would be moved out to Belmont, just seven miles east. Genting would also buy up Belmont's gaming rights, but not make use of them. So Belmont would have only horses, no casino. Gambling at Aqueduct, horses at Belmont: very simple.

Hayward and Duncker were stunned by the scheme. They pointed out to Kok Thay that by NYRA's lease with the state, extending to 2033, they had the right to approve or veto any change with the track. All else aside, was Genting prepared to ante up the money it would take to do all this? Kok Thay nodded. He'd costed it out: he was prepared to pay up to $700 million to make it all happen, including changes to Belmont's track and grounds. NYRA, a public/private partnership, would get some of that; the state would get quite a lot. Later, it would seem that perhaps Andrew didn't want NYRA to get *any* of that take. Another possible motive had nothing to do with money. The first governor Cuomo had tried, in his time, to take over NYRA and send its board members packing. He loathed horse owners with their money to blow on Thoroughbreds, their women in fancy hats; he felt they'd profiteered from the tracks. Mario's efforts had failed; now, perhaps, Andrew would show his father how to bring the issue to resolution.

For Hayward, the beginning of the end came in late April 2012, with a scathing report from the Racing and Wagering Board, the same state entity whose chairman had warned that Andrew was out to get Hayward. At issue was NYRA's share of "exotic bets." Instead of betting on just one horse, a bettor could wager on, say, which horse would win, which one would place, and which would show. Or he might try picking the winners of successive races. If he picked those multiple winners correctly, he won big.

Traditionally at its three tracks, NYRA took 25 percent of each winning exotic bet. For a brief period, from 2008 until 2010, it had been allowed to increase its "take-out rate" to 26 percent—an inducement to bettors during the recession. As of September 15, 2010, it should have reduced its take-out rate back to 25 percent. But it didn't. It kept taking out 26 percent until Hayward announced the error and took action, on December 21, 2011. That 1 percent difference on all those exotic bets over those fifteen months added up to nearly $8.5 million. This was the amount improperly kept from those winning exotic bettors.

Hayward was adamant that this was an honest mistake, and certainly he had no motive. None of the money went to him or any other NYRA official. Most of it didn't even go to NYRA. After publicly acknowledging the error, Hayward managed to locate enough of the shortchanged bettors to return half of the $1.2 million that NYRA had taken in as its share.

Neither Hayward nor any other NYRA managers were interviewed for the Racing and Wagering Board report. Instead, some fifteen thousand documents were seized and sifted. Hayward read the results, like everyone else, in the *New York Times*. The report said that Hayward and others had knowingly withheld the nearly $8.5 million due bettors for those exotic bets.

Days later the NYRA board formally met, and voted to fire both Hayward and his general counsel, Patrick Kehoe. According to one board member, Del Giudice suggested that firing Hayward and Kehoe would make the governor go away.

It didn't.

Instead, NYRA's executive board came, as summoned, to the governor's office on May 9. Initially, Andrew seemed composed. He showed them some of the governors' portraits that hung in the refurbished corridors beside his office. Then he steered them into a conference room. Just as everyone sat down, Andrew's secretary came in to announce he had a call from the White House. One NYRA board member rolled his eyes at that. "One of my favorite routines," he muttered to a colleague.

When he returned, Andrew dropped his veneer of joviality. "You know," he began, "this dispute is not something that began yesterday." The board members thought they knew what he was talking about. He was alluding to Mario's clash, years before, with the NYRA board. "That never sat well with Andrew," one board member explained, "and he remembered it."

"We can do this the easy way or the hard way," Andrew reportedly said. "The easy way is you turn over control of the board, and we'll reconstitute the board, and we'll say I'll give it back to you in two years."

The hard way involved a lot of scrutiny that the board members really didn't want to invite.

"This is ludicrous," one board member managed.

"You're welcome to your own opinion," the governor reportedly replied, "but the reality is that it doesn't matter."

"He didn't say, 'I can ruin your reputation,'" one board member recalled drily, "because it was obvious that he was already doing that."

At least those board members had a choice about what to do. For Hayward and Kehoe, the game was over. They were smeared already in the Racing and Wagering Board's report for "knowingly" colluding in what, to restless newspaper readers, appeared to have been a nefarious plot to steal $8.5 million. Along with the report was a referral to the inspector general of possible criminal activity. Eager to show they had nothing to hide, the members of NYRA's executive board hired the well-known Washington law firm Williams & Connolly to investigate. On August 31, 2012, four of the firm's lawyers issued their findings. "Not a single NYRA employee was aware that the exotic takeout rate was out of compliance with the racing law until the discrepancy was identified in a December 2011 audit," the report concluded. "Nor did NYRA attempt to mislead the public." As if to dispel any doubts, the report reiterated that finding in even stronger terms. "Despite whatever 'interim' conclusions the [Racing and Wagering Board] reached—without reviewing all of the relevant documents or interviewing a single witness—no one at NYRA intended to steal from bettors or to flout the law. The one-percent takeout error was an inadvertent mistake."

The report was sent not just to NYRA, but to the inspector general. The IG declined to make it public. Instead, she embarked on her own two-year investigation. Her own report, released in the summer of 2014, would find no evidence of any criminal activity, and no knowing disregard on the part of Hayward or Kehoe. All she could accuse them of was "inexcusable inattention to the [sunset provision of the legislation] and dereliction of their duties" for not finding the overcharge sooner.

By then, Hayward had fought for, and won, severance payment from NYRA. He asked for about a year's pay: in his case, $460,000. He was granted $20,000.

NYRA was still an independent entity, with a lease to run its three Thoroughbred tracks until 2033. But its board was now thoroughly cowed by the wrathful governor, and so when Andrew declared he was taking it over, he got not a peep of protest. Out with the old board, in with the new: Andrew's "reorganization board" would oversee NYRA for three years, putting its house back in order. The board would then likely revert to private control, the governor decreed. "We know that long term this is not a venture for government to run."

Whether the state would willingly give up control of such a gusher would have to be seen. What was clear was that Andrew had just redirected untold riches from NYRA to the state. Genting's Resorts World Casino at Aqueduct, with its forty-five hundred video lottery terminals, was making as much as $73 million a month: one former NYRA board member estimated NYRA's take of that lucre at $130 million a year. Now Andrew would control that money. With NYRA sidelined, Genting could also more easily realize its grand scheme of building the country's largest convention center with full-fledged casino at Aqueduct and moving Aqueduct's racing to Belmont. That, too, Andrew would control, without any interference from NYRA.

But there was more. Together, NYRA's three tracks had acreage worth $1 billion. With NYRA under his control, Andrew could do with that land as he wished.

Full-scale gaming was, of course, not yet legal outside the Indian casinos. Not until the fall of 2013 could Andrew hope to hold a public vote on the issue. But the path was clear—or seemed to be, until a mortifying revelation two weeks later after his takeover of NYRA threw the grand scheme into limbo and handed the governor his first crisis.

At some point in the last days of May 2012, the second floor fielded a jarring call from a *New York Times* reporter. Was it true, the reporter asked in so many words, that in late 2011 Genting had made a $400,000 contribution to the Committee to Save New York, the nonprofit set up to tout Andrew's agenda? Was it also true that the New York State Gaming Association, a trade group with close ties with Genting, had given the CSNY $2 million? Was there any connection, the reporter asked in so many words, between those contributions and the governor's decision to push Genting's $4 billion convention center in his State of the State speech?

Not for the first time, and not for the last, Andrew responded to imminent bad news by getting a jump on the story. On June 1, 2012, he appeared on former governor David Paterson's radio show to announce that, sadly, talks with Genting had broken down over development costs. "The conversations haven't really worked out," the governor said, declining to go into detail. This was, in one sense, a positive turn, he added. Now the plan was to get the constitutional amendment passed, then hold a competitive bidding process. Other gaming companies had already indicated that they wanted to vie for the right to build one of the planned six or seven casinos. "They want to be here," Andrew told Paterson. "They're excited." On June 4, 2012, came the story the governor had hoped to get a jump on, and to defuse, run as the *Times*' lead of the day.

The governor's top press aide, Richard Bamberger, came charging out with a statement vehemently denying any quid pro quo. "To try to suggest an improper relationship between the governor and gaming interests is to distort the facts in a malicious or reckless manner," he declared. "To malign, distort or intimidate CSNY supporters or cast suspicion on their efforts is wrong on the facts, law and effect. To report CSNY's lobbying efforts without reporting the context, history and totality is misleading. We understand the *Times*' desire to win awards for breaking scandals, but that is different than trying to manufacture them."

Bamberger's basic points—which was to say, those of the governor, breathing down the back of his neck—were valid as far as they went. Andrew had supported gaming publicly before Genting and the New York Gaming Association had given that money to the CSNY. For its part, the CSNY had acted entirely within its legal rights, using the money to promote gaming. But the *Times* was just as much within its rights to question the propriety of $2.4 million in gaming money given to promote the governor's agenda just weeks before the governor announced Genting would get the go-ahead to build the nation's largest convention center.

For all the second floor's rage and denials, the story got worse the next day. Now came details of a cozy fund-raiser for the governor the previous October at the Westchester estate of Barry Gosin, a commercial property dealer. There, Genting's Kok Thay had given Andrew much the same presentation he gave NYRA's Hayward and Kehoe, flipping open his laptop and operating a slide show as he made his pitch.

The context, according to one participant, was a bit more nuanced than that.

Jeffrey Gural, a real estate executive who owned two upstate "racinos"—racetracks with those video lottery terminals—had helped pull together the living room fund-raiser at Gosin's home. Most but not all of the guests were in the gaming industry, eager to keep the governor focused on bringing casinos to the state.

Westchester was blanketed by a snowstorm that early afternoon, and so most of the guests wore flannel shirts, faded jeans, and boots. The event was nearly over when the Genting group arrived, slowed down in Queens by the snow. They were in suits and ties—a culture clash—and seemed not to have mastered the art of mingling. Not long after they arrived, one guest left, only to return moments later with an announcement: a sizable tree limb had come down across the driveway. Moments later, the power went out. There was still daylight—no need for candles—but the remaining guests stole glances at one another, wondering how long it would be before they could leave.

That was when Kok Thay popped open his laptop on the dining room table and gave the governor his pitch.

According to one gaming industry source, the Malaysian company didn't offer to make a campaign contribution at the fund-raiser. The *Times* reported that "a few weeks after the fund-raiser, the gambling association, of which Genting is a member, contributed $2 million to the Committee to Save New York, the private lobbying group that Mr. Cuomo pushed to be set up."

Kathryn Wylde of the CSNY was happy to take those checks. "If you want to have a good working relationship with the governor, it was wise to make [a contribution to the CSNY]," the gaming industry source observed.

With his pummeling in the press, Andrew couldn't distance himself fast and far enough from Genting. One source close to the governor found that remarkable. "You would have thought these people ambushed Andrew and tried to stuff cash in his pockets." As the source noted, Andrew might have disarmed the press by freely acknowledging the contributions: they were, after all, entirely legal. Instead, he looked for others to blame—in this case Genting. Politically, the source noted, that might not be smart in the long run for the governor and his circle. "They're so absolute, they can't walk it back later on if they change their minds."

Barely forty-eight hours after the Genting revelation, the earnest commissioners of JCOPE convened the first of two meetings to address the greater issue that Genting had now raised. Many millions of dollars in secret donations had come pouring in to the Committee to Save New York and other 501(c)(4)s. Yet in accordance with Andrew's ethics bill of the previous year, donor disclosure was to begin. The question was: when?

Ravi Batra thought he knew where this was going. Horrified by the headlines, he had plowed through a pile of documents sent by JCOPE in advance of the meetings. At about 3 a.m. he had what he later called his eureka moment.

"The recent disclosures of this week have left me stunned," Batra declared as the hearing got under way. He was appalled by the Genting donations to the CSNY. But also, had his fellow commissioners stopped to consider the implications of Genting's foreign ownership? Expanded disclosure rules were called for, he declared, or else citizens would need "night goggles" to see who donated and what the special interests might be after.

Most of the commissioners, Batra soon realized, hadn't read the pile of papers they were sent the day before. He didn't blame them for that, but it did mean none had seen what he did at 3 a.m.

Batra's eureka moment was about the starting date of disclosure for anonymous donors: the meeting's main matter of business. In accordance with the ethics bill, a first disclosure report for donors was to be published in July 2012, looking back over the year's first six months. After that, there would be reporting periods of disclosure every six months—again retrospective, like income taxes or a student's report card. What Batra had noticed was that Janet DiFiore proposed to start the clock for donor disclosure on July 1, 2012.

This was no small thing. July 1 would fall in the year's *second* reporting period, from July 1 to December 31, 2012. All donors *before* July 1, 2012, could stay under the cloak of darkness. The CSNY's tax filings for 2011 had revealed that $12 million of the $17.5 million donated to it in 2011 had come from just twenty donors. Yet the names of these and the rest of about seventy-five donors to the CSNY that year had been redacted, and neither these nor donors for the first half of 2012 would ever be known if JCOPE changed the starting date of disclosure to July 1, 2012. Indeed, as Batra saw, starting July 1 not only protected those donors. It also gave them one last chance—until the end of June—to make *more* anonymous contributions. After July 1, they could stop writing checks and the CSNY could quietly expire.

Batra was so stressed by the end of the hearing that when he reached over to pick up his heavy briefcase, he pulled a chest muscle. Worried, his fellow commissioners and staff called an ambulance over his objections: a fitting end to a dreadful hearing. A month later at the public meeting, the commissioners did just as Batra feared, starting the clock for donor identity on July 1, 2012. A spokesman for JCOPE gave no explanation for why donor disclosure should start July 1 when the law itself called for disclosure to start June 1. It was, Batra told friends, one of those things that only happened in "Alice in Wonderland"—or Albany.

Publicly, Batra declared his intent to sue JCOPE for illegality. Privately, he reached out to federal authorities to make them aware of what he felt was rank corruption on the part of JCOPE.

For a governor who had campaigned on greater transparency, Genting was the latest story to belie that promise. Even as his men were working the phones to shake loose the rap, the Albany *Times Union* revealed that two of its reporters, Jimmy Vielkind and James Odato, had made a trip to the state archives and learned how secretive the governor could be.

The two had begun with a routine Freedom of Information Law request. They wanted to know if any more of Andrew's papers from his term as attorney general had arrived at the state archives. Somewhat to their surprise, an archivist came back with thirty boxes of documents they hadn't seen before.

The reporters made several trips to the archives to look through the boxes and found one particularly intriguing document. That was a memo from Linda Lacewell, in the summer of 2007, noting with seeming concern that then-senator Bruno had done *no* state business on one of the travel days recorded in the Troopergate report, and the report had failed to note that. For a moment it looked like a smoking gun.

When the reporters called the second floor to ask about the memo, the reaction was swift. Lacewell rushed over to the archives and spent nearly eight hours in the records room, as the reporters later noted from sign-in sheets. She pulled numerous documents from the case files—documents the reporters had seen on their earlier visits—including the daily calendars and notebooks of Ellen Biben, the former top prosecutor in Andrew's AG office, now executive director of JCOPE. All this, despite the fact that the smoking gun was no gun at all. Bruno's travel day of no state business *had* been noted in the final Troopergate report, and it was, in fact, a day in which the speaker flew back from New York to Albany after a day with business meetings. The man had to get home, after all.

When the reporters wrote up their experience in the paper, Andrew's top press aide, Richard Bamberger, sent another blistering letter, this one nearly thirteen hundred words long, castigating the *Times Union*'s "fixation" on the records and arguing that "sending records to the Archives is about preservation for future generations, not access for today." Why records should be accessed later than sooner was left unexplained.

Ironically, Andrew censored even the lighter and more humorous side of himself that might have helped offset his yen for secrecy. "Governor

Andrew Cuomo is clever, artful and funny—but all of that's a secret," observed the AP's Michael Gormley. Back in May, for the 112th annual Legislative Correspondents Association show, Andrew had contributed a video skit shot in the governor's mansion, starring himself and his top aides. It was seen by hundreds of Albany insiders and was reportedly quite funny. Yet when Gormley requested a copy he was stonewalled. Nine weeks after he requested it under the Freedom of Information Law, it still had not been released. Any sense of the evening could only be gleaned from the reporters' own skits. The show, titled "iGov," played off Andrew's declaration "I am the government," and imagined a future in which he became just that. "Albany! Albany!" sang a reporter playing Andrew, in a reworked version of "C'est Moi" from *Camelot*: "*I am the new Louis XIV / Kneel to me! Kneel to me! / Who is the government? It's me! / The branches are nice, but do we need all three? / It's time for a new transparency.*"

Amid the fallout from Genting, Andrew's second season ended anticlimactically. Quietly, even. His influence over the Republican senators had ebbed, now that he had given them the golden apple of redistricting, and if only to show they were no longer under his thumb, they rebuffed his call for decriminalizing small amounts of marijuana, blocked any rise in the minimum wage, and waved away any talk of campaign finance reform—Democratic issues all, taken up late in the term by Andrew with no real expectation they'd pass, more to appease his own party than anything else. He did win a major reorganization of care for the mentally and physically disabled, which let him check off the social justice box for the year. But for all the drama of the Big Ugly, the legislature actually passed fewer bills than in any session since 1914. The governor's poll ratings were still high, but his sophomore slump had begun.

Perhaps sensing that his son needed a boost, Mario supplied it at an eightieth birthday celebration in the executive mansion he knew so well, telling the crowd of about a hundred that his son had proved himself "the best governor in modern times," and that he might one day "have an opportunity to serve at a higher level, to serve the people of the United States." The White House nod might have been spontaneous, the musing of an aging father. Then again, Team Cuomo did not as a rule do off the cuff. To Cuomo watchers, it fit the game plan. When he was running strong, Andrew stayed clear of 2016: no talk, no walk. Silence put him above the fray, and kept curiosity high. But let the media's attention start to wander, and up would pop the hint from some unnamed person in the know that Andrew might just...could just...run if the times were right.

As an eightieth birthday present, Andrew gave his father the gift he deserved but hadn't wanted: an official portrait of the fifty-second governor, to be hung in the Hall of Governors at last. Mario had refused to sit for one after his governorship, nor had he sat for one now: the likeness was based on a 1989 photograph. There was an odd sort of vanity in shunning that honor, an insecurity too, all manifested in those two political moments that defined his public life more than any others: the indecision about whether to run for the White House himself, and whether to accept the invitation to become a U.S. Supreme Court justice. Harold Holzer, the historian and family friend, was among the well-wishers at the executive mansion, and recounted one other comment Mario made. He quoted Mario saying, "The difference between Andrew and me is that I made plenty of mistakes. Andrew learned from all of my mistakes and he doesn't make any."

Andrew needed more than a little soft soap from his father. He needed a new, galvanizing mission. "What's next?" he would ask close aides. "I don't see it out there." What he needed was another marriage equality. For now, he threw his restless ambitions into the kind of project that Robert Moses, the all-powerful New York builder of bridges and highways, would have admired: replacing the Tappan Zee Bridge.

As any commuter could attest, the rickety cantilever bridge made for a jarring ride. From its western side, a driver skimmed along just above the water, a queasy experience, then rose and rolled on, and on, across nearly three riverine miles. Its placement at the Hudson's second-widest point was a matter of ancient but still-relevant politics: it sat just north of the Port Authority's twenty-five-mile range of jurisdiction, so that its tolls flowed instead to the New York State Thruway Authority, a new creation back in 1955 when the Tappan Zee opened. Now the bridge was six years past its fifty-year life span.

Andrew's three predecessors had spent $88 million in studies on what to do about the Tappan Zee, held 430 public meetings, and weighed 150 proposals. Eventually a massive bridge of two separate spans—four lanes one way, four lanes the other—had emerged, larded with light rail, bus lanes, and much more. The only problem was its cost: as much as $16 billion. So nothing had been done. But something had to be. To pare its cost, Andrew simply lopped off the mass transit from it. That, he declared, would cut its cost to $5.2 billion: building the two new spans, and hauling the old one away.

This was still the kind of big-scale project that states didn't do anymore, as Andrew noted. Nelson Rockefeller had built Albany's Empire State Plaza. The new Tappan Zee would be just as necessary and monumental. "The new Tappan Zee," Andrew declared, "is not just going to be about repairing that bridge. It's going to be about making the statement that government can work and society can work and we can still do big things." Like the Empire State Plaza, it would also be a monument to the governor who built it. Mario, as Andrew well knew, had never managed anything of the kind.

Robert Moses, both brilliant and brutal, might have recognized a bit of himself in the young governor. Like Moses, Andrew drew up plans for his amended version of the Tappan Zee with virtually no public input at first. Like Moses, he waved off mass transit—bus or rail line—as too expensive to include. And like Moses, he got his great work under way with only a fraction of the funds he needed to complete it. But also like the great builder, he ran into a buzzsaw of opposition. Stripping mass transit from the master plan proved too extreme for a wide array of townships. Opposition grew, until Andrew felt impelled to make a small concession. The new bridge *would* be designed to accommodate rush-hour buses in emergency lanes. Any more, he said, would double the new bridge's projected $5.2 billion cost.

A cadre of TZBers—Tappan Zee Bridge activists and bloggers, along with local politicians—questioned that assumption. Andrew, they argued, was taking his mass transit numbers from the lavish plans of earlier eras, drawn up by governors who didn't want the headache of building a new bridge and used the hyped figures to put off any action at all. By one more moderate estimate, putting in mass transit would cost between $1 billion to $2.5 billion. Andrew shook his head. "You can build whatever you want," he told local officials. "You then have to pay for what you build."

It was advice that he might have taken himself. A new bridge of one span, rather than two, would have cost much less, and with car traffic on the bridge diminishing every year now as a younger generation rejected commuting, the one span might have served. But that would have meant starting anew, with a new design that had to go through the years-long approval process again. The governor wanted his monument now. Better to take the gargantuan two-span bridge off the shelf, strip out mass transit, and pay $5.2 billion—or whatever the cost rose to—to get the damned thing done.

After much back-and-forth, Andrew won a federal loan of $1.6 billion to get the work started. Where would the state find the rest? Where bridge money always came from: state bonds, backed by future tolls.

Early that August, Larry Schwartz predicted that when the new Tappan Zee opened in 2018, round-trip fare might be fourteen dollars, nearly triple the current five dollars. Trucks with three or four axles would pay that much more. Up from the editorial pages of Westchester and Rockland Counties came howls of dismay. After a suitable interval, the governor pledged that he would do all he could to assure tolls were lower than that. How much lower? Maybe eleven dollars.

It was a ploy, one that Andrew had reportedly used the previous August with New Jersey governor Chris Christie in raising tolls on the Port Authority's bridge and tunnel crossings. First had come the bad news: tolls at the George Washington Bridge and other Port Authority crossings would rise by an immediate four dollars, then by another two dollars, to raise E-ZPass lanes to fourteen dollars by 2014. Next came cries of alarm from the outraged public, followed by shock and surprise from both governors, in their roles as coheads of Port Authority. Then, after whip-cracking by both on behalf of the public, there was good news: E-ZPass tolls would go up by just two dollars, at least for the next year or so. Money raised, motorists assuaged. Eventually, the *Bergen Record* would suggest that the Port Authority toll hike of 2011 had been choreographed from the start by both governors.

Through the summer of 2012, Andrew won over local lawmakers with assurances the Tappan Zee toll would stay low—or at least moderate. He neglected to note that for this massive, multi-billion-dollar project, he had no financial plan in place, only numbers pulled from the air. Two years later, there would still be no plan. Drills on barges would be hammering into the river bottom and the new four-lane spans would be starting to rise like dinosaurs from the primordial muck. But Andrew would still not have touched that $1.6 billion federal loan. Instead, the Thruway Authority would be issuing its own bonds to cover construction costs. Why? Because tapping the federal loan would obligate Andrew to say how the state planned to repay the money. That, in turn, would mean saying how much tolls would rise on the Tappan Zee to cover the payments. Best to tap other sources, and keep those numbers hidden until after Andrew's reelection in 2014.

As for the rest of the bridge's cost—something north of $3.5 billion—the governor had said nothing about where he expected to find this money. The answer could only be more bonds, more tolls, more bad news for commuters. Robert Moses had done just that: started bridges and highways with no idea where the money to complete them would come from. Once they were started, he knew, they would get done. They had to. The money would come.

In the year since Andrew had pushed through his Public Integrity Reform Act, or PIRA, public corruption had died down a bit, enough to let the governor hope he'd snuffed it out. But no. That August, three new tawdry tales hit the news, all involving downstate Democrats. An assemblywoman had allegedly used public funds to hire her boyfriends; a state senator had bilked a nonprofit. These paled beside Vito Lopez, a powerful Democratic assemblyman from Brooklyn who had sexually harassed two of his female staffers. After reading aloud a letter of censure, Shelly Silver stripped him of his committee chairmanship and seniority, and banned him from employing interns.

The story then took a dramatic turn. Earlier in the year, Lopez, seventy-one, had abused at least two *other* female staffers. Those women had brought suit against the state, and Silver, as head of the Assembly, had had to deal with their accusations. He had chosen not to disclose these women's charges, or even refer the matter to his ethics committee. Instead, he had kept the suit a secret from all but those who had to know, and reached a settlement with the victims. The AG's office had consulted on how such settlements were done; the comptroller's office had weighed in on how to process the money involved. In response to the women's demand for $1.2 million, Silver had bargained down their high-profile lawyer, Gloria Allred, to $135,080, and Lopez had lived to fight another day. But now, it seemed, his time was up.

Silver's alleged cover-up stirred almost more outrage than the creepy assemblyman's conduct. How could it be right for the Speaker to give state money to buy the women's silence and have no one the wiser, knowing the old lech would likely prey on more female interns? Andrew's first answer was lawyerly. "Well, that happens all the time, right? You have a car accident. The state driver was negligent, the state pays damages. So the state often pays for damages of public officials. Your question is, 'Well, how about in this case with these facts, is it proper?' I don't know the facts."

As JCOPE's commissioners anguished over how to proceed, Andrew played a brilliant hand of 2016: the game for presidential contenders pretending not to be. Charlotte, North Carolina, was the venue for the 2012 Democratic National Convention, and the anointing of Barack Obama for his run at a second term. Twenty-eight years before, an up-and-coming governor from New York had electrified the crowd, but Andrew would not be lured into replicating his father's role. Better to shun that stage, and the expectations it would raise too soon. Better to know, too, what Hillary Clinton planned to do before making a move of his own.

But that didn't mean skipping the convention altogether. On its last day, September 6, Andrew slipped down from New York to address the state's delegation at a breakfast gathering. Not from the big stage: rather, from a white tent in the parking lot of the Doubletree Hotel, a safe distance from the glare of national media. It was a stem-winder. His voice growing louder, almost shouting at points, Andrew threw big hunks of Democratic dogma at the delighted crowd. "When one of us is raised, we are all raised," he declared. "And when one of us is lowered, we're all lowered." The *New York Times* observed that Andrew sounded "unmistakably like a man with ambitions well beyond Albany," and noted how he kept sliding back and forth, addressing "New Yorkers," then "America."

JCOPE had held a private meeting on September 4 to address the Lopez matter, and while the results of that meeting were not made public, Andrew seemed to know what they were by the time he gave that speech. JCOPE had reached a painful decision. It would investigate Lopez, but leave Silver alone. Apparently the commissioners felt that Silver had acted within bounds, perhaps even appropriately. The problem was Lopez.

Of all the howls of indignation, the loudest now was Andrew's. A week before, he had told the press that as attorney general he had sanctioned confidential settlements, and that it was a normal way to settle cases like this. Now he was saying the opposite. JCOPE had an absolute duty to investigate the Speaker and the secret settlement, he declared. For that matter, it now had the same obligation to look into the attorney general and the comptroller for their roles. Andrew was too clever to chortle in public. But the Lopez affair was looking like a political godsend. Three of Andrew's political rivals—Silver, Schneiderman, and DiNapoli—had all been soiled by the secret settlement. Now they sat in the same little boat, targets all for JCOPE, and all Andrew had to do was call for justice. Yes, he now declared. JCOPE must get to the bottom of all this.

The JCOPE commissioners protested, none more so than Ravi Batra. The night of September 6, e-mails and calls began flying back and forth among them. Many felt conned by the governor. The "independent" commission they had joined back in late 2011 wasn't independent at all. That night, a handful of the angriest began talking about staging a coup. They asked Batra if he would lead it. Batra, though reluctant, was willing, but the insurgents numbered just six—two shy of a majority. With eight votes, they fantasized, they could fire the staff, redesign the commission so that it sat equidistant from all three branches, and let them decide who and who not to investigate. But they lacked those two votes.

The next day, Andrew went so far as to threaten a Moreland commission if the commissioners failed to do his bidding. Even the Andrew apologists on JCOPE were stunned. Batra called for a special prosecutor to take whatever steps were needed to make JCOPE independent at last. Andrew responded by calling Batra a grandstander. With that, Batra resigned, issuing a fierce proclamation as he did. "There is no independence in JCOPE," he declared. JCOPE had started as a beautiful experiment, he wrote. But the governor's own heavy hand had ruined its promise. Being on JCOPE, Batra concluded, was like "watching a glorious diamond being crushed by a sledgehammer."

Taking Andrew's heed, the glum commissioners widened their scope after all to include Silver, Schneiderman, and DiNapoli. The attorney general's office protested that all it had done was a cursory review of the settlement—pro forma for any state matter. The comptroller had merely stamped the disbursement as legitimate state business. In fact, that was all they *had* done. But while a cold early autumn settled over the capital, a blizzard of subpoenas engulfed the offices of the assembly Speaker, the attorney general, and the state comptroller. "They're trying to get every e-mail we have," Schneiderman seethed to a colleague. "The subpoenas they've sent are outrageous." None of the men in a boat—not even Silver—dared protest in public. "It's a no-win situation," said one top lobbyist. "Andrew has a giant megaphone and bully pulpit. You don't go at him because the response would be worse than whatever it is you're upset about."

Rex Smith, editor in chief of the Albany *Times Union*, mused on his editorial page in late September that all this was starting to feel familiar. A major investigation had been cranked up, and for what? Lopez was marginalized already, so why investigate him? Silver had chosen to make a secret payout in lieu of litigation: maddening, but hardly illegal. A trial might have ended up costing the state a good deal more than that. Schneiderman's office, and DiNapoli's, had done what they were supposed to do. It was a lot more smoke than fire, Smith opined, which was to say a lot like Andrew's first investigation: Troopergate. Smith's implication was that the Lopez investigation, like Troopergate, was tailored to benefit one person above all: Andrew M. Cuomo.

As one contretemps escalated, another came to a close: the fierce dispute between Andrew and Mayor Bloomberg over the 9/11 Memorial. Could the perceived snub of Mario at the last anniversary have led the son to delay the opening of the museum? In any event, the work had stopped when Andrew as cohead of the Port Authority, along with New Jersey's Chris Christie, the PA's other head, brought construction to a halt. The PA, its governors agreed, had spent way too much already on Bloomberg's legacy project. Bloomberg's 9/11 foundation would have to do more.

They had a point. The projected construction cost of $700 million had been meant to cover both the open memorial site, with its graceful pools, and the hundred-thousand-square-foot museum going seven floors down. Bloomberg's foundation would pay the lion's share of that; the Port Authority would kick in and do the construction. Now the budget had soared—to as high as $1.3 billion, by Andrew's reckoning—and Andrew wanted to be sure that the taxpayers of New York and New Jersey would not be forced to pay much of that extra cost. For that matter, might they be stuck with the site's $60 million annual operating cost? Andrew said the foundation owed the PA $300 million already; Bloomberg said the foundation had already done far more than its share, and that the PA was the party that owed the foundation, more than $100 million.

As always with Andrew, the crux was control. He wanted the Port Authority to take charge, both now and after the museum finally opened, to rein in the runaway costs that a billionaire mayor had let get the better of him. At the ten-year anniversary, so went the story as told in a biting *Esquire* feature, Governor Pataki had leaned toward Andrew and said, "Isn't this a great day? Just beautiful—and look how all this has turned out." To which Andrew had allegedly replied, "This is the biggest waste of money anybody's ever seen. Who would have ever spent this money? If we'd known what this was going to be like, nobody would have ever done this."

Month after month, into the spring of 2012, the whole 9/11 Museum sat still as a tomb, snuffing out hopes that it might be completed by the eleventh anniversary. In June, some two hundred families of victims wrote a bitter letter to the two governors, calling the delay "a betrayal."

Prodded into action, Andrew and the mayor tried to form an advisory committee, only to fall out over how much the foundation would pay for the museum's operating costs. More months passed. With the eleventh anniversary just days away—and with it the prospect of scorn heaped on all parties—the mayor's people and the governor's people spent a tense weekend negotiating. A deal was reached; work was restarted; the museum would open, at last, in 2014, thirteen years after 9/11.

As far as he was concerned, Andrew had acted to save toll-payers money by cutting the Port Authority's share of the costs. But always, under the facts of the matter, whatever that matter might be, was that palpable thirst for control. He couldn't just reach a gentleman's agreement with the mayor when the two of them disagreed. He had to have it his way, all his way, until he risked looking bad in the press. Then, and only then, did the deal get done, though even so, the governor got more than he gave. So widespread was his reach by now that lawmakers, colleagues, even ex-in-laws, were left wondering if the heat they'd just felt was his breath on their necks, or just a warm breeze wafting by.

To the Kennedy family known simply as the RFKs, two incidents that year seemed suspicious.

Douglas and Molly Kennedy were with their three-day-old son in the maternity ward of Northern Westchester Hospital in Mount Kisco on January 7, 2012, when Doug decided to take the infant for a first look at the night sky: there was a full moon. He did this with the permission of the doctor on duty—who happened to be Tim Haydock, one of Kerry's ex-boyfriends.

"So Tim gives me the okay," Douglas Kennedy recalled, "and our nurses give me the okay, and then when I started to walk out, two nurses who were not on duty said, 'No, you can't leave.'" Later, the nurses testified that they tried to stop him, and that when Kennedy reached a stairwell, a physical altercation ensued. One nurse said Kennedy twisted her arm. In fact, security camera footage would show a polite and calm Kennedy merely trying to push open the stairwell door with his back, as he held his son, and that one of the nurses then tried to grab the infant from his arms. The second nurse later said that Kennedy then kicked her in the pelvis, knocking her backward onto the floor. Dr. Haydock, who was with Kennedy, declared, "I witnessed the incident and I can state unequivocally that the nurses were the only aggressors. To charge Mr. Kennedy with a crime is simply incomprehensible to me."

The nurses filed a complaint with the Mount Kisco police. The police investigated and found no grounds to charge Kennedy. Child Protective Services investigated too, and cleared Kennedy completely. "Mr. Kennedy's decision to take a walk with his son did not place his child at imminent risk or harm. Mr. Kennedy had no ability to predict that one of the nurses would attempt to physically take the boy from his arms. His actions were only to protect his son."

Seven weeks after the incident, Kennedy was charged by the Westchester district attorney's office with endangering his baby and physically harassing the two nurses. Andrew had supported the DA in her campaign for office and had just named her chairwoman of JCOPE.

Kennedy was put on trial that November, and acquitted on both counts. He found it bizarre that the DA's office brought charges nearly two months after local police and Child Protective Services had found no grounds to pursue the case.

Kerry Kennedy's own legal travails began on the morning of July 13, 2012, when her car collided with a tractor-trailer. Instead of stopping, she kept driving, then pulled off the highway at the next exit. Police found her disoriented enough to charge her with drugged driving.

Kerry was in her gym clothes, headed to her gym at 8 a.m. on Interstate 684, when the incident occurred. The drug at issue was not alcohol, as blood tests soon determined, but Ambien. Kerry had a simple explanation: she had mistaken the sleep-inducing drug for her thyroid medication. Nevertheless, she was charged with driving under the influence of a drug.

The driving-while-impaired case hung over Kerry until February 2014, when a jury trial was held. Prosecutors argued that even if she had taken the Ambien by mistake—highly likely, given the time of morning and her attire—she knew that her judgment was impaired and kept driving anyway. That constituted a misdemeanor and could bring up to a year in jail. The six-person jury took just an hour to acquit her.

Janet DiFiore remained Westchester DA through this whole period, from Kerry's arrest and indictment through the jury trial. In July 2014, her husband, Dennis Glazer, was named to the state's new casino siting board, a position of considerable influence. To the Kennedys, the close ties between Andrew and DiFiore, and the way both Doug's and Kerry's legal travails had unfolded, left lingering suspicions that the warmth they felt on their backs of their necks was more than a breeze. "Kerry will never say a bad word about Andrew," her brother Douglas declared. "Literally to this day she will not. And Andrew will spend his life trying to take her down."

CHAPTER 25

Guns and Butter

Where was that Next Big Thing?

On October 28, 2012, it came roaring up the Atlantic Coast, the roughest storm in generations, headed straight for New York and New Jersey. Andrew canceled the southern campaign swing he'd agreed to take for Obama in the last days of the presidential campaign—likely with relief, given the lack of enthusiasm he showed for the president these days—and declared a state of emergency. "Do not underestimate this storm," he warned as Sandy approached.

Perhaps it traced to those late-night calls with the AAA tow truck: that passion for answering emergencies, taking control, and saving the stranded. Politically, big storms brought promise and peril. The challenge was to take all reasonable measures as soon as possible—and then get credit for taking them before anyone else could. Not by chance that Sunday, with Sandy a day away, did Andrew announce the closing of the New York City subways. He did it from outside the city, to underscore that this was in fact a governor's decision, not a mayor's. And he did it an hour before the mayor's own scheduled briefing. The governor and the mayor would work together, but let no one doubt it: the governor was in control.

As the full brunt of the storm hit Monday night, Andrew rode down the East Side in an SUV driven by a state trooper. With him was his top aide, Howard Glaser. He wanted to see how bad high tide really was. To their shock, the East River had surged over its seawall and inundated the streets west of First Avenue. Truly alarmed, Andrew had the driver head toward the World Trade Center site, with its sunken memorial plaza. The whole of lower Manhattan was pitch-dark, the power gone. Fighting the wind, the men made their way with flashlights in hand to a wall overlooking the memorial. Below was the excavation pit for the seven-story-deep 9/11 Museum. The pit was filled with water. The Hudson River had breached its seawall too. It was surging across the West Side Highway, rising toward them. But it hadn't reached them yet. How then was the pit already water-filled? "We didn't know if the wall had been cracked and the water was coming up from there," Andrew said later of the pit. "A little voice in your head is saying, 'Yeah, and what if it is?'" They might find themselves trapped, their escape route cut off.

By Tuesday, Andrew was everywhere—or seemed to be—giving on-camera interviews in a windblown rain slicker, reassuring New Yorkers the worst had passed. As governor, he was weathering the storm well, giving updates and stern advice: a leader in charge. Only later would a government report, apparently intended only for insiders, give a less admiring portrait of the governor as storm captain.

Early on, the report explained, Andrew decided to set up a Superstorm Sandy command post at his Manhattan offices on 40th Street and Third Avenue. That seemed wise—except that the state already had a crisis command post up in Albany. The post was poorly run, with dispirited employees manning a subterranean "Cold War relic" of a bunker below police headquarters. Andrew may have been right to want a command center in the eye of the storm. He certainly wanted to be in the storm himself, available for those on-camera interviews, not up in Albany letting Mayor Bloomberg get the press. But in setting up the second command center, the report went on, Andrew fostered a sense of bringing the A team down with him and leaving the B team upstate, which in turn created confusion and "inefficiencies." The move, concluded the report, was a likely "strategic mistake."

The way the report emerged said a lot about how the administration worked. Two drafts were produced on the same day. One included the negative comments in blue boldface—a draft apparently meant to be read only by the head of the state's Division of Homeland Security and Emergency Services, a Cuomo loyalist. The other was a sanitized version. Albany *Times Union* reporter Jim Odato, who got hold of the two drafts, asked why they were different, yet bore the same date. No one in the state's Homeland Security office could offer an answer.

Three days after Sandy's fierce impact, lower Manhattan remained without power, as did millions of residents in other parts of New York and New Jersey. Gas was scarce, and gas lines long. But the city's tunnels were being drained, and soon the subways would be working again. It was time for a victory lap. That Thursday afternoon, November 1, the state's top officials took one, gathering first for a look at the still-flooded Brooklyn-Battery Tunnel, then holding a news conference. Andrew dominated with a rousing speech about New York spirit. "They say sometimes that when it comes to personalities, your greatest strength can be your greatest weakness," he declared. "In some ways, that is true for this city also. What made this city and made this state was our proximity to the water. It was our port, it was the Hudson River, the Erie Canal—that's what made us... That becomes a great liability in the face of a storm, and that is what we have seen, in a way we haven't seen in decades, if ever."

As the officials clustered before the cameras—Senators Chuck Schumer and Kirsten Gillibrand, U.S. Homeland Security secretary Janet Napolitano, and more—a small, trim figure kept his distance, arms tightly crossed, clearly irked by Cuomo's remarks. There Mayor Bloomberg stayed, until Senator Schumer saw him. "It's called a photo op," Schumer said teasingly to the mayor. "After twelve years you ought to know how it works." Bloomberg rolled his eyes, but ventured closer. Andrew, still presiding, offered gushing words for the mayor's help these last tough days. Finally the mayor addressed the gathering. "Governor, thank you," he said of those words. "As Henry Kissinger would say, they have the added advantage of being true." Now Cuomo was the one to roll his eyes.

Through the storm, the governor and mayor had worked together, but not, perhaps, with brio. They gave separate briefings. If one put a press release out at 10 a.m., the other issued one at 1 p.m. Rumor had it that a state official had been strongly chastised by the second floor for appearing at a storm-related event with the mayor; the governor's office denied it. If polls were the yardstick, Andrew was the winner: his numbers were up even more than Bloomberg's when the skies finally cleared.

There was, however, an even bigger winner of the Sandy sweepstakes: Governor Chris Christie of New Jersey, who with his wide circumference seemed to spin like a gyroscope all over his state. Christie had been mentioned before the storm as a possible Republican rival for 2016; now, as he praised Obama for the president's own storm effort, and toured the state by helicopter with him, Christie looked like a leader who'd put politics aside to help his citizens take on a crisis. So, in these final days of the general campaign, did Obama, gaining as much from the glow of bipartisanship in his race against Mitt Romney as Christie did for the presidency next time. As columnist Frank Rich mischievously tweeted, "Maybe it turns out that Christie is the October Surprise."

Andrew wasn't finished, however. The hapless utilities still had New Yorkers in the dark, days after Sandy's passing. That was unacceptable. How could Con Edison and the Long Island Power Authority (LIPA) have failed to restore power when they had had Hurricane Irene the year before as a dress rehearsal? Andrew wanted answers, and he wanted them fast: only a Moreland commission would do. And so materialized the governor's first Moreland, which in retrospect would have certain earmarks of the more notorious one that followed.

One of the culprits, the commissioners realized, was Andrew Cuomo. Of the fifteen seats on LIPA's board, nine were to be filled by the governor. Yet three of those had stayed empty for the twenty-two months of Andrew's tenure. Three more board members were serving expired terms, just hanging on for replacements. One of those was the chairman. So far, Andrew had filled just one seat. The commissioners agreed to make a little note of that and moved on.

With just weeks to study the mess and come up with solutions, the Moreland commissioners weighed three options. The favorite was to privatize LIPA: let a private utility buy LIPA's assets and run the power grid itself, under state oversight. Not every commissioner was sold, however. Mark Green, the former New York public advocate, had doubts about privatization. So did Robert Abrams, the onetime New York attorney general. They asked for—and got—a promise that the interim report would say a *majority* of commissioners liked privatization.

The report did use the word "majority," and so did the press release accompanying it. But those drafts were then set aside. In the later version released to the press, "majority" was scrubbed. Based on the final version, *Newsday* duly noted, "The best resolution, the panel concluded, was to scrap LIPA and go with a private company."

That wasn't what the report said. It was what Andrew wanted it to say. For the first time, and not the last, Andrew would seemingly bend a powerful Moreland commission to abide by his choices, not the commissioners'.

Along with Barack Obama's reelection that November came, in the state of New York, a most confusing verdict. Democrats won back the Senate—only they didn't. They had a majority when the votes were counted, but then they lost it. Albany was a very strange place.

Back in June, when the session had ended and he could no more hold himself above the partisan fray, Andrew had been nudged by his own party to start stumping for Democrats as their campaigns ramped up. All members of the legislature, Senate and Assembly, were up for reelection every even-numbered year: that was how it worked in New York. With his still-stellar poll numbers, Andrew could do more than help a few candidates win. He could put the Senate back in Democrats' hands.

And why, the party faithful pleaded, would Andrew not want to do that? True, the governor had gotten a lot done with a Republican majority. But Senate Republicans had blocked any increase in the woefully low minimum wage. They were antiabortion; they put business needs above the environment; they kept campaign finance reform bottled up. Worst of all, they'd gerrymandered the district lines, consigning many voters, mostly black and Hispanic, to unequal representation for the next decade. Was this the party that ought to wield power? For Andrew—Democrat, self-described progressive, his liberal father's son—the answer was yes.

He didn't put it so baldly, of course. Did he want to see his own party regain the senate? "I want to see the best people in the state Senate that we can attract," he coolly replied. He hardly needed to add that some of the Senate's *worst* actors were downstate Democrats.

As his party waited to see their governor do something—anything—to help Democrats win, Andrew did what he could behind the scenes to help three Senate Republicans to whom he owed his greatest triumph: marriage equality. One of the Marriage Four, James Alesi, had chosen not to run for reelection. The others were struggling to keep their seats. All had paid a price, in the end, for supporting marriage equality—a price hardly offset by campaign contributions from grateful gay rights groups. Two would lose that fall; the third would hold on for one more term. In the aftermath, Andrew would applaud their political courage. "I don't believe we elect officials to always agree with us," he said somberly. "We elect officials to use their best judgment and to be people of character and integrity." He was perhaps talking not just about them but about the politician he tried to be.

Despite the Marriage Four's struggles, Republicans that fall had reason to hope they might cling to power in the Senate. After all, they had newly drawn districts—drawn their way—to maximize their chances. They also had tacit help from Andrew, who let them use grip-and-grin photos of them with the still-popular governor in their campaign literature: a show of bipartisanship, perhaps, but at the expense of Democratic candidates whose leader was supposed to be helping them.

When the votes were counted, though, Democrats could claim at least thirty-one seats, with two more likely to go their way in unresolved races. One of the toss-ups, to the statewide shock of Republicans, was that new sixty-third district, the one meant to provide an extra buffer for the endangered Republican Senate majority because its upper Hudson Valley constituents were so reliably Republican. A Democratic public school board mom named Cecilia Tkaczyk had given her generic Republican rival a far tougher fight than expected, and might just win after disputed votes were counted.

Republicans had won just thirty seats outright, shy a majority even with the old sixty-two districts, let alone sixty-three. That was it: the Democrats had won back the Senate. Only they hadn't, for that was when the games began, with string-pulling by the governor.

The first of the Republicans' postelection gains came when a newly elected conservative Democrat from Brooklyn declared he would caucus with them, possibly a surprise to some of the Democrats who had put him in office. Then came four more, as the Independent Democratic Conference, to their party's mortification, forged formal ties with the Republicans.

IDC founder Jeffrey Klein, the Democrat whose district covered parts of the Bronx and Westchester, had seen that the time was right to take advantage of the Republicans' vulnerability and boost his own hand. He proposed that the IDC be recognized as its own little fiefdom, a third, permanent Senate conference, creating in effect a coalition government. Klein and his IDC would acquire equal power with the Republicans to move legislation: the currency of the realm. He and Dean Skelos would even take turns presiding over the Senate. In the little hothouse of Albany politics, this was big.

Only later would Andrew emerge as an active participant in the process. "The governor and [top aide] Larry [Schwartz] made it very clear they wanted the IDC to work with the Republicans to run the Senate," a source would tell political reporter Blake Zeff. Andrew himself had "many, many conversations" with Republican leaders, clarifying just how the coalition would work—and how it would block the Democrats from the majority they'd just won. Yet when asked at the time when the IDC was forming if he had played any part in the drama, Andrew said no. "I haven't gotten involved in a leadership dispute or debate and the Assembly will pick a leader and the Senate will pick a leader. And I have no intention of getting involved in either situation." It was a clever bit of lawyerly equivocation. Strictly speaking, Andrew wasn't weighing in on who would lead either chamber—only on how the IDC would affect them both.

Even as Albany was absorbing this news, a black downstate Democrat, Malcolm Smith of Queens, announced he was joining the IDC too. So now even if the Democrats won both of those unresolved races, the GOP would be firmly in control—sharing power but in control—with thirty-six votes to the Democrats' twenty-seven.

That Smith was black was hardly a coincidence, at least not to the embittered downstate Democrats, most of whom were black and Hispanic. Smith was a token, they felt, so that no one could say the new ruling majority was all white. Nor could anyone say that this shift of power was racial politics, meant to disenfranchise blacks and Hispanics. After all, there was Smith! But to the downstate Democrats, this shift of power was *all* about race, and the puppet master was Andrew.

That race remained a factor in New York politics could be denied by none. For more than forty years, until 2008, the Senate had been ruled by white Republicans, with black and Hispanic downstate Democrats way at the back of the bus. The Democratic takeback of the Senate that year had been celebrated as a racial triumph by those same black and Hispanic downstaters. Sadly, the tawdry dealings that ensued, the brief-lived coup led by Pedro Espada, the failures to pass any meaningful legislation, and the loss of power with the next election—this too was seen as racial: the failure of those same black and Hispanic downstaters to govern. Most of the Democrats now being indicted and put on trial were lawmakers of color as well.

Racially, there was no coincidence between Andrew's ascension to governor in 2010 and the Republicans' return to power that year in the state senate. Blacks and Hispanics had blown their chance. The predominantly white Republicans were back in charge. The IDC that had helped ensure the new Republican majority was white too, right up until the defection of Malcolm Smith.

If asked why Andrew preferred working with Republicans, his aides, off the record, would note the ever-lengthening list of indicted downstate Democrats. Soon to join that list would be Malcolm Smith—to the embarrassment of both parties, each of which in a sense had now invested in him. The aides had a point.

Even as Jeff Klein was celebrating his victory, Andrew was plotting how to use the enhanced IDC for his own agenda. Klein was a rook on this newly configured chessboard. But Andrew was still the king.

Sandy was a crisis—and for all the intramural grumbling, a crisis well met. But it wasn't the kind of Next Big Thing for which Andrew had pined. It wasn't an issue of social justice, like marriage equality, or some transformation of the state. Andrew could see one such prospect, but he was damned if he was going to touch it. Of all the issues confronting him, fracking was the last thing he wanted to do next.

With polls consistently showing the state split on fracking, and each side as ardent as the other, Andrew had hoped to chart a middle course. The counties of the Southern Tier—poor aboveground but sitting atop vast reserves of natural gas below—were all too happy to take the environmental risks. No major watershed lay nearby, so Andrew could sanction fracking in those counties, on privately owned land whose owners had willingly sold their mineral rights, and the rest of the state could wait and see how things worked out from there: fracking lite.

But in the last fifteen months or so, a grassroots movement unlike any other had swept the state. Yoko Ono and Sean Lennon, Lady Gaga and Paul McCartney had led rallies; tens of thousands of antifrackers had sent in comments to push the governor into blocking the practice, which he alone with his pen could do. State senator Tony Avella, a leader of the antifrackers, put the political risk in stark terms. "Governor Cuomo, if you allow hydrofracking to occur in this state, you own it. And if you want to run for president, all it'll take is one incident, one contamination, that we know will happen, and your dream of running for president is over. It's over."

A deadline loomed in late November 2012. Either Andrew lifted the moratorium that had held back fracking until now, declaring the state was ready, or he didn't, in which case the regulatory clock would run out and the whole process would have to begin again: more study, more public hearings, more delay. As that date approached, spokesmen for the natural gas industry openly voiced their indignation with a governor who seemed to have lost his spine. They too warned Andrew of the implications for a presidential run. He was perhaps too late already if he hoped to avoid being punished by the issue as a presidential candidate for 2016 in the pro-drilling heartland. "It's going to be very difficult for a guy like Cuomo to go into Ohio with his record and say, 'I'm pro gas,'" one industry lobbyist warned. The *Wall Street Journal* weighed in too. "The man who would be president is ducking the premier energy debate of our time."

After months of silence, Andrew reached his decision at last. He would kick the can down the road. After four years of study, the state's Department of Environmental Conservation would study fracking some more. In addition, the state's Department of Health would study its impact on human health. "We've said all along that the decision will be made based on the science, right?" Andrew declared. So that's what he would do. The science would take as long as it needed.

And so began a study so patient and painstaking that it would still be going, cloaked in secrecy, two years later. Andrew's most contentious issue would as a result be gently sidelined for the entirety of his reelection campaign. It was perhaps a clever move, but a cynical one too. Political leaders didn't solve thorny issues by just putting them aside.

That fall, Andrew ran toward, not away from, another Next Big Thing. Of all the troubled upstate cities, Buffalo was the worst off—and so, Andrew declared, the most deserving of a big cash infusion. A "Billion for Buffalo" became his rallying cry. A sort of empowerment zone on steroids, Billion for Buffalo would fund mostly high-tech projects. It sounded great, but where, wondered Democratic senator Liz Krueger, was the $1 billion to come from? Mostly from long-existing programs, she discovered, simply slid under a new heading: Only $130 million was new money. "Yet he advertised it as a huge new chunk!" So was it real? "Like so much of what the administration did," Krueger observed, "what was real and what was not was sort of a trick question."

The true Next Big Thing came in the form of a horrible tragedy, one that cried out for sweeping reform: the killing of twenty-six people, including twenty children, on December 14, 2012, by a troubled youth wielding a high-capacity assault weapon called a Bushmaster in a grade school in Newtown, Connecticut.

As the nation reeled, Andrew spoke out. "Let this terrible tragedy finally be the wake-up call for aggressive action," he declared, "and I pledge my full support in that effort." He was serious. Top lawmakers home for the holidays began hearing from the governor. He wanted the toughest gun control bill in the land, and he wanted it now. New York already had a ban on assault weapons like the one used in Connecticut, but Andrew wanted it strengthened by restricting the sales of high-capacity magazines. New York and a handful of other states had already gone so far as to ban magazines holding more than ten rounds. So, said the governor, why not seven? And why not bring the legislature back—*right now*—to pass it?

The Republican leaders tried to steer a moderate course. They too were appalled by Newtown. They too saw room for improvement in gun control. Cracking down on illegal guns. Tightening oversight of the mentally ill and their access to guns of all kinds. Establishing a statewide gun registry, not just county by county. And yes, maybe smaller-capacity magazines. But this was complex stuff. They couldn't just jam a bill through before Christmas. Better to let the legislature start up on schedule, talk out the issues, and pass the right bill. Grudgingly, Andrew agreed, but he made very clear that what he wanted was the toughest assault weapon bill in the land. A bill to be proud of. And, perhaps, to run on in 2016.

The two sides were still talking on January 9, 2013, when Andrew gave his third State of the State speech and made gun control a major focus of it. "Stop the madness," the governor cried. "In a word, enough!" He ticked off half a dozen priorities for the bill he hoped to pass in the next days, from banning all civilian sales of assault weapons and large-capacity magazines to boosting penalties and jail time for illegal gun possession, especially for those who, as in Newtown, used such guns on school grounds.

Offstage, Andrew was holding tense meetings on gun control with senior Republicans and their staffers. He wanted to ban not just assault weapons but rifles with pistol grips. Surely no hunter used guns like that.

The Republican staffers spent hours one day trying to explain the differences between long guns and different pistol grips, how some were used for hunting, and for what kinds of game. "If you ban all pistol grips, you get into problems," one lawmaker observed. To Andrew they all looked like assault weapons; he wanted to ban them all.

How many bullets? That was the other debate. States at the vanguard of gun control law—including New York—had set ten-bullet-or-more maximums for gun magazines. So New York's maximum would be seven, Andrew ruled. The Republican staffers tried to explain the problem with that. Gun clips were designed to hold ten bullets at least. "So hunters would be illegal if they're carrying ten-bullet clips," the staffers noted.

"They can put seven in," the governor retorted.

"Yeah, but the clip holds ten. And hunters carry boxes of ammo." So they could *look* illegal by having those ten-bullet clips and the bullets to fill them, even if they had only seven bullets loaded.

"He just knew that nationally it was ten so he wanted to do seven," one Republican lawmaker recalled with a sigh. "No compromise there."

Politically, Andrew had the upper hand, and he knew it. Newtown had stirred one of those waves of public emotion that a smart politician knew to ride, and no one was better at sensing those swells than Andrew. Even the Republicans' moderate flank wanted stricter gun control after Newtown—including the Long Island townships ruled by Dean Skelos. The Senate majority leader could ill afford to ignore those horrified suburban families wondering if their schools were next. If Republicans did balk at the bill, Andrew would go to the downstate Democrats, bringing the IDC with him. After all, the IDC's band of five could hardly vote *against* gun control, not when street gangs and gun dealers wielded guns on the outer-borough streets of New York City. And the downstate Democrats, despite their ire at Andrew, were all for gun control. Andrew liked the Republicans, but the moment they stopped compromising with him, he would go across the aisle. "I was married," he told the Republicans by way of explanation. "And when you're married you have to do what your wife says. You have to go to the in-laws, you have to do all sorts of things. But when you're not married and you have a girlfriend, if you're not happy you find another girlfriend."

Andrew wanted his bill his way—and he wanted it fast. "We can't have an effective date thirty days from now," he told the Republican Senate's chief of staff. "That'll create a run on guns." Just that past weekend, a gun show had drawn anxious crowds, all wanting to buy guns that might soon be banned. Reluctantly, the Republicans took up the New York SAFE Act, as it was now called, and passed it later that day. It included the seven-bullet rule, along with a mandate that mental health professionals report to the authorities any patients "likely to engage in conduct that would result in serious harm to self or others." Both items would soon be struck from the bill as unworkable, and Andrew's advisers would start looking for others to blame.

Shrewd a judge as he was of public sentiment, Andrew seemed taken aback by the furious reaction of gun owners across the state, particularly upstate, to his New York SAFE Act. New York was too blue a state for the National Rifle Association to hold much sway: Democrats held all statewide posts. Andrew himself remained widely popular. Yet overnight, small armies of gun-owning Republicans who had come to admire the Democratic governor deserted en masse.

To the fascination of Albany watchers, the loudest voice protesting the bill was Fred Dicker's. In the days after its passing, the *New York Post*'s state editor and columnist had scathing words on his radio show for this grievous breach of the Second Amendment—and for the governor who had pushed it into law. "A major attack is under way," Dicker warned. "This is a Trojan horse. This is not about semiautomatic rifles. This is a sweeping set of gun laws... The governor is using the tragedy... as a justification for sweeping changes in gun laws including regulating every single gun millions of New Yorkers now own... It's another reason people are going to be leaving New York."

Dicker's admiration for Andrew had started to falter even before the SAFE Act. On his radio show, the dean of Albany's press corps had rapped Andrew for not throwing the gates open to fracking. But about guns, and the Second Amendment, Dicker felt far more strongly. Gamely, Andrew came on the show to debate the SAFE Act with him. The governor was calm and logical, his host somewhat less so. Once or twice more, Andrew tried to reason on air with Dicker, but the *Post*'s man would not be swayed. The honeymoon—Dicker's sixth with this latest of the six governors he had covered since 1982—was over.

To the rest of the press corps, the effect was breathtaking. Almost overnight, Dicker's column was rubbed clean of its glowing tone toward the governor. Back at the keyboard was Dicker the Rottweiler, his off-the-record sources now unfailingly critical of the governor, as if magnetically flipped.

Precipitous a change as this might be in a columnist, it seemed mind-bending in a biographer. How, Albany insiders asked, could a writer who now heaped public scorn on his subject be his Boswell? Andrew must have wondered the same. By April, he had called HarperCollins, Dicker's publisher. Though terms were kept confidential, Dicker abandoned his book, likely keeping the first half of his reported six-figure advance. Now Andrew would write his own book, with a collaborator, to be published by HarperCollins in the midst of his 2014 reelection campaign. He promised his publishers a full and candid account of key moments in his personal and political life. Clearly the pitch worked: HarperCollins reportedly agreed to pay him an advance of at least $700,000.

In his anger over guns, Dicker spoke for more voters than Andrew might have hoped. By the end of January 2013, the governor's poll numbers had dropped dramatically, from 74 percent to 59 percent. One of his close advisers, expecting a black mood, found the governor unfazed. "If I dropped as a result of that, good, I'm proud of that," Andrew said. "To have fought for that and taken a hit for it? Fine." Even after knowing Andrew for thirty years, the adviser was surprised by that. The governor was hypersensitive to polls; the drop of a point or two could rile him. That he was willing to squander nearly 15 points for gun control—that surprised the adviser too. Often in those thirty years, the adviser had wondered what Andrew's fundamental beliefs were; he could be, as the adviser put it, so fluid. Did he in fact have any? Seeing him across the desk that day, the adviser felt reassured. There *was* a political core to Andrew, and gun control, with all that it implied and involved, was it.

Perhaps. But with Andrew, politics was always part of the equation. It simply couldn't be taken out of the man. He had rushed his SAFE Act into law not only to head off a run on guns but to beat the president on his own federal gun law. And beat him he did, by one day: on January 16, 2013, Obama came out with a similar list of gun control proposals, vowing to make them the laws of the land. Three months later, to the president's chagrin, every one of those proposals would be defeated on the floor of the U.S. Senate. He had waited too long; the NRA had had time to kill the bills. Andrew, moving fast, had prevailed.

Unfortunately, speed had made for a flawed bill. The U.S. Department of Veterans Affairs declared it would not do the mental health reporting required by the law for fear of violating patient privacy and discouraging new patients from seeking treatment. More troublesome was the new seven-bullet magazine rule. Some law enforcement officials packed firearms with ten-bullet magazines. A "carve-out" in the bill would be needed to keep them exempt from it. For that matter no one else could follow the rule, since no seven-bullet clip existed. All the new rule did was turn gun owners into criminals for carrying guns that held ten bullets instead of seven. Eventually, a federal judge would strike it from the act as arbitrary, and Andrew would revise the SAFE Act accordingly. "There is no such thing as a seven-bullet magazine," he would admit. "That doesn't exist. So you really have no practical option."

Gun control was a high priority for Mayor Bloomberg too, one he had pushed for years, and his staff had happily kibitzed with the governor's advisers as the SAFE Act came together. So the mayor was surprised when his national initiative, Mayors Against Illegal Guns, was left out of a major *New York Times* account of how the bill was drawn up—an account clearly done with cooperation from the second floor. "The omission was glaring," recalled a mayoral staffer, "because [Mayors Against Illegal Guns] was by far the biggest player in the space."

That was annoying enough. But then in late March, after the seven-bullet clip had been roundly derided, Fred Dicker quoted an unnamed Cuomo aide on why the bill had flaws. "Much of what's in the law was drafted by people connected to Mayor Bloomberg and the Brady Center," the source explained, "not by the governor's staff."

That was why there were so many problems with it.

The SAFE Act was national news, whatever its flaws, and Andrew in pushing it had put himself back on the national stage. The timing was fortunate. Obama's second term was beginning, and with it, in this speeded-up media age, the first ruminations on who might succeed him in 2016.

Hillary Clinton, her tour of duty as secretary of state just concluded, seemed the inevitable front-runner, the one Democratic candidate Andrew wouldn't take on. But for Hillary there were suddenly health issues. Exhausted after four years of shuttle diplomacy, she had incurred a stomach virus that left her dehydrated, so much so that one night in mid-December 2012, she collapsed at home alone. When she finally got to a hospital, her doctors diagnosed a concussion and kept a close watch on it. On Sunday, December 30, 2012, they detected a blood clot in a vein called the right transverse sinus, behind her right ear, between the brain and the skull. Had the clot gone untreated, it might have caused a stroke or brain hemorrhage. Fortunately, this vein was one of a pair: the left transverse sinus could absorb the extra blood flow while anticoagulants eased the clot in the right one. Three days later, Hillary was released from New York–Presbyterian Hospital flanked by her husband and daughter, looking tired but relieved.

Inevitably, questions about her health would reemerge, but for now, Hillary at sixty-five remained the most experienced prospect in either party. Polls projected her trouncing all comers, from Vice President Joe Biden to the headline-grabbing governors of New Jersey and New York. And that, for Andrew, made for a maddening dilemma. Until Hillary declared herself in or out of the race, big-money Democratic donors would sit on their hands. "It's really a crazy situation," one Cuomo supporter admitted. "He's totally trapped by her." Yet if Andrew was to nurse any hopes for 2016, he would have to act on them sooner than later, building a national campaign. At some point, staying above the fray would mean sitting out the fight.

Gun owners might seethe and sign petitions, suits might be filed, but to at least 59 percent of his electorate, the instigator of America's toughest gun control law was off to a powerful start in his third legislative session. Behind the glowing articles and souped-up talk of 2016, though, there were warnings of trouble to come.

One came in the form of the candidate with the unpronounceable name. Back when she'd entered the race for the newly carved sixty-third district, Cecilia Tkaczyk had studied the demographics of her Hudson Valley area and found them... not so bad. True, the new district had a lot of Republican voters. But they weren't that conservative, and they cared as much as she did about public education. They deeply resented the education cuts that Andrew's first budget had imposed, and got no sympathy on that subject from Tkaczyk's Republican rival, George Amedore, a five-year assemblyman and builder. Fracking worried them too, and Amedore's wait-and-see attitude did nothing to ease their doubts. Tkaczyk was adamantly opposed to fracking, and embraced her region's rural roots; she was probably the only senatorial candidate who tended Jacob breed sheep and belonged to a local spinning and weaving guild.

Two weeks before election day, Tkaczyk had pulled close enough in the polls to be of sudden interest to a pair of political action committees funded by wealthy liberals. To her shock—and without any communication from them, in keeping with election laws—the PACs committed $500,000 to flood the airwaves with ads and blanket the district with mailers promoting her stances. Amedore had outspent Tkaczyk by $367,000 so far. Overnight, Tkaczyk became the heavy, and started closing the gap.

In those final days, Andrew ignored pleas to campaign for his fellow Democrat, and talked of letting the voters decide. Tkaczyk went on election night to her favorite Greek restaurant and heard Amedore claim victory. Yet by midnight she was back from the dead, ahead by 136 votes, and claimed the victory as her own. So began an agonizing, back-and-forth endgame, the lead shifting as absentee ballots were counted and contested ballots challenged in court. Not until January was the winner declared: Tkaczyk, by eighteen votes. Many Democrats called to congratulate her on her roller-coaster win. Andrew, the leader of her party, was not among them.

There was a lot in Tkaczyk's win for the governor to consider. The two PACs were dedicated to campaign finance reform—and freely acknowledged the glaring irony of spending big money to get candidates elected who would stop PACs like them from doing what they were doing. One of them was cofounded by Jonathan Soros, son of billionaire investor George Soros. The other was founded by Sean Eldridge and his husband, Facebook cofounder Chris Hughes. Here were three very rich liberals who saw New York's porous campaign rules as a root cause of its corruption. They had listened to Andrew's speeches as a candidate and hoped he was their man. Nothing they had seen since then had persuaded them that he was. He paid lip service to the issue, then took in millions from real estate moguls with an eye toward his own reelection in 2014. The latest to surface was Fisher Brothers, the Manhattan real estate and investment firm: word leaked that Fisher Brothers had given $500,000 to the Committee to Save New York. Fisher Brothers executives had also given $120,000 to Andrew's campaigns since 2008. For what? Who knew?

Whatever the facts of certain donations, the pattern was all too clear. Anyone could form an LLC, give $60,800 to a Democratic statewide candidate, and then form as many more LLCs as they wanted. That was a loophole big enough to drive a truck through—and for Andrew, a cavalcade of trucks had driven through it with money for his 2014 reelection campaign. Real estate developer Leonard Litwin led the procession with $625,000 donated through various holdings between December 1, 2010, and July 11, 2013. Further back in the wagon train for this same period were other developers like Peter Kalikow ($125,000), Roth & Sons Management ($120,800), Marathon Development ($75,000), and Tishman Speyer ($60,800). As the New York Public Interest Research Group (NYPIRG) noted in its dogged accounting of the figures, 80.18 percent of the money raised by Andrew in this election cycle had come from donors giving $10,000 or more. The system was to blame, no doubt about it, but Andrew was doing nothing to change it, just reaping its rewards from New York's richest voters: Governor One Percent indeed.

So far, the reform-minded PACs were merely working to elect reform-minded candidates, not working directly against Andrew. If the governor kept letting campaign finance reform slide, one day soon they would.

Another warning came on February 13, 2013, in an act of political courage.

Until that moment, few in state politics had spoken out about Andrew in any critical way. The governor was all-powerful, he ruled by fear, and woe to the lawmaker or lackey who questioned any of his edicts. When Mayor Stephanie Miner of Syracuse took to the op-ed page of the *New York Times* to explain how the state was killing her city, the whole state sat up and took notice.

It was budget time, and Andrew was once again tightening the screws. Desperate cities and counties were staggering under mandated costs—for their share of Medicaid, public education, essential services, and pensions. These costs were rising precipitously, and the local governments saw no way to pay them—not pinned down as they were by Andrew's 2 percent tax cap on property taxes.

Some months before, Miner and other mayors had gone to Albany to plead their case. Their costs were fixed; they had no cash to pay them. The state would have to help. From the second floor came a stern reply: they would have to learn to live within their means. Andrew himself put it in three words: "That's called life."

That was when Miner began to seethe.

A former labor lawyer who had started in Syracuse politics as a student stuffing envelopes, Miner was, at forty-three, the city's first woman mayor, admired across party lines for her straight-shooting style. She was also the recently named cochair of the state Democratic Party, appointed by the governor.

Miner presided from an oak-paneled suite in Syracuse's nineteenth-century city hall, a Romanesque limestone castle of towers and turrets that had backed onto the original Erie Canal. The building evoked Syracuse's former grandeur as the salt capital of the United States, but those days were long gone, and Miner felt anything but regal in her high-vaulted office. Often at her desk she squeezed a tight rubber ball to alleviate tension.

Soon after she took office in early 2010, Miner had crunched the numbers and realized that Syracuse was headed straight toward bankruptcy. Labor costs were high, thanks to pensions and earlier contracts that had given too much away. Municipal and school aid had been cut, and property taxes no longer covered those budgets, let alone police and firemen, sanitation, and other services. Big companies—Kodak in Rochester, Carrier Corporation in Syracuse—had slashed workforces and shut down plants. High school and college graduates had left; poor immigrants had arrived; tax receipts had fallen as the demand for social services rose. Cities all over America were suffering these problems, worsened by the Great Recession. Syracuse was merely worse off than most. Yet the governor's only advice was to cut costs. Cut what?

The protocol at budget time was for someone from the second floor, usually the lieutenant governor, to call each of the mayors of the state's major cities to warn what the numbers would be in the governor's proposal. Three or four days before Andrew was to issue his draft in January, Miner realized she hadn't gotten her call. She reached out to Joe Percoco, Andrew's ever-trusty enforcer. "What's in it for Syracuse?" she asked.

"You mean all you care about is Syracuse?" Percoco replied. He was perhaps trying to be humorous. Miner was not amused. Yes, she said, that was what she wanted to know.

Percoco said he would get back to her. He didn't, and nor did the lieutenant governor, Bob Duffy. Only when the press called did Miner hear that the budget had been released, and that it had a plan to lighten Syracuse's pension costs by $11 million. Miner was intrigued. She knew the city's budget very well. She had no idea where that $11 million would come from.

Soon Miner learned. The state was proposing that its hard-hit cities take advantage of future pension savings generated from Tier VI, Andrew's pension triumph of the previous year. Raising the retirement age for future state workers from sixty-two to sixty-three, trimming their benefits—all that could be booked now, and used to reduce current pension costs.

Miner was aghast. To her, this was simply a loan by another name. She said as much to reporters. In response, the lieutenant governor delivered a warning via the *Syracuse Post-Standard*'s editorial board. If Miner didn't want to realize these savings, Syracuse would be taken over by a state-led financial control board. The board would make the hard decisions that Miner appeared unwilling—or unable—to make. That was when Miner began drafting her *New York Times* op-ed.

The day before the piece was to run, Miner called Percoco to give him a heads-up. The enforcer wasn't happy. Driving home, Miner got a call from an assistant on the *Times*' op-ed page. "We just got a call from the governor's office, screaming at us, asking us to pull it." Later, Miner would hear on good authority that the governor himself had called Arthur "Pinch" Sulzberger, the *Times*' publisher, to try to kill the piece. Despite the calls, the piece went online that night.

In her op-ed, Miner called the governor's proposal "an accounting gimmick" that "would let municipalities push payment of today's ballooning pension costs into the future." It would merely put them deeper in debt. "We mayors have proposals on labor arbitration, pension rules, budget gimmicks and taxes," Miner wrote. "What we don't have, yet, is the leadership to arrive at a consensus on what will work. For that we need the governor."

Calls and e-mails began flooding in from around the state, congratulating Miner on saying what had to be said. For forty-eight hours there was silence from the second floor. Then one top aide called to ask why Miner had done this terrible thing. "Because I want you to pay attention to Syracuse's problems," she said. The top aide laughed. "And Syracuse reads the *New York Times*," he retorted. By which, Miner inferred, he meant she need not have bothered with her op-ed, since the citizens of Syracuse were too poor and ignorant to read the newspaper of record.

Over the next months, Syracuse reporters began asking the mayor how she felt about possible political retribution to "take her out" and "cut her off at the knees." The muttering died down when she won reelection that fall with 68 percent of the vote, and no one asked her to resign as cochair of the state Democratic Party, so she kept the post until April 2014. By then, Andrew was looking toward his own reelection; he deserved the cochair of his choice, Miner felt, so she stepped down.

At last came a call from Andrew. He said it was ridiculous that they were feuding. "I'm a lot older than you are," he said, "and I know that politics is about addition, not subtraction." They should have a good catch-up talk, he said. Joe Percoco would arrange it. Weeks passed, but finally, with the primary looming, the governor did call for a schmooze. He said he wanted to replicate the Buffalo Billion in other hard-hit cities, and urged Miner to submit a wish list for Syracuse. Think big, he told her. Miner said she would. Despite their differences, she would support him, she told him, and she did.

Soon after the election, Miner submitted her Billion for Syracuse list—everything from fixing failing water pipes to repairing crumbling roads. She heard nothing, until the mid-January day when she woke to the news that Rochester would be getting the Buffalo treatment. No one from the administration had even contacted her to give her a heads-up, much less address her list.

Meanwhile, several upstate cities borrowed against future pension saving, as the governor had advised. None of Miner's fellow mayors told her that had proved helpful. Miner declined to borrow that money for Syracuse. She calculated that the city had saved, as a result, $10 million.

In March 2013, Andrew put his third consecutive budget to bed on time—a feat long unequaled in the state of New York. There was much in that $135.1 billion package to admire.

As the new budget reaffirmed, Andrew had made hard cuts, and overall, the state was better for them—if better meant a balanced budget with whacks to social programs. Deeper, though, lay threats the state had not yet taken on. New York still had higher taxes than almost any other state.

A Washington-based think tank called the Tax Foundation ranked New York fiftieth of all states overall in its annual State Business Tax Climate Index. Change *had* come. Behind the shiny rhetoric, however, lay the upstate cities Stephanie Miner had invoked in her op-ed, punished by those sky-high taxes, poor and depressed as Appalachia. Their founding industries had left or languished years or decades before—the governor bore no blame for that. But if their troubles continued to grow, then they, not his triumphs, would be the story of Governor Andrew Cuomo. They were the millstones he pulled behind him, the true tests of his power to lead.

Clearly aware of the stakes, Andrew coined a new New York promotional campaign with a motto: "Open for Business." Regulations were being eased, the campaign stressed, business taxes cut. The meat of this new dish was Start-Up NY, an ambitious plan to lure start-up companies to the state by allying them with one or another of the sixty-four campuses in the State University of New York system, where they could be tethered to high-tech pods and nurture their start-ups tax-free for ten years.

It was a bold idea—an inspiring one, even—and one that Andrew would embrace wholeheartedly: well into 2014, television commercials for Start-Up NY would appear with ruthless regularity.

Still, with one after another of those upstate cities in bad or worsening shape, the best solution for a governor with his eye on higher office was perhaps to conjure up a few bright new programs like Start-Up NY, promote the hell out of them—and get out while the getting was good.

CHAPTER 26

Scandalmania

Even lawmakers who'd thought they'd seen it all—bribery, embezzlement, the whole kit and caboodle of public corruption—were stunned that winter and spring of 2013 as one after another of their colleagues were indicted, in a wave like none that any could remember. With every next headline, the governor who had passed an ethics bill and pronounced the problem solved looked more at sea.

Loath as always to take blame, Andrew focused on what he felt the lesson was here. Every one of the malefactors was a downstate Democrat. The liberal press had bashed him for not helping Democrats regain the Senate. Well, look who those Democrats were! To many in the capitol, characters like John Sampson, Malcolm Smith, and Shirley Huntley had seemed suspect long before they were nabbed. "You didn't need to know the specifics of whether they were currently under investigation," said Steve Cohen, the onetime prosecutor and former secretary to the governor. "The way they conducted themselves, there was no question they were squirrelly. Everything was what they could get. So the general attitude we had was: how can you campaign for these guys?"

As a former prosecutor himself, Andrew did wonder why the two separate, wide-ranging investigations, conducted by two U.S. attorneys, hadn't netted more crooks, given how corrupt he felt the downstate Democrats to be. Was it possible that Preet Bharara, the ambitious U.S. attorney for the Southern District of New York, had had an ulterior motive for bringing his cases to light when he did? To embarrass Andrew on ethics as the media began sizing up presidential prospects for 2016? After the *New York Post* published part of a Bharara speech rapping Albany's silence on corruption, one of Andrew's advisers voiced that very suspicion. Andrew said he'd had that thought too, and called Bharara directly. The U.S. attorney told Andrew he "ran with what he had," the aide later reported, and wasn't giving the governor any "pops." The governor took him at his word; a year later, relations between the two would be far more fraught.

Blame aside, Andrew hardly needed Preet Bharara to tell him he looked bad. His ethics bill of 2011, with JCOPE its centerpiece, had plainly done nothing to stamp out corruption. And so an important part of his narrative, as pollster Steven Greenberg put it, had fallen away. "He's floundering around," one high-level legislative official said. "He doesn't know what to do, how to react."

Unfortunately, the lawmakers pushing for ethics reform, especially campaign finance reform, were Democrats. That would mean working with the party so tarnished already, and upending the balancing act Andrew had struck with the Independent Democratic Conference and the Republicans, first informally, now officially. "He always wanted a bipartisan legislature to get things done," one adviser pointed out. "That's his big message for national office."

The Democrats hardly thrilled to the prospect of working with the governor whom they suspected of stealing their Senate majority from them. Andrew wasn't feeling a lot of love from Republican senators either—not after the SAFE Act. "After two years of giving in, the people are feeling their spines now," one GOP senator said of his colleagues. Guns, marriage—enough! "They see the governor is not nearly as popular as he was... We're not going to let this guy push us around anymore." A lot of this saber-rattling came now that the next decade's district lines had been drawn. Few Republicans, as a result, had any interest in helping the governor on ethics reform—especially campaign finance reform, which Dean Skelos viewed as a waste of taxpayer money. All Andrew could do was gin up the strongest new ethics reform bill he could, dare both houses to vote it down, and then, if they did—showing the voters who was really to blame—drop the M-bomb of a Moreland commission.

Clearly a first prong of this new ethics bill would have to be more powers for authorities to pursue more forms of corruption involving public officials. The logical official to take on those powers was the attorney general: the governor could grant them to the AG with a stroke of his pen. Andrew chose not to do that. Instead, he would ask the legislature to pass a bill that conferred those powers on the state's sixty-two county district attorneys: a bill unlikely to pass. Once again, Andrew's dealings with his AG seemed punitive—and personal. "Andrew doesn't trust Schneiderman," confided one of the governor's close advisers. "He thinks he hasn't been a good AG. Lawyers who were really experienced have all left under Schneiderman, they say he's too political."

One day that spring of 2013, the subject of Schneiderman came up in a second-floor meeting, and the governor smirked. Was it true, he asked. Was Schneiderman actually wearing eyeliner? For months afterward, the rumor wafted through Andrew's administration, seemingly fanned by the governor himself, until Schneiderman was asked directly about it at a news conference. He did not wear eyeliner, he replied, though he quickly added that he had no problem with anyone of either sex who did. The fact was that he had an eye condition for which he took drops—drops that had the side effect of making one's eyelashes longer and thicker. "My relationship with the governor is very strong," Schneiderman added. "My office represents his agencies, my lawyers talk to his people probably dozens of times every single day."

The lawyers talked, yes. But their leaders? Half a dozen people close to the two men begged to differ. There was no relationship between the governor and the AG who was, among other things, Andrew's government counsel.

By this time the same could be said of Andrew and virtually every other high-ranking official in the state.

Another prong of the Public Trust Act, as Andrew had come to call it, would clearly have to be campaign finance reform. Here he hesitated. Had a yarn-spinning schoolteacher put him off the issue? In the aftermath of her unlikely eighteen-vote victory, Cece Tkaczyk had become its champion, and the groundswell had grown. By May 2013, its funders included media and entertainment billionaire Barry Diller, David Rockefeller Sr., and restaurateur Danny Meyer, along with the three wealthy liberals whose money had clinched Tkaczyk's come-from-behind win, Facebook cofounder Chris Hughes, his husband, Sean Eldridge, and financier Jonathan Soros. Week after week the group pushed Andrew to bring out the toughest possible campaign finance reform bill as part of his Public Trust Act. But for all the money they threw at the problem, Andrew seemed unwilling to act.

The governor did want campaign finance reform, his former aide Steve Cohen argued. "He's the greatest shot at getting it passed!" Andrew was just up against a legislature that wouldn't pass the full-blown finance system the reformers wanted. Instead of blaming the governor for that, and playing into Republican hands, said Cohen, why not go for one piece at a time? "If I can get rid of the LLC loophole and lower campaign limits," he hypothesized, channeling the governor, "you're telling me that none of that is worthwhile without overall campaign finance reform?"

For that, though, the reformers had to trust that Andrew was on their side, not stalling reform as his campaign coffers swelled with old-fashioned loot. That was the problem. They didn't trust him at all.

Andrew was still cobbling together his Public Trust Act on the day in May 2013 that Albany was slimed again. Two investigations of Vito Lopez, the lecherous Brooklyn assemblyman, produced searing reports with graphic details. For Andrew, the headlines brought both danger and opportunity. He started with the obvious: lambasting Lopez. "This is a disgusting, sordid incident," the governor declared. "The man should resign, and he should be expelled by his colleagues if he doesn't." The reports, he said, only added more graphic detail to a "narrative we already knew."

Despite Lopez's reputation, Andrew as late as 2011 had thrown him a sizable bone. An Assembly seat in Brooklyn's 54th District had come vacant, presenting Andrew with a choice. He could do nothing, in which case a regular primary would be held, and voters would choose from whichever candidates signed on to run. Or he could call for a "special election," allowing the resident party boss to choose who would run on the Democratic Party line. Andrew had done the latter; the boss was Lopez. It was a favor, pure and simple, that put Lopez in the governor's debt, especially after Lopez's handpicked candidate won.

Castigating Lopez now was the obvious if overdue move. Shelly Silver was the conundrum. Editorial boards across the state were calling for the Speaker's resignation or replacement as party leader. He'd orchestrated the six-figure payoff in secret, and then, confronted by the second pair of accusers, merely issued a letter of censure.

Asked if he thought Silver should go, Andrew demurred. It was not his place to say who should be Assembly Speaker. If the Speaker was wondering what the governor really felt, a stinging column by Fred Dicker could be read as a hint. "Time's Up! Shameful Shelly Has Got to Go!" ran the *New York Post*'s headline. The Speaker, acknowledged one of his advisers, suspected that the governor had put Dicker to the task. "It's what Andrew has done numerous times in the past," the adviser explained. "A veiled—or not even veiled—threat."

In the kabuki dance that passed for Albany politics, the Speaker made no call to the governor in response to the *Post* story to question him directly. He pretended the *Post* piece didn't exist. "If he asks, say I didn't see the story," he told his adviser.

A day or two later, one of the governor's own advisers asked if the *Post* piece was in fact Dicker channeling the governor. Andrew denied it. "I haven't talked to Fred for two months," he protested. "When I call the house, Jean Miller gets on the phone." Jean Miller was Dicker's longtime girlfriend. "Fred thinks I've betrayed him, he doesn't want to talk to me." But such was the politics—and paranoia—of Albany that the governor's adviser went off wondering if the governor had just spun him too. Andrew had never lied to him, though on occasion he'd forgotten what he said and later revised it.

Certainly Andrew had reason to think that the second most powerful figure in Albany might be advised to step down. Lopez was only the latest in a long line of tainted Assembly Democrats. Circumspect though he might be in his personal life, Silver as their leader had shrugged at the wrongdoings, one after another. Arguably, that made him the cause of "Scandalmania," as the press had dubbed the lengthening scroll of shame, which had all but brought the legislature to a halt. A new Speaker would set a new tone. He might also prove more pliable.

But not now—not with a month in the 2013 session to go, and with so little of Andrew's agenda accomplished. "Throwing the Assembly into chaos would mean he couldn't get anything done," one adviser explained. "Also, there was no heir apparent." And as one lawmaker noted, "a weak Silver is probably better for him than a strong leader. It allows him to get what he needs."

Instead of pushing for Shelly's removal, Andrew spent that May weekend negotiating with him. Silver felt that Lopez's latest declaration—to resign at the end of session—might have to be tolerated. Absolutely not, Andrew retorted. If the assemblyman resigned any later than Monday, the Assembly would have to expel him—right away. The message was passed on to Lopez, and duly heard. On Monday, the old goat resigned.

That, Andrew told Silver, was just the start. New reforms were needed. The governor suggested some; the Speaker offered others; by that back-and-forth, one aide said later, the Speaker survived, and the Public Trust bill advanced.

Two other officials—the AG and the comptroller—had endured months of data dumps and inquisitions over the Lopez affair, but if Andrew had hoped to see them tarnished, he was disappointed. They came up clean. Wisely, he refrained from mentioning either Schneiderman or DiNapoli now.

In a radio interview the next week, Andrew was asked if he bore any of the blame for Scandalmania. He offered a classic Cuomo exercise in anthypophora. "Is the governor to blame for Vito Lopez' sexual [harassment]? No... Is the governor responsible when an assemblyman is bribed or when a legislator violates an escrow account or sexually harasses a staffer?... No, of course not. It's silly... Will you ever stop people from doing venal, stupid, criminal, illegal acts? Not in government, not in politics, not in the military."

Voters, said Andrew hopefully, understood he was doing all he could to clean up Albany. "Which is true," he said. "I am doing everything that I can do." Lopez was one kind of ethical transgression, bribery another, loose campaign money a third, but all were, to use Andrew's term, bad acts. For the first time, Andrew made explicit his warning of what he would do if the legislature failed to pass every one of his ethics reforms: convene a Moreland commission, and start by investigating every lawmaker's outside income, campaign contributions, following the money wherever it led.

After four consecutive months of decline, Andrew's poll ratings ticked up, from 62 percent approval to 64 percent. Perhaps his sophomore slump was over.

Andrew knew as well as anyone how he would be judged. He'd said it himself: jobs, jobs, jobs. Not in Manhattan, where Wall Street was recovering its losses and jobs were returning, but in that hardscrabble landscape called upstate, a world away, with its broken cities and desolate towns. Like many another American governor, Andrew had eyed legalized gambling as a game-changer, and gotten that first bill through the legislature. Soon, as required by the state constitution, a second successive legislature would vote on whether to change the law and allow gaming. If it voted yes, gaming's fate would be decided by public referendum that fall. But all might be for naught if the Native Americans weren't on board: the Senecas, the Mohawks, and the Oneidas, whose casinos stood fortresslike in the west, the north, and the center of the state, on reservation land. On May 1, the day that Andrew embarked on marathon sessions with the tribes, the Native Americans were definitely not on board.

Gaming had made Native Americans rich—some of them, anyway. But once again, the white man had broken his treaties. "Racinos"—video lottery terminal parlors next to horse-racing tracks—had cropped up near their reservations and had the nerve to call themselves casinos. The tribes viewed them as unfair competition and so withheld fees required by their compacts with the state—compacts that promised two of the tribes regional exclusivity. Now came a governor proposing to build at least three full-fledged casinos upstate, possibly near their own. The Native Americans didn't like that at all, and they had clout: millions of dollars for lobbyists to bury the governor's casino initiative.

Andrew considered the players involved: the tribes, the neighboring counties that resented the tribes, the state and its need for new casinos. The rough shape of a deal began to materialize in his mind, a way to make everyone a winner. On April 25, 2013, he called Ray Halbritter, leader of the Oneida Nation, and asked him to be in Albany on May 1 for the start of what he warned might be days-long talks. He hoped to get the tribes' sign-off on his casino plan and end decades of legal acrimony in the process. No one with any knowledge of the situation gave him a chance.

Andrew didn't start with the Oneidas by chance. In 1976, when the tribe was dirt poor and occupied a mere thirty-two acres without running water, a fire had killed Halbritter's aunt and uncle. Through profit-making bingo games allowed by the state, the Oneidas raised money for a fire department. Bingo then grew into a full-fledged casino called Turning Stone, for which the state and tribe signed a twenty-year compact in 1993. Governor Mario Cuomo was wary of gaming, but legally obligated to negotiate the compact, which to the Oneidas made him the hero of the story.

The compact was an early one of its kind, and somewhat flawed. It granted no exclusivity to the Oneidas, so they paid no exclusivity fees on their burgeoning casino revenues. Now the compact was close to expiring, giving the governor leverage.

Halbritter and Andrew met for ten-hour stretches in Albany and Manhattan. In exchange for having the Oneida Nation support his statewide casino plan, Andrew agreed not to site any of his upstate casinos within a ten-county range of Turning Stone. The Oneidas would then have to start paying exclusivity fees, and some of that would go to the counties that encompassed the Oneida Nation. The counties agreed to drop their suits in return. In a radio interview, Andrew was asked if some of the credit for this three-way deal should go to Mario for the original compact. "Of course he had a major contribution and it couldn't have happened without him," Andrew said impishly. "He birthed the current governor. Without Mario there would be no Andrew and without Andrew there would be no deal today."

It was a triumph, but either the Mohawks or the Senecas could still lobby the casino initiative to death. Both felt betrayed by the state, which had let racinos creep up to their turf and advertise as casinos. And so both had withheld millions of dollars in fees due to the state.

Days after the Oneida settlement, Andrew announced the Mohawk settlement. None of the new upstate casinos would be sited close to the tribe's northern turf. In return, the Mohawks would hand over $30 million of the $60 million in payments held up for the last several years.

Andrew had saved the hardest for last. The Senecas hated the three racinos that had sprung up in the western reach of their state and had withheld nearly $600 million of exclusivity fees.

The Senecas, like the Mohawks, were vulnerable: their own compact expired in 2016. But when Andrew, in an opening shot, warned that it might not be renewed, the Senecas' president, Barry Snyder, made clear that the threat wouldn't work. "Yet again he has chosen a path of playground bully tactics rather than one of maturity, dignity, and mutual respect," he fumed publicly.

Andrew had a backup plan. If the Senecas tried to kill the constitutional amendment on gaming, the governor would put racinos all over western New York. Video lottery terminals didn't need a constitutional amendment. They were legal already. By mid-June, Snyder had caved. The Senecas would keep $209 million of the $617 million they'd held back in fees. Their exclusivity would be extended too: no new casino in western New York, and no new VLTs. As for the three nearby racinos that had siphoned off business, they would stop calling themselves casinos. In addition to disgorging $408 million, the Senecas would resume paying 25 percent of their slot revenues to the state and surrounding counties.

With his tribe trifecta, Andrew's odds for getting his casino bill through the legislature a second time—en route to a constitutional amendment—shot up. Emboldened, he began calling for four casinos upstate, rather than three, in the only regions now open after the Indian deals—the Catskills, the Southern Tier, and the Albany area—and hammering home the point that the upstate casinos would have five years before New York City got any of its own. Not all of the gaming industry's major players were impressed. Michael Leven, president of the Sands, said, "It's twenty years past the time where the Catskills would have been the place to put an integrated resort." Leven saw no point in risking an investment upstate. Better to wait for New York City.

Jobs, jobs, jobs. Casinos would help, but Andrew's other proposal might do more in the long run, with none of gaming's risks: no siphoning money from people too poor to spend it on slot machines, no fostering gambling addictions.

By mid-May, Andrew was touring the state to highlight Start-Up NY as part of his "Open for Business" campaign. It was a catchy idea—who wouldn't like high-tech start-ups on university greens?—and mostly it got glowing reviews, though some curmudgeons had questions. Wouldn't all those tax-free enterprises need the services of firemen and policemen and teachers, and wouldn't their new college towns have to subsidize them by having everyone else pay their taxes for the ten years they were tax-exempt? And what would happen if the high-tech start-ups died, as start-ups often did?

Andrew waved off the naysayers. If just half the expected start-ups took root, he said, imagine how many jobs that would mean. A quixotic group called Unshackle Upstate was pleased, but wary. "We hope that what we don't see is the governor and the legislature clapping their hands, wiping them, and saying, 'We're all done here,'" said its executive director, Brian Sampson. "This is a piece of the puzzle. But the puzzle isn't put together yet."

A steady bombardment of ads was now appearing for Start-Up NY on television and radio, not just in state but nationwide. Many lawmakers thought they saw, behind the boosterism, a vehicle to promote the governor. None of the ads showed Andrew's face or mentioned his name. But they painted a picture of business in the state far rosier than the facts supported.

Early in the summer of 2013, the Albany bureau of the Gannett media chain submitted a Freedom of Information Law request asking for details on how much the administration's Empire State Development was spending altogether on its "Open for Business" campaign. Over the next year, the state made two evasive responses. Only when Tom DiNapoli announced an audit of the budget in mid-July 2014 did the administration issue a five-page memo describing the campaign, with some figures but no financial documents. It noted that the legislature had allocated $50 million a year for the "Open for Business" campaign, and that of the $200 million total for four years, about $124 million had been spent or committed by July 2014, with the balance to be carried over to the next year. About half of that had been spent promoting tourism; the other half had gone to three separate "New York Open for Business" campaigns and the Start-Up NY campaign.

None of this was done on the sly. The $200 million had been duly approved. The campaign, however, was reminiscent of those glossy booklets Andrew had ordered up at HUD, promoting himself as much as the agency. Now, as then, Andrew had bold ideas, packaged them smartly, and pitched them well. But he always seemed to be riding the plans to his own greater glory. As New York television watchers could wearily attest, the commercials for Start-Up NY appeared morning, noon, and night.

And what had they wrought? As of June 2014, according to the administration's own press release, they would generate exactly twelve start-ups in the leafy environs of New York's university system. The state expected these start-ups to invest $50 million in all, and generate about four hundred jobs. But these were projections, like those for the Erie Canal Corridor Initiative. Time would tell. In the interim, again according to the administration, Start-Up NY would cost an estimated $323 million by March 2017.

So Andrew had spent $124 million, out of $200 million, to get twelve start-ups that hoped to generate $50 million in investment and four hundred jobs. But who knew? Maybe one of those start-ups was the next Microsoft.

That June 2013, as the session hurtled to an end, a Women's Equality Act rocked the legislature almost exactly as Andrew had anticipated it would. No great outcry had provoked it; Andrew had simply seen a smart way to burnish his image with at least half the voters in New York State while taking a cudgel to Republicans. Its ten planks came as a package—all or nothing—and that, as Republicans immediately saw, made it a booby trap. Most Senate Republicans would happily endorse nine of the platform's ten points—equal rights in the workplace, enhanced protections for victims of domestic abuse, and so forth. Then there was that tenth one. Abortion rights were federal law thanks to *Roe v. Wade*, and federal law superseded state law. States did have their own differing abortion laws. New York's law was not as far-reaching as *Roe v. Wade*: it forbade abortions after twenty-four weeks of pregnancy unless the pregnant woman's life was at risk. Hence the tenth plank: bringing New York's freedom of choice rights in line with federal law.

Andrew could easily have set the tenth plank aside and gotten the other nine passed. There was hardly an abortion emergency. Even in the unlikely event that *Roe v. Wade* was struck down by the U.S. Supreme Court, abortion would then be an issue for states to decide, and a state as pro-choice as New York would all but certainly strengthen the language of its law at that time. Nevertheless, Andrew insisted that federal-style abortion rights be part of the bill. As a result, Republicans would have no choice but to vote down the whole package. That would put them on record as opposing abortion *and* other women's rights. "There is a simplicity and a clarity to this pro-choice language," Andrew declared. "The citizens of this state have a right to know where these elected officials stand."

Conservatives, especially of the Catholic persuasion, tarred the bill as "late-term abortion expansion," which was simply untrue. Aligning New York's law with federal law wasn't "expanding rights." But as the pro-life forces doubtless hoped, the distortion pressured Republicans in both chambers, even downstate moderates, to vote the act down. And so it died. For Andrew, that was almost as good an outcome as having the bill pass. What a rallying cry it would make in his reelection campaign.

One week before the end of the term, Andrew came out at last with his campaign finance reform bill, the other prong of his Public Trust Act. If nothing else, it showed he knew what the problems were, and how to solve them. It adopted New York City's six-to-one matching fund plan. It closed the LLC loophole, and limited contributions to "housekeeping" funds. It was a bold, sweeping agenda—and not just for New York State, either. This was what all states should do for state elections. There was just one lingering question. Did Andrew want it to pass?

Even as his advisers hastened to spin him as the champion of campaign finance reform, skeptics wondered why the governor had kept mum on the issue so long, only to unveil this mighty bill with just days left in the session. To lawmakers, the timing sent a message. The governor was just going through the motions. If he'd cared as much as he now said he did, he would have started fighting for it months before. Political columnist Blake Zeff felt sure he was seeing a trick in the works. "Pretend you want a bill," as he put it, "while you actually kill it."

With the session's end looming, the activists began to feel they were being played. They had only to look at Andrew's swelling campaign coffers for 2014: he had $22 million now, raised from dinners that cost $50,000 a seat, chipped in by mostly anonymous LLCs at $60,800 per LLC. Why had these hedge funders and real estate developers kicked in so much? Surely not for campaign finance reform and abortion rights. A pretty good guess was lower corporate taxes and keeping campaign money as fluid as it was. Andrew was benefiting from the system as it was: broken, inequitable, and, to some, corrupt on its face.

Despite some last-minute saber-rattling by Andrew, the bill died on the floor, taking the rest of the Public Trust Act with it.

For weeks, Andrew had warned that if his Public Trust Act went down in flames, he would convene a Moreland commission. Now the lawmakers had called his bluff. As the session ended, he made good on his threat. "It's going to be a real follow-the-money investigation," Andrew declared. "We want to see who gives you money, the legislation you introduce and your member items." How serious was he? Andrew was asked. "As serious as a heart attack," he replied. Already he was lining up current and former prosecutors as likely commissioners.

Nowhere mentioned in these public deliberations was the attorney general. Schneiderman's office might have helped the commission get up and running. Unlike the governor, he actually had the authority—and subpoena power—to go wherever his investigations took him, including the legislature. But he seemed frozen out; when asked to comment, his office declined.

Once before, a governor of New York had gone this route to smoke out corruption. His Moreland commission had found many instances of self-dealing, and recommended various reforms. "Many parts of the system that allowed the political scandals to take place remain intact, ripe for abuse in the decade ahead," the commission's report warned. "This in itself is a scandal."

That governor was Mario, who accepted the 1990 report's findings but did little to address them. Andrew had his own Moreland now. Making it work, to produce real change, was the challenge.

Andrew's third session ended, the *New York Times* declared, with a thud. That was not quite fair. Women's Equality and Public Trust had failed. New York's campaign finance rules were just as porous as before; U.S. Attorney Preet Bharara was warning publicly that more lawmakers would soon be charged. But this was a session that had started with the strictest gun control act in the nation. And if lawmakers had had second thoughts, forcing a legislative lull, Andrew had pulled them out of their torpor at the end with his upstate gambits: the Indian deals and Start-Up NY.

For a governor planning his reelection campaign, there might be little lost in the seeming failures of two major initiatives. "Let's say I'm him," suggested one of the governor's top advisers. "What do I want to be talking about in the year ahead? You want to rally your base: with women's issues and campaign finance reform and corruption." To the public, Andrew had fought the good fight for all three. Now on the hustings, he could rail against the Republicans who'd blocked both bills, and get them passed in an electoral year, winning points if he did and points if he didn't. As for the presidency, ever beckoning, weren't these the very issues a centrist Democrat might ride to the White House, waving the banner of bipartisanship? Perhaps it was cynical to suggest that Andrew had let both women's equality and the public trust act expire on purpose. Then again, given their last-minute appearance on the legislative stage . . . was it?

The wild card was Hillary, holed up working on her latest memoir. Tossing out teasers about whether she might run, only to wave off the thought, she kept all other possible candidates cornered. As she did, the Republican-led House Committee on Oversight and Government Reform held hearing after hearing on Benghazi, the tragic attacks on Libya's U.S. embassy compound on September 11, 2012. Republicans' efforts to blame Hillary for a cover-up seemed partisan. But the Benghazi pot was still bubbling. If nothing else, it would rally right-wingers and, along with mutterings about her health, complicate a presidential run once thought impossible for Hillary to lose.

With Hillary dominating the talk of 2016, all Andrew could do at this stage was burnish his own record and hope the presumed front-runner made some mistakes. It had happened before, in 2008. Perhaps it would happen again.

A nemesis of a different sort had reemerged, questioning whether his punishment fit the crime. Hank Morris, the convicted pension-fund placement agent, had paid to the state the entire $19 million he had earned illegally. He had been banned from the securities industry, banned from acting as a placement agent—and, as of February 2011, imprisoned for a period of up to four years. After as little as twelve months, however, he was entitled to a presumptive right of release, as long as he was deemed no threat to society and unlikely to commit his crime again. Now in the medium-security Hudson Correctional Facility in Hudson, New York, he had served those twelve months as a model prisoner, with not a single disciplinary infraction. Yet his request for parole in February 2012 was summarily denied. Nothing about his conduct in jail was considered, nor his presumptive right of release. The parole panel concluded there was a "reasonable probability" that Morris, a first-time offender of any kind, would "not live and remain at liberty without violating the law," and castigated him for the heinousness of his crime.

Morris spent the next months appealing, to no avail. He had a lawyer submit a petition for release; more months passed. Finally on March 29, 2013, a state supreme court judge ruled on the petition. The court was deeply disturbed that the parole board had willfully ignored Morris's inmate status report, which made clear there was no reasonable probability he would be any threat to society or commit his crime again. (In fact he couldn't, as his lawyer pointed out, since he was no longer licensed to be a placement agent.) The judge declared in an amended ruling that the board's denial of parole to Morris was "arbitrary and capricious" and "bordering on impropriety." Morris was released at last—after twenty-six months, more than twice the minimum sentence.

The New York State Commissioner of Corrections was, as always, appointed by the governor.

CHAPTER 27

Less Is Moreland

"It's an independent commission that is free to investigate whatever they believe needs to be investigated on the merits," Andrew declared of his newly convened Moreland commission. "It's not about the legislature. It's about enforcing the campaign finance laws in this state. It is not about any one branch or the other."

Standing beside Andrew at the requisite press conference was the attorney general; it was his press conference too. Andrew had realized he couldn't just shoulder the AG aside and launch the Moreland commission himself, not if he wanted to investigate more than the executive branch. The AG's participation meant the commission was "fully empowered," as Schneiderman put it, with a "broad mandate" to "investigate anything to do with public corruption and the enforcement of the laws related to public corruption." Meaning the legislature. Like Wyatt Earp, the AG was able to deputize the commission's twenty-five members, giving them the power to issue subpoenas and refer criminal charges. By following the money trail, they could shine a powerful light on Albany's pay-to-play culture and focus on cleaning it up.

Schneiderman had seen the Moreland as a terrific opportunity, but already he was having his doubts, as one of his staffers later explained. The AG had urged Andrew to keep the commission small—no more than six or seven members—and to exclude any elected officials in order to avoid even the slightest appearance of conflict of interest. Andrew's commission had twenty-five members, half of whom would soon be up for reelection. Nor was the AG happy at Andrew's flat-out declaration that the commission would look at the legislature. It raised a glaring separation-of-powers issue. "He could have walked away," the adviser said of Schneiderman at that point. "If he had, the Moreland would not have happened." Instead, the AG got the governor to stress, as he did at the press conference, that the Moreland would look at campaign finance irregularities wherever it found them. With that, a bit warily, the AG signed on.

In the commission's first two weeks, the members worked closely with the attorney general's office, getting help on how to proceed. Even then, the governor made his opinions known. Gently, the AG's staffers tried to ward him off. "We were saying, 'All you have to do is back off, and everything will be fine,'" one close observer recalled. Yet Andrew wouldn't—or couldn't—do that. One close observer sensed Andrew still vying with his father, set on steering this Moreland to bigger results than Mario's in the late 1980s. If so, the current Governor Cuomo seemed to take the wrong lesson from the first. Richard Emery, a lawyer who had served on the earlier Commission on Government Integrity, was aware of "zero" contact between the governor and his Moreland except for planning its budget needs.

His pledge of independence notwithstanding, Andrew wanted the Moreland to delve into lawmakers' outside income and conflicts of interest. Lawmakers had just divulged, for the first time, the sketchiest details of that income, thanks to Andrew's ethics reform bill of 2011. Some of the numbers begged for scrutiny. At the top of the heap was Shelly Silver, who in 2012 had earned between $350,000 and $450,000 to be "of counsel" to a Manhattan-based law firm. The new disclosure rules stopped short of requiring lawmakers to say who their outside clients were and what they'd done for them, and Silver declined to elaborate. For 2012, Silver's household income—legal work plus Speaker's salary plus other undisclosed fees—earned him between $763,000 and $1.1 million: the rules allowed such a range.

At Andrew's urging, the committee asked lawmakers for detailed disclosure on any outside legal income over $20,000. Both chambers refused. Dean Skelos went so far as to call the commission a "witch hunt." Asked about that, Andrew offered a most Mario-like reply. "The concept of 'witch hunt,' when you use that word, you suggest that you're looking for something that isn't there," he declared. "Because there really were no witches. You couldn't really search for the witch because the witch didn't exist... This is not about looking for something that's not there. We know it's there because we read in the newspaper about all these cases of corruption. So this isn't an idle mission where we're creating or fabricating the issue. The truth is the exact opposite."

Through the Board of Elections, the Moreland commissioners also began looking at major campaign contributions and where they led. More than a few put-upon lawmakers wondered if the Moreland commission would look at the contributions to New York's largest fund-raiser by far:

the governor. The Committee to Save New York had wound down after raising and spending that $17 million for Andrew's agenda; as soon as its donors could no longer give anonymously, it had simply vanished. A few of those donors had come into the public eye somehow—very intriguing ones, like Genting. Might the Moreland not uncover who the others were? Andrew as of September 2013 had $27.8 million socked away for his 2014 reelection campaign, much of it from large donations by big real estate developers. Would the commission look at those donations?

Quietly, the Moreland commission's cochairs decided to do just that. William J. Fitzpatrick, DA of Onondaga County, and Kathleen Rice, DA of Nassau County, put their investigators on the case and soon came up with some startling discoveries involving New York City developers and big donations, followed almost immediately by very big tax breaks on fast-rising residential towers.

One was Extell, which was building a needle-thin hotel condo tower, 1,004 feet high, called One57, rooted on 57th Street and overlooking Central Park. As the *New York Daily News*' Kenneth Lovett reported in a series of scoops, two checks to the Cuomo reelection campaign had been recorded on January 28, 2013, from two LLCs with the same address as Extell Financial Services, part of Extell Development. Each check was for $50,000. That very day, the Assembly passed a bill containing a major tax break that benefited Extell and four other developers.

That was neither the start nor the end of Extell's largesse to the governor. During Andrew's campaign for attorney general in 2006, and then through 2008, Extell's president, Gary Barnett, had given him a total of $147,100, routed through family members and linked corporations. In May and June 2012, just as the state legislature was starting to consider the request that would end in a bill giving Extell a tax break worth $35 million over ten years with One57, Barnett and his wife, Ayala, donated a total of $100,000 to the Cuomo reelection campaign. Shortly after the bill was signed, amid those twin contributions of $50,000, Barnett gave another $100,000 to a state Democratic Party campaign account, to which gifts without limit could be given. Then came another $100,000 from Barnett in April 2013, to the Democratic State Committee, and $15,000 to the Democratic Assembly Campaign Committee, in March and April. These gifts were followed by two more, for another total of $100,000, in July 2013 by LLCs also linked directly to Extell: West 33rd Street LLC and 112–118 West 25th Street LLC.

Fisher Brothers, which planned a high-rise residential tower at 22 Thames Street, got the same tax break after three partners gave $25,000 each to Cuomo weeks before the breaks were approved by the legislature.

If the timing of the sums was troubling, more so was the tax break the developers won. Known simply as 421-A, it had been on the books for decades as a way to encourage builders to put up housing in emerging neighborhoods. The whole point was to jump-start growth outside Midtown Manhattan, although sometimes developers, in return for building in the outer boroughs, got 421-A credit for Midtown parcels.

Apparently in 2012, the five developers had been shocked to learn they didn't qualify for 421-A tax breaks for their residential Manhattan towers. It was a complex business that had to do with air rights. Whether aware or not of the air rights problem, all five had gone ahead with their buildings, and sold apartments with reduced carrying charges—made possible by their 421-As. The new owners of these homes in the sky were not perhaps the sort for whom 421-A benefits had been intended. But there they were—potential victims of a high-class housing mix-up.

For help, the High-Rise Five had turned to the Real Estate Board of New York, the construction industry's lobbying arm, whose longtime president, Steven Spinola, had played a lead role in the Committee to Save New York. REBNY had come to Albany to lobby for the housing bill that would grant the five their 421-A tax breaks. To lawmakers, REBNY declared that 421-A tax breaks had been due the developers from the start. They were now just correcting an oversight. Edified, the lawmakers passed the bill and granted the tax breaks. Apparently none stopped to wonder why the break didn't apply to all other New York City developers building luxury residential towers in Manhattan. Where were their 421-As?

Intrigued by all this, the Moreland's cochairs had approved the sending of subpoenas to the five developers, as well as to REBNY, which perhaps not coincidentally had donated $2 million to Andrew in one way or another since the start of his term. The cochairs wanted to know more. That was when they learned just how independent their commission really was.

When word of those subpoenas reached Albany's second floor, Larry Schwartz got right on the phone with the Moreland's executive director, Regina Calcaterra, one of the members most closely allied with the governor. He wanted the five subpoenas reeled in. It was too late for that, but a subpoena to REBNY was still in draft form. The Moreland cochairs were told to drop it.

From then on, reported the *Daily News*' Kenneth Lovett—and later a team of three reporters, in great detail, for the *New York Times*—Team Cuomo was all over the Moreland commission. A subpoena to JCOPE, to learn more of what lawmakers had been accused of doing in the past? No go. Another to the Legislative Ethics Commission to see what that frail body might have learned of lawmakers' misdeeds? Forget about it.

The Moreland commissioners subpoenaed the Senate Republicans to learn if their "housekeeping account" had been used for partisan purposes. But when it drew up the same inquiries for the state Democratic Party, seeking details on the millions of dollars used to promote the governor's legislative agenda, that subpoena too was killed. Yet another, to an ad-buying firm called Buying Time that the Democratic Party and Cuomo had used extensively, was sent and then withdrawn.

There was simply no getting around it: the quashed subpoenas were a shocking display of raw power on Andrew's part. They made a mockery of his claims of independence for the commission; they all but ruined the whole enterprise.

Cochair William Fitzpatrick, district attorney from Onondaga County, did his best to salvage what dignity he could for the commission. "Press reports to the contrary, we have been independent since day one," he harrumphed. "There's a big difference between interference and input." A spokesperson added that the Moreland commission by original design reported on a weekly basis to the governor who had empaneled it and the AG who deputized its members. "The cochairs get input from the governor's office," Fitzpatrick said, "but it is their judgment and discretion that governs the commission and determines its action."

As editorial pages around the state took them to task, Fitzgerald and his cochairs reversed course. A subpoena would, after all, be sent to the state Democratic Party. The one sent to and withdrawn from the ad firm Buying Time would be sent again. As for the one sent to REBNY, it was held in check. The lobbying arm representing those five developers was now said to be cooperating with investigators.

For the Moreland's beleaguered commissioners, the back-and-forth was deeply embarrassing, and the governor was entirely to blame. "He sets up the panel, pretends he has no role, it gets out of control, then he asserts himself; it looks bad, then he has reverse himself and say, 'Investigate everyone!'" said one close observer. At each turn, the Moreland commissioners took the grief. "The cochairs have been beaten up in this process, they've been bullied," explained one close observer. "Both [Nassau County district attorney] Kathleen Rice and Fitzpatrick would have taken some level of guidance, they were there to play ball, but these guys were so overbearing." By that, the observer meant Andrew's advisers, particularly Larry Schwartz. "The way they behaved was shortsighted and thuggish. It's not long ball. I always assumed they had the best and brightest, and were outmaneuvering everyone."

One of the governor's advisers had a different take on the issue. He blamed Calcaterra. "That book should have been the tipoff," he said with a laugh. Back in November 2012, when Andrew had appointed her to head the commission, Calcaterra was finishing a memoir of her abusive childhood in Suffolk County and her searing experiences in the state's foster care system. She had gone on to become a securities lawyer and distinguished herself as the executive director of Andrew's Moreland commission on Superstorm Sandy. As this second Moreland got under way, sources say Calcaterra made clear that her allegiance was to the governor. That put her at potential loggerheads with the commission's chief investigator, Danya Perry, who felt the commissioners' only allegiance should be to the truth. Calcaterra was just very...intense. And there to underscore that was her memoir, published just as the Moreland got under way in August 2013, with the very intense title *Etched in Sand: A True Story of Five Siblings Who Survived an Unspeakable Childhood on Long Island.*

Increasingly, the commissioners pinned their hopes to their first scheduled report, due December 1. If they could make it as tough as they felt it should be, perhaps the months of second-floor hectoring would seem worthwhile.

In a quiet election year, Andrew's referendum on gaming moved like a submarine beneath the surface. Voters upstate were vaguely for it—anything for an economic boost. Downstate, a majority disapproved, but not too strongly, given that the casinos—the first ones anyway—would sprout upstate. Then came a Siena poll at the end of September, declaring the state's voters evenly split, 46 percent for and 46 percent against. The gaming industry had spent $11 million lobbying for passage of full-fledged gambling, a prodigious sum for Albany. To have won over no more than half the electorate was pretty underwhelming.

But Andrew had anticipated voter opposition, and during the summer his staffers had reworded the amendment before sending it to the Board of Elections. The revision stated that "the proposed amendment...would allow the Legislature to authorize up to seven casinos in New York State for the legislated purposes of promoting job growth, increasing aid to schools and permitting local governments to lower property taxes through revenues generated." When asked how they viewed the referendum after hearing that wording, 55 percent of poll responders said yes, just 42 percent no. That was about the split on election day too.

Andrew had won his amendment: gaming would come to New York. Whether his triumph would help the state was harder to say. Casinos generated tax revenue, but a host of social ills along with it. In urban areas like Atlantic City, they bred surrounding slums, sucking dry the stores and restaurants and auto dealers in their vicinity, spawning instead the sad little storefronts that gambling's miseries brought: pawn shops, auto-title lenders, and paycheck-cashing stores. How, too, would these new casinos draw tourists to some humdrum stretch of upstate New York, when up-and-running Indian casinos were as easy to reach from afar? *New York Post* columnist Bob McManus found the prospect ludicrous. "Anyone who thinks cash-flush foreign players will flock to, say, Binghamton for fun and games is either pipe-dreaming or hasn't driven north on Route 17 in the past 50 years or so." The new casinos, McManus added, were "a pig in a poke, meant largely to obscure Cuomo's sparse progress with upstate economic development."

With an eye toward his 2014 reelection campaign, Andrew wondered how else he might cut the state's still sky-high taxes. That October, he announced a new tax commission. It would look at a broad array of possible cuts, but focus on further reductions in property taxes. It would be headed by his old foes Carl McCall and George Pataki—a grand gesture of bipartisanship. Apparently the former governor was unaware that Andrew had convened another tax commission ten months before, because when he reached out to Peter Solomon, a well-known New York financier, he was startled to hear that Solomon had headed that one up, and that the first commission was about to issue its own tax-cut recommendations.

"What did the governor tell you, exactly?" Solomon pressed Pataki about Cuomo.

Pataki admitted he hadn't met with the governor, only his staff. The staff had made no mention of the other commission. He had been encouraged to pursue not only property tax cuts but a cut in the personal income tax that would take it down to where it had been when he left office in 1995.

Solomon was astounded. "Governor, do you know how much that would cost the state in today's dollars to do that?"

Pataki wasn't quite sure.

"Three point two billion dollars." The state couldn't afford that, Solomon said. So why had the governor convened this new tax commission? Solomon had no idea. E. J. McMahon of the Empire Center for New York State Policy felt he knew why: to generate headlines about tax cuts, and beam an image of bipartisanship across the state, creating nothing but fodder for Andrew's campaign.

Pataki kept his frustrations private. But when the McCall-Pataki commission published its recommendations that December with only a faint endorsement for ending the millionaires' tax after all, the former governor felt he had to weigh in. "The governor [Cuomo] has appropriately said that in 2018 the temporary income tax surcharge on personal income will expire, and one of the important recommendations of this commission is that in 2018 that temporary higher personal income tax go away. I believe that that is one of, if not the single most important thing we can do to get this state's economy growing the way it should be growing."

Pataki had learned that with Andrew, commissions didn't often do what they set out to do. "He would let them drift, manipulate them—very much as he was doing with the Moreland commission," one commission member observed said of Andrew. "In the end, with Moreland, he just got confused: he thought he could treat it the same way as he'd treated the others. He forgot that the attorney general's office had a say in it too."

Between the Moreland commission and the legislature that November, icy legal letters flew back and forth. Lawmakers from both parties refused to comply with the Moreland's demand for details on outside income. "It's total brinksmanship, heading into an election year," one of the governor's advisers declared. No one mistook the Moreland for anything but what it was: a stalking horse for Andrew. Its toughening stance against the lawmakers was Andrew's own, and there was, in that, some grit to admire. No Republicans wanted ethics reform. Nor did many Democrats. The governor had launched this campaign on his own. He was the one who had called the commission into being; he was the one who had brought on the AG to give it teeth. For that, he was now Albany's most hated man. Yet if he failed to turn this culture around, his governorship would fail.

As the commission raced to meet its deadline for that first report, most of its members were in agreement. The single best way to stem public corruption was campaign finance reform—of the New York City variety, with its six-to-one matching funds system. To the members' mystification, this was the one recommendation that Andrew wanted nowhere in the report. "Maybe he doesn't want the commission to recommend something he doesn't think he can pass," one observer suggested. Still, the vigor of his resistance to campaign finance reform was striking. Nowhere was it more evident than in the debate over who should write the section on campaign finance reform in the commission's report.

The commission had plenty of seasoned district attorneys who might have written the whole report. At Andrew's urging, the job went to a young Harvard Law graduate named Alex Crohn—or "Crohny," as the AG's staff began calling him—who had worked for Mylan Denerstein, the governor's counsel. Later, more than one commission source complained anonymously to *City & State* that Crohn's draft was riddled with grammatical mistakes and factual errors, and seemed aimed principally at promoting the governor's agenda, especially in the executive summary. In Crohn's hands, the section on campaign finance reform became so equivocal that "the pen was wrested from his hand," as one fellow lawyer put it.

The cochairs turned to a top investigator to rewrite the executive summary—the part most of the public would read. At first they withheld the new version from Calcaterra, whom they now perceived as a direct conduit to the second floor. Then came pressure from Larry Schwartz himself, demanding a copy. When the summary was handed over, the commission lost any last semblance of independence and fell into two warring camps. On one side were the three cochairs and most of their colleagues. On the other were Calcaterra, Crohn, and a few other second-floor loyalists.

Still in play was that critical section on public campaign financing. Andrew or one of his top advisers made friendly calls to all the commissioners they thought might be pliable on the issue. They found seven willing to say that public financing as a concept had its problems. With that, Andrew demanded that the section have a formal dissent. "That would give him the political cover he needed," an AG insider noted. The cover, that is, to pour cold water on campaign finance reform. With another nudge from the second floor, the lawyer chosen to write that dissent was... Alex Crohn.

The meddling continued right up to the night the report was officially released, on December 2, 2013. In the executive summary, the cochairs wanted a ringing endorsement of public financing. "*The commission recommends...*" That was how the commission as a body had decided to do it, notwithstanding the seven dissenting votes on the issue. To their fury, as *Daily News* reporter Kenneth Lovett learned, certain members of the press were sent a draft that read, in so many words, "A majority of the commission members recommend..."

Rubbed raw by the constant push and pull from Team Cuomo those last weeks, the cochairs exploded when they saw that draft. Calcaterra had agreed to show them the text a final time before it was printed to be sure the mentions of a "majority" on public financing had been removed. She had not. Fiercely, the cochairs made her change the text before the public saw it. Andrew was manipulating the report just as he had with the first Moreland. The same word—"majority"—was at stake! Only this time he wanted to assure it stayed in, rather than scheming to keep it out.

The next night, Andrew was down in Manhattan, attending a fifty-sixth birthday fund-raiser at the Roseland Ballroom with entertainment by a new friend, singer-songwriter Billy Joel. "*Have a birthday party, invite your friends and charge them fifty grand,*" Joel sang in a parody of his 1978 hit "Honesty." "*If you run for governor don't be too concerned / Make sure the unions are in place / Find a bunch of millionaires with lots of cash to burn / And make sure all your sex tapes hide your face.*" On his way out, Andrew was asked about public financing, and alluded to the "political division" it had caused among the Moreland commissioners. On other issues, he added, the commission had voted as one: those were issues where, as he said, "we can move forward."

It sounded familiar: conjure up an opposition, offer a few words of regret about "political division" and the need to be sensitive to it, then use that as the rationale for going the other way.

Despite the subpoenas quashed or withdrawn, the Moreland commission surprised almost everyone in Albany by putting out a first-rate report. Two hundred subpoenas had brought in millions of pages of documents. Multiple investigations were under way. No names were attached to those ongoing cases, but the various methods of public corruption were briskly explained, the overall picture well framed: Albany was a culture of money, plain and simple. In the executive summary, the commission quoted then New York City councilman Daniel Halloran, who in a secretly wired conversation had put it better than any prosecutor—or for that matter, playwright—could: "That's politics, that's politics, it's all about how much. Not about whether or will, it's about how much, and that's our politicians in New York, they're all like that, all like that. And they get like that because of the drive that the money does for everything else. You can't do anything without the fucking money."

Probing and impressive as it was, the Moreland's report now faced the dilemma that its predecessor had faced under Mario. Would any of its recommendations be taken up? And if so, how, and by whom?

In most respects, election day 2013 had been an uneventful one. It was an off year for Albany's lawmakers—an off year, too, for both of New York's Democratic senators. One race stood out: Bill de Blasio's landslide victory in the New York City mayoral race. At six foot six, the former New York City public advocate and liberal Democrat towered over the competition, more so above the term-limited and exiting mayor. No doubt his height helped—the shorter man rarely won in American politics—but so did his theme of two very different cities, one of billionaires like Bloomberg, and one of everyone else. De Blasio had learned from a master: the "two cities" theme was taken almost verbatim from Mario's 1984 convention speech.

In fact, the new mayor and the governor were close political allies of more than twenty years. "We started as young guys many wrinkles and many gray hairs ago, and we shared the good times and we shared the bad times," Andrew recalled of de Blasio. They had met in 1992 during the first Bill Clinton campaign, working on his New York primary win. "You could see a blueprint back in those days," recalled fellow campaign grunt Joe Ithier. "They were hungry and they each wanted to become somebody big in name recognition and job." When Andrew went to HUD, de Blasio became his regional director for New York and New Jersey. It was during Andrew's chaotic campaign for governor in 2002 that de Blasio, by then a Brooklyn councilman, proved his loyalty as one of the few city officials to stand by Andrew. That, and his mediating skills with the Carl McCall camp as Andrew withdrew from the race, had forged a bond.

The bond was still intact in 2010, when Andrew was running for governor the second time. Again Andrew called on de Blasio as a mediator, this time to win the endorsement—and ballot line—of the liberal Working Families Party. De Blasio was a staunch liberal himself, considerably to the left of Andrew, and was instrumental in getting the Working Families Party to buy in. Now, as mayor and governor, they would work wonderfully well together, rising above the built-in tensions of that complex relationship.

Or perhaps they would work exactly as well as it suited Andrew to have them work.

De Blasio's family story had resonated with liberal voters: the once openly lesbian black wife, the two handsome biracial children, son Dante's spectacular Afro. But more than a slogan and good optics had won the day. De Blasio had pledged to bring universal pre-kindergarten to New York's public schools, funded by a tax on the rich. It was a highly popular plan among New York City voters that put him squarely at odds with his old friend Andrew, whose top priority for his reelection campaign was to cut taxes, not raise them. And so unfolded the fascinating drama of de Blasio versus Cuomo, Part 1: protégé versus mentor, mayor versus governor, progressive versus faux-progressive. It was a standoff in which each had plenty to lose.

De Blasio's first visit to Albany since his towering win was to attend Andrew's fourth State of the State speech in January 2014. Greeted like a rock star wherever he went, he all but eclipsed the governor, who muted his own image with a centrist speech clearly meant to kick off his reelection campaign and position himself, if only hypothetically, for 2016. "The arrows are pointing up," Andrew began, never shy about taking credit for good news. The Cuomo administration had "given New Yorkers a government that costs less, taxes less, and actually does more for the people who are in need." The tax breaks were modest, arguably offset by the millionaires' tax that hadn't sunset after all; New York still ranked among the highest-taxing states in the nation. Rhetoric notwithstanding, Andrew clearly recognized that his top priority in this election year was to pass a $2 billion package of tax cuts.

Andrew made no mention of the new mayor whose presence galvanized the crowd, but he did mention universal pre-kindergarten. He was for it, he said; it would be done, and done that year. How it would be financed was a matter for another day. The phrase "tax the rich" failed to cross his lips.

Sometimes the dueling agendas of two politicians were so finely balanced, each one's relative power so perfectly offset by the other's, that their contest seemed a martial art, like tai chi. So it was with the governor and mayor over universal pre-K, as the state's political world looked on in fascination.

In one sense, Andrew had the upper hand. As Mayor Bloomberg had learned to his dismay, the city was a vassal to the state. The mayor went hat in hand to the governor for billions in state aid each year. City taxes could only be raised at the governor's and legislature's say-so. De Blasio, from his years in New York City government, had to have known that his campaign cry of "tax the rich" could only be enacted with the blessing of a governor who had no interest in doing so. Was it possible that the mayoral candidate and the governor had had a tacit agreement as old friends to let the candidate cry "tax the rich" without the governor pointing out that no such tax would pass in his administration?

But now de Blasio had a cudgel the governor hadn't counted on: a mandate from 73 percent of New York City's voters to follow through on that campaign pledge. That was power the governor could only ignore at his peril. The Democratic Assembly was behind de Blasio: public education and its unions were Shelly Silver's top constituency, and soaking the rich to pay for pre-K seemed right to him. Senator Jeffrey Klein and his IDC members were all for de Blasio–style pre-K too. Andrew needed their backing to pass his own agenda. In fact, de Blasio had the entire left wing of the Democratic Party. Andrew had alienated that wing time and again, reasoning that he could tack to the right on financial issues and pull the left along because it had nowhere else to go. The left's disenchantment with him was now approaching a danger point. If he killed universal pre-K, the left might just bolt and find a challenger to him in the gubernatorial primary.

Andrew, with his power of incumbency and a war chest now of $33.3 million, was still a shoo-in to win. Being "primaried" would be a major embarrassment, however. It would cost money better spent later on and very likely keep him from the landslide victory he sought as a message to the national Democratic Party. It might also keep him from matching his father's victory margin of 64 percent in Mario's own reelection campaign of 1986. If he needed any more inducement to make pre-K work, Andrew could get it from his largest campaign contributor, Leonard Litwin, a real estate developer who had given him $800,000. Litwin was all for universal pre-K—and for soaking the rich to fund it.

As if making his first move on that three-dimensional board of Triopoly that President Clinton had given him long ago, Andrew declared, days after his State of the State, that universal pre-K would be a reality that year. Only it wouldn't be funded by taxing the rich. That wasn't necessary. The governor had found $1.5 billion in his upcoming budget to phase in pre-K over the next five years.

The new mayor responded, in so many words, like Melville's Bartleby the Scrivener: "I would prefer not to." He was pleased that the governor had backed universal pre-K, but he wanted it paid for, as promised, by a tax on the rich.

At that, Andrew pounced. Why would de Blasio want a tax to pay for pre-K if it wasn't needed? Clearly, taxing the rich was, for the progressive mayor, a partisan agenda, an end in itself. "If it isn't pre-K," the governor declared, "it will be something else." Team Cuomo began working the phones, casting doubt on the mayor's capacity to get pre-K up and running by September, however it was funded.

Again, de Blasio demurred. Funding pre-K through the budget left it vulnerable to cuts the next year, or the year after that, far more so than a set tax on the rich.

By late January, the governor was declaring the mayor could have a "blank check" for pre-K funding—meaning as much of the budget as he needed. Just no new taxes. "Why do you need a tax for a service we're going to fully fund?" the governor said.

In public with the mayor, Andrew joshed and grinned. At an evangelical church in Albany one Sunday, he went so far as to sit with his old friend, singing hymns and clapping; the two took turns praising each other to the congregation. Behind the scenes, Team Cuomo was working the phones to chill support for de Blasio's rich-tax route to pre-K.

One politician, after endorsing the mayor's plan, got a call from Joe Percoco. Was he upset with the governor? Percoco asked. Percoco was clearly angry. "Basically the underlying message was, you know, 'We appreciate if you're not publicly out there actively supporting this.'"

For Andrew, the standoff with de Blasio wasn't just political. It was personal. "Tribal," as one of his big supporters put it. "I gave him his first job," the supporter quoted Andrew saying about his onetime protégé. "*And this is what he does to me.*"

There was something odd, when one stopped to think about it, about a governor sparring with his fellow Democrat and old friend, while treating with kid gloves a Republican governor across the river touted until now as a leading presidential rival for 2016. Yet with New Jersey's Chris Christie mired in scandal, fighting for his political life, Andrew was keeping a decorous silence. That just wasn't Andrew. What was up?

The story had hit the national news right about the time of Andrew's 2014 State of the State speech, and a strange little story it was. For five straight mornings the previous September, two of the three traffic lanes leading up to the George Washington Bridge in Fort Lee, New Jersey, had been closed, causing massive gridlock. Finally Patrick Foye, a New York official of the bistate Port Authority, blasted his New Jersey counterparts and ordered the lanes reopened. Their closing, he said, was a violation of federal and state law. At first, the Christie administration explained the closures as part of a traffic study. Over the next weeks, rumors of a political vendetta seeped out—a vendetta enacted by Christie aides against the Fort Lee mayor for not endorsing Christie in his 2013 reelection campaign. Christie laughed off the idea—until e-mails between two of his top staffers came to light. "Time for some traffic problems in Fort Lee," wrote Deputy Chief of Staff Bridget Kelly in what seemed an order to close the lanes. "Got it," replied Christie Port Authority appointee David Wildstein. With those two e-mails, the story exploded.

Andrew, when pressed, said he hadn't known about the lane closings until they made the news. Did he have any comment now? "I think Governor Christie made it clear," he said, "that he is very displeased with what happened."

For Andrew to be unaware of the closings for weeks was hard to imagine. He was, after all, cohead of the Port Authority with Christie. Perhaps at first he had not been made aware of Foye's e-mail of September 13, 2013, blasting New Jersey for closing the lanes. That was what Howard Glaser later implied. Glaser said Foye had forwarded his e-mail to him, and Glaser had chosen not to inform the governor. The odds of Foye writing that furious e-mail without second-floor supervision were slim to none, but never mind: maybe Andrew had had more important things to focus on that week.

On October 1, however, the *Wall Street Journal* ran an article on Foye as the hero of the story—the whistleblower for gridlocked commuters—and published rumors of a political vendetta. Very likely, Glaser or someone else on the second floor had leaked it to the *Journal*—no one on the PA's New Jersey side would have wanted it out, and who else knew about it? Yet Andrew still had no comment to make about Christie and the lane closings. The hands-off attitude suggested a policy of détente between the two governors. At this early stage in the race for 2016, the two had more to gain from working together than taking potshots at each other.

That seemed to change in November, when Christie and his wife met for more than an hour with a possible New York Republican rival for Andrew's job in 2014: Westchester County Executive Rob Astorino. Any Republican weighing a challenge to Andrew was David to Goliath, but of the prospects, Astorino might be the strongest: a moderate who had just won a powerful victory in his strongly Democratic county. Asked about the report in a conference call with reporters, Andrew bristled. "I can tell you this," he said. "I spoke to Governor Christie this morning, who told me the exact opposite. And I'll leave it at that."

Christie's meeting with Astorino posed a serious threat, as Andrew well knew. As head of the Republican Governors Association, Christie would have a lot of sway about which gubernatorial races the national Republican Party chose to back in 2014. For at least one member of Andrew's inner circle, the very mention of Astorino stirred molten rage. Back in 2005, Larry Schwartz had been on the other side of Astorino's first campaign, and helped defeat him by skewering him in the press as Westchester's "public enemy Number One."

Patrick Foye, the noble PA whistleblower, testified under oath on December 9 and blew the traffic-study story to smithereens. As the PA's top appointee on the New York side, Foye declared that he had been unaware of any such study. Top Christie aide David Wildstein had already resigned; now Foye's PA counterpart on the Jersey side, Bill Baroni, left too. Christie roundly denied any knowledge of his staffers' actions. They had disappointed him, he said, deceived and betrayed him. Almost no one believed him, especially after other New Jersey mayors came forward to say that they too had been punished for not endorsing Christie's reelection. As the portly governor tried to tough it out, the glittery talk of a White House run fell like snow around him.

Yet even now, Andrew kept his distance. "I don't know anything more than basically has been in the newspaper," he said in one typical answer, "because it's basically a New Jersey issue." Actually it wasn't, since the Port Authority was a bistate agency. But it suited Andrew to see it that way. As political columnist Blake Zeff noted, "There's an old press secretary maxim: If there's a story about bad news, stay out of it at all costs." Quite possibly, too, the scandal might cross the river. Investigators might start asking why the Port Authority's inspector general had not launched an investigation of "Bridgegate" and why the second floor had ignored Foye's e-mail. Didn't Andrew's own Public Trust Act, gone but not forgotten, ascribe as much blame to those who knew of a crime as those who perpetrated it? For that matter, might the e-mail trail on Bridgegate turn up some tacit awareness, on the New York side, of the closures before they occurred? Might it take investigators back to that funny business in 2011 with toll hikes coordinated clandestinely by Cuomo and Christie?

That winter, as the investigations ground on, Andrew said barely a peep more about the scandal consuming his New Jersey rival—the fellow governor who, as recently as New Year's, had bested him in a 2016 presidential poll by 47 to 42 percent. That left Christie, across the Hudson, to pace the halls of his executive mansion, wondering if Andrew, fellow micromanager that he was, had steered Foye from the start—perhaps even dictated the e-mail of outrage September 13—then leaked to the *Journal* and gently, ever so gently, brought the story to life.

No such mystery cloaked Andrew's role in his latest swipe at another bête noire, the AG with the long wet lashes. Back in November 2013, Eric Schneiderman had notched a real triumph. He had inked a $613 million settlement with JPMorgan Chase to compensate New Yorkers for losses incurred as a result of the bank's policies in the housing crisis. The money would be spent helping homeowners who had found themselves underwater or foreclosed upon when the bubble burst. As spelled out in the settlement, the AG would have sole discretion to allocate these monies. From the second floor came a chilly response. Why did the AG think this was his money to spend? Its proper place, the governor's aides declared, was in the state treasury, to be spent as the governor saw fit.

On January 13, 2014, the AG's solicitor general sent a lengthy legal memo to the governor's counsel, noting all the reasons why this was, in fact, the AG's money to spend on behalf of New York taxpayers. First, the wording in the settlement with JPMorgan Chase was crystal clear. Second, this was setting no precedent. Andrew himself, as AG, had settled a major case—the one about out-of-network medical reimbursements—for

$90 million. He had allocated that money himself, first as AG, then as governor. None of it had gone to the state treasury.

The solicitor general was, by her office, expressing the opinion of the state. Andrew was incensed. Why had the state not sought *his* opinion? The governor wanted that $613 million put into the state treasury to help pay for the $2 billion in tax cuts he was drawing up in his budget deliberations. There was, he felt, no comparison with the $90 million health care settlement. That was much less money.

Over the next days, the AG's office felt the full brunt of Andrew's wrath. "The threats were flying from Andrew," recalled one insider. "He actually said, 'I'll take the $600 million out of your budget.' Which was funny because we're a $300 million agency." The AG had the law on his side—and he had control of the first $163 million of that $613 million. The rest was to be doled out by Chase in three annual increments of $150 million each next November. But law seemed beside the point with a vengeful governor literally yelling in phone calls that week. This was hardball.

Finally on January 20, a truce was announced. That first tranche of $163 million would be split between the AG and the state. Both parties would spend it on housing-related projects—not, in the governor's case, on helping fund a reduction in the estate tax rate for the wealthy. They agreed to talk later about what would be done with the remaining $450 million.

Later, for the governor, meant secretly the following week. There in the fine print of a bill for the new budget was a provision stripping Schneiderman of any control over the remaining money. Instead, the money would be put in a new housing fund managed by the governor and legislative leaders. "We got the news ten minutes before the deal was announced," one AG staffer explained. "No negotiation. No *conversation*. Andrew stabbed us in the back." Worse, the legislation took away the right of the attorney general ever to direct settlement monies again. All Schneiderman could say, to save face, was that his intention from the start had been to use that money to help struggling homeowners. If the governor's new fund accomplished that, who was he to argue?

Andrew's move erased any last doubt Schneiderman might have had about what drove the governor. "For Andrew, there's just not space for two," a sympathetic insider declared, by which the insider meant two equal partners in any power-sharing situation. "He sees others' success as an encroachment on his own."

On Tuesday, March 4, 2014, Mayor de Blasio came to Albany to head a rally for statewide pre-K and the rich tax he hoped would fund it. About a thousand supporters, many urged to come by their teachers' unions, gathered at an armory near the state capitol. The mayor felt good about the turnout—until he realized what was happening outside the capitol itself.

A very different crowd of more than ten thousand had gathered in support of New York City's charter schools—those privately funded new arrivals to the public school system—and to knock the politician who had come to exemplify opposition to them: Mayor de Blasio. Specifically, they were there to protest de Blasio's decision to deny three new charters space in traditional public schools. Later, Andrew's staff would say he had had nothing to do with gathering this crowd to protest in Albany at the very time de Blasio was addressing *his* crowd a short distance away. Whether that was true or not, his appearance on that frigid March Tuesday electrified the crowd.

"They say it's cold out here," Andrew declared, "but I don't feel cold, I feel hot! I feel fired up!" The crowd roared its delight. "You are not alone," he said, his voice rising. "We will save charter schools."

It was, as the *New York Times* later noted, "a master class in political gamesmanship." Andrew made the mayor, for all his height, look puny, and stole his thunder with an education issue that stirred far deeper passions, across a far wider field, than statewide pre-K. A giddy spokesman for the governor led a press photographer through the capitol's musty upper reaches to a bathroom window with the widest view of the gathering, and Andrew below, in his best Bobby Kennedy style, mesmerizing the crowd.

This was a story that had begun just weeks before, when a clutch of charter school leaders had come to Albany seeking help in dealing with a new mayor who seemed dead set against charters. De Blasio in his campaign had talked of a go-slow approach to new charters, of making the existing ones pay rent to the city, and of putting more effort into shoring up the city's traditional public schools. He was, it was fair to say, close to the state's allied teachers' unions, which viewed charters as a threat. That day, after a few desultory talks with lawmakers, the charter school leaders had prepared to head back to Manhattan when they got an astonishing call from the governor's office. The governor wanted to see them.

The leaders were ushered into a private conference room. There they met with the governor for no less than forty-five minutes. He told them he shared their alarm about de Blasio's charter school stance. To their even greater surprise, he stayed in touch over the next days, and began urging them to stage a large rally in Albany. Having them hold it on the same day as de Blasio's rally was, of course, coincidental. In their phone talks, the governor said nothing about wanting to address the rally. That was just smart politics: he wanted to see how large the crowd would be. By then, he had a flash point to focus on: those three blocked charter schools.

In the fifteen years since New York's first charters had sprouted, they had inspired an odd alliance, from educational progressives to neoconservatives. Through his three terms, Mayor Bloomberg had nurtured the movement, letting charters "co-locate" rent free in traditional public schools, and making them part of the public school system. Now there were 183 of them throughout the five boroughs, all founded and run by nonprofits, in many cases backed by wealthy New Yorkers for whom public education had become a passionate cause.

Charters, with Mayor Bloomberg's blessing, had the right to try creative approaches, impose stern discipline, and fire underperforming teachers. Many now outperformed traditional schools on testing, and in the poor, often desperate neighborhoods where most were found, hundreds of families tried their luck in the lotteries that decided which of their children would attend. All this was anathema to the teachers' unions.

The three charters de Blasio had blocked were all started by Success Academy, a nonprofit run by a former Democratic councilwoman named Eva Moskowitz, backed by a board of wealthy Wall Streeters, including activist investor Daniel Loeb. De Blasio reportedly disliked Moskowitz, and charter advocates saw nasty politics in the move. A furious Moskowitz railed at the mayor for shortchanging "poor minority kids who want a shot at the American dream." Andrew's own speech echoed that line.

The truth was more nuanced. Presented with seventeen new charters that wished to take space in specific public schools, the new mayor had approved fourteen of the "co-locations," including five founded by Moskowitz. But de Blasio had issues with the three charter schools he chose to block. He objected to one's plan to place elementary school children in a high school with inner-city teens, and another's to swell the ranks of an already crowded Harlem school to an estimated 130 percent capacity. That charter would also displace a large number of autistic and emotionally disturbed children. The mayor chose not to displace them.

This was the crucible on which the governor's new cause was based.

With Andrew, there was never just one reason. Charters gave him a lance to unhorse the mayor from his moral high ground on pre-K. It also polled well: aside from the teachers' unions, many voters in both parties liked charters. Dean Skelos's Republicans would happily pass any pro-charter bill, dissing the teachers' unions as they did. In an election year, charters would also help Andrew in downstate Republican enclaves like Westchester, and pull the rug out under from Rob Astorino, the Westchester County executive who had just declared he would run as the Republicans' candidate against Cuomo in the fall. Most of all—and this, as Andrew would say, was the beauty of it—fighting for charters would endear him to the Wall Street hedge funders on all those charter school boards. Along with Dan Loeb, who chaired Success Academy's board, there was Loeb's archrival Bill Ackman, and Carl Icahn, Bruce Kovner, and Daniel Nir. There, too, was Ken Langone, now head of Republicans for Cuomo. "Every time I am with the governor, I talk to him about charter schools," Langone said. "He gets it." Of the $33.3 million that Andrew had now put in his campaign coffers, an appreciable fraction came from just this crowd. Championing charters would bring in that much more.

That March, in his new budget, Andrew included fixes for both charter schools and pre-K that had to madden New York's mayor, though as a seasoned pro, he kept his game face on. For any and all new charters, the city would be required to find space in public schools, or else pay their rent in private spaces. No charters, either new or established, would pay rent, as de Blasio had proposed. Specifically, the mayor would have to find space for those three blocked Moskowitz schools.

Most important, the state, not the city, would have the power to approve new charter schools—as many or as few as it liked. Yet the city would have to find ways to pay for them. Over time, there would be nothing de Blasio could do to stop dozens more charters from taking root. De Blasio had lost big.

On statewide pre-K, the budget struck what seemed at first a rather conciliatory note. The state would provide $300 million for pre-K in its first year, with numbers to rise each next year. The mayor had said he needed $340 million for state pre-K the first year: that was close enough for him to declare that he and his old friend Andrew had taken "an extraordinary and historic step forward for New York City." But this was funding from the budget, not from a tax on the rich. And it was up to the governor to say how much more de Blasio would get in coming years. It was, after all, a budget allocation. Budgets went up and down.

Behind the numbers, a far more consequential change had occurred. Early in his tenure, Mayor Bloomberg had persuaded the state to give him absolute power over the city's public and charter schools—nothing less would let him beat back the unions. Now the state was taking much of that power back. Once again, Andrew had found a rival in his path and thrown him over. *He* would call the shots on city schools. He knew no other way to proceed.

As the deadline for Andrew's fourth successive on-time budget bore down, tensions ran high among the state's Four Men in a Room: Silver, Skelos, the governor, and now Jeffrey Klein of the pivoting IDC. The afternoon of Friday, March 28, 2014, was ebbing; that evening, as on every Friday, Shelly Silver would be unreachable, observing the Sabbath until Saturday night. If he left before a deal was struck, the budget bills wouldn't be printed in time to be in circulation for three days before the deadline. Unless Andrew issued a message of necessity with them on Monday, the vote would be delayed until Tuesday—too late for Andrew to proclaim an on-time budget record for modern times, including Mario's time.

For Andrew's top priority, the ink was basically dry. Better times had brought higher tax revenues, and so the governor would get his $2 billion tax cut to brandish as he ran for reelection. If the leaders had fought bitter battles over what and where to cut, the public would be none the wiser for it, for once again, despite his pledge of transparency, the governor had closed the door to that room. In one of his less deft pronouncements, Andrew defended the system he once vowed to change. "Just because something is done behind closed doors," he declared, "doesn't mean the process isn't transparent."

All that remained was the really hard one: campaign finance reform. On it, like an inverted pyramid, rested Albany's whole culture of corruption. The Moreland commission, despite Andrew's meddling, was investigating in every direction. In February alone it had issued more than twenty subpoenas, focusing less now on lawmakers' outside income than how some used their campaign accounts as personal slush funds. Yet nothing it did would be worth a jot without campaign finance reform.

In the abstract, Andrew was open to a statewide version of New York City's six-to-one "multiplier" plan, with $6 of public money for each dollar raised, up to $175. He was all for putting an end to $60,800 individual gifts in limitless LLCs, as well as unregulated gifts to party "housekeeping" funds. He just knew what Dean Skelos thought about all this. Skelos had made himself clear: no taxpayer monies for political campaigns, end of story. If Skelos's Senate was adamantly opposed to the public financing of political campaigns, as one of his top aides suggested, what was the point of proposing it?

Still, Andrew had knocked some ideas around with Skelos, and in this last week of negotiations, the two had come up with a compromise. Neither time nor political reality allowed public financing for all of this year's legislative and statewide elections. But as an experiment—an earnest, good-faith first step by a governor with nothing but the people's best interests at heart—Andrew had proposed that the six-to-one multiplier be used in one or two upcoming elections. He had just the one or two in mind. One would be the comptroller's race, in which Tom DiNapoli was currently unopposed. Another was the attorney general's race, in which Eric Schneiderman as yet faced no rivals either.

Politics wasn't often deemed a humorous pursuit, but it was hard to imagine Andrew and his kitchen cabinet not laughing as they came up with this one. Both DiNapoli and Schneiderman had led the charge for public financing, so starting with their races did make a kind of sense. They were, however, too far along in the electoral cycle to commit to public financing. Both had raised sizable sums for their reelection campaigns—sums that would have to be put aside so they could start afresh on the six-to-one multiplier plan. Andrew's plan would level the field and invite Republicans to take them on. Why not, when they too could get six-to-one money and all be bound by the same cap? The fact that Andrew resented both DiNapoli and Schneiderman and hoped to see them defeated bore no relevance, of course, to the matter.

Schneiderman was able to fend off the governor's kind offer before it became official. But the final budget would formally declare the comptroller's race a test case in public financing—for one year only—forcing DiNapoli, the champion of campaign reform, to eat his words by waiving the six-to-one multiplier money and declaring that if anyone did run against him, he would campaign the old-fashioned way.

On that Friday afternoon, with Silver about to slip away for the Sabbath, the talk in the room was about whether that one test case would be enough. Fred Dicker later reported that Jonathan Soros, one of the strongest and deepest-pocketed proponents of public campaign financing, called each of the leaders that day to warn that without real reform—across the board—he would fund election-year attacks against them.

Jeff Klein might have embraced the one-race solution if not for the grumbling of his own liberal base down in the Bronx. Heading the Independent Democratic Conference had brought him a whole new measure of power, but it meant working with Republicans, and that, in turn, meant killing or ignoring issues of importance to his Democratic voters. One was the Dream Act, to give undocumented college students a shot at state aid. Klein had said he supported it but brought it to the floor before its votes were assured, and so the act had just died; many of Klein's Latino voters saw treachery there. That Friday, Klein wanted to be the guy who got public campaign financing passed in a serious way, and pleased his base after all. Skelos was adamant: no.

"The governor sat there with Klein and Skelos like a marriage counselor," one of Dicker's sources reported, "telling them that they had to resolve their difference or end their [political] marriage." Klein could either go with the one-race plan or end his power-sharing deal with Skelos and leave the room. The real power was Andrew's. His was the hand at the IDC tiller, pushing it toward the Republicans, or pulling it back, just as he had foreseen.

Andrew had his own dilemma. He knew his cute little test case of public campaign financing would hardly suffice as reform. To be called a reformer—for 2014 and, perhaps, for 2016—he needed his Moreland commission to follow through on its many investigations. Yet he faced a fierce and growing backlash from lawmakers of either party over the Moreland's subpoenas and demands. The legislature was feeling the heat, all right, and as a result, so was he.

Unhappy on the left, unhappy on the right. What did that suggest?

A deal.

That Saturday, March 29, at the last possible moment, Andrew announced that his budget would include key items of ethics reform. New enforcement powers to root out corruption. Tougher bribery laws. More disclosure. Chunks, that is, of the Public Trust Act that lawmakers had killed, back before the Moreland got them scared.

But there was more.

If the lawmakers agreed to that package, and passed it that day as a budget, then Andrew would give them a treat.

He would scuttle the Moreland commission.

The Albany press corps, getting this update from the governor himself, struggled to absorb what it had just heard. Kill the Moreland? Just when its team of investigators was zeroing in on all those possible illegalities?

Yes, Andrew replied, they had heard him right. The point of the Moreland had been to pursue corruption in the absence of vigorous laws. With the new laws, it simply wasn't needed anymore.

To the press corps, this sounded awfully familiar. Wasn't it exactly what Andrew had done with redistricting? Held it over the legislature, vowing to see it done the equitable way, only to trade it away for other concessions, ethics be damned? The governor had held those Moreland investigations over lawmakers' heads, gotten what he wanted in the budget, then made the Moreland go away. As far as the governor was concerned, the new reform measures put in the budget had the same weight of deterrence as Moreland. Almost no one else agreed. A few new statutes that might or might not be enforced seemed awfully light compared to twenty-five full-time commission members, and teams of investigators, working at least through 2015 to bring cases and reform across the board.

Too cute for their own good—that was the phrase an editorial writer had used about the governor and his advisers in another case of canny politicking. As his fourth on-time budget went to press, Andrew again looked too cute. This time, his maneuver would draw the attention of the one state official impervious to all of his carrots and sticks: the U.S. attorney for Southern District, Preet Bharara.

CHAPTER 28

Starting Again

By two of the numbers that counted most, Andrew looked like a reelection winner—a powerful, rival-crushing winner—in the spring of 2014. Donations would soon reach $35 million, far more than any other governor running for reelection in the United States that year. No one had dared mount a primary race against him—not yet, at least—and his recently declared Republican rival, Rob Astorino, was a virtual unknown outside Westchester. One poll showed Andrew beating him 65 percent to 25 percent. All was going according to plan: to win by such an electoral margin that party elders would urge him to run for the White House in 2016. *If* Hillary Clinton for some reason chose not to enter the race.

In the history of ifs, that was surely one of the largest ever, but it wasn't Andrew's only problem. As governor, his favorability rating remained high—about 63 percent—but was floating gently downward. A poll of Albany lawmakers and politicos would have ranked him much lower, for the truth was that Andrew had worn out his welcome on both sides of the aisle. Republicans still bridled at the Moreland's intrusions, at the gun control act they'd voted to pass despite their better instincts, at all the ways Andrew had held them up for the new district lines. Democrats hated the Moreland intrusions too, the mockery Andrew had made of campaign finance reform, redistricting, and a hundred other things, but above all the way he'd played the Republicans against them. To more than a few, he wasn't a Democrat at all, but instead some Darth Vader standing atop both parties with a boot on each one's neck.

Andrew had his own word for that. "Bipartisan." And a case might be made that he had done exactly what a strong-willed, bipartisan governor should have done. His wins were significant, his budgets on time. If all sides resented the dealmaker, wasn't that proof that the dealmaker was making good deals?

It hardly seemed fair, after all his smart moves, for Andrew to be blocked by the one person—the one politician in America—who could stop him cold. In fact, Hillary wasn't Andrew's only impediment to national office. In a Fox News poll that April, just 2 percent of New York Democrats called him their likely candidate for president in 2016. That was down from 4 percent the previous December. And that was his home state! In Iowa, which he'd pointedly declined to visit so far, he wasn't even a blip. How other parts of the country would view the scowling Italian with the Queens accent remained to be seen. All that could change, of course, and fast: the Bridgegate-plagued Governor Christie currently trailed Cuomo in a poll of preferred presidential candidates, 50 percent to 34 percent.

Andrew had a more immediate problem, however. A lot of people seemed quite upset by his shuttering of the Moreland commission. Among them was Preet Bharara, the U.S. attorney for the Southern District of New York, whose record of successful prosecutions for insider trading was about 80–0 and counting.

Days after the Moreland's closing was announced, Bharara issued a rare public rebuke of the governor, calling the shutdown "premature" and "difficult to understand." He was sure that Andrew did not intend it, Bharara said coolly, but the way it was handled left the impression that "investigations potentially significant to the public interest have been bargained away as part of the negotiated arrangement between legislative and executive leaders."

In other words, Andrew had sold justice for a political deal. Or so it appeared.

Andrew sharply disagreed. The Moreland commission, he said, had been intended from the start as a "temporary" device to compel legislative action. "It was created because the legislature wouldn't pass something called the Public Trust Act." The new package of reforms, he said, simply obviated the need for Moreland.

Yet much remained unchanged, starting with the biggest loopholes of New York's campaign finance system. Unlimited donations to housekeeping accounts? Check. Same $60,800 limit for individual donors through LLCs? Check. Same freedom to start additional LLCs and give $60,800 through each? Check again. As for disclosure of outside income, by the time Andrew finished negotiating with Skelos, Silver, and Klein in the days leading up to the budget deal, the new rules had been rubbed smooth. Surely it was no coincidence that the three legislative leaders were all lawyers whose outside income dwarfed that of most of their colleagues. Skelos, Silver, and Klein—it sounded like a law firm. Even Moreland cochair William J. Fitzpatrick, who had kept his own frustrations private, admitted that the commission had fallen short on that key issue. "I myself am still distressed that we as a commission were unable to force legislators to disclose exactly what it is they do to earn lucrative income."

More than new rules were thwarted. A dozen or more active investigations were put on ice too. Makau Mutua, law school dean at SUNY Buffalo and a Moreland commission member, said publicly that "more than a few cases...required further scrutiny." They were, he said, "the kind of things for which folks have been indicted or convicted before." Ethical lapses, in short. What would happen to those investigations now?

Preet Bharara had an answer: his office would take them over. Bharara was as interested in why the commission had closed when it did as in the investigations left hanging. Nine months might be the right length of time for a baby to gestate, he said drily, but not for an investigative panel to do its work. "Thinking people wonder why that happened," he said, "and want to get to the bottom of it."

One day that April, a team from the U.S. attorney's office showed up with a truck at the Moreland commission's Manhattan office to Hoover up all of the commission's files. The investigators would go down two tracks: following through on those open cases, and, as intriguing, looking into any actions that might have interfered with the Moreland commission's work. One possible subject of interest was Regina Calcaterra, the executive director. Another was Larry Schwartz.

In a sit-down with the editors of *Crain's New York Business*, Andrew flared when asked if he had crossed some legal line by interfering. "It's not a legal question," he exclaimed. "The Moreland commission was my commission. It's my commission. My subpoena power, my Moreland commission. I can appoint it, I can disband it...I can't 'interfere' with it because it's mine. It is controlled by me."

That wasn't how Andrew had characterized the Moreland the previous July, when he set it on its way as an "independent commission." And it wasn't how the commission had presented itself in court, when the legislature fought its subpoenas by arguing that the commission was a tool of the governor's office, and thus not entitled to investigate the legislative branch. Though created by the governor, the Moreland's lawyers had replied, the commission "had independent authority to make investigatory decisions that he does not control."

Now Preet Bharara could weigh such contradictions, and Andrew, for the first time in his governorship, would have no power to influence the outcome. "Cuomo can't investigate him," political columnist Blake Zeff observed. "He can't hurt him electorally, since Bharara is an appointee of the president. And Cuomo can't use state legislation to reduce his power, since Bharara works for the U.S. Department of Justice."

All these tactics Andrew had employed against one or another of his chosen enemies. Spitzer he'd investigated. Schneiderman he'd undermined with his AG-like Department of Financial Services, then by seizing the AG's $613 million JPMorgan settlement. DiNapoli he'd dispossessed of his power to audit state government contracts. Both Schneiderman and DiNapoli he'd tried to hurt with his public finance plan for their campaigns. None of that would work with Preet Bharara.

"Cuomo is entering this conflict without his usual leverage," as Zeff noted, "against someone he can't control, embarrass or investigate. Someone who also has subpoena power, and a potential interest in Cuomo's staff's communications."

As part of Bharara's investigation, a grand jury subpoena was sent to the disbanded Moreland commission, seeking e-mails, text messages, and other records from all commission members.

In response, the Moreland commission hired a white-collar defense lawyer. A spokesperson described this as a purely pro forma decision. Andrew in turn hired a lawyer who would represent the governor's office. As any lawyer knew, this indicated the possibility that the two parties' legal interests—the Moreland's and Andrew's—might diverge.

Soon others in the governor's office, including Larry Schwartz, would hire their own lawyers too.

In his first three years as governor, Andrew had kept his home life private. His weekends were for tinkering with his cars, spending time with Sandra and his daughters—and working. He never took a full day off: as with his father and grandfather before him, life was work and family, and almost nothing else.

The house was quieter now that the twins were up at Deerfield Academy. When he could, Andrew drove up to see their games—at least one was on the school soccer team—but as two Deerfield parents recalled, the way he did so was rather odd.

Andrew would drive up to the games in a black SUV. Instead of joining the other parents and cheering from the sidelines, however, he would drive to the far side of the field, roll down the driver's-side window, and watch the game from *inside the car,* never emerging to wave to the twins.

As for Andrew's relationship with Sandra Lee, it was all but invisible. Once in a great while Sandra granted a short interview as fluffy as her lemon meringue. Readers learned that her favorite meal was lasagna, cooked the semi-homemade way with canned tomato soup, cottage cheese, and ground chuck—a recipe that provoked a rare public squawk from Matilda. That, Matilda declared, was *not* how lasagna was made. Guests to the home Sandra shared with Andrew were asked to wear slippers to protect the all-white living room, with its ivory carpet, decorative polar bears, and mother-of-pearl coffee table. "Some people think I have an issue with cleanliness," Sandra admitted, "but to me it's just so pretty." A brief tour for a reporter led to the dining room, done in a Founding Fathers theme. "I like to create what I call tablescapes," Sandra explained. "It's so much more fun when you organize your table around a theme, don't you think?" Asked if marriage to the governor was in her plans, she said sweetly, "Right now I'm happy being a girlfriend. But someday Andrew and I will get there. When his kids say we need to, we will."

In the publishing world, Sandra had a reputation for brutal ambition and leaving coworkers bloodied behind her. A veteran of the publishing business called her "very dogged in the pursuit of her own name and career. She tends to get easily upset when there are problems. She can get vicious: 'How come you're not doing more for me?' 'Wait, we just talked an hour ago!'" Her relationship with Miramax had ended badly, her once bullish boosters disenchanted. How two such strong-willed people managed to live under the same roof was a mystery that no one outside the family could explain, though after nearly nine years, the relationship clearly worked. "Actually, I think they're perfect together," one former aide to Andrew said wryly. "They're both narcissists."

To the first couple's great annoyance, some of that fluffy coverage came back to bite them in mid-May 2014. Feature stories in *Vogue*, *Elle Decor*, and other publications had showcased Sandra's redecorating efforts at the six-bedroom white clapboard house she had christened Lily Pond. Sandra had "ripped out an 80s-era powder room and its 'icky' bunny wallpaper," reported *USA Today*. "She put parallel white marble islands in the kitchen. She joined two smaller, darker spaces and installed a wall of windows to create one big, bright living room." In a story on her, *New York* magazine had also noted that Sandra had remodeled the basement.

All this came as a surprise to Bill Maskiell, the town building inspector for New Castle, New York. He saw no records of a finished basement in town records for 4 Bittersweet Lane, nor for the additions of a gazebo and shed that he noted in driving by the property.

Through much of 2012, the inspector hounded Sandra to file building permits for the gazebo and shed. "I got no response from her people," Maskiell explained to the press in May 2014. "I finally spoke with his [Cuomo's] people. They sat down with me and said yes, yes, yes. Then they didn't get back to me. I finally sent a violation and got a response.

Finally, Larry Schwartz got in touch with me." With Schwartz's direct involvement, Sandra got town approval at last for the gazebo and shed.

The installation cost of those two additions was estimated at $11,000. Maskiell still had no way of assessing the redecorating inside, and whether it required a permit, because Sandra refused to let a town assessor do an interior inspection. Schwartz did respond by e-mail to a press inquiry. He noted that all the work done inside was decorative, requiring no building permits. "It was retiling, painting, wallpapering. It's like her line of work—decorative. I'm not aware of any rooms that were combined." Pressed on the issue of the remodeled basement, Schwartz replied, "Again, the key word is decorative—window treatments."

Since Sandra's purchase of the house for $1.2 million in 2008, its value had declined to $936,000, resulting in an annual property tax bill of $28,312. With her refusal in May 2014 to allow the interior inspection, and the resulting coverage in both the *New York Times* and *Wall Street Journal*, local tax assessor Phil Platz saw no choice but to presume that the work *had* increased the house's value. In mid-June, he declared that Lily Pond was now valued back at $1.2 million, and that Sandra, as its owner, would now pay $36,500 in annual property taxes.

To the governor's aides, the subtext was all too clear. This was a nasty trick, they felt, pulled by Republican Rob Astorino, the Westchester county executive now running for governor against Andrew. As one spokesperson put it, "This is just Rob Astorino playing his little Westchester political games about a gazebo when he should be doing his job."

Whatever Astorino's role in the kerfuffle, Andrew faced a more immediate political threat—from within his own party.

Between Andrew and the left wing of his party had stretched, from the start, an uneasy distance, bridged by expedience and hope that the son would become the father. For some time that distance had grown, as Andrew showed how little he had in common with Mario on fiscal policies. As ex–state assemblyman and political pundit Richard Brodsky put it, "There's a strong sense among the progressive grassroots that it's just not enough to be really good on gay marriage and abortion rights and guns if your economic philosophy reflects Paul Ryan and the Tea Party, and that's what's bubbling to the surface now."

Perhaps if Andrew had not pushed so hard to get his fourth budget done in record-making time, he could have held a hard line on public financing and not let the Moreland commission go down. Or maybe he had gotten exactly the deal he wanted. Either way, the left wing and its increasingly powerful Working Families Party were fed up. To hear Andrew say that "half a loaf" of campaign finance reform was better than none only irked them further. "The [one-race] plan is hardly half a loaf," declared Blair Horner of the New York Public Interest Research Group, whose admiration for Andrew had curdled since his stint in Andrew's AG office some years earlier. "A designed-to-fail public financing system is not even a slice of a loaf. More like a moldy crumb." And trading Moreland away was unforgivable. To the left, the real significance of Moreland was that it had promised to take on big money's role in politics. Andrew, in killing it, had sided with the rich, then helped the rich further with his $2 billion in tax cuts, most of which went to lower the estate taxes of people wealthy enough to have such problems. Once again, he began hearing that name, like an echo behind him: Governor One Percent.

Andrew bridled at the taunts, and on public financing, he had a point. All those Democrats who cried out for campaign financing caps—what about their so-called independent expenditure committees, the slush funds operated by unions? The Democrats were no better than the Republicans in that regard. "[If] David Koch wants to set up an independent expenditure committee, he can!" Andrew exclaimed. "[If] 1199 wants to spend $5 million, they can. Jonathan Soros wants to spend $10 million, he can! Teachers' union wants to spend $5 million, they can. Well then, what's the point of public financing?"

Nevertheless, the new rap on Andrew had taken hold. Democrats all over the country were pledging to narrow the gap between the One Percent and everyone else. In New York, Andrew's policies were widening it.

The Working Families Party wasn't yet strong enough to push an incumbent out of office, certainly not one as powerful as Andrew. But it could take the risk of endorsing a true progressive. One poll suggested that a spoiler might cut Andrew's margin of victory from 57 percent to 37 percent—enough to ruin his image of indomitability, and possibly forestall a White House run. The risk was sizable: like all independent parties, the WFP needed 50,000 votes on election day to keep its ballot line and ensure its political survival. It had backed Andrew, with deep misgivings, in 2010, and garnered 150,000 votes. If it stayed with Andrew it would live to fight another four years, but at what ethical cost?

As the WFP's May 31 convention loomed, Andrew turned to the mediator who had helped him twice before, unlikely as the choice now seemed. Bill de Blasio was the WFP's darling, the candidate of true liberal values whose victory was, to a very real extent, the WFP's doing. The new mayor of New York was one of the few friends Andrew had in the party—the one he least deserved after his rope-a-dope treatment of the mayor these last months. But friendship wasn't the only motivation for either man. Whatever his margin of victory, Andrew *would* win reelection, and de Blasio would have to work with him. Better to work with a governor who owed him rather than one who felt betrayed. De Blasio went to the WFP leaders to plead Andrew's case and keep them from endorsing a rival. Andrew was in his debt now, and both men knew it.

Good negotiator though he was, de Blasio was dealing with angry leaders. Angry rank and file too. Andrew had assumed that wouldn't matter, since he had the backing of several big unions on which the party depended, starting with his old dependable, 1199. As the endorsement hung in the balance, the unions flexed their muscles: they would walk if Andrew wasn't chosen. The whole party would be torn in half.

But Andrew had overplayed his hand. The unions might have the money; they might have the power. What they lacked were the votes. Among the party's voting members, anger against Andrew ran high—so high that they seemed all but certain to throw the endorsement to a forty-two-year-old Fordham professor named Zephyr Teachout, whose speech had stirred progressive passions. They would do that even if it meant losing the unions and giving the ballot line to a dark horse unlikely to garner fifty thousand votes in November. In other words, they would commit political suicide rather than give Andrew the endorsement. That was how strongly they resented the governor who had let them down so often. "If he had been a warm, open person," suggested Bill Samuels, the Democratic activist, "feelings might not run so high." But Andrew's harsh demeanor and bullying manner had alienated so many across the board that Samuels, for one, couldn't think of a Democrat he knew who *liked* Andrew, much less supported him with any enthusiasm.

Andrew had met a power greater than his own: the party's willingness to blow itself up. The WFP would lose—but so would he. At stake was that margin of victory, and possibly the path to higher office. Andrew's only choice, if he hoped to win by a landslide, was to give the WFP what it wanted: 180-degree turns on major issues.

As the convention lurched toward its Saturday night finale, Andrew made a series of concessions. He would work for the Dream Act, helping illegal immigrants get state aid for college. *Really* work—not just pay lip service to the act and let the Republican Senate kill it again. He would push for the decriminalization of small amounts of marijuana, which had sent so many black and Hispanic men to jail. He would work to raise the minimum wage to $10.10 an hour, in line with the president's goal. And he would work for public financing across the board, not just for one little race.

The party wanted to hear Andrew make those pledges in person. He demurred. The last thing he needed was to go to the suburban Albany hotel where the increasingly rowdy WFP members were gathered and have the crowd hoot him down. That Saturday afternoon, one speaker after another denounced him. One called him a liar. The realization surely dawned on him that even now, he might lose the endorsement and reap the embarrassment that would follow. And so at some point on that unnerving day, he made the ultimate concession.

Yes, Andrew agreed, he might be willing to help tip the Senate majority back to the Democrats. To do that, he would have to campaign directly against the renegade Democrats of the IDC unless they too came home to their party.

This was extraordinary.

The governor would, in other words, undo the coalition government he had worked with—and to a great extent formed behind the scenes. In pulling the IDC back to the Democrats, he would make a clean break with the Republican Senate he had worked so well with, and its leader Dean Skelos, whose straight-up style he'd frankly preferred to the querulous—and all too often corrupt—Democratic Party.

All this for the endorsement of a minor political party.

But Andrew didn't have that endorsement yet—and he was, understandably, leery of pledging to bring the Democrats back to power before he had it in hand. What if he gave these crazy left-wingers everything they wanted and they still rejected him out of sheer spite? It was at that point, as one senior member of the WFP put it, that Bill de Blasio saved the governor's ass.

The mayor had unprecedented leverage over the unions—contract talks were pending, and the unions wanted to play nice—and so the new mayor made a request. He asked them to support only Democrats in the fall Senate elections.

This was less obvious than it seemed. The unions backed Democratic senators and governors, but in legislative races they tended to side with whoever was in power, and often backed Republican incumbents. Which was why, when the unions acquiesced to the new mayor's request, the whole playing board shifted decisively. With Andrew *and* the unions supporting them, Democrats almost certainly would win back the Senate. That was bigger than all the bitterness the WFP members felt toward Andrew. And Andrew, in turn, could go public with his pledge knowing he had the votes.

But the drama wasn't over.

Sometime that day, as debate raged on about who the party should endorse, Andrew read a short speech into a video camera set up somewhere in what looked like a government file room. In it he ticked off his new pledges, working up to the largest. "The simple truth is, to make this agenda a reality, we must change the Senate leadership," he intoned. "We should start by telling the IDC that they must agree to return to the Democratic Party or face our unified opposition. And then we must tell senators who call themselves senators that they must support these items or we don't consider them Democrats and they will face our unified opposition. And then together we must go out and we must win a majority of the seats in the Senate. It is that simple, but it is that sweeping, because that is the obstacle to making this agenda a reality."

The video was sent to the hotel, to be shown at 10 p.m. as Andrew's official speech to the floor. Instead, as 10 p.m. came and went, the delegates were told there were "technical difficulties" downloading it. In fact, two senior women in the WFP had found the governor's pledges insufficient. That passage about minimum wage? Too vague. The women wanted Andrew to spell out exactly what he'd agreed to: not only the raise to $10.10 an hour across the board, but a raise that could be upwardly indexed for cost-of-living differences in one part of the state or another, up to 30 percent. This was a clause Andrew had previously rejected. He hadn't mentioned the index. The women were adamant. Either he reshoot the whole video, including those key details, or they would yank the endorsement.

Andrew, a WFP in-house memo later reported, was "mere minutes away" from losing the endorsement to Teachout. Resolutely, he reshot the video, stumbling a bit over the minimum-wage details but including them, as demanded. *Still* not all the party leaders were won over. Backstage, they studied the video intently, listening for lawyerly hedges. One made de Blasio's top aide call Andrew directly. She wanted to hear the governor tell her again, directly and personally, that he would do what he had just pledged to do. When he called back, the WFPer had her iPhone hooked up to the speaker system so everyone in the audience could hear. And *still* not every WFPer was satisfied. In a second phone call, this one with just half a dozen of them, the governor reiterated his pledges, like a schoolboy drawing them in chalk on a blackboard again and again.

Finally, at about midnight, the vote was held. Andrew won over Teachout, 59 percent to 41 percent.

The next day, while marching in a Celebrate Israel parade down Fifth Avenue, Andrew was asked how he felt about the bruising treatment he had endured the night before. He seemed to regard the whole thing as a bad dream best forgotten. "It's very simple at these political conventions: you either win or you lose," he said. "I won."

Andrew thought he'd won what he set out to get: a near guarantee of a wide victory margin that November. What he had lost was the image of invincibility, and with it, the rule by fear he had used to run the state. "The only way to overcome a bully like Cuomo is to stand up to him," Bill Samuels said. "The WFP convention proved that theory true."

Andrew all but conceded that nothing further would come from the end of his fourth legislative session. The issues he had now embraced to get his WFP endorsement were all opposed by the Republican Senate. Dean Skelos would hardly soften on them after hearing the governor pledge to end the Republicans' majority that fall. In the session's waning days, a deal on medical marijuana was reached. It would be legalized, though on more conservative grounds than almost any other state. An agreement on how teachers would be evaluated was settled as well. The rest would have to wait until November's elections, with the Senate's fate hanging over all.

Andrew's first term as governor was basically done, the tote sheet for his four legislative sessions there for all to judge. If the results were not quite as "historic" as his press releases claimed, they were still considerable. Budgets balanced, order restored: the ship of state's engines were thrumming back to life. Largely with his own muscle and moxie, Andrew had pushed through two major social reforms—marriage equality and enhanced gun control—that set standards for the nation to follow. Above all, he had worked with the legislature: brusquely, sometimes harshly, even, but worked nonetheless. He knew every lawmaker's strengths and needs, and like an LBJ of the North, used them with a stern dispatch to get things done. The contrast with a sitting president who seemed to disdain in-the-pit politics could not be more stark.

And yet so much remained to be done.

The overriding challenge remained that desolate country of empty storefronts and weather-beaten farms called upstate. Andrew, to his credit, had thrown one initiative after another at those cities and towns, and some might yet stick. His proclamations of progress were, however, premature. New York still had the nation's worst business climate according to the conservative-leaning Tax Foundation, with among the highest individual income tax and property tax rates, as well as high unemployment indicators. In the end, Andrew would be judged, fairly or not, by how he changed all that. So far, the jury was out.

Back in 2010, when he had won his governorship, Andrew had thought fracking might jump-start the state's economy. Then came the furious backlash. With the state divided on how to proceed, he had ducked a no-win issue, not just month after month, but year after year, until it had become an epic case of can-kicking down the road. As of mid-2014 it remained unresolved—presided over by a governor who clearly hoped fracking might just go away. Perhaps he had saved the state an environmental horror, though a go-slow approach, carefully monitored, might have at least demonstrated if fracking *could* be done safely, and if so, brought an enormous boost to upstate.

Instead, Andrew had gambled on gaming. By late April 2014, twenty-two companies, including Caesars and Genting, had paid $1 million application fees to bid on one or another of the four upstate sites, with formal bids due at the end of June and choices made by fall. "The cynics said, 'You're not going to get the applications...gaming is over the curve,'" Andrew crowed. "I think you've actually had more interest and it's gone better than people suspected it might early on." His old nemesis Tom DiNapoli, the comptroller, remained wary of the whole proposition. In a report, he worried that any jobs created by new casinos might lead to unemployment elsewhere as the economic landscape shifted in response to gaming.

Aqueduct, to be sure, was raking in money with its forty-five hundred video lottery terminals, and the state took a sizable cut, using its proceeds for education, among other community needs. But the story in Atlantic City, New Jersey, was very different. Since January 2014, four of the city's twelve casinos had warned they would go out of business if they didn't find buyers. "It comes down to saturation," Mayor Don Guardian lamented. "How many more casinos do you think you can build in the mid-Atlantic states?" The rest of his city's casinos were struggling in neighborhoods they'd blighted, amid abandoned buildings and vacant lots. How would Andrew's casinos fare in a state already saturated with Native American casinos, rising up in rural stretches en route to nowhere?

One answer—possibly surprising to those other companies that had just tendered million-dollar application fees to bid on upstate sites—was to sanction casinos closer to New York City after all. Andrew had stressed that the upstate four would enjoy seven years of competition-free business before the balance of three downstate casinos got built. Yet by April 2014, the Malaysian casino conglomerate Genting was busily drawing up plans for a site just one hour's drive from Manhattan—a site well known by the governor from his early days with Sheldon Goldstein.

A site at Sterling Forest.

In the decade after Andrew's foiled effort with his mentor to buy the whole of Sterling Forest, a hardy band of locals had fought for its permanent preservation—and won. As of 1998, the forest had become Sterling Forest State Park, the largest addition to the state park system in fifty years, run by the Palisades Interstate Parks Commission. Yet its private inholdings remained, along with an adjacent public ski resort that Genting was eyeing.

Black bears still roamed the forest, and rattlesnakes still slithered on its steep-sloped ridges, but Genting's pitch to the well-heeled citizens of Tuxedo, the town nearest the old ski resort, was that its complex would nestle gently in those woods, catering to an upscale clientele. The pitch was accompanied by some very sizable sums. Genting would pay Tuxedo about $47.5 million in various stages.

Once upon a time, Andrew had dreamed of making his fortune with Sterling Forest. Now, if Genting won its bid and profited as hoped, along with the other new upstate casinos, the governor might have a stirring story of pulling his state from recession with gaming—a story to tell on the presidential campaign trail of 2016. The governor's relations with Genting were said to have turned frosty after the disclosure of its contribution to the Committee to Save New York. But if a new casino helped the state—at least long enough for Andrew to run for president—he would curb his ire.

Andrew's fondest hope for upstate revival now seemed more feasible than it had when he launched it two years before. A kinder climate had let him add $855 million to his budget to ramp up Billion for Buffalo. Gone was the smoke and mirrors of old, existing programs, replaced with new ones that included a solar panel factory for Elon Musk, founder of Tesla electric vehicles. But as Investigative Post reporter Jim Heaney discovered, most of that $855 million was parceled out to three developers, all major contributors to Andrew's 2014 campaign. No one in the administration proved willing to share unredacted documents on how this taxpayer money was allocated, or return any of Heaney's calls.

There was, alas, still the impediment of Hillary. That June, *Hard Choices*, the 656-page memoir of her years as secretary of state, rolled out with global fanfare but to tepid reviews. Initially brisk sales plummeted by week two. On her book tour, Hillary offered teasing or coy answers to the overarching question of whether she would run. Some close friends swore she would, others that she might not. As always when she came back into the limelight, her favorability ratings fell: for all those who admired her, a lot of Americans still had contradictory feelings about the Clintons, and the prospect of another Clinton presidency—a twofer, with Bill also in residence—seemed possibly one too many. A cottage industry in anti-Hillary books did a lively business as summer unfolded, with one outselling her own book. As inexorable as Hillary for President seemed, there were hints in her book-tour interviews that she might just startle the world and choose a private life over a public one.

About all of this, Andrew, as powerful and wily as he was, could do nothing. He had spent his life working up to this moment, plotting each next step. Of his generation of American politicians, he had the single best résumé for a White House run: the time put in at each next station, the solid achievements scored. Yet there was Hillary, blocking his path, the one politician he couldn't fight.

Now, even as Andrew waited on Hillary, there was a new threat coming up in his rearview mirror. Massachusetts senator Elizabeth Warren had paid none of the dues that Andrew had. She hadn't started by stuffing envelopes and doing advance work. She hadn't spent her twenties helping the homeless. She hadn't gone to the White House to shake a moribund housing agency back to life. She hadn't suffered the pain of running for office and losing in the sorriest way. Yet there she was, edging up on him: the new hope for his party's liberal wing.

A year is a lifetime in politics. That much was true. The path to 2016 might yet come clear for Andrew Cuomo, and if it did, he would be ready: no Mario-like hand-wringing for him. If it didn't, a lifetime of striving might be stopped right there, though a governor of such rapacious ambition would not go gently into that good night.

CHAPTER 29

Full Circle

Dominant though he was in the polls, Andrew was taking no chances. By November 2014, more than half of his war chest—now $47 million—would be spent saturating the airwaves, first in a primary against a neophyte, then in a race against a rival who never pulled close. It was a campaign season as flat and placid as could be—just the kind Andrew liked—except in one sense almost certainly unnoticed by the governor: it highlighted all of his strengths and flaws, more sharply than ever before, like some twenty-first-century portrait of Dorian Gray.

Zephyr Teachout, the Fordham professor who had battled Andrew for the Working Families Party line and lost, was still gathering signatures to go the petition route on July 23, 2014, when Andrew was rocked by a devastating *New York Times* investigation of the Moreland commission. All the second-floor meddling was laid bare: the blocking of subpoenas, the steering of commissioners toward targets of the administration's choosing and away from others, the forming of factions with most of the commission's members on one side and a posse of Andrew loyalists on the other, and ultimately the shutting down of the commission at Andrew's behest. As interesting as all of that was what followed.

First, Andrew had his press office whip off a scathing thirteen-page broadside against the *Times*, arguing that the newspaper had missed the whole point. The commission was never independent. It was his to interact with as much as he liked; give-and-takes about whom to subpoena were par for the course. In its fiery tone, it echoed the letter he had sent two years before, when the *Times* reported gaming interests' $2.4 million contribution to the Committee to Save New York. There was in both letters more than a trace of self-righteousness and avoidance of blame.

Two days later, the first Governor Cuomo weighed in. "Andrew is as honest a politician as we have seen in New York," Mario declared.

"Whatever other difficulties people might find, I don't find 'em. I don't see them.... He's absolutely as straight as they come and as bright as they come." There was an echo here too: Mario querulously defending his son in 1986, after questions in the press about Andrew's legal work for big real estate developers while Mario was governor.

For five days, Andrew stayed out of sight, hoping the story might fade. When the clamor for his comments grew only louder, he scheduled a Monday morning press conference—in Buffalo. Was it a coincidence that Albany's press corps would have to hustle to be there?

Shortly before Andrew appeared, four of the Moreland's twenty-five members issued unsolicited public comments. One, cochair William Fitzpatrick of Onondonga County, put out a three-page letter saying "nobody interfered with me or my co-chairs." In his press conference, Andrew made repeated mention of Fitzpatrick's letter, declaring that Fitzpatrick "knows better than anyone else what happened with the Moreland Commission."

Reporters were quick to exhume an e-mail from Fitzpatrick the year before, in which he told a colleague that the governor's office "needs to understand this is an INDEPENDENT commission and needs to be treated as such." Apparently his feelings had changed.

So had Andrew's. Having said the week before that he ruled the commission, he now said it had been independent and that he and his advisers had never done more than offer advice. "If you had watched the movie to the end," he told one reporter, meaning if the reporter had seen the commission reach its natural end, "the name of the movie would have been 'Independence.' You named it 'Interference.'"

The Moreland would have reached that natural end, Andrew went on, if it hadn't accomplished its goals through the legislature. In fact, he said, the commission had had "phenomenal success," and the changes passed by lawmakers as a result had simply rendered it moot. This was revisionist history, a ploy used before. Declaring HUD off the high-risk agency list was one example; taking credit for twenty-seven thousand nonexistent jobs in the Erie Canal Corridor was another. The arc of Andrew's moral universe was long, and often bent toward dubious superlatives.

Letters in defense of some new version were another stock tactic. Just earlier that year, in the donnybrook between Andrew and Mayor de Blasio over universal pre-K, reporters had been inundated with unsolicited letters from public officials supportive of Andrew's approach. Back in the WestHELP days, local officials wary of Andrew's plan had gotten similar letters, and a pounding in the press if they didn't relent.

Within hours of the Buffalo press conference, reporters targeted Joe

Percoco as the instigator of those Moreland members' letters. Several members said Percoco had volunteered to provide drafts of what they might write. He also suggested they communicate with him by private e-mail, not their government e-mail accounts.

All this was of keen interest to the U.S. attorney for the Southern District of New York. Two days after the Buffalo press conference, Preet Bharara made public a letter of his own. "We have reason to believe a number of commissioners recently have been contacted about the commission's work, and some commissioners have been asked to issue public statements characterizing events and facts regarding the commission's operation," Bharara declared. As the prosecutor investigating Moreland, he regarded those commissioners as potential witnesses. Which meant that Joe Percoco's nudges might constitute witness tampering. "To the extent anyone attempts to influence or tamper with a witness's recollection of events relevant to our investigation... we must consider whether such actions constitute obstruction of justice or tampering with witnesses that violate federal law."

Larry Schwartz was high on Bharara's witness list, and rumors swirled about what he might or might not tell the U.S. attorney. Any suspicions that Schwartz might cast his boss in an unfavorable light were offset, however, by his rambling address that summer at a "Team Cuomo" alumni gathering under a white tent by the executive mansion. Eyes glistening, Schwartz spoke of the loyalty that defined the Cuomos, father and son. Never had he experienced anything like it. The loyalty, the loyalty... So emotional was he that even the Cuomo alums felt slightly embarrassed as he blathered on. Next up was Chris Cuomo. Flashing a grin, he nodded toward Schwartz. "Is that guy nuts, or what?" The crowd roared in relief.

And then to the microphone came Andrew, darker, more intense, more uncomfortable in public than his brother, even with this audience of Cuomo stalwarts. Not for the first time and not for the last, the contrast stirred in those true believers a thought that made them feel guilty, even... disloyal. Wasn't Chris the more natural inheritor of the mantle? Wouldn't *he* be the one with national appeal, more handsome, more at ease, more charismatic, shorn of that brooding demeanor and harsh Queens accent that would surely rub Kansans and Iowans the wrong way?

Until Preet Bharara announced his Moreland findings, a cloud of possible culpability would hang over the governor's head. For better or worse, that cloud would linger until after November 4: no U.S. attorney would risk influencing a state election with findings from an investigation if he could help it. As the Moreland press ebbed, few in Albany thought Andrew would be found guilty of anything but rough play. Most likely, the Moreland debacle had simply brought to light—again—his least appealing trait: that need to control everyone around him, ultimately to his own detriment. Under the character makeover—the humbled veteran of loss and divorce, Andrew 2.0—was the same old Andrew Cuomo. Mario had been just as controlling, but his intellect had leavened his style. Even as governor, Andrew was still the operational guy, his need to control unmitigated by literature.

Moreland notwithstanding, this was campaign season. Now as ever, Andrew fought with everything he had. At seventeen, he had shimmied up those phone poles with posters and a staple gun. At fifty-six, enthroned as the leader of his state, with all the power of incumbency and millions of dollars to spare, he still used ploys he'd learned in his father's first reelection campaign, back in 1986.

Now, as then, the Cuomo running for office made no mention of his primary rival. For Andrew, Zephyr Teachout didn't exist. He made no mention of his Republican rival either. Mario in reelection mode had been the same way.

Back in 1986, the Cuomos had dealt with whacky Abe Hirschfeld, whose bid for lieutenant governor put them in an embarrassing spot, by challenging his candidacy petitions in court. Teachout, unfortunately, had gathered forty-five thousand signatures where only fifteen thousand were needed. A challenge by two Cuomo-linked plaintiffs was quickly brushed aside.

Of potentially more use was Article IV, Section 2 of the state constitution, which called for the governor to have resided in New York five years prior to election. Teachout had joined the faculty at Fordham in 2009, but spent subsequent summers at a cabin in Vermont, held drivers' licenses from various states, and had not changed her address to New York for some time after she moved there. Did the law require *continuous* residency? The Cuomo campaign went to court to say it did.

At Teachout's campaign appearances, little posses of protesters started showing up, bearing posters with neat block lettering. COME CLEAN ON YOUR RESIDENCY, read one. ZEPHYR TEACHOUT (D-VT), read another. The protesters were young and neatly, even conservatively dressed. When reporters tried to photograph them, they hid their faces with their posters. When asked whom they represented, the protesters refused to answer.

Intrigued, reporters followed some of the protesters back to a Midtown office building that turned out to contain the Cuomo campaign headquarters. One protester carried an identification badge from a real estate firm that owned the building and had donated to Cuomo's campaign.

Social-media sleuthing showed several others with ties to the governor's political operation. Cornered, a Cuomo spokesman was forced to admit that the protesters were campaign workers. Was the governor aware of this laughable gambit? Perhaps not—but then, if there was one thing everyone who worked for him agreed on, it was that Andrew made every decision himself.

On August 11, 2014, a Brooklyn state supreme court judge ruled that Teachout met the minimum residency requirement. "Game on!" Teachout declared. Now, she added, it was time for Andrew to debate her "about the issues that real New Yorkers care about: schools, fracking, corruption and building a fair and strong economy." Instead, the Cuomo campaign appealed—and lost, on August 20.

Still, there would be no debate. Debates were for underdogs. Like his father in 1986, Andrew was the front-runner, and so remained in full Rose Garden mode. A bad unscripted moment, on or off the debate stage, might derail a campaign: for Andrew, it had happened before. Best just to keep ignoring the pesky professor.

That proved possible right up until the New York City Labor Day parade, when a smiling Teachout made her way through the front ranks of marchers toward Andrew. "How're you doing?" she called out. Like a dog to danger, Joe Percoco slid between the two of them, turning his back to Teachout so that he blocked her without seeming to do so. Still smiling, Teachout slid around to try another angle, only to be blocked by Percoco again. From a video of the scene—a video that went viral—the governor seemed to realize that his primary rival was not giving up. He turned away, scanning the crowd, to catch a welcome glimpse of America's tallest mayor. "Where's Mayor de Blasio?" Andrew shouted out. "Where's the mayor when you need him?" Into the frame swam the mayor at last, to be greeted by his on-again, off-again ally not just warmly but ecstatically. "I never saw her," Andrew said later when asked if he had failed a test in civility by turning his back on Teachout. "If anything I failed an eyesight test."

Teachout wasn't the only one the governor seemed loath to greet. Once again, the obligations of retail politics appeared onerous to him, if not painful. "While some politicians feed off handshakes, hugs and high-fives, Mr. Cuomo seems to avoid them," observed the *New York Times*' Thomas Kaplan. "When he speaks to an audience, listeners are rarely invited to speak to him. And when he finishes, he tends to leave immediately, often ducking quickly behind a curtain hung for the occasion, then out the door." Almost always, Andrew's appearances were tightly planned and controlled, the risk of spontaneous interactions kept in check. Even uptight Mayor Bloomberg had seemed to loosen up through his three-term tenure. Andrew seemed to be growing more uptight over time. "Before he was governor, he was out in the street," remarked John Quinn, a Democratic State Committee member from lower Manhattan. "Not anymore."

To the surprise of no one, Andrew beat Zephyr Teachout in the Democratic primary of September 9. To the shock of all, his heretofore unknown rival won 35.5 percent of the vote, the best showing against an incumbent governor since 1970, when New York gubernatorial primaries were established. Teachout carried many eastern and northern counties that Andrew had won in 2010. The whole Hudson Valley was Teachout territory, including the capital region. Teachout had shown pluck and charm, but clearly this was an anti-Andrew vote.

In the wake of what had to be a great humiliation, Andrew did his best to look pleased. "I am happy, happy, happy," he declared. "Where I come from, you win with 60 [percent], you say one thing: 'Thank you very much.'"

Days after the primary, Andrew got more bad news. His monument project, the epic rebuilding of the Tappan Zee Bridge, hit a serious snag. A loan of $511 million for bridge-related work from the U.S. Environmental Protection Agency was deemed improper. Therein lay a story that said a lot about how Andrew worked.

The new bridge was going up, but Andrew still hadn't touched the $1.6 billion federal loan that constituted his only known source of funding for the $5.2 billion project. He knew that tapping the loan would force him to say how high tolls would go to pay off the inevitable bonds. Better to do that after election day than before. But where was money to come from in the meantime?

Through an obscure government agency that he controlled, Andrew talked the EPA into granting that $511 million. This was Clean Water Act money, meant for environmental enhancement. No problem: the $65 million demolition of the old bridge, done through that loan, would involve ridding the river of toxic paint. Oyster beds would be restored for $1.2 million, a large marsh revived for $800,000. The $511 million was duly approved.

Then an EPA regional director, Judy Enck, took a closer look. The oyster beds and marshes were window dressing, she decided, the toxic paint a nonissue after many nontoxic coats. All but $29.1 million of the $511 million, in fact, was earmarked for plain old construction costs. It was a move reminiscent of the one Andrew had made early on as governor, putting all those separate agency piles of money for capital projects into one pile he controlled. The EPA loan was another instance of what admirers might call creative resource allocation—and critics "too cute by half." In mid-September, more than $480 million of that EPA loan was rescinded.

This was election season—the silly season, as Andrew called it—and higher bridge tolls on the Tappan Zee weren't the only bit of unpleasantness that seemed best put off until after election day. At almost every scheduled public appearance, the governor was met with throngs of loudly chanting antifrackers. No less irate were the legions who saw fracking as New York's great fiscal hope—if a somewhat less promising one now that natural gas prices had plummeted and farmers' dreams had dimmed. Still the state's health review of fracking remained undone, more than eighteen months from its inception. Clearly no decision would be made until Andrew's reelection.

Casinos were another hot topic that somehow slid off the calendar. The state gaming commission had pledged to announce the winning bids for upstate casinos by "early fall," as its website noted, but no such announcement had come. Meanwhile, casinos were closing right and left: Atlantic City's two-year-old Revel Casino Hotel, hailed by Governor Christie as a game-changer for New Jersey gaming, closed in September. The Trump Plaza and the Showboat, other Atlantic City mainstays, announced plans to close too, after several other Atlantic City closings earlier in the year. Massachusetts voters, having passed gaming legislation in 2011, were so appalled by gaming's collapse they were about to vote on undoing their referendum. More and more, Andrew's investment in gaming looked like an investment in Lehman Brothers in August 2008—a case of very bad timing.

As for the siting of New York's new upstate casinos, angry reactions would greet whatever choices the gaming commission made, from big operators who lost out, to gaming-wary townships that learned a casino would soon be rising near them. Two years earlier, Andrew had hailed gaming as the state's salvation. Now it looked like a bust. No wonder fall would come late this year—after election day.

Despite Rob Astorino's hopeful cries of an historic upset, the governor's race moved toward its end with all the inevitability of a royal coronation. The game to watch was the New York state senate, as Democrats fought to win back their majority. This was the game Andrew had pledged to join on behalf of the Working Families Party—and his own. Things hadn't quite worked out that way.

Well into October, Andrew had made virtually no effort to help the cause. Mayor de Blasio gave speeches firing up the base, reminding voters what was at stake if the Democrats won—or lost—the Senate. "We are so close to victory I can taste it," he cried. Andrew gave no such speeches. Instead, he said he would work with whatever legislature was elected—hardly fighting words.

So absent was Andrew from the fray that when at last he endorsed one Democratic candidate with a single declarative sentence on October 8, he made national news. Asked if he supported the Democratic challenger to Mark Grisanti, the Buffalo Republican who had overcome his doubts to vote for marriage equality, Andrew hesitated. The thought of working against this last of the Marriage Four was "personally difficult" for him, he said—an understandable sentiment, but less than helpful to his party, which needed every seat it could get to tip the Senate. Three Democratic incumbents predicted to be shoo-ins were down in the polls; two Republicans deemed vulnerable were up. Where was Andrew? "I can't name a swing district he's visited," said liberal activist Bill Samuels. "How many ads has he run for a Democratic majority? For higher minimum wage? For campaign finance reform?" In short, for all the issues Andrew had pledged to support in return for the Working Family Party's endorsement? "None."

Even as he let his fellow Democrats languish, Andrew put a scheme into play that seemed tailor-made to destroy the Working Families Party. Those left-wing loonies had infuriated him; now, perhaps, he would have his revenge, even as the WFP's ballot line helped elect him.

The scheme was both simple and clever—if, perhaps, too cute by half. Andrew formed a new political party: the Women's Equality Party. Its platform was the ten-plank Women's Equality Act Andrew had failed to push through in the last legislative session. In retrospect, was that not what he'd intended, keeping that fiery abortion plank to stoke flames for the new WEP? A Women's Equality Express bus made three tours around the state, filled on each swing by local Democratic officials. The pitch was for voters, women especially, to choose the Democratic slate, from governor on down, but to do so by voting through the new WEP. If fifty thousand women did that, the WEP would have its own ballot line in four years' time. That would give women a jolt of new political power; it would help pass the Women's Equality Act.

It might also eviscerate the Working Families Party. The more voters the new WEP siphoned, the more likely the old WFP would fail to muster its own minimum of fifty thousand votes. Without them, it would lose its ballot line and, like poor old Ray Harding's Liberal Party, cease to be. Asked if this was his motivation, Andrew scoffed at what he called "really tortured analysis." But no one in the Working Families Party harbored any doubts that this was exactly his aim. The WFP had deeply embarrassed the governor—all that groveling at the eleventh hour. No one treated Andrew Cuomo that way and got away with it.

The plan appealed to a fair number of state Democratic women candidates. A second, additional ballot line; why not? But each Democratic candidate, in order to qualify for the WEP ballot line, had to go the petition route for her district and garner fifteen thousand signatures. By late September, the Board of Elections had tossed out half a dozen candidates' petitions and struck their names from the WEP line. The Cuomo campaign had taken on the task of getting those signatures for upstate candidates, and struggled in rural areas where voters lived far apart. Apparently one or more of the canvassing groups had given up and gone the easier route of gathering signatures in New York City. Of the 4,444 signatures filed for the Hudson Valley's Senator Cecilia Tkaczyk, the sheep-shearing Democrat who'd won her first election by eighteen votes, 3,160 were invalid. Many of those were culled from Brooklyn and the Bronx. "While gerrymandering has led to the creation of some weird-looking districts," noted the Albany *Times-Union*'s Casey Seiler, "Tkaczyk's does not stretch from her native Duanesburg to either of those boroughs."

Still the WEP was a threat. Liz Krueger, the liberal Manhattan senator who never hesitated to speak her mind, found the whole scheme "disturbing." The plan, she declared, "will come back to bite women and Democrats in our derrieres." The similarity in acronyms, many WFPers felt, was Andrew's crowning touch, sure to generate confusion at the polls and steer that many more WFP voters to the WEP.

Like his father, Andrew had stayed close to home as governor, in Albany or Westchester. If he ventured any farther, he tweaked reporters, that talk would start again: the talk of a White House run in 2016. Now, with election day looming, he made his first trips abroad, back to back, with the inevitable result: more talk of 2016.

The first trip was a formal state visit to Israel, a natural for a governor wooing Jewish votes that included a one-on-one with Prime Minister Benjamin Netanyahu. "I thank you for coming here," Netanyahu told Andrew, "and standing on the right side of the moral divide." Next up: Afghanistan, where Andrew posed at the wheel of a formidable military vehicle and received counterterrorism briefings. "It's here," Andrew said soberly of the terrorist threat. "It may get a little bit better. It may get a little bit worse. But it's never going away. And it is very important to me to immerse myself in the topic." That, he stressed, was in the context of anticipating terrorist threats to New York. But the timing of his first two international trips could hardly be mistaken.

On cue, Hillary Clinton strode onstage at a late-October Midtown Manhattan rally for Andrew to cries of "2016." The cries were for Hillary, not Andrew. More than ever, the race seemed Hillary's to own if she wished. "They ask me all the time about Hillary Clinton: 'What's Hillary going to do?'" Andrew told the crowd. "I say, 'Well, Hillary Clinton is so good that whatever she does, she's going to be an overwhelming success. And I hope she does something really, really, really big.' That's what I hope."

Might there, for Hillary, be something really, really, really big *besides* the presidency? Something that allowed Andrew to seize it instead? That wistful hope seemed to hold him back from an early endorsement, though he denied it. "Hillary Clinton can't be endorsed," he said, "because Hillary Clinton hasn't said she's running for anything." Not true: Senators Chuck Schumer of New York and Tim Kaine of Virginia, among other prominent Democrats, had endorsed Hillary already.

Through the last weeks of his first term, Andrew did more than play out the campaign clock. He showed some grit as governor too.

In the almost two years since he'd passed his SAFE Act, Andrew had taken a lot of lumps from upstate gun owners. Another constituency, mental health workers, were also dismayed: they questioned their new duty, under the act, to report people deemed a danger to themselves or others to a state database that would deny them guns for at least five years. An investigation by the *New York Times* disclosed that October that no fewer than 34,500 citizens had been reported. Mental health experts found that number high, and worried the law might have swept up thousands of people not truly ill. Andrew thought it too low: as he observed, the state's mental hospitals treated 140,000 patients a year. The law might err on the side of caution, but on balance it seemed to be working as intended. No one would know how many Sandy Hook shootings it helped prevent. But surely one was enough.

With little more than a week to go before election day, Ebola came to New York City: a young doctor just back from West Africa tested positive for the terrifying disease. A swift response was needed, and Governors Cuomo and Christie provided it together—perhaps a bit too swiftly. In a joint news conference, they called federal prevention protocols inadequate, and declared that travelers arriving from West Africa who had had direct contact with Ebola patients would be subject to a twenty-one-day quarantine "at a government-regulated facility."

Soon, the two governors were fielding an onslaught of criticism from higher authorities, from the Centers for Disease Control and Prevention to the UN secretary-general. Quarantines were unnecessary and would only keep doctors in the United States from going *to* West Africa to fight the disease. The governors were letting politics trump science.

Andrew's peace pact with Governor Christie had held since Bridgegate, if not before. Now, though, he seemed to take advantage of a scheduled Florida trip by Christie. While the New Jersey governor was gone, Andrew reappeared before the cameras on his own with a modified plan that undercut his counterpart. To Cuomo-watchers, it was another tool from the toolbox: beat bad press by throwing colleagues under the bus. Gone from the rhetoric were "government-regulated facilities." High-risk travelers were instead encouraged to spend twenty-one-day quarantines at home. Gone too was the accusing tone. A quarantine, the governor implied, could be a kind of vacation. "Enjoy your family, enjoy your kids, enjoy your friends," the governor advised prospective quarantinees. "Read a book. Read my book," he said, referring to his just-published memoir, *All Things Possible.*

Federal authorities continued to simmer, but a *Wall Street Journal*/NBC 4 New York/Marist College poll brought happy Halloween news to the governor. New Yorkers by an overwhelming majority—82 percent—approved of twenty-one-day quarantine measures for anyone who'd come in contact with an Ebola patient. An overall 63 percent approved of Andrew's handling of the scare; among registered Democrats, the figure rose to 71 percent. Medical experts might quibble, but Andrew had come out fast and hard, and voters liked that. From those late-night AAA tow-truck runs to his coolheaded handling of Superstorm Sandy, he had had some of his best moments helping others at risk. That was saying a lot.

The verdict came within minutes of the polls' closing that Tuesday, November 4, 2014: Andrew had won his second term. Not by the 64 percent his father had mustered in 1986, not close: more like 54 percent. For an incumbent who had raised $47 million and spent much of that battling a rival with minimal name recognition, it was a C-plus performance at best.

Losing most of upstate was the real sting of it all. Ever since his Erie Canal campaign at HUD, Andrew had courted those flinty farmers and Dollar Store shoppers in New York's poorest counties. In 2010 he had won thirty-seven of those counties; this time he won only eight. From Wayne to Warren, Jefferson to Chautauqua, voters turned out en masse against him. The only county out west that went for Andrew was Erie, and how could it not, after Andrew's "Billion for Buffalo" infusion of cash?

To Andrew's former adviser Steve Cohen, the reason was all too clear. "You want to explain Andrew not getting 64 percent? It's guns, not Moreland." Arguably, the SAFE Act was the most personal gambit of Andrew's first term. Politically it was the costliest, as upstate gun owners had now shown at the polls. "Was his desire to pass the most comprehensive gun legislation a political calculation gone wrong," Cohen asked rhetorically, "or a willingness to expend political capital on something he believed in? I think it's both. Did he understand what the repercussions were? I don't think he did. We didn't understand how big marriage was going to be. We also didn't understand the impact of guns."

Still, it was victory, and for Andrew Mark Cuomo, it came with a poignant moment. In a packed banquet room in Midtown Manhattan, he took his father's hand and held it aloft, a boxer's sign of triumph. As all could see, Mario was fragile, his once-powerful frame diminished, the tentacles of age encircling him. One of Andrew's advisers asked the governor-elect if it felt like a last hurrah. "Yeah," Andrew said quietly. "It's all right." By which, the adviser knew, Andrew meant it was more than all right. Mario was seeing the dynasty he'd built get carried on. Andrew, the loyal but unintellectual son, had proven his mettle once again.

Across the country, Republicans had swept back into power, regaining the U.S. Senate and winning governorships east and west. The races, often close but tipping one after another away from the Democrats, were a sharp repudiation of President Obama. Pundits were divided on whether the newly unified U.S. Congress would find common ground with the administration and get bills passed, or bring two more years of gridlock.

For Andrew, the morning after the midterms brought news that seemed sure to enhance his power. The New York state senate had gone Republican again, by a whisker. The whole left wing of the Democratic Party was furious with Andrew. He had broken his pledge, as far as they were concerned; he had done almost nothing to help candidates of his own party, and the lost majority was his fault—his scheme, more like it.

The week after the election, Fred Dicker would have a scoop on that, with an actual on-the-record source. For months, Michael Lawler, manager of Rob Astorino's campaign, had wondered why Dean Skelos showed so little interest in the Republican candidate. When a top Long Island Republican in Dean Skelos's county went so far as to endorse Andrew instead of Astorino, Lawler called the Republican's aide. "What the fuck?" According to Lawler, the aide said, "When this is over, give me a call." Post-election,

Lawler did just that, or so he told Dicker. He said he learned a deal had been cut. In trade for the top Republican's endorsement, Andrew had desisted from any campaigning for Senate Democrats in Dean Skelos's Long Island. The deal helped tip the Senate to the Republicans, and fortify Skelos, even as it helped reelect Andrew. If Lawler was right, each leader had worked against his own party to advance himself.

Andrew denied he'd betrayed his party. Some of those sitting Democrats had lost by wide margins, like sheep-shearing Cece Tkaczyk. No amount of rhetoric from the governor would have tipped the race in her favor. Perhaps. But the other outcome that went the governor's way was all his doing. His Women's Equality Party had inched over the fifty-thousand-vote threshold, pulling votes from the Working Families Party that had dared to humiliate him in the spring. That was remarkable. The WEP would be a stalking horse for the governor now. At least the WFP had lived to fight another day, notching more than fifty thousand votes too. But the left-wingers of the WFP were under no illusions as to what Andrew had tried to do. "Governor Cuomo promised to take back the State Senate," fumed WFP director Bill Lipton. "Instead, he squandered millions on a fake party, and left millions more in his campaign account as New York Democrats in the legislature and in Congress withered on the vine." In this next term, Andrew would be trying to marginalize and ultimately kill off the WFP, even as the party worked to defeat him.

For Andrew, the second term would be very different from—and more challenging than—the first. The state was in better fiscal shape, with all that that entailed. But the governor had worn out his welcome. On the right, gun owners still simmered over the SAFE Act. On the left, even moderates saw betrayal on a host of issues: redistricting, the millionaires' tax, campaign finance reform, and letting the Senate slip through their fingers. From across the political spectrum, there was censure of the ill-fated Moreland commission. "What Cuomo is walking into is a seething, resentful mess," declared Richard Brodsky, the former assemblyman and fellow at a left-leaning think tank. "But he has the political skills to repeat the thing that everyone credits him for, which is making the government function."

Could that yet be Andrew's springboard to national office? "Every presidential election is a reaction to the style of the guy in the Oval Office," suggested one of Andrew's advisers. "If you have gridlock Obama, then the person who will replace him, Republican or Democrat, is the anti-Obama. Is it Hillary? Or could it be Andrew?" Andrew was a long shot, the adviser conceded. "But he's positioned himself. He can't contest Hillary for the left, but he can position himself as someone who can deal with the left *and* the right. He's viable in this cycle if people collectively say we can't put someone forward who's not a strongly moderate candidate.

"So you'll see Cuomo trying to move the party to the center going forward," the adviser suggested. "He can stake out his position and then embrace Hillary. If she wins, it makes sense. If she loses, it makes sense. I think his positioning is Clintonian. The irony is: who is more Clintonian, Hillary or Andrew?"

For Andrew, a unified Republican U.S. Congress could be far more beneficial than a divided one. If the party actually governed, instead of obstructed, it might be strong for 2016. Hillary as the Democrat might lose. Four years of a Republican presidency might set Andrew up as the perfect alternative: the seasoned, centrist, three-term governor with all those on-time budgets behind him. At the picture-perfect presidential age of sixty-three.

There was just that nagging question of character. Andrew was commanding, pragmatic, hardworking, personally incorruptible (so far), fierce in defense of his policies—and willing to compromise when absolutely necessary. In short, a strong leader. He was also vengeful, bullying, mean-spirited, conniving, not always true to his word, and very secretive.

That last was perhaps the most troubling in a potential chief executive. Andrew had come into office promising a much-needed transparency in Albany. In some ways, he had fulfilled that promise: lawmakers, for example, were now forced to disclose their outside income. In all too many others, he had been anything but transparent. Laws were still hammered out behind closed doors, printed up, and barely whisked under lawmakers' noses before message-of-necessity votes. Andrew and his circle still pinged each other with untraceable PIN-to-PIN messages on personal e-mail accounts. In a new, unpublicized policy, many of the e-mails sent by and to tens of thousands of state employees were purged after ninety days. Journalists making Freedom of Information Law requests for government documents had found the Cuomo administration violating the FOIL's spirit and practice. Many requests went unfulfilled for months if not years. Any possibly embarrassing request was immediately sent up to the governor's office to be studied; when a response was readied, it too was sent to the governor's office, as well as the governor's general counsel. "They're keeping information from the public they know the public may not like," declared Phillip Musegaas, the Hudson River program director at the environmental group Riverkeeper. His own group's requests for plans to monitor fish during the Tappan Zee Bridge construction had languished for months.

In his first years as governor, Andrew had often drawn comparisons to President Lyndon Johnson for his charm and cunning in getting bills passed. Now another president was sometimes evoked. Rex Smith, editor in chief of the Albany *Times Union*, had written that glowing editorial upon Andrew's inauguration, wondering if a tough, strong, no-nonsense leader was exactly what Albany needed after its years of chaos. Now he was struck by similarities between Andrew and Richard Nixon—ones that had only grown with Andrew's handling of the Moreland commission, and the investigation that hung over his head.

Nixon, like Andrew, had forged a path of political pragmatism, Smith observed, sometimes shocking his own party as he did. He had created the Environmental Protection Agency; he had opened the door to China. Like Andrew, he had nursed fierce ambition, and stood strong when under attack. But Nixon had trusted no one but himself, and let a yen for secrecy lead to his own undoing.

"Hmm," Smith wrote. "Do you know anybody else in public life who is a compulsive manipulator? Whose impressive roster of accomplishments, achieved through his prodigious political skills, is at risk of being overshadowed just now by questions involving ethics and credibility?" Moreland was no Watergate, Smith conceded. "But like the crisis that felled Richard Nixon," he wrote, "the political peril confronting Andrew Cuomo is rooted in the very behavior that enabled him to achieve success."

Unlike Nixon, Andrew had another chance: a whole new term in which to achieve great things. He made a first significant decision before the term even began: on December 17, 2014, flanked by state health officials, he issued a statewide, permanent ban on fracking. Antifracking activists were as stunned as the oil and natural gas industries. The governor had hidden for nearly two years behind an ongoing health study, and pushed the hard choice past election day, but in the end he'd come out flatly against fracking. Unproven as the health risks might still be, the list was just too long: birth defects, respiratory illnesses, air and water pollution from benzene, formaldehyde, and more. With that one stroke, much of the state's Democratic Party came back to his fold. They might not like Andrew Cuomo any more than they had the day before, but this, as Vice President Joe Biden had whispered to Obama when health care passed, was fucking big. Nationally, the fracking ban would weigh on other governors grappling with the issue. It also made Andrew, once more, a serious contender for 2016.

It was a double-barreled day: the other big news came, ostensibly, from the state board charged with choosing new upstate casino sites, though few doubted Andrew had had his say in the matter. To the great relief of Sterling Forest's defenders, Genting's Tuxedo plan was scotched. But Genting had had two backup plans for mega-casinos near New York City, and the board picked one: an $800-million resort casino complex in the hard-pressed Catskills, on the grounds of the old Borscht Belt Concord Hotel. Apparently Cuomo had made his peace with the Malaysian gaming giant. Genting seemed to have gotten over its own hurt feelings: in 2012–13, it spent more than any other gaming interest on lobbying ($2.5 million) and campaign contributions ($984,244).

Doubtless Andrew had hoped, with his first oath of office, that he would be starting his White House run now. Instead, he seemed consigned to four more years of Albany, of dickering with Shelly and Dean. He could see it as delay—or perhaps as opportunity, to strike a more open and moderating tone with both parties, to reintroduce himself: Andrew 3.0.

There was, one insider suggested, a sense of aloneness about Andrew that holiday season. Many of his closest advisers had gone or would soon leave, among them Larry Schwartz and Ben Lawsky; Howard Glaser had left months before. Apparently Andrew was spooked by the departures. Rationally, he knew his tribe had families to support, and only so much time to spend on government service. Still he seemed hurt, even abandoned. Also anxious about finding good people to replace them. Maybe *any* people to replace them. By now everyone knew how brutal a manager he could be. "He's just chewed through people," observed one unsympathetic colleague. Getting even Albany hacks to fill seats would be a challenge.

What was it about Andrew? All that drive, that mix of public service and personal glory: success at any cost. Maybe that was what fueled every American politician, but somehow in Andrew it all seemed deeper and more complex.

"Ultimately, this is a guy who is a solitary figure," one top aide conceded. "And this notion of wanting to surround himself with people he trusts—at the end of the day, can you trust anyone but yourself?" Aides would betray you, friends use you, wives abandon you; even children would eventually leave. Andrew, to protect himself, cut himself off and lived for his work: his work today and the upward climb.

Mario, for all his outward geniality, had been that way too. "Of course it goes back to Mario," one aide said with a sigh, "and yes, it was a much darker relationship than the camp would have you believe. Mario was a complicated, brilliant, sophisticated, loving father. But not much emotion."

Father and son: for Mario and Andrew, it had been the bond of ultimate trust, maybe the only bond that really held, no matter what. It was about loyalty and love, also competition and anger and hurt—on both sides. And then, on January 1, 2015, the very day of Andrew's second-term inauguration, the bond was broken.

Struggling with heart disease, Mario had gone to the hospital almost immediately after Andrew's election victory. Through December he had weakened, until his doctors advised there was no more to be done. It was time to go home, to surround himself with family and twenty-four-hour care until the inevitable end.

A first inauguration was, by tradition, done in Albany on New Year's Eve. So it had been for Andrew in 2010, and for his father before him. Now came word that Mario was fading. Andrew canceled the ceremony and rushed to his parents' Sutton Place apartment. At his father's bedside, he read aloud excerpts of the inauguration speech he was to give the next day at the new One World Trade Center in downtown Manhattan, to be followed by a second, somewhat different version in Buffalo—so that Andrew would be honoring both sides of the state.

The speech started strong and then got better. Consciously or not, Andrew wove in phrases and sentiments his father might have used. "We've seen the national unrest and the national discord," Andrew read. "The American promise itself is being questioned. The offer of fairness and opportunity that was the American compact is now in doubt... While American capitalism never guaranteed success, it did guarantee opportunity... For previous generations, our education system offered hope. It was the escalator out of poverty. The public education system could take an Italian immigrant's son from the back of a grocery store in South Jamaica to become the governor of New York State..."

Drawn and diminished, Mario listened to the familiar cadences, the images and rhythms taken up and given new life by the son he loved so much—the son who was, perhaps, so much like him that that was where the problems began. At the end he smiled. "Pretty good," he said, "for a second termer."

The next day, Andrew gave his first speech for a crowd at One World Trade Center that included all the state's dignitaries, Sandra Lee and his daughters, and a sea of Cuomo family loyalists. The speech wound its way to early-nineteenth-century governor DeWitt Clinton, whose vision of the Erie Canal had made New York the economic engine of the country. "They said it can't be done, it's too ambitious, but he did it on time and on budget. That's who we are! That's the stock we come from," Andrew said, his voice rising. "You give us adversity, we turn it into opportunity. You try to divide us, we come back more united and tighter than ever before."

The speech was bold and impassioned, maybe the best speech that Andrew Mark Cuomo had ever given. It ended on a grace note: E. B. White's image of New York to the nation as the white church spire was to the village, the visible symbol of aspiration and faith, a very Mario-like allusion. Mario, on his Sutton Place deathbed, was listening. That evening, not long after Andrew's second speech in Buffalo, the fifty-second governor died.

For a day or so, the family remained in seclusion. Then Andrew broke his silence. In what became the second termer's first public words, he said simply, "There is a hole in my heart that I fear is going to be there forever."

Outside the Frank E. Campbell Funeral Chapel on Madison Avenue, hundreds of mourners filed in one by one to pay their respects, with television cameras recording their solemn progression. The funeral was held a short walk away at St. Ignatius Loyola, the Catholic cathedral on Park Avenue at 84th Street. The full-to-brimming congregation included former president Bill Clinton and former secretary of state Hillary Clinton; Mayor Bill de Blasio and his wife, Chirlane; and former mayor Michael Bloomberg. Mario's oldest son, his proud successor, gave the eulogy. "At his core he was a philosopher," Andrew told the crowd. "He was a poet. He was an advocate. He was a crusader. Mario Cuomo was the keynote speaker for our better angels."

Mario, his son suggested, wasn't really a politician at all. "Mario Cuomo's politics were more a personal belief system than a traditional theory. It was who he was. Not what he did." That was gracious and true, if also perhaps imbued with a nuance—that as governor, Mario stood taller for his beliefs than his accomplishments. No matter: he was a rare and remarkable figure, passionate and inspiring. Andrew, in his eulogy, scoffed at the "dime-store psychoanalysis of our quote-unquote complex father-and-son relationship." The pundits' perceptions were "all a lot of hooey," Andrew declared. "And it's this simple: I was devoted to my father, from the time I was fifteen, joining him in every crusade. My dad was my hero, he was my best friend, he was my confidant and my mentor."

Andrew had spent more than half a century attached to this man who was his father, trying to please him even as he vied to outdo him, filled with love and admiration, resentment and hurt. Now, on his own, the fifty-sixth governor of New York State would press on, in mourning and, perhaps, free.

Notes

Chapter 1: The High Point

As the fifty-sixth governor: Michael Barbaro, "Behind N.Y. Gay Marriage, an Unlikely Mix of Forces," *New York Times*, June 25, 2011.

Cohen was a former: Danny Hakim, "Andrew M. Cuomo," *New York Times*, May 5, 2012.

Of the four: Nicholas Confessore and Michael Barbaro, "Once Against Gay Marriage, 4 Senators Say They Will Back It," *New York Times*, June 13, 2011.

"The only question": Author interview with a person familiar with the matter.

By Monday: Confessore and Barbaro, "Once Against Gay Marriage, 4 Senators Say They Will Back It."

Back in 2009: Ken Lovett, "Alesi: I Can Vote for a Gay Marriage Bill," *New York Daily News*, June 13, 2011.

Caught on camera: "New York NOW Exclusive—Alesi Agonizes over Vote," YouTube video, 0:11, posted by WMHT, December 2, 2009, http://www.youtube.com/watch?v=zwdCa5E6i8U.

The governor invited: Barbaro, "Behind N.Y. Gay Marriage, an Unlikely Mix of Forces."

"I'm not out": Jimmy Vielkind, "GOP Senator from Saratoga Becomes 31st Vote for Same-Sex Marriage Bill," Albany *Times Union*, June 15, 2011, http://www.timesunion.com/local/article/GOP-senator-from-Saratoga-becomes-31st-vote-for-1424481.php#ixzz1PMqXqoNl.

"I'm tired": Nicholas Confessore and Danny Hakim, "Gay Marriage Is One Vote Shy of Clearing State Senate," *New York Times*, June 14, 2011.

Descendant: Allison Hoffman, "Jewish Lawmaker Key to N.Y. Marriage Bill," *Tablet* (blog), June 17, 2011, http://www.tabletmag.com/scroll/70277/jewish-lawmaker-holds-key-to-n-y-marriage-bill.

"I need to know": Author interview with a person familiar with the matter.

That evening: *New York Post*, "Gov's Out There," June 16, 2011, http://pagesix.com/2011/06/16/govs-out-there/.

Whose thirty-one-year-old brother: Joshua David Stein, "The Semi Homemade World of Sandra Lee," *Out*, April 3, 2011, http://www.out.com/entertainment/television/2011/04/03/semi-homemade-world-sandra-lee.

That weekend: The following passage, including unattributed quotes, is based on author interviews with individuals familiar with the matter.

Charges of bribery: Michael Barbaro, Alison Leigh Cowan, and Ashley Parker, "A Senator's Shadow Family," *New York Times*, March 19, 2011. Kruger later pleaded guilty to federal corruption charges in December 2011 and was sentenced to seven years in prison.

"My intellectual and emotional journey": New York State Senate, "Senator Saland's Statement on Marriage Equality," news release, June 25, 2011, http://www.nysenate.gov/press-release/senator-salands-statement-marriage-equality.

"New York has finally": New York State Government, "Governor Cuomo Announces Passage of Marriage Equality Act," news release, June 24, 2011, http://www.governor.ny.gov/press/062411passageofmarriageequality.

It would double: Bill Keller, "A Decent Proposal," *New York Times*, June 26, 2011.

"The aggregation of power": The following passage, including unattributed quotes, is based on author interviews with individuals familiar with the matter.

The end of his marriage: Jennifer Steinhauer, "Kennedy-Cuomo Union Appears to Be Ending," *New York Times*, July 1, 2003. See also David Saltonstall, Celeste Katz, and Maggie Haberman, "Andy Figured It Out: He Took Suspicions to Other Man's Wife," *New York Daily News*, July 6, 2003.

"Very few politicians": Author interview with political consultant Robert Shrum.

Later his father: Author interview with a person familiar with the matter.

"We don't like negatives": The following passage, including unattributed quotes, is based on author interviews with individuals familiar with the matter.

Big real estate developers: Kenneth Lovett, "Gov. Cuomo Got $100,000 from Developer, Then Signed Law Giving It Big Tax Breaks," *New York Daily News*, August 9, 2013, http://www.nydailynews.com/new-york/cuomo-100k-developer-signing-tax-break-law-article-1.1422003.

Andrew shuts it down: Susanne Craig, William K. Rashbaum, and Thomas Kaplan, "Cuomo's Office Hobbled Ethics Inquiries by Moreland Commission," *New York Times*, July 23, 2014.

Chapter 2: The Men in the Family

Shortly after Andrew's birth: Robert S. McElvaine, *Mario Cuomo: A Biography* (New York: Scribner, 1988), 150.

Not by chance: Queens Borough Public Library, Bulletin 647, April 1939, archived on the Dunton family website, http://www.dunton.org/archive/DuntonQueens1939.htm.

"Puncha, puncha, puncha": Paul Grondahl, "A Political Legacy That's Steeped in the Bloodline," Albany *Times Union*, February 7, 2011.

"Andrea was fond": Author interview with George Haggerty Jr., a childhood friend of Andrew Cuomo.

Andrea was the patriarch: McElvaine, *Mario Cuomo*, 30–35.

The corner groceries: Author interview with Tony Gallo, a former classmate of Andrew Cuomo.

"Don't fool around": McElvaine, *Mario Cuomo*, 35.

"When he did start school": McElvaine, *Mario Cuomo*, 50.

He ended up in Brooklyn: Michael Oreskes, "Man in the News; Rising Voice in Democratic Ranks," *New York Times*, July 16, 1984.

Years later: Author interview with a person familiar with the matter.

The Cuomos returned one night: Personal journals of Mario Cuomo, entry for October 22, 1982, http://www.kimhill.com/other/cuomo/tree.html.

He published a children's story: Mario Cuomo, *The Blue Spruce* (Chelsea, Michigan: Sleeping Bear Press, 1999).

In 2009: Christine Haughney, "From Queens Roots, Cuomo Clan Branched Out," *New York Times*, May 3, 2010.

There were, as Matilda Cuomo acknowledged: McElvaine, *Mario Cuomo*, 155.

Mario had made his name: Eliot Brown, "Willets Point, a Development Waterloo?" *New York Observer*, February 19, 2008. See also Clayton Knowles, "City Faces Suit on World's Fair Parking Project," *New York Times*, September 25, 1963, and Thomas Buckley, "Junkmen Battle the Fair to Stay in Business," *New York Times*, April 12, 1964.

Once the site: "Mayor: Valley of Ashes in 'Great Gatsby' Was Inspired by Willets Point," WNYC, June 14, 2012, http://www.wnyc.org/story/216534-blog-mayor-valley-ashes-great-gatsby-was-inspired-willets-point/.

Corona, Queens, was threatened: Thomas L. Waite, "Corona '88: It's Schools Now, Not Homes," *New York Times*, July 10, 1988. See also Jack Newfield, "Corona Compromise," *Village Voice*, November 19, 1970, and Jonathan Mahler, *Ladies and Gentlemen, the Bronx Is Burning: 1977, Baseball, Politics, and the Battle for the Soul of a City* (New York: Picador, 2006), 104–108.

Andrew, now thirteen: Author interview with a person familiar with the matter. See also Joanna Molloy, "Andrew Cuomo: An Oral History," *Esquire*, May 13, 2010, http://www.esquire.com/features/andrew-cuomo-bio-0510.

"That was a big deal": Author interview with Tony Gallo.

As secretary of HUD: Author interview with a person familiar with the matter.

"My father": Steve Fishman, "The Cuomo Family Business," *New York*, August 1, 2010, http://nymag.com/news/politics/67397/#print.

When the journalist: Reporting notes of Ken Auletta from his coverage of the 1982 New York City mayoral campaign.

"Matilda was *the* formative influence": Author interview with Cuomo family friend Dino Amoroso.

"She did the family": Reporting notes of Ken Auletta from his coverage of the 1982 New York City mayoral campaign.

A self-educated carpenter: McElvaine, *Mario Cuomo*, 131.

"One day Andrew said": Author interview with Tony Gallo.

Bonus from the Pittsburgh Pirates: *Sports Illustrated*, "Back When Cuomo Was a Contender," June 20, 1988, http://www.si.com/vault/1988/06/20/117896/back-when-cuomo-was-a-contender.

The truth was darker: Author interview with a person familiar with the matter.

"I was the oldest boy": Lois Romano, "The Cuomo Behind Cuomo," *Washington Post*, August 8, 1986.

"The face on Andrew": Abigail Pogrebin, "Andrew Cuomo's Quest for Camelot," *Talk*, August 2001.

One colleague: Author interview with a CNN colleague of Christopher Cuomo.

Tony Gallo: Author interview with Tony Gallo.

One classmate: Author interview with a former classmate of Andrew Cuomo.

"I thought": Author interview with former Andrew Cuomo teacher John Diorio.

When Tony Gallo: Author interview with Tony Gallo.

At fourteen he launched: Pogrebin, "Andrew Cuomo's Quest for Camelot."

For fun: Author interview with Robert Caracciolo, a childhood friend of Andrew Cuomo.

"In mechanics": Michael Barbaro, "Indulging an Obsession with Motors and Muscle," *New York Times*, October 28, 2010.

After school and on weekends: Author interview with George Haggerty, a childhood friend of Andrew Cuomo.

A sky blue 1975 Corvette: Barbaro, "Indulging an Obsession with Motors and Muscle."

"You tend to deal": Ibid.

He had made a first: McElvaine, *Mario Cuomo*, 202.

"It's a lost art": Romano, "The Cuomo Behind Cuomo."

Crude: William B. Falk, "A Son to Be Reckoned With," *Newsday*, June 11, 1991.

Eagerly, John Diorio: Author interview with John Diorio.

Andrew signed on to work: Author interviews with childhood friends of Andrew Cuomo.

That fall, at his father's insistence: Falk, "A Son to Be Reckoned With."

Chapter 3: From Andy to Andrew

The first day: Author interview with former Andrew Cuomo classmate Rich Mulieri.

"Q-15": Author interview with George Haggerty, a childhood friend of Andrew Cuomo.

The ill-fated road trip: Author interviews with friends of Andrew Cuomo who went on the Florida trip.

Managing the Bronx: Anna Quindlen, "About New York; the Sudden Popularity of Andrew Cuomo," *New York Times*, November 6, 1982.

One night: Author interview with former Mario Cuomo aide Joe Spinelli. See also Grondahl, "A Political Legacy That's Steeped in the Bloodline."

Al Gordon: Author interview with Al Gordon, a former campaign staffer for Mario Cuomo.

Richard Starkey: Author interview with media consultant Richard Starkey.

A gentler view: Author interview with Abraham Lincoln scholar Harold Holzer.

"I know the kitchen table": Fishman, "The Cuomo Family Business."

Koch won the runoff: Frank Lynn, "Cuomo to Stay in Race," *New York Times*, September 20, 1977.

As political consultant Bruce Gyory: Author interview with political consultant Bruce Gyory.

"Every night": Author interview with a veteran political consultant.

Andrew denied: Jen Chung, "Ed Koch Held Decades-Long Grudge against Cuomos over 'Vote for Cuomo, Not the Homo' Posters," Gothamist.com, February 1, 2013, http://gothamist.com/2013/02/01/ed_koch_forgave_mario_and_andrew_fo.php.

One school of thought: Author interview with a person familiar with the matter.

Mario denied: McElvaine, *Mario Cuomo*, 251–252.

"The way in which": Edward I. Koch, *Mayor: An Autobiography* (New York: Simon & Schuster, 1984).

There weren't just a few: Sean Patrick Farrell, "Last Word: Ed Koch" (videotaped interview), *New York Times*, February 1, 2013, tape mark 07.00.

Later, Koch reversed: McElvaine, *Mario Cuomo*, 253.

Four days: Author interview with journalist Howard Blum.

That view was echoed: Farrell, "Last Word: Ed Koch," tape mark 07.00.

Honorable 42 percent: Lee Dembart, "Koch Starts Building Staff, with Costikyan as First Mayor," *New York Times*, November 10, 1977.

In a parking lot: Author interview with a person familiar with the matter.

This wasn't the end: Fishman, "The Cuomo Family Business."

"Andrew was my little man": Author interview with a person familiar with the matter.

One night on a dark street: Joe Klein, "The Meaning of Mario," *New York*, June 14, 1982.

Andrew was paying: Reporting notes of Ken Auletta from his coverage of the 1982 New York City mayoral campaign.

He and his father: Elizabeth A. Harris, "Cuomo's Albany Housing, from Old Hotel to Mansion," *New York Times*, January 1, 2011.

"Think of": Jennifer Senior, "The Name of the Father," *New York*, March 27, 2006.

Matilda would hear: Romano, "The Cuomo Behind Cuomo."

Gary Eisenman: Author interview with Gary Eisenman, a law school friend of Andrew Cuomo.

Andrew brought a bright green parrot: Senior, "The Name of the Father."

He hung a picture: Pogrebin, "Andrew Cuomo's Quest for Camelot."

To ward him off: Jeanie Kasindorf, "The Other Cuomo," *New York*, March 21, 1988.

On his first day: Author interview with Pete Schwarz, a law school friend of Andrew Cuomo.

"He was a good listener": Author interview with Bruce McKeegan, a law school friend of Andrew Cuomo.

Gary Eisenman: Author interview with Gary Eisenman.

Pete Schwarz's father: Author interview with Pete Schwarz.

One of his professors: Author interview with Albany Law School professor Michael Hutter.

"The way we used to study": Author interview with Gary Eisenman.

"He was down the court": Author interview with Bruce McKeegan.

One weekend: Author interview with Gary Eisenman.

"Soaking wet": Author interview with Pete Schwarz.

"He would work": Author interview with Pete Schwarz.

"He drove": Author interview with Gary Eisenman.

The firm, recently founded: Selwyn Raab, "At Andrew Cuomo's Firm, Politics and the Law Intersect," *New York Times*, August 27, 1986.

Lucille had come into Mario's orbit: Molloy, "Andrew Cuomo: An Oral History."

She was also beautiful: The following passage, including unattributed quotes, is based on author interviews with friends of Andrew Cuomo.

One night: Author interview with Gary Eisenman.

That July, Andrea Cuomo: "Father of Mario Cuomo Dies," *New York Times*, July 3, 1981.

Andrew inherited: Kasindorf, "The Other Cuomo."

Chapter 4: A Loyalty Like Heat

On January 15: E. J. Dionne Jr., "Carey Rules Out Race for 3d Term; Wide Field Likely," *New York Times*, January 16, 1982.

With Carey's withdrawal: Maurice Carroll, "Cuomo Vows 'Friendly' Run against Koch for Statehouse," *New York Times*, February 23, 1982.

A month later: "Koch, Announcing for Governor, Promises to Serve 'All the People,' *New York Times*, February 23, 1982.

"Politics is a game": Author interview with New York legislator Mel Miller.

One Cuomo worker: Author interview with a person familiar with the matter.

Family friends: Reporting notes of Ken Auletta from his coverage of the 1982 New York City mayoral campaign.

Auletta, who at the time: Dan Rattiner, "Who's Here: Ken Auletta, Writer," *Dan's Papers*, June 27, 2013.

At first: Kasindorf, "The Other Cuomo."

In a *Playboy* interview: Clyde Haberman, "Ridiculed Suburbs in Jest, Koch Says," *New York Times*, February 25, 1982. See also David Wallis, "Albany, Hub of the Empire State," *New York Times*, November 24, 2006.

Maureen Connelly: Author interview with media consultant Maureen Connelly.

Andrew would settle: Quindlen, "About New York; the Sudden Popularity of Andrew Cuomo."

A day or two: Author interview with Mark Gordon, a former campaign aide to Mario Cuomo.

The dingy walls: Quindlen, "About New York; the Sudden Popularity of Andrew Cuomo."

One was Gary: Author interviews with individuals familiar with the matter.

You have to divide: Quindlen, "About New York; the Sudden Popularity of Andrew Cuomo."

"Andrew didn't stand down": Author interview with Dino Amoroso.

"Andrew pushes his father": William Triplett, "Eyes on the Prize," *Washingtonian*, September 2000.

Erastus Corning II: M. A. Farber, "Erastus Corning 2d, Albany Mayor Since '42, Dies," *New York Times*, May 29, 1983.

Publicly: Author interview with a person who worked on Mario Cuomo's 1982 gubernatorial campaign.

On local television: Kasindorf, "The Other Cuomo."

Andrew was called over: Senior, "The Name of the Father."

All three: Richard J. Meislin, "Friedman Is Guilty with 3 in Scandal," *New York Times*, November 26, 1986. See also Richard D. Lyons, "Meade Esposito, 86, Former Power in Politics, Is Dead," *New York Times*, September 4, 1993, and Richard J. Meislin, "Manes's Death: A Frantic Call, a Fatal Thrust," *New York Times*, March 15, 1986. Stan Friedman was convicted on corruption charges in 1986 and Meade Esposito in 1987, while Donald Manes would commit suicide in 1986 before charges were even brought, when a friend who had pled guilty to related charges agreed to testify against him.

"You've got us beat": Senior, "The Name of the Father."

Andrew told them no: Kasindorf, "The Other Cuomo."

Mario Cuomo had not just reached: Frank Lynn, "The Democrats Designate Koch for Statehouse," *New York Times*, June 22, 1982.

He found: Quindlen, "About New York; the Sudden Popularity of Andrew Cuomo."

Every morning: Kasindorf, "The Other Cuomo."

Gotbaum loathed Koch: Author interview with Norman Adler.

Yet Adler: Grondahl, "A Political Legacy That's Steeped in the Bloodline."

"I like to think": Fishman, "The Cuomo Family Business."

"It went beyond": Author interview with a person familiar with the matter.

The Prince of Darkness: Grondahl, "A Political Legacy That's Steeped in the Bloodline."

"Mario bestowed power": Author interview with a person familiar with the matter.

"He has no real friends": Author interview with a person familiar with the matter.
Even Gary Eisenman: Author interview with Gary Eisenman.
One day: Author interview with Mark Gordon.
On another day: Author interview with Norman Adler.
That was power: Pogrebin, "Andrew Cuomo's Quest for Camelot."
Norm Adler: Author interview with Norman Adler.
A young, creative pollster: Author interview with election pollster Robert Sullivan.
A bit later that night: Author interview with a person familiar with the matter.
His family's Rite Aid: Leslie Wayne, "Lehrman's Path to Race for Governor," *New York Times*, October 21, 1982.
No television commercials: Michael Oreskes, "Lehrman Has Spent $8 Million on Campaign and Cuomo $1 Million," *New York Times*, October 5, 1982.
All told: Ken Auletta, "Profiles: Governor Mario Cuomo," *New Yorker*, April 9 and April 16, 1984.
"It was one": Author interview with journalist E. J. Dionne Jr.
Cuomo scored his best shot: Frank Lynn, "Cuomo Clashes with Lehrman in First Debate," *New York Times*, October 8, 1982.
Ads would cost money: McElvaine, *Mario Cuomo*, 301.
"You could see these slopes": Author interview with a person familiar with the matter.
"A key lieutenant": Author interview with a person familiar with the matter.
The race was tighter: E. J. Dionne Jr., "The Polls: A Look Back at the Fluctuations," *New York Times*, November 4, 1982.
"Everybody is after Andrew": Quindlen, "About New York; the Sudden Popularity of Andrew Cuomo."
The pay was small: Grondahl, "A Political Legacy That's Steeped in the Bloodline."

Chapter 5: The Enforcer

"The condition": Michael Oreskes, "Reporter's Notebook: Transition and Transit," *New York Times*, December 23, 1982.
Christopher Cuomo: Michael Barbaro, "Stately Home Awaits the Return of a Political Son," *New York Times*, November 3, 2010.
Ten days: Edward A. Gargan, "Cuomo Assumes a Key Role in the Ossining Prison Crisis," *New York Times*, January 10, 1983.
Governor Cuomo: "An Investigation of Allegations Arising from the Liberal Party Factional Dispute" (report), Temporary Commission of Investigation of the State of New York, March 1984.
At the big party meeting: Frank Lynn, "After 17 Hours of Tumult, Harding is Liberals' Boss," *New York Times*, January 31, 1983.
One profile: Grondahl, "A Political Legacy That's Steeped in the Bloodline."
"He was a nasty piece": Author interview with a reporter who covered Albany.
"He was just curt": Author interview with a former aide to Governor Mario Cuomo.
"I did not deal with Andrew": Romano, "The Cuomo behind Cuomo."
A more charitable view: Auletta, "Profiles: Governor Mario Cuomo."
Soon, he was having dinner: Author interview with journalist Ken Auletta.
At one point: Reporting notes of Ken Auletta from his coverage of Mario Cuomo's first year as governor of New York.
That March: "Cronyism, Inside and Out," *New York Times*, March 17, 1983.

Ten days after: Edward A. Gargan, "Cuomo's Nominee to Head U.D.C. Steps Aside Pending Confirmation," *New York Times*, March 17, 1983.

"The Little Cuomo": Falk, "A Son to Be Reckoned With."

"You have to understand": Romano, "The Cuomo Behind Cuomo."

Adam Nagourney: Author interview with journalist Adam Nagourney.

Another, George Arzt: Author interview with journalist and media consultant George Arzt.

By the early 1980s: John McDonald and Penny Loeb, "Influential Developer as Partner," *New York Newsday*, June 18, 1989, http://s3.documentcloud.org/documents/7293/influential-developer-as-partner.pdf.

Jerry Weiss: Frank Lynn, "Developer in the Andrew Cuomo Suit," *New York Times*, December 25, 1987.

Arco, a management company: McDonald and Loeb, "Influential Developer as Partner."

The state was moving: Temporary Commission of Investigation of the State of New York, "A Report on the World Trade Center Move-Out," May 1986.

He wanted Partridge: Kirk Johnson, "Major Contributor to Cuomo to Testify at a Bribery Trial," *New York Times*, November 25, 1987.

"Threatened to ruin": Lynn, "Developer in the Andrew Cuomo Suit."

Andrew was involved: Investigation Commission, "A Report on the World Trade Center Move-Out." Andrew Cuomo consistently maintained that he became involved in the Broome Street matter to protect the state's interests, citing the conclusions of the State Investigation Commission's May 1986 report for support. The commission had found that in leasing matters, several former General Services employees had "exhibited a general disregard of ethical concerns and conflicts of interest."

In late 1983: Lynn, "Andrew Cuomo Embroiled in Dispute."

Partridge soon found himself charged: Kirk Johnson, "Former Official Accused of Role in Leasing Case," *New York Times*, July 2, 1986.

Eventually he was found innocent: *People of the State of New York v. Joseph Siggia and Harry Partridge*, Appellant Division of the Supreme Court of the State of New York, First Department, July 10, 1990. 163 A.D. 2d, 113 (1990).

That November: Frank Lynn, "New York's Voters Give Approval to $1.25 Billion State Bond Issue," *New York Times*, November 9, 1983.

He seemed to trust: Author interview with a former staffer to Governor Mario Cuomo.

"He's like a guy": Reporting notes of Ken Auletta from his coverage of Mario Cuomo's first year as governor of New York.

That summer: Michael Oreskes, "Reporter's Notebook: Cuomo Goes His Own Way on A-Plants," *New York Times*, August 7, 1983.

He and Gary Eisenman studied together: Author interview with Gary Eisenman.

"He comes in with his guys": Author interview with a person familiar with the matter.

He would go to work: Michael Oreskes, "Son of Cuomo Will Join Staff of Prosecutor," *New York Times*, April 12, 1984.

Chapter 6: A Cause to Embrace

Charles Raffa: Leonard Buder, "Two Men Beat Father-in-Law of the Governor," *New York Times*, May 23, 1984.

Journalist Nick Pileggi: Nicholas Pileggi, "Cuomo and Those Rumors," *New York*, November 2, 1987.

The known facts: Buder, "Two Men Beat Father-in-Law of the Governor." See also Associated Press, "Cuomo Goes to See His Father-in-Law, a Victim of Beating," May 24, 1984.

***New York Times* reporter Selwyn Raab:** Selwyn Raab, "Unorthodox Steps in Inquiry on a Cuomo Relative," *New York Times*, October 28, 1987.

The incident was deeply upsetting: Author interview with a former staffer to governor Mario Cuomo.

At his World Trade Center offices: Author interview with a former staffer to governor Mario Cuomo.

An hour before: Romano, "The Cuomo Behind Cuomo."

Out at the podium: Mario Cuomo, 1984 Democratic National Convention Keynote Address (video and transcript), San Francisco, July 16, 1984, http://www.americanrhetoric.com/speeches/mariocuomo1984dnc.htm.

Andrew had won: Associated Press, "Son of Governor Quits as D.A. Aide to Join Law Firm," May 23, 1985, http://news.google.com/newspapers?nid=1917&dat=19850523&id=wgshAAAAIBAJ&sjid=mXIFAAAAIBAJ&pg=1302,1777261.

And yet among his peers: Author interview with a person familiar with the situation.

Later, though: Gerson Borrero, "Gerson Borrerro Sits Down with Wayne Barrett" (video interview), *City & State*, May 29, 2014, tape mark 6:55, http://www.cityandstateny.com/27/28/politics/gerson-borrero-sits-down-with-wayne-barrett-part-one.html#.VBl9Deemf3p.

Lucille Falcone was handling: Wayne Barrett, "The Cuomo Sleaze Team," *Village Voice*, August 16, 1988.

Andrew was installed on the board: Lynn, "Developer in the Andrew Cuomo Suit."

If Andrew wasn't on track: Frank Lynn, "Andrew Cuomo to Shift to Full-Time Housing Work," *New York Times*, October 18, 1988. See also Jonathan Mahler, "The Making of Andrew Cuomo," *New York Times*, August 11, 2010.

By now, the romance: Author interview with Gary Eisenman.

Among Andrew's girlfriends: Author interview with a person familiar with the matter.

She would also be linked: Ruth Graham, "Celebrating 10 Years of Aiding Public Schools," *New York Sun*, April 6, 2005, http://www.nysun.com/on-the-town/celebrating-10-years-of-aiding-public-schools/11802/.

Goldstein was a fascinating: McDonald and Loeb, "Influential Developer as Partner." See also Michael Winerip, "Local Role in H.U.D. Hearings," *New York Times*, August 6, 1989. Alfonse D'Amato has long maintained that he sought no favors from the U.S. Department of Housing and Urban Development.

Responding to a lawsuit: Robin Herman, "Pact Requires City to Shelter Homeless Men," *New York Times*, August 27, 1981.

One cold evening: "Our History," *Homes for the Homeless* website, http://www.hfhnyc.org/abouthfh/ourhistory.asp.

Stern envisioned: Jeffrey Schmalz, "Cuomo Backs Proposal to House 2,000 Families," *New York Times*, December 20, 1985.

Royce Mulholland: Author interview with real estate developer Royce Mulholland, a former aide to governor Mario Cuomo.

"Once Andrew got involved": Author interview with a homeless advocate in New York.

Robert Esnard: Author interview with former New York City deputy mayor Robert Esnard.

"How do you begin": Jeffrey Schmalz, "Families' Shelter Set for Brooklyn," *New York Times*, February 19, 1986.

"Andrew can look at a spoon": Author interview with Royce Mulholland.

"Here's my beef with Andrew": Author interview with a person who worked as a New York City homeless advocate in the 1980s.

Andrew was again profiled: Jeffrey Schmalz, "Younger Cuomo Steps from Father's Shadow," *New York Times*, March 14, 1986.

After the election: Michael Oreskes, "Cuomo's Solo Campaign Drive Leaves Undercurrent of Discontent in Party," *New York Times*, November 6, 1986.

Hirschfeld had gathered: Frank Lynn, "A Risky Challenge: Cuomo Push on Hirschfeld's Petitions Would Be an Expensive One to Lose," *New York Times*, August 12, 1986.

If they could show: Jane Gross, "City Voters to Testify in Suit over Hirschfeld's Petitions," *New York Times*, August 11, 1986.

Judge Vincent Bradley: Jeffrey Schmalz, "Cuomo Defending Aides' Efforts to Take Hirschfeld from Ballot," *New York Times*, August 22, 1986.

Pictures of Hirschfeld: Kiley Armstrong, "Lawyer Is Responsible for Petition Debacle, Tearful Hirschfeld Says," Associated Press, August 21, 1986.

He appealed: Frank Lynn, "Hirschfeld Loses in Top Court and Quits Race," *New York Times*, August 29, 1986.

"I'm not the arrogant one": Frank Lynn, "Politicians Find a Flaw in Cuomo Election Plan," *New York Times*, October 2, 1986.

A landslide, 65 percent: Oreskes, "Cuomo's Solo Campaign Drive."

"If anything could change my mind": Jon Margolis, "Mario Cuomo and the Ethnic Factor," *Chicago Tribune*, January 27, 1986.

Andrew had told the press: Michael Oreskes and Selwyn Raab, "At Andrew Cuomo's Firm, Politics and Law Intersect," *New York Times*, August 27, 1986.

***A New York Times* editorial:** "Why Do Clients Hire Andrew Cuomo?" *New York Times*, October 11, 1986.

An attack by columnist William Safire: William Safire, "The New Rainmaker," *New York Times*, August 28, 1986.

Weeks after his outsized win: Jeffrey Schmalz, "Cuomo and the Press: Time of Tension," *New York Times*, November 22, 1986.

Chapter 7: In Search of a Killing

Governor Cuomo's State of the State: Michael Oreskes, "Approval of Thruway Exit Revives 25-Year Dispute," *New York Times*, August 14, 1987.

A conglomerate: Ann Botshon, *Saving Sterling Forest: The Epic Struggle to Preserve New York's Highlands* (Albany: State University of New York Press, 2006), 20–30.

"My objection": Oreskes, "Approval of Thruway Exit Revives 25-Year Dispute."

Unconcerned, Governor Cuomo: Barrett, "The Cuomo Sleaze Team."

Investigative journalist Wayne Barrett: Ibid.

Bruce Bean: Author interview with Bruce Bean, a former lawyer for City Investing.

Sterling Forest manager: Author interview with Ken Heim, a Sterling Forest manager in the 1980s.

Andrew didn't say: Oreskes, "Approval of Thruway Exit Revives 25-Year Dispute."

The sewage: Robert Hanley, "Disputes Over Forest Turn Fierce," *New York Times*, November 22, 1988.

Interior took a serious look: Frank Lynn, "Building of Thruway Exit is Delayed," *New York Times*, October 17, 1987. This passage is also based on a letter from former U.S. National Park Service Regional Director James W. Coleman to Orin Lehman, the former commissioner of the New York State Office of Parks, Recreation and Historic Preservation, September 14, 1987.

Estimated cost: Frank Lynn, "Regan Opposes Thruway Exit at Sterling Forest," *New York Times*, December 28, 1988.

One day in December: Lynn, "Regan Opposes Thruway Exit at Sterling Forest."

Sam Dealey: Sam Dealey and James Ring Adams, "Banking on Andy Cuomo," *American Spectator*, January 1999.

First pair of lawsuits: *Oceanmark Federal Savings and Loan Association v. Andrew Cuomo et al.*, Circuit Court of the Seventeen Judicial Circuit, Broward County, Florida. Derivative Complaint for Money Damages, Injunctive Relief and Statutory Relief, December 22, 1987. Case 87-34662-CL. See also *Oceanmark Federal Savings & Loan Association v. Andrew Cuomo et al.*, U.S. District Court for the Southern District of Florida. Amended Complaint for Money Damages and Declaratory and Injunctive Relief, February 16, 1988. Case 87-cv-7020.

An Oceanmark board meeting: Minutes of July 21, 1987 meeting of the Oceanmark board of directors, 8-9.

They felt Oceanmark: *Oceanmark Federal Savings & Loan Association v. Andrew Cuomo et al.*, U.S. District Court for the Southern District of Florida. Affidavit of Plaintiff Lynn Fenster Smith in Support of Motion for Temporary Injunctive Relief, December 30, 1987, 4. Case 87-cv-7020.

In 1998: Sam Dealey's notes from his August 6, 1998, interview with Florida lawyer William Friedlander.

A key document: Unsigned, undated document submitted by plaintiff's lawyer in Oceanmark litigation.

"Members of the New York Group": *Oceanmark Federal Savings & Loan Association v. Andrew Cuomo et al.*, U.S. District Court for the Southern District of Florida. Amended Complaint for Money Damages and Declaratory and Injunctive Relief, February 16, 1988, 11-12. Case 87-cv-7020.

In a memo: Memo from developer Sheldon Goldstein to his then attorney, Andrew Cuomo, April 16, 1987.

Lynn Fenster Smith and her brother: Dealey and Adams, "Banking on Andy Cuomo."

That memo from Goldstein: Memo from developer Sheldon Goldstein to his then attorney, Andrew Cuomo, April 16, 1987.

In a memo: Memo from Andrew Cuomo to Goldstein et al., June 4, 1987.

In the federal complaint: *Oceanmark Federal Savings & Loan Association v. Andrew Cuomo et al.*, U.S. District Court for the Southern District of Florida. Amended Complaint for Money Damages and Declaratory and Injunctive Relief, February 16, 1988, 23. Case 87-cv-7020.

The New York Group declared: *Oceanmark Federal Savings & Loan Association v. Andrew Cuomo et al.*, U.S. District Court for the Southern District of Florida. Amended Complaint for Money Damages and Declaratory and Injunctive Relief, February 16, 1988, 47. Case 87-cv-7020.

In late November: Johnson, "Major Contributor to Cuomo to Testify at a Bribery Trial." See also Kirk Johnson, "Ex-New York Official is Convicted of Perjury," *New York Times*, January 15, 1988, and *People of the State of New York v. Joseph Siggia and Harry Partridge*, Appellant Division of the Supreme Court of the State of New York, First Department, July 10, 1990. 163 A.D. 2d, 113 (1990).

A group picture: A photograph shown to the author by a friend of Andrew Cuomo.

"If he's compartmentalized": Author interview with a friend of Andrew Cuomo.

Days before Christmas: Jeffrey Schmalz, "Housing for Homeless Families Opens in Brooklyn," *New York Times*, December 22, 1987.

"I don't want to see": Joyce Purnick, "Andrew Cuomo's Proposal for Shelter Runs into Snags," *New York Times*, September 23, 1986.

"This is my Christmas present": Schmalz, "Housing for Homeless Families Opens in Brooklyn."

"Andrew was very into the logo": Author interview with a former colleague of Andrew Cuomo.

Later that spring: Author interview with Royce Mulholland.

The suit alleged: *Oceanmark Federal Savings and Loan Association v. Andrew Cuomo et al.*, Circuit Court of the Seventeen Judicial Circuit, Broward County, Florida. Derivative Complaint for Money Damages, Injunctive Relief and Statutory Relief, December 22, 1987, 6-7. Case 87-34662-CL.

He said he no longer represented: Will Lester, "Thrift Files Civil Complaint over Allegations of Takeover," Associated Press, December 22, 1987.

He filed his own suit: Associated Press, "N.Y. Governor's Son Faces Suit over Thrift Dealings," December 23, 1987. Associated Press, "Andrew Cuomo Files Libel Suit in Florida," December 24, 1987. See also Don Melvin, "Cuomo's Son Files Suit Against Thrift Chairman," Fort Lauderdale *Sun Sentinel*, December 24, 1987.

"The stock is not for sale": United Press International, "Cuomo Son in Second Suit Thrift Files in U.S. Court," December 31, 1987.

In his later interview: Sam Dealey's notes from his August 6, 1998, interview with William Friedlander.

The two sides met: Don Melvin, "U.S. Investigating Andrew Cuomo Case," Fort Lauderdale *Sun Sentinel*, January 8, 1988.

On that next court date: Don Melvin, "Federal Court Ruling Favors Cuomo's Son," Fort Lauderdale *Sun Sentinel*, January 22, 1988.

The Fensters were indeed voted: Lane Kelley, "Fensters Removed from Thrift's Board," Fort Lauderdale *Sun Sentinel*, February 23, 1988.

On April 18: Jeffrey Schmalz, "Suit Involving Cuomo's Son over Savings-Loan Is Settled," *New York Times*, April 19, 1988. See also Associated Press, "Parties Settle Savings Lawsuits Involving Andrew Cuomo," April 19, 1988.

The Federal Home Loan: Melvin, "U.S. Investigating Andrew Cuomo Case."

On June 17, 1988: Agreement between the group of Oceanmark investors led by Sheldon Goldstein and the Federal Home Loan Bank Board, June 17, 1988.

Two years later: Dan Christensen, "Did Cuomo Come Clean?" *Miami Daily Business Review*, September 17, 1998.

Andrew's father had lashed out: Sam Roberts, "For Cuomo's Son, a Bold Venture to Aid the Poor," *New York Times*, December 24, 1987.

Chapter 8: Cuomolot

First on the list: James Feron, "Town Accepts Plan to Shelter the Homeless," *New York Times*, January 15, 1988.

A collective roar: Scott Raab, "The Perfect Prince of Cool," *Esquire*, November 1, 2000, http://www.esquire.com/perfect-prince-cool-0900.

700 residents: Sara Rimer, "Housing for Homeless Fuels Debate in Westchester Town," *New York Times*, January 23, 1988.

WestHELP would be financed: Feron, "Town Accepts Plan to Shelter the Homeless."

William O'Shaughnessy: Author interview with Westchester County broadcaster William O'Shaughnessy.

Late one night: Author interview with Westchester Country legislator Paul Feiner. See also Dealey and Adams, "Banking on Andrew Cuomo."

According to *Newsday*: Falk, "A Son to Be Reckoned With." When Andrew Cuomo's alleged threats against Feiner and DeMarco were first reported, Cuomo denied making them.

"He was a hard charger": Author interview with a friend of Andrew Cuomo.

Mayfair Knollwood: Sam Roberts, "In Westchester It May Become: Not in My Village," *New York Times*, November 10, 1988.

Mount Pleasant's supervisor: Kasindorf, "The Other Cuomo."

One night, Andrew met: Author interview with a Mount Vernon resident.

A profile in *New York* magazine: Kasindorf, "The Other Cuomo."

"He called them his monkeys": Author interview with a New York State politician.

In his five years as governor: Jeffrey Schmalz, "The Cuomo Years: The Words, the Deeds," *New York Times*, January 6, 1988.

"Leadership isn't a multiple-choice test": Jeffrey Schmalz, "The Mystery of Mario Cuomo," *New York Times*, May 15, 1988.

"You're telling me": Sam Roberts, "Mario Cuomo, Vocal Foe of Italian Stereotyping, Finally Sees 'The Godfather,'" *New York Times*, October 21, 2013.

He would die: "Charles Raffa, 84, Cuomo's Father-in-Law," *New York Times*, October 20, 1988.

Mount Vernon signed on: Michael Winerip, "How Mt. Vernon Avoided Racism: It Voted Yes," *New York Times*, September 30, 1988.

Andrew announced his departure: Lynn, "Andrew Cuomo to Shift to Full-Time Housing Work."

Tonio Burgos: Falk, "A Son to Be Reckoned With."

In making the switch: Lynn, "Andrew Cuomo to Shift to Full-Time Housing Work."

A *New York Times*: Ibid.

Kerry had just suffered: Author interview with a person familiar with the matter.

On their first date: Kevin Sack, "Andrew Cuomo," *New York Times*, March 2, 1994.

By the end of the tour: Pogrebin, "Andrew Cuomo's Quest for Camelot."

She did roll her eyes: Author interview with a person familiar with the matter.

"Andrew refused": Fishman, "The Cuomo Family Business."

The Cuomos, as one journalist noted: Mahler, "Making of Andrew Cuomo."

As Kerry later explained: Jennifer Steinhauer, "A Personality That Says Kennedy, in a Campaign by the Name of Cuomo," *New York Times*, August 28, 2002.

A messy estate battle: Peter Blauner, "All-Star Family Feud," *New York*, February 13, 1989.

"We had a picture": Author interview with political consultant Bill Lynch.
The couple spent the next year: Elizabeth Kolbert, "Wedding to Join a Cuomo and a Kennedy," *New York Times*, February 15, 1998.
Later, he described: Pogrebin, "Andrew Cuomo's Quest for Camelot."
The engagement was announced: Kolbert, "Wedding to Join a Cuomo and a Kennedy."
According to a new suit: Details of the 1990 lawsuit are recounted in *Oceanmark Bank v. Cuomo et al.*, Complaint for Declaratory and Ancillary Relief. U.S. District Court for the Southern District of Florida. 94-cv-6754.
The first time Andrew was deposed: Dealey and Adams, "Banking on Andy Cuomo." Another source is Sam Dealey's notes from his August 6, 1998 interview with William Friedlander.
The new agreement: Settlement agreement between Lynn and Jeffrey Fenster and the New York Group, May 1990.
The first time he visited: Author interview with a person familiar with the matter.
From the moment: Author interview with a person familiar with the matter.
Developer Donald Trump: Sack, "Andrew Cuomo."
The wedding: Maureen Dowd, "Cuomos and Kennedys Sit on Both Sides of the Aisle," *New York Times*, June 9, 1990.
Six-bedroom house: Haughney, "From Queens Roots, Cuomo Clan Branched Out."
Lucille, suggested a friend: Author interview with a friend of Andrew Cuomo.

Chapter 9: Waterloo in White Plains

A network of a thousand units: Falk, "A Son to Be Reckoned With."
Richard Motta: Author interview with Richard Motta, a former colleague of Andrew Cuomo.
Greenburgh scaled its last hurdle: James Feron, "Westhelp Wins but Faces a Delay," *New York Times*, April 29, 1990.
Andrew let a reporter: Falk, "A Son to Be Reckoned With."
Andrew had tried to charm: Author interview with Al Del Vecchio, the former mayor of White Plains, New York.
Andrew's shelter: Tessa Melvin, "White Plains Rejects Westhelp Project for Homeless," *New York Times*, September 8, 1991.
A videotape: Special meeting of the White Plains Common Council, September 3 and 4, 1991 (video), Public Access Channel 35 and the White Plains Cable Access Television Commission.
Mike Coffey: Author interview with former White Plains Common Council member Mike Coffey.
Rita Malmud: Author interview with former White Plains Common Council member Rita Malmud.
"Everything erupted": Author interview with Al Del Vecchio.
Andrew got a call: Author interview with a person familiar with the matter.
"I don't think it's necessary": Sam Roberts, "Same Challenges, Different Cuomo," *New York Times*, November 18, 1991.
Andrew went on to say: Sam Roberts, "Dinkins Plan for Shelters Dealt Setback," *New York Times*, November 19, 1991.
On October 11: Robin Toner, "In 'Waiting for Mario,' Only the Plot Goes On," *New York Times*, October 16, 1991.

All that morning: Author interview with a person close to New York governor Mario Cuomo.

At one such event: Author interview with a person familiar with the matter.

After one session: Author interview with homeless advocate George McDonald.

The report's findings leaked: Celia W. Dugger, "Report to Dinkins Urges Overhaul in Shelter System for the Homeless," *New York Times*, January 31, 1992.

The mayor waved off: Todd S. Purdum, "Pressure on Dinkins? Volatile Mix at City Hall Is Stirred by Panel's Proposals on the Homeless," *New York Times*, February 7, 1992.

In September 1992: Celia W. Dugger, "Placing Emphasis on Treatment, Dinkins Plans to Revamp Shelters," *New York Times*, September 22, 1992.

Bill Clinton had gone: CBS, *60 Minutes* episode, January 26, 1992, https://www.youtube.com/watch?v=5IpJUfy-Roo.

Flowers had then produced tapes: John J. Goldman, "Clinton Apologizes for Remarks About Cuomo," *Los Angeles Times*, January 29, 1992.

Andrew landed a spot: Triplett, "Eyes on the Prize."

"I got a call": Author interview with Henry Cisneros, a former secretary of the U.S. Department of Housing and Urban Development.

The names were announced: "Andrew Cuomo Named to a Post at H.U.D.," *New York Times*, February 3, 1993.

The Dinkins administration: Author interview with former New York senator Alfonse D'Amato.

Seven low-income housing projects: Kim I. Mills, "HUD's Ex-New York Regional Administrator Gets $125,000 Real Estate Job," Associated Press, July 27, 1989. See also Robert Pear, "U.S. Plans to Sell 7 Housing Projects in 3-State Region Without Bids," *New York Times*, May 12, 1982; John McDonald and Penny Loeb, "A Job for a Helpful HUD Official," *Newsday*, June 18, 1989; Michael Winerip, "Builders Helped by H.U.D. Aide Hired Him after He Left Agency," *New York Times*, July 28, 1989; Associated Press, "Congressman Accuses Ex-HUD Official of 'Cashing In,'" July 29, 1989; David Hess, "HUD Officer's Moves Aided Later Partners," *Philadelphia Inquirer*, July 29, 1989; and Penny Loeb, "All in the Family, HUD-Style," *Newsday*, December 29, 1989.

An ethics investigation: Lindsey Gruson, "Senate Panel Finds No Evidence to Warrant Action on D'Amato," *New York Times*, August 3, 1991.

"You could nitpick": Author interview with Alfonse D'Amato.

Chapter 10: Mr. Cuomo Goes to Washington

Hickory Hill: Author interviews with individuals who visited Hickory Hill at the time Andrew Cuomo moved in.

Art Agnos: Author interview with former HUD regional director Art Agnos.

HUD was an acronym: The website of the U.S. Department of Housing and Urban Development contains detailed information about the history of HUD and extensive archives, http://portal.hud.gov/hudportal/HUD?src=/about.

One cynical old-timer: Author interview with a person familiar with the matter.

"Almost any program": Author interview with a person familiar with the matter.

Watching television: Philip Shenon, "Samuel R. Pierce Jr., Ex-Housing Secretary, Dies at 78," *New York Times*, November 3, 2000.

"Ten floors of basement": U.S. Department of Housing and Urban Development, Prepared Remarks for Secretary of Housing and Urban Development Shaun Donovan at the HUD Summer Intern Event, June 24, 2009, http://portal.hud.gov/hudportal/HUD?src=/press/speeches_remarks_statements/2009/speech_06242009.

It had never once: Christopher Swope, "HUD the Unlovable," *Governing*, December 2002.

He had, as one observer: Sack, "Andrew Cuomo."

"Andrew was going 150 miles": This quote and other unattributed quotes that follow come from author interviews with former HUD staffers, unless otherwise noted.

"He does not rest easy": Lizette Alvarez, "It's Andrew Cuomo's Turn at Bat, and Some See Makings of Slugger," *New York Times*, January 4, 1998.

"He yelled at me": Pogrebin, "Andrew Cuomo's Quest for Camelot."

Andrew didn't deny: Raab, "The Perfect Prince of Cool."

"He wasn't necessarily": Author interview with Henry Cisneros.

Events at Hickory Hill: Author interview with a person familiar with the matter.

"Andrew wanted": Author interview with an adviser to former New York governor Mario Cuomo.

In his memoir: George Stephanopoulos, *All Too Human* (New York: Back Bay Books, 2000), 165–174.

According to a later account: Kevin Sack, "Cuomo Announces He Is Not Seeking Seat on High Court," *New York Times*, April 8, 1993.

Over the next several weeks: Stephanopoulos, *All Too Human*, 165–174.

The close adviser: Author interview with an adviser to former New York governor Mario Cuomo.

One staffer: Author interview with a former HUD official.

Andrew held a cocktail party: Sack, "Andrew Cuomo."

He had begun to regard: Author interview with Henry Cisneros.

He and Kerry were invited: Sack, "Andrew Cuomo."

Unfortunately, Andrew and Kerry: Author interview with a person familiar with the matter.

The president sent him: David M. Halbfinger and Nicholas Confessore, "Cuomo's Former Boss, Bill Clinton, Is an Admirer," *New York Times*, October 27, 2010.

Andrew, as one reporter: Michael Wolff, "Prince Andrew," *New York Times*, April 16, 2001.

At an event in 1994: Halbfinger and Confessore, "Cuomo's Former Boss, Bill Clinton, Is an Admirer."

The report: Jason DeParle, "Report to Clinton Sees Vast Extent of Homelessness," *New York Times*, February 17, 1994.

That first year: Author interview with an advocate for the New York City homeless.

Voters were tired: Fishman, "The Cuomo Family Business."

One of his staffers: Author interview with a former campaign staffer for Mario Cuomo.

"Mario wrote": Author interview with a New York State legislator.

"I would swear": Author interview with New York legislator Mel Miller.

Years later: Thomas Kaplan and Susanne Craig, "Cuomo Reflects in Memoir on Highs and Lows, Both Personal and Political," *New York Times*, October 8, 2014.

Pataki railed at Cuomo: Kevin Sack, "'Air Pataki' Replaces 'Air Cuomo,' as Family Members Ride," *New York Times*, May 11, 1995. See also Associated Press, "Air Pataki: Governor Is a Frequent Flier," August 16, 2001, http://www.recordonline.com/apps/pbcs.dll/article?AID=/20010816/NEWS/308169999&cid=sitesearch.

He railed: Author interview with a former aide to Mario Cuomo.

"It's very difficult to say": Kevin Sack, "Cuomo, a Mystery in an Enigma in a Politician, and His Final Race; in an Interview, No Excuses, No Regrets, Some Uncertainty," *New York Times*, November 13, 1994.

Chapter 11: Rise to Power

Two nonpartisan federal agencies: Alan L. Dean et al., "Renewing HUD: A Long-Term Agenda for Effective Performance," National Academy of Public Administration, July 1994. See also General Accounting Office, "GAO High-Risk Program," January 1994.

Some weeks: Guy Gugliotta, "Saving HUD: One Department's Risky Strategy for Radical Change," *Washington Post*, February 6, 1995.

"A lot of this": Author interview with Joe Shuldiner, a former assistant secretary at the U.S. Department of Housing and Urban Development.

Over time, that would allow: "Housing Dept. Plans Big Cut in Work Force," *New York Times*, January 8, 1995.

The recommendations: Author interview with Henry Cisneros.

Andrew had another, more personal triumph: Nadine Brozan, "Chronicle," *New York Times*, January 13, 1995.

Kerry hoped the twins: Author interview with a person familiar with the matter.

Judy England-Joseph: Author interview with Judy England-Joseph.

"Cuomo took an agency": Author interview with a Republican staffer on Washington D.C.'s Capitol Hill.

"From day one": Author interview with a person familiar with the matter.

"Illusory" transformation: Guy Gugliotta, "Critics See Unstated Motive for Restructuring HUD," *Washington Post*, January 13, 1995, http://www.highbeam.com/doc/1P2-816187.html.

A Lazio staffer: Author interview with a staffer to former U.S. Congressman Rick Lazio.

He found himself satirized: Anonymous, *Primary Colors* (New York: Random House, 1996).

The one on enterprise zones: "Audit of Empowerment Zone, Enterprise Community and Economic Development Initiative Grant Selection Processes," Office of Inspector General, U.S. Department of Housing and Urban Development, August 31, 1995, http://archives.hud.gov/offices/oig/reports/internal/ig5h0002.pdf.

Later, Gaffney recalled: Sean Paige, "Bad Blood Between Cuomo, Gaffney Continues at HUD," *Insight on the News*, December 4, 2000.

At some point: Dealey and Adams, "Banking on Andy Cuomo."

Back they went: Complaint for Declaratory and Ancillary Relief. *Oceanmark Bank, Federal Savings Bank v. Andrew Cuomo et al.*, Circuit Court of the Seventeen Judicial Circuit, Broward County, Florida. 94-007208-04.

The parties reached their new settlement: Compromise and Settlement Agreement, April 1996, in re: *Oceanmark Bank, Federal Savings Bank vs. Andrew Cuomo et al.*, Circuit Court of the Seventeen Judicial Circuit, Broward County, Florida. 94-007208-04.

That Cisneros had had a mistress: David Johnston, "Concluding That Cisneros Lied, Reno Urges a Special Prosecutor," *New York Times*, March 14, 1995.

"We strategized together": Author interview with lawyer Greg Craig.

The memo first calling: Jake Tapper, "Andrew Cuomo's Attitude Problem," *Salon*, September 3, 2002.

Another HUD staffer: Author interview with a HUD staffer who was there at the time of the Seattle audit.

In Cisneros's recollection: Author interview with Henry Cisneros.

Frank DeStefano: Author interview with Frank DeStefano, a former HUD staffer.

The numbers: Statement by former HUD secretary Henry Cisneros, Senate Committee on Banking, Housing and Urban Affairs, Confirmation Hearing on the Nomination of Andrew Cuomo to Become HUD Secretary, January 22, 1997, http://archives.hud.gov/testimony/1997/hrng0197.cfm.

As D'Amato somberly put it: Hearing of the Senate Banking, Housing and Urban Affairs Committee on the nomination of Andrew Cuomo to be secretary of the U.S. Department of Housing and Urban Development (transcript), Federal News Service, January 22, 1997.

Frank DeStefano: Author interview with Frank DeStefano.

Chapter 12: Mr. Secretary

When he rode over: Author interview with Todd Howe.

"Cuomo had one focus": This quote and other unattributed quotes that follow come from author interviews with former HUD staffers.

"He would say": Author interview with former HUD official Fred Karnas.

"He was tough": Author interview with former HUD official Julian Potter.

In his first appearance: Michael Janofsky, "Cuomo Says HUD Needs Added $5.6 Billion for Subsidies," *New York Times*, February 28, 1997.

Clarence Day: Author interview with Clarence Day, a former security officer for Andrew Cuomo.

"What is HUD?": Alvarez, "It's Andrew Cuomo's Turn at Bat."

"People looked at us": Author interview with Todd Howe.

The memo: Michael Powell and Raymond Hernandez, "Political Test May Loom for the Cuomos' Bond," *New York Times*, May 2, 2010.

"The brilliance of Cuomo": Author interview with former capitol hill staffer Joe Ventrone.

She seemed to come in: Author interview with a former HUD staffer.

"To me the message": Author interview with former HUD official Matt Franklin.

"He told his assistant secretaries": Author interview with a former HUD staffer.

He hated the gatherings: Author interviews with individuals familiar with the matter.

"The Kennedys are terrible singers": Author interview with Douglas Kennedy.

Andrew stopped going to Hyannis: Author interviews with individuals familiar with the matter.

A trip to Las Vegas: Art Nadler, "HUD Charges Area Landlord in Alleged Kickback Scheme," *Las Vegas Sun News*, April 16, 1998.

Operation Safe Home: U.S. Department of Housing and Urban Development, "HUD's Operation Safe Home Steps Up Effort to Rid Butler County, Ohio, Public Housing of Crime, Illegal Drugs" (press release), May 15, 1997, http://archives.hud.gov/news/1997/pr97-76.cfm.

"They were out": Author interview with former HUD official Saúl Ramirez.

To Gaffney: Testimony of Susan Gaffney, Hearing Before the Senate Committee on Governmental Affairs, September 9, 1998.

"On the other hand": Author interview with a former HUD staffer.

Later, senators at a subcommittee: Testimony of Susan Gaffney, Hearing Before the Senate Committee on Governmental Affairs, September 9, 1998.

The irony: The following passage, including unattributed quotes, is based on author interviews with former HUD staffers.

"Dirty tricks": Testimony of Susan Gaffney, Hearing Before the Senate Committee on Governmental Affairs, September 9, 1998.

She was also accused: Matt Rees, "Andrew Cuomo's Vendetta," *Weekly Standard*, May 17, 1999.

She went right: Testimony of Susan Gaffney, Hearing Before the Senate Committee on Governmental Affairs, September 9, 1998.

Gaffney did the only other thing: Judith Haverman, "Housing Officials Drop Complaint Against IG," *Washington Post*, September 15, 1997.

In July: Naftali Bendavid, "Chicago FBI Agent to Prove Fraud at HUD," *Chicago Tribune*, July 30, 1997, http://articles.chicagotribune.com/1997-07-30/news/9707300111_1_fbi-director-louis-freeh-housing-secretary-andrew-cuomo-violent-crime-investigations.

Eddie Eitches: Scott Greenberg, "When Rick Lazio Loved Andy Cuomo," *Village Voice*, May 25, 2010, http://blogs.villagevoice.com/runninscared/2010/05/when_rick_lazio.php.

Asked if that was true: Author interview with a former HUD staffer.

Andrew changed that: The following passage, including unattributed quotes, is based on author interviews with former HUD staffers.

The agency-wide overhaul: U.S. Department of Housing and Urban Development, "HUD 2020 Management Reform Plan," report, June 26, 1997, http://archives.hud.gov/reports/2020/mrindex.cfm.

The GAO'S Judy England-Joseph: Author interview with Judy England-Joseph.

That October: Mike Causey, "Keep an Eye on HUD," *Washington Post*, October 12, 1997.

"It was nerve-wracking": Author interview with a former HUD civil servant.

"You had directors": The following passage, including unattributed quotes, is based on author interviews with former HUD staffers.

To Susan Gaffney: Office of the Inspector General of the U.S. Department of Housing and Urban Development, "Interim Review of HUD 2020 Management Reform Plan" (audit), November 25, 1997, http://archives.hud.gov/offices/oig/reports/internal/ig8h0801.pdf.

In May 1998: Rochelle L. Stanfield, "HUD Ache," *Government Executive*, October 1, 1998, http://www.govexec.com/magazine/1998/10/hud-ache/6158/.

Chapter 13: A Nemesis to Contend With

On his one-year anniversary: Alvarez, "It's Andrew Cuomo's Turn at Bat."

On January 26: CNN All Politics, "Lewinsky Has Spoken: Makes Complete Statement to Starr; Clinton Issues Forceful Denial of Affair," January 26, 1998, http://www.cnn.com/ALLPOLITICS/1998/01/26/clinton.main/.

Wednesday night political gatherings: Halbfinger and Confessore, "Cuomo's Former Boss, Bill Clinton, Is an Admirer."

The meetings were held: Author interview with a person familiar with the matter.

Bruce Rozet: Melissa Healy, "U.S. Expands Fraud Case Against L.A. Developer," *Los Angeles Times*, April 16, 1998. See also Randolph E. Schmid, "HUD Charges Landlord with Fraud," Associated Press, April 15, 1998.

Insignia's chairman: David M. Halbfinger, "Bond with Past Foe Is Fodder for Attack on Cuomo," *New York Times*, October 14, 2010.

He was, however, on the verge: Author interview with a former HUD official.

More than $900 million: Wayne Barrett, "Andrew Cuomo's $2 Million Man," *Village Voice*, August 29, 2006.

Andrew paid an early visit: The following passage, including unattributed quotes, is based on author interviews with former capitol hill staffers.

Andrew started hiring: U.S. Department of Housing and Urban Development, "Community Builders Fellowship Program—Introduction," http://archives.hud.gov/initiatives/communitybuilder/combintr.cfm. See also Ernst & Young, LLP, "Report on the Community Builder Program" (report for the U.S. Department of Housing and Urban Development), http://archives.hud.gov/initiatives/communitybuilder/cbreport.cfm.

For a prototype: Author interview with Todd Howe.

That first HUD Next Door: Lawrence L. Knutson, "HUD Opens Storefront in D.C.," Associated Press, May 7, 1998.

"The context": Author interview with a former HUD staffer.

"You bring in people": Author interview with Judy England-Joseph.

"They were all 13s": Author interview with Eddie Eitches.

"How else": Author interview with Gary Eisenman.

But the results: Author interview with a former HUD staffer.

Andrew warned Gaffney: Testimony of Susan Gaffney before the U.S. Senate Committee on Governmental Affairs, September 9, 1998.

David Osborne: Author interview with former HUD consultant David Osborne.

On May 7, 1998: Testimony of Susan Gaffney, Senate Banking, Housing, and Urban Affairs Committee's Subcommittee on Housing and Opportunity and Community Development, May 7, 1998, http://www.banking.senate.gov/98_05hrg/050798/witness/gaffney.htm.

Gaffney talked to FBI investigators: U.S. General Accounting Office, "HUD: Review of Bucklin Report Prepared to Assist HUD in Defending Against EEO Complaint by HUD's Deputy Assistant Inspector General," report, August 3, 1999, http://www.gao.gov/assets/90/88999.pdf.

"I realized": Susan Gaffney Senate testimony, May 7, 1998.

The three black mayors: John B. O'Donnell, "Schmoke Takes Case to Clinton," *Baltimore Sun*, April 17, 1998. See also Michael Janofsky, "Black Mayors Protest Being the Focus of a Federal Housing Inquiry," *New York Times*, April 17, 1998; John B. O'Donnell, "Black Mayors' Group Urges Investigation of HUD Inspector General," *Baltimore Sun*, April 18, 1998; and Sam Fulwood III, "L.A. May Still Face HUD Investigation," *Los Angeles Times*, May 20, 1998.

Andrew now lined up: Fulwood, "L.A. May Still Face HUD Investigation."

Republican congressman Jerry Lewis: Janofsky, "Black Mayors Protest Being the Focus of a Federal Housing Inquiry."

One staffer recalled: Author interview with a former HUD staffer.

The discrimination complaint: U.S. General Accounting Office, "HUD EEO Investigation: Contracting and Process Irregularities in HUD's Investigation of the IG," report, September 1999, http://www.gpo.gov/fdsys/pkg/GAOREPORTS-OSI-99-6/pdf/GAOREPORTS-OSI-99-6.pdf. See also "Gaffney Readies Racial Data," *Housing Affairs Letter*, April 10, 1998; George Archibald, "Senate Chairman Champions HUD's Inspector General," *Washington Times*, September 10, 1998; "Patrick Readies Report on Gaffney," *Housing Affairs Letter*, December 4, 1998.

A report later done: U.S. General Accounting Office, "HUD EEO Investigation."

Andrew's top press officer: Judith Havemann, "HUD Inspector General Fans Feud with Cuomo," *Washington Post*, September 10, 1998.

The word the GAO: U.S. General Accounting Office, "HUD EEO Investigation."

Gaffney had warned: Testimony of Susan Gaffney, Hearing Before the Senate Committee on Governmental Affairs, September 9, 1998.

That December: "Patrick Readies Report on Gaffney," *Housing Affairs Letter*, December 4, 1998. See also Rees, "Andrew Cuomo's Vendetta."

The secretary's office, meanwhile: U.S. General Accounting Office, "HUD EEO Investigation."

The GAO's report: Ibid.

Newsome himself: Author e-mail exchange with former HUD official Philip Newsome.

The complaint has since been destroyed: Freedom of Information request filed by the author.

One IG staffer: Author interview with a former HUD staffer.

Newsome said: Author interview with Philip Newsome.

Newsome's lawyers did take: *Newsome v. Cuomo et al.*, U.S. District Court for the District of Columbia, case 99-cv-988, filed April 20, 1999.

Officers began subletting: Author interview with a former HUD staffer.

At a key conference: Author interview with a former Capitol Hill staffer.

Andrew and Kerry were talking divorce: Author interviews with individuals familiar with the matter.

Andrew's name: Bob Herbert, "The Succession Rush Is On," *New York Times*, November 12, 1998.

A Gore victory: "Speculation Is Rife on Cuomo's Future," *Housing Affairs Letter*, December 4, 1998.

Chapter 14: A Last Chance for Change

Over five days in August: U.S. Department of Housing and Urban Development, "Cuomo Announces $193.1 Million in Federal Aid to Upstate New York as Canal Corridor Tour Ends," press release, August 19, 1999, http://archives.hud.gov/news/1999/pr99-155.html.

In all, HUD was handing out: U.S. Department of Housing and Urban Development, "Vice President Gore Discusses Economic Development Efforts and Announces Success of New York Canal Initiative," press release, September 30, 1999, http://archives.hud.gov/news/1999/pr99-204.html.

Governor Mario Cuomo: "A Reborn Erie Canal," editorial, *New York Times*, August 18, 1997.

Steve Groat: Author interview with Clyde, New York, resident Steve Groat.

Andrew hired a Cornell professor: Cornell University, Department of City and Regional Planning, "Reclaiming a Regional Resource: A Progress Report on the Department of Housing and Urban Development's Canal Corridor Initiative,"

September 22, 1999, http://archives.hud.gov/news/1999/interior.pdf. See also U.S. Department of Housing and Urban Development, "Vice President Gore Discusses Economic Development Efforts and Announces Success of New York Canal Initiative," press release, September 30, 1999, http://archives.hud.gov/news/1999/pr99-204.html.

The next year: Cornell University, Department of City and Regional Planning, "Diversifying and Rebuilding Local Economies: A Second Progress Report on the U.S. Department of Housing and Urban Development's Canal Corridor Initiative," August 2000, http://archives.hud.gov/news/2000/canalcorridor/cornellreport.pdf.

Christopherson was a big fan: Author interview with Cornell University professor Susan Christopherson.

Still, the HUD press releases: U.S. Department of Housing and Urban Development, "Cornell Study Says HUD Canal Initiative Pumping $700 Million a Year into Upstate," press release, August 7, 2000, http://archives.hud.gov/news/2000/pr00-204.html.

In their inevitable audit: U.S. Department of Housing and Urban Development, Office of the Inspector General, "Canal Corridor Initiative," audit, March 30, 2001, http://archives.hud.gov/offices/oig/reports/internal/ig120001.pdf.

As Andrew sermonized: Bob Herbert, "Working on Poverty," *New York Times*, March 3, 1999.

"When you advocate": Michael Grunwald, "Cuomo Launches Anti-Poverty Campaign," *Washington Post*, May 29, 1999.

Andrew published: U.S. Department of Housing and Urban Development, "New HUD Report Shows Most Communities Doing Well in Strong Economy, But Some Cities Face New Urban Challenge," press release, April 28, 1999.

Then he enticed: Grunwald, "Cuomo Launches Anti-Poverty Campaign."

Andrew needed a guide: Author interview with Jackie Johnson, a former deputy assistant secretary for Native American programs at the U.S. Department of Housing and Urban Development.

Paul Iron Cloud: Author interview with Paul Iron Cloud, an Oglala Sioux Tribal Housing Authority official.

No president: Susan Page, "President Stops at S.D. Reservation That Prosperity Passed By," *USA Today*, July 8, 1999.

"We're coming from Washington": Peter T. Kilborn, "Clinton, Amid the Despair on a Reservation, Again Pledges Help," *New York Times*, July 7, 1999.

Jackie Johnson felt Andrew had delivered: Author interview with Jackie Johnson.

Paul Iron Cloud: Author interview with Paul Iron Cloud.

A gun buyback program: U.S. Department of Housing and Urban Development, "President Clinton Announces Violence-Prevention Initiative to Buy Up to 300,000 Guns," press release, September 9, 1999, http://archives.hud.gov/news/1999/pr99-185.html.

Clarence Day: Author interview with Clarence Day.

By July: Raymond Hernandez and Fox Butterfield, "2 Gun Companies in New York Talks," *New York Times*, July 21, 1999.

Andrew saw his chance: David Stout and Richard Perez-Peña, "Housing Agencies to Sue Gun Makers," *New York Times*, December 7, 1999.

"Eliot was the consummate": Author interview with a former aide to New York attorney general Eliot Spitzer.

When the news broke: Stout and Perez-Peña, "Housing Agencies to Sue Gun Makers."

Tensions heightened: Eric Lipton, "Duel for the Limelight: A Special Report; Behind Gun Deal, 2 Ambitious Democrats Wrestle for the Credit," *New York Times*, April 3, 2000.

"Would I put locks": Jeffrey L. Seglin, "The Right Thing: When Good Ethics Aren't Good Business," *New York Times*, March 18, 2001.

"Kevin and I": Author interview with former HUD lawyer Max Stier.

Spitzer was more than chagrined: Lipton, "Duel for the Limelight."

At the start: Author interview with a former HUD staffer.

More Americans: U.S. Department of Housing and Urban Development, "1999 Home Ownership Rate Hits Record Annual High of 66.8%," press release, January 27, 2000.

"This was going to be": Author interview with a former HUD staffer.

Fannie Mae and Freddie Mac: Jack M. Guttentag, "What Do Fannie Mae and Freddie Mac Do?" *The Mortgage Professor*, March 10, 2003, http://www.mtgprofessor.com/a%20-%20secondary%20markets/what_do_fannie_and_freddie_do.htm.

In April 1999: George Temkin et al., "A Study of the GSEs' Single-Family Underwriting Guidelines," Urban Institute, April 1, 1999. The report was commissioned by HUD.

There were heated words: Author interview with a former HUD staffer.

Two *New York Times* reporters: David M. Halbfinger and Michael Powell, "As HUD Chief, Cuomo Earns a Mixed Score," *New York Times*, August 23, 2010.

Andrew did bear blame: Wayne Barrett, "Andrew Cuomo and Fannie and Freddie," *Village Voice*, August 5, 2008, http://www.villagevoice.com/2008-08-05/news/how-andrew-cuomo-gave-birth-to-the-crisis-at-fannie-mae-and-freddie-mac/.

By March 1999: U.S. Department of Housing and Urban Development, Real Estate Settlement Procedures Act (RESPA) Statement of Policy 1999-1 Regarding Lender Payments to Mortgage Brokers; Final Rule, *Federal Register* 64, no. 39, March 1, 1999, http://www.gpo.gov/fdsys/pkg/FR-1999-03-01/html/99-4921.htm.

Brokers didn't even have to disclose: Halbfinger and Powell, "As HUD Chief, Cuomo Earns a Mixed Score."

Some 150 class action suits: Barrett, "Andrew Cuomo and Fannie and Freddie."

As political columnist: Michael Tomasky, "Loser Takes All," *New York*, May 27, 2002.

One assemblyman: Richard Perez-Peña, "For Democrats, Old Tensions and New Alliances," *New York Times*, May 17, 2000.

At the Los Angeles convention: Adam Nagourney, "New York Hopefuls Make the Rounds," *New York Times*, August 17, 2000.

By then the marriage: Author interview with a person familiar with the matter.

In his last year: Brian Blomquist, "Tax $$ Funded Air Cuomo—Made 25 Visits to N.Y. as HUD Chief," *New York Post*, April 1, 2001.

"He never, ever": Richard Perez-Peña, "Cuomo's Campaign Engine Is Young and Well Connected," *New York Times*, April 15, 2002.

On February 17: Testimony of Susan Gaffney before the U.S. House Budget Committee, February 17, 2000, http://www.hud.gov/offices/oig/data/kasichsg7.pdf.

Gaffney soon after filed: Associated Press, "HUD IG Files Harassment Complaint," October 18, 2000.

Andrew might have worked: Author interview with a person familiar with the matter.

***A Vision for Change*:** "Inside the Beltway," column, *Washington Times*, December 14, 2000, http://www.washingtontimes.com/news/2000/dec/14/20001214-013510-8032r/?page=all.

On his last week: U.S. Department of Housing and Urban Development, "Success of HUD Management Reforms Confirmed by GAO Department Removed from High-Risk List," press release, January 17, 2001.

A GAO follow-up: U.S. General Accounting Office, "HUD's High-Risk Program Areas and Management Challenges," report, July 24, 2002, http://www.gao.gov/assets/110/109525.pdf.

"In my business": Pogrebin, "Andrew Cuomo's Quest for Camelot."

A pair of professors: Michael J. Rich and Robert P. Stoker, *Collaborative Governance for Urban Revitalization* (Cornell: Cornell University Press, 2014).

On balance: Derek S. Hyra, *The New Urban Renewal: The Economic Transformation of Harlem and Bronzeville* (Chicago: University of Chicago Press, 2008).

"If you saw": Author interview with Betsy Julian.

The black investigator: Ellen Nakashima, "HUD's Inspector General Retiring After Racial-Bias Settlement," *Washington Post*, May 6, 2001, http://articles.sun-sentinel.com/2001-05-06/news/0105060155_1_inspector-settlement-susan-gaffney.

"Without going into specifics": Author e-mail exchange with former HUD investigator Philip Newsome.

As one of the last acts: Associated Press, "Marc Rich Dies at 78," June 27, 2013.

Kenneth Cole: Adam Nagourney, "A Cuomo Runs for His Father's Old Job in Albany," *New York Times*, January 30, 2001.

They could hardly help: Author interview with a person familiar with the matter.

Chapter 15: Running into the Ground

One early spring day: Michael Wolff, "Prince Andrew," *New York*, April 16, 2001.

"The whole family": Ibid.

Tax returns: Robert Hardt Jr., "Cuomo Hit Pay Dirt After HUD," *New York Post*, May 11, 2002.

Jack Newfield: Author interview with former Mario Cuomo aide Joe Spinelli.

"Andrew was naïve": Author interview with a person familiar with the matter.

"Andrew very much": Grondahl, "A Political Legacy That's Steeped in the Bloodline."

"The joy on people's faces": Author interview with a person familiar with the matter.

With McCall's credentials: Author interview with New York legislator Kevin Parker.

"I think": Author interview with George Arzt.

"He shoehorns his wife": Wolff, "Prince Andrew."

"It's rare": Joel Siegel, "Cuomo Can Count on Kennedy Clout," *New York Daily News*, February 11, 2001.

That was true: Author interview with a person familiar with the situation.

On the day he visited: Author interview with a person familiar with the situation.

Years later: Senior, "The Name of the Father."

***Daily News* reporter:** Nat Hentoff, "What's Next for the Left?" *Village Voice*, July 3, 2001.

As for Michael Wolff: Author interview with journalist Michael Wolff.

Bill Lynch: Author interview with political consultant Bill Lynch.

Four years after: Author interview with New York State Senator Liz Krueger.

One officeholder: Jake Tapper, "Andrew Cuomo's Attitude Problem," *Salon*, September 3, 2002, http://www.salon.com/2002/09/03/cuomo/.

Some time later: Author interview with a person familiar with the matter.

He remained fond: Author interview with a person familiar with the matter.

"He was a terrible candidate": Author interview with journalist Michael Wolff.

At one point: Author interview with a person familiar with the matter.

Probably the bulk: The following passage, including unattributed quotes, is based on author interviews with individuals familiar with the matter.

In early focus groups: Author interview with political adviser Richie Fife.

"That changed the dynamic": Author interview with Adam Nagourney.

"Andrew was totally closed out": Author interview with political adviser Bob Bellafiore.

"The more the people": Michael Powell, "Democrats' Snarls Make Pataki Purr," *Washington Post*, May 10, 2002.

In early 2002: Adam Nagourney, "Union Crosses Party Lines for Pataki," *New York Times*, March 20, 2002.

Mostly he railed: James C. McKinley Jr., "Andrew Cuomo Turns Pataki's Charge Against Him: Free Flights," *New York Times*, May 4, 2001.

In just four: Lloyd Constantine, "More of the Same from Cuomo," Albany *Times Union*, August 12, 2012, http://www.timesunion.com/opinion/article/More-of-the-same-from-Cuomo-3780369.php.

"I was on a number": Author interview with a person familiar with the matter.

Mario had agreed: Constantine, "More of the Same from Cuomo."

Andrew's campaign was stalling: Associated Press, "Pataki Raises $12.8 Million Over Six Months," July 15, 2002, http://www.foxnews.com/story/2002/07/15/pataki-raises-128-million-over-six-months/.

A chance meeting: Halbfinger, "Bond with Past Foe Is Fodder for Attack on Cuomo."

More than $300,000: Russ Buettner, "Andrew's Money Pot," *The Empire Zone* (blog), *New York Times*, November 7, 2006, http://empirezone.blogs.nytimes.com/2006/11/07/andrews-money-pot/.

By 2006: Barrett, "Andrew Cuomo's $2 Million Man."

John Belizaire: Perez-Peña, "Cuomo's Campaign Engine Is Young and Well Connected."

Often Kerry: George Rush, Fernanda Santos, and Joel Siegel, "It's Gettin' Ugly," *New York Daily News*, July 2, 2003.

"It was probably midafternoon": Author interview with a journalist who covered Andrew Cuomo's 2002 gubernatorial campaign.

"There was one leader": Adam Nagourney, "Cuomo's Criticism of Pataki's Role after 9/11 Sets Off Furor," *New York Times*, April 18, 2002.

Even his press aide: Author interview with a person familiar with the matter.

Adam Nagourney: Nagourney, "Cuomo's Criticism of Pataki's Role after 9/11 Sets Off Furor."

The coat-holder quote: Author interview with Adam Nagourney.

The irony: Author interview with a former adviser to Carl McCall.

Kevin Finnegan: Author interview with political adviser Kevin Finnegan.

"Let me tell you": Joe Mahoney and Joel Siegel, "Cuomo Pulls Out of Dem Convention," *New York Daily News*, May 23, 2002.

In their rousing introductory speeches: E. J. Kessler, "Andrew Cuomo's Risky Strategy in Gubernatorial Bid," Westchester County, New York, *Journal News*, May 29, 2002.

David Axelrod: Dan Balz, "In New York, Cuomo Runs to the Outside," *Washington Post*, May 24, 2002.

"We had like a thousand": Author interview with a person who worked on Andrew Cuomo's 2002 gubernatorial campaign.

"He wasn't a screamer": Author interview with a person who worked on Andrew Cuomo's 2002 gubernatorial campaign.

"We would send him up": Author interview with Kevin Finnegan.

That July: Shaila K. Dewan and Raymond Hernandez, "Schumer Endorses McCall as Clinton Remains Neutral," *New York Times*, July 23, 2002.

The Clintons: Richard Perez-Peña, "Silence of Clintons Speaks Loudly for McCall," *New York Times*, August 21, 2002.

On a tour: E. J. Dionne Jr., "Cuomo's Primary Problem," *Washington Post*, August 27, 2002.

In early July: Quinnipiac University, "McCall Takes Lead among Likely New York Dem Voters" (press release), August 15, 2002.

But in August: Fredric U. Dicker, "Carl Pulls Away from Andy by 16 Points," *New York Post*, August 16, 2002.

"If you were out": Randal C. Archibold, "McCall Criticizes Cuomo's Plans to Use His Father's Help in the Campaign," *New York Times*, August 1, 2002.

"Mario had this forty-page manifesto": Author interview with a person who worked on Andrew Cuomo's 2002 gubernatorial campaign.

"There were some very intense": Author interview with a journalist who covered Andrew Cuomo's 2002 gubernatorial campaign

Michael Wolff: Author interview with Michael Wolff.

"My staff": Author interview with a person who worked on Andrew Cuomo's 2002 gubernatorial campaign.

"If he goes through with this": Author interview with Kevin Finnegan.

In a Hail Mary move: Author interview with a person who worked on Andrew Cuomo's 2002 gubernatorial campaign.

His family, yes: Financial disclosure forms for Andrew Cuomo's 2002 campaign for the governorship of New York.

One August day: Richard Perez-Peña and Randal C. Archibold, "Personal Life of Candidate Ignites Dispute," *New York Times*, August 26, 2002. See also Joe Mahoney and Joel Siegel, "McCall Knew Mehiel Past," *New York Daily News*, August 27, 2002, and Wayne Barrett, "McCall's Mess," *Village Voice*, August 27, 2002.

McCall was ahead: Quinnipiac University, "McCall Tops 50% Among Likely NY Dem Voters" (press release), September 3, 2002.

"That was the exact": Bob Herbert, "Cuomo's Post-Mortem," *New York Times*, September 5, 2002.

Secretly that last weekend: Shaila K. Dewan, "Cuomo Quits Race and Backs McCall for Governorship," *New York Times*, September 4, 2002.

It came Saturday: Michael Powell, "Cuomo Ends Bid to Be Governor," *Washington Post*, September 4, 2002.

Andrew was in the parade: Randal C. Archibold, "Always in Charge, Even as He Bows Out," *New York Times*, September 4, 2002.

One of Andrew's emissaries: Dewan, "Cuomo Quits Race and Backs McCall for Governorship."

Specifically: Tapper, "Andrew Cuomo's Attitude Problem."

Three or four months earlier: Author interview with a former adviser to Carl McCall.

Many spent all of Monday night: Archibold, "Always in Charge, Even as He Bows Out."

"Today is a day": Dewan, "Cuomo Quits Race and Backs McCall for Governorship."

"While it's harder": Tapper, "Andrew Cuomo's Attitude Problem."

Later that same day: Herbert, "Cuomo's Post-Mortem."
Jake Tapper: Tapper, "Andrew Cuomo's Attitude Problem."
Norm Adler: Powell, "Cuomo Ends Bid to Be Governor."
A *New York Times*: Dewan, "Cuomo Quits Race and Backs McCall for Governorship."
"What a selfish motherfucker!": Author interview with a former aide to Bill McCall.
Now, too, the money: Author interview with political consultant Bill Lynch.
Some weeks: Author interview with journalist Ken Auletta.
Michael Wolff: Author interview with journalist Michael Wolff.
That fall: Author interview with political consultant Bob Shrum.
The day after: Author interview with a person familiar with the matter.
"One can live": Henri Troyat and Nancy Amphous, *Tolstoy* (New York: Grove, 2001), 152.

Chapter 16: Hitting Bottom

"Andrew was a Rottweiler": Author interview with a person familiar with the matter.
"On rare occasions": Author interview with a person familiar with the matter.
He gathered essays: Andrew Cuomo (editor), *Crossroads: The Future of American Politics* (New York: Random House, 2003).
The Cuomos and the Colleys: Jeane MacIntosh, "Angry Andrew Told Polo Playboy: Stay Away from My Kids," *New York Post*, July 5, 2003.
Andrew was growing suspicious: Saltonstall, Katz, and Haberman, "Andy Figured It Out."
What she said: The following passage, including unattributed quotes, is based on author interviews with individuals familiar with the matter.
A week later: Andy Geller and Fredric U. Dicker, "Cuomo & Kennedy Wife Kerry Separate," *New York Times*, July 1, 2003.
The Cuomos were convening: The following passage, including unattributed quotes, is based on author interviews with individuals familiar with the matter.
Within hours: Jennifer Steinhauer, "Kennedy-Cuomo Union Appears to Be Ending," *New York Times*, July 1, 2003.
Colley called: Brad Hamilton, "Kerry Crushed by Bruce's Kiss-Off," *New York Post*, July 6, 2003.
"Why is he denying": George Rush and Maggie Haberman, "Plays Polo, Calls Talk of Affair 'Nonsense,'" *New York Daily News*, July 5, 2003.
"I'm thinking": Joe McGurk, Jeane MacIntosh, Fred Dicker, and Richard Johnson, "This Is Hell for Our Kids: Andy Breaks Silence to Bare His Torment," *New York Post*, July 3, 2003.
At the local Fourth: Rush and Haberman, "Plays Polo, Calls Talk of Affair 'Nonsense.'"
From the Vineyard: Saltonstall, Katz, and Haberman, "Andy Figured It Out."
"He kind of thinks": Hamilton, "Kerry Crushed by Bruce's Kiss-Off."
"Ann was as mad": Jeane MacIntosh and Fredric U. Dicker, "Cheat's Wife Blasts Andrew," *New York Post*, July 10, 2003.
Shortly after learning: MacIntosh, "Angry Andrew Told Polo Playboy: Stay Away from My Kids."
Then, Colley told his friends: Author interview with a person familiar with the situation.
That next week: Celeste Katz and Dave Goldiner, "Cuomo Scandal Quartet Scatters," *New York Daily News*, July 7, 2003.

Kerry went to Italy: Fredric U. Dicker, "Kerry & Andy in Split-Up Sitdown," *New York Post*, July 29, 2003.

Before renting a two-bedroom: Haughney, "From Queens Roots, Cuomo Clan Branched Out."

The $910 million sale: John Holush, "Insignia Financial Group; Shedding Residential to Focus on Commercial," *New York Times*, May 24, 1998. See also Karush Rogers, "A Headline Deal Maker Stays Off the Beaten Path."

One stop was St. Thomas: Halbfinger, "Bond with Past Foe Is Fodder for Attack on Cuomo."

Watching in the wings: Maggie Haberman, "Yachts of Questions—Andy's Mystery Marina Job," *New York Post*, May 1, 2006. See also Business Wire, "Island Global Yachting (IGY) Partners with Nakheel to Build and Operate World-Class Marinas in Dubai," press release, December 5, 2005.

"He hated the job": Author interview with a person familiar with the matter.

$819,473 in 2004: Maggie Haberman, "Andy's Dandy Income; but Little to Charity," *New York Post*, June 3, 2006.

Norm Adler: Author interview with Norm Adler.

The first time he called: Author interview with a person familiar with the matter.

One close observer: Author interview with a person familiar with the matter.

Cunningham, asked directly: Author interview with Jennifer Cunningham.

Between the end: Leslie Eaton, "A Softer Cuomo, a Stronger Candidate," *New York Times*, October 27, 2006.

Another was Bobby Kennedy: Jonathan P. Hicks, "Only in New York: Kennedys, Cuomos and Voters, Oh, My," *New York Times*, January 18, 2005.

By late January: Jonathan P. Hicks, "Robert Kennedy Won't Run for State Attorney General," *New York Times*, January 25, 2005.

"It was a little like": Author interview with Jennifer Cunningham.

With the union's blessing: Michael Slackman, "Cuomo Gains Early Backing of Union for 2006," *New York Times*, April 17, 2005.

In the summer of 2005: Michael Barbaro, "A TV Cook's Next Serving? Cuomo Family Style," *New York Times*, May 14, 2010. See also Benjamin Wallace, "The Ravenous and Resourceful Sandra Lee," *New York*, March 27, 2011.

A daughter of teenaged, troubled parents: Sandra Lee, *Made from Scratch* (Des Moines: Meredith Books, 2007), 12.

Physical abuse: Lee, *Made from Scratch*, 34.

By the age of twelve: Lee, *Made from Scratch*, 39.

Bert Fields: Lee, *Made from Scratch*, 193.

Soon Karatz would be fighting: *USA v. Karatz*, U.S. District Court for the Central District of California, case 09-cr-203.

Found guilty: Stuart Pfeifer, "Former KB Home CEO Bruce Karatz Sentenced to Five Years' Probation," *Los Angeles Times*, November 11, 2010, http://articles.latimes.com/2010/nov/11/business/la-fi-karatz-sentence-20101111.

Karatz would earn: Scott DeCarlo, "CEO Compensation," *Forbes*, April 17, 2006, http://www.forbes.com/lists/2006/12/O29G.html.

"He walked in": Joanna Molloy, "Q&A: Food Network Host and Cookbook Author Sandra Lee on Attorney General Andrew Cuomo," *New York Daily News*, January 25, 2010.

As one mutual friend: Author interview with a person familiar with the matter.

Eventually they were outed: Jennifer Fermino, "Cuomo's Gal Talks About Life as the Governor's Girlfriend," *New York Post*, January 3, 2011, http://nypost.com/2011/01/03/cuomos-gal-talks-about-life-as-the-governors-girlfriend/.

Four-bedroom home: Haughney, "From Queens Roots, Cuomo Clan Branched Out."

"She really ran the campaign": Author interview with Kevin Finnegan.

Hank Sheinkopf: Author interview with media and political consultant Hank Sheinkopf.

Hank Sheinkopf: Ibid.

Green got less: Jonathan P. Hicks, "Three Democratic Attorney General Candidates, Rebuffed at Convention, Seek Ballot Spots," *New York Times*, June 7, 2006.

Charlie King: Jonathan P. Hicks, "Once Friends and Political Allies, Now Bitter Rivals in Race for Attorney General," *New York Times*, March 12, 2006.

As Mark Green put it: Elizabeth Benjamin, "On Stump, Humbler Cuomo Still Atones for '02 Debacle," Albany *Times Union*, February 21, 2006.

In late August: "Cuomo vs. Green," editorial, *New York Times*, August 27, 2006.

Andrew did better: Jonathan P. Hicks, "Harlem Leaders Support Cuomo in Race to Replace Spitzer," *New York Times*, August 22, 2006.

A week before: Jonathan P. Hicks and Patrick Healy, "As Rival Quits Race, Cuomo Business Link Is Topic of Questions," *New York Times*, September 6, 2006.

King would land: Author interview with Bill Lynch.

A stinging exposé: Barrett, "Andrew Cuomo's $2 Million Man."

Andrew won regardless: Kenneth Lovett, "Andy in Easy Victory over Faded Green," *New York Post*, September 13, 2006.

Her office: Jonathan P. Hicks, "Pirro Attacks Early, Questioning Cuomo's Qualifications," *New York Times*, June 15, 2006.

Her husband: Randal C. Archibold, "Husband's Crimes Are Not Expected to Hinder Pirro's Re-Election Bid," *New York Times*, November 2, 2001.

Two weeks: Patrick Healy, "Pirro Under Investigation over Plan to Tape Husband," *New York Times*, September 27, 2006.

"Andrew is a very lucky guy": Author interview with a person familiar with the matter.

A top aide: Author interview with a person familiar with the matter.

Andrew denied that: Patrick Healy, "In Son's Race, Father Sees Cuomo Comeback," *New York Times*, October 31, 2006.

That irked Mark Green: Author interview with New York politician Mark Green.

"A former governor": Michael Powell and Raymond Hernandez, "Political Test May Loom for the Cuomo's Bond," *New York Times*, May 2, 2010.

Chapter 17: Attorney General with a Vengeance

Who worked for Mario: Pei Shan Hoe, "Cuomo's Counselor Reveals Secrets Behind His Boss' Success," *New York World*, December 9, 2011.

Cohen had drifted away: Author interview with a person familiar with the matter.

"It didn't work": Author interview with a person who worked for Andrew Cuomo when he was New York State attorney general.

Steve Cohen was still unpacking: Author interview with a person familiar with the matter.

College student loans: Karen W. Arenson, "Some Lenders Are Setting Rates College by College," *New York Times*, June 19, 2007, and Sam Dillon, "Student Lender Discloses Ties to Colleges That Included Gifts to Officials," *New York Times*, April 21, 2007.

As soon as he got: Author interview with a person familiar with the matter.

Robert Hernan: Jacob Gershman, "Cuomo's Tight Rein Chafed Office's Lawyers," *Wall Street Journal*, October 10, 2010.

"There's this side of him": Author interview with a person who worked for Andrew Cuomo when he was New York State attorney general.

The Albany *Times Union*: Carol DeMare, "Court: Lift Shroud on Pork," Albany *Times Union*, October 25, 2006.

Joe Bruno: Mike McIntire, "Bruno Bought Stock with Campaign Funds," *New York Times*, January 13, 2007.

He would also enforce: Michael Cooper, "Budget Reform Pact Augurs a More Transparent Albany," *New York Times*, January 17, 2007.

He called in Jerry: Author interview with a person familiar with the matter.

For an assistant Manhattan district attorney: Author interview with a person familiar with the matter.

"She freaks people out": Author interview with a New York City defense attorney.

"Linda will bite": Author interview with a person who worked for Andrew Cuomo when he was New York State attorney general.

The fund was a pot: Danny Hakim and Mary Williams Walsh, "Hevesi's Sons and Aides Face Pension Fund Investigation," *New York Times*, July 15, 2007.

Until the previous December: Chris Dolmetsch, "Ex-New York State Comptroller Alan Hevesi Granted Parole," Bloomberg News, November 15, 2012.

Two decades before: Elizabeth Kolbert, "Regan, Under Fire, Comptroller Tends to Job, Not Image," *New York Times*, March 9, 1989.

"I want this": Author interview with a person familiar with the matter.

By May: Author interview with a person familiar with the matter.

He had used the power: Danny Hakim and William K. Rashbaum, "Hevesi Is Expected to Plead Guilty in Pension Case," *New York Times*, September 28, 2010.

On May 7: Nicholas Confessore, "Cuomo Announces Inquiry into Conflicts Under Hevesi," *New York Times*, May 8, 2007.

"Eliot has this fixation": Author interview with Steve Cohen, a former top aide to Andrew Cuomo.

Shortly after taking office: Ann Farmer, "Spitzer Backs a Democrat from Nassau for the Senate," *New York Times*, January 13, 2007.

Another special election: Michael Cooper, "N.Y. Assembly Democrats Settle on Comptroller," *New York Times*, February 7, 2007.

According to Bruno: Danny Hakim, "Bruno-Spitzer Relationship Sinks Even Lower," *City Room* (blog), *New York Times*, July 2, 2007.

On July 1: James M. Odato, "State Flies Bruno to Fundraiser," Albany *Times Union*, July 1, 2007.

Four days later: Fredric U. Dicker, "Gov's Trooper Snoop Job on Bruno," *New York Post*, July 5, 2007.

"It was an Alice": The following passage, including unattributed quotes, is based on author interviews with individuals who worked for former New York governor Eliot Spitzer.

Later, the office's style: Danny Hakim, "Cuomo Said to Dissuade Lawyer Use by Witnesses," *New York Times*, July 31, 2012.

The Troopergate report: State of New York Office of the Attorney General, "Report of Investigation into the Alleged Misuse of New York State Aircraft and the Resources of the New York State Police," July 23, 2007.

About Bruno: Ibid, 45–49.

Air Cuomo: Constantine, "More of the Same from Cuomo."

"There was no one": Author interview with an aide to former New York governor Eliot Spitzer.

A onetime AP reporter: Author interview with a person familiar with the matter.

Instead, the governor's lawyers: Danny Hakim and Nicholas Confessore, "2 Spitzer Aides Not Questioned Over Police Use," *New York Times*, July 24, 2007.

At a press conference: Danny Hakim, "Spitzer's Staff Misused Police, Report Finds," *New York Times*, July 23, 2007.

A Spitzer aide: Author interview with an aide to former New York governor Eliot Spitzer.

The state ethics commission: Danny Hakim, "Ethics Commission Begins Review of Spitzer's Office," *New York Times*, July 26, 2007.

In all: Constantine, "More of the Same from Cuomo."

Going so far as to call: Author interview with a person familiar with the matter.

Later, one insider: Author interview with a person familiar with the matter.

Chapter 18: Managing the Meltdown

"That would have been": The following passage, including unattributed quotes, is based on author interviews with individuals who worked for Andrew Cuomo when he was New York State attorney general.

"Project Sunlight": Nicholas Confessore, "Grant Holders Must Disclose Financial Ties," *New York Times*, March 23, 2007.

Now, from inside: Author interview with Blair Horner, who worked for Andrew Cuomo when he was New York State attorney general.

One old Mario hand: Author interview with a person familiar with the matter.

The well-known Carlyle Fund: Danny Hakim, "Pension Inquiry Scrutinizes Fees to a Hevesi Consultant," *New York Times*, August 29, 2007.

Spitzer invited Andrew: Author interview with a person familiar with the matter.

As a year-end profile: Rick Karlin, "Political Winds Shift Back to Cuomo," Albany *Times Union*, December 23, 2007.

Years later: Author interview with an aide to former New York governor Eliot Spitzer.

"The black thing is dead": Author interview with a person who worked for Andrew Cuomo when he was New York State attorney general.

"Not a focused guy": Author interview with a New York lawmaker.

The new governor declared: "Paterson Says He Tried Cocaine and Marijuana in 1970s," *New York Times*, March 25, 2008.

Had affairs: Sewell Chan, "Paterson Acknowledges Extramarital Affairs," *City Room* (blog), *New York Times*, March 18, 2008.

By early 2008: Vikas Bajaj, "In Deal with Cuomo, Mortgage Giants Accept Appraisal Standards," *New York Times*, March 4, 2008.

On the eve: Jenny Anderson and Vikas Bajaj, "New Trouble in Auction-Rate Securities," *New York Times*, February 15, 2008.

$330 billion: Anderson and Bajaj, "New Trouble in Auction-Rate Securities."
"What's the SEC": Author interview with a person familiar with the matter.
The attorneys general: Author interview with a person familiar with the matter.
At a press conference: Louise Story, "New York Sues UBS for Securities Fraud," *New York Times*, July 25, 2008.
Within days: Story, "New York Sues UBS for Securities Fraud." See also Liz Rappaport, "Auction-Rate Crackdown Widens," *Wall Street Journal*, July 25, 2008, and Michael McDonald and Karen Freifeld, "UBS Fined $150 Million, Agrees to Buy Auction Debt," Bloomberg News, August 8, 2008, http://www.bloomberg.com/apps/news?pid=newsarchive&sid=asdBwkzlyq5g&refer=home.
In fact, Massachusetts: Gretchen Morgenson, "Suit Claims UBS Misled Investors," *New York Times*, June 27, 2008.
Word came down: Gretchen Morgenson and Louise Story, "In Financial Crisis, No Prosecutions of Top Figures," *New York Times*, April 14, 2011.
"The settlements": Author interview with Joseph Fichera, CEO of the financial advisory firm Saber Partners, LLC.
A former prosecutor: Author interview with a prosecutor who worked for Andrew Cuomo when he was New York State attorney general.
In many cases: Author interview with a person familiar with the matter.
"It was really about stopping": Author interview with a person familiar with the matter.
In the summer of 2008: New York State Attorney General, "Attorney General Cuomo Announces Landmark Reform Agreements with the Nation's Three Principal Credit Rating Agencies," press release, June 5, 2008.
An in-depth report: Vikas Bajaj, "Post-Spitzer, a New Breed of Reformer," *New York Times*, June 27, 2008.
Financial writer Charles Gasparino: Charles Gasparino, "Behind Cuomo's Overblown Record," *New York Post*, October 21, 2009, http://nypost.com/2009/10/21/behind-cuomos-overblown-record/.
"Cuomo would just get an idea": Author interview with a prosecutor who worked for Eliot Spitzer when he was New York State attorney general.
"Spitzer was very happy": Author interview with a New York defense attorney.
"New York under Spitzer": Author interview with a prosecutor who worked for Eliot Spitzer when he was New York State attorney general.
When the appellate division: *People v. Grasso*, New York Supreme Court, Appellate Division, First Department, Order, May 8, 2007, http://www.nycourts.gov/reporter/3dseries/2007/2007_03990.htm. See also Patricia Hurtado and Edgar Ortega, "Grasso Wins Appeal of Lawsuit Over Stock Exchange Pay," Bloomberg News, May 8, 2007, http://www.bloomberg.com/apps/news?pid=newsarchive&sid=aomfesU4o0cU&refer=home.
One day in the spring: Diane Brady, "Kenneth Langone on Standing Up to Eliot Spitzer," Bloomberg News, July 26, 2012, http://www.businessweek.com/articles/2012-07-26/kenneth-langone-on-standing-up-to-eliot-spitzer.
On June 25: Anderson, "Ex-Big Board Chairman Wins Round in Pay Fight."
A week later: Jenny Anderson, "Stock Exchange's Ex-Chief Wins Battle to Keep Pay," *New York Times*, July 2, 2008.
According to a lawyer: Author interview with a lawyer familiar with the matter.

One of the four: *People v. Grasso*, New York Supreme Court, Appellate Division, First Department, Order, July 1, 2008, http://online.wsj.com/public/resources/documents/grasso.pdf.

When he called: Brady, "Kenneth Langone on Standing Up to Eliot Spitzer."

He would go on: Javier C. Hernández and Susanne Craig, "Cuomo Played Pivotal Role in Charter School Push," *New York Times*, April 3, 2014.

By early 2014: Charles Gasparino, "Republicans for Cuomo Sell Out Cheap," *New York Post*, February 27, 2014, http://nypost.com/2014/02/27/republicans-for-cuomo-sell-out-cheap/.

Between 2001 and 2009: Andrea Peyser, "Donald for Governor... Why Not?" *New York Post*, December 23, 2013, http://nypost.com/2013/12/23/donald-for-governor-why-not/.

In 2010, David Koch: Chris Good, "David Koch and Wife Gave Gov. Andrew Cuomo $87K," *Atlantic*, March 31, 2011, http://www.theatlantic.com/politics/archive/2011/03/david-koch-and-wife-gave-gov-andrew-cuomo-87k/73300/.

They were, he said: Vikas Bajaj and Graham Bowley, "S.E.C. Temporarily Blocks Short Sales of Financial Stocks," *New York Times*, September 19, 2008.

Back in August 2007: Gretchen Morgenson, "Behind Insurer's Crisis, Blind Eye to a Web of Risk," *New York Times*, September 27, 2008.

First $85 billion: "A.I.G. Rescue Grows to $150 Billion," *New York Times*. See also Zachary Tracer, "AIG Bailout Ends Four Years After Two-Year Plan," Bloomberg News, December 11, 2012.

A private meeting: Morgenson and Story, "In Financial Crisis, No Prosecutions of Top Figures."

Days after: Peter Whoriskey, "AIG Spa Trip Fuels Fury on Hill," *Washington Post*, October 8, 2008.

A partridge hunt: "A.I.G. to Help Cuomo Recover Millions in Executive Pay," *New York Times*, October 16, 2008.

Joseph Cassano: Michael Daly, "Pin AIG Woes on Brooklyn Boy," *New York Daily News*, March 17, 2009. See also Karen Freifeld, "AIG Agrees to Hold Back Pay for Former CEO Sullivan," Bloomberg News, October 22, 2008.

On a crisp fall day: Jonathan D. Glater and Vikas Bajaj, "Cuomo Seeks Recovery of Bonuses at A.I.G.," *New York Times*, October 15, 2008. See also Jonathan D. Glater, "A.I.G. to Suspend Millions in Executive Payouts," *New York Times*, October 22, 2008.

"The days": Jonathan D. Glater, "A.I.G. Agrees to Let New York Review the Propriety of Its Pay Packages," *New York Times*, October 17, 2008.

In late October: Jonathan D. Glater, "Cuomo Investigates Bonuses at Banking Companies," *New York Times*, October 29, 2008. See also Ben White and Jonathan D. Glater, "Cuomo Asks for Pay Data from Banks," *New York Times*, October 30, 2008.

The race should have ended: Author interview with a person familiar with the matter.

Having penned: Caroline Kennedy, "A President Like My Father," *New York Times*, January 27, 2008.

"He's not being helpful": Nicholas Confessore, "Much Talk of Cuomo for Clinton's Seat, but Who's Talking?" *New York Times*, November 26, 2008.

"It wasn't necessarily the case": Author interview with a top political operative.

Caroline set out: Adam Nagourney and Nicholas Confessore, "As Privacy Ends for Kennedy, a Rough Path Awaits," *New York Times*, December 16, 2008.

A flurry of calls: Nicholas Confessore, "Cuomo Aide Is Said to Try to Slow Kennedy Bid," *New York Times*, January 6, 2009.

They greeted Caroline: Nagourney and Confessore, "As Privacy Ends for Kennedy, a Rough Path Awaits."

She also had a bad case: Nicholas Confessore and David M. Halbfinger, interview with Caroline Kennedy (transcript), *New York Times*, December 27, 2008.

"It's driving him crazy": Danny Hakim and Raymond Hernandez, "Kennedy Brand Leaves Cuomo Feeling Stymied," *New York Times*, December 19, 2008.

She "has a tremendous relationship": Nicholas Confessore and Danny Hakim, "Kennedy Drops Bid for Senate Seat, Citing Personal Reasons," *New York Times*, January 21, 2009.

By another of the state's: Jacob Gershman, "Paterson's Latest Cuomo Quandary," *New York*, January 9, 2009.

The next afternoon: Kate Phillips, "Senate Confirms Clinton as Secretary of State," *The Caucus* (blog), *New York Times*, January 21, 2009.

The day before: Katharine Q. Seelye, "Live Blog: The Inauguration of Barack Obama," *The Caucus* (blog), *New York Times*, January 20, 2009.

Paterson was stunned: Author interview with a person familiar with the matter.

At 11 p.m.: Maggie Haberman and Fredric U. Dicker, "Tax and Nanny Issues Shoot Down Caroline Kennedy Senate Bid," *New York Post*, January 22, 2009. See also Fredric U. Dicker, "Paterson Lyin' King of State," *New York Post*, January 27, 2009; Chris Smith, "The Zany Adventures of (Senator) Caroline Kennedy," *New York*, January 24, 2009; and Larissa MacFarquhar, "Ms. Kennedy Regrets," *New Yorker*, February 2, 2009. The *New York Post* story of January 22, 2009, appears to have been removed from the newspaper's website.

"Andrew was in his office": Author interview with a person familiar with the matter.

Chapter 19: Man of the People

Andrew and his top investigators: Chris Smith, "The Political Art of Anger Management," *New York*, April 19, 2009.

Overall, Merrill would lose: Michael J. de la Merced and Louise Story, "Nearly 700 at Merrill in Million-Dollar Club," *New York Times*, February 11, 2009.

$3.57 billion: Ron Scherer, "New York Sues Bank of America over Merrill Lynch Merger," *Christian Science Monitor*, February 4, 2010.

Eventually, Andrew: *People of the State of New York v. Bank of America*, New York State Supreme Court in Manhattan, No. 450115/2010.

The suit would drag on: Christie Smythe, Chris Dolmetsch, and Greg Farrell, "Lewis, BofA Reach $25 Million Pact with N.Y. over Merrill," Bloomberg News, March 27, 2014.

Overall, the big banks' bonus pool: Ben White, "What Red Ink? Wall Street Paid Hefty Bonuses," *New York Times*, January 28, 2009.

Ben Lawsky spent Friday: Smith, "The Political Art of Anger Management."

Its CEO Edward Liddy: Tami Luhby, "AIG Freezes Ex-CEO Payments," CNNMoney.com, October 22, 2008.

Sending a letter: Letter from Andrew Cuomo to Congressman Barney Frank, March 17, 2009.

On Monday: "Cuomo Says Most Huge A.I.G. Bonuses Were Returned," *New York Times*, March 23, 2009.

"We have a very aggressive theory": Mary Williams Walsh and Carl Hulse, "A.I.G. Bonuses of $50 Million Will Be Repaid," *New York Times*, March 23, 2009.

Roughly seventy employees: Jackie Calmes and Louise Story, "Outcry Builds in Washington for Recovery of A.I.G. Bonuses," *New York Times*, March 17, 2009.

"Did anything get changed": Author interview with a person familiar with the matter.

David Loglisci: Danny Hakim, "Former Hevesi Aide Pleads Guilty in Pension Case," *New York Times*, March 10, 2010.

Loglisci's brother: Nicholas Confessore, "For a Low-Budget Comedy, an Unexpected Second Act, in Politics," *New York Times*, March 21, 2009.

When Andrew announced: Danny Hakim, "Hevesi Aides Indicted in Kickback Scheme," *New York Times*, March 19, 2009.

An admiring if wry: Michael Powell, Danny Hakim, and Louise Story, "For Cuomo, Financial Crisis Is His Political Moment," *New York Times*, March 20, 2009.

The powerful Carlyle Group: Danny Hakim, "Carlyle Settles with New York in Pension Case," *New York Times*, May 14, 2009.

Steven Rattner: Biography of Steven Rattner on his website, http://stevenrattner.com/bio/.

Rattner counted: Michael Wolff, "The Clark Kent Timesman," *New York*, November 10, 2003.

Rattner had met: Author interview with a person familiar with the matter.

$150 million: Karen Freifeld, "Hevesi Ex-Adviser Morris Pleads Guilty in Cuomo Pension Corruption Probe," Bloomberg News, November 22, 2010, http://www.bloomberg.com/news/2010-11-22/hank-morris-tells-new-york-judge-he-agrees-to-plead-guilty-to-felony-count.html.

When the AG's office asked him: The following passage, including unattributed quotes, is based on author interviews with individuals who worked for Andrew Cuomo when he was New York State attorney general.

One in particular: Cohan, "The Smartest Guy in the Room."

Rattner went so far: U.S. Securities and Exchange Commission v. Steven L. Rattner, U.S. District Court for the Southern District of New York, 10-cv-8699 (complaint).

The Republicans pulled a fast one: Danny Hakim and Jeremy W. Peters, "Door Is Locked, and Senate Is in Gridlock," *New York Times*, June 10, 2009.

A week later: Danny Hakim and Jeremy W. Peters, "Monserrate's Flip Creates Tie in New York Senate," *New York Times*, June 15, 2009.

On July 9: Danny Hakim, "Albany Impasse Ends as Defector Rejoins Caucus," *New York Times*, July 9, 2009.

Paterson went ahead: Danny Hakim, "Paterson Picks M.T.A. Figure as His No. 2," *New York Times*, July 8, 2009.

Mario had taken a dislike: Author interview with a person familiar with the matter.

Andrew based his objection: Jason Horowitz, "Cuomo Denounces a 'Ploy' That Would Empower Paterson," *New York Observer*, July 6, 2009.

When the inevitable suit: Jeremy W. Peters, "Judge Blocks Paterson's Lt. Gov. Pick," *New York Times*, July 21, 2009. See also Jeremy W. Peters, "Court Rejects Ravitch Appointment," *City Room* (blog), *New York Times*, August 20, 2009, and Jeremy W. Peters and Sewell Chan, "In 4-3 Vote, Court Says Paterson Can Appoint Lt. Governor," *City Room* (blog), *New York Times*, September 22, 2009.

Pedro Espada Jr.: Mosi Secret, "Ex-State Senator Guilty of Theft from Nonprofit," *New York Times*, May 14, 2012.

Hiram Monserrate: Fernanda Santos, "No Jail Time for Monserrate," *New York Times*, December 4, 2009.

"The Cuomo play": Jacob Gershman, "Cuomo's Gambit," *New York*, August 23, 2009.

The grapevine reverberated: Author interview with an aide to former New York governor David Paterson.

On the eve: Danny Hakim and Nicholas Confessore, "Resisting Obama, Paterson Vows to Seek Office," *New York Times*, September 20, 2009.

Through 1199: Danny Hakim, "Adviser to Cuomo Is Also Top Lobbyist," *New York Times*, April 29, 2010.

Rattner pleaded the Fifth: Michael Corkery and Michael Rothfeld, "Suit Seeking Wall Street Ban Spoils Ex-Car Czar's Big Day," *Wall Street Journal*, November 19, 2010.

That October: Danny Hakim, "Ex-Political Boss Pleads Guilty in Pension Case," *New York Times*, October 6, 2009.

At his sentencing: John Eligon, "No Jail Time for Ex-Political Boss in Pension Case," *New York Times*, May 18, 2011.

In late October: Fredric U. Dicker, "Gov's Yankee Freebie 'Foul,'" *New York Post*, November 2, 2009.

According to one Paterson aide: Author interview with an aide to former New York governor David Paterson.

David Johnson: William K. Rashbaum, Danny Hakim, David Koscieniewski, and Serge K. Kovaleski, "Question of Influence in Abuse Case of Paterson Aide," *New York Times*, February 24, 2009.

Ravi Batra: Author interview with attorney Ravi Batra.

Chapter 20: Going for Governor

Andrew announced: Danny Hakim and Nicholas Confessore, "Cuomo Opens Campaign for New York Governor," *New York Times*, May 22, 2010.

A war chest: Serge F. Kovaleski and Griffin Palmer, "Cuomo Accepts Millions from Interests He Assails," *New York Times*, June 23, 2010.

Kevin Finnegan: Author interview with Kevin Finnegan.

"He knew that Eric": Author interview with a political operative in New York.

Perhaps, as one friend: Author interview with a person familiar with the matter.

The Sulzbergers were German Jews: Jewish Telegraphic Agency, "Death of Cyrus Sulzberger," May 2, 1932.

"From the bottom up": Author interview with a person familiar with the matter.

Samuels was the first to admit: Author interview with Bill Samuels.

"The only guy": Author interview with an aide to Andrew Cuomo.

Formally, David Paterson: Author interview with an aide to former New York governor David Paterson.

A post-primary poll: Nicholas Confessore and Elizabeth A. Harris, "Bloomberg Backs Cuomo as Governor's Race Tightens," *City Room* (blog), *New York Times*, September 22, 2010.

The thinking: Author interview with an aide to Andrew Cuomo.

The burly developer: Michael M. Grynbaum and Michael Barbaro, "Paladino Is Taunting in a Letter to Cuomo," *New York Times*, September 19, 2010.

He circulated a flier: Joe Coscarelli, "State Politics: Carl Paladino Catches Andrew Cuomo Showering With His Chain On," *Runnin' Scared* (blog), *Village Voice*, September 19, 2010.

When a reporter: Michael Barbaro, "In New York Governor Race, Two Italian Identities," *New York Times*, October 10, 2010.

With his aides: Chris Smith, "How Andrew Cuomo Lost," *New York*, October 15, 2010.

The press learned: Jack Mirkinson, "Carl Paladino Threatens Reporter: 'I'll Take You Out,'" *Huffington Post*, September 30, 2010. See also video of press conference on YouTube: https://www.youtube.com/watch?v=uCn9yspCl_g.

Andrew had had affairs: Maggie Haberman, "Paladino Switches Gears and Course-Corrects," *Politico*, September 30, 2010.

In a TV ad: Carl Paladino TV ad, posted on YouTube, https://www.youtube.com/watch?v=YC-edyIDLIU.

"It is true": Author interview with an aide to former New York City mayor Michael Bloomberg.

"It was very specific": Author interview with an aide to former New York City mayor Michael Bloomberg.

"Where have you been": Nicholas Confessore, "Cuomo Facing Criticism from Blacks," *New York Times*, September 26, 2010.

Andrew headed for Harlem: Reid Pillifant, "Cuomo's Base-Solidifying Visit to Harlem Goes Poorly," *New York Observer*, September 27, 2010.

All appointments: Author interview with a person familiar with the matter.

As outgoing governor: Tom Zeller Jr., "New York Governor Vetoes Fracking Bill," *Green* (blog), *New York Times*, December 11, 2010.

Quadrangle had agreed: Louise Story, "Investment Firm Agrees to Settle Kickback Inquiry," *New York Times*, April 15, 2010.

By mid-October: Joshua Gallu, Karen Freifeld, and Bob Van Voris, "SEC Settles with Steven Rattner over Kickbacks; Cuomo Files New Lawsuits," Bloomberg News, November 17, 2010.

"Rattner comes back": Author interview with a person familiar with the matter.

Not long after the election: John Eligon, "Adviser Pleads Guilty in Pay-to-Play Pension Scheme," *New York Times*, November 22, 2010. See also Jacob Gershman, "After a Productive Two Years, Hank Morris Wins His Freedom," *Wall Street Journal*, April 23, 2013.

Andrew filed two civil suits: Gallu, Freifeld, and Van Voris, "SEC Settles with Steven Rattner over Kickbacks; Cuomo Files New Lawsuits."

He told Rattner's lawyer: Author interview with a person familiar with the matter.

He went on the *Charlie Rose*: Appearance of Steven Rattner on the *Charlie Rose* show (transcript), broadcast of November 22, 2010.

The next day: Author interview with a person familiar with the situation.

For Rattner, the AG suits: Author interview with a person familiar with the situation.

All in all, including Rattner's: Peter Lattman, "Rattner to Pay $10 Million in Settlement with Cuomo," *New York Times*, December 30, 2010.

New Year's Eve: Author interview with a person familiar with the matter.

The governor-elect's girlfriend: Javier C. Hernandez, "No Traditional First-Lady Role for Busy Sandra Lee," *New York Times*, December 30, 2010.

Chapter 21: A State in Need of Saving

Andrew was presiding: Author interview with a person familiar with the matter.

"It was the same thing": Author interview with a person familiar with the matter.

In his inaugural speech: "Full Text of Cuomo's Inauguration Speech," *New York Times*, January 1, 2011.

One pair of guests: Author interview at the same time with two individuals familiar with the situation.

Among those impressed: Author interview with Albany *Times Union* editor in chief Rex Smith.

Smith's editorial: Rex Smith, "A New Cuomo Takes the Key," Albany *Times Union*, January 2, 2011.

As attorney general: Author interview with a person familiar with the matter.

The chill: Elizabeth A. Harris, "Going to an Event Featuring Cuomo? Take a Coat, or Maybe a Blanket," *New York Times*, January 7, 2011.

The crisis, Andrew began: State of the State address by New York Governor Andrew Cuomo (transcript), January 5, 2011.

On December 22: Jacob Gershman, "Cuomo Keeps Grip on Funds in Settlement," *Wall Street Journal*, April 22, 2012.

Taming the budget: State of the State address by New York Governor Andrew Cuomo (transcript), January 5, 2011.

Lawmakers in each house: National Conference of State Legislatures, 2011 NCSL Legislator Compensation Table, http://www.ncsl.org/research/about-state-legislatures/2011-ncsl-legislator-compensation-table.aspx.

Many supplemented: "New York Legislators' Secret Income," editorial, *New York Times*, September 23, 2013.

Back in 1812: Robert Draper, "The League of Dangerous Mapmakers," *Atlantic*, September 19, 2012.

One looked like Abraham Lincoln: NY Constitution, "Redistricting," http://nyconstitution.org/issue-summary/Redistricting.

Sixty of the state's: Cara Matthews, "Battle Over Redistricting Continues," *Politics on the Hudson* (blog), Westchester County, New York, *Journal News*, March 14, 2011.

Within days: Nicholas Confessore and Thomas Kaplan, "Group Takes on Albany with Cuomo's Blessing," *New York Times*, January 17, 2011.

In that first year: John Eligon, "Group Allied with Cuomo Tops Albany Spending List," *New York Times*, March 27, 2012.

A few came forward: Confessore and Kaplan, "Group Takes on Albany with Cuomo's Blessing."

Blair Horner: Author interview with Blair Horner.

He invited the leaders: Author interview with a person familiar with the matter.

John Sampson: Charles V. Bagli, "Report Criticized Senators on Casino in Queens," *New York Times*, October 21, 2010.

In fact: Blake Zeff, "Another Cuomo Noninterference Story Falls Apart," *Capital New York*, September 2, 2014.

The budget would cut: "Gov. Cuomo's Budget," editorial, *New York Times*, February 2, 2011.

Back in the campaign: The following passage, including unattributed quotes, is based on author interviews with individuals familiar with the matter.

About $2 billion: "Medicaid and New York's Budget," editorial, *New York Times*, February 19, 2011.

For 24 hours: The following passage, including unattributed quotes, is based on author interviews with individuals familiar with the matter.

Norman Adler: Author interview with Norman Adler.

"He might leave at seven p.m.": Author interview with a person familiar with the matter.

He had warned them: "Within Our Means: Their Real Agenda," editorial, *New York Times*, February 7, 2011.

One night in late February: Jimmy Vielkind, "Cuomo Faces Critics," Albany *Times Union*, February 21, 2011.

As promised: Thomas Kaplan, "Cuomo Redistricting Bill Limits Lawmakers' Role," *New York Times*, February 17, 2011.

"When Cuomo stands up": Author interview with Hank Sheinkopf.

The only way to change the process: Thomas Kaplan and John Eligon, "New York Lawmakers Vote to Limit Public Pensions," *New York Times*, March 14, 2012. See also Teri Weaver, "Redistricting Up for Another Vote for New York Lawmakers," Syracuse *Post-Standard*, January 14, 2013.

"You stick up": Author interview with Hank Sheinkopf.

Big Ugly: "A Budget, and Just That," editorial, Albany *Times Union*, March 10, 2013.

"Message of necessity": Peter J. Galie and Christopher Bopst, " 'It Ain't Necessarily So': The Governor's 'Message of Necessity' and the Legislative Process in New York," *Albany Law Review*, 76, no. 4, http://www.albanylawreview.org/Articles/Vol76_4/76.4.2219%20Bopst%20Galie.pdf.

$132.5 billion: "Gov. Cuomo's Budget," editorial, *New York Times*, April 2, 2011.

"Cuomo has taken": Lawrence C. Levy, "Cuomo Seizes Control," Albany *Times Union*, March 27, 2011.

First on-time budget: Michael Oreskes, "Cuomo at Midterm," *New York Times*, January 7, 1985, and Al Baker, "Legislature Votes to Hold Referendum on On-Time Budgets," *New York Times*, May 5, 2005. See also Staff Report to the New York State Senate Select Committee on Budget and Tax Reform, April 2010, http://www.nysenate.gov/files/pdfs/FINALFiscalYearWhitePaper.pdf.

Budget gurus: E. J. McMahon, "First Glance at Cuomo Budget," *NY Torch* (blog), Empire Center for Public Policy, February 2, 2011.

Another expert: Author interview with a person familiar with the matter.

"I'm hoping": Casey Seiler, "Budget Plan Closes Deficit with No Tax Increase," Albany *Times Union*, March 28, 2011.

Four days later: Author interviews with individuals familiar with the matter.

The only one left out: "Gov. Cuomo's Budget," editorial, *New York Times*.

The property tax cap passed: Nicholas Confessore and Thomas Kaplan, "Albany Reaches Deal on Tax Cap and Rent," *New York Times*, June 21, 2011.

"That was unbelievable": Author interview with a New York legislator.

"I'll be judged": Author interview with a person familiar with the matter.

Chapter 22: Like Midas

Bill Smith: Author interview with gay-rights activist Bill Smith.

Later, one prominent Republican: Author interview with a person familiar with the matter.

In the months afterward: Danny Hakim, "Money Flows to Republican Backers of Gay Marriage," *New York Times*, January 17, 2012.

"The push of the people": Author interview with a person familiar with the matter.

On April 15: John Eligon, "Prison for Ex-Comptroller Convicted in Pension Scheme," *New York Times*, April 16, 2011. See also Jennifer Peltz, "Ex-NY Comptroller Hevesi Gets 1-4 Years in Prison," *USA Today*, April 15, 2011.

Even as the list: Nicholas Confessore and Michael Barbaro, "Graft Charges Depict Kruger's Lavish Lifestyle," *New York Times*, March 10, 2011.

JCOPE would have: Website of the New York State Joint Commission on Public Affairs, http://www.jcope.ny.gov/about/jurisdiction.html.

The veto rules: NYConstitution.org, "What's Wrong with the Joint Commission on Public Ethics" (JCOPE), http://nyconstitution.org/issue/Ethics. See also New York City Bar Association and Common Cause/New York, "Hope for JCOPE," report, March 14, 2014, 18, http://www2.nycbar.org/pdf/report/uploads/Hope-for-JCOPE-Report.pdf.

So as Blake Zeff: Author interview with political writer Blake Zeff.

"This reminds me": Author interview with a person familiar with the matter.

That June: Danny Hakim and Thomas Kaplan, "As Ethics Measure Emerges, So Do Questions About Its Teeth," *New York Times*, June 7, 2011.

By June 7: "Senator Gianaris Opening Remarks at Independent Redistricting Forum" (video at New York State forum on redistricting), June 7, 2011, http://www.nysenate.gov/video/2011/jun/13/senator-gianaris-opening-remarks-independent-redistricting-forum.

Currently, a donor: New York State Board of Elections, 2011 Contribution Limits, http://www.elections.ny.gov/NYSBOE/Finance/2011FamilyContributionLimits.pdf.

The plan would give "Well, It's a Start," editorial, *New York Times*, June 20, 2011.

Chipmunk Balls: Fredric U. Dicker, "Andy Has Uphill Fight to Win in '16: Top Dem," *New York Post*, August 15, 2011.

To Bill Smith: Author interview with Bill Smith.

That Sunday: John Leland, "Cheering a Gay Marriage Law, and Its Champions," *New York Times*, June 26, 2011.

"So, Governor": Maureen Dowd, "Utopia on the Hudson," *New York Times*, June 28, 2011.

In February: Thomas Kaplan, "A Call to Deny Communion to Cuomo," *New York Times*, February 22, 2011.

"I don't think": Author interview with Kevin Parker.

On July 1: Danny Hakim and Nicholas Confessore, "Cuomo Will Seek to Lift Ban on Hydraulic Fracking," *New York Times*, June 30, 2011.

Scary stories: Eliza Griswold, "The Fracturing of Pennsylvania," *New York Times*, November 17, 2011.

The hard-hit farmers: Jerry Zremski, "A Border Tale of Boom and Bust," *Buffalo News*, May 11, 2014, http://www.buffalonews.com/city-region/environment/a-border-tale-of-boom-and-bust-20140511.

He was using his bully pulpit: Danny Hakim, "Cuomo Takes Tough Stance on Nuclear Reactors," *New York Times,* June 28, 2011.

Andrew told his DEC commissioner: Hakim and Confessore, "Cuomo Will Seek to Lift Ban on Hydraulic Fracking."

"I think he overplays": Author interview with a person familiar with the situation.

Bob Shrum: Author interview with Robert Shrum.

But that, suggested a seasoned hand: Author interview with a person familiar with the matter.

Chapter 23: Making Enemies

He had raised roughly: Henry Goldman and Roger Runningen, "Obama Joining Families of 9/11 Victims to Dedicate Museum," Bloomberg News, May 14, 2014.

$15 million: David W. Dunlap, "$350 Million Raised to Date for 9/11 Memorial," *New York Times*, April 9, 2008.

The call came from Larry Schwartz: The following passage, including unattributed quotes, is based on author interviews with individuals familiar with the matter.

Early that Sunday morning: Josh Margolin, "9/11 Slight Fight," *New York Post*, June 18, 2012.

How, exactly: Author interview with a person familiar with the matter.

"They Fume and They Bicker": Michael M. Grynbaum, Thomas Kaplan, and Kate Taylor, "They Fume and They Bicker While Running City and State," *New York Times*, December 23, 2011.

Oddly, the governor refused: The following passage, including unattributed quotes, is based on author interviews with individuals familiar with the matter.

One of its major players: Michael M. Grynbaum, "Taxi Bill Has Potential Foe in Cuomo. Mario Cuomo," *City Room* (blog), *New York Times,* June 22, 2011.

With the livery car bill: The following passage, including unattributed quotes, is based on author interviews with individuals familiar with the matter.

Andrew signed: Michael M. Grynbaum, "Deal Struck to Broaden Taxi Service in the City," *New York Times*, December 20, 2011.

"The governor and I": Freeman Klopott and Henry Goldman, "Cuomo Agrees to Taxi Bill That Adds $1 Billion to NYC Revenue," Bloomberg News, December 21, 2011.

The push came via Larry Schwartz: Author interview with a person familiar with the matter.

By late October: Danny Hakim and Thomas Kaplan, "'Occupy Albany' vs. 'Governor 1 Percent,'" *New York Times*, October 27, 2011. See also Jimmy Vielkind, "At Camp, Heat Rises to Top," Albany *Times Union*, October 26, 2011, http://www.timesunion.com/local/article/At-camp-heat-rises-to-top-2233614.php.

Instead, he urged: Fredric U. Dicker, "Cuomo Is 'Preoccupied' Wall Street," *New York Post*, October 24, 2011, http://nypost.com/2011/10/24/cuomo-is-preoccupied-wall-street/.

Susan Lerner: Thomas Kaplan, "Albany Tax Deal to Raise Rate for Highest Earners," *New York Times*, December 6, 2011.

Brian Kolb: Author interview with a person familiar with the matter.

On the anniversary: Thomas Kaplan, "At Open House, Visitors Bear Praise for Governor," *New York Times,* January 1, 2012.

Andrew was presiding: Thomas Kaplan, "A Cuomo Microscope on Capitol Renovation," *New York Times*, January 3, 2012. See also Jesse McKinley, "A Jewel in Albany Regains Its Luster," *New York Times*, March 9, 2013.

The mayor found himself: Author interview with a person familiar with the matter.

Andrew explained: 2012 State of the State Address (transcript), Office of New York Governor Andrew Cuomo, https://www.governor.ny.gov/assets/documents/Building-a-New-New-York-Book.pdf.

Six Indian casinos: Charles V. Bagli, "Plan for Indian Casino in the Catskills Is Rejected," *New York Times*, February 18, 2011.

$500 million renovation: Charles V. Bagli, "Replace Javits with Center in Queens? Too Far from Sights, Convention Experts Say," *New York Times*, February 21, 2012.

Without competitive bidding: "Andrew's Bad Bet," editorial, *New York Post*, January 9, 2012.

In a memo: James M. Odato, "Tax Chief Deputizes IG Staff to Permit Use of Returns," Albany *Times Union*, February 5, 2012. See also Thomas Kaplan, "Drawing Fire, Deal Gives Agency Staff Power to See State Workers' Tax Files," *New York Times*, February 6, 2012, and Michael Gormley, "NY Legislators Cite Tax-Records Privacy," Associated Press, February 6, 2012.

Later, a court ruling: James M. Odato, "A Matter of Sharing," Albany *Times Union*, March 16, 2014.

To Ravi Batra: Author interview with Ravi Batra.

JCOPE would report: Associated Press, "Appointees to New York Ethics Board Question Whether Panel Is Under Jurisdiction of Cuomo or Legislature," February 28, 2012.

Batra's concern: Author interview with Ravi Batra.

Lawmakers were startled: John Eligon, "Budget Provision Raises Worries About Cuomo's Reach," *New York Times*, January 19, 2012.

Money authorized: Kenneth Lovett, "Controller DiNapoli Warns That Cuomo's Budget Blueprint Is a Power Grab," *New York Daily News*, February 7, 2012.

Pressed by seventeen: Environmental Advocates of New York, "Groups Call on Governor Cuomo to Drop Transfer Language from NYS Budget," press release, March 8, 2012, http://www.eany.org/our-work/press-release/groups-call-governor-cuomo-drop-transfer-language-nys-budget.

The governor instead: Jon Campbell, "Transfer Language Clarified in Final State Budget," Westchester County, New York, *Journal News*, March 27, 2012.

The Department of Financial Services: Reid Pillifant, "Ben Lawsky Audits DiNapoli, Who Audited Cuomo," *Capital New York*, August 20, 2013.

"Meanwhile," said an observer: Author interview with a person familiar with the matter.

As the *New York Times* noted: "Not What Albany Needs," editorial, *New York Times*, March 1, 2012.

"I *am* the government": Glenn Blain, "Gov. Andrew Cuomo Says 'I *Am* the Government,'" *New York Daily News*, November 10, 2011.

Instead of having them: Erik Kriss, "Gov Rips Union Man DiNap on Pensions," *New York Post*, February 17, 2012.

"The comptroller is irrelevant": Rick Karlin, "Cuomo, DiNapoli Spat Continues," Albany *Times Union*, February 27, 2012.

Andrew again threatened line: Kenneth Lovett, "Cuomo's Ultimatum," *New York Daily News*, February 22, 2012.

He had nixed: Author interview with a person familiar with the matter.

"If there were acceptable lines": Azi Paybarah, "Again, Cuomo Outlines Conditions Under Which He'd Abandon His Redistricting-Veto Promise," *Capital New York*, March 2, 2010.

By Andrew's new plan: Josh Benson, "Andrew Cuomo's Promise to Fix Redistricting Isn't What It Once Was," *Capital New York*, February 20, 2012. See also Casey Seiler, "Details Emerge on Possible Constitutional Change," *Capitol Confidential* (blog), Albany *Times Union*, March 1, 2012; Office of the Governor of New York, "Governor Cuomo Announces Passage of Constitutional Amendment and Legal Statute That Permanently Reform Redistricting Process," press release, March 15, 2012; and "Gov. Cuomo Succumbs," editorial, *New York Times*, March 16, 2012.

The governor got Tier VI: Office of the Governor of New York, "Governor Cuomo Announces Passage of Major Pension Reform," press release, March 15, 2012.

One victory: Joan Gralla, "NY State Lawmakers to Allow Casino Gambling," Reuters, March 15, 2012.

A plan at last: "Gov. Cuomo Succumbs," *New York Times*.

Andrew lost his bid: Thomas Kaplan and Danny Hakim, "Cuomo and Top Legislators Near Accord on the Budget," *New York Times*, March 26, 2012.

"Sleep deprivation": Thomas Kaplan, "After Albany All-Nighter, Lawmakers Say: No More," *New York Times*, March 16, 2012.

This new sixty-third: Jimmy Vielkind, "Panel Makes Case for New District," Albany *Times Union*, January 30, 2012.

As lawmakers pored: Thomas Kaplan, "Albany Redrawing Political Map with Old Lines of Thought," *New York Times*, March 12, 2012.

"Have you no shame?": Associated Press, "Gov. Andrew Cuomo, GOP Senate Come Up Winners in Big Deals," March 15, 2012.

In the Senate: Website of the office of New York State Senator Liz Krueger, "Senate Democrats Walk Out to Protest Stop to Redistricting Debate," March 15, 2012, http://www.nysenate.gov/news/senate-democrats-walk-out-protest-stop-redistricting-debate.

The vote: Nick Reisman, "Senate Democrats Stage Walk Out over Redistricting," *New York State of Politics*, March 15, 2012.

To Mayor Ed Koch: Thomas Kaplan, "Albany Redrawing Political Map with Old Lines of Thought," *New York Times*, March 12, 2012.

Andrew distrusted: Fredric U. Dicker, "Dems O(k) with 401 for Selves," *New York Post*, Marcg 19, 2012.

"In a Senate": Author interview with Kevin Parker.

"I'll tell you": Author interview with a person familiar with the matter.

"The truth is": "Gov. Cuomo Succumbs," *New York Times*.

"I failed": Danny Hakim, John Eligon, and Thomas Kaplan, "Cuomo, Admitting Setbacks, Says He Asked for the Moon," *New York Times*, March 15, 2010.

Recently announced: Thomas Kaplan, "Governor Cuomo to Be Subject of a Biography," *City Room* (blog), *New York Times*, January 19, 2012.

Liz Benjamin: Ben Smith, "Cuomo Aide Slammed Reporter in Dossier," *BuzzFeed*, April 15, 2012.

Andrew boasted: Jimmy Vielkind, "Cuomo Won't Give AG Election Enforcement Powers," *Capitol Confidential* (blog), Albany *Times Union*, April 16, 2012.

One FOIL request: Jimmy Vielkind, "Delay Hurts Public Access," Albany *Times Union*, March 12, 2012.

When a reporter: James M. Odato, "Lots of Black Ink on Travel Records," Albany *Times Union*, August 15, 2011.

Requests for his schedules: Vielkind, "Delay Hurts Public Access."

***Washington Post*:** Aaron Blake, "The Nation's 10 Most Popular Governors—and Why," *Washington Post*, April 11, 2012.

***Time* put him on its new:** Ed Rendell, "Andrew Cuomo," *Time*, April 18, 2012.

"I've seen this movie before": Chris Smith, "Andrew Cuomo Says 2016 Presidential Speculation Is 'Fascinating,' and He's Right," *New York*, April 26, 2012.

Early that May: Associated Press, "President Obama Visits Albany High-Tech Center with Gov. Andrew Cuomo," May 8, 2012.

One Wall Street dealmaker: Author interview with a person familiar with the matter.

Chapter 24: The Great Allure of Gaming

He was a book guy: Roger Cohen, "Schuster Executive to Head Little, Brown," *New York Times*, July 25, 1991.

Hayward had felt: Author interview with a person familiar with the matter.

Andrew fired off a sizzling letter: Office of the Governor of New York, "Governor Cuomo to NYRA: Jobs Must Be Based in New York," press release, April 28, 2011, http://www.governor.ny.gov/press/042811nyrajobs.

"Look," said Michael: Author interview with a person familiar with the matter.

The first governor Cuomo: Tom Precious, "NYRA Has History of Run-ins with Cuomo Family," *Blood-Horse*, May 7, 2012. See also Andrew Beyer, "New York Racing's Imminent Takeover by the State Is Cause for Worry," *Washington Post*, August 25, 2012, http://www.washingtonpost.com/sports/new-york-racings-imminent-takeover-by-the-state-is-cause-for-worry/2012/08/25/5f91db5c-ee14-11e1-afd6-f55f84bc0c41_story.html.

In late April 2012: Danny Hakim, "State Report Says Racing Association Knowingly Withheld Millions," *New York Times*, April 29, 2012. See also James M. Odato, "NYRA Overcharged by a Nose," Albany *Times Union*, December 22, 2011.

Traditionally at its three tracks: Author interview with a person familiar with the matter.

***New York Times*:** Hakim, "State Report Says Racing Association Knowingly Withheld Millions."

Days later: Jerry Bossert, "New York Racing Association Fires President Charles Hayward Amid Report of Exotic Wagering Scam," *New York Daily News*, May 5, 2012.

According to one board member: The following passage, including unattributed quotes, is based on author interviews with individuals familiar with the matter.

Eager to show: Letter from four Williams & Connolly attorneys to Catherine Leahy Scott, who was at the time acting inspector general for the state of New York, August 31, 2012.

Her own report: Office of the New York State Inspector General, "NYS Inspector General Scott Finds New York Racing Association, Failing to Heed Statute, Overcharged Bettors By Millions" (press release), August 25, 2014, http://ig.ny.gov/pdfs/NYRAPR8-25-14.pdf.

Hayward had fought for: Justin Mason, "NYRA Details Payout Given to Executives It Fired," Schenectady, New York, *Daily Gazette*, May 13, 2014, http://www.dailygazette.com/news/2014/may/13/0513nyra/?print.

Andrew declared: Michael Gormley, "Cuomo, NYRA Agree to Smaller, 3-Year Board," Associated Press, May 22, 2012. See also Joe Drape, "New York Seizes Control of Horse-Racing Board," *New York Times*, May 22, 2010.

One former NYRA board member: Author interview with a person familiar with the matter.

At some point: Nicholas Confessore, Danny Hakim, and Charles V. Bagli, "Gambling Group Gave $2 Million to a Cuomo Ally," *New York Times*, June 4, 2012.

On June 1: Thomas Kaplan and Danny Hakim, "Cuomo's $4 Billion Plan for Project in Queens Falls Apart," *New York Times*, June 1, 2012.

On June 4: Confessore, Hakim, and Bagli, "Gambling Group Gave $2 Million to a Cuomo Ally."

The governor's top press aide: Jon Campbell, "Cuomo's Office Releases 2,200-Word Letter on Lobbying Group," Westchester County, New York, *Journal News*, July 20, 2012. The full text of Bamberger's letter surfaced in response to a FOIL request by the *Journal News*.

A cozy fund-raiser: Jacob Gershman and Eliot Brown, "Casinos Wagered Early on Cuomo," *Wall Street Journal*, June 5, 2012.

Jeffrey Gural: Author interview with a person familiar with the matter.

According to one gaming industry source: Author interview with a person familiar with the matter.

One source close to the governor: Author interview with a person familiar with the matter.

Ravi Batra thought he knew: Author interview with Ravi Batra.

"The recent disclosures": Associated Press, "New York Ethics Board Member 'Stunned' by Gambling Donations to Pro-Cuomo Lobbying Group," June 7, 2012.

The CSNY's tax filings: Nicholas Confessore and Thomas Kaplan, "$12 Million to Help Cuomo Came from Just 20 People," *New York Times*, May 12, 2012.

Batra was so stressed: Author interview with Ravi Batra.

The Albany *Times Union*: Jimmy Vielkind and James M. Odato, "Cuomo Control of Information Includes Screening, Redaction of Records at State Archives," Albany *Times Union*, July 23, 2012. See also Vielkind, "The 'Troopergate' Memo Cuomo Wants to Keep Hidden," and Vielkind, "Delay Hurts Public Access."

"Governor Andrew Cuomo is clever": Michael Gormley, "Analysis: Gov. Cuomo at a Crossroads on Open Government," Associated Press, July 28, 2012.

The show: Associated Press, "New York Gov. Cuomo on Menu at the Longest-Running Annual Political Satire Show in the Nation," May 23, 2012.

Mario supplied it: Danny Hakim, "Cuomo for President? Who Said That? Well, Dad," *New York Times*, July 8, 2012.

As an eightieth birthday present: Office of the Governor of New York, "Governor Andrew M. Cuomo, Cuomo Alumni Present Governor Mario M. Cuomo with a Surprise Birthday Gift: A Portrait to Hang in the Hall of Governors," press release, June 23, 2012, http://www.governor.ny.gov/press/06232012cuomoportrait.

Harold Holzer: Hakim, "Cuomo for President? Who Said That? Well, Dad."

Its placement: David Kestenbaum, "A Big Bridge in the Wrong Place," *Planet Money* (blog), National Public Radio, August 19, 2011.

The new Tappan Zee: Jim O'Grady, "NY Gov Cuomo Offers No Details on Tappan Zee Bridge Funds," *Transportation Nation*, website of WNYC, the New York City NPR station, May 3, 2012.

Any more: Peter Applebome, "Faulting a Plan to Replace the Scorned Tappan Zee," *New York Times*, June 26, 2012.

"You can build whatever you want": Kate Hinds, "Cuomo Says Mass Transit System for Tappan Zee Would Double Costs," WNYC, July 10, 2012.

Andrew won a federal loan: Krista Madsen, "New Tappan Zee Bridge Secures Largest TIFIA Loan Ever," *Tarrytown-Sleepy Hollow Patch*, December 20, 2013.

Early that August: CBS New York, "Officials: $14 Toll Expected for New Tappan Zee Bridge; Commuters Go Ballistic," August 3, 2012.

Eventually, the *Bergen Record*: Shawn Boburg, "Top Christie Port Authority Appointees Devised Toll-Hike Plan to Bolster Image of NJ, NY Governors," *Bergen Record*, March 2, 2014.

Vito Lopez: Danny Hakim, "Lawmaker Is Censured over Sexual Harassment," *New York Times*, August 24, 2012.

In response to the women's demand: Danny Hakim, "2 Women Received $32,000 from Assemblyman, Beyond Money from State," *New York Times*, August 29, 2012.

"Well, that happens": Reid Pillifant, "Cuomo Declines a Chance to Comment on the Assembly's Vito Lopez Bailout," *Capital New York*, August 27, 2012.

On its last day: Michael Barbaro, "Cuomo, in Convention City, Gives Spirited Speech from Small Stage," *New York Times*, September 6, 2012.

It would investigate Lopez: Danny Hakim, "New York Ethics Inquiry Won't Look at Speaker's Actions," *New York Times*, September 6, 2012.

The JCOPE commissioners protested: Author interview with Ravi Batra.

Batra resigned: Thomas Kaplan and Danny Hakim, "Cuomo Is Open to 'Tweaks' in Ethics Panel," *New York Times*, September 11, 2012.

"There is no independence": Associated Press, "NY Ethics Board Member Who Quit Strikes at Board," September 9, 2012.

Being on JCOPE: Liz Benjamin, "Ravi Batra Explains His JCOPE Resignation to Cuomo in 3,430 Words," *New York State of Politics*, September 10, 2012, http://www.nystateofpolitics.com/2012/09/ravi-batra-explains-his-jcope-resignation-to-cuomo-in-3430-words/.

Commissioners widened their scope: Joseph Spector and Jon Campbell, "Silver, Assembly Knocked in Lopez Scandal," Rochester, New York, *Democrat and Chronicle*, May 14, 2013.

"They're trying to get": Author interview with a person familiar with the situation.

"It's a no-win situation": Author interview with a person familiar with the situation.

Rex Smith: Rex Smith, "Smith: What Kind of Scandal Is This?" Albany *Times Union*, September 22, 2012.

A spokesman for Andrew: Margolin, "9/11 Slight Fight."

Bloomberg's foundation: Charles V. Bagli, "Dispute over Costs Delays Opening of 9/11 Museum," *New York Times*, September 8, 2012.

At the ten-year anniversary: Scott Raab, "The Truth about the World Trade Center," *Esquire*, September 2012.

In June: David Seifman, "9/11 Kin Tell Govs: PA 'Betrayed' Victims," *New York Post*, June 28, 2012.

A deal was reached: Charles V. Bagli, "Agreement Will Restart Work on Sept. 11 Museum," *New York Times*, September 10, 2012.

Douglas and Molly: Jim Fitzgerald, "Douglas Kennedy Invokes Father's Assassination During Court Appearance," *Huffington Post*, April 13, 2012. See also Associated Press,

"Kennedy Cleared in Westchester Hospital Tussle," November 20, 2012, and Lee Higgins, "Kennedy Sues N.Y. Nurses, Hospital after Newborn Case," Westchester County, New York *Journal News*, January 9, 2013.

"So Tim gives me the okay": Author interview with Douglas Kennedy.

Dr. Haydock: Janon Fisher, "RFK's Son Douglas Kennedy Charged for Endangering 3-Day-Old Son after Tussle at Westchester Hospital," *New York Daily News*, February 26, 2012. See also Associated Press, "Security Video Shows Struggle Between RFK Son, Nurses," February 26, 2012.

Kerry Kennedy's own legal travail: Peter Applebome, "Private Lives of Kennedys, Played Out in Public," *New York Times*, July 15, 2012. See also Wendy Ruderman and Michael Schwirtz, "Kerry Kennedy Cites Possible Seizure, Not Drugs, in Car Crash," *New York Times*, July 17, 2012, and Joseph Berger, "Fast Acquittal for Kennedy, Whose Name Put Prosecutors in Bind," *New York Times*, February 28, 2014.

Chapter 25: Guns and Butter

Canceled the southern: Richard Dunham, "Hurricane Sandy Prompts Obama, Romney to Cancel Campaign Appearances; Biden, Bill Clinton Pick Up the Slack," Albany *Times Union*, October 29, 2012.

Declared a state of emergency: Office of the Governor of New York, "Governor Cuomo Declares State of Emergency in New York in Preparation for Potential Impact of Hurricane Sandy," press release, October 26, 2012.

"Do not underestimate": Juliette Kayyem, "Politicians Push Back," *Boston Globe*, November 1, 2012.

Andrew rode down the East Side: Chris Smith, "Foul-Weather Friends: Bloomberg and Cuomo, Bonded in Crisis," *New York*, November 3, 2012.

"We didn't know": Freeman Klopott, "Trade Center Construction Resumes on Generator Power," Bloomberg News, November 2, 2010.

Only later: James M. Odato, "Report Rips State Handling of Superstorm Sandy Response," Albany *Times Union*, February 10, 2014.

A news conference: Matt Chaban, "Governor Cuomo Declares New York's Greatest Strength Also Its Greatest Weakness," *New York Observer*, November 1, 2012.

As the officials clustered: Smith, "Foul-Weather Friends."

Rumor had it: David Seifman, "Andy, Mike Fight for Spotlight," *New York Post*, December 2, 2012.

Toured the state by helicopter: Julie Pace, "Obama, Chris Christie Tour Damage Left by Hurricane Sandy in New Jersey," *Huffington Post*, October 31, 2012.

Columnist Frank Rich: Tweet by columnist Frank Rich, https://twitter.com/frankrichny/status/263336480716492800.

And so materialized: Dana Rubinstein, "Cuomo Launches a Moreland Commission, Finally Moving to Take Charge of the Utilities Issue," *Capital New York*, November 13, 2012.

With just weeks to study: Author interview with a person familiar with the matter.

In the later version: Moreland Commission on Utility Storm Preparation and Response, Interim Report, January 7, 2013, http://moreland.ny.gov/sites/default/files/MAC-Interim-Report1-7-2013.pdf.

Based on the final version: Yancey Roy, "Moreland Commission: Scrap LIPA after Sandy Performance," *Newsday*, January 7, 2013.

"I want to see": Glenn Bain, "Gov. Andrew Cuomo, a Democrat, Hints That He Might Support Some of the Republican Candidates for State Senate," *New York Daily News*, July 10, 2012.

Two would lose: Thomas Kaplan, "Primary Results Close for 2 G.O.P. Legislators Who Voted for Same-Sex Marriage," *New York Times*, September 13, 2012. See also Thomas Kaplan, "After Defeat, Senator Says He Won't Try Third-Party Bid," *New York Times*, September 27, 2012.

"I don't believe": Thomas Kaplan and Michael M. Grynbaum, "Governor and Mayor Are Upset That 2 Backers of Gay Marriage May Fall," *New York Times*, September 19, 2012.

One of the toss-ups: Thomas Kaplan, "Groups Push to Highlight Campaign Finance Reform," *New York Times*, October 21, 2012.

Only later: Zeff, "Another Cuomo Noninterference Story Falls Apart."

A black downstate Democrat: Jon Campbell, "Malcolm Smith to Join Independent Democratic Conference," Westchester County, New York, *Journal News*, December 4, 2012.

Soon to join that list: Jim Dwyer, "Jumping from Party to Party to Bribery Charge," *New York Times*, April 2, 2013. In June 2014, Malcolm Smith was granted a mistrial in his trial for bribery and wire fraud. As this book went to press, a new trial was scheduled for January 2015.

State senator Tony Avella: Dan Rosenblum, "Lawmaker Says Fracking Could Ruin Cuomo 2016: 'All It'll Take Is One Incident,'" *Capital New York*, July 10, 2012.

"It's going to be very difficult": Freeman Klopott, "Cuomo's Fracking Dilemma Poses Political Risk Beyond New York," Bloomberg News, October 9, 2012.

The *Wall Street Journal*: "Cuomo's De-Fracking," editorial, *Wall Street Journal*, October 3, 2012.

After months of silence: Mireya Navarro, "New York State Plans Health Review as It Weighs Gas Drilling," *New York Times*, September 20, 2012.

"We've said all along": Danny Hakim, "Shift by Cuomo on Gas Drilling Prompts Both Anger and Praise," *New York Times*, September 30, 2012.

That fall, Andrew ran: Author interview with senator Liz Krueger.

"Let this terrible tragedy": Office of New York Governor Andrew Cuomo, "Statement from Governor Andrew M. Cuomo on Shooting at Sandy Hook Elementary School," press release, December 14, 2012.

"Stop the madness!": Erik Kriss, "NY Gov. Cuomo Pushes Strict Gun-Control Measures in Wake of Shootings," *New York Post*, January 10, 2013.

Offstage, Andrew was holding tense meetings: Author interview with a person familiar with the matter.

"If you ban": Author interview with a person familiar with the matter.

"I was married": Author interview with a person familiar with the matter.

Along with a mandate: New York State Psychiatric Association, "NYSPA Issues Press Release on SAFE Act Reporting Requirements," press release, undated.

The loudest voice: Azi Paybarah, "Andrew Cuomo's Favorite Columnist Is Up in Arms," *Capital New York*, January 15, 2013.

Gamely, Andrew came on the show: Casey Seiler, "Cuomo Takes to the Air to Defend SAFE Act," *Capitol Confidential* (blog), Albany *Times Union*, January 17, 2013.

Six-figure advance: Keith J. Kelly, "Dicker Gets Deal to Write Bio of Cuomo," *New York Post*, April 13, 2012.

With a collaborator: Erica Orden, "Cuomo Hires Writer, Moves Book Ahead," *Wall Street Journal*, August 7, 2013.

HarperCollins reportedly agreed to pay: Jimmy Vielkind, "Cuomo's Book Deal Worth at Least $700,000," *Capital New York*, May 23, 2014.

By the end of January: Quinnipiac University, "Gun Bill Knocks GOP Support for New York's Cuomo, Quinnipiac University Poll Finds; Most Republicans Say Gun Bill Went Too Far," press release, January 30, 2013.

One of his close advisers: Author interview with a person familiar with the matter.

Three months later: Jonathan Weisman, "Senate Blocks Drive for Gun Control," *New York Times*, April 17, 2013.

Eventually, a federal judge: Thomas Kaplan, "U.S. Judge Upholds Most New York Gun Limits," *New York Times*, December 31, 2013.

The mayor was surprised: Author interview with a person familiar with the matter.

Hillary Clinton: Helene Cooper, "Clinton's Blood Clot Is Located Near Her Brain, Doctors Say," *New York Times*, December 30, 2012. See also Denise Grady and Mark Landler, "Clinton out of Hospital After Treatment for Clot," *New York Times*, January 2, 2013.

"It's really a crazy situation": Maggie Haberman, "Andrew Cuomo's New Problems: Bad Headlines, Hillary Clinton," *Politico*, February 24, 2013.

Tkaczyk was adamantly opposed: Jimmy Vielkind, "Democratic Chairs Beg Cuomo to Back Tkaczyk," *Capitol Confidential* (blog), Albany *Times Union*, November 4, 2012.

Two weeks before election day: Thomas Kaplan, "Groups Push to Highlight Campaign Reform," *New York Times*, October 21, 2013.

Heard Amedore claim victory: Anne Hayden, "Amedore, Tkaczyk Both Claim Victory," *Altamont Enterprise & Albany Post*, November 8, 2012.

Not until January: Thomas Kaplan, "Democrat Ekes Out Senate Win," *New York Times*, January 18, 2013.

The latest to surface: Danny Hakim, "Lobbying Group That Backs Cuomo Gets Big Donations from Firm He Investigated," *New York Times*, November 26, 2012.

Real estate developer: Casey Seiler, "NYPIRG Breaks Down Cuomo's 2013 Big-Money Donors," *Capitol Confidential* (blog), Albany *Times Union*, July 15, 2013.

Another warning: Stephanie A. Miner, "Cuomo to Cities: Just Borrow," *New York Times*, February 13, 2013.

Some months before: Author interview with Syracuse mayor Stephanie Miner.

"That's called life": Karen DeWitt, "Cuomo Tells Local Governments: Make Tough Calls," WNYC Radio, October 22, 1012.

A former labor lawyer: Office of the Mayor of Syracuse New York, "Mayor's Biography," http://www.syrgov.net/Mayors_Biography.aspx.

In response, the lieutenant governor: Danny Hakim, "Syracuse's Democratic Mayor Gets Under Governor's Skin," *New York Times*, January 23, 2013.

The day before: Author interview with Stephanie Miner.

Over the next months: Author interview with Stephanie Miner.

She won reelection: Michelle Breidenbach, "Syracuse Mayor Stephanie Miner Wins Election to a Second Term," Syracuse Media Group, November 5, 2013.

She stepped down: Glenn Blain, "State Democratic Party Co-Chairwoman Stephanie Miner—Who Has Clashed with Gov. Cuomo—Resigns," *New York Daily News*, April 17, 2014. See also Fredric U. Dicker, "Dems Won't Support Cuomo for President in 2016: Sources," *New York Post*, April 21, 2014.

At last came a call: Author interview with Stephanie Miner.

Finally, with the primary looming: Liz Benjamin, "Miner & Cuomo Bury the Hatchet," *New York State of Politics*, September 5, 2014, http://www.nystateofpolitics.com/2014/09/miner-cuomo-bury-the-hatchet/.

A Washington-based think tank: Scott Drenkard and Joseph Henchman, "2013 State Business Tax Climate Index," report, Tax Foundation, October 9, 2012, http://taxfoundation.org/article/2013-state-business-tax-climate-index.

Open for Business: Office of the Governor of New York State, "Governor Cuomo Launches 'New York Open for Business' Marketing Initiative" (press release), August 24, 2011.

Start-Up NY: Office of the Governor of New York State, "Governor Cuomo and Legislative Leaders Announce Agreement on Start-Up NY Legislation That Will Implement Tax-Free NY Initiative," press release, June 19, 2013.

Chapter 26: Scandalmania

John Sampson: Mosi Secret, "Senator in Corruption Case Spoke of Silencing Witnesses, Prosecutors Say," *New York Times*, May 6, 2013. John Sampson pleaded not guilty to corruption charges, and as this book went to press, the prosecution was still pending.

Malcolm Smith: Dwyer, "Jumping from Party to Party to Bribery Charge." In June 2014, Malcolm Smith was granted a mistrial in his trial for bribery and wire fraud. As this book went to press, a new trial was scheduled for January 2015.

Shirley Huntley: John Marzulli and Greg B. Smith, "Ex-State Senator Shirley Huntley Sentenced to Year and Day in Prison," *New York Daily News*, May 10, 2013.

"You didn't need to know": Author interview with Steve Cohen.

After the *New York Post*: "Deafening Silence from Albany Pols," *New York Post*, April 5, 2013.

One of Andrew's advisers: Author interview with a person familiar with the matter.

An important part: Associated Press, "32 New York Officials Snared for Corruption in 7 Years," May 6, 2013, http://www.syracuse.com/news/index.ssf/2013/05/32_ny_officials_snared_for_cor.html.

"He's floundering": Kenneth Lovett, "Gov. Andrew Cuomo Sees Bills and Ratings Slip Up," *New York Daily News*, May 6, 2013.

"He always wanted": Author interview with an individual familiar with the matter.

After two years: Lovett, "Gov. Andrew Cuomo Sees Bills and Ratings Slip Up."

More powers for authorities: Thomas Kaplan, "Cuomo Offers Plan to Fight Corruption After Arrests," *New York Times*, April 9, 2013.

"Andrew doesn't trust": Author interview with a person familiar with the matter.

Wearing eyeliner: Susanne Craig, "Cuomo and Schneiderman Prepare to Fight over JPMorgan Settlement," *New York Times*, January 16, 2014.

"My relationship": Ross Barkan, "Schneiderman Says He Doesn't Wear Eyeliner, Not That There's Anything Wrong with That," *New York Observer*, February 13, 2014.

By May 2013: Thomas Kaplan, "Wealthy Group Seeks to Reform Election Giving in New York," *New York Times*, April 11, 2012.

The governor did want: Author interview with Steve Cohen.

Graphic details: Danny Hakim, "Report Finds Lawmaker Was Shielded by Leaders," *New York Times*, May 15, 2013.

"This is a disgusting, sordid incident": Associated Press, "NY Assembly Speaker to Propose Lopez Removal," May 16, 2013.

As late as 2011: Liz Robbins, "Democratic Party Pick Wins Brooklyn Race," *New York Times*, September 14, 2011. See also Bill Samuels, "Filling Vacancies," NYConstitution.org, undated, http://nyconstitution.org/issue/Vacancies.

Asked if he thought: Thomas Kaplan, "Scrutiny of Silver Continues as Lopez Is Set to Resign," *New York Times*, May 19, 2013.

A stinging column: Fredric U. Dicker, "Time's Up! Shameful Shelly Has Got to Go," *New York Post*, May 16, 2013.

One of the governor's own advisers: Author interview with a person familiar with the matter.

Jean Miller: Joe Mahoney, "Pol Blasts Postie as 'Slime' over Baby Story," *New York Daily News*, January 13, 2005.

"Throwing the Assembly": Author interview with a person familiar with the matter.

As one lawmaker noted: Author interview with a person familiar with the matter.

Instead of pushing: Author interview with a person familiar with the matter.

On Monday, the old goat: "No Public Office for Vito Lopez," editorial, *New York Times*, May 20, 2013.

They came up clean: Nick Reisman, "DiNapoli and Schneiderman React to Lopez Report," *New York State of Politics*, May 15, 2013, http://www.nystateofpolitics.com/2013/05/dinapoli-and-schneiderman-react-to-lopez-report/. See also State of New York Joint Commission on Public Ethics, "Substantial Basis Investigation Report: In the Matter of an Investigation of Assemblyman Vito Lopez," http://www.jcope.ny.gov/enforcement/2013/lopez/Lopez%20Substantial%20Basis%20Investigation%20Report.pdf.

In a radio interview: Jill Colvin, "Governor Cuomo Talks Scandals and Sex," *New York Observer*, May 20, 2013.

After four consecutive months: Erica Orden, "After Months of Decline, Cuomo's Rating Ticks Upward: Poll," *Wall Street Journal*, May 20, 2013.

Gaming had made: New York State Task Force on Casino Gambling, Report to the Governor of New York, August 30, 1996, http://gaming.ny.gov/reports.php.

On April 25: Glenn Coin and Michelle Breidenbach, "How Gov. Cuomo, the Oneida Indian Nation and Two Counties Made Historic Deal in Record Time," Syracuse *Post-Standard*, May 19, 2013.

In 1976: Bruce Entelisano, "Death Drives Life for Oneida Nation Leader Ray Halbritter," *Rome Observer*, June 23, 2010, http://www.romeobserver.com/articles/2010/06/23/news/doc4c22b5983b152519017657.txt?viewmode=fullstory.

In exchange: Office of the Governor of New York, "Governor Cuomo Announces Landmark Agreement Between State, Oneida Nation, and Oneida and Madison Counties," press release, May 16, 2013, http://www.governor.ny.gov/press/05162013-agreement-with-state-oneida-nation-and-oneida-and-madison-counties.

Days after the Oneida settlement: "Cuomo Signs Deal with Mohawks to Protect Casino Territory," *New York Times*, May 21, 2013. See also Jon Campbell, "Mohawks, Cuomo Reach Deal on Casino Revenue," Rochester, New York, *Democrat and Chronicle*, May 21, 2013.

For their own three casinos: Justin Sondel, "Cuomo Gives the Senecas an Ultimatum," *Niagara Gazette*, May 9, 2013, http://www.niagara-gazette.com/news/local_news/article_f4120676-0f75-52b5-980f-a9569d4fa37f.html.

When Andrew: Associated Press, "Seneca Head: Cuomo Acts Like Bully with Casinos," May 17, 2013.

The Senecas would keep: Charles Bagli, "Seneca Tribe Reaches Deal with Cuomo on Gambling," *New York Times*, June 13, 2013. See also Office of the Governor of New York, "Governor Cuomo and Seneca Nation of Indians Announce Landmark Agreement," press release, June 13, 2013, https://www.governor.ny.gov/press/06-13-2013/Landmark-Agreement.

Michael Leven: Christopher Palmeri and Freeman Klopott, "Cuomo Casino Plan Called a Loser by Las Vegas Sands," Bloomberg News, June 5, 2013.

"We hope that what": WXXI-AM Radio, "Cuomo's Tax-Free Zones Draw Mixed Reviews," May 24, 2013, http://innovationtrail.org/post/cuomos-tax-free-zones-draw-mixed-reviews.

Early in the summer: Joseph Spector, "After a One-Year Delay, NY Comes Clean on Ad Spending," Rochester, New York, *Democrat and Chronicle*, July 17, 2014, http://www.democratandchronicle.com/story/news/local/2014/07/17/one-year-delay-ny-comes-clean-ad-spending/12813427/. See also Joseph Spector, "Astorino Says Cuomo Should Halt 'Open for Business' Ads," Westchester County, New York, *Journal News*, July 18, 2014, http://www.poughkeepsiejournal.com/story/news/local/new-york/2014/07/18/astorino-says-cuomo-halt-open-business-ads/12865297/.

As of June 2014: Office of the Governor of New York, "Governor Cuomo Announces First Wave of Businesses to Expand or Locate in New York State Under Start-Up NY," press release, June 4, 2014, http://www.governor.ny.gov/press/06042014-first-wave-businesses-start-up-ny.

In the interim: Jon Campbell, "In Budget Update, Cuomo's Office Revels Cost of Start-Up NY," Westchester County, New York, *Journal News*, August 5, 2013, http://polhudson.lohudblogs.com/2013/08/05/in-budget-update-cuomos-office-acknowledges-cost-of-start-up-ny/.

"There is a simplicity": Jimmy Vielkind, "Finally, the Women's Equality Bill Is Released," *Capitol Confidential* (blog), Albany *Times Union*, June 4, 2013.

And so it died: Thomas Kaplan, "All-or-Nothing Strategy on Women's Equality Legislation Ends with Nothing," *New York Times*, June 23, 2013. See also Casey Seiler and Rick Karlin, "Women's Bill Falls Short," Albany *Times Union*, June 22, 2013.

Andrew came out at last: Thomas Kaplan, "Cuomo Pushes Legislators on Elections Financing," *New York Times*, June 11, 2013. See also Jimmy Vielkind, "Cuomo Bill Eyes Public-Financed Elections," Albany *Times Union*, June 10, 2013.

Political columnist Blake Zeff: Blake Zeff, "Andrew Cuomo Pretends to Want Public Financing Really Badly," *Salon*, June 13, 2013.

The bill died on the floor: Aaron Short, "A Hostile Campaign Finance Amendment Dies in the Senate," *City & State*, June 21, 2013, http://archives.cityandstateny.com/a-hostile-amendment-dies-in-the-senate/.

"It's going to be": Michael Goodwin, "Finally, It's Bums Away," *New York Post*, June 26, 2013.

Nowhere mentioned: Michael Gormley, "Legality of Cuomo's Lawmaker Corruption Probe Questioned, Associated Press, June 21, 2013, http://www.troyrecord.com/general-news/20130621/legality-of-cuomos-lawmaker-corruption-probe-questioned.

Once before: Bill Hammond, "Fumigate the Capitol? You Wish," *New York Daily News*, June 25, 2013.

Andrew's third session: Thomas Kaplan, "Action on Expanded Gambling as Albany's Legislative Session Sputters to End," *New York Times*, June 21, 2013.

"Let's say I'm him": Author interview with a person familiar with the matter.

A nemesis: *Henry "Hank" Morris v. New York State Department of Corrections et al.*, Supreme Court of the State of New York, Columbia County, case 5696-13. Judge's decision/order of March 29, 2013 and amended decision/order of April 15, 2013.

Chapter 27: Less Is Moreland

"It's an independent commission": Albany *Times Union*, "Watch Live: Cuomo Announces Moreland Commission Panel at 10 a.m.," July 2, 2013, http://blog.timesunion.com/capitol/archives/190510/watch-live-cuomo-announces-moreland-commission-panel-at-10-a-m/.

Schneiderman had seen: Author interview with a person familiar with the matter.

Gently, the AG's staffers: Author interview with a person familiar with the matter.

Richard Emery: Casey Seiler, "Hands-On, Hands-Off Cuomos Differ," Albany *Times Union*, October 10, 2013, http://www.timesunion.com/local/article/Hands-on-hands-off-Cuomos-differ-4883465.php.

Shelly Silver, who in 2012: Thomas Kaplan and Danny Hakim, "Legislators Reap Benefits of Part-Time Jobs at Law Firms, Filings Show," *New York Times*, July 3, 2013.

Dean Skelos: Colin Campbell, "Andrew Cuomo Discusses Albany Corruption and Witches," *New York Observer*, July 2, 2013, http://observer.com/2013/07/andrew-cuomo-discusses-albany-corruption-and-witches/.

Had wound down: Thomas Kaplan, "Business Leaders' Committee That Backed Cuomo Finishes Its Business and Shuts Down," *New York Times*, August 30, 2013.

As of September 2013: Erica Orden and Derek Kravitz, "Cuomo Stockpiles Cash," *Wall Street Journal*, November 17, 2013.

One was Extell: Kenneth Lovett, "Gov. Cuomo Got $100,000 from Developer, Then Signed Law Giving It Tax Breaks," *New York Daily News*, August 9, 2013.

That very day: New York State Assembly, "Assembly Passes Landmark Legislation to Give Hundreds of Thousands of New York City Homeowners Property Relief," press release, January 28, 2013, http://assembly.state.ny.us/Press/20130128a/.

Then came another $100,000: Jimmy Vielkind, "Cuomo Real Estate Donors among Moreland Subpoena Targets," Albany *Times Union*, August 14, 2013, http://www.timesunion.com/local/article/Cuomo-real-estate-donors-among-Moreland-subpoena-4730494.php.

These gifts were followed: Kenneth Lovett, "Gov. Cuomo's Long-Time City Developer Donor Got More Generous When It Stood to Get $35 Million in Tax Breaks," *New York Daily News*, August 10, 2013, http://www.nydailynews.com/news/politics/cuomo-donor-generous-stood-save-35m-article-1.1423003.

Fisher Brothers: Kenneth Lovett, "Gov. Cuomo Received $76,000 from Real Estate Investors Weeks Before Giving Their Property a Tax Break on Bill," *New York Daily News*, August 15, 2013.

Donated $2 million: Yancey Roy, "Watchdog: Lobby Group Gave Cuomo Nearly $2M Since 2011," *Newsday*, October 11, 2013, http://www.newsday.com/news/region-state/watchdog-lobby-group-gave-cuomo-nearly-2m-since-2011-1.6241879.

From then on: Kenneth Lovett, "Gov. Cuomo Leans on 'Independent' Corruption Panel," *New York Daily News*, September 30, 2013. See also Craig, Rashbaum, and Kaplan, "Cuomo's Office Hobbled Ethics Inquiries by Moreland Commission."

Yet another: Craig, Rashbaum, and Kaplan, "Cuomo's Office Hobbled Ethics Inquiries by Moreland Commission."

Cochair William Fitzpatrick: Kenneth Lovett, "Anti-Corruption Commission Co-Chair William Fitzpatrick Denies Governor's Office Interference," *New York Daily News*, October 22, 2013.

A spokesperson added: Jimmy Vielkind, "A 'Disheartened' Advocate on Cuomo's Role in Steering an Anti-Corruption Panel," *Capital New York*, October 7, 2013.

A subpoena would, after all: Thomas Kaplan, "Panel to Investigate State Democratic Party," *New York Times*, October 15, 2013.

"He sets up the panel": Author interview with a person familiar with the matter.

One of the governor's advisers: Author interview with a person familiar with the matter.

Her memoir: Regina Calcaterra, *Etched in Sand: A True Story of Five Siblings Who Survived an Unspeakable Childhood on Long Island* (New York: William Morrow, 2013).

Then came a Siena poll: Dan O'Regan, "Referendum Language Sways Support for Casinos, Poll Shows," *Legislative Gazette*, September 30, 2013, http://www.legislativegazette.com/Articles-Top-Stories-c-2013-09-30-85258.113122-Referendum-language-sways-support-for-casinos-poll-shows.html

But Andrew had anticipated: Michael Gormley, "Judge Rejects NY Casino Referendum Challenge," Associated Press, October 16, 2013. See also Associated Press, "NY Casino Referendum: Before and After," November 6, 2013.

***New York Post* columnist:** Bob McManus, "Andrew Cuomo's Casino Charade," *New York Post*, September 30, 2013.

That October: Yancey Roy, "Cuomo Appoints Pataki, McCall to Lead New Tax Commission," *Newsday*, October 2, 2013.

Apparently, the former governor: Author interview with a person familiar with the situation.

Solomon had headed that one: Office of the Governor of New York, "Governor Cuomo Announces Tax Commission Members," press release, December 11, 2012, https://www.governor.ny.gov/press/12112012taxcommissionmembers.

The former governor: E. J. McMahon, "First Take on Pataki-McCall Commission," Empire Center for Public Policy, December 10, 2013, http://www.empirecenter.org/publications/first-take-on-pataki-mccall-commission/.

"He would let them drift": Author interview with a person familiar with the matter.

"It's total brinksmanship": Author interview with a person familiar with the matter.

"Maybe he doesn't want": Author interview with a person familiar with the matter.

Alex Crohn: Morgan Pehme, Jon Lentz, and Matthew Hamilton, "Co-Chairs' Picks to Write Moreland Report Were Nixed for Second Floor Insider," *City & State*, April 15, 2014, http://www.cityandstateny.com/2/politics/second-floor-nixed-commission-report-writer-for-internal-candidate.html#.VD-Zb-emf3o.

The cochairs: Author interview with a person familiar with the matter.

The meddling: Kenneth Lovett, "A Moreland Commission 'Whoops' Moment Has Left Some Angry," *New York Daily News*, December 3, 2013, http://www.nydailynews.com/blogs/dailypolitics/moreland-commission-whoops-moment-left-angry-blog-entry-1.1697389.

The next night: Erica Orden, "Billy Joel Serenades Gov. Andrew Cuomo at His Birthday Fundraiser," *Wall Street Journal*, December 4, 2013.

On his way out: Zack Fink, "Billy Joel Helps Celebrate Governor Cuomo's Birthday," Watertown, New York, Time Warner Cable News, December 3, 2013, http://watertown.twcnews.com/content/politics/political_news/707481/billy-joel-helps-celebrate-governor-cuomo-s-birthday/.

In the executive summary: State of New York, Commission to Investigate Public Corruption, Preliminary Report, December 2, 2013, http://publiccorruption.moreland.ny.gov/sites/default/files/moreland_report_final.pdf.

"We started": Henry Goldman and Freeman Klopott, "De Blasio's 20-Year Friendship with Cuomo Facing Test," Bloomberg News, November 15, 2013.

It was during Andrew's chaotic campaign: Kenneth Lovett, "De Blasio and Cuomo's Tight Bond to Be Tested," *New York Daily News*, November 9, 2013.

"The arrows are pointing up": Erica Orden, "Cuomo Pushes Tax Relief Proposals in Speech," *Wall Street Journal*, January 9, 2014.

The Cuomo administration: Jon Campbell, "Gov. Cuomo's State of the State Calls for Tax Cuts, Education Boost," Rochester, New York, *Democrat and Chronicle*, January 8, 2014, http://www.democratandchronicle.com/story/news/local/2014/01/08/cuomos-state-of-the-state-calls-for-tax-cuts-education-boost/4373703/.

Leonard Litwin: Kenneth Lovett, "Gov. Cuomo's Reelection Being Bankrolled by Big-Bucks Buddies, Group Finds," *New York Daily News*, January 16, 2014.

Andrew declared: Michael M. Grynbaum and Thomas Kaplan, "Pre-K Plan Puts Cuomo at Odds with de Blasio on Funding," *New York Times*, January 21, 2014.

By late January: Thomas Kaplan, "Cuomo Sweetens Pre-K Deal: 'Whatever' Mayor Needs, " *New York Times*, January 23, 2014.

In public with the mayor: Susanne Craig, "De Blasio Strikes Conciliatory Note on Pre-K," *New York Times*, February 16, 2014.

For Andrew, the standoff: Author interview with a person familiar with the matter.

New Jersey's Chris Christie: N. R. Kleinfeld, "A Bridge to Scandal: Behind the Fort Lee Ruse," *New York Times*, January 12, 2014.

Andrew, when pressed: Laura Nahmias, "Asked about Christie's Scandal, Cuomo Says Little," *Capital New York*, January 18, 2014.

Howard Glaser later implied: Zack Fink, "Bridgegate Scandal's New Front? Andrew Cuomo, Pat Foye and What the New York Side Knew," *Salon*, May 2, 2014, http://www.salon.com/2014/05/02/bridgegate_scandals_new_front_andrew_cuomo_pat_foye_and_what_the_new_york_side_knew/.

On October 1: Ted Mann, "Port Chief Fumed Over Bridge Jam," *Wall Street Journal*, October 1, 2013.

In November, when Christie: Fredric U. Dicker, "Christie Ready to Back Cuomo Challenger," *New York Post*, November 25, 2013. See also Edward-Isaac Dovere, "Andrew Cuomo's Cameo in Bridge Mess," *Politico*, January 18, 2014, http://www.politico.com/story/2014/01/andrew-cuomo-chris-christie-bridgegate-102352.html.

Asked about the report: Maggie Haberman, "Andrew Cuomo-Chris Christie Ties in Spotlight," *Politico*, November 25, 2013, http://www.politico.com/story/2013/11/andrew-cuomo-chris-christie-2016-election-100345.html.

Back in 2005: Erica Orden, "New York Governor's Race Highlights an Old Feud," *Wall Street Journal*, July 7, 2014.

Patrick Foye: Ted Mann, "Port Authority Chief Testifies in George Washington Bridge Flap," *Wall Street Journal*, December 9, 2013.

Wildstein: Ed O'Keefe and Karen Tumulty, "Chris Christie Slams David Wildstein in E-mail to Supporters," *Washington Post*, February 1, 2014.

Andrew kept his distance: Blake Zeff, "Why Cuomo Isn't Touching Bridgegate," *Salon*, January 21, 2014.

That winter: "Cuomo Would Lose to Christie in NY in 2016 Vote for President, According to Poll," *Huffington Post*, November 18, 2013, http://www.huffingtonpost.com/2013/11/18/cuomo-christie-2016-president-_n_4296063.html.

He had inked: U.S. Department of Justice, "Justice Department, Federal and State Partners Secure Record $13 Billion Global Settlement with JPMorgan for Misleading Investors About Securities Containing Toxic Mortgages," press release, November 19, 2013, http://www.justice.gov/opa/pr/2013/November/13-ag-1237.html.

On January 13: Michael Powell, "New York's Mortgage Bank Hunter May Not Be Able to Direct His Spoils," *New York Times*, January 13, 2014. See also memo from New York solicitor general Barbara Underwood to Mylan Denerstein, counselor to New York governor Andrew Cuomo, January 13, 2014, posted on the *Capital New York* website, http://www.capitalnewyork.com/sites/default/files/140113_Underwood_to_Denerstein.pdf.

"The threats were flying": Author interview with a person familiar with the matter.

Finally on January 20: Susanne Craig, "Cuomo and Attorney General Agree on Division of JPMorgan Funds," *New York Times*, January 20, 2014.

There in the fine print: Author interview with a person familiar with the matter.

"For Andrew, there's just not space": Author interview with a person familiar with the matter.

On Tuesday, March 4: Freeman Klopott and Henry Goldman, "De Blasio Hits Albany with Rally for Tax on NYC Wealthy," Bloomberg News, March 4, 2014.

"They say it's cold": Office of the Governor of New York, transcript of Governor Andrew Cuomo's speech at a charter school rally, March 4, 2014, https://www.governor.ny.gov/press/03042014-charter-school-rally.

As the *New York Times*: Thomas Kaplan, Susanne Craig, and Michael M. Grynbaum, "Cuomo Burnishes His Political Brand, Using de Blasio as His Foil," March 6, 2014.

This was a story: Javier C. Hernández and Susanne Craig, "Cuomo Played Pivotal Role in Charter School Push," *New York Times*, April 3, 2014.

A furious Moskowitz: Jill Colvin, "Eva Moskowitz Goes on Media Tour Bashing 'So-Called Progressive' Bill de Blasio," *New York Observer*, March 5, 2014.

Presented with seventeen: Juan Gonzalez, "Gonzalez: Parents, Educators Fed Up with Special Treatment of Charter Schools," *New York Daily News*, October 11, 2013. See also Ginia Bellafante, "How de Blasio's Narrative Got Hijacked," *New York Times*, March 6, 2014, and Javier C. Hernández, "Gentler Words About Charter Schools from de Blasio," *New York Times*, March 23, 2014.

Along with Dan Loeb: Hernández and Craig, "Cuomo Played Pivotal Role in Charter School Push."

On statewide pre-K: Thomas Kaplan and Javier C. Hernández, "State Budget Deal Reached; $300 Million for New York City Pre-K," *New York Times*, March 29, 2014.

Early in his tenure: Valerie Strauss, "What de Blasio's Win in New York City Means for School Reform," *Washington Post*, November 6, 2013. See also Eliza Shapiro, "What the State's Charter Push Did to Mayoral Control," *Capital New York*, April 4,

2014. In 2014, Mayor de Blasio denied the claim that Governor Cuomo had abrogated his authority over New York City schools.

If he left: Kaplan and Hernández, "State Budget Deal Reached; $300 Million for New York City Pre-K." See also *New York State of Politics,* "'Tremendous Progress' but Silver a No-Show for Budget Meeting," March 24, 2014, http://www.nystateofpolitics.com/2014/03/tremendous-progress-but-silver-a-no-show-for-budget-meeting/.

In February alone: Mike Vilensky, "New York Assembly Speaker Silver Sounds Off on Investigation," *Wall Street Journal*, February 25, 2014.

Fred Dicker later reported: Fredric U. Dicker, "Soros' Son Pushed Cuomo, Legislature into Campaign Funding," *New York Post,* March 31, 2014.

That Saturday: Kaplan and Hernández, "State Budget Deal Reached; $300 Million for New York City Pre-K." See also New York State Board of Elections, "Independent Expenditure Reporting," undated, http://www.elections.ny.gov/IndependentExpenditureReporting.html.

"Too cute": "How About It, Gov. Cuomo?" *New York Post*, April 13, 2014.

Chapter 28: Starting Again

Donations would soon reach: Joseph Spector, "Cuomo Reports $35 Million in Campaign War Chest," *Journal News,* July 14, 2014, http://www.lohud.com/story/news/politics/albany-watch/2014/07/15/cuomo-reports-million-campaign-war-chest/12718187/.

More than any other: Ibid.

One poll: Erica Orden, "New York Gov. Cuomo's Approval Ratings Drop Sharply in New Poll," *Wall Street Journal*, March 5, 2014.

In a Fox News poll: Dicker, "Dems Won't Support Cuomo for President in 2016: Sources."

Christie currently trailed: Quinnipiac University, "Cuomo Thumps Trump, Astorino in New York Gov Race, Quinnipiac University Poll Finds, Clinton Runs Better Against Christie in 2016 Race," press release, February 13, 2014, http://www.quinnipiac.edu/news-and-events/quinnipiac-university-poll/new-york-state/release-detail?ReleaseID=2007.

About 80–0: Ben Protess and Matthew Goldstein, "Appeal Judges Hint at Doubts in Insider Case," *New York Times*, April 22, 2014.

Days after the Moreland's: William K. Rashbaum and Susanne Craig, "U.S. Attorney Criticizes Cuomo's Closing of Panel," *New York Times*, April 9, 2014.

The Moreland commission, he said: Laura Nahmias, "Cuomo Responds to Moreland Rebuke," *Capital New York*, April 10, 2014, http://www.capitalnewyork.com/article/albany/2014/04/8543554/cuomo-responds-moreland-rebuke.

Yet much remained unchanged: Jesse McKinley and Thomas Kaplan, "Capitol Corruption Panel's Demise Angers Watchdogs," *New York Times*, March 31, 2014. See also Theodoric Meyer, "Cuomo's Unclosed Loophole," *Syracuse New Times*, July 16, 2014, http://www.syracusenewtimes.com/cuomos-unclosed-loophole/.

As for disclosure: Thomas Kaplan, "With Panel Gone, a Move to Monitor New York Lawmakers' Income Is Thwarted," *New York Times*, April 16, 2014.

Makau Mutua: Kenneth Lovett, "Ex-Ethics Commission Member Says There Are Cases of Potential Government Corruption That Need Review," *New York Daily News*, May 2, 2014, http://www.nydailynews.com/news/politics/ex-ethics-member-dirt-find-state-government-corruption-probe-article-1.1776527.

Nine months: Erica Orden, "Preet Bharara Criticizes Gov. Cuomo for Closing Corruption Commission," *Wall Street Journal*, April 10, 2014.

"Thinking people": Thomas Kaplan and William K. Rashbaum, "Cuomo Caught Up in Rare Conflict with Prosecutor," *New York Times*, April 10, 2014.

In a sit-down: Chris Bragg, "Cuomo on Moreland Tampering: It's My Commission," *Crain's New York Business*, April 24, 2014, http://www.crainsnewyork.com/article/20140424/BLOGS04/140429924/cuomo-on-moreland-tampering-its-my-commission#.

The previous July: Craig, Rashbaum, and Kaplan, "Cuomo's Office Hobbled Ethics Inquiries by Moreland Commission."

"Cuomo can't investigate him": Blake Zeff, "Cuomo Gets a Critic His Own Size," *Capital New York*, April 14, 2014, http://www.capitalnewyork.com/article/albany/2014/04/8543657/cuomo-gets-critic-his-own-size.

DiNapoli he'd dispossessed: Alan S. Chartock, "Declawing the State Comptroller," NY Press, July 11, 2012, http://nypress.com/declawing-the-state-comptroller/.

"Cuomo is entering": Zeff, "Cuomo Gets a Critic His Own Size."

As part of Bharara's investigation: William K. Rashbaum and Susanne Craig, "U.S. Said to Seek Records from Anticorruption Panel's Members," *New York Times*, May 6, 2014.

The Moreland commission hired: Erica Orden, "Lawyer Hired for Ethics Panel Disbanded by Cuomo," *Wall Street Journal*, May 22, 2014.

Andrew in turn hired a lawyer: Kenneth Lovett, "Attorney Representing Governor's Office in Federal Probe Has No Contract," *New York Daily News*, August 1, 2014, http://www.nydailynews.com/blogs/dailypolitics/attorney-representing-governor-office-federal-probe-contract-blog-entry-1.1888547.

Readers learned: Annie Karn, "Sandra Lee and Andrew Cuomo: A Love Story," *New York Post*, December 4, 2009. See also Benjamin Wallace, "The Ravenous and Resourceful Sandra Lee," *New York*, March 27, 2011, http://nymag.com/news/features/sandra-lee-2011-4/#print.

Guests to the home: Gully Wells, "Sandra Lee: The Woman in White," *Vogue*, February 22, 2011, http://www.vogue.com/865456/sandra-lee-the-woman-in-white/.

A veteran of the publishing business: Author interview with a person familiar with the matter.

"Actually, I think": Author interview with a former aide to Andrew Cuomo.

Feature stories: David McKay Wilson, "Gov. Cuomo Girlfriend Sandra Lee Skips Permits," Westchester County, New York, *Journal News*, May 11, 2014, http://www.democratandchronicle.com/story/news/2014/05/11/tale-cuomo-clintons-taxes/8960455/.

All this came as a surprise: Mara Gay, "Cuomo's Girlfriend Got State Help with Permits," *Wall Street Journal*, May 11, 2014. See also Corey Kilgannon, "Decorating and Design Meet Taxation and Politics Where Cuomo Lives," *New York Times*, June 13, 2014, and David McKay Wilson, "Sandra Lee-Cuomo Home Assessment Raised 29%," Westchester County, New York, *Journal News*, June 12, 2014, http://www.usatoday.com/story/news/nation/2014/06/12/sandra-lee-cuomo-home-assessment-raised-29/10358829/.

Since Sandra's purchase: Wilson, "Sandra Lee-Cuomo Home Assessment Raised 29%."

$1.2 million: Kilgannon, "Decorating and Design Meet Taxation and Politics Where Cuomo Lives."

In mid-June: Wilson, "Sandra Lee-Cuomo Home Assessment Raised 29%."

As one spokesperson put it: Gay, "Cuomo's Girlfriend Got State Help with Permits."

As ex-state assemblyman: Alex Seitz-Wald, "Why Can't Andrew Cuomo and New York Democrats Play Nice?" *National Journal*, April 10, 2014, http://www.nationaljournal.com/magazine/why-can-t-andrew-cuomo-and-new-york-democrats-play-nice-20140410.

"The [one-race] plan": Casey Seiler, "Casey Seiler: The Second Law of Cuomo," Albany *Times Union*, April 5, 2014, http://www.timesunion.com/opinion/article/Casey-Seiler-The-2nd-Law-of-Cuomo-5379233.php.

One poll suggested that a spoiler: Quinnipiac University, "Liberal Dem Would Hurt Cuomo in New York Gov Race, Quinnipiac University Poll Finds; But Gov, DiNapoli, Schneiderman All Have Big Leads," press release, May 21, 2014, http://www.quinnipiac.edu/news-and-events/quinnipiac-university-poll/new-york-state/release-detail?ReleaseID=2044.

"If he had been a warm": Author interview with Bill Samuels.

That Saturday afternoon: Laura Nahmias, "At W.F.P. Convention, An Endorsement and Plenty of Anger," *Capital New York*, June 1, 2014, http://www.capitalnewyork.com/article/albany/2014/06/8546354/wfp-convention-endorsement-and-plenty-anger.

Sometime that day: Author interviews with three leaders of the Working Families Party.

Andrew, a WFP in-house memo: Jon Campbell, "Internal Memo: What Else Was the WFP Supposed to 'Get'?" Westchester County, New York, *Journal News*, June 4, 2014, http://polhudson.lohudblogs.com/2014/06/04/internal-memo-else-wfp-supposed-get/.

He reshot the video: Video of Governor Andrew Cuomo's speech to the New York State Working Families Convention (video post on YouTube), June 28, 2014, http://uneditedpolitics.com/andrew-cuomo-video-speech-working-families-party-nominating-convention-53114/.

When he called back: Thomas Kaplan and Susanne Craig, "As Antics Subside, Both Cuomo and the Left Claim the Last Hurrah," *New York Times*, June 1, 2014. See also Erica Orden, "Last-Minute Deal in Albany," *Wall Street Journal*, June 2, 2014.

Andrew won: David Klepper, "Despite Dustup, NY Gov Cuomo Gets Liberal Backing," Associated Press, June 1, 2014.

The next day: Azi Paybarah, "Cuomo Explains the Limits of His W.F.P. Alliance," June 1, 2014, http://www.capitalnewyork.com/article/city-hall/2014/06/8546353/cuomo-explains-limits-his-wfp-alliance.

"The only way to overcome": Joseph Spector, "Samuels Won't Run for Lieutenant Governor," Westchester County, New York, *Journal News*, June 2, 2014, http://polhudson.lohudblogs.com/2014/06/02/samuels-wont-run-lieutenant-governor/.

New York still had: Scott Drenkard and Joseph Henchman, "2014 State Business Tax Climate Index" (report), Tax Foundation, October 9, 2013, http://taxfoundation.org/article/2014-state-business-tax-climate-index.

By late April: Jesse McKinley and Charles V. Bagli, "22 Companies Apply to Open 4 Casinos in New York State," *New York Times*, April 24, 2014.

His old nemesis: Jesse McKinley, "In Report, State Comptroller Is Cautious about Benefits of Casinos," *New York Times*, May 29, 2014.

But the story in Atlantic City: Charles V. Bagli, "Atlantic City Strives to Rise as Casinos Fail," *New York Times*, July 14, 2014.

As of 1998: Joseph Berger, "For $55 Million, New York Acquires Sterling Forest," *New York Times*, February 11, 1998.

Federal authorities weighed in: Lynn, "Building of Thruway Exit Is Delayed." See also letter from former U.S. National Park Service Regional Director James W. Coleman to Orin Lehman, the former commissioner of the New York State Office of Parks, Recreation and Historic Preservation, September 14, 1987.

Still, by early fall: "Don't Gamble Away Sterling Forest," editorial, *New York Times*, October 7, 2014.

Genting would pay: Hema Easley, "Tuxedo, Genting Americas Casino OK Benefits Pact," *Times Herald-Record*, July 2, 2014, http://www.recordonline.com/apps/pbcs.dll/article?AID=/20140702/NEWS/407020320.

Andrew's fondest hope: Jim Heaney, "Suppression of Buffalo Billion Spending Records," Investigative Post, December 22, 2014.

Initially brisk sales plummeted: Philip Bump, "'Hard Choices' Is Bombing, Especially If You Ask Hillary's Critics," *Washington Post*, June 18, 2014.

One outselling her own book: Amy Chozick and Alexandra Alter, "A Provocateur's Book on Hillary Clinton Overtakes Her Memoir in Sales," *New York Times*, July 10, 2014.

Chapter 29: Full Circle

On July 23, 2014: Craig, Rashbaum, and Kaplan, "Cuomo's Office Hobbled Ethics Inquiries by Moreland Commission."

Andrew had his press office: "Governor Cuomo's Office Responds," *New York Times*, July 23, 2014.

The letter: Campbell, "Cuomo's Office Releases 2,200-Word Letter on Lobbying Group."

"Andrew is as honest": Annie Karni, "Mario Cuomo Defends His Son: 'Andrew's as Honest a Politician as We Have Seen,'" *New York Daily News*, July 28, 2014.

Defending his son: Safire, "The New Rainmaker."

One, co-chair William Fitzpatrick: Jon Campbell, "Moreland Co-Chair: 'Nobody 'Interfered' with Me or My Co-Chairs,'" *Politics on the Hudson* (blog), Westchester County *Journal News*, July 28, 2014.

In his press conference: Susanne Craig, Thomas Kaplan, and William K. Rashbaum, "U.S. Attorney Warns Cuomo on Moreland Commission Case," *New York Times*, July 31, 2014.

"If you had watched": Thomas Kaplan and Susanne Craig, "Defiant, Cuomo Denies Interfering with Ethics Commission," *New York Times*, July 28, 2014.

Just earlier that year: Thomas Kaplan, "Cuomo Aides Use Allies to Shore Up the Governor's Image," *New York Times*, August 4, 2014.

Reporters targeted Joe Percoco: Brendan J. Lyons, "Cuomo Aide Urged Spin," Albany *Times Union*, August 1, 2014.

Preet Bharara made public: Craig, Kaplan, and Rashbaum, "U.S. Attorney Warns Cuomo on Moreland Commission Case."

His rambling address: Author interview with a person familiar with the matter.

Article IV, Section 2: Thomas Kaplan, "Cuomo Contests New York Residency of Teachout Before Primary," *New York Times*, August 6, 2014.

At Teachout's campaign appearances: Hunter Walker, "Cuomo Campaign Admits Its Volunteers Staged Mysterious Protests Against Rival," *Business Insider*, July 25, 2014.

On August 11: Thomas Kaplan, "A Cuomo Primary Opponent Can Run, a State Judge Rules," *New York Times*, August 11, 2014.

"Game on": Matthew Hamilton, "Teachout Keeps Spot on Ballot," Albany *Times Union*, August 11, 2014.

The New York City Labor Day parade: Video of a scene from the New York City Labor Day parade, September 6, 2014, posted on Vimeo, http://vimeo.com/105433950.

"I never saw her": Celeste Katz, "Gov. Cuomo Shrugs Off Underdog Foes Teachout and Wu as Inexperienced...and Maybe Invisible?" *New York Daily News*, September 8, 2014.

"While some politicians": Thomas Kaplan, "Handshakes and Hugs, Hallmarks of the Stump, Are Rare with Cuomo," *New York Times*, August 29, 2014.

His heretofore unknown rival: Thomas Kaplan, "Cuomo Defeats Teachout, Liberal Rival, in the Democratic Primary," *New York Times*, September 9, 2014.

"I am happy": Thomas Kaplan, "Cuomo Says He's 'Fine with 60%' in Primary and Looks to General Election," *New York Times*, September 10, 2014.

A loan of $511: Joseph Berger, "E.P.A. Cuts Size of Loan New York Sought for Tappan Zee Bridge," *New York Times*, September 16, 2014.

The $65 million demolition: Joseph Berger, "Environmental Agency Approves $511 Million Loan for Tappan Zee Replacement," *New York Times*, June 26, 2014.

Most of the $511 million: Joseph Berger, "Loan Sought for Tappan Zee Work Is Faulted," *New York Times*, June 25, 2014. See also Joseph Berger, "E.P.A. Cuts Size of Loan New York Sought for Tappan Zee Bridge."

Two-year-old Revel Casino Hotel: Charles V. Bagli, "Revel Casino in Atlantic City Is Sold to Real Estate Company," *New York Times*, October 1, 2014.

Mayor de Blasio gave speeches: Matt Flegenheimer and Thomas Kaplan, "As de Blasio Aids Bid for Democratic Senate, Cuomo Is a Nearly Invisible Man," *New York Times*, October 9, 2014.

He endorsed one Democratic candidate: Thomas Kaplan, "Cuomo Endorses Democrat for State Senate," *New York Times*, October 12, 2014.

"I can't name a swing district": Author interview with Bill Samuels.

Andrew scoffed: Ken Lovett, "Cuomo: Women's Equality Line Isn't About Punishing Working Families Party," *New York Daily News*, October 31, 2014.

By late September: Casey Seiler, "Casey Seiler: WEP Flops Upstate," Albany *Times Union*, September 27, 2014.

Liz Krueger, the liberal Manhattan senator: Liz Benjamin, "Sen. Krueger: Cuomo WEP Push 'Disturbing,'" *New York State of Politics* (blog), October 31, 2014.

The first trip: Thomas Kaplan and Jason Horowitz, "Cuomo, Visiting Israel, Joins Growing U.S. List," *New York Times*, August 13, 2014.

"It's here": Erica Orden, "New York Gov. Andrew Cuomo Travels to Afghanistan," *Wall Street Journal*, September 27, 2014.

Hillary Clinton strode onstage: Amy Chozick and Thomas Kaplan, "Another Twist in the Drama of the Clintons and the Cuomos," *New York Times*, October 23, 2014.

Mental health workers: Anemona Hartocollis, "Mental Health Issues Put 34,500 on New York's No-Guns List," *New York Times*, October 19, 2014.

An onslaught of criticism: Kate Zernike and Thomas Kaplan, "Cuomo's and Christie's Shifts on Ebola Are Criticized as Politics, Not Science," *New York Times*, October 27, 2014.

"Enjoy your family": Erin Durkin, "Gov. Cuomo Defends Ebola Policy, Suggests People Under Quarantine Read His Book," *New York Daily News*, October 27, 2014.

A *Wall Street Journal*/NBC: Erica Orden, "Poll: New Yorkers Support Mandatory Ebola Quarantines," *Wall Street Journal*, October 30, 2014.

More like 54 percent: Thomas Kaplan, "Cuomo Says Obama's Woes Hurt Democrats in New York Races," *New York Times*, November 6, 2014.

To Andrew's former adviser: Author interview with Steve Cohen.

One of Andrew's advisers: Author interview with a person familiar with the matter.

The week after the election: Fredric U. Dicker, "Cuomo Had a Secret Re-Election 'Pact' with Republicans," *New York Post*, November 20, 2014.

CeCe Tkaczyk: John W. Barry, "Amedore Defeats Tkaczyk in Race for 46th Senate District," *Poughkeepsie Journal*, November 5, 2014.

"Governor Cuomo promised": Nick Reisman, "WFP and Cuomo: It's Complicated," *New York State of Politics* (blog), November 5, 2014.

"What Cuomo is walking into": Andrew J. Hawkins, "Cuomo Faces Shaky Second Term," *Crain's New York Business*, November 3, 2014.

"Every presidential election": Author interview with a person familiar with the matter.

In a new, unpublicized policy: James Odato, "Meter's Running on Email," Albany *Times Union*, June 30, 2013.

"They're keeping information": Michael Virtanen, "Cuomo's Office Tightly Controls Public Records," Associated Press, October 24, 2014.

Rex Smith: Rex Smith, "Rex Smith: A Lesson of Watergate, 40 Years On," Albany *Times Union*, August 6, 2014.

But Genting had had: Jesse McKinley and Charles V. Bagli, "Board Backs Casinos in the Catskills," *New York Times*, December 18, 2014.

There was, one insider suggested: Author interview with a person familiar with the matter.

"He's just chewed through people": Author interview with a person familiar with the matter.

"Ultimately, this is a guy": Author interview with a person familiar with the matter.

Acknowledgments

The first person I have to thank will be surprised to hear it. Back in December 2011, I happened to hear former New York governor David Paterson give a talk about his successor. For all sorts of reasons, Paterson might have spoken grudgingly of Andrew Cuomo. Instead, he marveled at Cuomo's political savvy, how in his first year in office Cuomo had done everything right. I found that intriguing. That Cuomo was being touted as a presidential candidate in 2016 made him that much more compelling. And so one thing led to another. Also thanks to Kelly Vickery.

Esther Newberg, my extraordinary agent, needed no persuading that Cuomo's story was now worth a book. Deb Futter, my peerless editor at Twelve, saw the story too, right from the start, and has cheered it on ever since. I am grateful to her whole team at Twelve for helping turn it into a book.

I've had a wonderfully dedicated fact-checker in Cynthia Cotts, and an always-ready researcher in John Surico. I think together we've untangled most of the snags, but if any mistakes remain, they are solely my fault.

In the nearly three years that I reported and wrote this book, I conducted more than three hundred interviews with people who knew Andrew Cuomo one way or another: childhood friends, college mates, ex-staffers and colleagues, loyalists and critics. Many of them, unfortunately, cannot be listed here because they felt obliged to speak off the record. Andrew Cuomo is not only the most powerful person in the state, but an intimidating figure too, known to be vindictive and unforgiving. Not many choose to be on his bad side.

At the start of this project, I called the governor's press office with the earnest if naïve hope of interviewing him first. The governor demurred, but word did come down that at some point a "sit-down," as meetings are referred to on the second floor of Albany's capitol building, would be arranged.

In the meantime, the governor assigned one of his top advisers, Steve Cohen, to be my minder. This was a smart and useful arrangement for the governor as well as for me, one for which I remain grateful. It gave the governor some sense of what I was doing, and it gave me a conduit into the administration. Steve eventually set up quite a few good interviews for me, and always made himself available to give me his take on the latest developments—a take that, I came to realize, was channeling the governor.

Darren Dopp, a well-known Albany hand who has aided, in one capacity or another, three governors—Mario Cuomo, Eliot Spitzer, and, less formally, Andrew—also steered me to sources and provided a running commentary. I knew Darren's name as I started this book, and was delighted to get his call out of the blue. But of course it wasn't out of the blue. Like Steve, Darren gave me a running discourse on events from the governor's perspective. Both Steve and Darren were as candid as loyalists can be, for which I am grateful. I even think most of what they told me is true.

Despite indications right up until the end that the governor would speak with me, the sit-down never came. This put me in league with just about every reporter covering Albany. In a way, I have come to feel that Andrew did me a service, forcing me to widen my circles of sources—forcing me, in fact, to work harder than I might have if I had had hours of taped talks with him to fill the pages. Andrew is a wonderful subject, complex and contradictory, but disinclined to reveal much of value about himself.

I owe a huge debt of thanks to Sam Dealey, a Washington-based writer and editor who shared with me his many boxes of court documents from the Oceanmark lawsuits that entangled Andrew in his youth. As per protocol in the Florida federal courts, those documents from the mid-1980s were destroyed at some point, but Sam had reported on the case while they were extant, and saw fit to keep them. I spent several happy afternoons at his gracious home poring over them, enjoying the added benefit of his company. Thanks also to Rex Smith, editor in chief of the Albany *Times Union*, for opening his paper's archives to me, and sharing his own thoughts on Andrew. Thanks to Jon Cowan, Andrew's former chief of staff at HUD, for sharing his thoughts and introducing me to several of his ex-HUD colleagues.

Thanks above all to Gayfryd Steinberg, my wife and partner, who endured more talk about Andrew Cuomo than anyone should have to, and who read the final manuscript with a sharpened pencil and a gimlet eye.

Index

About the Author

Michael Shnayerson became a contributing editor at *Vanity Fair* in 1986 and has since written more than seventy-five stories for the magazine. He began his career in 1976 as a reporter at the *Santa Fe Reporter* and moved to *Time* as a staff writer in 1978. In 1980 he became editor in chief of *Avenue*, and he has been a consulting editor at *Condé Nast Traveler* since its inception in 1987. Shnayerson is the author of *Irwin Shaw: A Biography* and *The Car That Could: The Inside Story of GM's Revolutionary Electric Vehicle*, which was named one of the best business books of 1996 by *BusinessWeek*; and he is the coauthor, with Mark J. Plotkin, of *The Killers Within: The Deadly Rise of Drug-Resistant Bacteria* and coauthor of Harry Belafonte's memoir *My Song*.

ABOUT TWELVE

TWELVE

TWELVE was established in August 2005 with the objective of publishing no more than twelve books each year. We strive to publish the singular book, by authors who have a unique perspective and compelling authority. Works that explain our culture; that illuminate, inspire, provoke, and entertain. We seek to establish communities of conversation surrounding our books. Talented authors deserve attention not only from publishers, but from readers as well. To sell the book is only the beginning of our mission. To build avid audiences of readers who are enriched by these works—that is our ultimate purpose.

For more information about forthcoming TWELVE books, please go to www.twelvebooks.com.